Contents

CW00508803

Contents

Contents

Contents

Abbreviations and References

FA 1993	=	Finance Act 1993
FA 1994	=	Finance Act 1994
FA 1995	=	Finance Act 1995
FA 1996	=	Finance Act 1996
FA 1997	=	Finance Act 1997
F(No 2)A 1997	=	Finance Act (No 2) 1997
FA 1998	=	Finance Act 1998
FA 2000	=	Finance Act 2000
DR	=	The Exchange Gains and Losses (Deferral of Gains and Losses) Regulations 1994
ER	=	The Exchange Gains and Losses (Excess Gains and Losses) Regulations 1994
ESCR	=	The European Single Currency (Taxes) Regulations 1998
ICR	=	The Exchange Gains and Losses (Insurance Companies) Regulations 1994
ICTA 1988	=	Income and Corporation Taxes Act 1988
LR	=	The Local Currency Elections Regulations 1994
MR	=	The Exchange Gains and Losses (Alternative Method of Calculation of Gain or Loss) Regulations 1994
Reg	=	Regulation
s	=	Section
Sch	=	Schedule
SSAP 20	=	Statement of Standard Accounting Practice 20
TCGA 1992	=	Taxation of Chargeable Gains Act 1992
TMA 1970	=	Taxes Management Act 1970
TR	=	The Exchange Gains and Losses (Transitional Provisions) Regulations 1994

Table of Statutes

Table of Statutory Instruments

Table of Cases

Chapter 1

Introduction to the Taxation of Foreign Exchange Gains and Losses

Introduction

1.1   The *Finance Act 1993* and its associated regulations produced a completely new regime for the taxation of foreign exchange gains and losses (from 23 March 1995). It has changed the way in which UK companies must deal with the taxation of transactions denominated in non-sterling currencies and cannot be ignored by any company engaging in any aspect of international trade or borrowing, or being part of an international group.

1.2   The old system of taxing exchange differences was complex and full of anomalies and uncertainties. The new system is even more complex, but has relatively few anomalies and uncertainties.

1.3   Subsequent chapters of this book set out the system introduced by the *Finance Act 1993* in a way which will provide most UK companies with a framework within which to plan transactions and prepare their tax computations.

1.4   This chapter gives a brief history of the development of the taxation of exchange gains and losses and a summary of the position immediately before the new legislation becomes effective. This is required for understanding and applying the transitional provisions, for dealing with tax liabilities arising before Commencement Day and for individual taxpayers who are not covered by the new rules. It also gives a brief outline of the new regime.

Position prior to 1970

1.5   Until the 1970s, when the Bretton Woods system broke down, exchange differences were not a common problem in the accounts of UK companies. There had only been two major devaluations of sterling: that by Stafford Cripps in September 1949, which took the value of the pound down from $4.03 to $2.80 and the Wilson government devaluation of November 1967 which reduced the value from $2.80 to $2.40.

1976: First Inland Revenue Consultative Document

1.6   By 1976, exchange movements had become the rule rather than the exception and in his Budget speech, Denis Healey undertook to initiate consultation on the subject of tax relief for foreign currency losses with a view to introducing legislation the following year.

1.7   The Inland Revenue paper which followed set out its view on the current state of the law. Broadly, the paper said that whether the exchange loss could be allowed as a trading deduction depended on the nature of the loan and whether it was to be properly regarded as on fixed or circulating capital account. The paper expressed the opinion that the distinction between fixed and circulating capital was based upon principles well-established in tax case law, so that no difficulty was envisaged in drawing the distinction.

1.8   However, the paper went on to suggest that there could be some scope for extending and more closely defining the way in which relief for exchange losses was given and opened for discussion whether bringing exchange differences on particular loans into account for tax should be mandatory or optional, the way in which relief would be given and whether the tax treatment would be on accruals or realisation basis.

1.9   Interested parties duly made representations to the Inland Revenue, but in the 1977 Budget, the Chancellor decided that 'the arguments for general relief for exchange losses' were 'finely balanced'. Overall, he wished to use his available budgetary spending on income tax reliefs and so did nothing on the tax treatment of exchange losses.

1.10   During that consultation process, the first major modern case on exchange differences was being heard. This was *Firestone Tire & Rubber Co Ltd v Evans, 51 TC 615*, relating to capital v revenue distinctions in a current account between the UK subsidiary and its US parent. It concluded that a single account could be regarded as split between capital and revenue balances and that only the exchange losses on the revenue part were tax deductible.

Marine Midland case

1.11   However, the more significant case was to be *Pattison v Marine Midland Ltd, 57 TC 219*, which reached the House of Lords in 1983.

1.12   Marine Midland was a UK bank which borrowed dollars by way of subordinated loan stock, did not convert the dollars into sterling and lent them on in the course of its business. For accounts purposes, the monetary assets and liabilities denominated in dollars were valued in sterling at the year end exchange rate, but to the extent that liabilities were matched by assets, no profit or loss was shown. Only the profit or loss on the unmatched dollars was taken to income.

1.13   The Court of Appeal and the House of Lords held that where there was matching, no profit or loss arose for tax purposes. The unmatched position was always on current account and thus was taxable or tax allowable depending on whether it was a profit or a loss.

1.14   This 'matching' concept thus departed from the Inland Revenue view of the law which would have looked separately at the capital account and the revenue account items and would thus have disallowed the losses on capital account borrowing, but taxed the profits on current account assets. The Commissioners and the High Court considered the capital v revenue definition and found in favour of the Inland Revenue. However, this point was not considered at the Court of Appeal or House of Lords.

1985: Statement of Practice

1.15   In response to this decision, on 25 January 1985, the Inland Revenue issued a provisional Statement of Practice setting out the way in which it would aim to deal with the exchange gains and losses for tax purposes. Taxpayers were invited to settle open assessments on the basis of the provisional statement but were not compelled to do so. After many representations and discussions, on 17 February 1987, a new Statement of Practice (SP 1/87) was published.

1.16   The Inland Revenue stated that this Statement of Practice was a practical guide to the settlement of the computations of trading taxpayers, but accepted that it could not be expected to apply in all circumstances. The Statement, in making its opening definitions, continued to take the view that the distinction between capital and current liabilities was based upon principles well-established in case law. It stated that the distinction was essentially between loans providing temporary financial accommodation and loans which could be said to add to the capital of the business. The answer in any particular case was said to turn on its facts and circumstances, which would have to be considered in detail.

1.17   The Statement made it quite clear that only single currency matching was included and went on to set out the rules to be applied in a range of circumstances.

1.18   It also made it clear that it did not apply to non-trading companies, nor could groups of companies be regarded as a single entity for matching purposes. It had no application to capital gains, where the decision in *Bentley v Pike, 55 TC 590* established that a gain or loss on an asset should be computed by comparing the sterling value at the date of sale of the consideration received with the sterling value at the date of acquisition of the acquisition cost. This decision was subsequently upheld in *Capcount Trading v Evans [1993] STC 11*. A Special Commissioners hearing on 2 May 1996 (*Poseidon Inc v Inspector of Taxes (SpC 82), [1996] SSCD 273*) did not apply the *Bentley v Pike* principle. It held that when consideration for a chargeable asset disposal was received in instalments, exchange losses arising (due to spot rates changing from the rate on the contracted date of disposal) were deductible as irrecoverable consideration under *TCGA 1992, s 40(2)*. This decision was overturned by the decision in *Goodbrand v Loffland Brothers North Sea Inc* (see 1.38 below).

1.19   During the representations which were made on the provisional Statement of Practice, considerable pressure was exerted to clarify the position by introducing new legislation. When the Statement was issued, Norman Lamont, then Financial Secretary to the Treasury, invited institutions to prepare detailed proposals suggesting tax law changes. On 27 July 1987, nine bodies (now known as 'The Group of Nine') issued a report with such proposals. The nine were the Confederation of British Industry, The Institute of Directors, The Law Society, The Institute of Chartered Accountants in England & Wales, The Association of Corporate Treasurers, The International Chamber of Commerce, The Association of British Insurers, The British Bankers Association and the Institute of Taxation. Their reports sought 'urgent action ... to deal with the serious anomaly that capital gains and losses on foreign currency borrowing are neither taxed nor relieved'.

1.20   There was no immediate response to this request from the legislature. However, matters did move on in the courts. Two further cases relating to foreign exchange losses were being heard around this time.

Overseas Containers and Woolworth cases

1.21   *Overseas Containers (Finance) Limited v Stoker (Inspector of Taxes), 61 TC 473*, was heard in the High Court in June and July 1987 and subsequently in the Court of Appeal in February and March 1989.

1.22   Overseas Containers Limited ('OCL') was formed by four major UK shipping companies as the vehicle by which they would enter the container shipping market. In 1967 contracts were entered into by OCL for the construction in Germany of five container ships. The price was payable in stages and OCL also entered into loan agreements with the German shipyards concerned to meet the stage payments. These loans were then repayable over a period of six and a half years from the date of delivery of the ships.

1.23   Shortly after the placing of these contracts, it became clear that a devaluation of sterling was imminent. A major loss on exchange on these loans was felt by OCL to be unlikely to result in a tax deduction in its hands and this, possibly amongst other factors, led to the loans being transferred into another group company, Overseas Containers (Finance) Limited. This was to be established as a finance company with other loan transactions also entered into. In this way, the loans in question would, it was hoped, be regarded as part of its trading activity and thus any exchange losses would be deductible for tax purposes.

1.24   The deciding element in this case was that the loans had been transferred for a purely tax avoidance motive rather than for some greater commercial purpose. For this reason, the transfer was disregarded and the exchange losses which arose on the Deutschmark loans were disallowed for tax purposes.

1.25   The courts did, however, conclude that loans entered into by the company when properly established as one with a Schedule D Case I finance trade, gave rise to exchange losses which were taxable or deductible. The court also accepted that the real cost of funds is the sum of interest and exchange differences, the two being interdependent. However, it was felt that this was not relevant to the determination of the correct tax treatment.

1.26   The more significant case was *A P Beauchamp (HM Inspector of Taxes) v F W Woolworth Plc, 61 TC 542.* This was heard in the High Court in April 1987, the Court of Appeal in June and July 1988 and the House of Lords in May and June 1989.

1.27   In 1971, F W Woolworth, although a UK publicly quoted company, was 52.7% owned by the US Woolworth corporation. Under the Exchange Control regulations in force at that time, such a UK company was required to raise a pro rata proportion of its loan finance outside the UK, such foreign currency borrowing had to be for a minimum period of five years and contracts for the forward purchase of foreign currency could only be made with a maturity date of no more than six months.

1.28   Thus, when the company wished to extend its general credit facilities to finance the cash flows arising from the steady expansion of its trading activity, it had no option but to raise five-year loans from overseas. It did this by taking out two Swiss Franc loans each of SF50 million, each with a five-year term. They were at fixed interest rates, one of them at 6% and one at 7%. Each loan could be repaid early at the option of the borrower although a premium was payable in the event of this option being exercised. One of the loans was in fact repaid early.

1.29   The loan proceeds were converted into sterling immediately upon receipt and then used for the general business purposes of the company. The loans were repaid out of general funds. As a result of the repayment, the company suffered exchange losses totalling £11.4 million.

1.30   The taxpayer company claimed that these exchange losses were allowable deductions for tax purposes, given that the loans were to deal with short-term cash flow problems and thus represented temporary facilities rather than part of the structure of the capital account borrowing of the company. The Special Commissioners agreed with this view and found in favour of Woolworth.

1.31   The High Court, on appeal, found in favour of the Inland Revenue, the Court of Appeal then reversed this and found in favour of the taxpayer and finally the House of Lords gave judgment in favour of the Revenue.

1.32   The basis of the decision was that the question as to whether a loan transaction entered into by the taxpayer was of a revenue or capital nature was a question of law to be determined in the light of the facts found by the Commissioners. A loan was a revenue transaction only if it was temporary and fluctuating and incurred in meeting the ordinary running of the business. The nature of the loans involved in this case, being fixed in amount for a definite period of greater than one year, was sufficient to determine that in law they should be regarded as transactions of a capital nature. This meant that the exchange differences on them were regarded as 'nothings' for tax purposes – exchange losses failing to achieve tax relief, but any exchange gains on such items similarly being tax free.

1.33   During the course of the House of Lords hearing, one of their Lordships commented that although the law as it stood clearly gave the result that such losses were not tax allowable, this appeared to be an entirely unreasonable approach and the Inland Revenue should give urgent consideration to changing the law.

1989: Inland Revenue Consultative Paper

1.34   Some steps towards making such a change had been explored in the Inland Revenue consultative paper of March 1989 entitled 'Tax Treatment of Foreign Exchange Gains and Losses'. Following the responses to this consultation, a further consultative document was published in March 1991 and the response to that led to the publication of a press release on 11 August 1992 expressing the firm intention to introduce legislative changes and outlining the nature of these. The new draft clauses were published in February 1993 and incorporated into the *Finance Act* later that year.

1.35   This legislation, together with its associated regulations, forms the subject matter of the later chapters of this book and is outlined briefly in 1.44 *et seq.*, below.

Whittles v Uniholdings

1.36   Shortly before the new legislation was finally brought into effect by the laying of the Regulations, a further tax case was heard by the High Court on 25 November 1994. The circumstances in *Whittles (Inspector of Taxes) v Uniholdings Ltd (No. 3) [1995] STC 185* were considered to give rise to an extension of the Marine Midland matching principle, so that the two sides of the transaction should be taken together to establish the tax result. These two were a dollar loan (the proceeds of which had been converted into sterling) and a dollar forward contract to fund the loan repayment. After much dispute on the nature of the facts, the Court held that the loan and forward contract were part of a single composite transaction, so that the effect of the two combined should be the basis for computing the tax liability of the company.

1.37   The case was overturned (with no further right of appeal granted) in the Court of Appeal on 14 May 1996. Thus the *Marine Midland* matching principle has not been extended.

Goodbrand v Loffland Brothers North Sea Inc

1.38   Since the introduction of the new legislation, one case on foreign exchange has gone through the courts. *Goodbrand v Loffland Brothers North Sea Inc [1996] STC 102* considered whether in capital gains computations a taxpayer can claim relief under *TCGA 1992, s 48* for an exchange loss that arises on deferred consideration (i.e. when consideration actually received in currency and translated into sterling at the spot rate on receipt is less than the sterling equivalent of the deferred consideration calculated at the time of disposal in accordance with *TCGA 1992, s 48*). The Inland Revenue won the case on appeal to the Chancery Division with the result that the consideration must be calculated as the sterling equivalent of the currency amount at the date of disposal and no claim is possible under *TCGA 1992, s 48* for any exchange loss.

Taxation of foreign exchange gains and losses for individuals

1.39   The tax treatment of exchange gains and losses under the old rules continues to apply to sole traders and partnerships of individuals and continues to be relevant whilst the tax computations of companies for periods pre-Commencement Day are being settled and during the transitional period of the new legislation.

Summary of the old rules (still applying to individuals)

1.40   The 'old' rules may be summarised as follows, in as far as they apply to traders:

	Type of transaction	*Tax treatment of exchange difference*
1.	Ordinary trade debtors.	Sch D Case I – accruals basis.
2.	Ordinary trade creditors.	Sch D Case I – accruals basis.
3.	Foreign currency bank current accounts (assets).	Sch D Case I – accruals basis if held for trade purposes. Otherwise, capital gain.
4.	Foreign currency overdrafts.	Sch D Case I – accruals basis.
5.	Interest payable or receivable.	Follows the tax treatment of the interest itself – convert at spot rate on the payable/receivable date.
6.	Currency swaps.	If for trading transactions, then follows Sch D Case I treatment of swap. Otherwise taxed as a part of the capital gain on the settlement of the swap.
7.	Borrowing of over one year and not entirely of an 'overdraft' nature.	Nothings – no tax relief for losses – gains tax free.
8.	Loans which are 'debts on security', including debentures.	Capital gain/loss on realisation.
9.	Simple loans – not 'debts on security'.	Nothings.
10.	Foreign currency denominated share capital of the taxpayer.	Nothings.
11.	Investment in foreign currency denominated shares.	Capital gain/loss on realisation.
12.	Foreign currency denominated shares held by a share dealer.	Sch D Case I – probably on a realisation basis – treatment varies depending on accounting treatment and other factors.
13.	Currency options	If for trading transactions then follow Sch D Case I treatment for option. Otherwise taxed as part of capital gain or under *TCGA 1992, s 143*.

1.41 Investment companies will get no tax relief for losses which are relieved under Schedule D Case I in trading companies in the table above.

1.42 Where there are 'matched' transactions, reference should be made to Marine Midland (see 1.11 above).

1.43 It is the nothings in the table which give rise to the problems under the old rules, particularly if they occur on items which are hedging a corresponding asset or liability, the exchange difference on which is fully brought into tax.

Overview of foreign exchange tax rules (for corporates)

1.44 As explained in 1.1 above the new foreign exchange legislation ('the foreign exchange tax rules') is enacted to have effect from 23 March 1995 (the 'Appointed Day'). Each company is brought into the legislation from the beginning of its first accounting period starting on or after 23 March 1995.

1.45 Basically the rules tax the accounting exchange differences accruing on monetary assets, liabilities and currency contracts of companies. The precise application of the legislation has, however, been altered by *Finance Act 2000*. With effect from 1 January 2000, the currency in which a company makes up its accounts will affect the currency in which the corporation tax computations must be prepared. The foreign exchange legislation applies equally to companies preparing corporation tax computations in a currency other than sterling and those computing their taxable profits in sterling itself, but the reference currency against which movements are measured will be different.

1.46 *FA 2000, s 105(1)*, substitutes new *ss 92–95* into *FA 1993*.

1.47 New *FA 1993, s 92* states the basic principle that a company carrying on any type of business must compute its profits chargeable to corporation tax in sterling. The section encapsulates in statute a rule that had previously applied only by virtue of a combination of legislative provision and case law. This basic rule is, however, subject to the further provision now contained in *FA 1993, s 93*, which makes it mandatory for a company to compute its chargeable profits (other than capital gains/losses) in a currency other than sterling in certain prescribed circumstances (see Chapter 10, Part I).

1.48 The exchange differences arising on application of the rules are taxed as income:

(*a*) under Schedule D Case I if the monetary items are used for the purposes of the trade; or (*b*)   under special Schedule D Case III rules (exchange differences, together with financial instrument profits/losses and loan relationship debits/credits, go into a separate category within Schedule D Case III with quite flexible relief for losses) if the items are not for the purposes of a trade (see Chapters 3, 4 and 5).

1.49   There are detailed definitions of the assets, liabilities and currency contracts which fall within the foreign exchange tax rules. The rules do not generally apply to shares or debt convertible into shares (assets only), so these items continue to be taxed under capital gains tax rules (see Chapters 3 and 4).

1.50   There are complex transitional rules to cope with monetary assets, liabilities and currency contracts entered into before commencement of the foreign exchange tax rules which continue to exist after commencement. These transitional rules are needed to move from the 'old' rules treatment (see 1.40 above) to the new accruals based income treatment (see Chapters 4 and 6).

1.51   There are a number of anti-avoidance provisions within the foreign exchange tax rules which can mean in certain circumstances that the ability to deduct an exchange loss is restricted (see Chapter 7).

1.52   Where a company has borrowed in a foreign currency, or entered into a currency contract, to hedge an equity investment in an overseas subsidiary, the borrowing or currency contract falls inside the foreign exchange tax rules but the matching shares do not. This could lead to a company paying tax on a large unrealised exchange gain (on the borrowing or contract) when overall the company's net foreign exchange difference is nil. The foreign exchange tax rules therefore include a 'matching election' under which companies can (if certain conditions are met) elect to defer taxing exchange differences on such hedging transactions until the matching shares are sold (see Chapter 9).

1.53   When first introduced, the new regime provided for trading companies which were effectively operating in a foreign currency to elect (if certain conditions were met) to calculate their relevant taxable trading profits before capital allowances in the appropriate foreign currency. This was known as the 'local currency election' (see Chapter 10, Part II). Now that certain companies are required by law to compute their chargeable profits (other than capital gains/losses) in a currency other than sterling, the facility for making a local currency election has been removed (by substitution of *FA 1993*, old *s 93* with new *s 93*). The new rules have wider application: whereas the local currency election was only available to qualifying trading companies, the new functional currency rules apply in the circumstances prescribed irrespective of the nature of the company's business (see Chapter 10, Part I).

1.54   As outlined in 1.48 above the foreign exchange tax rules tax exchange differences as they accrue. The legislation does, however, include the ability subject to certain restrictions to defer taxing un-realised exchange gains on long-term capital assets and liabilities (the deferral of unrealised exchange gains provisions – see Chapter 8).

1.55   There are special rules within the foreign exchange tax rules to deal with their application to controlled foreign companies, insurance companies, oil companies and partnerships involving both individuals and companies (see Chapter 12).

1.56   All these provisions are covered in more detail in the remaining chapters of this book.

Chapter 2

Legal Framework of the 1993 Finance Act Foreign Exchange Provisions

2.1   The legislative provisions for the taxation of exchange gains and losses are extremely complex and lengthy. In order to attempt to achieve the objective of greater certainty of UK fiscal law, many matters are set out in great detail and the Inland Revenue have published a substantial Explanatory Statement giving their interpretation of the legislation in a variety of circumstances identified during the consultation process.

Primary legislation

2.2   The primary legislation is contained in *FA 1993, ss 92–96, 125–170* and *15–18 Schs*, with additional provisions in *FA 1994, ss 114–116, FA 1995, s 131, FA 1996, ss 82, 83* and *8 Sch, 9 Sch 4, 14 Sch 42, 43, 67–74* and *15 Sch 22–24* and *FA 2000, ss 105–106*.

2.3   However, this primary legislation does not contain many of the detailed aspects of the new rules, which are contained in seven (formerly eight) sets of regulations laid under the provisions set out in the primary legislation. These regulations have the force of law.

2.4   The foreign exchange legislation and regulations deal with the exchange differences on the principal elements of currency contracts. The tax treatment of periodic payments under those contracts is dealt with under the financial instruments legislation, which is contained in *FA 1994, ss 147–177* and *18 Sch*.

2.5   Even after some years of consultation, drafting and redrafting, the Inland Revenue accepted that there are still areas of doubt on interpretation of the foreign exchange and financial instruments legislation and issued an Explanatory Statement covering both of these and running into some 54 pages.

2.6   The *Finance Act 1993* provisions deal with the following areas:

(*a*)   the currency to be used for corporation tax purposes;

(*b*)   the basis on which foreign exchange gains and losses accrue;

(*c*)   trading exchange gains and losses;

(*d*) non-trading exchange gains and losses, including loss relief;

(*e*) anti-avoidance provisions;

(*f*) deferral of tax on unrealised exchange gains;

(*g*) exchange differences on irrecoverable debts;

(*h*) currency contracts – early termination and reciprocal contracts;

(*j*) excess (i.e. non-exchange) gains and losses;

(*k*) local currency to be used;

(*l*) exchange rates to be used;

(*m*) interpretation and definitions; and

(*n*) outline provisions in other areas and the powers to lay regulations to introduce the detailed rules for these.

2.7   By comparison to this massive tranche of legislation, the additions in *FA 1994* were modest. The three sections dealing with foreign exchange differences merely deal with perceived shortcomings in the 1993 legislation.

2.8   *FA 1995* introduced an anti-avoidance provision to prevent groups of companies containing members with different year ends exploiting the capital gains transitional provisions.

2.9   *FA 1996* introduced various changes (mostly by amending the earlier legislation) to align the foreign exchange tax rules with the new corporate and government debt rules included in that *Act*. In particular, it introduced different non-trading loss relief rules applicable to all accounting periods ending on or after 1 April 1996. It also introduced some prospective amendments for the introduction of self-assessment by companies.

2.10   *FA 2000* introduced the changes referred to at 1.45 above and prescribes circumstances in which companies are required to compute and express their profits chargeable to corporation tax in a currency other than sterling.

Regulations

2.11   The eight regulations, which were laid on 16 December 1994 cover many of the important practical aspects of the legislation and are as follows:

(*a*) The Exchange Gains and Losses (Transitional Provisions) Regulations 1994;

(*b*) The Exchange Gains and Losses (Alternative Method of Calculation of Gain or Loss) Regulations 1994;

(c)   The Exchange Gains and Losses (Deferral of Gains and Losses) Regulations 1994;

(d)   The Exchange Gains and Losses (Excess Gains and Losses) Regulations 1994;

(e)   The Local Currency Elections Regulations 1994;

(f)   The Exchange Gains and Losses (Insurance Companies) Regulations 1994;

(g)   The Exchange Gains and Losses (Debts of Varying Amounts) Regulations 1994; and

(h)   The Currency Contracts and Options (Amendment of Enactments) Order 1994.

The Local Currency Elections Regulations 1994 were made under powers which are no longer contained in *FA 1993, ss 93–95*, as those sections are substituted by *FA 2000, s 105*, and so they have lapsed.

2.12   Three further sets of regulations were issued on 21 May 1996 as follows:

(a)   The Exchange Gains and Losses (Transitional Provisions) (Amendment) Regulations 1996;

(b)   The Exchange Gains and Losses (Alternative Method of Calculation of Gain or Loss) (Amendment) Regulations 1996; and

(c)   The Exchange Gains and Losses (Deferral of Gains and Losses) (Amendment) Regulations 1996.

These regulations came into force on 30 June 1996 and have effect from various dates. The original 1994 regulations reproduced in Appendix 4 of this book have been amended for the 1996 regulations with notes on the effective dates.

2.13   In August 2000 the Treasury laid a further set of regulations which make consequential amendments to the Transitional Regulations and the Matching Election Regulation to take account of the provisions of *FA 2000, ss 105–106*. These regulations remain in draft but the modifications (will) have effect in relation to any accounting period of a company beginning on or after 1 January 2000 and for which *ss 105–106* have effect.

Explanatory Statement

2.14   The final set of documentation, The Explanatory Statement, does not have legislative effect. It cannot thus be relied upon in all circumstances and in particular it cannot be taken to apply where taxpayer companies enter into transactions which may be within the letter of the legislation and the Statement but that are outside the spirit of one or both, i.e. a transaction which the Inland Revenue would regard as tax avoidance.

2.15   However, the Statement should be regarded as a reliable basis on which to enter into commercially founded transactions where there may be some doubt or ambiguity in the interpretation of the primary legislation or regulations.

Inland Revenue Tax Bulletins

2.16   Since publication of The Explanatory Statement, the Inland Revenue have issued further guidance on the foreign exchange tax rules in Inland Revenue Tax Bulletin Issue 17 (on controlled foreign companies), Issue 21 (on deep discount and qualifying indexed securities) and Issue 24 (matched assets and liabilities).

Appendices

2.17   For ease of reference, the following text is reproduced as appendices to this book.

Appendix 1   The relevant provisions of *TMA 1970, ICTA 1988, FA 1993, FA 1994, FA 1995, FA 1996* and *FA 2000*

Appendix 2   Inland Revenue Statement of Practice 9/94, Inland Revenue Statement of Practice 4/98 and Inland Revenue Statement of Practice 2000 (Draft), all dealing with the application of the rules to corporate partnerships

Appendix 3   The Inland Revenue Explanatory Statement

Appendix 4   The Regulations

Appendix 5   Extracts from Inland Revenue Bulletin Issues 17, 21 and 24

Appendix 6   Statement of Standard Accounting Practice 20

Appendix 7   Inland Revenue Press Releases

Chapter 3

Basic Rules

Introduction

3.1   The legislation sets out the framework for taxing exchange gains and losses by defining the scope of the new regime in terms of:

● Qualifying Companies.

● Qualifying Assets.

● Qualifying Liabilities.

● Currency Contracts.

● Currency Options.

● Translation Times.

● Accrual Periods.

3.2   It then sets out in detail how exchange gains and losses on qualifying assets, liabilities and currency contracts are to be calculated for tax purposes. Currency options are slightly different because they fall within the 'qualifying payments' rules for interest and currency risk financial instruments, which rely partly on the accounting treatment to determine the taxable profit or loss in a particular accounting period.

Interaction with corporate and government debt rules

3.3   The new corporate and government debt rules state that for accounting periods ending after 31 March 1996 taxable exchange differences should be calculated in accordance with the foreign exchange tax rules in *FA 1993* (as amended by *FA 1996*) and not included in the debits and credits arising on loan relationships [*FA 1996, 9 Sch 4(1)*].

Qualifying companies

3.4   For accounting periods ending before 1 April 1996, any *company* is a 'qualifying company' except:

(*a*)   a company set up for charitable purposes only; and

(*b*) a company which is approved under *ICTA 1988, s 842* as an investment trust. [*FA 1993, s 152*].

For accounting periods ending on or after 1 April 1996, any company is a qualifying company except a company which is approved under (*b*) above.

Also excluded are the trustees of an authorised unit trust (who are deemed by *ICTA 1988, s 468* to be a company for the purpose of taxing the income arising to them). Individuals, and partnerships of individuals, are outside the scope of the legislation and will therefore continue to be subject to tax on the basis of the old rules. The exclusion of companies set up for charitable purposes only under (*a*) above was removed by *FA 1996* on the introduction of the corporate and government debt tax rules. [*FA 1993, s 152(2)* repealed by *FA 1996, 41 Sch, Part V(3)*]. Such companies fall within the foreign exchange tax rules (and the corporate and government debt rules) for accounting periods ending on or after 1 April 1996. See 3.46 below for details of some exemptions from tax for such charitable companies.

Partnerships involving companies and individuals

3.5   There is no special provision under the foreign exchange tax rules for partnerships involving both qualifying companies and individuals or other non-qualifying persons. However, *ICTA 1988, s 114(1)* requires the profits and losses of the trade carried on by such a partnership to be computed *for the purposes of corporation tax* as if the partnership were a company, with the company's share in the profits or losses of the accounting period of the partnership being treated as if it were a separate trade [*ICTA 1988, s 114(2)*] (see 12.55 *et seq.* below). The partnership's profits will therefore be required to take account of the foreign exchange tax rules in order to determine a qualifying company's share of profits or losses. This leaves open the question of how partnership trading profits should be computed for the purposes of assessing the profits or losses of the partners who are individuals. The Inland Revenue Statement of Practice SP 4/98 [see Appendix 2] provides for separate partnership tax computations to be prepared:

(*a*) for partners which are qualifying companies, on the basis that the foreign exchange tax rules apply to the company; and

(*b*) for partners which are not qualifying companies, such as individuals, on the basis that the old rules for taxing exchange gains and losses apply to the company.

The results of each computation are then to be apportioned to the partners in proportion to their profit shares. For the purposes of the financial instrument rules in *FA 1994* there is a provision which explicitly requires this approach: [*FA 1994, s 172*].

Non-resident companies

3.6   If a non-UK resident company is subject to corporation tax in respect of a trade carried on in the UK through a branch or agency, exchange differences on qualifying assets, liabilities or contracts of the branch or agency will be subject to tax under the new rules. In all other circumstances the Inland Revenue regard non-UK resident companies as outside the charge to tax in respect of exchange gains and losses, on the basis that the legislation is expressed in terms of profits attributable to accounting periods and therefore has no application outside the field of corporation tax (see Inland Revenue Explanatory Statement, para 2.5).

3.7   Where the non-resident company draws up its own accounts in a currency other than sterling and

(*a*)   makes a return of accounts for its branch in the UK in the same currency [*FA 1993, s 93(2)(b)*], *or*

(*b*)   makes a return of accounts for its branch in sterling but prepared from financial statements maintained in a foreign currency [*FA 1993, s 93(3)(b)*],

the profits subject to corporation tax must be computed in foreign currency.

Qualifying assets

3.8   A qualifying asset is defined as:

(*a*)   a right to settlement under a 'qualifying' debt (subject to the exceptions mentioned below);

(*b*)   a unit of currency; and

(*c*)   a share or convertible debt held in 'qualifying circumstances'.

[*FA 1993, s 153(1)*].

3.9   A 'qualifying' debt is a debt which is to be settled by payment in money or by the transfer of another debt which is to be settled by monetary payment. [*FA 1993, s 153(11)*]. The definition of qualifying asset broadly corresponds with the definition of 'monetary asset' used in Statement of Standard Accounting Practice 20 ('SSAP 20').

3.10   Assets which are *not* qualifying assets include:

(*a*)   shares in a company *not* held in 'qualifying circumstances' (see 3.11 below);

(*b*)   convertible debt (see 3.12 below);

(*c*)   an amount receivable under a currency contract (currency contracts are dealt with separately in *FA 1993, s 126*);

(*d*) for accounting periods ending before 1 April 1996, interest accrued (but not yet payable) in respect of a debt; and

(*e*) assets representing loan relationships linked to the value of chargeable assets (see 3.15 below).

3.11 Shares and convertible debt held in 'qualifying circumstances' are shares and convertible debt held as trading stock (e.g. by banks and securities dealers) and accounted for as monetary assets denominated in the currency in which the debt is to be settled or the shares were issued. [*FA 1993, s 153(11)*].

Convertible debt

3.12 The definition of convertible debt was amended by *FA 1996, 14 Sch 70* with effect from 1 April 1996. [*FA 1996, 15 Sch 22(4)*]. The revised definition of convertible debt assets that are excluded from the foreign exchange tax rules (and the corporate and government debt rules, except in respect of interest) is to be found in *FA 1996, s 92*. This defines convertible assets as convertible debts where

(*a*) at the time of the debt coming into existence there was more than a negligible likelihood of conversion;

(*b*) conversion is not into a specified cash value of shares (including a value defined by a formula); and

(*c*) the disposal of the asset would not be a trading transaction of the company.

3.13 The most difficult aspect of this definition is the 'cash value' condition, contained in *FA 1996, s 92(1)(c)*. Taken literally, the words would prevent almost any convertible security from qualifying within this legislation. The Inland Revenue Manual, at page CT 12131, gives an extreme example of conversion into shares of the issuer (or any other company) worth a specified value. It appears that, following the cases of *CIR v McGuckian [1994] STC 888* and *Jenks v Dickinson Sp C [1996] SSCD 299 (Sp C 86)*, the Courts would follow a 'purposive' approach to the interpretation of legislation where the literal meaning of the words appears to give an anomalous result. The 'purpose' of *section 92* seems to be to include only those securities which give a genuine equity risk and return to the holder as qualifying convertibles and, in the absence of further clarification from the Inland Revenue or litigation on the point, this is probably the best test to apply.

3.14 Relevant discounted securities (as defined in *FA 1996, 13 Sch 3*) are also incapable of being excluded as convertible debt assets. Before 1 April 1996, convertible debt was defined as a debt on a security which, under the terms of the issue, carried a right of conversion into shares or securities, or the right to acquire additional shares or securities *unless* it was a deep gain security or it was held in qualifying circumstances. [*FA 1993, s 153(4)* and *(11A)* as introduced by *FA 1995, 24 Sch 4*]. For a debt which from 1 April 1996 no longer meets the revised convertible debt definition, the company is treated as having acquired the debt at its market value on 1 April 1996. This establishes the opening basic valuation of the debt for the foreign exchange tax rules. [*FA 1996, 15 Sch 22(4)*].

3.15   With effect from 1 April 1996, the monetary assets excluded from the foreign exchange tax rules are broadened to cover loans linked to the value of chargeable assets as defined by *FA 1996, s 93*. [*FA 1996, 14 Sch 70* and *15, Sch 22(4)*]. Thus, for example, an investment in a loan the repayment amount of which is linked to the value of a property is excluded from the foreign exchange tax rules (and the corporate and government debt rules, except in respect of interest).

Acquisitions and disposals of assets

3.16   There are detailed rules for determining when a company is treated as acquiring or disposing of an asset for the purposes of the foreign exchange tax rules. [*FA 1993, s 154*]. The general rule is that a company acquires or disposes of an asset when it becomes unconditionally entitled to the asset or ceases unconditionally to be entitled to it. However:

(*a*)   any transfer of the asset by way of security is ignored;

(*b*)   an asset which is acquired or disposed of under a contract is acquired or disposed of on the contract date (or the time at which a conditional contract becomes unconditional), without regard to the time the asset is transferred;

(*c*)   where the acquisition is accounted for at an earlier time than the contract date and the company is following normal accounting practice, the accounting treatment overrides the above rule; and

(*d*)   where the company accounts for the acquisition or disposal of a debt on a security or a share at a time which is later than the contract date (e.g. on completion of the contract), and the company is following normal accounting practice, the accounting treatment is followed.

3.17   Where a company has made several acquisitions and disposals of debts on securities, or shares held in qualifying circumstances, of the same kind, holdings acquired at different times are treated as different assets. If the identification of disposals with acquisitions used in the accounts follows normal accountancy practice it will be respected in determining for the purpose of the foreign exchange tax rules the identity of the debts or shares held at a particular time. Exceptions to this will be required to adopt a 'first in first out' approach. [*FA 1993, s 154(9)–(11)*].

Qualifying liabilities

3.18   A qualifying liability is defined as:

(*a*)   a duty to settle a qualifying debt (as defined in 3.9 above);

(*b*)   a provision made by a company in respect of a contingent liability, provided that

    (i)   if the company became subject to the liability, it would be a qualifying debt owed for the purpose of the trade, and

    (ii)   the provision is deductible under normal Schedule D Case I principles; and

(*c*)   a duty to transfer a qualifying debt on a security, or share held in qualifying circumstances, which the company does not own (intended to cover exchange differences on 'short sales' of qualifying assets).

[*FA 1993, s 153(2)*].

3.19   Liabilities which are *not* qualifying liabilities include:

(*a*)   up to 1 April 1996, convertible debt, i.e. a debt on a security which, under the *terms of issue* carries a right of conversion into shares or securities, or a right to acquire additional shares or securities, *unless* it is a deep gain security. [*FA 1993, s 153(6)* and *(11A)* as introduced by *FA 1995, 24 Sch 4*] (see 3.20 below);

(*b*)   an amount payable under a currency contract; and

(*c*)   for accounting periods ending before 1 April 1996, interest accrued in respect of a debt.

3.20   Convertible debt liabilities as defined above were excluded from the foreign exchange tax rules before 1 April 1996. From 1 April 1996, to bring the foreign exchange tax rules into line with the corporate and government debt rules, such liabilities are brought into tax within the foreign exchange tax rules. [*FA 1996, 14 Sch 70(2)* and *15 Sch 22(5)*]. The company is treated as having issued such liabilities on 1 April 1996 at their accounting basic valuation on that day. This establishes the opening basic valuation of the liabilities for the foreign exchange tax rules. [*FA 1996, 15 Sch 22(5)*].

3.21   As in the case of assets, when a company acquires or disposes of a liability by way of transfer, the acquisition or disposal date is the date of the contract (or the date it becomes unconditional, in the case of a conditional contract), and not the transfer date. However, if the liability is recognised at an earlier time in the accounts, and this is in accordance with normal accountancy practice, the earlier date will apply.

3.22   A provision is recognised as a qualifying liability from the time the company makes the provision to the time when it releases it, provided this is in accordance with normal accountancy practice.

3.23   Liabilities in respect of short sales of debts on securities and shares held in qualifying circumstances are treated as ceasing when the company acquires the corresponding debts or shares (i.e. the contract date – see Qualifying assets at 3.8 *et seq.* above). From the date of the sale there will have been a debtor in respect of the agreed sale proceeds, usually in the currency of the debts or shares which were the subject of the sale contract. This will be matched by the 'short sale liability' until the asset is acquired, i.e. an exchange gain on the debtor will be cancelled out by a loss on the 'short sale liability'. When the asset is acquired it will be treated as sold immediately (under the short sale contract) so exchange differences will arise only on the debtor, until settlement of the sale.

Currency contracts

3.24   A currency contract is a contract under which a company becomes entitled to a right and subject to a duty to:

(*a*)   *receive* payment at a specified time of a specified amount of one currency; and

(*b*)   *pay* in exchange and at the same time a specified amount of another currency.

[*FA 1993, s 126(1)* and *FA 1994, s 150(2)*].

3.25   This definition includes forward contracts to buy or sell currency, currency futures and currency swap agreements which involve an exchange of principal at the maturity date. *FA 1993, s 126(1A)* and *FA 1994, s 150(9)* make it clear that the rules for currency contracts also apply to agreements which provide for settlement by means of a single payment representing the difference in value between the two currencies in place of an actual exchange of the currencies specified in the contract. Currency *options* are outside the scope of this definition of 'currency contract'.

3.26   The tax treatment of currency contracts, which is covered partly by the foreign exchange tax rules and partly by the financial instrument rules, and of currency options, is dealt with separately in Chapter 4.

Calculation of exchange gains and losses

3.27   Although the legislation sets out in considerable detail precisely how exchange gains and losses are to be measured for tax purposes, in many situations where a company follows SSAP 20 in accounting for foreign currency transactions the basis used for calculating such gains and losses for accounts purposes will be followed for tax purposes.

Qualifying assets and liabilities of fixed amount

3.28   For qualifying assets and liabilities whose amounts do not vary, an exchange gain or loss is found by calculating the difference between the *local currency equivalent* of the *basic valuation* of the asset or liability at the beginning and end of an *accrual period*. Generally this means finding the change in the local currency equivalent of the foreign currency book cost of the asset or liability in each accounting period, or part of an accounting period, for which the asset or liability was held by the company. The terms used have the following meanings:

(*a*)   *Basic valuation*
This is the underlying value which a company, following normal accountancy practice, puts on the asset or liability when it becomes entitled or subject to it. This will normally be opening book value expressed in the *nominal currency* of the debt or shares (i.e. normally the currency in which a debt is to be settled or shares are denominated). [*FA 1993, s 159*].

(*b*)   *Local currency*
This is the currency in which a company is required to prepare and express its profits subject to corporation tax, i.e. sterling or relevant foreign currency (see 10.18).

Before the introduction of the functional currency rules in *FA 2000*, 'local currency' meant sterling, except in the case of transactions connected with a trade in respect of which a local currency election had been made. Where a local currency election is in force, the 'local currency' is the elected currency. [*FA 1993, s 149*]

(*c*)   *Local currency equivalent*
This is the value of an asset or liability expressed in sterling or relevant foreign currency. It is found by translating the basic valuation (see (*a*) above) into the local currency at the exchange rate appropriate to the translation time. [*FA 1993, s 164(5)*]

(*d*)   *Translation time*
A 'translation time' is a time at which a translation into sterling (or other local currency) must be made in respect of a qualifying asset, liability or currency contract. There will be a translation time:

(i)   immediately after the company becomes entitled to the asset or currency contract or becomes subject to the liability;

(ii)   immediately before the company ceases to be entitled to the asset or currency contract or subject to the liability; and

(iii)   at the time when each intermediate accounting period ends.

[*FA 1993, s 158*].

(*e*) *Accrual period*
An 'accrual period' in relation to a particular asset, liability or currency contract is the interval between one translation time and the next. Except in the accounting period of acquisition or disposal of the asset etc, it will therefore coincide with the company's own accounting period. [*FA 1993, s 158*].

Basic valuation of assets and liabilities

3.29   Exchange gains and losses are calculated for the purposes of the foreign exchange tax rules by translating into local currency the *basic valuation* of a qualifying asset or liability. The general rule is that the basic valuation is the value placed on the asset or liability for accounts purposes immediately after the qualifying company acquired or became subject to it. The main exceptions to this rule are as follows:

(*a*)   If the valuation used by the company does not comply with normal accountancy practice, the valuation required by normal accounting practice will be used.

(*b*)   If the company expresses the value in a currency other than the *nominal currency* of the asset or liability (see below), it must be translated into the nominal currency using the London closing exchange rate for the date of acquisition.

(*c*)   The basic valuation of a liability in respect of a short sale of a qualifying debt on a security or a share or shares held in qualifying circumstances' (i.e. on trading account) is the consideration specified in the short sale contract.

(*d*)   If a qualifying asset is a debt on a security which is subject to the accrued income scheme as a result of a transfer before 1 April 1996 [*ICTA 1988, s 710*] the basic valuation is the consideration payable for the security, adjusted to exclude the interest element included in the price as calculated under *ICTA 1988, s 713(2)(b) or (3)(b)*. In calculating the basic valuation any sterling amounts are to be translated into the nominal currency using the London closing rate for the date of the contract to acquire the security. The accrued income scheme ceased to have effect from 1 April 1996. From that date the basic valuation of an asset transferred with accrued interest is the total consideration for the transfer less the accrued interest transferred (the exchange differences on the interest are dealt with as a separate item, see 3.48 below). [*FA 1996, 14 Sch 73*].

[*FA 1993, s 159*].

Nominal currency and settlement currency

3.30   The *nominal currency* of a debt, whether an asset or a liability, is the *settlement currency* of the debt. *Settlement currency* is normally the currency in which ultimate settlement of the debt falls to be made. However, if the amount of the currency to be paid in settlement is to be determined by reference to an amount of another currency, the settlement currency is the other currency. [*FA 1993, s 160* and *161*].

Example 1

A company borrows €50m under an agreement which provides for repayment in sterling, the amount repayable being the sterling equivalent of €50m, calculated using the €/£ spot exchange rate in force at close of business two days before the due date for repayment of the debt. Although the debt is repayable in sterling, its 'settlement currency' is the euros because the amount of sterling to be repaid is calculated by reference to an amount of euros.

Sterling assets and liabilities

3.31   The definitions of 'qualifying asset' and 'qualifying liability' make no reference to foreign currency, and include sterling debts which are within the terms of the definition. If, as is usually the case, sterling is the company's local currency, there will be no change in the local currency equivalent of the basic valuation of the sterling asset or liability, and therefore no taxable exchange gain or loss can arise. The position is different, however, if a company borrows sterling for the purpose of a trade which has, say, a US dollar local currency, e.g. because it makes up its accounts in US dollars. The local currency (US dollar) equivalent of the sterling borrowing would then depend on the £/US$ exchange rate and taxable US dollar exchange gains and losses could arise. Sterling assets and liabilities may be affected by the transitional rule for trading assets and liabilities taxed on a realisation basis pre-commencement (see 6.44 below).

Exchange rate to be used

3.32   Where foreign currency items are translated into sterling (or another local currency) for accounts purposes at an arm's length rate of exchange, that rate will also be used to determine the local currency equivalent at a translation time of:

(*a*)   the basic valuation of an asset or liability;

(*b*)   the nominal amount of a debt outstanding; and

(*c*)   an amount of currency.

[*FA 1993, s 150* and *151*].

3.33   An 'arm's length rate' is an exchange rate which might reasonably be expected to be agreed between person's dealing at arm's length. It is not defined in terms of a spot rate of exchange and where, in accordance with normal accountancy practice, an item has been translated in the accounts at a forward exchange rate that rate will be used to calculate the taxable exchange gain or loss, provided it is an arm's length rate.

3.34   Where an arm's length rate is not used in the accounts, the 'London closing exchange rate' for the two currencies for the day on which the translation time falls is to be used. [*FA 1993, s 150(7)*]. 'London closing exchange rate' is not defined, although it appears elsewhere in the Taxes Acts (for example, *ICTA 1988, s 716(6)* in relation to the application of the accrued income scheme to foreign currency securities). In practice a published rate of exchange based on rates applying at the close of business on the London markets is likely to be accepted. The Inland Revenue Explanatory Statement, para 2.4 refers to rates published by 'reputable independent bodies' such as Reuters, the Bank of England and the *Financial Times*.

3.35   For translation times occurring within an accounting period, an average rate of exchange which is used for accounts purposes may also be used for the calculation of taxable exchange gains and losses, provided the following conditions are met:

(*a*)   the rate used represents the average of arm's length rates for *all* the days in a period; and

(*b*)   the arm's length rate for any given day in the period (other than the first) is not significantly different from the arm's length rate for the previous day.

[*FA 1993, s 150(9)*].

3.36   These conditions are broadly consistent with SSAP 20, which permits the use of an average rate to translate individual transactions into local currency using the 'temporal method' of accounting for foreign currency transactions for a period if the rates do not fluctuate significantly in the period (SSAP 20, para 46). The average rate used for tax and accounting purposes can be for any period, including the whole of the accounting period.

3.37   Where a company's normal accounting practice is to use an average rate of exchange for a period, but it does not satisfy condition 3.35(*a*) above, the average of the London closing exchange rates for all the days in the period is to be used (provided the rates do not vary significantly from one day to the next). [*FA 1993, s 150(12)*]. This would apply where, for example, the company used the mean of the arm's length exchange rates at the beginning and end of each month to translate transactions undertaken in the month.

Example 2

A company makes up its accounts to 31 December. On 30 June 1996, when £1 = $1.50, it borrows $150,000, and records the liability in its books at £100,000. The $150,000 are placed on deposit and on 7 July 1996, when £1 = $1.51, they are used to purchase a piece of equipment. On 31 December, when £1 = $1.4, the borrowing is retranslated into sterling at the closing rate of exchange and is shown in the balance sheet as £107,143. The cost of the equipment is recorded at the historical exchange rate (£1 = $1.51) and appears in the balance sheet at £99,338. Exchange gains and losses calculated under the foreign exchange tax rules are the same as those which are recognised in the accounts. i.e.:

	£
$150,000 borrowing	
Translation time 2: Sterling value at 31.12.96 $150,000 @ $1.40	(107,143)
Translation time 1: Sterling value at 30.6.96 $150,000 @ $1.50	(100,000)
Exchange loss	(7,143)
$150,000 bank deposit	
Translation time 2: Sterling value at 7.7.96 $150,000 @ $1.51	99,338
Translation time 1: Sterling value at 30.6.96 $150,000 @ $1.50	100,000
Exchange loss	(662)

Example 3

A UK trading company sells goods in October 1996 for $225,000. The debt is outstanding at 31 December 1996, the company year end. The company accounts for the sale using the average exchange rate for October, when £1 = $1.50, and retranslates the unpaid debtor for balance sheet purposes at the closing exchange rate of £1 = $1.40.

The average exchange rate for October is the average of the daily closing exchange rates (mid price) for the month, and there were no dramatic exchange rate movements in the year, so the exchange gain recognised in the accounts will be the same as taxable gain calculated under the foreign exchange tax rules:

	£
Translation time 2: debtor at closing rate $225,000 @ $1.40	160,714
Translation time 1: debtor at October average rate $225,000 @ $1.50	150,000
Exchange gain	10,714

Exchange gains and losses on debts whose amounts vary

3.38   There are special rules for calculating exchange gains and losses on debts which increase or decrease in amount during an accrual period.

3.39   The local currency equivalent at the start of the accrual period of the amount of a debt which is a qualifying asset is adjusted by adding to it the local currency equivalent of any increases in the debt (at the time of the increase) and deducting from it the local currency equivalent of any decrease. The adjusted figure is deducted from the local currency equivalent of the debt at the end of the accrual period to give the exchange gain or loss attributable to the accrual period. [*FA 1993, s 127*].

Example 4

DM bank account (qualifying asset).

Date	Amount	Exchange Rate	Increase/ (decrease)	£ equivalent
	DM	DM/£	DM	
1.1.96	150,000	3.0	–	50,000
31.3.96	175,000	2.9	25,000	8,621
31.7.96	120,000	2.6	(55,000)	(21,154)
31.12.96	120,000	2.7	–	44,444

The exchange gain is calculated as follows:

		£
Local currency equivalent 31.12.96		44,444
Less local currency equivalent 1.1.96,	50,000	
adjusted for increases and decreases	8,621	
	(21,154)	
		37,467
Exchange gain		6,977

If the company prepares accounts under SSAP 20 using the 'temporal method' of translation, this will be equal to the accounting exchange gain. The rules work in the same way for debts which are qualifying liabilities except, of course, that the signs are reversed.

Example 5

US$ current account with overseas parent company.

Date	Amount	Exchange Rate	Increase/ (decrease)	£ equivalent
	$	$/£	$	
1.4.97	(100,000)	2.0	–	(50,000)
30.6.97	(75,000)	1.9	25,000	13,158
31.10.97	(180,000)	1.8	(105,000)	(58,333)
31.3.98	(180,000)	1.75	–	(102,857)

The exchange loss is calculated as follows:

		£
Local currency equivalent 31.3.98		(102,857)
Less local currency equivalent 1.4.97	(50,000)	
adjusted for increases and decreases	13,158	
	(58,333)	
		(95,175)
Exchange loss		(7,682)

3.40   With effect from 1 April 1996, debts on which a discount or premium accrues are treated as variable debts in respect of which the rules outlined above apply. [*FA 1996, 14 Sch 67* and *15 Sch 22(2)*]. Hence the rules in respect of deep discount securities, deep gain securities and qualifying indexed securities (see 3.54 below) do not apply from 1 April 1996. The debt is considered to increase or decrease each time the premium or discount is accrued. The value of such debts held on 1 April 1996 is determined on the assumption that the amendment has always had effect. [*FA 1996, 15 Sch 22(3)*].

Example 6

A company invested in a zero coupon deep discount security issued at $100m on 1 January 1996 and redeemable at $121m on 31 December 1997. The discount is accrued on a straight line basis i.e. $10.5m in each year's accounts.

Exchange rates are:

1 January 1996	£1 = $1.55
31 December 1996	£1 = $1.6
31 December 1997	£1 = $1.5

The taxable exchange differences are as follows:

1996	$m
Basic valuation 1 January 1996	100
Basic valuation 1 April 1996	100
Basic valuation 31 December 1996	110.5
Taxable exchange difference 1996:	
$110.5m/1.6	69.06
$100m/1.55	(64.50)
$10.5m /1.6	(6.56)
Exchange loss in 1996	(2.00)

1997

Basic valuation 31 December 1996	110.5
Basic valuation 31 December 1997	121

Taxable exchange difference 1997:

$121m/1.5	80.67
$110.5m/1.6	(69.06)
$10.5m/1.5	(7.00)
Exchange gain in 1997	4.61

Trading exchange gains and losses

3.41   There are different rules for the tax treatment of exchange gains and losses which relate to transactions undertaken for the purpose of a trade, and those which do not. If, throughout an accrual period, a qualifying asset, liability or contract is held or owed solely for the purpose of the company's trade:

(*a*)   an exchange gain calculated in accordance with the rules outlined above is treated as a taxable trade receipt of the accounting period in which the accrual period falls; and

(*b*)   an exchange loss is treated as a deductible trading expense of the accounting period. [*FA 1993, s 128*].

3.42   If the asset, liability or contract is held or owed partly for the purpose of the trade and partly for some other purpose, a gain or loss is to be apportioned on a 'just and reasonable' basis, and the proportion relating to the trade treated as described above. The non-trade proportion is dealt with under the rules for 'non-trading' exchange gains and losses described below. The rules apply to both capital and revenue transactions, and therefore disapply both the capital/revenue distinction [*ICTA 1988, s 74(f)*] and the non-deductibility of dual purpose expenditure. [*ICTA 1988, s 74(a)*]. *FA 1993, s 128(10)* makes it clear that the provisions of *ICTA 1988, s 74* are overridden for this purpose.

3.43   Many exchange gains and losses which arise on transactions of a revenue nature undertaken for the purpose of a trade are taken into account in calculating taxable trading profits under the general principles of Schedule D Case I. To avoid double counting, any exchange gain or loss arising on a qualifying asset or liability or on a currency contract is excluded from the computation of trading profits, except by virtue of being taxable under *FA 1993, s 128*.

3.44   There is no definition in the legislation of 'for the trade'. Whether or not a qualifying asset, qualifying liability or currency contract is for a trade has to be decided on the case law principles on what is trading. The Inland Revenue Manual on Foreign Exchange asks Inspectors to consider whether the transactions are ancillary to the trade of the company (and hence are trading) or, if not, to consider the purpose of the transactions on the basic case law principles of what is trading. For example, a forward contract to hedge the purchase price of trading supplies would be ancillary to the trade and so exchange differences could be trading whereas a loan to hedge the value of some foreign currency shares held as an investment would not be trading.

Non-trading exchange gains and losses

3.45   For accounting periods ending after 31 March 1996, any part of an exchange gain or loss calculated in accordance with the rules of *FA 1993, ss 125–127*, described above, which is not treated as a trade receipt or expense is subject to tax under the rules for 'non-trading' exchange gains and losses:

(*a*)   All non-trading exchange gains and losses which have accrued in an accounting period are aggregated with non-trading profits and losses under the financial instrument rules and non-trading loan relationship credits/debits.

(*b*)   If the net result is a gain, it is chargeable to tax as income under Schedule D Case III.

(*c*)   If the net result is a loss (a 'non-trading deficit'), this is deductible under special rules which provide for:

 (i)   offset against the company's profits of the accounting period of any description;

 (ii)   group relief against profits of other companies in the group;

 (iii)   carry back against Schedule D Case III profits (from the same categories); and

 (iv)   carry forward against non-trading income of later periods.

[*FA 1996, s 83* and *8 Sch*].

3.46   The rules for non-trading losses are described in more detail in Chapter 5 below. Companies set up for charitable purposes are only taxed on trading exchange differences because they are exempted from taxation under Schedule D Case III by *ICTA 1988, s 505(1)(c)(ii)* and they do not get relief for non-trading deficits. [*FA 1996, s 83(5)*].

3.47   The treatment outlined in 3.45 above for non-trading exchange differences (introduced by *FA 1996*) only applies to accounting periods ending after 31 March 1996. For accounting periods ending on or before 31 March 1996 the rules are as follows:

(*a*)   All non-trading exchange gains and losses which have accrued in an accounting period are aggregated together with non-trading profits and losses under the financial instrument rules.

(*b*)   If the net result is a gain, it is chargeable to tax as income under Schedule D Case VI.

(*c*)   If the net result is a loss, this is deductible under special rules which provide for:

   (i)   offset against the company's profits of the accounting period of any description;

   (ii)   group relief against profits of other companies in the group;

   (iii)   carry back against non-trading exchange gains of the preceding three years; and

   (iv)   carry forward against non-trading exchange gains of later periods.

There are transitional provisions to deal with losses brought forward from or carried back to accounting periods ending on or before 31 March 1996. These are described in more detail in Chapter 5.

Exclusion of debts representing income or charges on income

3.48   For accounting periods ending before 1 April 1996, there are several provisions which are intended to prevent double counting of debts representing income or charges on income:

(*a*)   interest accrued in respect of a debt is not part of the debt [*FA 1993, s 153(12)*];

(*b*)   a company acquires an asset or becomes subject to a liability representing interest at the time by which the interest has to be paid [*FA 1993, s 153(4B)* and *(5B)*];

(*c*)   where a non-trading asset comprises a right to receive income of any description (e.g. interest, dividends), any non-trading exchange gain or loss is ignored [*FA 1993, s 129(7)*]; and

(*d*)   where a qualifying liability is a debt for which relief is allowed as a charge on income under *ICTA 1988, s 338*, or for which relief would be allowed as a charge if the debt was settled (e.g. annual interest), the exchange gain or loss is ignored [*FA 1993, s 128(10A)* and *(10B)* (as introduced by *FA 1995, 24 Sch 2*) and *s 129(8)*].

3.49   For accounting periods ending on or after 1 April 1996 (in line with the introduction of the corporate and government debt rules) exchange differences on accrued interest are taxable under the foreign exchange tax rules. Exchange differences are similarly taxable from when interest becomes due and payable (if it is not paid) if the company recognises interest on a mark to market basis in its accounts. [*FA 1996, 14 Sch 71* and *72*]. Thus the foreign exchange differences are taxed over the same period as the interest itself is taxable under the corporate and government debt rules.

3.50 There is one exception to the accruals or mark to market treatment of the exchange differences. This arises when interest may only be deducted under the corporate and government debt rules when it is paid. This occurs when interest on a loan from a connected party not within the corporate and government debt rules is paid more than twelve months after the end of the accounting period in which it is recognised for accounts purposes. In such a case the interest is deductible only when paid and the foreign exchange tax rules follow this treatment. Thus the exchange differences on the accruing interest are not taxable and the eventual interest payment is translated for tax purposes at the spot rate on the date of payment. [*FA 1996, 9 Sch 2* and *14 Sch 72*].

Irrecoverable debts

3.51 Where all or part of a debt is irrecoverable, no taxable or deductible exchange gains or losses are accrued on the irrecoverable portion of the debt. [*FA 1993, s 144*]. The detailed rules for irrecoverable debts are dealt with in Chapter 11.

Qualifying assets which are unremittable

[*MR3* under *FA 1993, 15 Sch*].

3.52 The treatment of qualifying assets which are overseas debts which cannot be remitted to the United Kingdom is described in Chapter 11.

Prevention of double counting under chargeable gains rules

3.53 A number of qualifying assets within the foreign exchange tax rules could also be subject to tax on exchange movements under general chargeable gains principles. For currency, this double counting is prevented by *FA 1993, 17 Sch 2* and *3*. For debts and debts on securities, the double counting is prevented by *FA 1993, 17 Sch 4–6* for accounting periods ending on or before 31 March 1996. For accounting periods ending after 31 March 1996, all 'loan relationships' (as defined in *FA 1996, s 81* for the corporate and government debt rules) are defined as qualifying corporate bonds (*CGTA 1992, s 117* as amended by *FA 1996, 14 Sch 61*). Debts and debts on security which are qualifying assets under the foreign exchange tax rules and which could potentially be subject to chargeable gain taxation (i.e. such assets which are not trading items) meet the loan relationship definition and so are excluded from chargeable gains taxation by this provision. (*FA 1993, 17 Sch 4–6* is thus repealed for accounting periods ending after 31 March 1996.) The foreign exchange movement part of any gain or loss on the disposal of non-qualifying assets (e.g. shares not held in qualifying circumstances) continues to be taxed under the principles established in *Bentley v Pike, 55 TC 590* (see 1.18).

Deep gain, deep discount and qualifying indexed securities

3.54   Before 1 April 1996, deep gain securities fell within the scope of the definitions of qualifying assets and liabilities. There are special provisions in *FA 1989, 11 Sch 5A* which ensure that there is no double counting of exchange differences by excluding them from the amount treated as income on the transfer or redemption of such a security. There are similar provisions for deep discount securities (see 3.40 above).

3.55   The basic valuation of deep gain, deep discount and qualifying indexed securities for the purposes of calculating exchange differences before 1 April 1996 will usually be the issue price or cost of acquisition (see Explanatory Statement, paras 2.8–2.10 and 3.40 above).

Introduction of the euro

3.56   The European Commission indicated that the transition to single currency should be a tax neutral event. However, the application of existing tax principles to items arising as a result of the conversion process gives rise to anomalies and additional potential liabilities in both participating and non-participating States.

3.57   The existing UK corporate tax rules can accommodate the transition to the euro better than those in many of the other EU States. Nevertheless, on 21 January 1998 the Inland Revenue issued a Press Release (PR 5/98) which clarified some areas of potential difficulty and noted that any remaining anomalies would be resolved shortly. In a further Press Release dated 29 July 1998 (PR 110/98) the Government confirmed its approach was to ensure that, as far as possible, the introduction of the single currency in other Member States would not give rise to a charge or loss in the UK which would not otherwise have arisen. Various points of detail are addressed in these press releases which are reproduced in Appendix 7.

3.58   The *Finance Act 1998* made provision for the Inland Revenue to issue regulations where necessary in respect of the introduction of the euro. These regulations were published in December 1998 and are reproduced in Appendix 4. They appear largely to have made the technical changes necessary to give effect to many of the anomalies addressed in the press releases.

3.59   From the UK's perspective, the euro must be treated like any other foreign currency, and the foreign exchange tax legislation therefore applies equally to euro-denominated transactions. The following points are worth noting:

(*a*)   the table of exchange rates irrevocably fixing the rate at which participating currencies convert to the euro is an arm's length rate for the purposes of *FA 1993, s 150*;

(*b*) any foreign exchange movements arising in the accounts of a company on substitution of the euro for participating national currencies are taxable following normal rules;

(*c*) the introduction of the euro is, of itself, not generally a 'realisation' event for UK tax purposes, and the regulations confirm that no gains or losses will crystallise simply as a result of the redenomination of existing assets, liabilities or contracts into euros [*ESCR 7–11*];

(*d*) receipt of cash payments made on redenomination (or renominalisation) of shares and securities will not be treated as a part disposal of the security, provided that the cash payment is small as compared with the value of the security concerned; instead the amount will be deducted from the base cost on eventual disposal [*ESCR 39*];

(*e*) local currency elections made by reference to participating currencies automatically convert to euros (see 10.36);

(*f*) relief for the costs of redenominating *existing* securities into euros is available to both traders (under Schedule D Case I) and investment and life insurance companies [*ESCR 4–6*].

3.60 It is important to note that since 1 January 1999 all participating currencies have provided a perfect economic hedge for each other as they are irrevocably linked to each other via the euro. A liability in any participating currency can therefore be used to formally match an asset in any other participating currency. The detailed provisions for matching assets and liabilities are discussed in Chapter 9.

Chapter 4

Currency Contracts and Options

Introduction

4.1   Foreign currency financial instruments such as forward sales and purchases of currency, currency futures and currency swap agreements are dealt with partly under the *FA 1993* foreign exchange legislation ('the foreign exchange tax rules') and partly under the rules for the taxation of interest and currency risk financial instruments contained in *FA 1994* ('the financial instrument rules'). In general, the foreign exchange tax rules deal with the taxation of principal receipts and payments, and the financial instrument rules deal with periodic payments made under the contracts. Currency options are dealt with only in the financial instrument rules.

4.2   The rules dealing with these transactions determine:

(*a*)   how to calculate the taxable exchange gain or loss for an accounting period on a currency contract; and

(*b*)   when, and to what extent 'qualifying payments' under a currency contract or option should be recognised as a taxable profit or deductible loss under the financial instrument rules.

4.3   The basis of taxing profits and allowing relief for losses which have been calculated in this way is the same as that applying to exchange gains and losses of qualifying assets and liabilities (see Chapter 3):

(*a*)   If the contract or option was held for the purpose of a trade the gain or loss is treated as a receipt or expense of the trade.

(*b*)   If the contract was not held for the purpose of a trade, the gain or loss is included in the calculation of the Schedule D Case III income or 'non-trading deficit'. For accounting periods ending before 1 April 1996, the gain or loss is included in the calculation of the overall 'non-trading exchange gain or loss' of the accounting period, and taxed or relieved under the special rules for such gains and losses.

4.4   The taxable profit or deductible loss to be recognised in a particular accounting period on a currency contract or option which is undertaken on arm's length terms will usually be the profit or loss recognised in the accounts, provided 'normal accounting practice' has been followed in relation to the currency contract or option in question. [Inland Revenue Explanatory Statement, para 7.2].

Financial instrument rules

Acceptable accounting methods

4.5   The financial instrument rules in *FA 1994, ss 147–177* allow the profits and losses on instruments within those rules to be based on the accounts profits and losses provided the basis of accounting is either:

(*a*)   a mark to market basis, or

(*b*)   an accruals basis

which satisfies the requirements of *FA 1994, s 156*. The key requirement is that the company has followed normal accountancy practice in its choice of accounting method for a particular financial instrument. If the accounting treatment adopted does not meet the requirements of *FA 1994, s 156*, the company must calculate taxable profits and losses on the basis of an accounting treatment which does come within *FA 1994, s 156*.

Calculation of taxable profits and losses

4.6   Although the financial instrument element of the taxable profit or loss on a currency contract or option would normally be given by the accounts profit or loss, *FA 1994, s 155* sets out specific rules for calculating the taxable profit based on the accounts figures. The profit or loss is

'Amount A' − 'Amount B'

with Amounts A and B having different definitions depending on the accounting treatment. It is important to be aware of the meaning of Amounts A and B because many of the provisions requiring adjustments to the accounts figures are expressed in terms of additions to, or deductions from, Amount A or Amount B.

Mark to market basis of accounting

4.7   Where a company adopts an acceptable mark to market basis of accounting:

(*a*)   Amount A is the aggregate of

- qualifying payments (see 4.14 below) *receivable* which fall due in the accounting period; and

- any increase in the accounts value of the contract during the accounting period; and (*b*)   Amount B is the aggregate of

- qualifying payments *payable* by the company which fall due in the accounting period; and

- any reduction in the accounts value of the contract during the accounting period.

Taken together, the above amounts are equal to the mark to market profit or loss of the accounting period.

Accruals basis of accounting

4.8   Where a company adopts an acceptable accruals basis of accounting:

(*a*)   Amount A is the aggregate of amounts accrued in the accounting period in respect of qualifying payments receivable by the company (i.e. income accruals); and

(*b*)   Amount B is the aggregate of amounts accrued in the accounting period in respect of qualifying payments payable by the company (i.e. expense accruals).

Again, it will be seen that a net result equals the profit or loss accrued in the accounting period in respect of the contract.

Currency contracts

Definitions of currency contract

4.9   The term 'currency contract' is defined in both the foreign exchange tax rules and the financial instrument rules and includes:

(*a*)   forward contracts to buy, sell, or exchange amounts of foreign currency at a specified future date;

(*b*)   exchange traded currency futures; and

(*c*)   currency swap agreements.

Definition under foreign exchange tax rules

4.10   A 'currency contract' is a contract under which a qualifying company:

'(*a*)   becomes entitled to a right and subject to a duty to receive payment at a specified time of a specified amount of one currency (the first currency); and

(*b*)   it becomes entitled to a right and subject to a duty to pay in exchange and at the same time a specified amount of another currency (the second currency).'

[*FA 1993, s 126(1)*].

4.11   Although this definition is expressed in terms of an exchange of amounts in two currencies, it also includes 'net payment' contracts which are settled by a payment to or by the qualifying company of an amount designed to represent any difference in value at the specified time between the two amounts of currency. [*FA 1993, s 126(1A)*].

4.12   A 'contract for differences' which provides for a payment representing the difference in value between specified amounts of different currencies, but no right or obligation to actually exchange those currencies, will also be a currency contract under the foreign exchange rules. Taxable exchange gains and losses will be calculated as if the contract provided for the relevant exchange of currencies. [*FA 1993, s 126(6) and (7)*].

Definition under the financial instrument rules

4.13   An agreement which meets the definition of 'currency contract' under the foreign exchange tax rules will also be a 'currency contract' under the financial instrument rules provided that the only transfers of money (or money's worth) provided for under the contract in addition to the exchange of currencies referred to in the foreign exchange rules definition (the final exchange of currencies) fall within the following categories [*FA 1994, s 150(1)*]:

(*a*)   *Exchange of interest-based payments*
'A right to receive at a time specified in the contract a payment, the amount of which falls to be determined (wholly or mainly) by applying a specified rate of interest to a specified amount of the first currency,' and 'a duty to make at a time specified in the contract a payment, the amount of which falls to be determined (wholly or mainly) by applying a specified rate of interest to a specified amount of the second currency'. [*FA 1994, s 150(3)*].

(*b*)   *Earlier exchange of currency*
The receipt at a specified time (which is before the final exchange of currencies is to take place) of a specified amount of the second currency in exchange for payment at the same time of a specified amount of the first currency. [*FA 1994, s 150(4)*].

(*c*)   *Contract fees and costs*
This includes:

   (i)   a payment as consideration for entering into the contract;

   (ii)   a 'reasonable fee for arranging the contract';

   (iii)   'reasonable costs incurred in respect of a contract';

(iv) 'a payment for securing, or made in consequence of, the variation or termination of a contract'; and

(v) compensation for failing to comply with the terms of the contract.

[*FA 1994, s 151*].

(*d*) A single payment in settlement of the obligation to exchange amounts of the first and second currencies at the end of the contract or during the life of the contract under (*b*) above. [*FA 1994, s 150(9)*].

4.14 Payments and receipts within (*a*) and (*c*) above, and single payments based on the difference in value of the specified amounts of currency are 'qualifying payments' which are taxable under the financial instrument rules. Payments within category (*c*) above are also 'qualifying payments' whether or not made under the currency contract, as are payments for the acquisition or disposal of the contract. Exchanges of amounts of currency both at the end of the contract, and during the life of the contract under (*b*) above are 'currency contracts', the exchange gains and losses on which are dealt with under the foreign exchange tax rules for currency contracts.

4.15 Where a currency contract agreement provides for payments which fall outside categories (*a*) to (*d*) above, it will not be a 'qualifying contract' under the financial instrument rules and will therefore not be subject to taxation in accordance with those rules. However, 'non-qualifying' terms may be disregarded for this purpose if the present value of the non-qualifying term is small compared with the present value of the qualifying payments at the time the contract is entered into (or if appropriate, the time that its terms are varied). The Standing Committee debate on this provision indicates that 'small' for this purpose will include an amount which is less than 5% of the aggregate value of qualifying payments, without precluding a larger amount from being regarded as 'small'. For this purpose, the aggregate value of qualifying and non-qualifying payments is based on gross value (i.e. negative values are treated as positive values).

4.16 A 'contract for differences' which provides for a payment representing the difference in value between specified amounts of different currencies, but no right or obligation to actually exchange those currencies, will also be a currency contract under the financial instrument rules provided that the only other transfers of money (or money's worth) provided for under the contract are those referred to in 4.13 above. [*FA 1994, s 150(11)*].

Forward currency market transactions

4.17 The most common form of currency contract is the forward purchase or sale of currency, in which a company contracts with a counterparty, usually a bank, to buy or sell a specific amount of foreign currency at a pre-determined price for delivery on a future date. For example, the company may agree to purchase US$1,600,000 for £1m, for delivery in twelve months' time, when the current spot exchange rate is US$1.608/£. The difference between the exchange rate in the forward contract (forward rate) and the current rate of exchange (spot rate), known as the forward discount or premium, reflects the difference in interest rates in the two currencies. The only payment and receipt under a forward contract are the exchanges of currency at the end, but the accounting treatment may give rise to a deemed 'qualifying payment' which is dealt with under the financial instrument rules (see 4.21 below).

Calculation of taxable exchange gain or loss under FA 1993, s 126

4.18   *FA 1993, s 126* contains the rules for calculating the taxable exchange gain or loss on a currency contract. The contracts will provide for the receipt of an amount of one currency (the first currency) and the payment of an amount of another currency (the second currency). As in the case of qualifying assets and liabilities, there will be a 'translation time' when the company enters into the contract, when the contract matures, and at the end of any accounting period which falls within the term of the contract. [*FA 1993, s 158*]. The taxable exchange gain or loss of an 'accrual period' (i.e. the interval between two consecutive translation times – *FA 1993, s 158(4)*) is the aggregate of:

(*a*)   the difference between the local currency equivalent of the amount of the first currency at the first and second translation times; and

(*b*)   the difference in the local currency equivalent at the two translation times of the amount of the second currency.

4.19   The 'local currency' of a company is normally sterling. [*FA 1993, s 149(1)*]. An exception to this is where a company has made a local currency election to compute the taxable profits of a trade, or part of a trade, in a foreign currency (see Chapter 10). If a currency contract is held for the purpose of that trade (or part of the trade), the 'local currency' will be the currency in which taxable trading profits are calculated.

4.20   A 'local currency equivalent' of a currency amount is found by translating that amount into the local currency. The result will depend on the exchange rate which is used in the accounts, and whether that is an arm's length rate of exchange. [*FA 1993, s 150*]. Provided the company is following normal accounting practice, the following exchange rates used for accounts purposes may be used for calculating the local currency equivalent of the currency amounts:

(*a*)   The forward rate appropriate to the time of translation and the remaining life of the contract.

(*b*)   The spot rate appropriate to the time of translation.

(*c*)   The exchange rate implied in the currency contract.

(*d*)   For translation other than at the end of an accounting period, the average rate of exchange for a period of time which includes the translation time.

In these circumstances, the taxable profit or loss on the contract will be the amount recognised in the accounts.

Example 1 – Translation using spot exchange rates

Company A Ltd, which has $ sales and $ trade debtors entered into a twelve-month forward contract to sell $ for sterling as a general hedge against its $ sales. Its accounting policy is not to recognise exchange rate movements on forward contracts used for hedging foreign currency sales until the earlier of the year end and the maturity date of the contract, when the foreign currency payable under the contract is translated into sterling at the spot rate of exchange at the year end or maturity. Details of the forward contract and relevant exchange rates are as follows:

	Spot exchange rate
Contract entered into on 1 July 1996	$1.6/£
End of accounting period 31 December 1996	$1.7/£
Contract matures on 30 June 1997	$1.65/£

Contract details:
> Sell $1,550
> Buy £1,000
> Settlement date 30 June 1997

On 1 July 1996 the contract is not recognised in the accounts, in accordance with normal accounting practice, so the rate implied in the contract is used for the purpose of finding the local currency equivalent under *FA 1993, s 150(11)*. On 31 December 1996 the accounts profit on the contract is calculated as follows:

	£
£1,000 receivable under contract	1,000
Less $1,550 payable under contract @ $1.7/£	(912)
Unrealised profit on contract per accounts	88

1996

Applying *section 126* we have:

First currency amount £1,000 receivable – no difference in local currency equivalent at translation times.

	£
Second currency amount $1,550 payable	
Local currency equivalent at second translation time $1,550 @ $1.7/£	912
Less	
Local currency equivalent at first translation Time $1,550 @ $1.55/£ (rate implied in contract)	(1,000)
Decrease in period	88
Taxable exchange gain for 1996 (= accounts profit)	£88

1997

In 1997 the accounts loss on the contract is as follows:

	£
£1,000 receivable under contract	1,000
Less $1,550 payable under contract @ $1.65/£	(939)
Profit realised on contract	61
Less unrealised profit per 1996 accounts	(88)
Accounts loss on contract in 1997	£(27)

FA 1993, s 126

First currency amount £1,000 receivable – no change

	£
Second currency amount $1,550 payable	
Local currency equivalent at second translation time (30 June 1997) $1,550 @ $1.65/£	939
Less	
Local currency equivalent at first translation time (31 December 1996) $1,550 @ $1.7/£	(912)
Increase in period	£27
Tax relievable exchange loss for 1997 (= accounts loss)	£(27)

	£
Total profit taxable over life of contract: (1996) £88 less (1997) £27 =	£61

4.21   In some circumstances companies account for forward contracts by valuing them using the spot rate of exchange to translate the under-lying currencies, while accounting separately for the forward discount or premium. This may be an appropriate accounting treatment when, for example, the forward contracts hedge interest bearing liabilities or assets. In such cases the discount or premium will be included in the figure for the company's net interest expense or income. The use of spot exchange rates is permitted by *FA 1993, s 150* but this means that the forward discount or premium is not reflected in the taxable exchange differences calculated under *FA 1993, s 126*. In such a case, the forward discount or premium is treated as a deemed qualifying payment under the financial instrument rules. [*FA 1994, s 153(4)*]. This treats as a qualifying payment, deemed to be payable at the maturity of the contract, any difference in the local currency equivalent of the two currency amounts specified in the currency contract, calculated at the time the contract is entered into. 'Local currency equivalent' is determined by the foreign exchange tax rules. At the time the contract is entered into, there will be no difference in the local currency equivalent amounts if the accounting treatment uses the rate implied in the contract, or forward rate of exchange. However, if the spot rate is used the difference will be equal to the forward discount or premium on the contract. The separate treatment for tax purposes of the forward discount or premium and the underlying exchange rate movement on the contract mirrors the accounting treatment and enables it to be followed for tax purposes.

Example 2 – Separate recognition of forward premium

Company B Ltd accounts for forward contracts entered into for hedging purposes by translating the foreign currency amounts at the spot rate of exchange. The forward discount or premium on the contract and exchange rate movements on the underlying currencies are accounted for separately, with the forward discount or premium being amortised over the life of the contract. On 1 July 1996 it enters into a twelve-month forward contract to sell $1,550 for £1,000. The facts are the same as for Example 1 above.

Assuming that this accounting treatment is normal accounting practice in the circumstances in which the forward contracts have been entered into, and provided the exchange rates used in the accounts are arm's length rates of exchange, the tax treatment of the forward contract will follow the accounting treatment.

1996

Finance Act 1993, s 126	£
First currency amount £1,000 receivable – no change	0
Second currency amount $1,550 payable	
Local currency equivalent at second translation time (31 December 1996) $1,550 @ $1.70/£	912
Local currency equivalent at first translation time (1 July 1996) $1,550 @ $1.60/£	(969)
Decrease in period treated as taxable exchange gain	(57)

	£
Finance Act 1994, s 153(4)	
At start of contract (1 July 1996)	
Local currency equivalent of first currency amount	1,000
Less	
Local currency equivalent of second currency amount $1,550 @ $1.60/£	(969)
Difference	<u>31</u>
Deemed qualifying payment receivable	31
Amount attributable to accounting period ended 31 December 1996	

$$£31 \times \frac{6}{12} = \qquad 15.5$$

Total profit taxable in 1996: £57 plus £15.5 =	£72.5

1997

	£
Finance Act 1993, s 126	
First currency amount £1,000 receivable – no change	
Second currency amount $1,550 payable	
Local currency equivalent at second translation time (30 June 1997) $1,550 @ $1.65/£	939
Less	
Local currency equivalent at first translation time (31 December 1996) $1,550 @ $1.70/£	(912)
Increase for period	<u>27</u>
Tax relievable exchange loss	(27)

Finance Act 1994, s 153(4)

Deemed qualifying payment receivable attributable to accounting period ended 31 December 1997

$$£31 \times \frac{6}{12} = \qquad 15.5$$

Total loss deductible in 1997: £27 less £15.5 =	£(11.5)
Total profit taxable over life of contract: (1996) £72.5 less (1997) £11.5 =	£61

The above figures will be equal to the accounts profit or loss recognised in each accounting period, which are as follows:

4.21   *Currency Contracts and Options*

1996   £

Accrual of forward premium £31 $\times \frac{6}{12}$ =   15.5

Exchange gain on contract, based on spot
exchange rates   57.0

Total profit per accounts   £72.5

1997

Accrual of forward premium £31 $\times \frac{6}{12}$ =   15.5

Exchange loss on contract, based on spot
exchange rates   (27.0)

Total loss per accounts   £(11.5)

Example 3 – Translation at forward rate

Company C Ltd manages the group's foreign currency transaction exposures. All group companies hedge their foreign currency transactions
by entering into forward contracts with company C, which hedges the net
exposure by entering into forward contracts with third party banks to the
extent that the treasurer considers it appropriate. Open forward contracts are valued for accounts purposes using the forward rate for a
period equal to the remaining life of the contract. The facts and exchange
rates are as for Example 1, and the relevant forward rates are as
follows:

   12-month forward rate on 1 July 1996 $1.55/£

   6-month forward rate on 31 December 1996 $1.66/£

1996

Finance Act 1993, s 126   £

   First currency amount £1,000 receivable – no change

   Second currency amount $1,550 payable

   Local currency equivalent at second translation time
   (31 December 1996) $1,550 @ £1.66/£   934

   Less

   Local currency equivalent at first translation time
   (1 July 1996) $1,550 @ $1.55/£   (1000)

   Decrease in period   (66)

   Taxable exchange gain for period   66

Finance Act 1994, s 153(4)	£
Local currency equivalent of first currency amount	1,000
Local currency equivalent of second currency amount $1,550 @ $1.55/£	(1,000)
Difference	Nil
Deemed qualifying payment	Nil
Total profit taxable in 1996	£66

1997

Finance Act 1993, s 126	£
First currency amount £1,000 receivable – no change	
Second currency amount $1,550 payable	
Local currency equivalent at second translation time (30 June 1997) $1,550 @ $1.65/£	939
Less	
Local currency equivalent at first translation time (31 December 1996) $1,550 @ $1.66/£	(934)
Increase in period	5
Tax relievable exchange loss for period	(5)
No deemed qualifying payment under *FA 1994, s 153(4)*	
Total loss deductible in 1997	(5)
Total profit taxable over life of contract: (1996) £66 *less* (1997) £5 =	£61

Example 4 – Use of rate implied in the contract

Company D Ltd takes out specific forward contracts to hedge individual trade debtors and creditors. As permitted under SSAP 20, it uses the forward rate in the contract to translate the trading transaction into sterling for accounts purposes, and does not recognise any exchange profit or loss in its accounts on the forward contracts. On 1 July 1996 it makes a sale of $1,550 which is receivable on 30 June 1997. This is hedged by a twelve-month forward contract to sell $1,550 for £1,000. The sale is therefore booked at £1,000 and no exchange gain or loss appears in the accounts.

The forward contract is with an independent third party, and is therefore at an arm's length rate. It is normal accounting practice not to translate the forward contract for accounts purposes where the rate implied in the contract is used to translate the underlying transaction. It is therefore permissible to value the contract using the rate implied in the contract with the result that no taxable exchange gain or loss under *FA 1993, s 126* will accrue [*FA 1993, ss 150(6)* and *150(11)*]. The Inland Revenue state in the Explanatory Statement that the use of the contract rate in valuing the related trade debtor is the use of an arm's length rate to translate this item for accounts purposes. [*FA 1993, s 150(5)–(10)*]. It is therefore not necessary to recognise an exchange gain or loss for tax purposes on either the trade debtor or the currency contract.

Currency futures

4.22   A currency future is simply a forward contract to sell or purchase a specified amount of foreign currency, which is traded on a financial futures exchange. The main differences between a currency future and a conventional forward contract (the 'over the counter' equivalent of a currency future) are as follows:

Future	OTC forward contract
Standard maturity dates and periods only.	Maturity date or period is agreed between counterparties.
Each contract is for a standard amount of currency.	Wide range of contract size.
Cash or other collateral must be deposited with futures exchange as 'initial margin' and 'variation margin'.	No collateral (but uses credit lines).

4.23   A future may therefore be used for hedging purposes in the same way as a forward contract, although the standardised terms may result in a less precise hedge than a forward contract of the required size and maturity. The tax treatment of the contract itself will be exactly the same as for a forward contract, i.e. exchange gains and losses will be accrued following the rules for currency contracts contained in *FA 1993, s 126*. Additional features also need to be taken into account, however, as follows.

Consideration paid or received

4.24   If the futures contract is acquired or disposed of part way through its term, the consideration will be a 'qualifying payment' for the purposes of the financial instrument rules. In general the tax treatment of such qualifying payments will follow the accounting treatment, and will effectively increase or decrease the exchange gain or loss to be recognised under *FA 1993, s 126*. The treatment of qualifying payments is considered in more detail below in relation to currency swaps.

Margin payments

4.25   If a currency future requires a margin payment in a foreign currency (or, in the case of a future acquired for the purpose of a trade for which a 'local currency election' has been made, a currency other than the 'local currency'), this will be a qualifying asset for the purposes of the foreign exchange tax rules, and taxable gains or losses will accrue on the outstanding balance.

Currency swap agreements

4.26   Most currency swap agreements include the following features:

(*a*)   *Periodic payments*
These are annual or more frequent payments payable to and receivable from the swap counterparty. Usually there is an amount payable found by applying an interest rate to a notional amount in one currency and an amount receivable found by applying an interest rate to a notional amount in the second currency.

(*b*)   *Final exchange of principal amounts*
At the end of the agreement one party will pay a specified amount of one currency to the other and receives in exchange a specified amount of the second currency. Typically these are equal to the notional amounts on which the periodic payments are calculated.

4.27   The final exchange of principal is a currency contract for the purposes of the foreign exchange tax rules. Provided all other payments under the agreement either:

(*a*)   involve an exchange of amounts of the currencies specified in the final exchange of principal, but in the opposite direction to the final exchange and at an earlier time; or

(*b*)   are qualifying payments for the purposes of the financial instrument rules,

then the currency swap will also be a currency contract for the purposes of the financial instrument rules (see 4.13 above). Small non-qualifying payments are ignored for the purposes of applying this test [*FA 1994, s 152*] so that contracts cannot be removed artificially from the rules with ease. Before the Commencement Day from which the foreign exchange and financial instrument rules became effective for a company, the final exchange of principal amounts may have been taxable as a capital gains transaction, in the same way as a forward currency contract. Periodic payments made by a company were deductible as a trading expense or, under Extra Statutory Concession C17, as a charge on income. Other payments associated with this swap agreement, such as initial fees, variation fees and termination payments may have been deductible only as a capital loss or may have been disregarded for tax purposes altogether if the swap was undertaken for non-trading purposes or if it was a capital transaction of a trading company. The financial instrument rules treat all such payments as qualifying payments, giving rise to expenses which are ultimately deductible as expenses of a trade or from total profits. The timing of recognition of qualifying payments is determined under the financial instrument rules, but should follow the accounting treatment where this is based on normal accounting practice for the circumstances of the particular swap transaction.

Example 5 – Accruals basis

E Ltd, an investment company for tax purposes, enters into a 3-year currency swap agreement on 1 January 1997, to hedge its investment in its German subsidiaries. The terms of the swap are as follows:

Arrangement fee to broker £5,000
Initial fee to swap counterparty £60,000
Initial exchange of principal: notional
Periodic payments due 30 June and 31 December:

  – pay 6-month DM LIBOR on DM25,000,000
  – receive 6-month sterling LIBOR on £10,000,000

Final exchange of principal on 31 December 1999:

  – pay DM25,000,000
  – receive £10,000,000

Spot exchange rate	1 January 1997:	£1 = DM 2.500
	31 March 1997:	£1 = DM 2.400
6-month LIBOR	1 January 1997:	DM – 4%
		Sterling – 6%

As the following analysis shows, the total taxable profit or deductible loss in each accounting period will be the amount recognised in the accounts.

Accounting treatment

E Ltd prepares accounts to 31 March. At each year end it values the obligation to exchange principal amounts using the year end spot exchange rate and takes the gain or loss to reserves to offset exchange gains and losses which result from the translation into sterling of the book value of its German subsidiary. In the year ended 31 March 1997:

	£	£
Closing values		
£ receivable	10,000,000	
DM payable: DM25m @ DM2.400/£	(10,416,667)	
		(416,667)
Less values 1 January 1997		
£ receivable	(10,000,000)	
DM payable: DM25m @ DM2.500/£	10,000,000	
		0
		(416,667)

The broker's fee and initial fee to the bank are amortised evenly over the life of the swap and the LIBOR-based payments are accrued evenly over each 'interest period'. In the year ended 31 March:

	£
Brokers fee (£5,000) $\times \frac{3}{36}$	(417)
Initial fee £60,000 $\times \frac{3}{36}$	(5,000)
DM LIBOR payable:	
$25{,}000{,}000 \times \frac{3}{12} \times 4\%$ @ DM2.400/£	(104,167)
£ LIBOR receivable	
$10{,}000{,}000 \times \frac{3}{12} \times 6\%$	150,000
Net credit to profit and loss account	£40,416
Total loss recognised in the accounts (including reserves movement above)	£(376,251)

Tax treatment
The final exchange of principal is a currency contract for the purpose of the foreign exchange tax rules, and exchange gains and losses are calculated under *FA 1993, s 126*. The 'translation times' for the first accrual period (which falls in the accounting period ended 31 March 1997) are 1 January 1997 and 31 March 1997. The foreign currency amounts under the contract are translated for accounts purposes at the

arm's length spot rate of exchange on the relevant day, so that rate is also used for tax purposes. [*FA 1993, s 150(5)–(10)*]. Applying *FA 1993, s 126* in the accounting period ended 31 March 1997 gives the following result:

		£
First currency:	sterling receivable so no change in local currency equivalent	0
Second currency:	DM25,000,000 payable	

Local currency equivalent 31 March 1997: DM25,000,000
@ DM2.400/£   10,416,667

Less

Local currency equivalent 1 January 1997: DM25,000,000
@ DM2.500/£   (10,000,000)

Increase over accrual period – taxable exchange loss   416,667

[*FA 1993, s 126(5)(b)*]

Because the swap was not undertaken for the purpose of a trade carried on by E Ltd the taxable exchange gain or loss is a 'non-trading exchange loss' [*FA 1993, s 129(3)*] to be relieved in accordance with *FA 1993, s 129*.

All the other payments under the swap agreement are qualifying payments under the financial instrument rules, so the swap is also a currency contract for the purposes of those rules:

Brokers fee – *FA 1994, s 151(2)(a)*;
Initial fee – *FA 1994, s 151(1)(b)*;
LIBOR-based payments – *FA 1994, s 150(3)*.

The basis of accounting adopted for these qualifying payments should be regarded by the Inland Revenue as an 'acceptable accruals basis' for the purpose of *FA 1994, s 156(4)*, so the accrual of qualifying payments for tax purposes [*FA 1994, s 155*] would be based on the accruals in the accounts (see 4.5 *et seq.* above). Under the terms of *section 155*;

	£
Amount A (accrued amounts of qualifying payments to be received)	
Total LIBOR receivable	150,000
Total = Amount A	150,000

Amount B (accrued amounts of qualifying payments to be made)

Brokers fee	417
Initial fee	5,000
DM LIBOR payable	104,167
Total = Amount B	109,584

Profit on the contract accrues to the company equal
to the excess of amount A over amount B *FA 1994,
s 155(1)* =   40,416

The currency swap was not undertaken for the purpose of a trade carried
on by E Ltd, so the profit on the contract is a 'non-trading profit' which is
treated as if it were a non-trading credit in respect of a loan relationship
for the purposes of *FA 1996, s 82*. [*FA 1994, s 160*].

If E Ltd has no other transactions which give rise to gains and losses
which are taxable or relievable under *FA 1996, s 82*, the overall loss on
the contract will be relievable as a non-trading deficit in the accounting
period ended 31 March 1997:

	£
Tax relievable exchange loss on final exchange of principal	(416,667)
Profit on contract under financial instruments rules	40,416
Net non-trading deficit under *FA 1996, s 82*	(376,251)

The rules for relieving a non-trading deficit are described in detail in
Chapter 5.

In summary, the deductible loss is the net expense recognised in the
accounts, found by aggregating the loss taken to reserves and the net
income taken to the profit and loss account. In practice the company may
choose to make a matching election (see Chapter 9) to match the
exchange movement on the exchange of principal with the investment in
the German subsidiary.

Example 6 – Mark to market accounting

The facts are as in Example 5, but the swap is undertaken by F plc, which
is a bank undertaking currency swaps in the course of trade and which
receives an initial fee of £60,000 for entering into the swap and does not
pay or receive a broker's fee. At the end of each day it marks to market
all outstanding swap transactions taking any profit or loss to the profit
and loss account. As in Example 5, the complex rules give an overall
result for the taxable profit or deductible loss which is the same as that
recorded in the accounts.

F plc values the swap described in Example 5 as follows:

	£
1 January 1997	
Initial fee recovered	60,000
Present value of future swap payments and receipts	(10,000)
Net profit taken to profit and loss account	50,000
31 March 1997	
Present value of future swap payments and receipts	(325,000)
Less opening present value	10,000
Loss taken to profit and loss account	(315,000)
Net loss recognised in accounting period ended 31 March 1997	£(265,000)

It is assumed that the basis of accounting is an 'acceptable mark to market basis' for the purposes of *FA 1994, s 156(3)*, so that it will be used to calculate taxable profits and losses under *FA 1994, s 155(4)*. The taxable profit or deductible loss is then the excess (or deficiency) of amount A over amount B calculated as follows:

Amount A	£
Qualifying payments receivable by F plc in the period to 31 March 1997	60,000
Increase in value of the swap in the period to 31 March 1997	nil
Amount A	60,000
Amount B	
Qualifying payments payable by F plc in the period	nil
Decrease in value of the swap in the period to 31 March 1997 treating the initial value as nil [*FA 1994, s 150(7)*]	325,000
	325,000
Less exchange loss under *FA 1993, s 126* (See *FA 1994, s 162*)	(416,417)
Amount B (negative amount)	(91,417)
Amount A	60,000
Less amount B	(91,417)
Excess of amount A over amount B	151,417

The contract was undertaken for the purpose of the trade of F plc, which means it is treated as having:

	£
Trading profit equal to the excess of amount A over amount B [*FA 1994, ss 155(1) and 159*]	151,417
Trading loss equal to the deductible exchange loss on the final exchange of principal [*FA 1993, s 128(6)*]	(416,417)
Net trading loss to be recognised	(265,000)

The overall result is to recognise the same loss for tax purposes as for accounts purposes (there are rules to prevent profits and losses from being double counted under the foreign exchange tax rules and general Schedule D Case I principles – see below). In practice it will not be necessary to compute the profit or loss on such a contract separately where the result would be exactly the same as the figure included in the accounts profit, which forms the starting point for calculating the taxable profit of the trade.

Example 7 – Use of exchange rate implied in the currency contract

On 1 January 1998, G Ltd, an investment company for tax purposes, borrows for five years US$40,000,000 at fixed interest rate of 8% per annum (payable in equal instalments on 30 June and 31 December) by issuing a Eurobond. The issue price is 101%, and the $400,000 premium over the redemption price exactly equals the issuing costs, so the liability to be recognised in the accounts will be the net proceeds (equal to the redemption price) of US$40,000,000. On the same day G Ltd enters into a five-year currency swap with the following terms:

Initial exchange of principal
    G Ltd pays US$40,000,000
    G Ltd receives £20,000,000

Periodic payments on 30 June and 31 December
    G Ltd pays 6-month sterling LIBOR plus 0.1% on £20,000,000
    G Ltd receives 6/12 of 8% on US$40,000,000

Final exchange of principal on 31 December 2002
    G Ltd pays £20,000,000
    G Ltd receives US$40,000,000

Accounting treatment
The swap cashflows meet all the US$ obligations under the Eurobond to create a 'synthetic' floating rate sterling loan at LIBOR plus 0.1%. This is reflected in the accounting treatment:

The principal of the loan is translated into sterling at the exchange rate implied in the swap agreement ($2.00 = £1).

The interest on the loan and the periodic payments under the swap are accrued on a straight line basis over each interest period, and the net result (equivalent to sterling 6-month LIBOR plus 0.1%) is taken to the interest payable line in the profit and loss account.

Tax treatment

For accounts purposes, the US$ liability has been translated into sterling using the exchange rate implied in the contract, and the exchanges of principal under the currency swap agreement (currency contracts taxable under the foreign exchange tax rules including *FA 1993, s 126*) are not recognised in the accounts at all. The Inland Revenue will accept this accounting treatment (see Explanatory Statement, para 7.9), on the basis that:

(*a*)   the loan is translated using an arm's length exchange rate [*FA 1993, s 150(5)–(10)*]; and

(*b*)   the swap is 'off balance sheet' in accordance with normal accounting practice [*FA 1993, s 150(6) and (11)*].

The periodic cashflows will be recognised on an accruals basis under the financial instrument rules, as described in Example 5 above, matching the tax treatment of the bond interest under the corporate and government debt rules (for accounting periods ending after 31 March 1996), so the overall tax treatment of the swap and bond will be equivalent to that of a sterling loan at the interest rate given by the swap agreement.

Early termination and cash settlement of currency contracts

4.28   A currency contract can be effectively terminated before maturity in several ways including:

(*a*)   entering into a market rate contract in the opposite direction so as to lock into the unrealised gain or loss on the original contract;

(*b*)   cancellation of the agreement in consideration for a payment made between the counterparties; and

(*c*)   acquiring a contract with exactly reciprocal rights and obligations to the original contract – usually this will involve a payment between the counterparties to the new contract.

4.29   The tax rules for early termination depend on the mechanism used, and are complex, but the overall effect is to ensure that the total profit or loss on the original contract is recognised by the time of 'termination' while avoiding double counting of gains or losses accrued in earlier periods. The rules also apply where a currency contract is settled for a cash payment at maturity, instead of the exchange of currencies which may be provided for under the contract.

Close out with a market rate contract

4.30   There are no special rules where a currency contract is closed out by entering into a market rate contract, but the basic rules of the foreign exchange and financial instruments legislation will ensure that the economic profit or loss is recognised because exchange rate movements on the two contracts will cancel out for the remainder of the period to maturity.

Example 8 – Forward sale contract closed out early with a market rate forward purchase contract

H Ltd accounts for forward contracts by translating the currency amount receivable and payable using the forward exchange rate applicable at the date of valuation for the maturity date of the contract in question (like C Ltd in Example 3). It prepares accounts to 31 December and on 1 April 1997 enters into a twelve-month forward contract to sell French Francs for sterling. On 1 September 1997 it closes out the contract by entering into a six-month forward contract to buy French Francs for sterling. Both contracts are revalued at the three-month forward rate on 31 December 1997 for accounts purposes. Details of the contracts and exchange rates are as follows:

   1 April 1997 sell FFr800,000 buy £100,000 for settlement on 31 March 1998

   1 September 1997 buy FFr800,000 sell £80,000 for settlement on 31 March 1998.

Exchange rates	FFr/£
1 April 1997 12-month forward rate	8.00
1 September 1997 6-month forward rate	10.00
31 December 1997 3-month forward rate	9.00

The economic effect is to lock into a profit of £20,000, which will be realised on 31 March 1998, by contracting to sell FFr800,000 for £100,000 and buy FFr800,000 for £80,000. This is recognised in the 1997 accounts as follows:

	£
First contract:	
FFr800,000 payable @ FFr9.00/£ (3-month forward rate)	(88,889)
£100,000 receivable	100,000
Second contract:	
£80,000 payable	(80,000)
FFr800,000 receivable @ FFr9.00/£	88,889
Net profit year to 31 December 1997	20,000

4.30   *Currency Contracts and Options*

Clearly further exchange movements on the two contracts will cancel out for accounts purposes in the period from 1 January 1998 to 31 March 1998.

As was illustrated in Example 3 above, because the contracts are translated for accounts purposes at a forward exchange rate, the whole of the gain or loss will be recognised under *FA 1993, s 126*, and there will be no deemed qualifying payments under *FA 1994, s 153(4)* to be considered under the financial instrument rules. The taxable profit is the same as the accounts profit, as follows:

1997

	£
First contract 1 April 1997	
First currency is sterling – no change in value	
Second currency Fr800,000 payable:	
Local currency equivalent 31 December 1997 Fr800,000 @ 9.0/£	88,889
Less	
Local currency equivalent 1 April 1997 Fr800,000 @ 8.0/£	(100,000)
Decrease in accrual period = taxable exchange gain (1)	(11,111)
Taxable exchange gain (1)	11,111
Second contract	
First currency Fr800,000 receivable	
Local currency equivalent 31 December 1997 Fr800,000 @ 9.0/£	88,889
Less	
Local currency equivalent 1 September 1997 Fr800,000 @ 10.0/£	(80,000)
Second currency is sterling – no change in value	
Increase in accrual period	8,889
Taxable exchange gain (2)	8,889
Total of taxable exchange gains in period: (1) plus (2)	20,000

1998

Because both contracts have identical local currency equivalents at 31 December 1997 it is clear that no net taxable exchange gain or loss will accrue in 1998.

Settlement of a currency contract in exchange for lump sum payment

4.31   When a currency contract is cancelled or settled at maturity in exchange for a lump sum payment, this brings into play some complicated rules to prevent double counting. These are required largely because exchange movements on the underlying currencies are dealt with under the foreign exchange tax rules whereas a termination payment is a qualifying payment which is dealt with under the financial instrument rules. [*FA 1994, s 153(2)*]. Where the contract is accounted for on an accruals basis, an adjustment is also required to ensure that qualifying payments which have been accrued but not paid, and will therefore be reflected in the value of the lump sum payment, are not double counted. The relevant provisions are *FA 1993, s 146* and *FA 1994, s 161*. These two provisions:

(*a*)   Reverse out all exchange gains and losses recognised under *FA 1993, s 126* up to the date of termination of the contract. [*FA 1993, s 146*].

(*b*)   If the accruals basis of accounting applies, reverse out all accruals of qualifying payments which have not become due and payable by the time of termination. [*FA 1994, s 161*].

4.32   As a result, for a company following an acceptable accruals basis of accounting the overall taxable gain or loss recognised in the accounting period in which the contract is terminated is equal to:

Termination receipt/(payment)		V
Add	Qualifying payments received in final period	W
Less	Net unrealised exchange gain or loss up to end of previous accounting period	(X)
	Qualifying payments accrued in previous accounting periods and unpaid at start of final period	(Y)
Net taxable gain or loss in period of termination		N

This will normally be equal to the total profit or loss recognised on the contract in the accounts for the accounting period in which the contract is terminated.

4.33   *FA 1993, s 146* applies whenever a currency contract is settled for a lump sum, regardless of whether or not such settlement is covered by the original terms of the contract, and regardless of whether settlement takes place at maturity or before the contract maturity date. Under *section 146* it is necessary to calculate the *net contractual gain or loss* on the contract and this is the amount that has to be reversed out as described above. This is the aggregate of the taxable exchange gains and losses which have been recognised under the foreign exchange tax rules in respect of the contract for all accounting periods up to and including the period in which it is terminated. If the exchange gains and losses have been treated as trading income and expense under *FA 1993, s 128* the net contractual gain or loss is referred to as a 'net contractual gain or loss of a trade'. If the exchange gains and losses have been recognised as non-trading gains and losses under *FA 1993, s 129* the net contractual gain or loss will be a 'net contractual non-trading gain or loss'. If the currency contract has given rise to both trading and non-trading exchange gains and losses, the trading and non-trading amounts have to be aggregated separately and there may be a net contractual trading gain or loss and also a net contractual non-trading gain or loss. Each net contractual gain or loss is recognised in the accounting period in which the contract was terminated, as follows:

Net contractual trading gain P – Trading expense P
Net contractual trading loss Q – Trading receipt Q
Net contractual non-trading gain R – Non-trading loss R
Net contractual non-trading loss S – Non-trading gain S

4.34   If the company has a net contractual gain or loss of a trade and

(*a*)   the trade concerned has ceased before the contract is terminated, or

(*b*)   the company carries on 'exempt activities' immediately before the time of termination,

the net contractual gain or loss is instead treated as if it were a net contractual non-trading gain or loss [*FA 1993, s 146(12)* and *(13)*]. 'Exempt activities' are:

(i)   Long-term insurance business.

(ii)   Mutual insurance business.

(iii)   The occupation of commercial woodland in the UK.

(iv)   Activities of a company which is a housing association approved under *ICTA 1988, s 488* or a self-build society approved under *ICTA 1988, s 489.*

Items (i) and (iii) are defined in *FA 1993, s 143(6).* There are special rules to deal with situations where exchange gains and losses of a trade are expressed in a currency other than sterling.

4.35   *FA 1994, s 161* provides that where the accruals basis of accounting applies, the gain or loss calculated under the financial instrument rules for the accounting period in which the contract is terminated is to be adjusted to reverse out any part of a qualifying payment which has accrued under the financial instrument rules but does not become due and payable by the time the contract is terminated.

4.36   Examples 9 to 11 below illustrate the fact that, provided an 'acceptable' accruals or mark to market basis of accounting is used, the detailed rules result in a taxable gain or loss equal to the total gain or loss recognised in the accounts for the accounting period in which the contract is terminated.

Example 9 – Early termination of currency contract for lump sum payment – accruals basis accounting

The initial facts are as set out in Example 5. E Ltd, an investment company for tax purposes, has entered into a three-year currency swap on 1 January 1997 and recognised the following non-trading gains and losses under *FA 1993, s 129*, in the accounting period ended 31 March 1997:

	£
Deductible exchange loss on final exchange of principal	(416,417)
Profit on contract under financial instrument rules	40,416
Net non-trading loss under *FA 1993, s 129*	(376,001)

On 30 June 1997 the following periodic payments are made:

E Ltd receives £ LIBOR on £10,000,000
£10,000,000 × 6/12 × 6% =   £300,000

E Ltd pays DM LIBOR on DM25,000,000
DM25,000,000 × 6/12 × 4% =   DM500,000

Spot exchange rate DM 2.40/£ so the payment is
equivalent to   £208,333

6-month LIBOR rates for the period beginning 1 July 1997 are
DM − 4%
Sterling − 6%

On 30 September 1997 the company pays the counterparty £178,000 and the swap agreement is terminated. The spot exchange rate on 30 September 1997 is DM2.45/£. In its accounts E Ltd accrues the periodic payments and exchange difference on the exchange of principal to the date of termination, and then writes off to the profit and loss account the balance of the initial and brokers fees and the termination fee, net of amounts already accrued, as follows:

Exchange gain on final exchange of principal	£	£
DM25,000,000 @ 2.40/£	10,416,666	
Less		
DM25,000,000 @ 2.45/£	(10,204,081)	
		212,585
		c/f 212,585

		b/f 212,585
Sterling LIBOR received 30 June 1997	300,000	
Less accrued 31 March 1997	(150,000)	
		150,000

Sterling LIBOR accrued to 30 September 1997

£10,000,000 × 3/12 × 6%		150,000
DM LIBOR paid 30 June 1997	(208,333)	
Less accrued 31 March 1997	104,167	
		(104,166)

DM LIBOR accrued to 30 September 1997		
DM25,000,000 × 3/12 × 4% @ 2.45/£		(102,041)
Net profit accrued before termination		306,378

Termination payment		178,000
Less: Unrealised loss 1996/97	(416,417)	
Unrealised gain 1997/98	212,585	
DM LIBOR payable accrued	(102,041)	
£ LIBOR receivable accrued	150,000	
		(155,873)
Loss on termination		22,127

Balance of broker's fee written off (5,000 *less* 417)	(4,583)
Balance of initial fee written off (60,000 *less* 5,000)	(55,000)
Overall accounts profit on swap in year to 31 March 1998	224,668

Under *FA 1994, s 155(5)*, which deals with currency contracts accounted for on the accruals basis, the whole of the termination payment, which is a qualifying payment, is attributed to the accounting period ended 31 March 1998. The taxable gains and losses before any adjustments under the termination provisions are therefore:

	£	£
Taxable exchange gain under *FA 1993, s 126*		212,585

Loss on contract under financial instrument rules

Amount A:

Balance of June £ LIBOR receipt	150,000	
Accrual of December £ LIBOR receipt	150,000	
		300,000
		c/f 300,000

b/f 300,000

Amount B:

Balance of June DM LIBOR payment	(104,166)
Accrual of December DM LIBOR payment	(102,041)
Broker's fee	(4,583)
Initial fee	(55,000)
Termination payment	(178,000)
	(443,790)
Excess of amount B over amount A	(143,790)

The net contractual non-trading loss under *FA 1993, s 146* is

Loss in period ended 31 March 1997	(416,417)
Gain in period ended 31 March 1998	212,585
Net contractual non-trading loss	203,832

This is treated as a non-trading gain of the period ended 31 March 1998.

Under *FA 1994, s 161(2)* amounts A and B are adjusted for amounts accrued which had not become due and payable:

	£
Amount A as above	300,000
Less accrual for £ LIBOR receipt due December 1997	(150,000)
Revised amount A	150,000
Amount B as above	(443,790)
Less accrual for DM LIBOR payment due December 1997	102,041
Revised amount B	(341,749)
Revised loss on contract	(191,749)

This means that the overall taxable amount in the second accounting period is:

	£
Taxable exchange gain	212,585
Adjustment for net contractual loss	203,832
Revised loss on contract	(191,749)
Net taxable gain (= accounts profit)	224,668
In the first accrual period there was a net tax deduction of	(376,001)
Net loss relief given over life of swap	151,333

The actual payments and receipts were:

	£
Broker's fee	(5,000)
Initial fee	(60,000)
June £ LIBOR received	300,000
June DM LIBOR paid	(208,333)
Termination payment	(178,000)
Net loss on swap	(151,333)

Example 10 – Early termination of a currency contract for a lump sum – mark to market accounting

The facts are as in Example 6, in which F plc, a bank, accounted for a DM/£ currency swap on a mark to market basis. A loss of £265,000 on the swap was recognised for both accounts and tax purposes in the accounting period ended 31 March 1997.

On 30 June 1997 the following periodic payments are made:

F plc receives £ LIBOR on £10,000,000

£10,000,000 $\times$ 6/12 $\times$ 6% =   £300,000

F plc pays DM LIBOR on DM25,000,000

DM25,000,000 $\times$ 6/12 $\times$ 4% =   DM500,000

Spot exchange rate DM2.40/£ so the payment is equivalent to   £208,333

6-month LIBOR rates for the period beginning 1 July 1997 are

DM – 4%
Sterling – 6%

In the accounting period ended 31 March 1998 a profit of £238,667 is recorded in the profit and loss account, calculated as follows.

	£
Sterling LIBOR received 30 June 1997	300,000
Less	
DM LIBOR paid 30 June 1997	(208,333)
Termination payment	(178,000)
Less value of swap at 31 March 1997 (negative)	325,000
Profit on termination of swap	238,667

The taxable amounts before any adjustments under the termination provisions are as follows:

FA 1993, s 126   £

First currency: sterling receivable so no change
in local currency value

Second currency: DM25,000,000 payable

Local currency equivalent 30 September 1997:

DM25,000,000 @ DM2.450/£   10,204,081

Less

Local currency equivalent 31 March 1997:
DM25,000,000 @ DM2.50/£   (10,416,417)

Decrease over accrual period
   – taxable exchange gain   (212,336)

[*FA 1993, s 125(5)(a)*].

This will be treated as a trading receipt under *FA 1993, s 128(4)*.

Adjustments for termination – net contractual gain or loss

Trading exchange gain in current period   212,336

Less

Trading exchange loss of accounting period
ended 31 March 1997   (416,417)

Net contractual loss of the trade [*FA 1993, s 146(7)*]   (204,081)

Deemed gain equal to net contractual loss   204,081

Add trading exchange gain taxable in current period   212,336

Overall exchange gain taxable in current period   416,417

FA 1994, s 155(4)

Value of contract immediately before termination:
treated as nil [*FA 1994, s 155(7)*]   0

Less

Value of contract at start of accounting period (negative)   325,000

Increase in value for the period   325,000

Amount A

Qualifying payments receivable in period –
   sterling LIBOR   300,000

Increase in value of contract over period   325,000

Less total exchange gain accrued
in the current period [*FA 1994, s 162*]   (416,417)

Total – Amount A   208,583

Amount B

Qualifying payments payable in period –	
DM LIBOR	208,333
Termination payment	178,000
Total – Amount B	386,333
Loss on the contract to F plc, equal to excess of amount B over amount A [*FA 1994, s 155(2)*]	(177,750)
Overall position	
Gain under foreign exchange tax rules	416,417
Loss under financial instrument rules	(177,750)
Overall gain recognised in accounting period ended 31 March 1998 (equal to accounts profit)	238,667

The practical consequence is that, provided the basis of accounting adopted by the company is an 'acceptable' accruals or mark to market basis, the profit or loss recognised in the accounts in the accounting period in which termination occurs is the profit or loss to be recognised for accounts purposes. It should not be necessary in such cases to prepare separate calculations of the taxable and deductible amounts under the foreign exchange and financial instruments rules for each transaction. (See Inland Revenue Explanatory Statement).

Example 11 – Early termination of a currency contract by entering into a reciprocal contract

The facts are as in Example 2, in which B Ltd accounts separately for the forward discount or premium on a forward currency contract, which is amortised over the life of the contract on a straight line basis. On 1 July 1996 it entered into a twelve-month forward contract to sell $1,550 for £1,000. In the year ended 31 December 1996 B Ltd has recognised for tax and accounts purposes:

	£
Exchange gain under *FA 1993, s 126*	57.0
Qualifying payment receivable under *FA 1994, s 155(5)*	15.5
	72.5

On 31 March 1997, when the spot rate of exchange is $1.65/£, B Ltd enters into a three-month forward contract to buy $1,550 for £1,000, for settlement on 30 June 1997 for which it receives an immediate payment from the counterparty bank of £55. In the accounts it recognised a loss of £17.5, calculated as follows:

	£
Payment received for reciprocal contract	55.0
Less profit on original contract recognised in 1996 accounts	(72.5)
Loss in 1997 accounting period	(17.5)

For tax purposes it is necessary to look separately at the termination provisions in the foreign exchange and financial instrument rules.

Foreign exchange

The company is treated as if, on 31 March 1997 (the date it entered into the reciprocal contract), the original contract was terminated without any payments of currency being made in respect of it. As a result, the early termination provisions of *FA 1993, s 146* are applied. The reciprocal contract is ignored, so no exchange gain or loss accrues on either contract from 1 April 1997 to 30 June 1997 when both contracts mature.

[*FA 1993, s 147*].

Finance Act 1993, s 126	£
First currency amount £1,000 receivable – no change	0
Second currency amount $1,550 payable	
Local currency equivalent at second translation time (31 March 1997) $1,550 @ $1.65/£	939
Less	
Local currency equivalent at first translation time (31 December 1996) $1,550 @ $1.70/£	(912)
Increase in period treated as deductible exchange loss	27

Finance Act 1993, s 146	
Exchange loss of current period	(27)
Exchange gain of accounting period ended 31 December 1996	57
Net contractual gain	30
Deemed loss equal to net contractual gain	(30)
Add exchange loss of current period	(27)
Overall exchange loss of accounting period ended 31 December 1997	(57)

4.37   *Currency Contracts and Options*

Financial Instruments

Finance Act 1994, s 155(5)

The Inland Revenue regards the closing out of a currency contract by entering into a reciprocal contract as a termination event for the purpose of *FA 1994, s 161*, so an adjustment to amount A or amount B under *section 161(2)* is required. (See Inland Revenue Explanatory Statement, para 7.5.)

	£
Amount A	
Forward premium accrued to 31 March 1997	
$£31 \times \frac{3}{12}$	7.8
Less s 161(2) adjustments:	
current period	(7.8)
previous periods	(15.5)
Termination payment receivable	55.0
Total – Amount A	39.5
Amount B	0
Profit on the contract accrues to the company, equal to the excess of amount A over amount B	39.5
The overall result is recognition for tax purposes of the loss of £17.5 which is recognised in the accounts, i.e.	
Exchange loss under *FA 1993, ss 126* and *146*	(57.0)
Profit on contract under *FA 1994, s 155(5)*	39.5
Net deductible loss	(17.5)

Net settlement where a matching election is in place

4.37   The rules contained in *Finance Act 1993, s 146* are defective where a currency contract is a qualifying liability involved in a matching election. As discussed above, the effect of *s 146* is to adjust the amount of the settlement payment taxable/relievable under the Financial Instrument rules by bringing into charge to tax in the same period an amount equal and opposite to those amounts which have already been taxed/relieved under the foreign exchange rules up to the date of termination.

4.38   For example, consider the simple situation of a swap giving rise to the following amounts:

Period 1	FX loss	60
Period 2	FX gain	(30)
Period 3 (up to date of settlement)	FX gain	(10)
		20
Period 3 Termination payment		20

where the termination payment essentially reflects the net foreign exchange loss over the cumulative period.

4.39   In this basic case, the effect of the sections described above is that the termination payment of 20 is relievable under *FA 1994* but the FX loss is reversed by taxing 20 under *FA 1993*. The company has already had relief on an accruals basis for cumulative foreign exchange losses of 20, so the total relief given over the life of the transaction is 20, reflecting the economic position.

4.40   If, however, the swap had been a qualifying liability involved in a matching election, the foreign exchange movements falling to be taxed under *FA 1993* would have been (reduced to) nil in each accrual period – providing for them to be brought into charge to tax on ultimate disposal of the matched asset instead. Thus the termination payment of 20 is relievable under *FA 1994* as above but the amount to be brought in under *FA 1993* is nil. Loss relief is therefore potentially doubled up, but gains are double counted too.

4.41   In August 2000, draft regulations were laid which include a provision that seeks to remedy this anomaly. Regulation 10 of the *Exchange Gains and Losses (Miscellaneous Modifications) Regulations 2000* (see Appendix 4) provides for the necessary adjustment to be made under *s 146 FA 1993* where the liability is the subject of a matching election. These regulations do not yet have the force of law and the change is expected to be effective only on the date that they come into force.

Currency options

4.42   The tax treatment of currency options is contained entirely within the financial instruments legislation in *FA 1994*. The foreign exchange legislation applies only to currency contracts and qualifying assets and liabilities. However, when a currency option is exercised this will normally result in the company becoming subject to a currency contract, or acquiring or disposing of foreign currency, the profit or loss on which will be taxable under the foreign exchange tax rules.

Definition of currency option

4.43   The 'qualifying contracts' to which the financial instruments rules apply include a 'currency option'. [*FA 1994, s 147(1)(b)*]. For the purposes of *section 147*, 'currency option' is defined in *FA 1994, s 150* as:

(*a*)   an option to enter into a currency contract, or

(*b*)   an option to enter into such an option

provided that the only transfers of money or money's worth which may be made under the option agreement come within the following categories:

  (i)   A payment receivable or payable for entering into the option.

 (ii)   A reasonable fee for arranging the option.

(iii)   Reasonable costs incurred in respect of the option.

(iv)   A payment for the variation or termination of the option.

 (v)   A compensation payment if the option terms are not complied with.

4.44   Payments under the currency contract which is created if the option is exercised will be treated for tax by reference to the new contract alone. The following agreements are also currency options, provided that the only payments which may be made are within the categories listed above:

(*a*)   An option, the exercise of which at any time would result in a company immediately receiving a specified amount of one currency and paying a specified amount of another currency.

(*b*)   A contract which is subject to a condition precedent which, on its fulfilment, would result in the company immediately receiving a specified amount of one currency and paying a specified amount of another currency. In this case the contract before the fulfilment of the condition is regarded as a currency option and fulfilment of the contract is treated as exercise of the option.

4.45   The currency contract which arises as a result of exercising the option may provide for, or require, 'net settlement', i.e. a single payment representing the difference in value of the two currency amounts to be exchanged under the contract, rather than an actual exchange of amounts in the two currencies. [*FA 1994, s 150(9)*]. An option which is to be settled in this way would come within the scope of the financial instrument rules. Similarly, a 'contract for differences' which provided for a settlement payment to be made equivalent to the amount payable in net settlement of a currency option as defined would also be taxed under the financial instrument rules as a currency option. [*FA 1994, s 150(11)*].

4.46 As in the case of currency contracts, if an option agreement also provides for non-qualifying payments this will not prevent it from being a qualifying contract provided the aggregate of the present values of the non-qualifying payments is small in comparison with the aggregate of the present values of the 'relevant payments'. In the case of options 'relevant payments' include qualifying payments under the option contract itself and qualifying payments which would arise if the option were exercised. The definition covers virtually any kind of currency option which does not have special 'non-currency' features, including the following:

(*a*) *'Plain vanilla' currency option* – an option which gives the purchaser the right to convert a specified amount of one currency into another currency at a specified exchange rate, either on a specific future date or at any time in a specified period.

(*b*) *Option on a currency future* – an option to acquire or sell at a specified price a specific exchange-traded currency future.

(*c*) *Compound currency option* – an option to acquire or write a currency option on a future date for a specified premium and term.

(*d*) *Currency swaption* – an option to enter into a currency swap agreement at a future time on specified terms.

Taxation of currency options

4.47 As in the case of currency contracts,

(*a*) All qualifying payments relating to the currency option are taxable or deductible under the financial instrument rules.

(*b*) The timing of recognition of the qualifying payments will be determined by the accounting treatment and whether this is an 'acceptable accruals basis' or an 'acceptable mark to market basis'.

Example 12 – Currency option accruals basis

Company J Ltd pays £1,000 on 1 July 1997 for an option to purchase US$ for sterling on the following terms:

Exercise date: 30 June 1998

Strike price: $2.00/£

Amount of US$: $50,000

The spot exchange rate on 1 July 1997 is $2.00/£, the same as the option strike price. J Ltd prepares accounts to 31 December and writes off the option premium to profit and loss account on a straight line basis, but does not value the option at the year end. This accounting treatment follows normal accountancy practice for the circumstances in which the option was acquired.

1997

Part of the premium is written off to profit and loss account

$$£1,000 \times \frac{6}{12} = £500$$

This is an 'acceptable accruals basis' and the amount written off is 'amount B' for the purpose of *FA 1994, s 155(5)*. It will therefore be deductible as a trading expense if the option was undertaken for the purpose of J's trade, and as part of the non-trading exchange gain or loss of the accounting period if it was not. The option premium is the only 'qualifying payment' and there is no amount A to consider.

1998

On 30 June 1998, when the spot exchange rate is $1.6/£, J Ltd exercises the option and pays £25,000 to acquire $50,000. It immediately converts the $50,000 into sterling. The profit shown in the accounts is as follows:

	£
Proceeds of disposal of $50,000 @ $1.6/£	31,250
Less:	
Cost of $50,000 under currency option	(25,000)
Balance of option premium written-off	(500)
Profit	5,750

The £500 balance of the option premium written off is deductible under the financial instrument rules in the same way as for 1997, and there are no other qualifying payments to consider. The currency acquired under the option and immediately sold for sterling is a qualifying asset under the foreign exchange tax rules [*FA 1993, s 153(1)(b)*] and therefore produces a taxable exchange gain under *FA 1993, s 125* as follows:

	£
Local currency equivalent of $50,000 at end of accrual period (spot rate as per accounts): $50,000 @ $1.6/£	31,250
Less	
Local currency equivalent of $50,000 at start of accrual period (contract rate as per accounts): $50,000 @ $2.0/£	(25,000)
Taxable exchange gain equal to increase in accrual period	6,250

Overall, therefore, the tax treatment will follow the accounts.

Example 13 – Currency options – mark to market

The facts are as Example 12, but Company J Ltd accounts for currency options by marking them to market. At the end of 1997, when the spot rate of exchange was $2.5/£, it valued the contract at £100, which was the market price for a six-month option to buy $50,000 for £25,000 at that time. It therefore recognises the following profits and losses in its accounts.

1997	£
Closing value of option	100
Less cost	(1,000)
Loss to profit and loss account	(900)

1998	
Profit on currency acquired under option	6,250
Less value of option brought forward	(100)
Profit to profit and loss account	6,150

Assuming that the method of valuation adopted for accounts purposes is an 'acceptable mark to market basis', the analysis for tax purposes is as follows:

1997

	£	
Amount A (i) No qualifying payments receivable in period		
(ii) Closing value of option	100	
Less		
Opening value of option (nil – *FA 1994, s 155(7)*)	0	
Increase in value over period		100
Amount B (i) Qualifying payments payable in period		1,000
Loss accruing to J Ltd equals excess of amount B over amount A [*FA 1994, s 155(2)*]		(900)

1998		£
Amount A		0
Amount B		
Opening value of option	100	
Closing value of option nil – [*FA 1994, s 155(7)*]	0	
Decrease in value		100
Loss accruing to J Ltd equal to excess of amount B over amount A [*FA 1994, s 155(2)*]		(100)
Exchange gain on currency acquired under option (as per Example 12)		6,250
Overall profit for tax purposes		£6,150

Linked currency options

4.48   If a currency option is a 'linked currency option', the taxable profit or loss in each accounting period must be calculated on a mark to market basis, regardless of how it is treated in the accounts. [*FA 1994, s 157(1)*]. A currency option is a 'linked currency option' when it is one of a pair of currency options which satisfy the following conditions:

(*a*)   They are undertaken by the same company.

(*b*)   They are both with the same counterparty.

(*c*)   One option is exercisable *by* the qualifying company and the other is exercisable *against* the qualifying company.

(*d*)   The options must be exercised at substantially the same time.

(*e*)   Whichever option is exercised, the result is the same.

4.49   A pair of linked currency options, as defined, is equivalent in economic terms to a forward currency contract.

4.50   Mark to market treatment cannot be avoided by undertaking 'matching' options in two different companies in a group. Two options will also be linked currency options if they are undertaken by the qualifying company and an 'associated company' of the qualifying company, and/or the counterparties to the two options are two companies which are 'associated companies'. For this purpose 'associated company' has the meaning defined in *ICTA 1988, s 416*. [*FA 1994, s 157(5)*].

Example 14

K Ltd enters into the following linked currency options with XYZ plc.

> K Ltd pays XYZ plc £100 on 1 August 1997 for an option allowing K Ltd to sell US$20,000 to XYZ plc for £10,000 on 31 October 1997. XYZ plc pays K Ltd £100 on 1 August 1997 for an option allowing it to buy US$20,000 from K Ltd for £10,000 on 31 October 1997.

If sterling is weaker than US$2.0/£ on 31 October 1997 K Ltd will exercise its option to sell US$20,000 for £10,000. If sterling is stronger than US$2.0/£ on 31 October 1997, XYZ plc would exercise its option to purchase US$20,000 from K Ltd for £10,000. One of the two options is therefore almost certain to be exercised and the same result would have been achieved if K Ltd had entered into an unconditional contract to sell US$20,000 to XYZ plc for £10,000.

If K Ltd prepares accounts to 30 September and the options are marked to market for tax purposes at that date, the overall unrealised profit or loss will reflect exchange movements from the time the contract was entered into. The profit or loss will be close to the exchange gain or loss which would be recognised under *FA 1993, s 126* in the case of the equivalent forward contract.

If the company does not account for the options on an acceptable mark to market basis, a suitable basis of accounting must be agreed between the Inspector and the company. If no such agreement is reached, the basis of accounting can be specified in a notice served on the company by the Inspector.

Transitional rules

4.51   All the currency contracts and currency options which a company holds on its Commencement Day are taxable under the foreign exchange tax rules and/or financial instrument rules. This may be contrasted with pre-commencement interest rate contracts and options, which are subject to the financial instrument rules only by election. This is because the company is treated as if it had entered into a currency contract or option at the start of Commencement Day for the purpose of the financial instrument rules [*FA 1994, s 147(2)(b)*] and, in the case of currency contracts also for the purposes of the foreign exchange tax rules. [*FA 1993, s 165(3)*]. There are transitional rules to deal with situations where the basis of taxation changes from Commencement Day. In broad terms, the position may be summarised as follows:

(*a*)   From Commencement Day, the taxable profits and deductible losses accruing on currency contracts and options will be the profits and losses which are recognised in the accounts, provided the accounting treatment follows normal accountancy practice.

(*b*)   If before Commencement Day any sums have been taken into account in respect of the currency contract or option in computing trading profits, either as trading receipts or expenses, these amounts will be left undisturbed.

(*c*)   Any pre-commencement accrued gain or loss on the currency contract or option which has not been taken into account in computing trading profits will generally be taxable or deductible after Commencement Day, so that the whole of the economic profit or loss on the contract will be recognised under the foreign exchange tax rules and/or financial instrument rules.

Where are the transitional rules to be found?

4.52   The transitional provisions are scattered through the financial instrument rules in *FA 1994*. The relevant provisions are as follows:

FA 1994, s 153(4)

There is a deemed qualifying payment under a currency contract when there is a difference in the local currency values of the two currencies at the time the contract is entered into, or in some cases, the time it is deemed to have been entered into under *FA 1994, s 147(2)(b)*.

FA 1994, s 158(6)

This provides for Commencement Day to be treated as if it were a change in the basis of accounting, in relation to a pre-commencement currency contract or option. The wording of *section 158* is modified to provide for an adjustment in the accounting period beginning with Commencement Day to pick up amounts which would otherwise escape taxation and to prevent double counting under the old rules and foreign exchange tax rules.

FA 1994, s 175

This contains specific rules modifying the way the above provisions apply to pre-commencement contracts, depending on whether or not the profits or losses on such contracts are taken into account in computing trading profits.

Basis of translation for currency contracts held before Commencement Day

4.53   TR 5 provides that the exchange rate to be used in respect of the currency contract is the rate used in the accounts on the day immediately before the company's Commencement Day. This means that in general exchange gains and losses which accrue in the accounts from commence-ment will be the amounts recognised for tax purposes. Depending on the accounting treatment, the opening exchange rate could be:

(*a*)   The spot exchange rate on the pre-commencement balance sheet date.

(*b*)   An appropriate forward exchange rate applicable on the pre-commencement balance sheet date.

(*c*)   The rate implied in the contract, where the contract is off-balance sheet immediately before Commencement Day.

Provided the rate used is in accordance with normal accountancy prac-tice, it will determine the starting point for calculating exchange gains and losses under the foreign exchange tax rules.

Currency contracts and options held on trading account before Commencement Day

Forward contracts and currency futures on trading account

4.54   If a currency contract held at commencement is held for the purpose of the company's trade, and any unrealised gain or loss has already been included in taxable trading profits, the deemed qualifying payment under *FA 1994, s 153(4)* will be the actual forward premium or discount which is recognised in the accounts.

4.55   There will thus be no deemed qualifying payment if the company accounts for the contract at a forward exchange rate, or the contract is off-balance sheet at commencement (see Examples 2, 3 and 4 above) because in these cases no forward discount or premium is recognised for accounts purposes. If the company translates the contract at spot exchange rates, and accounts separately for the forward discount or premium as in Example 2, it would normally spread the forward discount or premium over the life of the contract. The post-commencement portion will therefore be taxable or deductible under the financial instrument rules in the same way as a contract entered into after commencement. The part of the forward premium or discount which accrues before commencement may be included in pre-commencement trading profits, in which case no transitional adjustment is needed. If the part of the forward discount or premium which is attributed to the pre-commencement period is not taken into account in computing the profits of the trade, *FA 1993, s 158* will treat it as a taxable or deductible amount in the first accounting period of the foreign exchange tax rules.

If the currency contract is marked to market for accounts purposes, *FA 1994, ss 155* and *158* together ensure that the profit or loss which has been recognised in the accounts by the end of the first post-commencement accounting period has also been fully taken into account for tax purposes by that time.

4.56   If the contract has been taxed on a mark to market basis in pre-commencement accounting periods, no adjustment is required. If it is taxed on a realisation basis, the pre-commencement market movement will be recognised as part of the financial instrument profit or loss for the accounting period which starts on the company's Commencement Day.

4.57   If the currency contract is not marked to market for accounts purposes, but the profit or loss on the contract is taxed on a realisation basis, either as part of the trading profit or, if it is on capital account, as a chargeable gain or allowable loss, *FA 1994, s 153(4)* is applied as if the company had entered into the contract at commencement. There will therefore be a deemed qualifying payment, found by comparing the values of the two currencies under the contract immediately before the start of Commencement Day. The exchange rates to be used (spot rate, forward rate or the rate implied in the contract) will be determined by the accounting treatment used by the company. The deemed qualifying payment is treated as accruing over the remaining life of the contract, so that the whole of the economic profit or loss on the contract will be taken into account post-commencement, under the foreign exchange tax rules and financial instrument rules.

Currency swaps on trading account

4.58   The transitional rules apply to currency swaps in exactly the same way as they do to forward contracts, but with the added complexity of various additional payments which may be associated with the swaps. When these additional payments are qualifying payments, *FA 1994, s 158* will operate to ensure that they are neither double counted under the old rules and the financial instrument rules, nor left out of account altogether. For example:

(*a*)   If the periodic interest-related payments have been treated as taxable or deductible on a paid basis under the old rules, the unpaid amounts accrued at Commencement Day will be recognised in the accounting period beginning on Commencement Day.

(*b*)   An initial fee or broker's fee paid at the commencement of the swap and disallowed for tax purposes is deductible in the accounting period beginning on Commencement Day, to the extent that it will not be accrued in post-commencement periods and therefore deducted under the basic rules.

(*c*)   A non-deductible termination payment made before commencement would not be affected by the transitional rules unless the company remained subject to the swap agreement at commencement. If the swap was still in place at commencement, the termination fee would be deductible in the accounting period beginning on Commencement Day.

Currency options on trading account

4.59   If the option is marked to market for accounts purposes, the accounting profits and losses in the post-commencement accounting periods will be included in trading profits. In addition, *FA 1994, s 158* will ensure that any difference between the pre-commencement profit or loss recognised for accounting and tax purposes is brought into the financial instrument rules in the accounting period which begins on Commencement Day.

4.60   If the option is not accounted for on a mark to market basis, the option premium paid or received will be taxable or deductible to the extent that it is accrued in the post-commencement accounts. *FA 1994, s 158* ensures that any part of the premium that has been recognised for accounts purposes in pre-commencement accounting periods, but not for tax purposes, will be brought into the computation of taxable trading profits for the period beginning on Commencement Day.

Currency contracts and options which are not on trading account

4.61   Under the old rules, if a currency contract or currency option was entered into by a company for a purpose not connected with its trade, and the transaction was not itself taxable as a trading transaction, or if it was a capital transaction undertaken for the purpose of the trade, it would be governed by the capital gains rules and taxed either as:

(*a*)   an acquisition or disposal of foreign currency, which is a chargeable asset under *TCGA 1992, s 21(1)(b)*; or

(*b*)   a transaction in financial futures or financial options and therefore dealt with under *TCGA 1992, s 143*.

4.62   The foreign exchange and financial instrument rules remove such transactions from the capital gains rules through the following mechanisms:

(*a*)   *FA 1993, 17 Sch 2* provides that where there is a disposal of foreign currency by a qualifying company on or after its Commencement Day, the gain or loss which is realised on the disposal is not a chargeable gain or an allowable loss.

(*b*)   *FA 1994, s 173* gives priority to amounts which are taxable under the financial instrument rules, and these cannot also be taken into account in computing chargeable gains or allowable losses under *TCGA 1992*.

(*c*)   *TCGA 1992, ss 38* and *39* require amounts which have been taken into account in computing income for tax purposes (e.g. under the foreign exchange rules for currency contracts) to be excluded from the calculation of any chargeable gain or allowable loss under the capital gains rules.

4.63   As a result, the whole of the profit or loss on a currency contract or currency option which, had it been disposed of before commencement, would have been taxable under the capital gains rules, will now be brought into the 'income treatment' afforded by the foreign exchange tax rules and financial instrument rules. This can be the case even where, under the capital gains rules, there is a disposal giving rise to a chargeable gain or allowable loss before commencement. This is dealt with by the financial instrument rules, [*FA 1994, s 158(3)*] ensuring that an equivalent income loss (equal to the earlier capital gain) arises at commencement (see Explanatory Statement, Annex II to Section 7).

Forward contracts and currency futures not on trading account

4.64   The currency contract is deemed to be entered into at the beginning of Commencement Day and if there is a difference in the local currency equivalent of the two currency amounts specified in the contract, this will be a deemed qualifying payment for the purposes of the financial instrument rules. [*FA 1994, s 153(4)*]. If the company does not account for the contract on a mark to market basis, qualifying payments (both deemed and actual) have to be recognised for tax purposes on an 'acceptable accruals basis' under *FA 1994, s 155(5)*. The Inland Revenue interprets this as a requirement to treat the deemed qualifying payment as accruing over the remaining life of the contract, on a straight line basis.

4.65   If the contract is marked to market, the fact that there is a deemed qualifying payment at maturity does not affect the basis of valuation. However, *FA 1994, s 155(7)(a)* treats the value of the contract as nil at the start of Commencement Day (the deemed acquisition time), so the whole of the pre-commencement gain or loss on the contract is brought into the accounting period beginning on Commencement Day.

Currency swaps not on trading account

4.66   The principles described above in relation to forward contracts apply equally to currency swaps, but it is also necessary to consider the additional payments which can be associated with currency swaps.

Initial exchange of principal amounts

4.67   If there is an actual exchange of principal amounts at the outset of the contract, this will be a currency contract potentially in the foreign exchange tax (not financial instrument) rules. As this exchange will have occurred pre-commencement its tax effects will have been dealt with entirely under the old rules in the pre-commencement accounting period.

Final exchange of principal

4.68 This is treated in exactly the same way as a conventional forward contract. If the accounting treatment results in a pre-commencement exchange gain or loss, this will be a deemed qualifying payment to be accrued post-commencement over the remaining life of the swap.

Initial fees and other initial payments

4.69 In general these would not be deductible for tax purposes, but would be amortised over the life of the swap for accounts purposes, assuming that the swap was accounted for on an accruals basis. The financial instrument rules would allow relief for the proportion of such payments which has accrued in post-commencement accounting periods. *FA 1994, s 158* ensures that the proportion which is accrued in pre-commencement accounting periods is deductible in the accounting period beginning on Commencement Day.

Periodic interest-related payments

4.70 Again, these are qualifying payments which are deductible on an accruals basis under the financial instrument rules and *FA 1994, s 158* ensures that amounts accounted for pre-commencement but not recognised for tax purposes are recognised in the accounting period beginning on Commencement Day.

Variation payments

4.71 If such a payment is made before Commencement Day, it will be fully taxable or deductible under the financial instrument rules either under the basic rules, or to the extent that it is accrued in pre-commencement accounting periods, as an adjustment under *FA 1994, s 158*.

Currency options not on trading account — holder

4.72 If the option is marked to market for accounts purposes, the accounting profits and losses in the post-commencement accounting periods will be taxable as part of the 'non-trading exchange gain or loss' of each period. In addition, *FA 1994, s 158* will ensure that any difference between the pre-commencement profit or loss recognised for accounting and tax purposes is brought into the financial instrument rules in the accounting period which begins on Commencement Day.

4.73   If the option is not accounted for on a mark to market basis, the option premium paid or received will be taxable or deductible to the extent that it is accrued in the post-commencement account. *FA 1994, s 158* ensures that any part of the premium that has been recognised for accounts purposes in pre-commencement accounting periods (but not recognised for tax purposes) will also be taxable or deductible in the accounting period beginning on Commencement Day.

Currency options not on trading account — grantor

4.74   Under the capital gains rules, if a company receives a premium for granting an option, that is treated as a disposal of an asset. A chargeable gain therefore arises on the day the option is granted (although this is cancelled if the option is exercised against the grantor, when the option transaction is treated as part of the transaction which results from the option being exercised). [*TCGA 1992, s 144(1)*]. A chargeable gain can therefore arise pre-commencement in respect of an option to which the company is subject post-commencement. Double counting is prevented by the operation of *FA 1994, s 158*.

For example, if the option is accounted for on an accruals basis, any part of the option premium which was accrued in the accounts for post-commencement accounting periods will be taxable as accruals of qualifying payments, but the premium will already have been taken into account in computing taxable profits in a pre-commencement accounting period and *FA 1994, s 158(3)* will operate to cancel the amounts taxable under the financial instrument rules, to prevent double counting. The overall effect is to leave the capital gain undisturbed.

4.75   If the option is exercised, the initial capital gain is cancelled and the tax treatment of the premium will be determined by the treatment of the currency contract or option which results from the exercise of the original option. The overall effect will be to recognise the whole of the profit or loss on the option under the new rules.

Rules affecting currency contracts and currency options

Change in basis of accounting

4.76   Because the taxation of qualifying payments under the financial instrument rules is based on the accounting treatment adopted for the currency contract or currency option, a change of accounting treatment from one accounting period to the next could result in an amount being taxed twice or not being recognised at all for tax purposes. To overcome this, a 'prior year adjustment' is made to the taxable profit or deductible loss of the accounting period immediately following the change. [*FA 1994, s 158*].

4.77   The adjustment brings into the accounting period the net income or expense which would otherwise be ignored as a result of the change, and deducts any amount which would otherwise be double counted. The mechanism for calculating and giving effect to this is as follows. Amounts A and B of *FA 1994, s 155* (see 4.7 and 4.8 above) are adjusted in the first accounting period in which the new basis of accounting is adopted as follows:

(*a*)   Amount A is increased by the amounts which would have been included in amount A for earlier periods under the new basis of accounting but were not included under the old basis.

(*b*)   Amount B is increased (or amount A decreased, as appropriate) by amounts which have been included in amount A for earlier accounting periods but would not have been included had the new basis of accounting applied in those periods.

(*c*)   Amount B is increased by the amounts which would have been included in amount B in earlier accounting periods had the new basis of accounting been adopted, but which were not included under the old basis.

(*d*)   Amount A is increased (or amount B is decreased, as appropriate) by amounts which have been included in amount B for earlier accounting periods but would not have been included, had the new basis of accounting been adopted for those periods.

Prevention of double counting

4.78   There are several rules designed to prevent amounts being taxable, or tax deductible, more than once under different parts of the *Taxes Acts*. Priority is given to amounts taxable or deductible under the financial instruments legislation. *FA 1994, s 173* provides that:

(*a*)   Any amount which is chargeable to corporation tax as profits of a qualifying company, or which is taken into account as a receipt in computing the profits or losses of a qualifying company, for the purposes of the financial instrument rules cannot be:

  (i)   chargeable to corporation tax as profits of the company, except under the financial instrument rules;

  (ii)   taken into account in computing taxable profits other than for the purposes of the financial instrument rules; or

  (iii)   included in consideration for the disposal of assets in calculating gains for the purposes of *TCGA 1992*.

(*b*)   Any amount which is tax deductible under the financial instrument rules cannot be:

  (i)   deducted in computing taxable profits for any other purpose;

(ii)   treated as a charge on income for the purpose of corporation tax; or

(iii)   included in the amounts deductible under *TCGA 1992, s 38* for the purpose of computing chargeable gains.

4.79   However, it should be noted that in the case of a currency contract which is accounted for on a mark to market basis, the exchange gain or loss which is taxable under the foreign exchange rules takes priority, and is deducted from the mark to market profit or loss. [*FA 1994, s 162*].

4.80   In addition, where a company makes a disposal of foreign currency on or after Commencement Day, and it did not hold the currency in 'exempt circumstances', no chargeable gain or allowable loss arises.

4.81   Taking these provisions together, the result is that:

(*a*)   Financial instruments which meet the definitions of 'currency contracts' and 'currency options' cannot be taxable under the capital gains rules.

(*b*)   Profits and losses on such instruments held for trading purposes will be taxable under the financial instrument rules and these will take priority where the results are at variance with the tax treatment under general Schedule D Case I principles.

Anti-avoidance

4.82   There are several anti-avoidance provisions which can apply to currency contracts and options.

Arm's length test

4.83   Where a company enters into a currency contract which:

(*a*)   is not on arm's length terms; or

(*b*)   would not have been entered into at all had the parties been acting at arm's length

the Board of Inland Revenue can issue a direction to 'ring fence' an exchange loss on the contract. Such a loss may then be offset only against an exchange gain accruing on the same contract in a later accounting period. [*FA 1993, s 137*]. (See Chapter 7).

Transfers of value

4.84   This applies where a company enters into a currency contract or currency option, or the terms of such a contract or option are varied, or such an option expires, so that there is a transfer of value to an associated company (either directly, or indirectly via a third party – for example back to back 'off-market' transactions with a bank). The transfer of value is reversed by adjusting 'Amount A' or 'Amount B' in the calculation of the profit or loss to be recognised under the financial instrument rules in respect of the contract or option in the accounting period in which the transaction was entered into, or its terms varied, or the option expired. [*FA 1994, s 165*].

Arm's length test – financial instrument rules

4.85   Where, on or after Commencement Day, a qualifying company enters into a currency contract or option, or the terms of a currency contract or option are varied, and

(*a*)   the transaction is not on arm's length terms; or

(*b*)   the transaction would not have been entered into at all had the parties been dealing at arm's length

the Board of Inland Revenue can issue a direction to restrict relief under the financial instruments rules for losses on the transaction. In broad terms, the effect of the direction is to adjust 'Amount A' and 'Amount B' under the financial instruments rules so that, on a cumulative basis, a net deduction is denied, but a net profit is taxed. [*FA 1994, s 167*].

Non-resident counterparties

4.86   If a company enters into a currency contract or currency option with a counterparty which is not resident in the UK, it is treated as a transaction which is not on arm's length terms for the purposes of *FA 1994, s 167* unless:

(*a*)   the counterparty is resident in a country with which the UK has a double taxation treaty which contains an interest article; or

(*b*)   the contract or option is with a trading branch in the UK of the non-resident counterparty.

4.87   If the contract is caught by this provision, tax relief is denied for a net loss on the contract calculated under the financial instrument rules, but a net profit is taxable, looking at the cumulative position over the life of the transaction. [*FA 1994, s 168*].

4.88   The anti-avoidance provisions of the foreign exchange tax rules are considered in more detail in Chapter 7 below.

Chapter 5

Non-Trading Exchange Losses

Introduction

5.1   As explained earlier in 3.45, there are different rules for the tax treatment of exchange gains and losses which relate to transactions undertaken for the purposes of a trade, and those which do not (the 'non-trading exchange gains and losses'). The rules for taxing non-trading exchange gains and losses depend on the accounting period in which the gains and losses arise. For accounting periods ending on or after 1 April 1996 the exchange gains and losses are taxed under the corporate and government debt rules (see 5.2 to 5.27 below). For earlier accounting periods the rules in *FA 1993* (before amendment by *FA 1996*) apply (see paragraphs 5.28 to 5.44 below). There are rules to deal with the transition from one regime to the other (see 5.45 to 5.47 below).

Accounting periods ending on or after 1 April 1996

Treatment as non-trading credit/debit

5.2   If a non-trading exchange gain arises on an item (under *FA 1993, s 129*) in an accounting period ending on or after 1 April 1996, it is treated as a 'non-trading credit' for the purposes of the corporate debt rules. [*FA 1993, s 130(1) as inserted by FA 1996, 14 Sch 69; FA 1996, s 105(1)*].

5.3   If a non-trading exchange loss arises in an accounting period ending on or after 1 April 1996, it is treated as a 'non-trading debit' for the purposes of the corporate debt rules. [*FA 1993, s 130(2) as inserted by FA 1996, 14 Sch 69*].

Aggregation with non-trading financial instruments and loan relationships

5.4   Similar rules apply to treat financial instrument non-trading gains and losses as non-trading credits/debits. The non-trading credits and debits arising from foreign exchange differences and financial instruments are then aggregated with all the non-trading credits and debits on loan relationships for the accounting period.

5.5   If the aggregate of non-trading credits is greater than the aggregate of non-trading debits, the net amount is taxable under Schedule D Case III. [*FA 1996, s 82(4)(a)*]. If the aggregate of non-trading debits is greater than the aggregate of non-trading credits, the net amount is the 'non-trading deficit' for the accounting period. [*FA 1996, s 82(4)(b)*]. The non-trading deficit may be relieved in a number of ways as discussed below.

Relief for non-trading deficit

5.6   The whole, or any part of, the non-trading deficit for an accounting period may be relieved in one of four ways:

(*a*)   By offset against the company's other taxable profits for the accounting period. [*FA 1996, s 83(2)(a)*].

(*b*)   By group relief against profits of other companies in the group. [*FA 1996, s 83(2)(b)*].

(*c*)   By carry back against Schedule D Case III profits. [*FA 1996, s 83(2)(c)*].

(*d*)   By carry forward and offset against non-trading profits of the 'next accounting period'. [*FA 1996, s 83(2)(d)*].

Any amount of the non-trading deficit for the year not subject to the claims above is treated as a non-trading debit of the 'next accounting period'. [*FA 1996, s 83(3)*]. However, the amount cannnot be offset against non-trading credits without a specific claim being made.

5.7   Each of the claims listed above will be considered in turn below followed by consideration of how they work together.

Time limits

5.8   The claims in 5.6(*a*)–(*c*) above must be made within two years of the end of the accounting period in which the deficit arose. The claim in 5.6(*d*) above must be made within two years of the end of the accounting period in which the non-trading deficit is to be offset against non-trading income. [*FA 1996, s 83(6) and (7)*]. The time limits can be extended at the discretion of the Inland Revenue. [*FA 1996, s 83(6)*].

Example 1

A company with a non-trading deficit in the year ended 30 June 1997 wishes to make a group relief claim under *FA 1996, s 83(2)(b)* and a claim to carry forward against non-trading income to the next accounting period (under *FA 1996, s 83(2)(d)*) which is to be the six months ended 31 December 1997.

5.9   *Non-Trading Exchange Losses*

The time limits for the two claims are:

FA 1996, s 83(2)(b) claim   30 June 1999

FA 1996, s 83(2)(d) claim   31 December 1999

Offset against other profits of the company

5.9   The claim to set off the deficit against other profits for the period must identify the profits to be reduced. [*FA 1996, 8 Sch 1(2)*].

5.10   Any claim under this provision applies *after* relief for any trading losses brought forward from earlier accounting periods. [*FA 1996, 8 Sch 1(3)(a)*]. There are rules to preserve double tax relief (see 5.23 below).

5.11   Any claim under this provision must be applied *before* any relief under *ICTA 1988, s 393A(1)* for current or subsequent year trading losses against the other profits of the company. [*FA 1996, 8 Sch 1(3)(b)(i)*].

5.12   Similarly a claim to offset a current year non-trading deficit against other profits of the company for the year takes priority over a claim to carry back a non-trading deficit from subsequent years for offset against profits of the current year. [*FA 1996, 8 Sch 1(3)(b)(ii)*].

5.13   A claim under this provision cannot be used to offset ring fence profits of the company (i.e. profits of oil and gas business – see *ICTA 1988, Pt XII, Chap V*). [*FA 1996, 8 Sch 1(4)*].

Example 2

	Year ended 31.12.97
Company A	£
Schedule D Case I profit	10,000
Trading loss b/f	(2,000)
Non-trading deficit	(15,000)
Capital gain	5,000
Taxable income:	
Schedule D Case I	10,000
less: trading loss b/f	(2,000)
	8,000
less: s 83(2)(a) claim	(8,000)
	Nil
Capital gain	5,000
less: s 83(2)(a) claim	(5,000)
Taxable income	Nil

Utilisation of non-trading deficit	£
Non-trading deficit for the year	(15,000)
s 83(2)(a) claim	13,000
Non-trading deficit remaining for other possible claims	(2,000)

Group relief

5.14   Group relief may be used to relieve all, part or none of the non-trading deficit of an accounting period. The part of the non-trading deficit that is subject to this group relief claim is treated as if it were a trading loss available for group relief. [*FA 1996, 8 Sch 2(2)*]. Thus this relief is very flexible allowing relief for some, all or none of the non-trading deficits against the total taxable profits of one or more other companies in the same group relief group.

Example 3

The information is the same as for Company A in Example 1, except that another group company (Company B) has taxable profits of £4,000.

	£
Non-trading deficits left after s 83(2)(a) claim	(2,000)
s 83(2)(b) group relief claim	2,000
Non-trading deficit left	Nil
Taxable income of Company B	

	£
Taxable income before group relief	4,000
less: s 83(2)(b) claim	(2,000)
Taxable income	2,000

Carry back of deficit to earlier accounting periods

5.15   A claim can be made to carry back some or all of the non-trading deficit to earlier accounting periods. This is not as flexible a claim as the others already described, as it is effectively 'all or nothing'. The claim has to be for an amount equal to the lower of:

(*a*)   the non-trading deficit for the period as reduced by any group relief or current year offset claim and as reduced by any amount of carried forward debit (see *FA 1996, s 83(3) and (4)* and further discussion in 5.20 *et seq.* below); and

(*b*)   the total profits available for relief under this carry back provision (see 5.16 below). [*FA 1996, 8 Sch 3(2)*].

5.16   The profits in earlier accounting periods that are eligible for a carry back of non-trading deficit claim are the profits taxable under Schedule D Case III as profits and gains incurred on the company's loan relationships in the 'permitted period'. [*FA 1996, 8 Sch 3(4)*].

Subject to the transitional provisions described below, the 'permitted period' is

(*a*)   for deficit periods ending on or after 2 July 1997, the twelve months immediately preceding the beginning of the deficit period; and

(*b*)   for deficit periods ending before 2 July 1997, the three years immediately preceding the beginning of the deficit period except to the extent that the three year period falls before 31 March 1996.

[*FA 1996, 8 Sch 3(7); F(No 2)A 1997, s 40(2) and (7)*].

See also 5.45 to 5.47 below.

For deficit periods that straddle 2 July 1997, the permitted period is the period from 1 April 1996 to immediately before the start of the deficit period for the 'pre-commencement part' of the deficit. The 'pre-commencement part' of the deficit is calculated on a time apportionment basis unless this does not give a just and reasonable result (in which case a just and reasonable basis is to be used). [*F(No 2)A 1997, s 40(8)–(12)*]. The provisions obviously only have effect if there are more than twelve months from 1 April 1996 to the start of the accounting period that crosses 2 July 1997. The operation of the rule in an accounting period crossing 2 July 1997 is best understood by an example.

Example 4

Company X has a year end of 31 May. Its non-trading Schedule D Case III profits/non-trading deficits are as follows:

		£
1 April 1996 to 31 May 1996	Schedule D Case III	30,000
1 June 1996 to 31 May 1997	Schedule D Case III	100,000
1 June 1997 to 31 May 1998	Non-trading deficit	120,000

Non-trading deficit carry back [*FA 1996, s 83(2)(c)*]

	£
Against 1 June 1996 to 31 May 1997 (Twelve months permitted period)	100,000

Against 1 April 1996 to 31 May 1996
    (Pre-commencement part)
    Pre-commencement part of deficit = £120,000/12 =
	10,000

Maximum carry back possible	110,000

5.17   This carry back claim is further restricted by the fact that a number of other reliefs are to be given against the Schedule D Case III profits before relief for a non-trading deficit carried back. The reliefs which have priority are:

(*a*)   relief for trading charges on income such as royalties (under *ICTA 1988, s 338*);

(*b*)   relief for any loss or deficit incurred in accounting periods earlier than the deficit period in question (i.e. relief for earlier losses take priority);

(*c*)   relief for trading losses against profits of the same or earlier accounting periods (under *ICTA 1988, s 393A*);

(*d*)   relief for a non-trading deficit by way of current year offset against other profits of the company or group relief; and

(*e*)   for an investment company, any relief for capital allowances, management expenses and/or business charges.

[*FA 1996, 8 Sch 3(6)*].

These reliefs reduce the profits eligible for the carry back claim (i.e. they reduce the size of 5.15(*b*) above).

5.18   The carry back claim, once quantified under the comparison in 5.15 above, reduces the eligible Schedule D Case III profits, on a later periods first (i.e. LIFO) basis. [*FA 1996, 8 Sch 3(3)*]. The carry back claim can displace double tax relief against Schedule D Case III profits (e.g. withholding tax on interest) as it is an all or nothing claim. If the carry back claim is restricted to 5.15(*b*) above, then there will be some non-trading deficit left to carry forward (see 5.20 *et seq.* below). If the claim is not so restricted (i.e. 5.15(*a*) above applies) then on a claim no carry forwards are possible – hence the 'all or nothing' character of this claim.

5.19   There are provisions to cater for an accounting period that is only partially within the permitted period. These require the Schedule D Case III profits from loan relationships of the accounting period to be time apportioned between the parts before and after the start of the permitted period. [*FA 1996, 8 Sch 3(5)*]. In practice the non-trading profits in the accounting period that crosses 31 March 1996 would be available for carry back offsets as follows (see Inland Revenue Manual).

(*a*)   Loan relationship net debits would be offset against the non-trading net credit equal to

    (i)   all non-trading loan relationship profits other than interest; plus

    (ii)   interest net credits of the accounting period which are time apportioned to the period after 31 March 1996; plus

    (iii)   transitional interest adjustments if treated as paid or received after 31 March 1996.

5.20 *Non-Trading Exchange Losses*

(*b*) Foreign exchange and financial instrument net debits can be offset against the overall net non-trading profit from foreign exchange and financial instruments for the whole accounting period (due to a combination of the carry back as far as 31 March 1996 and the transitional rule in *FA 1996, 15 Sch 23* (see 5.46 below).

Example 5

Year ended 31 March	1997 £	1998 £	1999 £	2000 £
Schedule D Case I	5,000	10,000	(20,000)	1,000
Schedule D Case III from loan relationships	1,000	15,000	3,000	–
Trading charges	–	(1,000)	–	–
Non-trading deficit				(12,000)
Taxable income:				
Schedule D Case I	5,000	10,000	Nil	1,000
s 393A c/back claim		(10,000)		
s 83(2)(a) claim				(1,000)
Schedule D Case III	1,000	15,000	3,000	
s 393A current and c/back claim		(7,000)	(3,000)	
s 83(2)(c) claim	(1,000)	(8,000)	Nil	Nil
Taxable income	5,000	Nil	Nil	Nil
Non-trading deficit				(12,000)
s 83(2)(a) claim				1,000
				(11,000)
Compare to eligible profits (1,000 + 8,000) so claim lower (s 83(2)(c))				9,000
Non-trading deficit left to carry forward under s 83(2)(d) and/or s 83(3)				(2,000)

Carry forward of deficit to future accounting periods

5.20 The non-trading deficit relief rules cater for flexible carry for-wards of non-trading deficits. A company can choose that all, some or

92

none of its non-trading deficit for a period is carried forward to the next accounting period and used to relieve 'non-trading profits' of that period. [*FA 1996, s 83(2)(d)*]. If no such claim is made then, to the extent that the non-trading deficit for the period has not been utilised by claims under *FA 1996, s 83(2)(a)–(c)*, it is carried forward to the next and subsequent accounting periods (the 'carried forward' deficit). [*FA 1996, s 83(3)*]. If a partial *s 83(2)(d)* claim is made, the balance of the non-trading deficit after the *s 83(2)(a)–(d)* claim is carried forward as a non-trading deficit as described above. The company must make a claim to utilise the non-trading deficit in future periods.

Carry forward under FA 1996, s 83(3) and utilisation of carry forward by making a claim under s 83(2)(d)

5.21   The Finance Act 1998 amended *s 83(3)* and *(4)* retrospectively, bringing the rules clearly into line with the Inland Revenue interpretation of the non-trading deficit carry forward rules.

(*a*)   Where a non-trading deficit is to be set against non-trading profits of the next accounting period under *s 83(2)(d)* it is necessary to make a specific claim, even in the case of offset against net loan relationship income of the future period.

(*b*)   Where no claim is made the carry forward under *s 83(3)* will operate. However, an amount of non-trading deficit carried forward to the next period in this way cannot be surrendered as group relief, set off against non-trading profits by means of a claim under *s 83(2)(a)* (although it can by means of a claim under *s 83(2)(d)*), or carried back against profits of earlier periods, nor will it be amalgamated with non-trading credits of the subsequent period.

(*c*)   An amount carried forward under *s 83(3)* can be made the subject of a *s 83(2)(d)* claim in respect of a third period. Thus, for example, if a non-trading deficit arises in period 1, and no claim is made, it will be carried forward under *s 83(3)* and treated as a deficit of period 2. If the taxpayer wishes to set the deficit against non-trading profits in period 3, it will need to make a claim under *s 83(2)(d)* in respect of period 2 (i.e. the rules are similar to those for brought forward management expenses).

5.22   The time limit for such a claim is two years from the end of the period in which the non-trading deficit is to be offset against non-trading income (see *s 83(6)* and *(7)(b)*). Thus, in the case of a claim to use the deficit in period 3, this would be two years from the end of period 3. Care must be taken to avoid overlooking such claims. If no claim is made to offset the deficit against period 3 non-trading profits, it will be carried forward under *s 83(3)* to period 3 and will be available to offset period 4 non-trading profits by virtue of a claim under *s 83(2)(d)*, and so on. This is best illustrated by an example.

Example 6

	Year 1 £'000	Year 2 £'000	Year 3 £'000
Trading income	10	20	–
Non-trading credits	200	–	30
Non-trading debits	(300)	–	(10)
Capital gain	–	–	30
Taxable income:			
Capital gain	–	–	30
less: s 83(2)(d) claim	–	–	(30)
Schedule D Case III	–	–	20
less: s 83(2)(d) claim	–	–	(20)
Schedule D Case I	10	20	–
less: s 83(2)(a) claim	(10)	–	–
	Nil	20	Nil
Non-trading deficit c/f *s 83(3)*	(90)	(40)	(40)
Non-trading deficit c/f *s 83(2)(d)*		(50)	

Double tax relief implications

5.23   *FA 1996, 14 Sch 42* and *43* introduce amendments to the foreign tax credit relief rules in *ICTA 1988, s 797* to allow credit relief to be preserved when making non-trading deficit relief claims. The new subsections *ICTA 1988, s 797(3A)* and *(3B)* allow companies to make flexible current year offset claims and carry forward claims whereby the company allocates the deficit for offset against whatever categories of income it chooses. The company can thus choose to avoid setting off the deficit against income on which it has suffered creditable foreign tax. This is illustrated by the following example.

Example 7

	Year 1 £'000	Year 2 £'000
Schedule D Case V dividend income (overseas tax suffered)	100	100
Chargeable gain	–	20

Schedule D Case I trading income	80	80
Non-trading deficit	(150)	–
Taxable income:		
Schedule D Case V dividend income	100	100
Chargeable gain	–	20
s 83(2)(d) claim	–	(20)
Schedule D Case I trading income	80	80
less: s 83(2)(a) claim	(80)	–
	100	180
Non-trading deficit	(150)	
s 83(2)(a) claim Year 1	80	
s 83(2)(d) claim Year 1		
s 83(3) carry forward	20	
	(50)	

There is no offset in Year 2. £50 is carried forward to Year 3.

5.24   *FA 1996, 14 Sch 43* inserts *ICTA 1988, s 797A* on credit relief which helps preserve credit relief when overseas tax has been suffered on interest income. The principle behind the provision is to allow the company to choose how much of its aggregate non-trading debits to offset against its aggregate non-trading credits so that sufficient net non-trading credits (being the overseas taxed interest income) are left to utilise the creditable foreign tax suffered on foreign source interest income.

5.25   The steps to follow in the calculations under *ICTA 1988, s 797A* are as follows.

(*a*)   Determine whether there are any interest non-trading credits in respect of which credit relief is available. If so, continue.

(*b*)   Compute the company's non-trading credits (this is the gross credits – debits are dealt with separately below) i.e. all non-trading credits from loan relationships, foreign exchange and financial instruments.

(*c*)   Compute the company's non-trading debits i.e. all non-trading debits from loan relationships, foreign exchange, financial instruments.

(*d*)   Compute the 'adjusted amount of the non-trading debits' being (*c*) above less the sum of:

   (i)   any group relief, carry forward and carry back claims made in respect of any non-trading deficit for the period;

(ii) any amount of any non-trading deficit for the period carried forward as a debit under *FA 1996, s 83(3)*; and

(iii) any amount carried forward to this accounting period under *FA 1996, s 83(2)(d)* (i.e. deficit for offset against non-trading profits).

(e) The 'adjusted amount of the non-trading debits' can then be offset against profits of the company for the year as the company sees fit (assuming there is a Schedule D Case III profit equal to the non-trading credits under (b) above). The Schedule D Case III profit should be split by source to separate the 'relevant income' for *ICTA 1988, s 797* purposes. Thus the company can choose to preserve double tax relief.

(f) If the company has a non-trading deficit for the period that is not fully accounted for by the items in (d)(i)–(iii) above, the excess left may be subject to a claim under *s 83(2)(a)* to offset it against current year profits. In applying (e) above, the amount subject to the current year offset claim will be allocated against the profits as specified in the *s 83(2)(a)* claim documentation.

This application of *ICTA 1988, s 797A* is illustrated by the following example.

Example 8

	£'000
Schedule D Case I	30
Chargeable gains	50
Non-trading credits	120
(100 foreign taxed interest, withholding tax 30)	
Non-trading debits	(180)
Taxable profits of other group company	20

Following the steps indicated above

(a) Yes

(b) Non-trading credits = 120

(c) Non-trading debits = 180
(Non-trading deficit = (b) – (c) = 60)

(d) Adjusted amount of non-trading debits = 180 less the sum of

(i) 20 (group relief)

(ii) Nil

(iii) Nil

= 160 (of which 40 is non-trading deficit)

(e)(f)	Schedule D Case I	Chargeable gains	Schedule D Case III(1)	Schedule D Case III(2)
	30	50	20	100
s 83(2)(a) offset rest of adjusted non-trading debits	(30)	(10)		
	____	(40)	(20)	(60)
	Nil	Nil	Nil	40

Corporation tax attributable to income subject to foreign tax: 40 @ 31%	12.40
Foreign tax attributable to income	30.00
Wasted foreign tax	17.60

DTR not fully preserved.

Depending on the income of the next period, the company could instead carry forward 40 of non-trading deficit as a debit (s 83(3)). If so steps (d) and (e) become

(d) Adjusted amount of non-trading debits = 180 less the sum of

(i) 20 (group relief)

(ii) 40

(iii) Nil

= 120

(e)(f)	Schedule D Case I	Chargeable gains	Schedule D Case III(1)	Schedule D Case III(2)
	30	50	20	100
s 83(2)(a)	(30)	(50)	(20)	(20)
	Nil	Nil	Nil	80

Corporation tax attributable to income subject to foreign tax: 80 @ 31%	24.80
Foreign tax attributable to income	30.00
Wasted foreign tax	5.20

There is better but not complete DTR preservation.

5.26   Non-Trading Exchange Losses

Interaction with other claims

5.26   Claims under *FA 1996, s 83* take priority over group relief claims for the accounting period in question. [*ICTA 1988, s 407(1)(b)*as amended by *FA 1996, 14 Sch 22(1)*]. Group relief takes priority over claims to carry back a non-trading deficit to the accounting period in question. [*ICTA 1988, s 407(2)(c)* as amended by *FA 1996, 14 Sch 22(2)*]. The scope of *ICTA 1988, s 242* claims is expanded to allow offset of surplus franked investment income against non-trading deficits under *FA 1996, s 83* claims. The time limit for such *s 242* claims is two years from the end of the relevant accounting period (i.e. two years from the end of that accounting period unless it is a *s 83(2)(d)* claim in which case it is two years from the end of the next accounting period). [*ICTA 1988, s 242(2)(f)* as substituted by *FA 1996, 14 Sch 12*]. *ICTA 1988, s 242* was not amended to reinstate non-trading deficits where a company pays ACT in respect of excess franked payments in a later accounting period. The Inland Revenue Manual asks Inspectors to let FID (loan relationships) know if this causes difficulties in practice.

Comprehensive example

5.27   To illustrate how all the claims work together there follows a comprehensive example on non-trading deficit relief.

Example 9

Year ended 31 March	1997	1998	1999	2000
	£	£	£	£
D Case I income	10,000	10,000	10,000	10,000
D Case V dividend income (overseas tax paid)	20,000	20,000	20,000	20,000
Capital gain	–	–	–	3,000
D Case III profits (loan relationships)	5,000	5,000	–	–
Non-trading deficit			(25,000)	(5,000)
Taxable income:				
D Case I income	10,000	10,000	10,000	10,000
less: s 83(2)(a) claim			(10,000)	(5,000)
D Case V income	20,000	20,000	20,000	20,000
D Case III profits	5,000	5,000		
less: s 83(2)(c) claim	(5,000)	(5,000)		
Capital gain				3,000
less: s 83(2)(d) claim				(3,000)
	30,000	30,000	20,000	25,000

Non-trading deficit utilisation:

	£	Time limit
Year ended 31.3.99 non-trading deficit	(25,000)	
s 83(2)(a) claim	10,000	31.3.2001
	(15,000)	
s 83(2)(c) claim (limited to 10,000)	10,000	31.3.2001
	(5,000)	
s 83(2)(d) claim	3,000	31.3.2001
Carried forward debit from year ended 31.3.99	(2,000)	
Year ended 31 March 2000 non-trading deficit	(5,000)	
	(7,000)	
s 83(2)(a) claim (restricted to current year amount of 5,000)	5,000	31.3.2002
Balance left	(2,000)	

Accounting periods ending before 1 April 1996

5.28   If a company has an accounting period within the foreign exchange tax rules but ending before 1 April 1996 the non-trading exchange loss relief rules as originally enacted in *FA 1993* apply. This means the non-trading exchange loss relief rules apply to all accounting periods beginning on or after 23 March 1995 and ending before 1 April 1996.

Example 10

Company C draws up accounts for calendar year to 31 March.

Company C has one year (to 31 March 1996) subject to the non-trading exchange loss relief rules.

Example 11

Company D (year end usually 30 June) is sold to a new owner and draws up accounts for the nine months ended 31 March 1996.

Company D has one nine month period subject to the non-trading exchange loss relief rules.

The non-trading exchange loss relief rules are outlined in 5.29 to 5.44 below. The rules to deal with the transition to the non-trading deficit rules are described in 5.45 to 5.47 below.

5.29 *Non-Trading Exchange Losses*

Determination of the aggregate non-trading exchange gain/loss to tax/relieve

5.29 Non-trading exchange gains and losses arising in a company for an accounting period ending before 1 April 1996 are aggregated in accordance with *FA 1993, s 129(5)* to give A (total gains) and B (total losses). The aggregation includes non-trading profits and losses under the financial instrument rules.

5.30 If A equals B then there is no net amount to tax or relieve. [*FA 1993, s 129(6)*]. If A exceeds B then A minus B is a gain chargeable to tax as income under Schedule D Case VI. [*FA 1993, s 130*]. If B exceeds A then this is known as 'the relievable amount' [*FA 1993, s 131(1) and (2)*] which is deductible in a number of ways described in more detail below.

Methods of deducting the relievable amount

5.31 The relievable amounts may be deducted in the following ways:

(*a*) By group relief against profits of other companies in the group. [*FA 1993, s 131(3)*].

(*b*) By offset against the company's other taxable profits for the accounting period. [*FA 1993, s 131(4)*].

(*c*) By carry back against non-trading exchange gains of the preceding three years. [*FA 1993, s 131(5)–(11)*].

(*d*) By carry forward against non-trading exchange gains in future years. [*FA 1993, s 131(12)*].

5.32 Each of these methods will be considered in turn below. All of them (apart from (*d*)) require a claim to be made within the period of two years immediately following the accounting period to which the relievable amount relates [*FA 1993, s 131(14)*] or within such further period as the Board may allow. A company can make some, all or none of the claims detailed under (*a*) to (*c*) above.

Group relief [*FA 1993 s 131(3)*]

5.33 Group relief is a totally flexible method as it may be used to offset all or part (or none) of the relievable amount against the total taxable profits of one or more other companies which are within the same group relief group. (In general terms these are companies within the same 75% UK group).

Offset against other profits of the company [*FA 1993, s 131(4)*]

5.34   As with group relief, the company can choose the quantum of the relievable amount (all, part or none) which will be offset against the other profits of the company for that accounting period. There is however, a restriction in this case. This claim for offset against other profits cannot displace relief for a trading loss brought forward from an earlier accounting period. A claim for offset against other profits can be made where the 'other profits' are franked investment income under *ICTA 1988, s 242(2)(f)*.

5.35   Any claim under this provision applies before any relief for current year trading losses against other profits of the company for the accounting period [*ICTA 1988, s 393A(1)*] in accordance with *FA 1993, s 133(1)*.

5.36   A claim under *FA 1993, s 131(4)* cannot be used to offset ring fence profits of the company (i.e. profits for oil and gas business – see *ICTA 1988, Pt XII, Chap V* in accordance with *FA 1993, s 133(2)*).

5.37   A claim under *FA 1993, s 131(4)* cannot be used to offset the policy holders' share of profits arising from life assurance business (as defined in *FA 1989*). [*ICR 6*].

Carry back against three preceding years' non-trading exchange gains [*FA 1993, s 131(5)–(11)*]

5.38   The carry back claim is not as flexible as the two claims already described as this claim is effectively 'all or nothing'. If a carry back claim is made in respect of the relievable amount this claim must be for all of that amount or that amount as reduced by group relief and current period offset claims made (if any). The other major restriction on the size of the carry back claim is the quantum of the 'relevant exchange profits' in the period of three years immediately preceding the accounting period in which the relievable amount arose. [*FA 1993, s 131(5) and (6)*]. Obviously the carry back claim has limited application because of the introduction of the non-trading deficit rules. It could be needed where a company has more than one accounting period within the foreign exchange tax rules ending before 1 April 1996. The transitional rules can also result in this claim being relevant (see 5.45 below).

5.39   The 'relevant exchange profits' are the total net non-trading exchange gains (taxable under Schedule D Case VI) in the three preceding years after deduction of:

(*a*)   any reliefs for earlier losses; and

(*b*)   any relief for trading or business charges in those years [under *ICTA 1988, s 388*].

5.40   The deduction (*a*) above implies that claims to carry back trading losses from earlier years of part/all of a 'relievable amount' for earlier accounting periods must be dealt with before claims for carry back of part/all of a 'relievable amount' from later accounting periods.

5.41   The carry back claim offsets the relievable amount against the latest period's non-trading exchange gains first (i.e. LIFO basis).

5.42   If there are trading losses in the accounting period in which the relievable amount arises the carryback claim for the non-trading exchange losses only applies after any claim under *ICTA 1988, s 393A(1)* (i.e. the exchange profits of a year must offset trading losses carried back – if claimed before they can be used for an exchange loss carryback claim). [*FA 1993, s 133(3)*].

5.43   The carry back claim provisions cater for circumstances when the permitted three-year carry back period includes accounting periods falling partly within and partly outside the three years allowed. To calculate the 'relevant exchange profits' the net non-trading exchange profits of the accounting period falling partly within the three-year permitted period are time apportioned so that only the proportion for the time within the three-year period is included. [*FA 1993, s 131(8)(b)*].

Carry forward against future years' non-trading exchange gains [*FA 1993, s 131(12)*]

5.44   Any part of the relievable amount left after the three claims outlined above is automatically carried forward for relief against future non-trading exchange gains. This is achieved by treating the amount carried forward as a non-trading exchange loss arising in the next succeeding accounting period. Amount B in that year is thus increased accordingly. The loss carried forward is, however, ignored for the purposes of calculating the amounts available for group relief and current year set off claims (under (*a*) and (*b*) in 5.31 above) in future accounting periods. As for the carry back claim, the automatic carry forward has very limited application because of the introduction of the non-trading deficit rules.

Transition from the non-trading exchange loss rules to the non-trading deficit rules

5.45   The application of the non-trading exchange loss rules may leave an amount of non-trading exchange loss (and/or non-trading financial instrument loss) which would be carried forward (under *FA 1993, s 131(12)*) but for the fact that it needs to be carried forward to an accounting period ending on or after 1 April 1996. *FA 1996, 15 Sch 24* provides that such an amount is treated as a carried forward debit (as per *FA 1996, s 83(3)*) in the accounting period ending on or after 1 April 1996.

5.46   It is also possible to carry back foreign exchange (and financial investment) non-trading losses from accounting periods ending on or after 1 April 1996 to earlier accounting periods under the provisions of *FA 1996, 15 Sch 23*.

5.47   The carry back works as follows:

(*a*)   Determine whether there is a 'relievable amount' (see 5.29 above) in the accounting period ending on or after 1 April 1996.

(*b*)   Determine whether a carry back claim is possible for the accounting periods beginning before 1 April 1996 (see 5.38 to 5.43 above) using the *FA 1993* rules before amendment by *FA 1996*.

(*c*)   Any amount so claimed reduces the profits of the relevant accounting period beginning before 1 April 1996 and an equal non-trading credit is deemed to arise in the accounting period ending on or after 1 April 1996 from which the loss was carried back. This is to prevent double counting as the loss carried back will be included as a non-trading debit in the relevant accounting period ending on or after 1 April 1996. [*FA 1996, 15 Sch 23(2)*].

Example 12

Year ended 31 March	1996 £	1997 £	1998 £	1999 £
Schedule D Case VI (exchange gains)	3,000			
Non-trading exchange loss		(3,000)	(3,000)	(3,000)
Non-trading financial instrument gain/(loss)		5,000	5,000	(2,000)
Relievable amount				(5,000)
Aggregate non-trading credits on loans		10,000	15,000	8,000
Taxable income				
Schedule D Case III		12,000	17,000	3,000
Schedule D Case VI	3,000			
less: FA 1993, s 131(5) claim	(3,000)			3,000
Taxable income	Nil	12,000	17,000	6,000

Carry backs and interest on tax

5.48   When non-trading foreign exchange losses are carried back against non-trading exchange gains of an earlier period the tax liability for that earlier period is reduced. This potentially adjusts the amount on which interest on overdue tax or tax overpaid is due. Special provisions introduced by *FA 1993, 18 Sch 1* and *5* and *FA 1995, 24 Sch 8–12* amend

5.48 *Non-Trading Exchange Losses*

TMA 1970, s 87A and *ICTA 1988, s 826* to ensure that for such interest purposes the tax liability is not treated as reduced from the outset but only from when the carryback claim is made. These provisions were further amended by *FA 1996, 14 Sch 1* and *48* to give the same result for the carry back of non-trading deficits against Schedule D Case III income of an earlier period.

Chapter 6

Commencement and Transitional Rules

Introduction

6.1   This chapter deals with the rules governing the introduction of the foreign exchange tax rules including:

(*a*)   the date ('Commencement Day') from which a company becomes taxable under these rules;

(*b*)   the initial 'basic valuation' of assets and liabilities held immediately on or before Commencement Day, which forms the basis for calculating taxable exchange gains and losses; and

(*c*)   transitional rules for calculating taxable exchange differences on transactions which straddle the Commencement Day.

6.2   A number of different transitional rules exist, reflecting the variety of treatment of exchange gains and losses prior to the introduction of the foreign exchange tax rules. The appropriate choice depends both on the nature and terms of the transaction, for example, whether it is a debt which is fixed or variable in amount and term, and the purpose for which it was undertaken. One consequence of this variety of transitional rules is that transactions which give rise to equal and opposite exchange gains and losses for accounts purposes may not produce equal and opposite taxable exchange gains and losses.

6.3   The transitional rules for currency contracts are dealt with in Chapter 4.

Commencement

6.4   The 'Appointed Day' from which the new rules come into operation is 23 March 1995, the date determined by the Treasury Order made on 15 December 1994 under the provisions of *FA 1993, s 165(7)(b)*.

6.5   The effective date from which the rules apply to a particular company – referred to in this book as the company's 'Commencement Day' – will coincide with the beginning of an accounting period (as defined in *ICTA 1988, s 12*) for that company. A company's Commencement Day is the first day of its first accounting period which begins on or

6.6 *Commencement and Transitional Rules*

after the Appointed Day. Taxable exchange gains and losses are calculated under the rules by reference to accounting periods, and normally these would coincide with the periods for which the company makes up its accounts.

6.6 This is illustrated by the following examples.

Example 1

Company A prepares accounts annually to 31 December. Its Commencement Day is therefore 1 January 1996.

Example 2

Company B prepares accounts to 31 March. The first accounting period beginning on or after the Appointed Day is the year ended 31 March 1996, so its Commencement Day is 1 April 1995.

Example 3

Company C normally makes up accounts to 31 March, but is acquired in February 1995 by a group which prepares accounts to 30 June. It therefore prepares accounts for the 15-month period 1 April 1994 to 30 June 1995. There will be two corporation tax accounting periods: the 12 months ended 31 March 1995 and the period 1 April 1995 to 30 June 1995. The first accounting period beginning on or after the Appointed Day is the period 1 April 1995 to 30 June 1995, so its Commencement Day is 1 April 1995.

Example 4

Company D makes up accounts to the last Saturday in September. Its 1993/94 accounting period therefore ended on 24 September 1994 and it prepares accounts for the 53-week period 25 September 1994 to 30 September 1995. There are two corporation tax accounting periods: the year ended 24 September 1995 and the period 25 September to 30 September 1995. The first accounting period beginning on or after the Appointed Day is the period 25 September 1995 to 30 September 1995, so its Commencement Day is 25 September 1995. However, if the company has entered into a 'mean accounting date' agreement with the Inland Revenue, under which each period of account is treated as a corporation tax accounting period ending on 30 September, the Commencement Day will be treated as 1 October 1995, the beginning of the first period of account which begins on or after the Appointed Day.

6.7   There is an anti-avoidance rule to prevent companies changing their accounting date for the purpose of obtaining a more favourable Commencement Day (see 7.44 below).

Qualifying assets, qualifying liabilities and currency contracts held before Commencement Day

6.8   The foreign exchange tax rules apply to all qualifying assets, qualifying liabilities and rights and duties under currency contracts to which a company becomes entitled or subject on or after its Commencement Day. However, where such transactions have been entered into before Commencement Day and a company is still entitled or subject to them on Commencement Day they are brought into the foreign exchange tax rules at the start of Commencement Day, subject to the effects of the transitional rules.

Commencement Day values – 'basic valuation'

6.9   Taxable exchange gains and losses on qualifying assets and liabilities are calculated by finding the sterling (or local currency) equivalent of the 'basic valuation' of the asset or liability (see Chapter 3). There are detailed rules for determining the basic valuation of qualifying assets and liabilities which straddle the company's Commencement Day, as follows.

A qualifying asset which was within the chargeable gains regime prior to Commencement Day

6.10   This includes foreign currency debts on a security, other second-hand foreign currency debts, foreign currency bank accounts and holdings of foreign currency (except where these items are circulating assets of a trade and therefore not subject to the capital gains rules prior to Commencement Day). The basic valuation of such an asset is its market value, expressed in the nominal currency of the asset, immediately before the company's Commencement Day. [*TR 6(3)*].

Any other qualifying asset or qualifying liability

6.11   The basic valuation is the valuation which the company puts on it immediately before the company's Commencement Day [*FA 1993, s 159(1)(a)* as modified by *TR 6(1)*]. This will normally be the figure used in preparing the accounts for the period ended immediately before the Commencement Day. Where, exceptionally, this valuation is not in accordance with normal accountancy practice, the basic valuation is the valuation which would be adopted under normal accountancy practice. [*FA 1993, s 159(1)(b)*].

6.12   In both cases if the valuation is not expressed in the nominal currency of the asset (as defined in *FA 1993, s 160*) it must be translated into the nominal currency (see 3.30 above).

6.13   However, a company may elect to adopt the original book value (i.e. normally cost) in place of the pre-commencement book value in respect of all its qualifying assets which are:

(*a*)   debts on a security, and

(*b*)   shares

if the profits and losses on such shares and debts on securities are taken into account in computing the profits of the trade. [*TR 6(2)*].

6.14   The election had to be made before 30 September 1996 and could be withdrawn before that date. Any election made has effect from the beginning of the company's Commencement Day and is irrevocable from 30 September 1996. [*TR 6(2)* and *(2A)* as amended by *SI 1996 No 1349*]. Under the original provisions any election had to be made within 92 days beginning with the company's Commencement Day and was irrevocable. [*TR 6 (2)* before amendment]. This election could be relevant to a general insurance company or a financial trader, for example, where debts on security are held as part of the trade.

6.15   For currency contracts, the starting point is simply the amount of currency specified in the contract. [*FA 1993, s 126*]. The concept of basic valuation is not relevant and there are therefore no special rules for the opening value of currency contracts.

Opening exchange rate to be used

6.16   The appropriate exchange rate for the day immediately preceding the company's Commencement Day is to be used as the opening exchange rate for assets, liabilities and currency contracts held at Commencement Day and will be:

(*a*)   In the case of a qualifying asset formerly within the chargeable gains regime, the London closing rate for that day;

(*b*)   In other cases:

  (i)   the exchange rate used for accounting purposes, if that is an arm's length rate; or

  (ii)   if no rate was used in the accounts for a currency contract, the rate implied by the contract if it is an arm's length rate (see Chapter 4); or

  (iii)   if neither of these apply, the London closing rate for the day.

[*TR 50*].

6.17   This means that in most cases the exchange rates used to prepare the closing balance sheet for the accounting period immediately preceding Commencement Day will be the starting point for calculating exchange differences taxable under the foreign exchange tax rules.

Irrecoverable debts

6.18   A debt which was wholly irrecoverable immediately before commencement is treated under the foreign exchange tax rules as having ceased to exist on the company's Commencement Day with no exchange gain or loss accruing (see 11.14 below).

Transitional rules

Introduction

6.19   There are different transitional rules to cover the variety of treatments of exchange gains and losses pre-commencement. The various treatment and the appropriate transitional rules are:

(*a*)   'fixed' assets and liabilities on which exchange differences were ignored pre-commencement (the 'fixed nothings') – the kink test transitional rule (see 6.21–6.37 below);

(*b*)   'fluctuating' nothings – the grandfathering transitional rule (see 6.21–6.28 and 6.38–6.42 below);

(*c*)   assets and liabilities of a trade for which exchange differences were taxed on a realisation basis pre-commencement (see 6.44–6.52 below);

(*d*)   assets which were within the chargeable gains regime pre-commencement – the capital gains transitional rule (see 6.53–6.75 below); and

(*e*)   currency contracts and options within the chargeable gains regime pre-commencement (see 4.48–4.70 above).

Order of application of provisions

6.20   In general, any calculation to be made under the transitional rules is to be made before the application of certain provisions:

(*a*)   the arm's length test (see 7.10 below);

(*b*)   the deferral of unrealised gains on long-term capital assets and liabilities (see Chapter 8); and

(*c*)   the matching election (see Chapter 9).

[*TR 2*].

6.21   *Commencement and Transitional Rules*

The transitional rules for nothings

6.21   These transitional rules apply to the types of asset and liability which will be qualifying assets and liabilities, but which previously would have produced exchange gains or losses which would be completely ignored for tax purposes. Examples include:

(*a*)   foreign currency borrowing by an investment company;

(*b*)   capital foreign currency liabilities of a trading company; and

(*c*)   loans and advances to companies in a group, made by a group member which is not carrying on a trade of making such loans and advances, where the debts are not debts on a security.

6.22   Such assets and liabilities are referred to in this book as 'nothings'. A particular point of difficulty is where exchange differences on nothings have affected the calculation of taxable trading profits through the application of the matching principle introduced by the decision in *Pattison v Marine Midland Limited, 57 TC 219* or the matching formula described in the Inland Revenue Statement of Practice SP1/87 (see Chapter 1). This difficulty is discussed in 6.43 below.

6.23   There are two possible transitional rules which can apply to a nothing:

(*a*)   *Debts of fixed term and amount*
Any debt which has both a fixed term *and* a fixed amount, as defined in *TR 3*, will be subject to the 'kink test' transitional rule. [*TR 17–22*].

(*b*)   *Fluctuating debts*
This term includes any debts which do not come within the definitions of both 'fixed term' *and* 'fixed amount'. They are subject to the 'grandfathering' rules. [*TR 3*].

Fixed-term debt

6.24   A debt is defined as having a fixed term if (and only if) it is provided that:

'(*a*)   the principal is to be repayable–

(i)   in total on one specified date; or

(ii)   in specified amounts or proportions on specified dates; and

(*b*)   any part of the principal once repaid cannot be redrawn; and

(*c*)   any interest which if not paid when due is to be capitalised or rolled-up, is to be added to the principal on the due date and repayable on the same terms as the principal.'

[*TR 3(6)*].

6.25   Many loan agreements which have a fixed term also allow the lender to require early repayment 'in various circumstances that are neither certain nor likely to occur' such as default by the borrower or changes in applicable tax or other law. This does not prevent them from meeting the definition of 'fixed term'. [*TR 3(7)*]. Some agreements also allow prepayment in whole or in part at the borrower's option. Provided any amounts prepaid cannot be redrawn, the ability to prepay does not prevent a loan which satisfies condition 6.24(*a*) above from being regarded as fixed term. [*TR 3(7)*].

Debts of fixed amount

6.26   A debt is defined as having a fixed amount if (and only if):

(*a*)   'the maximum amount of the principal is specified at the commencement of the term of the debt'; and

(*b*)   'the principal cannot be increased beyond that maximum amount,' except through the capitalisation of unpaid interest.

[*TR 3(8)*].

6.27   In determining whether a debt falls within this definition, clauses requiring principal or interest to be 'grossed up' for withholding or other taxes are to be ignored. [*TR 3(8)*].

Example 5

Company A agrees to borrow DM1m from a bank. Under the terms of the loan agreement it may draw down DM1m in one sum within thirty days of the date of the agreement and this must be repaid in full on the fifth anniversary of the date of the draw down. The only provision for prepayment is at the instigation of the lender if the borrower fails to meet its interest obligations. The loan is both fixed term and fixed amount, and therefore subject to the 'kink test'.

Example 6

Company B arranges a three-year overdraft facility of US$5m. During this period, the company can draw down and repay any amounts it wishes, up to the overdraft limit and the balance on the account varies between zero and $2.5m over the three-year period. This is a debt which is not fixed in amount or term, and is therefore subject to the grandfathering provisions.

Example 7

The facts are as in Example 6, except that the company draws down the full US$5m on the day the facility is granted and the debt remains at the same level until it is repaid at the end of the three-year period. Although this is a debt which is fixed in amount, as defined, it is not fixed in term because the company could repay part of the debt and subsequently draw it down again. It is therefore subject to the grandfathering provisions.

Deep gain securities, qualifying indexed securities and deep discount securities

6.28   The 'kink test' also applied up to 31 March 1996 to a qualifying asset (if it was not a chargeable gains asset) or qualifying liability which was:

(*a*)   a deep gain security (as defined in *FA 1989, 1 Sch 1*) and the amount payable on redemption was payable on one specified date; or

(*b*)   a qualifying indexed security as defined in *FA 1989, 11 Sch 1*; or

(*c*)   a deep discount security within *ICTA 1988, 4 Sch 1*,

as these were specifically defined as having a fixed term and fixed amount. The kink test ceased to apply to such securities on 31 March 1996 by assuming that the company ceased (for the purposes of the kink test only) to hold the asset or be subject to the liability. See also 3.40 above. [*TR 3(9)*].

Debts of fixed term and amount – the 'kink test'

6.29   The kink test prevents the exchange gains or losses taken into account under the foreign exchange tax rules exceeding the exchange gains or losses which have actually accrued over the life of the asset or liability. For any accounting period after Commencement Day the exchange gains or losses to be taken into account for tax purposes in relation to any such asset or liability will be arrived at as follows:

(*a*)   the gain or loss of the period (which may arise on translation at the balance sheet date or on realisation during the period) is to be aggregated with the exchange gains or losses which have accrued (ignoring these transitional provisions) in any previous accounting periods since the Commencement Day to give the 'post-commencement net exchange gain or loss';

(*b*)   the result is to be compared to the 'overall exchange gain or loss' which has accrued between the date the asset or liability came into existence and the balance sheet date – or, if the item was realised during the accounting period, the date of realisation;

(*c*)   the exchange gain or loss of the current period is adjusted so that the cumulative amount taxed or relieved since commencement is limited to the lower of the 'post-commencement net exchange gain or loss' and the 'overall exchange gain or loss' (if one of these two amounts is nil the result of the comparison is always nil); and (*d*)   where the 'post-commencement net exchange gain or loss' is a gain and the 'overall exchange difference' is a loss, or vice versa, the exchange gain or loss for the period will be the figure which reduces the total cumulative amount taxed or relieved since commencement to nil.

[*TR 18–21*].

This calculation must be carried out every year until the item is fully repaid. This rule is best illustrated by numerical examples and graphs.

Example 8 – pre-commencement gain

On 1 January 1992 A Ltd, an investment company, makes a seven-year loan of Fr12,000 to an overseas subsidiary on terms which mean that it is not a debt on a security, which is repaid on the maturity date of 31 December 1999. The loan is fixed term and fixed amount as defined. A Ltd prepares accounts to 31 December, and its Commencement Day is 1 January 1996. Exchange rates and balance sheet values are as follows:

Date	Exchange rate Fr/£	£ equivalent per accounts
1.1.92	10.0	1,200
31.12.95	8.0	1,500
31.12.96	7.5	1,600
31.12.97	9.0	1,333
31.12.98	12.0	1,000
31.12.99	8.57	1,400

	1996	1997	1998	1999
1. Pre-commencement gain (loss)	300	300	300	300
2. Post-commencement net gain or (loss)	100	(167)	(500)	(100)
3. Overall exchange gain or (loss)	400	133	(200)	200
4. Cumulative taxed gain or (loss) brought forward	None	100	Nil	(200)
5. Cumulative taxed gain or (loss) at end of year (lower of 2 and 3)	100	Nil	(200)	Nil
6. Deemed taxable exchange gain or (loss) for the year (5–4)	100	(100)	(200)	200

This is illustrated in Figure 1 below.

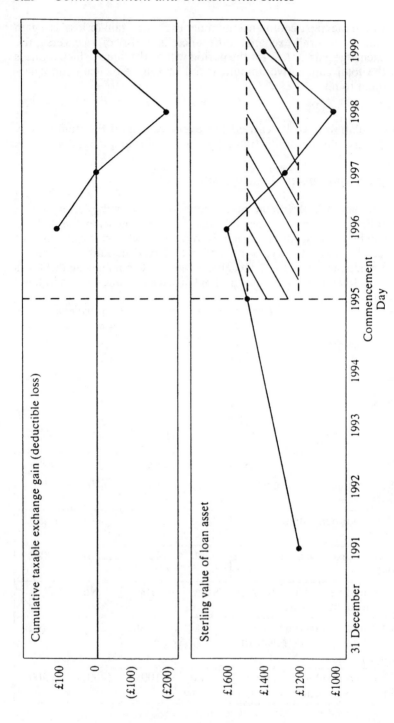

Figure 1 – Kink test, Example 8: a pre-commencement gain

Example 9 – pre-commencement loss

On 1 January 1994 B Ltd, an investment company, makes a five-year loan of Kr12,000 to an overseas subsidiary, which is repaid on the maturity date of 31 December 1998. The loan is fixed term and fixed amount as defined in *TR 3*, and is not a debt on a security. B Ltd prepares accounts to 31 December and its Commencement Day is 1 January 1996. Exchange rates and balance sheet values are as follows:

Date	Exchange Rate Kr/£	£ equivalent per accounts
1.1.94	8.0	1,500
31.12.95	10.0	1,200
31.12.96	9.0	1,333
31.12.97	9.5	1,263
31.12.98	12.0	1,000

	1996	1997	1998
1. Pre-commencement gain or (loss)	(300)	(300)	(300)
2. Post-commencement net gain or (loss)	133	63	(200)
3. Overall exchange gain or (loss)	(167)	(237)	(500)
4. Cumulative taxed gain or (loss) brought forward from prior year	None	Nil	Nil
5. Cumulative taxed gain or (loss) at end of year (lower of 2 and 3)	Nil	Nil	(200)
6. Deemed taxable exchange gain or (loss) for the year (5–4)	Nil	Nil	(200)

This is illustrated in Figure 2 below.

Effect of the kink test

6.30   Figures 1 and 2 illustrate the effect of the kink test on the extent to which exchange differences accruing after commencement are recognised for tax purposes. In broad terms, an unrealised exchange gain at commencement will mean restricted relief for post-commencement losses, but unrestricted taxation of post-commencement gains, on a cumulative basis. Similarly, an unrealised exchange loss at commencement will lead to restrictions on the taxation of post-commencement exchange gains,

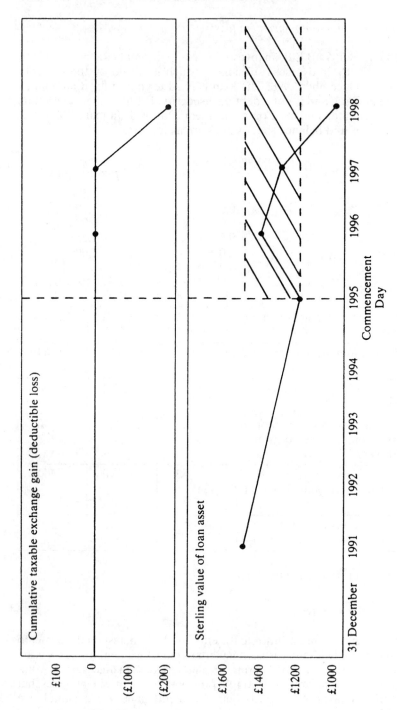

Figure 2 – Kink test, Example 9: a pre-commencement loss

116

but no restriction on relief for losses, again on a cumulative basis. Both Figures 1 and 2 illustrate that:

(*a*) Provided the exchange rate stays within the range between the rate when the asset or liability was first acquired and the rate at commencement (shaded in the diagrams), no taxable exchange gain or loss will accrue.

(*b*) If the exchange rate moves outside this range, taxable exchange gains or deductible losses will start to accrue.

(*c*) If the exchange rate moves back into the shaded range, all previous taxable exchange differences will be reversed.

(*d*) The overall effect of the kink test is determined by the exchange rate at the time the debt is settled (subject to the effects where a debt is repaid early and replaced – see 6.35 below).

Pre-commencement gain or loss – debts which vary in amount before commencement

6.31 When the pre-commencement gain or loss is calculated, it is necessary to disregard realised exchange differences. [*TR 18(3)*]. There are no specific rules for determining how much of the overall exchange gain or loss which has accrued on an asset or liability is a realised gain or loss so it is necessary to give the term its everyday meaning. The realised exchange gain or loss to be excluded from the pre-commencement gain or loss will therefore be the exchange gain or loss which has arisen on the part of the debt which is repaid before Commencement Day. In other words, the pre-commencement gain or loss is the exchange gain or loss which has accrued on the part of the debt which remains at the start of Commencement Day.

Example 10

A company borrows $100,000 when $2.0 = £1 and repays $40,000 when $2.5 = £1. It has a liability of $60,000 on Commencement Day and the closing exchange rate on the day before Commencement Day is $1.75 = £1. The pre-commencement loss is calculated as follows:

	£
Value of $60,000 immediately before Commencement Day	
$60,000 @ $1.75/£	34,286
Value of $60,000 at start of loan	
$60,000 @ $2.0/£	30,000
Increase, which is pre-commencement loss	4,286

6.32 The position is less straightforward if a debt has both increased and decreased before Commencement Day. It is then necessary to decide how to identify advances at different exchange rates with one or more repayments and the balance of the loan left at commencement. It is suggested that a 'first in first out' approach is adopted. This is consistent with *TR 21(5)*, which identifies a partial repayment after Commencement Day of a debt which has increased after Commencement Day first with the Commencement Day balance of the debt (see below).

Example 11

A company with a Commencement Day of 1 April 1995 borrows DM360,000 on terms which are fixed term and fixed amount as defined in *TR 3*, and which is drawn down and repaid by instalments as follows:

Date	Drawdown (repayment) DM	Balance DM	Exchange Rate DM/£
1.1.93	180,000	180,000	3.00
1.1.94	180,000	360,000	2.50
1.1.95	(120,000)	240,000	2.70
31.3.95		240,000	2.75

On a 'first in first out' basis the Commencement Day balance of DM240,000 is identified with the drawdowns as follows:

DM180,000 drawn on 1.1.94
DM60,000 drawn on 1.1.93

The pre-commencement gain or loss is calculated as follows, using the principles set out in *FA 1993, s 127* (accrual on debts whose amounts vary).

	£
1.1.93 DM60,000 @ DM3.00/£	20,000
1.1.94 DM180,000 @ DM2.50/£	72,000
Less	
31.3.95 DM240,000 @ DM2.75/£	(87,273)
Decrease, which is pre-commencement gain	4,727

Kink test when debt increases after commencement

6.33   If a debt which is subject to the kink test increases in amount on or after the company's Commencement Day, the Commencement Day balance of the debt ('the original debt') and any post-commencement increases in the amount of the debt are treated as two separate debts. [*TR 21*]. If there is a partial repayment of the debt after it has increased, the repayment is set firstly against the original debt, so as to reduce the amount which is subject to the kink test, in preference to reducing the amount which falls outside the kink test.

Example 12

A company with a Commencement Day of 1 January 1996 makes a loan to its US subsidiary which is subject to the kink test and which has the following movements.

Date	Drawdown (repayment) $	Balance $
1.1.95	100,000	100,000
31.12.95		100,000
31.3.96	150,000	250,000
31.12.96		250,000
30.6.97	(150,000)	100,000
31.12.97		100,000

In the accounting period ended 31 December 1996 taxable exchange gains and losses are calculated as if there were two separate assets:

- A loan of $100,000 made on 1 January 1995 and subject to the kink test.

- A loan of $150,000 made on 31 March 1996 and subject only to the basic rules.

In the accounting period ended 31 December 1997 the repayment of $150,000 is identified first with the 'original debt' of $100,000 and taxable exchange gains and losses are calculated on the basis that:

- the $100,000 loan made on 1 January 1995 is wholly repaid on 30 June 1997.

- $50,000 of the $150,000 loan made on 31 March 1996 is repaid on 30 June 1997.

Kink test when debt decreases after commencement

6.34   There are no special provisions to modify the kink test when a debt is partly repaid after commencement. This means that, for example, there is no reduction in the pre-commencement gain or loss which is included in the calculation of the overall exchange gain or loss for accrual periods following the reduction of the amount of a debt.

Example 13 – Pre-commencement loss and debt reduced after commencement

The facts up to Commencement Day are the same as in Example 9. On 1 January 1994, B Ltd, an investment company, makes a five-year loan of Kr12,000 to an overseas subsidiary. The loan is fixed term and fixed amount as defined in Regulation 3, and is not a debt on a security. B Ltd prepares accounts to 31 December and its Commencement Day is 1 January 1996. On 1 January 1997 Kr6,000 of the loan is repaid and the balance is repaid at the maturity date of 31 December 1998. Exchange rates and the loan balance at relevant dates are as follows:

Date	Balance of loan Kr	Exchange Rate Kr/£	£ equivalent £
1.1.95	12,000	8.0	1,500
31.12.95	12,000	10.0	1,200
31.12.96	12,000	9.0	1,333
1.1.97	6,000	9.0	667
31.12.97	6,000	9.5	632
31.12.98	6,000	12.0	500

Pre-commencement loss (as per Example 9)	(300)
1996	
Closing value of asset	1,333
Less opening value of asset	(1,200)
Exchange gain in year	133
Post-commencement gain	133
1997	
Opening value of asset	1,333
Less sterling equivalent of decrease (Kr6,000 @ Kr9.0/£)	(666)
	667
Closing value of asset	632
Exchange loss in year	(35)
Post-commencement net gain (133 *less* 35)	98
1998	
Closing value of asset	500
Less opening value of asset	(632)
Exchange loss in year	(132)
Post-commencement net loss (133 *less* 35 *less* 132)	(34)

	1996	1997	1998
Pre-commencement gain or (loss)	(300)	(300)	(300)
Post-commencement net gain or (loss)	133	98	(34)
Overall exchange gain or (loss)	(167)	(202)	(334)
Cumulative taxed gain or (loss) brought forward	None	Nil	Nil
Deemed taxable exchange gain or (loss) for the year	Nil	Nil	(34)

Anti-avoidance – replacement loans

6.35   There are anti-avoidance rules to prevent companies from opting out of the kink test by repaying and renewing loans. [*TR 22*]. If a qualifying asset or liability to which the kink test applies (whether an asset or a liability) is wholly or partly repaid early, and the company *owing* the original debt incurs another debt in a currency other than sterling within the period beginning 30 days before and ending 30 days after settlement of the first debt, the kink test applies to the 'replacement' debt in the same way as it applied to the original debt, up to the date on which the original debt would have been settled had it run to term. The kink test rules will apply to the new debt even if it is in a different currency (other than sterling) to the currency of the old debt. The company which is the *creditor* in respect of the replacement debt is affected by this rule only if it is the company which was the creditor in respect of the original debt. If a company has a debt due to it which is repaid and it reinvests the proceeds in another monetary asset which is not a loan to the original debtor, the new monetary asset is outside the kink test.

6.36   Any debt which is for goods or services supplied to or by the company in the course of its trade will not be treated as 'replacement' debt for the purpose of applying this rule. In the case of a company which has made a local currency election to compute the taxable profits of a trade, or part of a trade, in a currency other than sterling, 'replacement' debt:

(*a*)   does not include debts incurred for the purpose of the trade which are in the local currency of the trade;

(*b*)   includes debts denominated in sterling incurred for the purpose of the trade; and

(*c*)   includes debts not incurred for the purpose of the trade which are in a currency other than sterling.

6.37   Where the new debt exceeds the old debt in amount, the overall gains and losses and any post-commencement exchange gains and losses on the old debt will be treated as if they had accrued on that part of the new debt which is equal to the whole of the original debt. Where the new debt is less than the old, a corresponding proportion of both the historic exchange differences and the post-commencement exchange differences on the original debt will be attributed to the new debt.

Example 14

X plc and its subsidiaries, A Ltd and B Ltd, are UK-resident companies. It also has a US-resident subsidiary, C Inc. The group prepares accounts to 31 December, so the Commencement Day for X plc, A Ltd and B Ltd is 1 January 1996. At commencement, there are the following loans which will be subject to the kink test.

Currency and amount	From	To	Maturity date
$100,000	P Bank plc	X plc	31.12.98
$50,000	A Ltd	C Inc	31.7.97
DM100,000	B Ltd	A Ltd	30.6.99

The following transactions take place in 1996.

1.10.96	X plc borrows $150,000 from R Bank plc
5.10.96	X plc repays $100,000 to P Bank plc
5.10.96	X plc lends $50,000 to C Inc
12.10.96	C Inc repays $50,000 to A Ltd
1.11.96	B Ltd lends $100,000 to A Ltd
30.11.96	A Ltd repays DM100,000 to B Ltd

As a result, all the loans which were subject to the kink test have been repaid and all new loans started after Commencement Day, so in the absence of the anti-avoidance rule the kink test would cease to apply. The effect of the anti-avoidance rule is as follows:

X plc
New $ borrowing within 30 days of repayment of old $ borrowing, so the kink test applies to $100,000 of borrowing from R Bank plc as if the original borrowing from P Bank plc had continued to maturity on 31 December 1998. The exchange difference on the balance of $50,000 borrowing from R Bank plc is subject to tax under the basic rules. Although the $50,000 loaned by X plc to C Inc replaces the loan by A Ltd to C Inc within 30 days, this does not affect the tax treatment in X plc because X plc was not party to the original borrowing by C Inc.

A Ltd

C Inc has borrowed $50,000 within 30 days of repaying the $50,000 loan from A Ltd, so the basic requirement to invoke *TR 22* is met. However, A Ltd does not acquire the replacement debt asset and is therefore not affected by the anti-avoidance rule in respect of the $50,000 loan to C Inc.

A Ltd has borrowed in a currency other than sterling ($100,000) within the 30-day period preceding the date on which it repays its DM100,000 loan to B Ltd, so the kink test will apply to part of the $100,000 borrowing from B Ltd until 30 June 1999, the original maturity date of the DM100,000 loan. The part of the US$100,000 new loan which is subject to the kink test will be the amount equivalent to DM100,000 at the time the new debt was incurred. [*TR 22(5)*].

B Ltd

B Ltd is party to both the new loan to A Ltd ($100,000) and the original loan to A Ltd (DM100,000), so the kink test will apply to the relevant part of the $100,000 loan, as in the case of A Ltd.

Fluctuating nothings – the 'grandfathering' rule

6.38   Nothings which are not both fixed in term *and* fixed in amount, as defined, and therefore do not qualify for the kink test, will be subject to the 'grandfathering' provisions. [*TR 3*]. Such debts are kept out of the new rules ('grandfathered') until six years (or full repayment if earlier) after the company's Commencement Day, with the result that the exchange differences will continue to be ignored for tax purposes for this period.

6.39   It is worth noting that, as *FA 1993* applied to accounting periods commencing on or after 23 March 1995, the six-year grandfathering period will end during 2001 for most companies, e.g. assets and liabilities which have been grandfathered in companies making up accounts to 31 March annually will cease to be grandfathered at the end of the accounting period ended 31 March 2001. Companies may therefore need to reorganise their affairs if they wish to ensure that they continue to be hedged on an after tax basis.

6.40   Where the amount of the debt fluctuates, it is only the balance which was outstanding on Commencement Day or, if the balance is subsequently reduced, the reduced balance, which is grandfathered at any time. If there is an increase in the amount of the debt after the beginning of Commencement Day, the rules change so that exchange differences on the post-commencement increase in the debt are subject to tax under the foreign exchange tax rules. The treatment of debts which increase is as follows:

(*a*)   The company is treated as if it became entitled to the asset or subject to the liability at the beginning of the day on which the debt was first increased (whether or not the increase represents the reversal of a post-commencement decrease). This is therefore a 'translation time' and taxable exchange differences are calculated on the debt as if it were a new debt undertaken at the time of the increase.

(*b*)   In that and each subsequent accounting period, it is necessary to calculate the exchange gain or loss which would have accrued in the accrual period on a debt equal to the lowest amount of the debt at any time between Commencement Day and the end of the accrual period (the grandfathered balance).

(*c*)   The taxable exchange gain or loss on the debt for the period is the exchange difference accruing in the period as reduced by the exchange gain or loss which is calculated on the grandfathered balance.

6.41   On the sixth anniversary of a company's Commencement Day, any part of a debt which is treated as grandfathered at that time is treated as a new debt acquired by the company at the start of that day.

Example 15

Company P prepares accounts to 31 March, so its Commencement Day will be 1 April 1995. On 1 January 1995 it advances $100,000 to its US subsidiary on intercompany account (not a debt on a security). Subsequent movements on the account, and the exchange rates at the time of the movements are as follows:

Date	Advances (repayments)	Balance on account	Exchange rate
1.1.95	$100,000	$100,000	$1.8/£
31.3.95		$100,000	$2.0/£
30.9.95	($20,000)	$80,000	$2.2/£
31.3.96		$80,000	$2.1/£
30.6.96	($30,000)	$50,000	$2.0/£
31.12.96	$20,000	$70,000	$2.1/£
31.3.97		$70,000	$2.2/£
30.6.97	($40,000)	$30,000	$2.1/£
30.9.97	$90,000	$120,000	$2.0/£
31.3.98		$120,000	$1.9/£
31.3.00		$120,000	$1.7/£
1.1.01	(120,000)	0	$1.6/£

The amount owing on the intercompany account is a variable debt and there are no specified terms for repayment, so the Commencement Day balance on the account will be grandfathered under *TR 3*.

Accounting period ended 31 March 1996

The balance on the account has not increased, so the whole of the debt is grandfathered, i.e. no taxable exchange gains or losses accrued. The grandfathered amount is reduced to $80,000 by 31 March 1996.

Accounting period ended 31 March 1997

The debt is grandfathered until 31 December 1996 and exchange differences accruing up to that point in time are ignored. Because the debt is increased from $50,000 to $70,000 on 31 December 1996 the company is treated as if a new loan of $70,000 was made on 31 December 1996. [*TR 3(2)(a)*]. 31 December 1996 and 31 March 1997 are the relevant translation times. The lowest amount of the debt between Commencement Day and 31 March 1997 is $50,000, so the exchange difference on $50,000 is excluded from the taxable exchange difference. [*TR 3(3)*].

		£	£
31.3.97	Translation of basic value $70,000 @ $2.2		31,818
31.12.96	Translation of basic value $70,000 @ $2.1		(33,333)
Exchange loss			1,515
Regulation 3(3) adjustment	$50,000 @ $2.1	23,809	
Less	$50,000 @ $2.2	(22,727)	
			1,082
Deductible exchange loss			(433)

Accounting period ended 31 March 1998

In this accounting period the amount of the debt varies so the exchange gain or loss must be calculated in accordance with *FA 1993, s 127*. During this accounting period, the lowest value of the debt is $30,000 so this is the amount on which the grandfathering adjustment is based.

		£	£
31.3.97	$70,000 @ $2.2		31,818
30.6.97	($40,000) @ $2.1		(19,048)
30.9.97	$90,000 @ $2.0		45,000
First amount			57,770
Second amount			
31.3.98	$120,000 @ $1.9		63,158
Less first amount			(57,770)
Taxable exchange gain before grandfathering rule effect			5,388

Grandfathering adjustment

	$30,000 @ $2.2	13,636
Less	$30,000 @ $1.9	(15,789)
		(2,153)
Taxable exchange gain		3,235

Accounting periods ended 31 March 1999 to 2000
In these accounting periods there is no change in the amount of the debt or in the grandfathered balance. Taxable exchange differences will therefore accrue on $90,000 of the total $120,000 borrowing.

Accounting period ended 31 March 2001
In this accounting period the balance falls to nil. However, the Inland Revenue have confirmed their view that if a loan is repaid during an accounting period, the lowest amount of the debt will be the lower of:

(*a*)   the outstanding balance immediately before the loan was repaid; and

(*b*)   the lowest amount of the loan since the company's commencement day, and is *not* nil.

Hence, as in the previous two accounting periods, taxable exchange differences will accrue on $90,000 of the total $120,000 borrowing.

The amount of the debt which is grandfathered is illustrated in Figure 3 below.

Election to disapply grandfathering rules

6.42   A company may elect that the grandfathering rules should not apply to any of its assets or liabilities. The election must be made by giving a notice in writing to the Inspector within the period of 92 days beginning with the company's Commencement Day (or, if later, within the period of 183 days beginning with the Appointed Day). If the election is made, all the company's fluctuating nothings which would otherwise have been grandfathered are treated as if the company had become entitled to the assets and subject to the liabilities at the beginning of its Commencement Day. Taxable exchange differences will therefore accrue, based on the sterling (or local currency) value of the debt immediately before the company's Commencement Day. [*TR 5*]. The grandfathering rules cannot be disapplied selectively by a company, but the decision whether to disapply the grandfathering rules can be made independently for different companies in the same group.

Marine Midland matching and the application of Inland Revenue Statement of Practice SP1/87

6.43   Exchange differences on nothings can affect the computation of taxable trading profits through the application of the matching principle

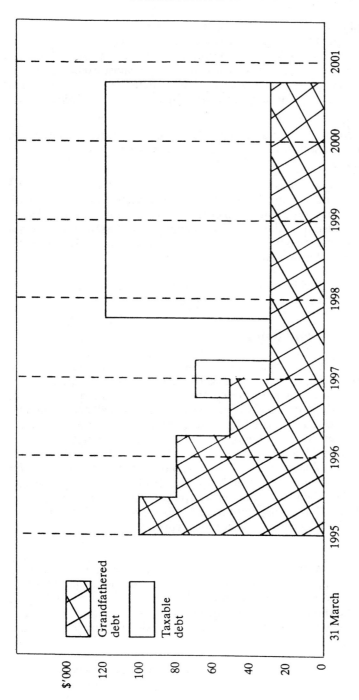

Figure 3 – Grandfathered part of fluctuating debt

introduced by the decision in *Pattison v Marine Midland Limited, 57 TC 219*, or the matching formula described in SP1/87. The Inland Revenue is understood to take the view that, to the extent that exchange differences on capital assets or liabilities have been offset against exchange differences on current liabilities or assets of a trade in this way, they have been taken into account for tax purposes. This has the following consequences.

(*a*)   A fluctuating nothing which has been wholly or partly matched with a current asset or liability of a trade cannot be grandfathered. [*TR 3(1)(a)*].

(*b*)   A nothing which is fixed in term and amount will be subject to the kink test but any exchange difference which has been matched with an exchange difference on a current asset or liability of a trade will be excluded from the 'overall exchange gain or loss' to be compared with the 'post-commencement net exchange gain or loss' in applying the kink test. [*TR 18(3)*].

There are no specific rules for identifying which nothings have been matched with trading items and which have not.

Trading assets and liabilities

6.44   There is no transitional provision for assets and liabilities of a trade where exchange differences on the assets or liabilities are included in taxable trading profits for pre-commencement accounting periods. In such cases all the profits and losses accruing on these balances should be taxed on an accruals basis under general Schedule D Case I principles before commencement and under the basic foreign exchange rules post-commencement. Transitional rules are, however, required for pre-commencement qualifying assets and liabilities, the profits and losses on which are taxed on a realisation basis, as part of the trading profits e.g. foreign currency bond investments held by general insurance companies. [*TR 8* and *10–13*]. It is important to remember that qualifying assets and liabilities include sterling (or other local currency) assets and liabilities. See 3.31 above.

6.45   The transitional rule for realisation basis items is intended to prevent the company obtaining immediate relief for losses that represent a reversal of the gain that has accrued up to commencement (and has not yet been taxed) on the asset (and vice versa). Instead such losses reduce the gain (calculated at Commencement Day) which is taxable when the asset is eventually sold.

6.46   The steps involved in the application of this transitional rule are:

(*a*)   Aggregate the gain or loss for the period on the asset (which may arise on translation at the balance sheet date or on realisation during the period) with all the exchange gains or losses on the asset which have accrued since Commencement Day (ignoring these transitional provisions); this is the 'cumulative gain or loss'.

(*b*)   Calculate the profit or loss which would have arisen if the asset was sold for its basic valuation immediately before Commencement Day (i.e. usually a sale at its book value in the last balance sheet before Commencement Day but can elect for original book value – see 6.13 above) – the 'attributed gain or loss'.

(*c*)   If there is an attributed gain and a cumulative gain (or an attributed loss and a cumulative loss) the taxable exchange gain (or loss) for the period will be the figure which makes the total cumulative amount taxed or relieved since commencement (the 'cumulative taxed gain or loss') equal to the cumulative gain (or loss).

(*d*)   If there is an attributed loss and a cumulative gain, (or vice versa) the attributed loss (or gain) is offset against the cumulative gain (or loss) to arrive at the cumulative taxed gain (or loss) but not so as to convert a cumulative taxed gain into a cumulative taxed loss (or vice versa).

(*e*)   The taxable exchange gain (or loss) for the period will be the difference between the cumulative taxed gain (or loss) of the period and the cumulative taxed gain (or loss) at the end of the previous period.

(*f*)   At the time of disposal of the asset the attributed gain or loss is reduced to the extent that it has been offset against the cumulative gain or loss under (*d*) above.

Thus if there is an attributed gain relief for cumulative exchange losses up to the amount of this gain will not be given. Instead the losses will reduce the attributed gain. When the asset is eventually sold the attributed gain crystallises to the extent it has not been offset by exchange losses. The same applies in reverse if there is an attributed loss.

6.47   The effects of this transitional rule for realisation basis trading assets may be summarised as:

(*a*)   A cumulative exchange loss will not be deductible unless it exceeds any attributed gain, when only the excess is deductible.

(*b*)   A cumulative exchange gain will not be taxable unless it exceeds any attributed loss, when only the excess is taxable.

(*c*)   If there is no attributed gain or loss the cumulative exchange gain or loss is fully taxable or deductible.

(*d*)   If there is a cumulative exchange gain and an attributed gain, or a cumulative exchange loss and an attributed loss, the cumulative gain is fully taxable, or the cumulative loss is fully deductible.

6.48 When an attributed gain or loss eventually crystallises this will normally be treated as a receipt or expense of the company's trade. However, if during the last accrual period before disposal the asset or liability has been to any extent held in exempt circumstances, the initial exchange gain or loss representing the balance of any attributed gain or loss is to be treated as a 'non-trading gain or loss'. [*TR 13*].

Example 16

Company X holds a US$10,000 Treasury bond from 1 January 1994 (when it was bought for $9,000) to 1 July 1998 when it is sold for $10,000. The profits on such sales are taxed on a realisation basis as part of the trading profit of Company X. The company's year end is 31 December. Exchange rates and balance sheet values are as follows:

Date	Exchange rate $/£	Book value $	£ equivalent
1.1.94	1.6	9,000	5,625
31.12.95	1.5	10,000	6,667
31.12.96	1.7	10,000	5,882
31.12.97	1.65	10,000	6,061
1.7.98	1.45	10,000	6,897

	1996	1997	1998
1. Attributed gain	1,042	1,042	1,042
2. Cumulative gain/(loss)	(785)	(606)	230
3. Cumulative taxed gain/ (loss) brought forward	Nil	Nil	Nil
4. Cumulative taxed gain/ (loss) at end of year (2 reduced by 1)	Nil	Nil	230
5. Deemed taxable gain/ (loss) for the year (4–3)	Nil	Nil	230

	1996	1997	1998
6. Cumulative adjustment to attributed gain	(785)	(606)	Nil
7. Residue of attributed gain left at end of year (1 + 6)	257	436	1,042*

* As cumulative position since Commencement Day is a net exchange gain, the full attributed gain arises on the sale of the bond.

Interaction with Schedule D Case I rules

6.49   At the time of disposal or settlement of the realisation basis asset, the profit or loss which is realised will be taken into account in computing the profits of the trade, following normal Schedule D Case I principles. To the extent that the realised profit or loss is attributable to exchange rate fluctuations, it will have already been taken into account under the foreign exchange tax rules, including the transitional rules. *FA 1993, s 128(11)* requires exchange differences to be deducted from the trading profit, in order to prevent double counting.

Election to spread attributed gains over six-year period

6.50   The application of the above transitional rule to realisation basis assets and liabilities can be complicated, particularly where a holding of a particular security has been acquired over a period and there are regular part disposals of the holding. There is an alternative, simpler treatment. A company could elect not to apply the above rule and instead to spread the attributed gains and losses over the six-year period beginning with its Commencement Day. [*TR 15*].

The election applies to all of the company's realisation basis qualifying assets and liabilities including those denominated in sterling (see 6.44 above).

6.51   The election, which has effect from the beginning of the company's Commencement Day:

(*a*)   had to be made by notice in writing to the Inspector of Taxes before 30 September 1996 (under the original provisions any election had to be made within 92 days beginning with the company's Commencement Day) [*SI 1996 No 1349*];

(*b*)   could be withdrawn by notice to the Inspector of Taxes before 30 September 1996 but is irrevocable from that date;

(*c*)   applies to realisation basis assets;

(*d*)   divides each attributable gain or loss into six equal parts, each of which is deemed to be an annual taxable exchange gain or loss;

(*e*)   the six taxable exchange gains or losses are treated as accruing on Commencement Day and the next five anniversaries of Commencement Day;

(*f*)   the above applies both before and after the actual disposal of the asset; and

(*g*)   exchange gains and losses which accrue to the company from commencement are therefore calculated under the basic rules, translating either the pre-commencement book value or book cost (if there is an election under *TR 6(2)*, see 6.13 above).

The realisation basis transitional rule is considered further in 12.44 *et seq.* below.

Variable debts

6.52   If the asset or liability is partly repaid, so that taxable exchange gains and losses are calculated under *FA 1993, s 127*, the remaining debt and the amount by which it has been reduced is treated as two separate debts for the purposes of applying the transitional rules. [*TR 13(6)*]. The attributed gain or loss and the cumulative figures for preceding accounting periods are apportioned between the two parts of the debt for this purpose.

Qualifying assets which are taxable under chargeable gains tax rules prior to commencement

6.53   These include:

(*a*)   foreign currency debts on a security which are not deep gain securities or convertible into shares;

(*b*)   foreign currency bank accounts;

(*c*)   holdings of foreign currency; and

(*d*)   second-hand foreign currency debts which are not debts on a security

so long as these assets have not been dealt with in computing trading profits. Sterling debt issued by one group company to another is also within this category as such debt was not a qualifying corporate bond before the foreign exchange and corporate debt regimes [*TCGA 1992, s 117(10)* before repeal by *FA 1996*] and so was a chargeable asset. Deep discount securities and qualifying indexed securities could fall within (*a*) above and so this transitional rule applies to these items (see Inland Revenue Bulletin Issue 21). The chargeable gains transitional rule ceased to apply to deep discount securities with effect from 1 April 1996. [*TR 10(3) inserted by SI 1996 No 1349*]. The rule is terminated by the company being deemed for the purpose of the transitional rule to cease holding the asset on 31 March 1996. The residual chargeable gain or allowable loss (see 6.58 below) is not crystallised until the actual disposal of the asset.

6.54   There are separate transitional rules, described in Chapter 4, in the financial instruments legislation, which deal with forward currency contracts, currency futures, currency swaps and currency options.

6.55   The transitional rules for qualifying assets which were chargeable assets taxable under capital gains tax rules prior to commencement are based on the rules described above for Schedule D Case I 'realisation basis' assets. The basic valuation of what were chargeable assets (other than currency contracts) is defined as the *market value* of the asset immediately before the company's Commencement Day, expressed in the nominal currency of the asset.

Transitional rule calculations for chargeable assets (other than currency contracts)

6.56   The first stage is to calculate the chargeable gain or allowable loss which would have arisen if the chargeable asset had been disposed of at market value immediately before the company's Commencement Day [*TR 8*] – the 'attributed gain or loss'. This rule is modified where the asset has been held by a company at a time when it was not resident in the UK (or was acquired from such a company via one or more no gain/no loss disposals). Such an asset is treated as having been acquired by the company at market value on the first day on which a disposal of the asset would have been subject to the UK capital gains rules.

6.57   It is then necessary to calculate, for each accrual period:

(*a*)   the cumulative gain or cumulative loss; and

(*b*)   the cumulative taxed gain or cumulative taxed loss

applying the rules described above for realisation basis assets, to determine the deemed taxable exchange gain or loss for the accrual period.

Example 17

On 1 July 1993, Company Y (an investment company) lends its French subsidiary FFr10,000 at fixed interest on terms which mean the loan is a debt on security. Company Y's year end is 31 March and the market value of the debt at 31 March 1995 is FFr10,500. The debt is sold for

FFr10,500 on 1 July 1997 when Y sells its French subsidiary to a third party.

Date	Exchange rate	£ equivalent
1.7.93	8.6	1,162 (of Fr10,000)
31.3.95	10.0	1,050 (of FFr10,500)
31.3.96	9.0	1,166
31.3.97	8.5	1,235
1.7.97	8.7	1,207

	31.3.96	*31.3.97*	*31.3.98*
1. Attributed (loss) at 31.3.95	(112)	(112)	(112)
2. Cumulative gain/(loss)	116	185	157
3. Cumulative taxed gain/(loss) brought forward	Nil	4	73
4. Cumulative taxed gain/(loss) at end of year (2 reduced by 1)	4	73	45
5. Deemed taxable gain/(loss) for the year (4–3)	4	69	(28)
6. Cumulative adjustment to allowable loss	112	112	112
7. Residue of allowable loss at end of year (1 + 6)	Nil	Nil	Nil

Note: this example has an attributed loss. If there is an attributed gain then indexation relief is available to reduce the attributed gain.

Disposals of chargeable assets

6.58   As in the case of Schedule D Case I realisation basis assets and liabilities, any part of the attributed gain or loss of a chargeable asset which has not been offset against post-commencement exchange losses or gains is recognised for tax purposes at the time of disposal.

On disposal:

(*a*)   An attributed gain (or, if there is a cumulative loss at the time of disposal, the excess of the gain over the loss, if any) will be a chargeable gain arising at the time of disposal (the 'residual gain').

(*b*)   An attributed loss (or, if there is a cumulative gain at the time of disposal, the excess of the loss over the gain, if any) will be an allowable loss arising at the time of disposal (the 'residual loss').

6.59   If a chargeable gain or allowable loss has been rolled over pre-commencement into a foreign currency debt on security which is held at Commencement Day, then this chargeable gain or allowable loss is part of the attributed gain or loss on the security. The rolled over gain or loss is crystallised when the company is no longer entitled to the security. Thus, it is not possible to have a further roll over if the debt disposal is within *TCGA 1992, s 127–130* or deemed to be within those sections by *TCGA 1992, s 135 or 136*. Similarly it is not possible to make a no gain/no loss transfer of the debt with the rolled up gain or loss.

6.60   There will be no chargeable gain or allowable loss under capital gains rules, other than the residual gain or loss referred to above, at the time of disposal, because from Commencement Day:

(*a*)   the disposal by a qualifying company of a debt on a security which is a qualifying asset is treated as a disposal of a qualifying corporate bond and therefore does not give rise to a chargeable gain or allowable loss [*FA 1993, 17 Sch 5*]; and

(*b*)   the disposal by a qualifying company of foreign currency or a foreign currency debt which is a qualifying asset but is not a debt on a security (which includes a foreign currency bank account) does not give rise to a chargeable gain or allowable loss. [*FA 1993, 17 Sch 1 and 4*].

6.61   Up to 31 March 1996, if the market value of a chargeable asset, on which there is an attributed gain, falls between Commencement Day and the time of disposal, the transitional rules could result in the company being taxed on more than the overall economic gain on the asset. The transitional rules provide for adjustments to the residual gain or loss intended to mitigate this effect (see 6.62 and 6.63 below). For disposals of assets on or after 1 April 1996, no adjustment is made as the market value movement will be taxable under the corporate and government debt rules. [*TR14(2)–(4)* deleted by *SI 1996 No 1349, Reg 7*].

6.62   The rules for calculating the adjustment to be made are complex [*TR 14*]:

(*a*)   If there is an attributed *gain*, and the market value at disposal is *less* than the market value at commencement, the residual gain (if any) is reduced or converted to an allowable loss by deducting the lower of:

    (i)   the sterling equivalent of the drop in market value (translated at the London closing rate for the day before Commencement Day); and

    (ii)   the residual gain, plus any post-commencement taxable exchange gains less any post-commencement deductible exchange losses.

(*b*)   If there is an attributed *loss*, and the market value at disposal is *greater* than the market value at commencement, the residual loss (if any) is reduced or converted into a chargeable gain by adding the lower of:

(i)   the sterling equivalent of the increase in market value (translated into sterling at the London closing rate for the day before Commencement Day); and

(ii)   the residual loss, plus any post-commencement deductible exchange losses less any post-commencement taxable exchange gains.

Example 18

A company buys a $ bond for $1,000 when it is equivalent to £500. It holds the bond at commencement and sells it in the accounting period which begins on Commencement Day. There is an attributed gain at commencement of £100 (ignoring indexation relief). The $ market value of the bond on disposal is less than the $ market value at commencement. The following table shows the adjustment for the fall in market value for different exchange rates and market values.

Scenario			*1*		*2*		*3*
Cost		$	1,000		1,000		1,000
	$2 = £1	£	500		500		500
Commencement Day market value = Basic Valuation		$	1,100		1,100		1,100
	$1.83 = £1	£	600		600		600

Scenario			*1*		*2*		*3*
Disposal Day Basic Valuation		$	1,100		1,100		1,100
		$1.72 = £1	638	$2.29 = £1	480	$1.57 = £1	700
Disposal Day market value		$	1,000		1,050		800
		$1.72 = £1	580	$2.29 = £1	458	$1.57 = £1	509

Scenario		1	2	3
Fall in market value ('Excess') in nominal currency	$	100	50	300
Fall in market value ('Excess') in £ at Commencement Day rate $1.83 = £1	£	55	27	164
		£	£	£
Attributed Gain		100	100	100
Exchange gain (loss) on Basic Valuation	A	38	(120)	100
Scenario		1	2	3
Taxable exchange gain (deductible loss)	B	38	(20)	100
Residual chargeable gain	C	100	0	100
Maximum 'excess' which can be deducted	B + C	138	(20)	200
Deductible excess	D	55	0	164
Residual gain less 'excess'	C − D	45	0	(64)
Taxable exchange gain (deductible loss)	B	38	(20)	100
Total gain (loss) recognised		83	(20)	36

6.63　The above adjustments to the residual gain or loss are not made if *FA 1993, s 127* (accrual on debts whose amounts vary) has been applied to the asset for any accounting period. [*TR 14(1)(b)*].

6.64　The Excess Gains and Losses Regulations, which are described in Chapter 11 (see 11.2–11.13 below) can also lead to an adjustment when there is a disposal of a pre-commencement chargeable asset and:

(*a*)　a gain is realised on the asset in terms of its nominal currency, and there has been a net deductible exchange loss on the asset since commencement; or

(*b*)　a loss is realised on the asset in terms of its nominal currency and there has been a net taxable exchange gain on the asset since commencement.

Interaction with corporate and government debt rules

6.65 The transitional rule for chargeable assets generates a chargeable gain/allowable loss (subject to any offset for post-commencement cumulative exchange losses/gains (respectively) on disposal). The corporate and government debt rules tax the market value movement since the start of the corporate debt rules on 1 April 1996. Without an additional provision *(FA 1996, 15 Sch 11)* this could result in double counting. The operation of this provision is best understood by an example.

Example 19

A company has a commencement date of 1 January 1996 and holds a regulation 6(3) asset

	£ equivalent
Cost	£100
Market value 1 January 1996	£110
Market value 1 April 1996	£120
Redeemed in 1997	£100

	£
Attributed gain (ignoring indexation)	110
	(100)
	10

Under corporate and government debt no profit recognised:

Redemption	100
Less: accruals value at 1.4.96	
(FA 1996, 15 Sch 4)	(100)
	nil

Thus if there are no exchange losses to reduce the attributed gain this debt which is redeemed at no profit gives a taxable chargeable gain on disposal of £10.

FA 1996, 15 Sch 11 adjustment needs to be made.

Opening accruals value on 1.4.96	100
Less: market value used in attributed	
gain calculation	(110)
Debit	(10)

This non-trading debit arises in the accounting period in which the debt is sold/redeemed and so (ignoring indexation) offsets the attributed gain.

(There was an election under *FA 1996, 15 Sch 12* with a time limit of 30 September 1996 which allowed a company to substitute the market value on 1 April 1996 for the market value at commencement day in the *FA 1996, 15 Sch 11* adjustment.)

Conversion of residual capital loss into exchange loss

6.66   If an allowable loss (i.e. a residual loss) accrues to a company under the above transitional rule in respect of what was a chargeable asset pre-commencement, this may be offset under the normal capital gains rules only against chargeable gains of the company which are realised in the same or later accounting periods. However, the company may elect instead to offset the loss against any exchange gains accruing to the company in the accounting period in which the disposal takes place or in subsequent accounting periods. The election:

(*a*)   must be made by notice to the Inspector of Taxes;

(*b*)   must be made within two years of the end of the accounting period in which the disposal takes place;

(*c*)   is irrevocable; and

(*d*)   cannot be made in respect of an asset if *FA 1993, s 127* (accrual on debts whose amounts vary) has been applied to the asset for any accounting period.

[*TR 14(5)*].

6.67   There are rules to prevent an allowable loss on non-qualifying assets such as shares from being converted into a loss which may be offset against exchange gains by means of such an election. [*TR 14(6)–(9)*]. This could occur where the loss has been 'rolled over' into qualifying assets by means of a reorganisation or other transaction under *TCGA 1992, s 127* which took place before Commencement Day. In such a case, the loss available under the election is reduced by the amount of the loss which arose originally on non-qualifying assets and arose on the former charge-able asset as a result of the application of *TCGA 1992, s 127*.

Conversion of pre-commencement capital losses into exchange losses

6.68   A company may by election offset allowable losses realised before commencement on certain types of chargeable assets against post-commencement exchange gains on similar assets. [*TR 16*].

6.69   The losses which qualify for the election ('available losses') are allowable losses which:

(*a*)   arose before Commencement Day;

(*b*)   arose when the company was within the charge to corporation tax; and

(*c*)   related to assets which would have been qualifying assets if they were held on Commencement Day (i.e. assets that were chargeable assets) *or* arose by virtue of *TCGA 1992, s 143* in respect of a currency contract, a currency option, an interest rate contract or an interest rate option (as defined in the financial instruments rules).

6.70   The election is irrevocable and:

(*a*)   is made by giving notice to the Inspector of Taxes;

(b)   must be made within the period of 92 days beginning with the company's Commencement Day (or, if later, the period of 183 days beginning with the Appointed Day);

(c)   may be made either in respect of the whole of the available losses or a specified smaller amount.

6.71   If the allowable loss arose on an asset which had been held by a company at a time when it was not resident in the UK (or was acquired from such a company via one or more no gain/no loss disposals) the 'available loss' is the allowable loss less any loss attributable to the period of ownership by a non-resident company. This is found by calculating the allowable loss (if any) which would have been realised if the company had disposed of the asset at market value on the first day on which a disposal would have been subject to the UK capital gains rules. [*TR 16(6)*]. There are special rules to prevent the election applying to a loss on a non-qualifying asset which has been 'rolled over' into a qualifying asset under the reorganisation provisions of *TCGA 1992, s 127*. [*TR 16(3)*].

6.72   Clearly, a company which has no allowable losses carried forward at Commencement Day cannot have any 'available losses'. If a company has unused allowable losses at commencement, and in pre-commencement periods has incurred allowable losses on assets which could give rise to available losses and assets which could not, the available losses are determined by:

(a)   setting allowable losses which are potential available losses against gains on the same type of assets; and

(b)   setting other losses against gains on assets which could not have given rise to available losses.

Example 20

A company prepares accounts to 31 December and had no allowable losses carried forward at the end of 1991. In the next four years various chargeable gains and allowable losses arose. These are summarised below to show the application of the identification rules in determining the available losses which are included in the allowable losses carried forward at the end of 1995.

	Assets in respect of which election possible	Other assets	Total
1992 Disposal of land		(50,000)	(50,000)
1993 Debt on security	(10,000)		(10,000)
Shares		5,000	5,000
	(10,000)	(45,000)	(55,000)

1994 Currency contracts	(2,000)		(2,000)
Land		50,000	50,000
Transfer of loss	5,000	(5,000)	
	(7,000)	0	(7,000)
1995 Foreign currency			
bank a/c	1,000		1,000
Shares		(7,000)	(7,000)
Allowable loss pool at			
31.12.95	(6,000)	(7,000)	(13,000)
Available losses 1			
January 1996 thus			£6,000

6.73   Losses in respect of which an election is made are offset against *taxable exchange gains* which accrue to the company from Commencement Day, on:

(*a*)   foreign currency assets (other than currency contracts or options) which would have been chargeable assets had they been held by the company immediately before commencement; or

(*b*)   currency contracts which would have been chargeable assets within *TCGA 1992, s 143* had they been held by the company immediately before commencement; but

(*c*)   *not* on currency options, interest rate contracts and options.

6.74   The loss is deducted from an exchange gain before the gain is treated as a trade receipt or taken into account as a non-trading exchange gain. It does not therefore offset profits on currency contracts which are found under the financial instrument rules, such as periodic receipts on a currency swap. The taxable exchange gain to be reduced by the available loss is first calculated taking account of:

(*a*)   transitional rules for chargeable assets (described above);

(*b*)   anti-avoidance rules (see Chapter 7);

(*c*)   deferral relief (see Chapter 8); and

(*d*)   the matching election (see Chapter 9).

6.75   Any allowable loss which has been the subject of an election ceases to be available to offset chargeable gains. Where the election is made in respect of part of a company's available losses, the election is treated as referring to the available losses which arose on earlier disposals rather than later disposals to determine the allowable loss which is available to offset chargeable gains.

Chapter 7

Anti-Avoidance

7.1   No modern tax legislation would be complete without anti-avoidance provisions designed to ensure that tax payers are unable to exploit the rules in a way which the Inland Revenue regard as unreasonable. The foreign exchange legislation is no exception and has a general provision described as the 'main benefit test', in addition to specific provisions dealing with non-arm's length transactions, changes of accounting date designed to exploit the switch from old to new rules and subsequent currency movements and using non-coterminous year ends within a group to avoid the capital gains transitional provisions. The consequences of each provision are rather different.

Main benefit test

7.2   The main benefit test is the most widely drawn of the anti-avoidance provisions and is contained in *FA 1993, s 135*. This disallows for tax purposes any exchange loss accruing to a company if:

(*a*)   it arises on an asset or liability which is a qualifying debt (whether or not a debt on security); and

(*b*)   that debt is denominated in a currency chosen so that the main benefit or one of the main benefits arising from the debt is expected to be making the exchange loss.

7.3   The section originally only applied by direction of the Board of Inland Revenue, so that companies did not have to volunteer adjustments under this provision in submitting their returns and such returns will not be considered incorrect for the purposes of the Pay and File legislation if an adjustment is subsequently made. However, with effect for accounting periods ending on or after 1 July 1999, the need for Board Direction has been removed. [*FA 1998, s 109*]. Thus under Corporation Tax Self-Assessment it is necessary for companies to consider whether an adjustment is required under *FA 1993, s 135* and to include an appropriate amount in the tax return.

7.4   The exchange losses covered are those related to a trade, part of a trade and to non-trading items.

7.5   It is difficult to see how making a real economic loss on foreign exchange can be described as a 'benefit' under any circumstances, unless it is part of a transaction where the total economic benefits outweigh the exchange loss disadvantage. For example, if a UK company chooses to borrow in Japanese Yen for a five-year fixed term at a low fixed interest rate, one of the inherent economic assumptions in the way that the market sets that interest rate is that the Yen will rise against sterling. In perfect economics, the sum of the interest paid and exchange loss suffered by the company will be the same as the interest cost if they had borrowed in sterling for the same period from a similar type of lender. However, the company will not have to fund the exchange loss until the end of the five-year term and this thus represents a clear advantage compared to paying the appropriate sterling interest rate at regular intervals throughout. The company will also benefit after Commencement Day because it will claim a tax deduction for the exchange loss as it accrues rather than on realisation at the expiry of five years. (There will, in most circumstances, be no tax relief on the exchange loss before Commencement Day.)

7.6   In the example given above, the pre-tax cash flow alone is a significant advantage of entering into the Yen borrowing. However, it may be that the post-tax cash flow (i.e. the acceleration of tax relief) is a crucial deciding factor when the company comes to choose between the Yen borrowing and the sterling borrowing.

7.7   Inland Revenue Explanatory Statement, para 3.6 states clearly that *section 135* will not catch commercial transactions. The provision is said to be widely drafted to ensure that transactions do not escape merely because the company can show some commercial purpose for the transaction, even if, in the eyes of the Inland Revenue, this purpose is a spurious one. It is stressed that the provision will apply only where obtaining tax relief for the exchange loss is the main benefit or one of the main benefits of the transaction and thus clearly implies that if the economic effect of early tax relief is a factor which adds to the benefits in a modest way, even if crucial in tipping the balance of the decision on nominal currency, then the tax payer company need not be concerned about the prospects of direction for the disallowance of the exchange losses.

7.8   However, if a company or a group of companies enters into a number of transactions, which, taken together, result in little or no economic cost, but one element of which will give rise to a substantial exchange loss for tax purposes, then the Inland Revenue have the powers within *section 135* to deny tax relief for that loss.

7.9   In view of this power, companies should document with great care the commercial rationale for any foreign currency assets or liabilities where a significant exchange loss is likely to arise, in order to ensure that innocent transactions cannot be successfully challenged under these provisions.

Arm's length test

7.10   There are three separate sections of the *Finance Act 1993* which apply the arm's length test to different aspects of the foreign exchange legislation. It is important to note that the two parties to a transaction do not need to be in any way connected with one another in order for a transaction between them to be regarded as non-arm's length. This enables the Inland Revenue to challenge 'offset trading' and similar transactions between third parties where the effect may be the accruing of a tax deductible exchange loss in the UK. The sanction under these provisions is to 'ring fence' any loss, as described below, rather than to disallow it totally.

FA 1993, s 136

7.11   The first of these anti-avoidance tests is contained in *section 136* and relates to qualifying assets and liabilities which have something in their nature which would not have been present if the transaction had been undertaken between independent third parties acting at arm's length and in the absence of any related transaction.

7.12   The first circumstance to consider here [*s 136(1)*] is those assets and liabilities which arise from transactions which would not have taken place or would have taken place on different terms under arm's length conditions. This covers matters such as inappropriate interest rates, repayment terms, or security. The entire exchange loss on such items can be dealt with as set out in para 7.22 below.

7.13   The second set of circumstances [*s 136(4)*] is where parties dealing at arm's length would have advanced a smaller amount by way of debt, bearing in mind the generally accepted debt:equity ratios for the territory concerned. In this case, the exchange loss on the excess debt over the arm's length amount falls to be dealt with as in para 7.22 below.

ICTA 1988, s 770 adjustments

7.14   The third set of circumstances [*s 136(8)–(10)*] apply where a UK company has advanced a loan denominated in foreign currency to a connected party on non-arm's length terms and the Inland Revenue have applied the intercompany pricing legislation contained in *ICTA 1988, s 770A* and *28AA Sch* to deem that company to have received interest or a higher rate of interest.

7.15   If the interest rate is the only non-arm's length feature and a *28AA Sch* adjustment has been made in respect of the entire loan, so that the company is paying tax on an arm's length rate of interest for the whole of that loan, then there will be no restriction under *section 136* to the company's ability to take a tax deduction for exchange losses accruing on the loan.

7.16   If, however, the *28AA Sch* adjustment has only been applied to a part of the loan, then only the exchange losses on that part of the loan in respect of which interest or additional interest is deemed to accrue and on which tax has thus been paid, will be freely available as a tax deduction. Exchange losses on the balance of the loan will fall to be dealt with in accordance with paragraph 7.22 below.

7.17   Such an adjustment under *28AA Sch* in respect of a part of a loan most commonly occurs when a UK company advances monies interest free to a thinly capitalised overseas subsidiary. The UK company is often able to argue successfully that a part of the loan should be regarded as quasi-equity and thus is appropriate to be advanced interest free. The amount involved will depend upon the appropriate thin capitalisation measures for the overseas territory in which the subsidiary is resident.

Exclusion from the arm's length test

7.18   There is an exclusion from the arm's length test for assets and liabilities where both parties involved in the transaction are members of the same UK group so that any 'advantage' which may be gained by one will be fully offset by a corresponding 'disadvantage' which will be suffered by the other, both within the charge to UK corporation tax. The exemption from the arm's length test is not however as simple as determining whether the two companies that are parties to the transaction are in the same capital gains tax group. There are a number of conditions to meet before the exemption applies. [*FA 1993, s 136(11)* and *(12)*].

7.19   Both companies must be members of the same chargeable gains group for the whole of the accounting period. There must also be an exchange loss in the company potentially caught by the arm's length test and an equal and opposite exchange gain accruing in the tax computation of the other party to the transaction. In addition, this exchange gain must accrue for an accrual period co-terminous with the accrual period of the loss-making company. The two companies involved must also hold the assets (or liabilities) for the purpose either of one trade or for non-trading purposes. These detailed requirements mean that if there is a loss in one company and there is no gain in the other company because of a local currency election then the arm's length test is in point. The arm's length test exemption will apply, however, if the exchange gain in the other company is not in fact currently taxable due to the effects of the matching election (*MR 12*). Thus, an intra-group loan to a company which then makes a matching election should not be within the arm's length test in the hands of the lender.

7.20 *Anti-Avoidance*

Debts of varying amounts – arm's length test

7.20 The basic legislative provisions excluded variable non-arm's length debts from any of the relieving provisions. However, the *Exchange Gains and Losses (Debts of Varying Amounts) Regulations 1994 (SI 1994 No 3232)*, introduced a new *section 136A* which contains broadly similar relieving provisions but of additional complexity to deal with debts which vary in amount.

Board direction – application of the arm's length test

7.21 As with the main benefit test, the arm's length tests originally applied only if the Board of Inland Revenue directed and thus no adjustment needed to be shown on the tax return initially submitted. However, with effect for accounting periods ending on or after 1 July 1999, the need for Board Direction has been removed. [*FA 1998, s 109*]. Thus under Corporation Tax Self-Assessment it is necessary for companies to consider whether an adjustment is required under this anti-avoidance provision and to include an appropriate amount in the tax return.

7.22 If the Board does make a direction, or where under self-assessment a company considers that an adjustment is required, then the amount of loss concerned will not be available to reduce profits of any kind in the current year, nor to carry back to earlier years. However, it will be available to carry forward and be offset against any future exchange profits arising on the *same asset or liability*. If the asset or liability was held on Commencement Day then the amount of the exchange gain or loss brought into this ring fencing calculation is the taxable amount as calculated for the period under the transitional rules. [*TR 2*]. See 6.20 above.

7.23 This approach to 'ring fencing' the exchange losses on non-arm's length transactions would initially appear to have unfortunate consequences if, for example, a company had a two year loan caught by *section 136* which made an exchange gain in year one and an exactly equal and opposite exchange loss in year two, following which it was repaid. There would have been no economic exchange difference over the life of the loan, but the ring fence on the year two loss would have given rise to a net tax liability on the year one gain. Inland Revenue Explanatory Statement, para 3.10 makes it clear that the Inland Revenue will not restrict loss relief in such circumstances, except to the extent that the loss exceeds profits on the same loan which have previously been taxed. Then, only the excess loss will be 'ring fenced' and the company will not overall pay tax on exchange profits when none were realised.

7.24 One of the most common circumstances in which *section 136* is likely to apply is advances by a UK parent company to its thinly capitalised overseas subsidiaries. The Inland Revenue have said (see

Inland Revenue Explanatory Statement, para 3.13) that they will not apply these provisions if the UK company receives a market rate of interest on such loans (unless the loan is part of a UK tax avoidance scheme), but in many jurisdictions such a full interest bearing loan to a thinly capitalised company will give rise to major overseas tax problems.

Example 1

A UK company makes an interest free loan of PTA 1,000m to its thinly capitalised Spanish subsidiary. The exchange differences on the loan in the first three years are as follows.

	Gain/(loss) £'000
1996	300
1997	(500)
1998	400

The effect of ring fencing under the arm's length test is as follows.

	Taxable gain/ (deductible loss) £'000	
1996	300	
1997	(300)	(note (*a*))
1998	200	(note (*b*))

Notes
(*a*)   200 ring fenced.

(*b*)   400 – 200 ring fenced loss carried forward.

7.25   Where a loan to a thinly capitalised overseas subsidiary is interest free or bears interest at a very low rate, the argument which is normally taken to resist an imputed interest charge under *ICTA 1988, s 770* is that the loan is quasi-equity. If this is the case, then it is entirely within the spirit of the foreign exchange legislation that exchange differences on such equity investment should be outside the scope of the charging and relieving provisions. However, *section 136* only restricts losses and does not exclude from tax exchange gains. Companies may thus wish to consider whether they can make such quasi-equity investments in a form which will be excluded from the definition of qualifying assets for foreign exchange purposes, provided that the ability to obtain repayment of the sums involved is retained.

7.26   The existence of a parental guarantee in respect of a loan made to a subsidiary will not be regarded of itself as evidence that the loan is not on arm's length terms. However, it will be necessary to demonstrate that an independent company in similar circumstances could have borrowed on similar terms and that the parent company guarantee is merely a result of the lender choosing to obtain enhanced security where it may be available (see Inland Revenue Explanatory Statement, paras 3.11 and 3.12).

7.27 For accounting periods prior to the introduction of Corporation Tax Self-Assessment, the Board uses its powers to direct that *section 136* applies to each separate accrual period taken alone. The fact that a direction has or has not been given in one year does not mean that the same course of action will be followed in a later year. This covers not only circumstances where a loan shows a fluctuating pattern of profits and losses, so that some years may be excluded from direction to ensure that the taxed profit does not exceed the economic profit, but also loans where the surrounding circumstances may change. However, it is the transaction by which the company became subject to the liability or entitled to the asset which is relevant in determining whether a direction will be made, not the circumstances applying in a subsequent period.

7.28 No direction will be given by the Board where:

(*a*) a company has matched borrowing and lending (either for the purpose of making a matching election or otherwise) so that it makes no exchange gain or loss on the two sides of the transaction taken together and there is a clear linkage between borrowing and lending, but one or both of them is on non-arm's length terms (see Inland Revenue Explanatory Statement, para 3.14); or

(*b*) the transaction's terms differ, but not materially, from those which would have been agreed at arm's length; or

(*c*) the substantive terms of the transaction are at arm's length, but are not documented in the same detail or manner as would be expected between parties acting at arm's length; or

(*d*) given the particular facts and circumstances, the Inland Revenue believe that it would be unreasonable or inappropriate for a direction to be made (see Inland Revenue Explanatory Statement, para 3.8).

7.29 Inland Revenue Explanatory Statement, para 3.7 does, however, make it clear that a direction will be given in respect of 'circular, loss-multiplying, or otherwise abusive transactions'.

7.30 Once companies become subject to Corporation Tax Self-Assessment, it would seem sensible for them to bear in mind the above points when deciding whether an adjustment should be made in the tax return for accounting periods ending on or after 1 July 1999.

FA 1993, s 137

7.31   Currency contracts are brought within the arm's length test by *section 137*. The basic provisions are similar to those in *section 136(1)*, ring fencing applying to the entire exchange loss on a non-arm's length transaction. Such exchange losses on currency contracts are thus only available to carry forward against future profits on the same contract.

7.32   The section also originally only applied by direction of the Board but contains none of the relieving provisions which appear in *section 136*, because the Inland Revenue do not believe that they are relevant to currency contracts. However, with effect for accounting periods ending on or after 1 July 1999, the need for Board Direction is removed [*FA 1998, s 109*]. Thus under Corporation Tax Self-Assessment it is necessary for companies to consider whether an adjustment is required under this anti-avoidance provision and to include an appropriate amount in the tax return.

7.33   However, if a company could show that the circumstances of an exchange loss arising on a non-arm's length currency contract were broadly equivalent to those set out above in describing the relieving provisions on assets and liabilities, then it was stated policy that no direction would be made by the Board of Inland Revenue under *section 137* (see Inland Revenue Explanatory Statement, para 3.16). Presumably this will also be an acceptable approach for companies to adopt under Corporation Tax Self-Assessment.

FA 1993, s 138

7.34   The final element of the arm's length test concerns the carry forward of ring fenced exchange losses under *sections 136* or *137*, the first two parts of the arm's length test described above, to a subsequent accounting period where there is a change in the conversion currency used (for a local currency election) in the later accounting period.

7.35   This provision, contained in *section 138*, clarifies the way in which subsequent exchange gains are to be calculated for the purposes of offsetting against these ring-fenced losses brought forward.

7.36   To ascertain the offsettable amount of brought forward loss, the loss is recomputed into the currency of the subsequent gain at the rate applying on the first day of the accrual period in which the gain arises.

7.37   The translation between those two foreign currencies is to be made at the London closing exchange rate for that day. This rate is one of the rates published by a 'reputable independent body' such as Reuters, The Bank of England or the *Financial Times*.

Use of currency other than sterling

7.38   The Inland Revenue are concerned to ensure that the new local currency provisions (see Chapter 10, Part I) are not open to abuse. *FA 2000, s 106(7)*, introduces new anti-avoidance rule, *FA 1993, s 135A*, to deny any tax advantage which would arise from artificial selection of a particular foreign currency for accounting purposes. As enacted, the new section requires computations to be adjusted to include any foreign exchange gain which would arise if the accounts had been produced in sterling. It is not, however, entirely clear when such adjustments fall to be made.

7.39   The section provides that, if the main benefit that might be expected to result from using the non-sterling currency is the elimination of net exchange gains on transactions in that currency, the gain which would have arisen by reference to sterling must be brought into charge to tax.

7.40   It is difficult to envisage a situation in which the use of a non-sterling currency would not be expected to eliminate gains on transactions in that currency. However, it would equally expect to eliminate losses. It is therefore unclear how it should be determined whether 'the main benefit that might be expected to accrue' is the avoidance of net gains.

7.41   The reference to 'net' gains appears to be deliberate: a company which has a balanced position should not be liable to attack under this section. However, it is worth noting that the definition of 'net' is by reference to *initial exchange gains* less *initial exchange losses,* i.e. *taxable* foreign exchange and losses. [*FA 1993, s 135A*].

7.42   A company which was previously entitled to make a local currency election (see Chapter 10, Part II) would certainly have expected one of the main benefits of making such an election to be the elimination of gains arising on transactions in its local currency. Even where the election was lodged for administrative convenience, it is likely that elimination of foreign exchange movements would have been one of the main benefits envisaged, although some losses would have been forfeited along the way, i.e. the election enabled foreign exchange movements against the selected currency to be ignored for tax purposes. This was not considered unacceptable, and so it is unlikely that, under the new rules, adjustments to non-sterling computations will be required unless the Inland Revenue consider the company to be engaged in unacceptable tax planning structures.

7.43   Nevertheless, adjustments under *s 135A* must be self-assessed, and companies must therefore take the section into consideration when preparing computations. The original wording of the section was amended during the legislative process and the Secretary to the Treasury made some helpful comments at Report Stage (see Hansard 18 July 2000). She confirmed that the rule is intended to be an anti-avoidance measure and should not catch any truly commercial situation. The Inland Revenue have promised some further clarification of the intended scope of this provision in the autumn. The combined guidance will hopefully help companies to determine their correct return position.

Change of accounting period

7.44   The fourth area of anti-avoidance provision in the foreign ex-change legislation is designed to stop companies manipulating the date at which the provisions of *FA 1993* first apply to them, or exploiting subsequent currency fluctuations, by changing their accounting date.

7.45   A company with a 31 December year end may, for example, monitor the exchange movements on its major foreign currency denomi-nated assets and liabilities through its year commencing 1 January 1995 and take the view that, for example, at 30 September 1995 its non-taxable exchange gains were at a maximum, so that a combination of refinancing and terminating the accounting period could give it a permanent tax advantage, with a new accounting period starting on 1 October 1995 producing large tax deductions on future exchanges losses.

7.46   The provisions of *section 166* are designed to counter this. The Inspector of Taxes may, if he believes that such manipulation of taxable profits and losses on foreign exchange was the reason for the change of accounting date, ignore the change in order to arrive at the taxable exchange gains and losses for that company.

7.47   To do this, the Inspector would require the company to compute exchange differences on all items in its accounts by reference to its original accounting date, 31 December in the example above, rather than the new accounting date.

7.48   The administrative complexity involved in such a procedure is likely to be very considerable and this alone will act as a substantial deterrent to companies considering changing their accounting date in the period shortly after the Appointed Day.

7.49   Although this provision is likely to have the greatest impact on changes of accounting date which change the company's Commence-ment Day, it is not restricted to this circumstance and continues to apply for all future periods. Thus, if a company wishes to draw up a short accounting period to realise a tax deduction for a large loss which it could offset by way of group relief or carry back, then the provisions of *section 166* could be applied.

7.50   A company which objects to the decision of an Inspector of Taxes to ignore a change of accounting date in respect of exchange gains and losses may appeal to the Commissioners, who will then decide the matter, making such adjustments to the company's corporation tax liability as is 'just and reasonable'.

7.51   It is quite clear that any company changing its accounting date for whatever reason on or after the Appointed Day should carefully and thoroughly document the reasons for doing so in order to be able to demonstrate to the Inspector of Taxes that the change was not for the purpose of foreign exchange tax planning, nor did it include this as one of its purposes.

Capital gains transition

7.52   The fifth area of anti-avoidance provision is designed to stop groups of companies containing members with different year ends from exploiting the foreign exchange tax rules at Commencement Day to avoid the impact of the capital gains transitional provisions. This was a late addition to the legislation designed to counter a very specific scheme and is contained in *FA 1995, s 131*. The transitional rules which apply to items which were chargeable assets under the old rules but are qualifying assets under the foreign exchange tax rules apply to assets held by a company at its Commencement Day (see 6.56 above). Perhaps the most common example of this is a debt instrument which would have been a qualifying corporate bond, and thus outside the capital gains regime, were it not denominated in foreign currency.

7.53   If company A with a 31 December year end, owning a foreign currency bond standing at a substantial gain were to transfer that bond to a member of the same 75% group, company B, with a 30 September year end, there would be scope for exploiting the foreign exchange tax rules if that transfer were to be made between 1 October and 31 December 1995. Company A would at that time still be in the old foreign exchange regime, whereas company B would be in its first year of the new regime. The transfer of the bond by company A would fall within the scope of *TCGA 1992, s 171* and thus be tax free. In the hands of company B, assuming that the bond fulfilled the appropriate conditions, it would be a qualifying asset and outside the scope of the capital gains provisions. The bond could then be sold to a third party, realising the gains without crystallising any tax liability, if there were no anti-avoidance provisions to prevent this.

7.54   The effect of the anti-avoidance provision is to deny the relief from tax on the disposal by the company which is still in the old foreign exchange regime to another group member which is in the foreign exchange tax rules. Thus, full tax is collected at this stage, whether or not the asset is then sold on outside the group. The provision in this way catches not only transactions aimed at tax avoidance but also reorganisations and transfers of assets between group companies with non-coterminous year ends where there is a purely commercial motivation.

Great care therefore needed to be taken with any such transactions during the first year of the new tax rules.

7.55 The transactions covered by this provision are not only transfers within a group under *TCGA 1992, s 171*, but also the transfer of a UK branch or agency under *section 172*, reconstructions or amalgamations involving transfers of business under *section 139*, transfers of a UK trade under *section 140A*, and exempt transfers involving building societies, friendly societies, industrial and provident societies and cooperative associations under *TCGA 1992 ss 215, 216* and *217A* and *ICTA 1988, s 486(8)*.

Interaction with corporate and government debt rules

7.56 The corporate and government debt rules contain a number of anti-avoidance provisions. These rules do not have any impact on the deductibility of foreign exchange losses because foreign exchange differences are calculated under *FA 1993* not under *FA 1996*. [*FA 1996, 9 Sch 4(1)*]. Thus the unallowable loans provisions in *FA 1996, 9 Sch 13* cannot deny deductions for exchange losses.

Restriction of interest deductions on particular foreign currency debts

7.57 The Inland Revenue introduced an anti-avoidance provision in *FA 1993, s 60* that impacts on foreign currency borrowings. The provision denies interest deductions for the excess of interest payable over a commercial return on the capital repayable (where the capital is expressed in its settlement currency). The purpose is to prevent excessive interest deductions calculated in one currency when the debt is settled in a different currency (in respect of which interest rates are lower).

7.58 The Inland Revenue Manual asks Inspectors to 'look critically at any borrowing or advance where exchange differences are computed by reference to one currency but interest is computed by reference to another currency'. The Inspectors are asked to notify International Division if they make an adjustment under *FA 1993, s 60*.

Chapter 8

Deferral of Unrealised Exchange Gains

Introduction

8.1   The basic principle of the foreign exchange tax rules is that exchange gains and losses are taxable as income/deductible as expenses on an accruals basis. The legislation does, however, include the ability for a company to claim to defer the taxation of unrealised trading or non-trading exchange gains on certain items to the next accounting period.

8.2   *FA 1993, ss 139–143* detail the basic rules under which a single company can claim to defer unrealised exchange gains. These provisions are discussed in 8.4–8.15 below.

8.3   Regulations issued under *FA 1993, s 143(7)* modify the effect of these basic provisions for:

(*a*)   the settlement and replacement of an asset or liability [*DR 2*] (see 8.16–8.25 below);

(*b*)   situations where a company's profits include income or gains on which foreign tax credit relief is available [*DR 3*] (see 8.26–8.28 below); and

(*c*)   UK groups of companies [*DR 4*] (see 8.29–8.37 below)

Basic single company rules

8.4   A company may claim to defer an unrealised exchange gain accruing on a long-term capital asset or liability. [*FA 1993, s 139(1)–(3)*]. The deferral is for one year but as long as the deferred gain remains unrealised it can be included in a deferral claim for the accounting period to which it is deferred, and so on. The exchange gain is treated as not accruing for the period in question but is treated as accruing in the next accounting period. The exchange gain so deferred is taxed as trading, non-trading or partly trading and partly non-trading depending on the purpose of the asset or liability in that second accounting period. [*FA 1993, s 140(3)–(10)*].

8.5   Exchange gains are 'unrealised' if the asset or liability in question is still held by the company at the end of the relevant accounting period [*FA 1993, s 143(1)*] so gains can be deferred from all except the

154

last accounting period in which the item is held. For debts which vary in amount, only that part of the exchange gain which relates to the balance outstanding at the end of the period may be deferred. [*FA 1993, s 143(2)*].

Long-term capital assets and liabilities

8.6 The asset or liability for which the claim is made must be a right to or duty of settlement under a qualifying debt (see 3.9 above) with a settlement date of at least one year from the date the debt was set up (under the original terms of that debt). [*FA 1993, s 143(4)*]. In addition, the asset or liability must be capital (as defined by case law) throughout the accounting period for which the claim is made.

Example 1

A three-year loan to company A to buy plant for use in its trade would be a long-term capital liability of company A with exchange differences taxable as trading income/expense.

Example 2

A five-year loan by company B (an investment company) to its overseas subsidiary would be a long-term capital asset of company B with exchange differences categorised as non-trading for tax purposes.

Amount available for deferral

8.7 A company may claim to defer all or part of the unrealised gain on a long-term capital asset or liability. [*FA 1993, s 139(3)(a)*]. The amount actually available to be deferred to the next accounting period is however restricted to a maximum being the lower of:

(*a*) the net unrealised exchange gains for the accounting period on all of the company's long-term capital assets and liabilities; and

(*b*) the net exchange gains of the company for the accounting period on all of its rights to and duties of settlement under qualifying debts and currency contracts;

less:

(*c*) 10% of the company's taxable profits (after all reliefs and deductions) before group relief and the deferral claim itself.

[*FA 1993, ss 139(2)* and *141*].

If either (*a*) or (*b*) is a net exchange loss then no deferral is possible. The transitional rules (see 6.19 above), matching provisions, arm's length test,

8.8 *Deferral of Unrealised Exchange Gains*

irrecoverable debt provision and unremittable income provisions take priority over the deferral provisions. Thus all exchange gains/losses brought into the deferral calculations must be the amounts as calculated after the application of all of these rules.

8.8   If the long-term capital asset or liability is a variable debt then only the unrealised gain on the part of the debt not repaid during the year is available for deferral. Apportioning the gain between the remaining balance and the amount repaid during the year is to be done on a just and reasonable basis. [*FA 1993, s 143(2)*]. If the gain to be deferred arises on a capital asset against which it is possible to offset pre-commencement capital losses (see 6.68 and 6.74 above), the deferral applies before the converted capital losses are offset.

8.9   The effects of deferral claims on a single company are illustrated in Example 3 below.

Example 3

C Ltd (not a member of a UK CGT group) borrowed DM3m on capital account for five years at the end of 1996 (it makes up accounts for calendar years).

	End of year		
	1996	*1997*	*1998*
Exchange rate DM/£	3	3.3	3.5
Loan (in £'000)	1,000	909	857
Net exchange gains for company on advances, borrowing and currency contracts	n/a	100	44
Profits of company chargeable to corporation tax	n/a	540	245

How much of the unrealised exchange gains in 1997 and 1998, if any, may be deferred on the DM loan?

1997

	£'000
Available for deferral	
Lower of – unrealised exchange gain on long-term capital liability (1,000–909)	91
– net exchange gains	100
Therefore lower is	91
Less: 10% × 540	(54)
Deferral claim possible	£37
Thus taxable profits for 1997 if claim made (540 − 37)	£503

156

1998

Available for deferral

Lower of – unrealised gain (909 − 857 + 37)*	89
– net gains (44 + 37)*	81
Therefore lower is	81
Less: 10% × (245 + 37)*	(28)
Deferral claim possible	£53

Taxable profits for 1998 if the claim is made:

Taxable profits in year (245 + 37)*	282
Less: exchange gain deferred this year	(53)
	£229

* The gain deferred from 1997 accrues in 1998 as the deferral is for one year and so must be included in the calculations.

Non-sterling trades deferral claims

8.10   The deferral claim rules have to be adjusted for situations where the company has made a local currency election (see Chapter 10) for all or part of its trade as such an election may give rise to trading exchange differences measured by reference to the elected currency rather than by reference to sterling.

8.11   The first situation to deal with is where the gain being deferred, or any gains or losses within the deferral restriction calculation, is expressed in a non-sterling currency. In this case the foreign currency amounts are translated into sterling for the deferral claim calculations at the rate used in the local currency election (i.e. the year end rate or the average rate for the year whichever the company has chosen). [*FA 1993, s 142(1)* and *(2)*].

8.12   The rules also need to cover the calculation of the exchange gain that accrues in the second year if part of a trading exchange gain of a local currency elected trade or part trade is deferred. In this case the sterling equivalent of the part of the gain not deferred is taken into account after the basic profits of the trade for the period are found in sterling. The gain deferred is brought into the second year's local currency trading profits as the local currency equivalent of the sterling amount deferred, translating into the local currency at the London closing rate for the end of the second year (or the date of settlement of the asset/liability if earlier). [*FA 1993, s 142(3)–(6)*].

8.13   *Deferral of Unrealised Exchange Gains*

Mechanism for making the deferral claim

8.13   The claim must give the following information:

(*a*)   the amount of the gain being deferred;

(*b*)   how the amount deferred is to be allocated to trading and non-trading categories in the next accounting period; and

(*c*)   details of the asset or liability concerned.

[*FA 1993, s 139(4)*].

8.14   One claim may be made per accounting period, so where more than one gain is being deferred the claim must provide the details outlined above for all the gains being deferred. [*FA 1993, s 139(5)*].

8.15   A deferral claim may be made or withdrawn within two years of the end of the relevant accounting period even if the company has been assessed to corporation tax for the period and that assessment is final and conclusive. Beyond that, two-year threshold claims cannot be made or withdrawn if the corporation tax assessment for the period is final and conclusive. Where no such assessment has been issued, claims can be made or withdrawn for up to six years from the end of the accounting period. The Board of the Inland Revenue may at its discretion allow deferral claims outside these time limits. [*FA 1993, s 139(6)–(8)*].

Example 4

Company D wishes to defer an unrealised exchange gain from the year ended 31 December 1996. A final assessment is issued for 1996 on 10 December 1997. Any deferral claim lodged by 31 December 1998 will be valid.

Settlement and replacement of an asset or liability

8.16   It is possible in certain circumstances to treat an exchange gain as unrealised (and hence available for deferral) for the accounting period in which a long-term capital asset/liability is settled and replaced by another long-term capital asset/liability ('the replacement debt'). The provision works by treating the exchange gain on the original debt as not accruing on it. Instead the gain is treated as accruing on the replacement debt. [*DR 2(2)*]. It is not necessary for the whole debt to be replaced, but the detailed rules must be followed with care if part of the original debt is replaced and part remains in existence. If there is a gain on the original debt and a loss on the replacement (or vice versa), but a gain overall, deferral is still possible, by taking the net result.

8.17   The conditions to be met are as follows:

(*a*)   The replacement debt must either be:

(i)   of a fixed amount (see 8.19 below); or

(ii)   a deep gain security with the redemption amount payable on one specified date, a qualifying indexed security, or a deep discount security.

(*b*)   The date on which the company becomes entitled or subject to the replacement debt must fall in the period beginning 30 days before the day when the original debt is settled and ending 30 days after that settlement date.

(*c*)   The replacement debt in question must meet the rules on allocation of debts to the original debts (see 8.20 and 8.21 below). [*DR 2(3)*].

8.18   There is no condition that the replacement debt must be in the same currency as the original debt.

8.19   The condition in 8.17(*a*)(i) is met for a replacement debt if:

(*a*)   the debt has a specified maximum principal (defined at the start of the debt) which cannot be subsequently increased; and

(*b*)   once wholly or partly repaid the principal repaid cannot be re-drawn; and

(*c*)   in circumstances where the debt has a provision to capitalise unpaid interest, the capitalised interest is to be added to the principal on the day the interest is due and is repayable on the same basis as the principal.

Clauses requiring a gross-up for withholding (or other) taxes are ignored in determining if this condition is met. [*DR 2(10)*].

Example 5

Company E has a $100m five-year bank loan to buy plant and machinery due to expire in December 1999. Company E changes bankers in March 1997 and takes out a new three-year loan on 1 March 1997. The original loan is repaid on 2 April 1997. Any exchange gain arising on the original loan in 1997 cannot be deferred as it was replaced more than thirty days before repayment.

More than one replacement debt or original debt

8.20   It may be the case in applying conditions 8.17(*a*) and (*b*) above that there is more than one debt that could be treated as replacing the original debt. In these circumstances a first in first out rule is applied; the

8.21 *Deferral of Unrealised Exchange Gains*

first debt to which the company becomes entitled or subject is taken as the first tranche replacing the original debt. Later debts are then allocated in chronological order as replacing the original debt up to a maximum of the quantum of the original debt. [*DR 2(7)(a)*].

Example 6

Company F has a ten-year FFr100m loan to finance its investment in shares in its French subsidiary. The loan expires on 1 April 1998. Company F takes out two new long-term fixed amount loans as follows:

	FFr m
15 March 1998	60
2 April 1998	50

The original loan is thus replaced by all of the 15 March 1998 loan plus FFr40m of the 2 April 1998 loan. Hence any exchange gain on the original loan is unrealised and available for deferral.

8.21   A similar first in first out rule applies where there is more than one original debt that a debt could be seen as replacing. A debt is taken as first replacing the original debt that is settled first and then replacing later debts in chronological order to the extent there is any quantum of the 'replacing' debt left. [*DR 2(7)(b)*].

Example 7

Company G repays two long-term capital loans in 1999:

1 June 1999	DM100m
15 July 1999	DM30m

It takes out a new DM120m long-term capital loan on 22 June 1999.

The new loan replaces the DM100m loan and DM20m of the DM30m loan.

8.22   The company may notify the Inspector if it considers the facts of the replacement to be otherwise than implied by the rules outlined in 8.20 and 8.21 above. For accounting periods ending before 30 June 1996, if the Inspector accepts the company's contention the debt replacement allocation will follow the facts rather than the rules outlined above. [*DR 2(8)*]. For later accounting periods the Inspector's acceptance is not required under the transition towards self assessment [*DR 2(8)* as amended by *SI 1996 No 1348, Reg 3*].

Original debt only partly replaced

8.23   If the original debt is not fully replaced then the exchange gain on the original debt for the settlement accounting period is split between realised and unrealised. The amount treated as realised (i.e. arising on the part of the debt not replaced) is:

$$\frac{(\text{Reduction in original debt less Replacement debt amount})}{\text{Replacement debt amount}} \times \begin{array}{c} \text{total} \\ \text{exchange gain} \\ \text{on original debt} \end{array}$$

The balance is treated as unrealised and hence available for deferral. [*DR 2(4)*].

Example 8

In 1999 Company G which has a year end of 31 December (see Example 7 above) incurs an exchange gain of £500,000 on a DM30m long-term capital loan that is repaid on 15 July 1999. This loan is replaced by a loan of DM20m.

$$\text{Realised exchange gain} = \frac{30 - 20}{20} \times £500,000 = £250,000$$

Unrealised exchange gain available for deferral = £250,000

Settlement and replacement in different accounting periods

8.24   If the replacement debt is taken out in an accounting period (accounting period one) and the original debt is repaid in a later accounting period (accounting period two) the exchange gain on the original debt in accounting period two is treated as unrealised accruing on the replacement debt in accounting period two. [*DR 2(5)*].

8.25   In the reverse situation where settlement of the original debt is in accounting period one the gain on the original debt is treated as unrealised in period one and thus available for deferral to period two where it is treated as part of the total gain on the replacement debt. [*DR 2(6)*].

Effect on deferral calculations of income or gains on which foreign tax credit relief is available

8.26   The calculation of the maximum amount available for deferral requires the deduction of 10% of the company's taxable profits before group relief (see 8.7 above). Where these profits include income or chargeable gains on which foreign tax credit relief is available, an

8.27 *Deferral of Unrealised Exchange Gains*

element of the profits of the company is disregarded for the purposes of the deferral calculation.

8.27   The profits are reduced for the purposes of the deferral calculation by X minus Y where:

(*a*)   X is the amount of the income and chargeable gains subject to foreign tax credit relief ('the relevant income and gains'); and

(*b*)   Y is the 'gross amount (if any) of income and gains on which . . .' the 'net corporation tax would be charged'.

[*DR 3(2)* and *(4)*].

8.28   The net corporation tax is:

(*a*)   the amount of corporation tax that would have been charged on the relevant income and gains if there was no foreign tax credit relief; *less*

(*b*)   the foreign tax credit relief allowed.

[*DR 3(3)*].

Example 9

Company F has the following taxable income in a year:

	£
Unrealised exchange gain (on long-term capital asset)	200
Schedule D Case V (gross of 10% withholding tax)	100
	300

Deferral calculations are thus:

(1)   X = 100
Pay tax at 20% on X (i.e. 30% − 10%)

(2)   Thus Y = 100 × 20/30 = 66.7
(i.e. 66.7 at 30% = 20 = 100 at 20%)

(3)   Reduce taxable profits for deferral calculation by X − Y
(i.e. by 100 − 66.7) = 33.3

(4)   Thus deferral calculation is:

Lower of: Unrealised exchange gain	200
and	
Net exchange gain	200
Lower of: i.e.	200
Less: 10% × (300 − 33.3)	(27)
Deferral possible	173

Thus taxable profits in year: 300

                                                                    (173)

                                                                    £127

The Inland Revenue Foreign Exchange and Financial Instruments Manual (at paragraph 9.1.7) clarifies that the reduction (X minus Y) is the foreign tax credit grossed up at the relevant corporation tax rate. Using the definition in the above example:

Reduction in taxable profits $= 10 \times 100/30 = 33.3$

Deferral for UK groups of companies

8.29   The amount available for deferral under *FA 1993, s 141* (as discussed in 8.7 above) for a company which is a member of a chargeable gains group (as defined in *TCGA 1992, s 170*) is calculated under modified rules set out in *DR 4*. These rules are very complex.

8.30   These modified rules apply for any accounting period during which the company is at any time in a chargeable gains group. The claim submitted by such a company must state that it is a member of a group. [*DR 4(2)*].

Effect on amount available for deferral

8.31   The regulations change the comparison of net unrealised exchange gains in the company to net exchange gains in the company to a comparison of the claimant company's share of group equivalents of these amounts.

8.32   The steps in the calculation are as follows:

(*a*)   Calculate for each group company the net unrealised exchange gain/loss on long-term capital assets and liabilities for the accounting period.

(*b*)   Aggregate all the net unrealised gains and losses found under (*a*) to give the group net unrealised gain or loss. If the result is a net loss no deferral claims are possible for the group companies. If the result is a net gain continue to step (*c*).

(*c*)   Calculate the group total gross unrealised exchange gain, being the sum of all the net unrealised *gains* found under (*a*).

(*d*)   Calculate for each group company the net exchange gain/loss on all of its rights to and duties of settlement under qualifying debts and currency contracts apart from those gains/losses arising on revenue trading debts and currency contracts. This change from the single company definition was added by the Inland Revenue to simplify the group calculation. It is designed to save companies having to separately analyse exchange differences on revenue trading items which may be included in many different lines of a company's profit and loss account. Companies still need to be able to find the exchange differences on capital items used in the trade for this calculation. The exchange differences on revenue trading items of the claimant company *cannot* however be ignored as described above and so must be included in the calculation of the net exchange gains of the claimant company.

(*e*) Aggregate all the net exchange gains and losses to give the group net exchange gain or loss. If the result is a net loss no deferral claim is possible for the claimant company. If the result is a net gain continue to step (*f*).

(*f*) Find the following fraction for the claimant company:

$$\frac{\text{net unrealised exchange gain of claimant company } ((a) \text{ above})}{\text{group total gross unrealised exchange gain } ((c) \text{ above})}$$

(*g*) take the lower of:

(i) the group net unrealised exchange gain ((*b*) above)

(ii) the group net exchange gain ((*e*) above).

(*h*) apply fraction (*f*) above to result of (*g*)

i.e. $\dfrac{(a) \times (g)}{(c)}$

(*j*) The maximum amount available for deferral by the claimant is then equal to

(i) the amount found in (*h*) above; *less*

(ii) 10% of the claimant company's taxable profits (after all reliefs and deductions) before group relief and the deferral claim itself.

The amount available for deferral is further restricted if the amount in (*h*) is greater than or equal to half of the claimant's taxable profits (after all reliefs and deductions) but before group relief and the deferral claim (see 8.33 below).

[*DR 4(4)–(6)*].

Example 10

Company G is a member of a UK chargeable gains group (made up of companies G, H and I). Data on exchange differences is given below. No capital assets or liabilities were settled during the year ended 31 March 1996 and the unrealised gains/losses indicated below arose on the only capital items held by the companies. What is the maximum amount of unrealised exchange gain that G can defer from the year ended 31 March 1996 to the year ended 31 March 1997?

Company G	£
Net unrealised gain on long-term capital items	150,000
Net trading exchange loss	(60,000)
Net non-trading exchange gain (including above unrealised gain)	200,000
Taxable profits for year (before group relief)	540,000

Company H

Net unrealised loss on long-term capital items	(20,000)
Net trading exchange loss (including above unrealised loss)	(15,000)

Company I

Net unrealised gain on long-term capital items	10,000
Net non-trading exchange gain (including above unrealised gain) 50,000	

Note that the only qualifying items held by all the companies are rights of and duties to settle under qualifying debts and currency contracts.

Using steps (*a*) to (*j*) above, the calculation for companies G, H and I is as follows.

	G £	H £	I £	Total £
(*a*) net unrealised gain/ (loss) on long-term capital items	150,000	(20,000)	10,000	
(*b*) group net unrealised gain				140,000
(*c*) group total gross unrealised gain				160,000
(*d*) net exchange gain/ (loss)	140,000 (Note 1)	(20,000) (Note 2)	50,000	
(*e*) group net exchange gain				170,000

$$(f) \quad = \frac{150,000}{160,000}$$

(*g*) = the lower of: £

    (*b*) =   £140,000
    and
    (*e*) =   £170,000
    i.e (*g*) =   140,000

8.33 *Deferral of Unrealised Exchange Gains*

(*h*) $= \dfrac{150,000}{160,000} \times 140,000\ ((f) \times (g))$

$= 131,250$

(*j*) Maximum amount available for deferral by Company G
$= 131,250 - (10\% \times 540,000)$

$= £77,250$

Notes:

1. As G is the claimant all exchange differences on its qualifying items are included.

2. As H incurs a trading exchange loss of £20,000 on all of its capital items, the rest of its trading exchange differences are revenue and so are ignored for this calculation i.e. (15,000) = (20,000) re capital plus 5,000 re revenue so result for (*d*) = (20,000).

Restriction where deferral amount is more than half taxable profits

8.33 Where the amount found in 8.32(*h*) above is half or more of the claimant company's taxable profits (after all reliefs and deductions but before group relief and the deferral claim) the calculation in 8.32(*j*) above (10% of taxable profits threshold) is changed as discussed further below.

8.34 For accounting periods ending before 30 June 1996, the 10% of taxable profits threshold is changed to being 10% of the aggregate taxable profits of particular group companies (but not the claimant company). The group companies included are those where (at any time during the accounting period in question) either:

(*a*) the group company owes the claimant company amounts (other than amounts due under debts for goods or services supplied to the group company in the course of its trade) equal to at least 10% of the total debts (excluding trade creditors as outlined above) owed by that group company; or

(*b*) the claimant company owes that group company amounts (other than debts for goods or services supplied by the claimant company in the course of its trade) equal to at least 10% of the total debts (excluding trade creditors as outlined above) owed by the claimant company.

[*FA 1993, s 141(3A) and (3B) inserted by DR 4(5)*].

Note that sterling debts are qualifying assets and liabilities, and will therefore come into these calculations provided that they are not debts for goods or services provided to or by the company in the course of its trade.

Example 11

Consider again Company G from Example 10 but this time on the assumption its taxable profits are only £200,000.

Company G's maximum intercompany loan position with H and I during the accounting period ended 31 March 1996 is as follows:

	£
Due by G to H (loan by H of surplus cash)	10,000
Due to G from I (loan by G of surplus cash)	20,000
Total debts owed by G (excluding trade creditors)	50,000
Total debts owed by I (excluding trade creditors)	60,000

Group company taxable profits:

Taxable profits of H (before group relief)	300,000
Taxable profits of I (before group relief)	400,000

What is the maximum amount available for deferral in Company G for the year ended 31 March 1996?

- From example 10 amount (h) = £131,250
  50% of G's taxable profits = £100,000
- Thus as £131,250 is greater than £100,000 the alternative profit threshold rules have to apply.
- Which companies' profits are included?
  – H as G owes H £10,000, being more than 10% of G's total debts (of £50,000).
  – I as I owes G £20,000 being more than 10% of I's total debts (of £60,000).
- Profit threshold is thus:
  10% (300,000 + 400,000) = 70,000
- Maximum amount available for deferral by G
  = 131,250 − 70,000 = £61,250

(compared to 131,250 − 20,000 = £111,250 if no intercompany loans to and from company G).

8.35   For accounting periods ending on or after 30 June 1996, the 10% of taxable profits threshold is changed to being 10% of the aggregate taxable profits of particular group companies and the claimant company. The group companies included are those where, at any time during the accounting period in question, either 8.34(*a*) or (*b*) above applies.

8.36 *Deferral of Unrealised Exchange Gains*

[*FA 1993, s 141(3)* as inserted by *DR 4(5)* and as amended by *SI 1996 No 1348, Reg 4*]. This corrects a drafting error in the original regulations.

Example 12

Consider again the facts in Example 11 but this time assume all the figures relate to the year ended 31 December 1996. What is the maximum amount available for deferral in company G for the year ended 31 December 1996?

- Amended 10% of profits threshold applies as in Example 11.

- Which companies' profits are included?
  H and I as under Example 11 and G as the accounting period ended on or after 30 June 1996.

- Profit threshold is thus:
  10% (300,000 + 400,000 + 200,000) = £90,000

- Maximum amount available for deferral by G =
  131,250 − 90,000 = £41,250

(Compared to £111,250 if no inter company loans to and from company G.)

Companies joining or leaving the group

8.36   If a company joins or leaves the group during an accounting period then the amounts to be included in the above calculations in respect of that company are calculated on a time apportioned basis (unless this gives an unreasonable or unjust result in which case a just and reasonable method may be used). [*DR 4(6)*]. Similar rules apply where the accounting periods of group companies do not coincide.

Group deferral claims in practice

8.37   The provisions enabling a group to defer taxing an unrealised exchange gain on a long-term capital item are very complex. It is not obvious how much of such a gain can be deferred without doing the detailed calculations. These calculations require detailed information on each company's exchange differences and intercompany loan position. The absolute maximum amount any claimant company in a group can ever defer is (all the gains referred to below being gains on long-term capital items):

$$\frac{\text{net unrealised exchange gain of claimant company}}{\text{group total gross unrealised exchange gain}} \times \text{group net unrealised exchange gain}$$

Less: 10% of taxable profits of claimant company (before group relief).

It may be useful to do this calculation first to assess whether it is financially worthwhile doing all the calculations. Note that this calculation is only the absolute maximum if the deferral amount is less than or equal to half the taxable profits of the claimant. If the deferral amount is more than half the taxable profits the maximum could be lower than this calculation.

Chapter 9

The Matching Election

The purpose of the matching election

9.1 Multinational groups often use foreign currency borrowing and other foreign currency liabilities to hedge against the risk of currency fluctuations reducing the value of their overseas assets. For example, a UK company with subsidiaries in the US may choose to denominate some of its borrowing in US$, in order to protect the US$ part of the group balance sheet from fluctuations in the US$/£ exchange rate. Before commencement of the foreign exchange tax rules exchange gains or losses on the US$ borrowing were ignored for tax purposes, and unrealised exchange movements on the $ assets were also ignored. A company which hedged its balance sheet in this way was likely to reflect this in the consolidated group accounts, which would be prepared in accordance with Statement of Standard Accounting Practice 20 ('SSAP 20'). Exchange gains or losses on the US$ borrowing and on translation into sterling of the US$ assets were both taken to reserves in the consolidated accounts, and resulted in offsetting movements in reserves. To the extent that the amount of the liability matched the amount of the asset there was no net exchange gain or loss recognised in the accounts and, as described above, there was no net exchange gain or loss recognised for tax purposes under the old rules. However, if the UK company sold the shares in its US subsidiary the capital gain or loss on disposal was calculated taking account of the exchange rate movement over the period of ownership, following the principles set out in *Bentley v Pike, 53 TC 590*. There was therefore the potential for a mismatch between the tax and accounting treatment, but only when there was a disposal of the shares which were hedged by the foreign currency borrowing.

9.2 In contrast, under the basic provisions of the foreign exchange tax rules, exchange gains are taxed, and relief is given for exchange losses, which accrue in each accounting period on the US$ liability, whether they are taken to reserves or to the profit and loss account. The shares in the subsidiary remain taxable under the capital gains rules, so no exchange gain or loss is recognised for tax purposes until the disposal of the shares. This creates a fundamental mismatch between the tax and accounting treatment, which could leave the UK company with a substantial tax liability on an unrealised exchange gain that does not appear in the consolidated group profit and loss account.

9.3   The matching election is designed to deal with this mismatch. Where a matching election is made, exchange gains and losses on the matching liability are not taxed on an accruals basis, but are held in suspense until the asset is disposed of. At the time of disposal, the deferred exchange gains and losses on a liability which is matched with shares will be recognised as a capital gain or loss. This not only overcomes the mismatch caused by the foreign exchange tax rules, but also means that the effect of balance sheet hedging is taken into account in calculating the overall capital gain or loss on a disposal of the shares. The detailed conditions for matching are set out in Regulations (*SI 1994 No 3227*) and their effect is illustrated by the following example.

Example 1

The consolidated balance sheet of UK group has net assets in the US, valued at US$250m, representing the net assets of its US subsidiary. It has borrowings of US$180m throughout the accounting period. The exchange rate is US$1.8/£ at the start of the accounting period and US$2.0/£ at the end.

	Asset	*Liability*
US$m	250	(180)
£m equivalent at year end	£m 125	£m (90)
£m equivalent at start of year	139	(100)
Exchange gain or (loss) for year	(14)	10

	Accounting treatment under SSAP 20	*Tax treatment old rules*	*Tax treatment new rules without matching election*	*Tax treatment new rules with matching election*
Liability	Exchange gain £10m taken to reserves	Not recognised	Taxable income Schedule D Case III £10m. Tax payable £3.0m	Taxable exchange gain £10m held in suspense until shares are sold
US assets	Exchange loss £14m taken to reserves	Not recognised, but reflected in capital gain or loss if shares in US subsidiary are sold.	Not recognised, but reflected in capital gain or loss if shares in US subsidiary are sold.	Not recognised, but reflected in capital gain or loss if shares in US subsidiary are sold.

	Accounting treatment under SSAP 20	Tax treatment old rules	Tax treatment new rules without matching election	Tax treatment new rules with matching election
Result		• No current mismatch between tax and accounts • Mismatch when US subsidiary sold	• Mismatch between tax and accounts	• No mismatch between tax and accounts, currently or on sale of shares

Assets eligible for the matching election

9.4   A 'sterling' company may make a matching election in respect of assets in the following categories ('eligible assets') [*MR 5(6)*] (but see also 9.6 and 9.7 below):

(*a*)   Shares in a non-UK resident associated company.

The non-resident is an associate of the company making an election if the UK company directly controls 20% or more of the voting power in the non-resident company. [*MR 5(9)(a)*].

(*b*)   Shares in a UK-resident 90% subsidiary which has made a local currency election (but see 9.5 below).

The UK-resident company must be trading in the UK, and have made a local currency election to compute taxable trading profits of the trade, or part of the trade, in a currency other than sterling (see Chapter 10 for details of the local currency election). For the purpose of the matching election a company is a 90% subsidiary if not less than 90% of its ordinary share capital is owned directly or indirectly by the company making the election. [*MR 5(7)*]. A company may make an election only in respect of its direct shareholding, but that direct shareholding does not need to represent 90% of the ordinary share capital provided the company making the election holds directly and indirectly 90% in total.

(*c*)   A debt on a security which under the terms of issue can be converted into or exchanged for shares in a non-resident associated company or a UK-resident 90% subsidiary which has made a local currency election.

For accrual periods ending on or after 30 June 1996, this definition is tightened up, stating that the convertible debt must not be a qualifying asset. [*MR 5(6)(c)* as amended by *SI 1996 No 1347, Reg 4(5)*]. The definition of convertible debt that is not a qualifying asset

[*FA 1993, s 153(4)*] was amended with effect from 1 April 1996 (see 3.12 above).

Only a company which holds shares in a debt issuing company representing at least 20% of voting power may make the election in respect of convertible debt. In the case of convertible debt of a UK resident company, an election may be made only by a company of which it is a 90% subsidiary.

(*d*) Chargeable assets of an overseas branch of the company, in respect of which a local currency election has *not* been made (but see 9.5 below).

This arises where a trading company has an overseas trading branch which holds assets which are not qualifying assets, and on which a chargeable gain would arise if the company wishing to make the election sold the assets. [*MR 5(8)*].

(*e*) The company's net investment in an overseas branch for which a local currency election has been made (but see 9.5 below).

Where a trading company makes a local currency election in respect of an overseas branch, allowing it to compute taxable trading profits in a currency other than sterling, it may make a matching election in respect of its 'net investment' in the branch. It cannot elect to match chargeable assets of the overseas branch. The 'net investment' of a company in a branch is the value of the assets of the branch less the liabilities of the branch and less any other liabilities owed by the company for the purpose of the branch's trading activities. [*MR 5(9)(b)*]. This means, for example, that if an overseas branch borrows from the 'head office' of the company in the UK, and the head office has external borrowings in the same currency of at least that amount, the net investment in the branch will be reduced by the intracompany loan between head office and the branch.

(*f*) A ship or an aircraft.

9.5   In August 2000, the Inland Revenue issued draft Regulations to modify the Regulations originally made under the provisions of *FA 1993* in order to accommodate the changes introduced in *FA 2000, ss 105–106* in respect of the use of a currency other than sterling (see Chapter 10, Part I). The definition of 'eligible asset' as discussed at para 9.4 above is amended to eliminate references to trades in respect of which a local currency election has been made and to substitute instead references to businesses which are compelled (by new *section 93* of *FA 1993*) to use the 'relevant foreign currency' to compute and express their profits chargeable to corporation tax. These Regulations have not yet been passed but when they are they will be deemed to have been in effect for as long as, and to apply to the same accounting periods as, *FA 2000, ss 105–106.*

9.6   The draft new Regulations amend *MR 5(6)* so that it now applies to companies which make up their accounts in sterling. Regulation 5(6) paragraphs (*b*), (*d*) and (*e*) are altered to delete references to a local currency election and replace it with references to businesses to which *FA 1993, s 93* applies.

9.7   A new Regulation [*MR 5(6A)*] is introduced to provide for companies which make up their accounts in a currency other than sterling to make a matching election in respect of the items which correspond to those set out in Regulation 5(6) for sterling companies.

9.8   Essentially these new Regulations ensure that a company's ability to make a matching election is not diminished by the change to the local currency rules. It is worth noting that due to the effective extension by *FA 2000* of the local currency rules to all businesses (and not just trading activities), the number of circumstances in which a company can now make a matching election is potentially increased.

Liabilities which may be matched with assets

9.9   For a liability to be matched with an asset, so that exchange gains and losses on the liability are held in suspense until the asset is disposed of, the liability must be owed by the company holding the asset. Qualifying liabilities and the liability side of a currency contract may be matched with an eligible asset provided they satisfy the necessary conditions. A liability is *not* eligible to be matched with an asset if:

(*a*)   it is a debt of accrued interest, or

(*b*)   it is a debt in respect of 'goods or services supplied to the company in the ordinary course of its trade'.

[*MR 5(4)(a)*].

Eligible liabilities – economic requirements

9.10   A liability is eligible to be matched with a particular asset if the nominal currency of the liability or the currency contract is such that it 'could reasonably be expected to eliminate or substantially reduce the economic risk of holding the asset which is attributable to fluctuations in exchange rates'. [*Reg 5(4)(b)* and *(5)*]. This is a broader condition than simply requiring the liability to be in the same currency as the asset (which may in fact be difficult to ascertain in the case of assets such as shares). Where an asset is only partly matched, either because the value of the asset is greater than the value of the liability or because there has been a partial matching election, this condition is applied by reference only to the part of the asset which is matched. [*MR 5(4)* and *(5)*].

9.11   Where a company borrows in a currency which has a formal linkage to the currency which is most closely linked to the value of the asset, the liability will be an eligible liability. For example, a company which has a subsidiary resident in Hong Kong whose assets and trading activities are primarily denominated in HK$ could regard borrowing in US$ as an eligible liability, as long as the link between the US$ and HK$ remains.

Eligible liabilities – accounting requirements

9.12   An eligible liability may be matched with an asset, other than a ship or an aircraft, only if the matching is reflected in the accounting treatment of the asset and liability in the entity accounts of the company which makes the matching election.

9.13   First of all a liability is only matched by an asset 'to the extent that the value of the liability at that time is matched by the value of the asset at that time'. [*MR 4(4)*]. The values referred to here are the values in the company's *entity* accounts at that time. [*MR 4(5)*]. If at any time the sterling value of the liability for accounts purposes exceeds that of the asset, the excess cannot be treated as matched under the matching election. The maximum liability which can be matched with an asset is therefore determined by the *book value* of the shares or other asset in the *entity accounts* of the company making the election. The values used for the purposes of the consolidated accounts are not relevant.

Example 2

An investment company holds shares in a direct subsidiary in its accounts at a value of €100m. It also has a loan due to the bank of €120m in its accounts.

If it meets the other accounting condition (see below) this company could make a matching election in respect of only €100m of the bank loan.

9.14   Secondly the accounting treatment of exchange differences on the asset and liability must reflect the fact that the liability is hedging the asset. A matching election thus has no effect unless any exchange differences on the assets are taken to reserves in the company's *entity* accounts together with exchange differences on the liability (to the extent the liability hedges the asset). [*MR 10(4)*]. The matching election rules effectively require companies to adopt entity matching under SSAP 20, paragraph 51 rather than just matching in group consolidated accounts.

9.15   In any accounting period, if an exchange gain on a borrowing (to the extent that the gain arose on the matched element of the borrowing) were taken to profit and loss account rather than to reserves, it would be taxed as income in the normal way notwithstanding that a matching election had been made. If, however, a loss is taken to the profit and loss account no relief will be available. This effectively forces companies to follow SSAP 20, paragraph 51, and account for the foreign currency borrowing as a hedge against the investment in the overseas subsidiary or branch in the company's entity accounts, and not just in the group consolidated accounts.

Form of the matching election

9.16   An election is made in respect of an asset, or part of an asset, which is eligible to be matched. It must be made by the company which owns the asset and owes the liability which is to be matched with the asset. The election, in the form of a notice to the Inspector of Taxes must contain the following information:

(*a*)   The asset to be matched.

(*b*)   If the election is not to be made for the whole of the asset either –

   (i)   a fixed percentage of the asset which is to be available for matching; or

   (ii)   a specific amount which is less than the whole value of the asset (the value of the whole asset as at the time the election is made must also be supplied); or

   (iii)   a proportion or part of the asset which is to be available for matching where this is given by reference to a formula or other method of calculation specified in the election (and may therefore vary over time).

(*c*)   The provision in the Matching Regulations under which the asset is eligible for the matching election.

[*MR 10(2)* as amended by *SI 1996 No 1347, Reg 5*].

Matching election for part of an asset

9.17   The different ways in which an election can be made for part of an asset are illustrated by the following examples.

Example 3

The election could specify that 60% of the company's investment in its French subsidiary, France SA [*MR 10(2)(c)(i)*] is to be matched.

Example 4

The company values France SA in its accounts at cost, €50m. The company could therefore make a matching election in respect of €30m of the value of the asset. [*MR 10(2)(c)(ii)*].

Example 5

A UK company has a Dutch subsidiary, Holdings BV, which owns all the shares in two operating companies based in Australia and Hong Kong. The matching election could specify that it applied to the proportion of Holdings BV which was represented by that company's investment in its Australian subsidiary. [*MR 10(2)(c)(iii)*].

9.18   An election in respect of a fixed percentage of an asset or a specific amount may be varied by subsequent election so as to *increase* the percentage or amount which is specified in the election. An election which specifies a percentage or amount cannot be amended to reduce the amount of the percentage which is available for matching. In the case of a 'formula' election there is no provision for varying the formula, but the proportion of the asset which is matched can vary upwards and downwards in accordance with the formula. [*MR 10(3)*].

9.19   For accrual periods ending on or after 30 June 1996, there is an anti-avoidance provision in respect of partial matching elections. [*MR 5(3A)* inserted by *SI 1996 No 1347, Reg 4(4)*]. If as a result of a partial matching election:

(*a*)   a liability is not wholly matched with the asset, or

(*b*)   there is a liability which could have been included in the election but was not,

relief is deferred for any exchange loss in the reserves of the company on the unmatched liability until the disposal of the asset. The Inland Revenue clarified the application of *MR 5(3A)* in the August 1996 Tax Bulletin. They stated that *MR 5(3A)* would only be applied to defer relief for exchange losses 'to the extent that such losses relate to the excess of:

● the amount of such liabilities which hedge or fund that asset (and in respect of which exchange differences are consequently taken to reserves in accordance with SSAP 20); over

● the amount of such liabilities matched for tax purposes'.

9.20   If *MR 5(3A)* is read literally, it does not seem to work properly when the partial matching election is put in place part of the way through the accounting period. However, in practice, the Inland Revenue have allowed its application.

Timing of the matching election

9.21   In general, a matching election is effective from the day on which it is made, and is irrevocable. [*MR 10(1)*]. The election can be made retrospective, however, in the following circumstances.

(a) Commencement Day.
If an election is made within the period of 92 days beginning with the company's Commencement Day (or, if later, within the period of 183 days beginning with the Appointed Day) in respect of an asset which the company held on its Commencement Day, the company can specify in the election that it is to be effective from Commencement Day. If it does not specify that the election is to be effective from Commencement Day, it will be effective from the day it is made. [*MR 11(4)*].

(b) New asset.
An election made in respect of a newly acquired asset can be made retrospective to the acquisition date provided the election is made not more than 92 days after the date of acquisition and the election specifies that it should be retrospective to the acquisition date. [*MR 11(2)*].

(c) Increase of partial matching election.
When an election for part of an asset is varied, the election can specify that the variation is effective from any day which is not more than 92 days earlier than the date of the new election. [*MR 11(3)*].

Effect of the matching election – interaction with the basic rules

9.22   If the whole of a liability is the subject of a matching election throughout an accounting period then the exchange differences accruing on that liability are totally ignored for tax computation purposes for that year. A liability may however be matched with an asset for part of an accrual period of the liability. For example, a company may be subject to the liability for the whole of an accounting period, but make a matching election which is effective from a date part way through the period. The taxable exchange gain or loss of the liability for any accrual period which includes the period when it is matched with an asset under the matching election is generally found using what is known as 'the alternative method' of calculation. This treats the exchange gain or loss of the accrual period as if it accrued evenly on a daily basis through the period. The exchange gain or loss on the liability is then adjusted by reducing the amount accrued each day in proportion to the amount of the liability which is matched. [*MR 5(2)*].

Example 6

In 1996 A Ltd borrowed US$100,000 for 10 years. On 1 July 1997 it acquired all the issued share capital of a trading company, T Inc, which operates in and is resident in the United States. A Ltd accounts for the shares in T Inc in its own accounts at cost ($60,000). It prepares accounts to 31 December and on 31 July 1997 makes a matching election (effective from 1 July 1997) in respect of the whole of its investment in T Inc. In the year to 31 December 1997 it accounts for the investment in T Inc and $60,000 of the borrowing by taking the exchange differences on the asset and 60% of the exchange differences on the liability to reserves. The exchange rates are as follows:

31 December 1996	US$1.60/£
1 July 1997	US$1.66/£
31 December 1997	US$1.70/£

For *accounts purposes* it treats $60,000 of the liability as matching the shares in T Inc from 1 July 1997 onwards, and takes exchange differences on the asset and part of the liability to reserves:

	£	£
Liability:		
1.1.97 to 30.6.97		
$100,000 @ $1.60/£	62,500	
Less		
$100,000 @ $1.66/£	(60,241)	
		2,259
1.7.97 to 31.12.97		
$40,000 @ $1.66/£	24,096	
Less		
$40,000 @ $1.70/£	(23,529)	
		567
Exchange gain taken to P/L account		2,826

For *tax purposes* the matching election is effective from 1 July 1997, and the 'alternative method' will therefore apply to the liability as shown below. The exchange gain for the period 1 January to 31 December 1997 before adjusting for the matching election is as follows:

9.23   *The Matching Election*

	£
$100,000 @ $1.60/£	62,500
Less	
$100,000 @ $1.70/£	(58,824)
Exchange gain before matching election	3,676

This is treated as accruing at a daily rate over the year.

Up to 30 June 1997 none of the liability was matched.

From 1 July to 31 December 1997 (184 days) $60,000 was matched with the T Inc shares, so the gain must be reduced as follows:

$$£3,676 \times \frac{184}{365} \times \frac{\$60,000}{\$100,000} \qquad (1,112)$$

Adjusted exchange gain = taxable exchange gain in 1997   £2,564

This is not the same figure as the gain taken to the profit and loss account because the actual exchange rate at the time the shares were acquired has been used for accounts purposes.

9.23   If the proportion of a liability which is matched remains constant, in practical terms it is simply necessary to reduce the exchange gain or loss for the accrual period in proportion to the level of matching. The 'alternative method' is only of significance when the extent to which a particular liability is matched varies during an accrual period of that liability.

9.24   The transitional rules take priority over the matching rules. [*TR2*]. See 6.20 above. Thus the exchange difference treated as accruing evenly on a daily basis under the alternative method described above is the exchange difference after application of the transitional rules. For example, a loan held on Commencement Day which is fully matched may be subject to the kink test. The exchange differences held in suspense (which may eventually crystallise, see 9.28 below) on this loan are the taxable amounts calculated under the kink test transitional rule (see 6.21 to 6.37 above).

9.25   In Example 6 above, the taxable exchange gain differed from the exchange gain taken to the profit and loss account because the 'alternative method' did not take account of the exchange rate at the time the asset was acquired and matching became effective for accounts purposes. The 'alternative method' is modified where its application to the matching election would cause significant discrepancies between the exchange differences recognised for accounts and tax purposes. If at any time during the accrual period of a matched liability:

(*a*)   there is a major change in the extent to which the liability is matched, and (*b*)   there is a significant change in the relevant exchange rate in the accrual period,

the 'alternative method' is applied as if the time at which the extent of matching changed was a translation time, effectively splitting the accrual period into two. [*MR 5(3)*]. This does not, however, create two separate accrual periods. The application of the modified alternative method is best illustrated by example.

Example 7

In 1996, C Ltd borrowed US$100,000 for ten years. On 1 July 1997 it acquired all the issued share capital of a trading company, W Inc, which operates in and is resident in the United States. C Ltd accounts for the shares in W Inc in its own accounts at cost ($100,000). It prepares accounts to 31 December and on 31 July 1997 makes a matching election (effective from 1 July 1997) in respect of the whole of its investment in W Inc. In the year to 31 December 1997 it accounts for the investment in W Inc, and the borrowing, by taking exchange differences which accrue on the asset and the liability from 1 July 1997 to reserves. The exchange rates and the sterling equivalent of $100,000 are as follows:

		£ equivalent of $ loan
31 December 1996	US$1.60/£	62,500
1 July 1997	US$2.0/£	50,000
31 December 1997	US$1.55/£	64,516

The accounts show an exchange gain of £12,500 on the liability in respect of the period to 30 June 1997, which is taken to the profit and loss account. The subsequent exchange loss of £14,516 on the liability is carried to reserves and offset against the corresponding exchange gain of £14,516 on the asset.

The basic rules ignoring matching would give a deductible loss of £2,016 (£64,516 *less* £62,500) on the loan for the accounting period ended 31 December 1997. Applying the 'alternative method', one would expect half of this loss to be attributed to the period before the asset was acquired, and remain deductible, and the other half to be attributed to the six months during which the liability was matched with the asset. In this case the exchange rate moved significantly during the period and the liability went from no matching to full matching. The 'alternative method' is therefore modified to bring the tax treatment in line with the accounting treatment, calculating taxable exchange gains and losses as if there had been a translation time at 30 June 1997. This results in:

(*a*)   an exchange gain of £12,500 in respect of the period 1 January to 30 June 1997, which would be taxable because the liability is not matched in this period; and

(*b*)   an exchange loss of £14,516 for the period 1 July to 31 December 1997, which is held in suspense as a result of the matching election.

Permanence of election and replacement loans

9.26   Once made, a matching election is irrevocable [*MR 10(1)(c)*], and an election to match part of an asset can be increased but not decreased. The exchange differences on the matching liabilities, which are excluded from the foreign exchange tax rules as a result of the matching election, are deferred for as long as the company holds the asset. They are *not* brought into taxation when the matching liability is repaid.

9.27   If a matched liability is settled, any other liabilities of the company which could be matched with the asset will be treated as matching in place of the original liability. [*MR 10(5)* as amended by *SI 1996 No 1347, Reg 5*]. Where there is more than one liability which could be matched with the asset, the liability which is treated as matching the asset is to be decided on a 'just and reasonable basis'. [*MR 10(7)*]. This means that liabilities in appropriate currencies will automatically be matched with the asset unless they are in respect of trading transactions or accrued interest as long as the company takes exchange differences on the matched liability to reserves. [*MR 5(4)(a)*]. If the loan matches the asset and exchange differences on the loan are not taken to reserves, exchange gains will be taxable and exchange losses not relieved. This is particularly worth bearing in mind given the introduction of the European single currency on 1 January 1999. Whereas previously a French franc borrowing would only be drawn into a matching election to match a French franc investment (or investment in another currency linked to the franc), it could now be pulled automatically into an election to match, for example, a Deutschmark investment due to the elimination of foreign exchange exposure between participating currencies. Particular care therefore needs to be taken where matching elections are in place in respect of eurozone assets.

Disposal of the matched asset – crystallisation of deferred exchange gains and losses

9.28   The exchange gains and losses on liabilities which are excluded from the foreign exchange tax rules as a result of a matching election are held in suspense until there is a disposal of the asset with which the liability was matched. However, the exchange gains and losses held in suspense are not crystallised on such a disposal in the following circumstances:

(*a*)   if the asset is reacquired by the company under a contract made not more than 30 days before or 30 days after the time of disposal [*MR 7(2)(a)*]; or

(*b*)   if the asset is disposed of at no gain/no loss which, for this purpose, includes a disposal under the following provisions of TCGA 1992 [*MR 8*]:

(i)   *s 139*: transfer of business to another UK resident company;

(ii) *s 140A*: transfer of business between companies resident in EU member states;

(iii) *s 171*: transfer of assets within a group;

(iv) *s 215*: amalgamation of building societies; and

(v)   *s 216*: transfer of building society business to a company; or

(c)   where there is no disposal because the transaction forms part of a reorganisation within *TCGA 1992, s 127*, or would do so but for the application of *TCGA 1992, s 116*. [*MR 9*].

9.29   If the matching election is made in respect of an overseas branch for which a local currency election has been made, the exchange gains and losses which are left out of account as a result of the matching election are never recognised for tax purposes. This is consistent with the treatment of the net investment itself – exchange gains and losses on the branch assets, which are taken to reserves for accounts purposes, are also ignored under the foreign exchange tax rules as a result of the local currency election.

9.30   Where there is a disposal of a matched asset which is not within one of the exceptions referred to above, it is necessary to calculate the aggregate of all the exchange gains and losses which have been eliminated from the foreign exchange tax rules by the matching election. This amount must take into account the effects of the transitional rules on the liability (i.e. the kink test, the grandfathering rules or the currency contract transitional rule if applicable – see Chapter 6). The net figure is treated as gain or loss which is deemed to accrue at the time that the disposal of the asset takes place. The tax treatment of the deemed gain or loss is as follows [*MR 7(3)–(7)*]:

Asset	*Tax Treatment*
shares in non-resident subsidiary or associate	CGT: chargeable gain/allowable loss
shares in resident 90% subsidiary	CGT: chargeable gain/allowable loss
convertible debt	CGT: chargeable gain/allowable loss
chargeable asset of overseas branch (no local currency election)	CGT: chargeable gain/allowable loss
ship or aircraft	Income: taxable exchange gain or loss under foreign exchange tax rules

9.31   The Matching Election

9.31   Where there is a part disposal of the asset, the amount of the deemed gain or loss to be recognised as above is reduced proportionately. [*MR 7(8)*].

No gain/no loss disposals

9.32   Where there is a no gain/no loss disposal of an asset, the matched exchange gains and losses remain in suspense but are transferred with the asset. As a result, the deemed chargeable gain or loss, or income exchange gain or loss, is deemed to accrue to the company which makes the first disposal of the asset which is not a no gain/no loss disposal, at the time of that disposal. [*MR 8*].

Reorganisations

9.33   There are special rules [*MR 9*] where a company ceases to hold the shares or convertible debt which was the subject of a matching election but there is no disposal of the shares or securities for capital gains purposes either:

(*a*)   because the company parts with the matched shares or securities in a transaction which comes within the reorganisation of share capital rules [*TCGA 1992, s 127*], e.g. a reorganisation of share capital, a conversion of securities or a share for share exchange; or

(*b*)   because the reorganisation etc. involves a qualifying corporate bond, *section 127* does not apply but *TCGA 1992, s 116(10)* provides that there is no capital gains disposal of the original matched shares or securities.

Transactions within TCGA 1992, s 127

9.34   Matching comes to an end when the company no longer holds the matched assets, but the deferred exchange gains and losses on the matching liabilities remain in suspense until there is a disposal of the 'new holding' which has replaced the original matched assets. At the time of this disposal, the aggregate exchange gain or loss which has been deferred by the matching election is incorporated into the capital gains computation of the new holding, as an adjustment to the consideration received. [*MR 9(3)* and *(4)*].

Transactions within TCGA 1992, s 116(10)

9.35   In a case where the matched asset is replaced by a qualifying corporate bond, *TCGA 1992, s 116(10)* operates in place of *TCGA 1992, s 127* to deem there to be no disposal, and also requires the capital gain on the matched asset to be calculated as if there had been a disposal at market value at the time of the reorganisation. The gain or loss on the original asset is then treated as arising at the time of the disposal of the qualifying corporate bond which replaced it. In this case, the capital gain or loss on the original asset is adjusted by the aggregate exchange gain or loss which has been deferred under the matching election, and it is the adjusted capital gain or loss which crystallises when the qualifying corporate bond is disposed of. [*MR 9(3)* and *(4)*].

9.36   The rules for no gain/no loss transfers and reorganisations can be applied in any combination to deal with a complex series of transactions. If there is a part disposal of an asset which comes within the reorganisation provisions described above, the deferred exchange gain or loss is apportioned between the part disposed of and the part retained and the rules above are applied as appropriate to the part retained and the part disposed of.

Practical issues

Borrowing and asset not in the same company

9.37   In order for a matching election to be effective, the asset, and the liability which hedges the asset, must be in the same company. This is often not the case in multinational groups, particularly where the borrowing is hedging equity investments in overseas subsidiaries and associates. Such groups often borrow in the group parent company but hold shares in overseas subsidiaries in an intermediate UK-resident holding company.

9.38   Simply transferring the borrowing to the shareholding company, or transferring the shares to the borrowing company, is not an attractive option, because it may lead to a loss of double taxation relief. An alternative is for the borrowing company to make an *interest free* loan in the appropriate currency to the shareholding company. The Inland Revenue Explanatory Statement, paragraph 2.24, makes it clear that where an interest free loan is made within a group primarily for the purpose of the matching arrangements or where the main reason for no interest being charged is to maximise the use of foreign tax credits the Inland Revenue will not seek to apply the transfer pricing legislation in *ICTA 1988, ss 770* and *773* to impute interest income in the lending company. This also applies where there is a foreign currency interest-free loan to the company holding the shares and a sterling interest-free loan back to the group lending company which has the original foreign currency borrowing or currency contract.

Example 8

R plc has a US subsidiary, T Inc, the shares of which are held by a UK-resident intermediate holding company S Ltd. The shares in T Inc cost $100m and are held by S Ltd at cost. T Inc has net assets of $180m and these are partly hedged by a loan of $70m which R plc had borrowed from a bank. The group wishes to make a matching election, but cannot because S Ltd, which holds the eligible asset (shares in T Inc) has no $ liabilities. The bank loan was taken out after commencement of the foreign exchange tax rules.

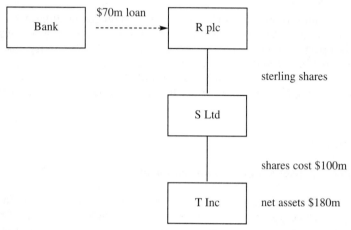

The current exchange rate is $2 = £1. The following interest-free loans are set up:

R plc lends $70m to S Ltd
S Ltd lends £35m to R plc

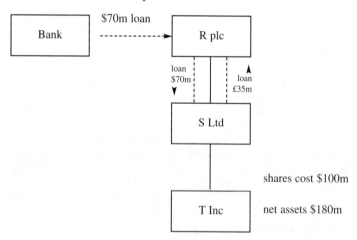

S Ltd now has a liability of $70m which is eligible for matching with the shares in T Inc. R plc has a qualifying liability of $70m and a qualifying asset of $70m, so the exchange differences which accrue on the asset and liability under the foreign exchange tax rules will be equal and opposite and will cancel each other out.

9.39 Relief for a loss which accrues on a loan which is not on arm's length terms can be restricted under the arm's length test (see Chapter 7, Anti-Avoidance). An interest-free loan made between the borrowing company and the company eligible to make a matching election is clearly not on arm's length terms and if loss relief were to be restricted in the lending company, this would leave the corresponding exchange gain on the borrowing as net taxable income. The arm's length test does not, however, apply to foreign currency loans between two UK-resident members of the same UK-chargeable gains group provided there is a taxable gain in one of the companies which is a party to the loan equal to the deductible loss in the other company. This criterion is to be applied without regard to the matching election [*MR 12*], so the fact that an exchange gain in the borrowing company is matched with an eligible asset, and is therefore not subject to tax as income of the accounting period in which it accrues, does not prevent this exemption from being satisfied. Losses which accrue in the lending company on interest-free intercompany loans made for the purposes of the matching election cannot therefore be restricted under the arm's length test.

Distributable profits

9.40 If a company has a foreign currency liability, an exchange loss on the liability can in some circumstances reduce the distributable profits of the company. If intercompany loans are used to provide an intermediate holding company with a foreign currency borrowing, to enable it to make a matching election, exchange losses on the borrowing could restrict its ability to pay dividends out of its dividend income from overseas subsidiaries.

Overseas holding companies – multicurrency assets

9.41 Groups often hold shares in overseas subsidiaries operating in a number of different countries through one or more overseas intermediate holding companies. If UK-resident companies borrow in foreign currency to hedge these overseas investments, the matching which is reflected in the group consolidated accounts can be made effective for tax purposes only if a matching election is made in respect of the shares in the overseas holding company. This raises a number of practical issues.

9.42 The first question is whether borrowing in one or more of the currencies of the operating companies can satisfy the matching election requirement that it eliminates or substantially reduces the economic risk, attributable to exchange rate fluctuations, of holding the asset. The example in the Inland Revenue Explanatory Statement, paragraph 2.22 illustrates the ways in which this test could be satisfied.

9.43 The other major practical issue is how to reflect the matching in the entity accounts of the company making the election. The matching is reflected in the group consolidated accounts by translating the under-lying assets of the operating company into sterling and taking exchange gains and losses to reserves to be matched with exchange differences on the corresponding borrowing. In order to match the investment with the borrowing for entity accounts purposes, the shares in a Dutch holding company must be treated for accounts purposes as a multicurrency asset, with a multicurrency carrying value in 'appropriate' currencies. This could be achieved, for example, by equity accounting for the investment in the Dutch holding company, so that its carrying value is based on the underlying net assets in each currency.

Borrowing and on-lending in a matching company

9.44 The provisions on replacement loans (see 9.27 above) mean that care should be taken when a matching company borrows and on-lends in foreign currency. If the currency is such that the borrowing could be used to match an asset held by the company, relief for an exchange loss on the borrowing could be lost or deferred whilst an exchange gain on the on-lending is taxable if the borrowing is automatically pulled into the matching election. This could happen, for example, if a whole asset matching election is made (with a fully matched liability) and a few years later the matched liability is wholly or partially repaid. If there happens to be another eligible liability (for example a borrowing that is on-lent) in the company at any time after the repayment, that liability will be pulled into the matching election and exchange loss relief on an accruals basis will be denied.

Chapter 10

Use of Local Currency

PART I : USE OF CURRENCY OTHER THAN STERLING

Introduction

10.1   *FA 2000, s 105(1)* substitutes new *ss 92–95* into *FA 1993*. These rules govern the currency in which profits chargeable to corporation tax must be computed and expressed.

10.2   First, statutory provision is made for the total profits or losses of a business subject to corporation tax to be computed and expressed in sterling. [*FA 1993*, new *s 92*].

10.3   Next, the new legislation sets out prescribed circumstances, most notably where a company makes up its accounts in a currency other than sterling, in which it is now mandatory for the chargeable profits and losses (other than capital gains/losses) of a company to be computed and expressed in foreign currency ('the relevant foreign currency'). [*FA 1993*, new *s 93*].

10.4   These new provisions are intended:

(*a*)   to cover all those cases where a local currency election would previously have been possible (see Chapter 10, Part II), and

(*b*)   to broaden the scope of the local currency election and extend its effect to a greater number of taxpayers.

10.5   The facility for making a local currency election has therefore been withdrawn with effect for accounting periods beginning on or after 1 January 2000, subject to limited transitional provisions. The local currency provisions are, however, still described and discussed in Part II of this Chapter as they continue to have some relevance.

Background to new rules

10.6   On 14 January 2000, the Government announced its intention to bring forward legislation in the next Finance Bill to improve the tax position of companies making up their accounts in a foreign currency. On

8 February 2000, the Inland Revenue published draft clauses for consultation. The response to the consultation process led to there being a number of amendments to the original provisions when the Finance Bill was published. Further alterations were made during the Bill's passage through Parliament.

10.7 The new rules replace the existing regime of local currency elections with an automatic system for computing chargeable profits (other than capital gains/losses) in foreign currency in certain prescribed circumstances. The scope of the new provisions is wider than that of the local currency regulations so that investment holding companies and traders who were not previously eligible to make a local currency election will now be able to prepare non-sterling computations.

10.8 The rules also extend to branches, both within and outside the UK, and some care is needed when determining whether these are actually caught by the new provisions.

10.9 The new regime is not a perfect replacement for the local currency election. It would appear that certain companies which had previously made a valid local currency election for all or part of a trade (or trades) may not now strictly meet the precise (and different) requirements for preparing tax computations in a foreign currency.

10.10 Moreover, some companies which had local currency elections in place may have non-trading activities which were outside the scope of the election but which will now also fall to be dealt with in the relevant foreign currency.

10.11 Finally, a new and broadly worded anti-avoidance provision, *FA 1993, s 135A,* has been introduced to make sure that companies do not secure unintended tax advantages from being able to compute taxable profits in a currency other than sterling (see 7.38 above).

10.12 The Inland Revenue hope to provide further clarification of the application of the new functional currency rules, and the anti-avoidance provision, later this year.

Effective date

10.13 The new rules apply to accounting periods beginning on or after 1 January 2000 if they also end on or after 21 March 2000 (Budget Day). They will have retrospective effect in many cases, i.e. to accounting periods starting before the rules were finalised.

10.14 Any company which did not make, or was not able to make, a local currency election for its last accounting period under the previous rules was able to defer the application of the new rules until its first accounting period beginning on or after 1 July 2000. This concession was, however, a one-off election which had to be filed by 31 August 2000.

10.15   The provisions do not alter the regime applicable to Controlled Foreign Companies.

Detailed provisions

10.16   A company must compute its profits or losses subject to corporation tax (other than capital gains/losses falling within *TCGA 1992*) in a currency other than sterling where:

(*a*)   the accounts of the company as a whole are prepared in a currency other than sterling in accordance with normal accounting practice [*FA 1993, s 93(2)(a)*]; or

(*b*)   the accounts of the company as a whole are prepared in sterling but insofar as an individual part of the business is concerned are prepared using the closing rate/net investment method (as per SSAP 20) from financial statements prepared in a currency other than sterling [*FA 1993, s 93(3)(a)*]; or

(*c*)   the return of accounts for the UK branch of an overseas company is prepared in a currency other than sterling [*FA 1993, s 93(2)(b)*]; or

(*d*)   the return of accounts for the UK branch of an overseas company prepared in sterling using the closing rate/net investment method (as per SSAP 20) from financial statements prepared in a currency other than sterling [*FA 1993, s 93(3)(b)*].

10.7   For this purpose, the 'accounts' of a company are:

(*a*)   the annual accounts of the company prepared in accordance with the Companies Act 1985 (or Part VIII of the Companies (Northern Ireland) Order 1986); or

(*b*)   if not required to make up accounts under (*a*) above, the accounts which it is required to keep under the law of its home State; or

(*c*)   if not required to keep accounts, whatever records of the company most closely correspond to the accounts which it would have been required to prepare if the Companies Act did apply to it [*FA 1993, s 93(7)*].

10.18   In these circumstances the computation must be prepared in the currency of the accounts, the 'relevant foreign currency'.

10.19   The consequences of these basic rules are:

(*a*)   any UK company, whether trading or not, which prepares its accounts in a foreign currency, is required to prepare its corporation tax computation in that currency;

(*b*)   UK companies which aggregate the results of overseas branches by means of the closing rate/net investment method under SSAP 20 must compute the chargeable profit/loss of *each* branch separately in the relevant foreign currency for each; and

(*c*)   a UK branch of an overseas company which makes up its accounts in a currency other than sterling must prepare its corporation tax computation in the currency used by the parent company, unless the branch prepares its branch return in sterling other than by applying the closing rate/net investment method from non-sterling accounts of the company.

10.20   Where a company carries on its business through different branches and these rules would apply differently if the branch were a separate business, then the rules must be applied to the branches separately. This provision removes the need for separate legislation to deal with ring fence trades.

10.21   A 'branch' for this purpose includes any collection of rights and liabilities and so may be smaller than the sort of operation conventionally thought of as comprising a branch. This is to fit in with the SSAP 20 definition which allows the closing rate/net investment method to be applied to a separate activity which falls short of a branch, e.g. a (fleet of) aircraft. [*FA 1993, s 93(7)*].

10.22   The profit or loss for corporation tax purposes is found by:

(i)   taking the chargeable profit/loss computed and expressed in *relevant foreign currency* (see 10.18 above);

(ii)   deducting management expenses (under *ICTA 1988, s 75(3)*), trading losses brought forward (under *ICTA 1988, s 392(B)* or *s 393*) and non-trading deficits (under *s 83, FA 1996*) also computed and expressed in *relevant foreign currency*;

(iii)   computing the sterling equivalent of the resultant amount by converting it at the London closing exchange rate on the last day of the accounting period (see 3.34).

10.23   Where branch returns are prepared using the average rate, that rate must be used in determining the sterling equivalent at (iii) above.

10.24   Losses brought forward and expressed in sterling should be converted into the relevant foreign currency at the closing rate for the last day of the immediately preceding accounting period. [*FA 1993, s 94(4)*].

10.25   Items denominated in any other currency should be converted into the relevant foreign currency using the London closing rate on the day on which the company became entitled to the receipt or incurred the expense. [*FA 1993, s 94(1) and (2)*]. However, an average arm's length rate should be used in the case of a business whose results are amalgamated into sterling accounts at an average arm's length rate.

10.26 Where a company prepares non-sterling accounts, it may elect – at any time during an accounting period – that, with effect from the first day of the accounting period in which the election is made, an average arm's length rate will be used. [*FA 1993, s 94(5)(a)*]. It may withdraw such an election with effect from the first day of the accounting period beginning after the date of the election. [*FA 1993, s 94(5)(b)*]. It may not then make another average rate election for three years. [*FA 1993, s 94(6)*].

10.27 Capital allowances are also to be computed in relevant foreign currency [*FA 1993, s 93(5)*]:

(*a*) new assets acquired in another currency are to be brought into the pool at the closing rate on the date of acquisition;

(*b*) monetary limits (e.g. expensive cars) are converted into the relevant foreign currency at the closing rate;

(*c*) pool balances should be converted into relevant foreign currency at the closing rate for the last day of the immediately preceding accounting period and brought into the new regime;

(*d*) there is no guidance on the maximum amount which can be taken out of the capital allowances pool on the disposal of an asset acquired at a time when the pool was carried in sterling.

10.28 The Inland Revenue are concerned to ensure these new provisions are not open to abuse. *FA 2000, s 106*, has therefore introduced a new anti-avoidance rule, *FA 1993, s 135A*, to deny any tax advantage which would arise from artificial selection of a particular foreign currency for accounting – and thus for tax – purposes (see 7.38).

PART II : LOCAL CURRENCY ELECTIONS

Introduction

10.29 Prior to *FA 2000*, i.e. for accounting periods beginning before 1 January 2000, the foreign exchange tax rules generally required sterling to be the reference currency for the calculation of taxable exchange differences. [*FA 1993, s 149(1)*]. A currency other than sterling could only be used as the reference currency in respect of assets, liabilities and currency contracts used in a trade/part of a trade where a 'local currency' election had been made for that trade/part of a trade. [*FA 1993, s 149(2)–(7)*].

10.30 This election was allowed by regulations under *FA 1993, ss 93, 94* and *94A*. It meant the trading profits before capital allowances of the elected trade/part of a trade were calculated in the 'local currency' (i.e. the chosen foreign currency) and then translated into sterling. This part of this chapter discusses the conditions that had to be met for a valid local currency election and the practical effects of such an election.

Scope of election

10.31 A local currency election could be made (if the conditions described later in this chapter are fulfilled) for either [*LR 3* and *4*]:

(*a*)   a whole trade of a company; or

(*b*)   a specified part of the trade of a company.

10.32 For 10.31(*b*) above to apply, the 'specified part of the trade' must be either:

(*a*)   a trade carried on wholly or partly through one or more branches outside the UK; or

(*b*)   a ring fence trade which meets the condition in *FA 1993, s 94A(2)*, (see 10.35 below).

10.33 Hence an election could be made for one or more overseas branches of a UK company or for one or more UK branches of an overseas company.

10.34 If a company carried on a trade through more than one branch in an overseas country then the same local currency must be used for all the branches in that country. [*LR 4(5)*]. A company could make a local currency election specifying a number of different currencies for different parts of a trade. [*LR 4(3)*]. Any part of a trade for which no election is made must use sterling as its reference currency. [*LR 4(6)*].

Ring fence trade elections

10.35 *FA 1993, s 94* and related regulations allowed elections for *parts* of the trade of a UK company carried on through overseas branches. This section was disapplied for petroleum extraction companies carrying on a ring fence trade (as defined in *ICTA 1988, s 492*). Such a company could make a local currency election for part of its trade *if* that part consisted of activities relating to oil or gas carried on under a petroleum licence in the UK or a designated area. [*FA 1993, s 94A* and *LR 4(2)(b)*].

Conditions for a valid election

10.36 A currency may be specified as a local currency in an election if it meets two conditions [*LR 5(2)*]:

(*a*)   the primary economic environment condition; and

(*b*)   the accounting condition.

Primary economic environment condition

10.37 A currency is only valid for a local currency election if it is 'the currency of the primary economic environment in which the trade or part of the trade is carried on'. [*LR 5(2)(a)*]. 'Primary economic environment' is not defined in the regulations. Instead *LR 6* states that in determining the primary economic environment 'regard shall be had to all relevant circumstances'. This regulation goes on to list five particular factors which will be taken into account if relevant.

10.38 The factors listed are [*LR 6*]:

(*a*) the currency in which the net cashflows of the trade or part are generated or expressed in the relevant accounting records;

(*b*) the currency in which the company manages the profitability of the trade or part so far as it is affected by currency exposure;

(*c*) in the case of a company that is resident in the United Kingdom, the currency in which the company's share capital and reserves are denominated;

(*d*) the currency to which the company or, where the trade or part is carried on through a branch, that branch, is exposed in its long-term capital borrowing (of any kind whatsoever); and

(*e*) the currency which is the generally recognised currency in which trading in the principal market of the trade or part is carried on.

10.39 Given that 'all relevant circumstances', in particular the above factors, have to be considered it may be difficult to determine whether a trade or part of a trade meets the economic environment condition. The Inland Revenue recognised this as a problem and so included a section (section 4) in the Explanatory Statement outlining how they would interpret this regulation.

10.40 The guidance in the Explanatory Statement explains that there is no requirement for a trade or part trade to meet a particular number of the listed factors. The five factors will have varying degrees of relevance and importance in cases considered.

10.41 The statement then considers each factor in turn and indicates circumstances when that factor will be relevant and important in deciding if the primary economic environment condition is met. The comments in the following paragraphs outline the guidance given by the Inland Revenue in the statement.

Net cashflows factor (a)

10.42 This factor is included as it derives from the SSAP 20 definition of local currency. The statement indicates that the currency in which net

10.43   *Use of Local Currency*

cashflows are generated would not be relevant if a significant proportion of its income was in one currency, with the rest of the income in a variety of currencies and expenses in sterling. The factor may become relevant if such non-local currency cashflows are immediately translated in the accounting records into the local currency (due to the inclusion in this factor of the currency in which the cashflows are 'expressed in the relevant accounting records'). Where a company uses multi-currency accounting the relevance of this factor depends on the contribution the cashflows in each set of records makes to the overall net cashflow. This factor is not relevant if records are kept of the same cashflows in a number of currencies operating in parallel (e.g. same cashflows recorded in both sterling and euros).

Profitability factor (b)

10.43   The Inland Revenue consider that this factor will probably be relevant for all companies. It may even be the only relevant factor. They emphasise that what is considered here is the currency in which profitability is managed not just measured. For example a company could measure its profits in sterling but hedge all its currency exposures into dollars. It would thus seem to manage its profits in dollars. The Inland Revenue expect companies to be able to provide evidence to back-up their contention that they manage profitability in a particular currency.

Share capital factor (c)

10.44   This factor is considered relevant for companies but obviously not for branches. It is not important when a company is thinly capitalised.

Long-term capital borrowings factor (d)

10.45   If a company has significant borrowings then the currency of these borrowings is considered a relevant factor (taking into account whether the borrowings are effectively converted into another currency by currency contracts). If the borrowings hedge currency assets there will be no net exposure to that currency and so the factor is not considered relevant. The currency for this factor is likely to be the same as the profitability factor currency. The Inland Revenue consider long term in this case to be a period of more than one year.

Principal market factor (e)

10.46   Some trades have a global market operating in one particular currency (e.g. oil) so obviously this currency is relevant for such trades.

Local currency type election already in place

10.47 The local currency election legislation enacted what had already been happening on an extra statutory basis in many instances. The Inland Revenue indicated (see Inland Revenue Explanatory Statement, para 4.10) that the economic environment condition was likely to be met where the local Inspector had agreed pre-commencement to what is tantamount to a local currency election.

Accounting condition

10.48 To meet the accounting condition one of the following must apply to the local currency for which the election is being made:

(*a*)   it is the currency used to prepare the company's accounts in accordance with normal accounting practice (accounts being UK statutory accounts or for overseas companies the closest equivalent to UK statutory accounts); or

(*b*)   for a UK company, the financial statements for the relevant trade/ part of the trade are prepared in that local currency and then these statements are included in the UK accounts by translation into sterling using the closing rate/net investment method (as outlined in SSAP 20); or

(*c*)   for a company not resident in the UK, the financial statements for the relevant trade/part of the trade are prepared in that local currency in accordance with normal accounting practice. [*LR 5(3)–(5)*].

10.49 A UK company carrying on a trade wholly in the UK but in a non-sterling currency is likely to meet condition (*a*) (although it could meet condition (*b*) instead). A UK company with overseas branches will usually meet condition (*b*) for those branches. A UK branch of an overseas company will usually meet condition (*c*).

10.50 The accounting condition is also satisfied for any election for an overseas branch if:

(*a*)   the trade/part of the trade is within the charge to corporation tax immediately before Commencement Day; and

(*b*)   the trading profits (before capital allowances) for accounting periods ending in the two years up to Commencement Day were computed in that local currency.

Such an election must however be made before the end of 92 days beginning with the company's Commencement Day. [*LR 5(6)* and *(7)*].

10.51   *Use of Local Currency*

Timing of election

10.51   A local currency election is effective for all accounting periods beginning on or after the date on which the election is made. [*LR 9(1)*].

Example 1

An election made on 12 December 1996 for the UK branch of an overseas company with accounting year end 31 December will be effective from 1 January 1997.

10.52   For trades/part trades within the charge to corporation tax immediately before Commencement Day, an election made before the end of 92 days beginning with Commencement Day will be effective for all accounting periods beginning on or after Commencement Day. [*LR 9(2)*].

Example 2

A UK company with Commencement Day 1 April 1995 making a local currency election for its French trading branch on 1 July 1995 will have a valid election from 1 April 1995 (an election made on 2 July 1995 would only be valid from 1 April 1996).

10.53   Similarly an election made for a trade/part trade coming within the charge to corporation tax on or after Commencement Day will be effective from the day it comes within the charge if the election is made before the end of 92 days beginning with that day. [*LR 9(3)*].

Example 3

A UK trading company (year end 31 December) sets up a new branch in Germany and the branch starts to trade on 1 October 1997. If the local currency election is made before 1 January 1998 it will be valid from 1 October 1997, as long as the company is not already within the charge to corporation tax in respect of its existing trade. If the company is already within the charge to tax, then strictly the election is only valid from the beginning of the accounting period following the date on which the election is made.

10.54   The election once made applies to all future accounting periods (subject to the exceptions outlined above) unless the local currency specified no longer meets the conditions of the election. See 10.63 below.

Information required in the election

10.55   The election must include:

(*a*)   the reasons why the conditions (see above) are met;

(*b*)   information on the nature of the trade/part trade and its location; and

(*c*)   the fact that the company wishes to translate the local currency elected profits into sterling (for the overall tax computation) at the average arm's length exchange rate for the accounting period (if applicable). [*LR 8(1)* – see also 10.57 below].

[*LR 10(1)*].

Effects of making the election

10.56   If a valid local currency election has been made then the UK trading profits (before capital allowances) of the trade/part of the trade affected are calculated in the specified local currency. [*FA 1993, ss 93* and *94*]. The resulting taxable profits are then translated into sterling for inclusion in the main corporation tax computation.

10.57   The translation into sterling will be at the London closing rate for the last day of the accounting period concerned [*FA 1993, ss 93(6)* and *94(11)*] unless the company has stated in the election that the translation should be at the average arm's length exchange rate for all the days in the accounting period. [*LR 8*]. Such a statement may be revoked for future accounting periods by notice to the Inspector. [*LR 8(4)*].

10.58   The calculation of taxable trading profits for the elected trade or part trade must follow all UK tax rules for Schedule D Case I. Hence exchange differences on qualifying assets, liabilities and currency contracts used for the trade must be included in the trading profits. These exchange differences will be measured using the local currency as the reference currency for translation.

Example 4

A UK company has a French branch for which a valid euro local currency election has been made. Exchange differences will only arise in the French branch trading profits computation if it has non-euro trade debtors, creditors or long-term funding of that trade.

10.59   The inclusion of all the assets/liabilities connected with the trade within the local currency election means that any liability of the company for the purpose of the branch trade is included in that election regardless of whether the loan is owed by the branch or the Head Office. The Inland

10.60 *Use of Local Currency*

Revenue have clarified in the Inland Revenue Explanatory Statement at paragraphs 2.17 to 2.19 that when a company borrows externally and passes on those funds to the branch then so much of those real external borrowings as correspond to that intra-company loan is covered by the local currency election. Thus, exchange differences on those borrowings are computed by reference to the branch local currency. (Usually this will mean there would be no exchange differences as the borrowings will be in that local currency.) As explained in paragraph 2.19 of the Inland Revenue Explanatory Statement, this treatment is likely to mean that head office will not need to make any adjustments in their computations for such external borrowings if they are on-lent to the branch as the exchange movement in head office on the branch asset loan will offset the exchange movement on the external liability. No adjustments should also be required of the branch as its profits are already calculated for tax purposes in the local currency.

10.60   If a branch or company has a local currency election for its trade, all other elements of its corporation tax computation must continue to be calculated by reference to sterling.

Example 5

A UK oil futures trading company has made a local currency election to use the US dollar for its whole trade. It has surplus funds which it lends in US dollars to its US parent under arm's length terms.

The debtor owed by the US parent is a qualifying asset which is not for trading purposes.

Exchange differences on revaluing the US dollar loan to the sterling equivalent each year end will be taxable as non-trading exchange gains/losses (even though no exchange differences are recognised in the (US dollar) accounts).

Invalid elections

10.61   If a local currency election is invalid, then profits should be calculated with sterling as the local currency. The Inland Revenue Foreign Exchange and Financial Instruments Manual gives guidance to Inspectors on how the taxable profits should be calculated in such circumstances.

10.62   For overseas branches, the Manual guidance is that the branch trading profit (as included in the company profit and loss account at the average exchange rate for the accounting period under the closing rate/net investment method of accounting) will be taxable. Exchange differences in respect of the branch's net assets taken to the company's reserves under the closing rate/net investment method will also be taxable. For a UK company submitting non-sterling accounts, the Inspectors are told to calculate the profit for the year by comparing opening and closing net assets (translated at the opening and closing exchange rates to sterling). They are then told to adjust for non-monetary items, non-trade income and disallowable expenditure translating these adjustments at the rates ruling on the particular day of a transaction or at the average rate for the period for non-trade income and disallowable expenditure. As Inspectors are following these calculation methods for invalid elections it seems possible to use these methods for foreign currency overseas branches and UK companies with non-sterling accounts where no election is made.

Example 6

Comparison of the taxable result when a local currency election is made for an overseas branch with the result when no such election is made.

	31/12/96 FFrm	31/12/97 FFrm
Net assets of branch (all trading monetary items)	<u>100</u>	<u>150</u>
Profit for year		<u>50</u>

Exchange rates
average for year ended 31 December 1997: FFr 8.5 = £1
on 31 December 1996: FFr8.4 = £1
on 31 December 1997: FFr8.6 = £1

Taxable profit if election made

FFr50m/8.5 =	£5.88m

Taxable profit if no election made

Exchange differences take to reserves:		
Revaluation of opening net assets:		
FFr100m @ 8.4 =	11.90	
FFr100m @ 8.6 =	<u>11.63</u>	
Exchange loss:		(0.27)
Revaluation of profit to closing rate:		
FFr50m @ 8.5 =	5.88	
FFr50m @ 8.6 =	<u>5.81</u>	
Exchange loss		(0.07)
Exchange loss taken to reserves		(0.34)
Profit taken to profit and loss account		
50/8.5		<u>5.88</u>
Net taxable profit (no election made)		£5.54m

10.63 *Use of Local Currency*

Currency ceasing to meet conditions

10.63   If the currency specified in a local currency election ceases to meet the conditions of the election (i.e. the accounting and/or primary economic environment conditions are no longer met) during an accounting period, then the election ceases to have effect at the end of that particular accounting period (*LR 10(4)*). If this occurs, the company is required to let the Inspector know as 'as soon as is reasonably practical after becoming aware of' this change (*LR 10(5)*).

Introduction of the euro

10.64   The *Finance Act 1998* introduced provisions enabling the Inland Revenue to issue regulations regarding the application of UK tax legislation to the introduction of the euro.

The European Single Currency (Taxes) Regulations were published in December 1998 and are reproduced in Appendix 4. As a result:

(*a*)   a local currency election made by a company in respect of trading activities carried on in a currency which joins EMU will automatically have effect in euro, assuming all other conditions continue to be fulfilled [*ESCR 43*];

(*b*)   a local currency election made by a company in respect of trading activities carried on in a currency which is not joining EMU may be replaced by an election in euro if the company adopts euro as its functional currency and assuming all other conditions are fulfilled;

(*c*)   where there is currently no election, the company may make an election in euro in the same way that it would for any other currency;

(*d*)   part trade elections in eurozone currencies are aggregated and an election had to be made by 3 April 1999 if the company wished to use an average exchange rate to translate the profits into sterling, whether or not this was specified in the original elections. [*ESCR 44* and *46*].

10.65   The Inland Revenue did not relax the time limit for lodging a local currency election in respect of the euro. An election to specify the euro as the local currency, whether as a replacement to an existing election or for the first time, must therefore be made *before the beginning* of the accounting period to which it is to apply (unless the company is commencing to trade). However, the Inland Revenue did accept elections before 1 January 1999 for accounting periods commencing on or after that date.

10.66   Pan-European groups may wish to adopt the euro as their reporting currency, and some UK companies may therefore adopt the euro as their functional currency to facilitate the preparation of group accounts. For accounting periods beginning after 31 December 1999, such companies do not need to file a local currency election. They will automatically have to prepare their tax computations in euro (see Chapter 10, Part I).

10.67 There has been no relaxation of the existing rules to allow investment companies to file a local currency election, but the new rules governing the use of currencies other than sterling to prepare tax computations (see Chapter 10, Part I) apply equally to non-trading entities.

Chapter 11

Other Special Provisions

Introduction

11.1   This chapter deals with the following special provisions under the foreign exchange tax rules:

(*a*)   Excess gains and losses (see 11.2–11.13 below).

(*b*)   Irrecoverable debts (see 11.14–11.21 below).

(*c*)   Unremittable income (see 11.22–11.26 below).

Excess gains and losses

11.2   The basic foreign exchange tax rules tax exchange differences arising on monetary assets and liabilities on an accruals basis. For accounting periods ending on or before 31 March 1996, it was also possible that a company would make a non-exchange gain or loss on the settlement of such a monetary asset or liability (e.g. buy a US Treasury bond for $1,000 and sell it for $1,200 making a non-exchange gain of $200). This gain or loss would only be taxable if the company dealt in such assets or liabilities as part of its trade. If the asset or liability was not a dealing item then the non-exchange gain or loss would not be taxable (from Commencement Day foreign currency assets are exempt from taxation under the chargeable gains rules – see 3.53 above). There are special rules (the excess gains and losses regulations) to cover situations where such non-exchange gains or losses arise.

11.3   The corporate and government debt rules resulted in the non-exchange gains or losses on loan relationships (as defined in *FA 1996, s 81*) being taxed on an accruals or mark to market basis. All loan relationships are qualifying assets or liabilities under the foreign exchange tax rules so the excess gains and losses regulations have no effect for loan relationships for accounting periods ending after 31 March 1996. There are items which are qualifying assets and liabilities and are not loan relationships (i.e. units of currency, rights and duties to settle under debts for goods and services, provisions, shares and short sales of shares held on trading account). The excess gains and losses regulations continue to apply to such items for accounting periods ending after 31 March 1996. The regulations should have limited application in such accounting periods as non-exchange gains and losses are unlikely to arise on such

204

items since most of them are fully taxable as part of the Schedule D Case I profit or loss.

Non-exchange loss

11.4   If a company makes a non-exchange loss on an asset or liability and this is not a tax deductible loss then that company may (subject to 11.8 below) claim relief (as a deemed exchange loss) in the disposal accounting period for an amount equal to the lower of:

(*a*)   the net taxable exchange gain on the asset or liability from acquisition to disposal; and

(*b*)   the non-exchange loss.

[*ER 2(1)*].

If a net tax deductible exchange loss has arisen over the life of the asset or liability no relief is possible. [*ER 2(1) and (5)*].

Example 1

*   Company A (an investment company) buys a US$ treasury bond for $1,000 on 1 April 1995 (when $1.6 = £1).

*   At 31 March 1996 $1.4 = £1.

*   Company A sells the $ bond for $910 on 31 March 1996.

*   Company A's year end is 31 March.

*   What is the tax position for the year ended 31 March 1996?

Solution:

(*a*)	Taxable exchange gain on asset	
	($1000/1.4)	£714
	($1000/1.6)	£(625)
		£89
(*b*)	Non-exchange loss on asset	$910
		$(1,000)
		$(90)
	at $1.4 = £1	£(64)

Claim possible: lower of (*a*) and (*b*) i.e.	£(64)

Tax position for year ended 31 March 1996

Taxable exchange gain	£89
less: deemed deductible exchange loss	£(64)
Net taxable exchange gain	£25

11.5   Other Special Provisions

11.5   The claim is all or nothing (e.g. in the example in 11.4 above Company A cannot claim for say £20 of the non-exchange loss to be treated as an exchange loss, it must claim £64 or not claim). It must be made within two years of the end of the accounting period in which the non-exchange loss accrued to the company. [*ER 2(7)*].

11.6   The amount of any non-exchange loss has to be reduced for the purposes of any claim by the amount of any compensation due to the company in respect of the loss if that compensation is not itself taxable. [*ER 2(3)*].

Non-exchange gain

11.7   If a company makes a non-exchange gain on an asset or liability and this is not a taxable gain then a taxable gain (a deemed exchange gain) arises in the accounting period in which the asset or liability is disposed of equal to the lower of:

(*a*)   the net tax deductible exchange loss on the asset or liability from acquisition to disposal; and

(*b*)   the non-exchange gain.

[*ER 2(4)*].

If a net taxable exchange gain has arisen over the life of the asset or liability no taxable gain arises. It is important to note that this non-exchange gain rule is mandatory and is not applied at the Revenue's direction.

Example 2

- Company B (an investment company) buys a DM bond for DM3,000 on 1 April 1995 (DM2.5 = £1).

- At 31 January 1996 DM2.7 = £1.

- Company B sells the bond on 31 January 1996 for DM3,200.

- Company B's year end is 31 March.

- What is the tax position for the year ended 31 March 1996?

Solution:
(*a*)   Tax deductible exchange loss
        (DM3,000/2.7)   £1,111
        (DM3,000/2.5)   £(1,200)
                                                                    ─────────
                                                                      £(89)
                                                                    ─────────

(*b*) Non-exchange gain		DM3,200
		DM(3,000)
		DM200

At DM 2.7 = £1	£74
Relief clawed back: lower of (*a*) and (*b*) i.e.	£74

Tax position for year ended 31 March 1996

Tax deductible exchange loss	£(89)
Deemed taxable exchange gain	£74
New deductible exchange loss	£(15)

Non-arm's length transactions

11.8   A claim cannot be made in respect of a non-exchange loss if the asset or liability in question was acquired or disposed of in a transaction that was not on arm's length terms. [*ER 2(1)(b)* and *(2)*]. The clawback of previous deductible exchange losses does, however, occur where a non-exchange gain arises even if the acquisition or disposal was on non-arm's length terms.

Part disposals

11.9   If a non-exchange gain or loss arises on a part disposal or settlement of an asset or liability the provisions above apply with the deemed exchange gain or loss arising in the period in which the part disposal or settlement occurs.

Subsequent recovery of non-exchange loss

11.10   There are special rules to cover the situation where a company claims relief in respect of a non-exchange loss and this loss is subsequently recovered.

11.11   A deemed exchange gain arises in the original non-exchange loss making company if some or all of the non-exchange loss is recovered by that original loss making company or by another (chargeable gains) group company (if the loss making company still has an accounting period when the recovery occurs). [*ER 3(1)*].

11.12   The amount of gain that is deemed to arise is equal to:

(*a*)   the amount of the non-exchange loss recovered (translated into sterling using the London closing rate for the date of recovery)

Less

(*b*) the amount of the non-exchange loss minus the amount of tax deductible exchange loss that was deemed to arise under the claim.

[*ER 3(3)*].

Example 3

- Company C incurs a non-exchange loss of £1,000 in 1997 and makes a claim for £500 deemed exchange loss to accrue in that year.
- In 1998 Company C recovers £600 of the non-exchange loss.
- In 1998 a deemed exchange gain of:

	£	£
(*i*) the amount recovered		600
less:		
(*ii*) the non-exchange loss	1,000	
less: deemed exchange loss	(500)	
		(500)
Deemed exchange gain in 1998		£100

11.13 There are detailed rules [*ER 3(4)*] to cover situations where parts of the loss are recovered at different times.

Irrecoverable debts

11.14 Where all or part of a debt is irrecoverable, no taxable or deductible exchange gains or losses are accrued on the irrecoverable portion of the debt. [*FA 1993, s 144*].

11.15 In detail this applies as follows:

(*a*) for the debt or part of the debt to be excluded the Inspector must be satisfied that the relevant part of the debt could at the end of an accounting period reasonably have been regarded as irrecoverable;

(*b*) if the application of this rule becomes the subject of an appeal, the Commissioners have to be satisfied in place of the Inspector;

(*c*) the provision does not require a claim and the Inspector could disallow an accrued exchange loss if he was satisfied that it arose on an irrecoverable debt; and

(*d*) the rule is not confined to trade debts. Exchange differences on any qualifying asset or liability which is shown to be irrecoverable will be excluded from taxation.

11.16   The term 'irrecoverable' is not defined in *FA 1993, s 144*. The Inland Revenue Company Taxation Manual Volume VI Foreign Exchange (see paragraph 13383) implies that Inspectors will define 'irrecoverable debts' as bad and doubtful debts. Thus the Inspectors will consider the same issues as they will do under *ICTA 1988, s 74(1)(j)* and *FA 1996, 9 Sch 5* in considering whether a debt is wholly or partly irrecoverable for the purposes of the foreign exchange tax rules.

11.17   If the Inspector (or, in the case of an appeal, the Commissioners) is satisfied that at the end of an accounting period a debt could reasonably be regarded as wholly irrecoverable the company is treated as if it ceased to hold the asset or liability immediately before the end of the accounting period, with the result that no taxable exchange differences would accrue in subsequent accounting periods. [*FA 1993, s 144(1)*]. If only part of the debt is shown to be irrecoverable, the company is treated as if that part of the debt had been repaid at the start of the next accounting period, so that its 'nominal value' decreased. [*FA 1993, s 144(3)*]. Exchange differences are subsequently calculated on the reduced amount.

11.18   Where the Inspector becomes satisfied that a debt which has been treated as wholly or partly irrecoverable subsequently ceases to be irrecoverable, or the irrecoverable part reduces, an appropriate proportion of the debt ignored comes back into tax. [*FA 1993, s 145*]. If there is an appeal, the Commissioners must be satisfied that the relevant part of the debt could reasonably be regarded as recoverable.

11.19   A debt previously treated as wholly irrecoverable is treated as a new debt equal to the recoverable amount, to which the company has become entitled (asset) or subject (liability) at the time from which the debt had ceased to be wholly irrecoverable. [*FA 1993, s 145(1)* and *(2)*].

11.20   Where a debt has previously been treated as partly irrecoverable, and the Inspector is satisfied that at a later time the amount which was recoverable could reasonably have been regarded as having increased, the nominal amount of the debt is treated as having increased, at the time of the change, to the new recoverable amount. [*FA 1993, s 145(3)–(5)*].

11.21   There are prospective amendments to the claims procedure under *FA 1993, s 144* and *145* which become effective with the introduction of self assessment for companies. [*FA 1996, 20 Sch 68* and *69; FA 1996, 41 Sch, Part V (10)*]. For accounting periods ending on or after 1 July 1999, the requirement for the Inspector to be satisfied as to the irrecoverable nature of a debt is removed and instead the position must be assessed by the company concerned.

Example 4

X plc is owed $100,000 by a customer. It sets up a 50% provision against the debt on 30 June 1996 and the provision remains at 50% at the end of its accounting period on 31 December 1996 and its accounting period ended 31 December 1997. The Inspector is satisfied that the debt was 50% irrecoverable on 31 December 1996 and during all of 1997. On 30 June 1998 the company determines that the likely recovery is $75,000 and reduces the provision to 25%. The Inspector is satisfied that the debt was 25% irrecoverable from 30 June 1998. How much of the exchange differences accruing in 1996, 1997 and 1998 are taxable?

31 December 1995 £1 = $1.52
30 June 1996 £1 = $1.5
31 December 1996 £1 = $1.45
31 December 1997 £1 = $1.42
30 June 1998 £1 = $1.46
31 December 1998 £1 = $1.48

Up to 31 December 1996, the exchange difference will be calculated on $100,000. After this, for tax purposes exchange differences will be calculated on the recoverable part of the debt of $50,000.

Date	Debt $	Debt £	Taxable exchange (loss)	Year
31 December 1995	100,000	65,789		
31 December 1996	100,000	68,966		
			3,177	1996
1 January 1996	50,000	34,483		
31 December 1997	50,000	35,211		
			728	1997
30 June 1998	50,000	34,247		
			(964)	
1 July 1998	75,000	51,370		
31 December 1998	75,000	50,676		
			(694)	
			(1,658)	1998

Unremittable income

11.22   Income which cannot be remitted to the UK, for example because of overseas exchange controls, may be left untaxed if a claim [*ICTA 1988, s 584*] is made to the Board of Inland Revenue. Where the Board is satisfied that the conditions of *section 584* are met, such income is referred to as 'unremittable income'. [*FA 1993, 15 Sch 3(4)*]. In the case of a company which has unremittable income, the income is treated as arising, and therefore taxable, on the date it ceases to be unremittable. If the income is denominated in foreign currency, it is translated into sterling at the exchange rate in force when it ceases to be unremittable.

11.23 No taxable exchange gain or loss will accrue on a qualifying debt which is a right to receive income. [*FA 1993, s 129(7)*]. However, in the case of unremittable income the income will generally have been received overseas and will now be represented by a debt such as a balance on a bank account. Without special provisions for debts representing unremittable income, therefore, taxable exchange gains and deductible exchange losses would accrue in each accounting period and these exchange differences would also be included in the amounts assessable when the income actually arose.

11.24 Under the special rules for unremittable income [*FA 1993, 15 Sch 3* and *MR 3*] a qualifying debt or a holding of currency which represents unremittable income is to be dealt with under the 'alternative method'. This means that the taxable exchange gain or loss accruing on the asset, as calculated under the basic rules, is treated as accruing in equal amounts on a daily basis. The amount of the exchange gain attributed to each day is reduced, to take account of the extent to which the income was unremittable on that day. [*MR 3(3)*]. The resulting accrued exchange gains and losses are aggregated for all the days in the accrual period to arrive at the overall taxable exchange gain or loss on the debt for the accrual period.

11.25 This method is modified when income which was previously unremittable becomes remittable. The accrual period is then divided into two sub-periods which begin and end at the time that the income ceases to be unremittable. The effect is that exchange gains and losses are computed for the accrual period by:

(*a*)　computing the exchange gains and losses which would have arisen under the basic rules if an accrual period ended, and a new one had begun, at the time the income ceased to be unremittable;

(*b*)　applying the 'alternative method' to each notional accrual period, so that each exchange gain or loss, calculated under (*a*) above, is divided by the number of days in each notional period;

(*c*)　reducing the amount attributed to each day to take account of the extent to which the income was unremittable on that day; and

(*d*)　aggregating the resulting accrued exchange gains and losses for all the days in the overall accrual period, to arrive at the taxable exchange gain or loss for the accrual period.

11.26 There are no special rules to exclude from the foreign exchange tax rules exchange gains and losses which accrue on qualifying assets which represent unremittable capital gains, or unremittable capital with no underlying tax liability attaching to it. Similarly, there is no special provision for unremittable trade debts, although in practice it should be

11.27 *Other Special Provisions*

possible to bring exchange rate fluctuations into the scope of Extra-Statutory Concession B38 ('Tax Concessions on Overseas Debts').

11.27 There are prospective amendments to the definition of un-remittable income in *FA 1993, 15 Sch 3 (4)* which become effective with the introduction of self assessment for companies. [*FA 1996, 20 Sch 70*]. For accounting periods ending on or after 1 July 1999, it is no longer necessary for the Board to be satisfied that the conditions of *ICTA 1988, s 584* are met in order for income to be considered to be unremittable.

Chapter 12

Controlled Foreign Companies and other Special Companies

Introduction

12.1   The foreign exchange tax rules have particular unique implications for a number of special companies. This chapter discusses these issues, the companies affected being:

(*a*)   Controlled foreign companies (see 12.2–12.28 below).

(*b*)   Insurance companies (see 12.29–12.51 below).

(*c*)   Oil companies (see 12.52–12.54 below).

(*d*)   Partnerships which include companies (see 12.55–12.70 below).

Controlled foreign companies ('CFCs')

Introduction

12.2   The foreign exchange tax rules bring into the measure of income under UK tax law many exchange gains and losses which were under the old rules treated as capital gains and losses, or ignored for tax purposes completely. The CFC rules are designed to bring into the UK tax net income, arising in non-resident subsidiaries of UK companies, which has suffered a low rate of taxation. It is not at present applied to capital gains. The extension of the meaning of 'income' to include most exchange gains and losses therefore has a material effect on the profits which are effectively subject to UK taxation through the CFC rules.

This is especially important for CFCs that have to distribute 90% of their chargeable profits (calculated in accordance with *ICTA 1988, 24 Sch*) in order to meet the acceptable distribution test and avoid a CFC direction. This 90% test applies to:

(*a*)   non-trading CFCs for accounting periods ending on or after 30 November 1993, and

(*b*)   trading CFCs for accounting periods beginning on or after 28 November 1995.

12.3 *CFCs and Other Special Companies*

12.3 The way in which the foreign exchange tax rules are applied in calculating chargeable profits of a CFC is summarised below. There are special rules [*FA 1993, s 168A*, introduced by *FA 1995, 25 Sch 7*] which deal with a CFC which subsequently becomes UK-tax resident, to ensure a proper application of the transitional rules.

Reference currency

12.4 The foreign exchange tax rules, which take effect for accounting periods beginning on or after 23 March 1995, mean that chargeable profits of both trading and non-trading CFCs are calculated in the currency in which the company prepares accounts. [*ICTA 1988, s 747A*, introduced by *FA 1995, 25 Sch 2*].

12.5 There are additional rules to prevent a change of currency for calculating chargeable profits. If there has been a CFC direction for a pre-commencement accounting period, chargeable profits will always be calculated in the currency in which the accounts for the period beginning on Commencement Day are prepared. This is the 'first relevant accounting period' of such a company. [*ICTA 1988, s 747A(6)*, inserted by *FA 1995, 25 Sch 2*].

12.6 If there has been no pre-commencement CFC direction, chargeable profits are calculated in the currency of the accounts until the accounting period:

(*a*) in respect of which there is a CFC direction; or

(*b*) in respect of which it can reasonably be assumed that a direction would have been made, had it not pursued an acceptable distribution policy.

This is the 'first relevant accounting period' of such a company. For trading CFCs the condition (*b*) above does not apply to accounting periods beginning before 28 November 1995.

[*ICTA 1998, s 747A* as inserted by *FA 1995, 25 Sch 2* and amended by *FA 1996, 36 Sch 1*].

12.7 Chargeable profits for subsequent accounting periods must always be calculated in the currency in which the accounts for the period of the direction (or acceptable distribution policy) were prepared. [*ICTA 1988, s 747A(2)*].

12.8 This means in particular that exchange gains and losses under the foreign exchange tax rules will be computed by reference to the accounting currency of the CFC (subject to the rules mentioned above where the reporting currency is changed). The chargeable profits so calculated are translated into sterling at the London closing exchange rate for the last day of the accounting period concerned. [*ICTA 1998, s 748(4) and (5)*, introduced by *FA 1995, 25 Sch 4*].

214

Introduction of the euro

12.9   Chargeable profits can be computed in the reporting currency but there can be no change in currency after the first relevant accounting period. [*ICTA 1988, s 747A*]. Where the relevant reporting currency is replaced by the euro due to the introduction of the European single currency on 1 January 1999, the currency to be used in computing future profits switches automatically to the euro [*ESCR 40*].

Transitional rules

Currency contracts

12.10   In computing the chargeable profits of a CFC, the transitional rules for the exchange of currency under currency contracts (see Chapter 4) will always apply. This means that in the case of currency contracts which would qualify for capital gains treatment under current law if the company was UK-resident, the unrealised exchange gain or loss at Commencement Day (measured in the CFC's accounting currency) is:

(*a*)   deemed to be a qualifying payment under the financial instrument rules, payable on the maturity date of the currency contract; and

(*b*)   treated as income or expense which accrues over the period from Commencement Day to the maturity date of the contract.

Qualifying assets and liabilities

12.11   The transitional rules for assets and liabilities will apply as if the company was resident in the UK for all accounting periods if [*TR 1(5)*]:

(*a*)   a CFC direction has been given in respect of the accounting period *which ends immediately before the CFC's Commencement Day*; or

(*b*)   it can reasonably be assumed that such a direction would have been given *for that accounting period* but for the fact that the company pursued an acceptable distribution policy (for trading companies, this second condition only applies to accounting periods beginning on or after 28 November 1995).

12.12   If there has never been a CFC direction in respect of a company, then for the purposes of computing chargeable profits it is treated as resident in the UK from the start of the accounting period in question but not for any earlier period. [*ICTA 1988, 24 Sch 1(4)*]. The transitional rules for qualifying assets and liabilities will therefore not apply to such a company unless it has avoided a direction by following an acceptable distribution policy in the *last accounting period before its Commencement Day.*

12.13   If a direction is made in respect of a CFC, for the purpose of computing chargeable profits it is assumed to have become resident in the UK at the beginning of the accounting period of the direction and for all subsequent accounting periods for which it is a CFC. This means that a CFC direction *for any pre-Commencement Day accounting period* will bring the transitional regulations into play, but a post-Commencement direction will not. The Inland Revenue, however, take the view that the transitional regulations apply only if 12.11(*a*) or (*b*) above applies.

12.14   If the transitional rules apply to a CFC, it will be necessary to determine whether a qualifying liability is fixed term and fixed amount, as defined. If it is, it will be subject to the kink test (see 6.29 above) but if it fails to meet this definition, exchange differences will not contribute to chargeable profits at all as the liability will be grandfathered subject to the special rules where such debts increase after Commencement Day (see 6.38 above). However, a CFC could elect for all its 'fluctuating' debts to be brought into the foreign exchange regime (see 6.42 above).

12.15   Because CFCs are outside the capital gains regime, a qualifying asset held immediately before commencement cannot be subject to the transitional rules for former chargeable assets. If the transitional rules for qualifying assets and liabilities apply to the CFC (see 12.12 above) the asset will be either grandfathered or subject to the kink test. Relief under *TR 16(1)* for pre-commencement capital losses will not be available to a CFC (see 6.68 above).

Overseas finance companies – transitional rule mismatch

12.16   Where a CFC is an overseas finance company which borrows in one currency, enters into a currency swap agreement and on-lends the borrowed funds in the second currency of the swap, the different transitional rules which apply to debts and currency contracts could create a mismatch in tax terms when the position is matched in accounting terms.

This problem has been recognised by the Inland Revenue and is referred to in the June 1995 edition of the Inland Revenue Tax Bulletin at page 222. If a CFC might otherwise become subject to a CFC direction under *ICTA 1988, s 747*, in the first accounting period which is subject to the foreign exchange and financial instrument rules purely because *FA 1994, s 153(4)* and *(5)* operate to impute a deemed receipt in respect of pre-commencement exchange gains, the Board of Inland Revenue 'will take this factor into account when deciding whether a direction should be made'.

Unmatched positions – risk of chargeable profits

12.17   Whether or not the transitional rules apply, there is a high risk of chargeable profits on unmatched positions. Particular points to note are:

(*a*)   If exchange rates fluctuate significantly, an exchange profit in an accounting period could reverse in a later period and then be unavailable for distribution, preventing the company following an acceptable distribution policy.

(*b*)   An exchange loss on a loan which is grandfathered will reduce accounts profits (and therefore distributable profits) but will not reduce chargeable profits, so the company may have insufficient reserves to follow an acceptable distribution policy.

(*c*)   Even if the kink test makes taxable gains unlikely on a cumulative basis (large unrealised loss at commencement), the CFC rules look at each year in isolation if there has not been a direction or one has not only been avoided by an acceptable distribution policy. [*ICTA 1988, 24 Sch 19*, introduced by *FA 1995, 25 Sch 6(5)*]. Reversal of last year's deductible loss will therefore create chargeable profits. Suppose there is a pre-commencement loss of £50. This will prevent gains of up to £50 from contributing to chargeable profits. However, if there is a post-commencement loss of £30 in the first year and a post-commencement gain of £40 in the second year there will be a taxable gain of £30 in year two (reversal of deductible loss of £30 in year one, which cannot be carried forward to year two) to bring the cumulative taxed loss back to zero.

(*d*)   If there has been a CFC direction or if there would have been a direction but for an acceptable distribution policy, the company is treated as UK-resident thereafter for the purpose of computing chargeable profits, so it should be possible to carry foreign exchange losses forward.

12.18   The treatment of exchange gains and losses as income items increases the likelihood that a company in a high tax territory could become a CFC through differences in the UK and overseas measure of taxable profits.

International holding companies

12.19   One of the requirements for an international holding company to satisfy the exempt activities test [*ICTA 1988, 25 Sch 6(4)*] is that at least 90% of its gross income during the accounting period in question is derived directly from 'qualifying companies' which it controls. The Inland Revenue takes the view that gross income is the gross income shown in the accounts so no problems should arise with this test as a result of the introduction of the foreign exchange tax rules.

Anti-avoidance

12.20   If a swap is with a counterparty resident in a territory which does not have a double tax treaty with the UK containing an interest article, the Inland Revenue could deny relief for any net periodic payments by the CFC, for the purpose of computing its chargeable profits. [*FA 1994, s 168(1)*].

12.21   It is also open to the Inland Revenue to apply the arm's length test [*FA 1993, s 136–148*] (see 7.10 above) effectively to deny relief on exchange losses which arise on debts and currency contracts which:

(*a*)   are not on arm's length terms, or

(*b*)   would not have been made between two parties at arm's length.

12.22   The Inland Revenue has indicated (Explanatory Statement, para 3.14) that it would not apply this provision to a UK-resident company in respect of a matched borrowing and lending. It is therefore possible that they will take a similar approach with a CFC.

Deferral of unrealised gains on long-term assets and liabilities

12.23   Where an unrealised exchange gain accrues to a CFC on a capital asset or liability with a minimum maturity of twelve months, part of the exchange gain could be deferred (see Chapter 8). Unlike a UK-resident company, the CFC can be looked at in isolation without aggregating exchange gains and losses with those of other companies in the group. This is because the CFC rules require that in computing chargeable profits the company is assumed for the purpose of any provision of the Tax Acts not to be a member of a group of companies. [*ICTA 1988, 24 Sch 5*]. A CFC will be assumed for the purpose of computing chargeable profits to have claimed available reliefs, including the deferral of un-realised gains (see 12.27 below).

12.24   An exchange gain or loss which accrues to a CFC in an account-ing period earlier than its 'first relevant accounting period' (see 12.5 and 12.6 above) is deemed not to have arisen for the purpose of calculating chargeable profits of a later accounting period. As well as preventing the bringing forward of losses, this also operates to prevent a gain treated as deferred in the preceding accounting period from being treated as arising in the current period under the deferral rules. [*ICTA 1988, 24 Sch 19, introduced by FA 1995, 25 Sch 6*].

12.25   From the 'first relevant accounting period' onwards, a deferred gain will be carried forward and included in the chargeable profits of the next accounting period (subject to any further deferral relief).

Matching elections

12.26　A UK company, which alone or with other UK companies, has a majority interest in a CFC, may make matching elections on behalf of the CFC for the purposes of computing the chargeable profits of the CFC. [*MR 6*]. The election is effective from the date made [*MR 10(1)*] unless expressed as made under *MR 11(5)*. A CFC matching election may be made under *MR 11(5)* if:

(*a*)　a CFC direction has been made on or after 23 March 1995 in respect of the CFC (and no CFC direction has been made for an earlier accounting period); and

(*b*)　(for elections made on or after 30 June 1996) where a CFC direction is made on or after 1 April 1996 and no earlier accounting period is an 'ADP exempt period' (as defined in *MR 11(6)*).

If a matching election is made under *MR 11(5)*, it must be made within 92 days of the date of the CFC direction. [*MR 11(5)(b)*]. An election under *MR 11(5)* is effective from the latest of:

(i)　the first day of the first accounting period affected by the CFC direction;

(ii)　the first day of the first accounting period beginning on or after 23 March 1995; and

(iii)　the day on which the (matched) asset is acquired by the company.

Other claims and elections by a CFC

12.27　CFCs are assumed to have made all claims and elections which maximise relief from tax. [*ICTA 1988, 24 Sch 4(1)*]. The following claims will therefore be assumed to have been made by the CFC:

(*a*)　Deferral of unrealised gains on long-term capital assets and liabilities.

(*b*)　Offset of non-trading deficit against other income (and non-trade exchange losses for pre-corporate debt periods).

(*c*)　Carry back and, in appropriate cases, carry forward of non-trading deficits (and non-trade exchange losses for pre-corporate debt periods).

12.28　The Inland Revenue is understood to take the view that the following elections must be claimed.

(*a*)　Opt out of grandfathering for fluctuating debts.

(*b*)　Matching election (see 12.26 above).

(*c*)　Excess gains and losses relief.

(*d*)   Elections under *TR 6(2)* and *15(1)* by *ICTA 1988, 24 Sch 4(2)*.

The normal time limits for (*a*), (*c*) and (*d*) are extended to a requirement to make them by the earlier of:

(i)   60 days after the making of a CFC direction in respect of the relevant accounting period; or

(ii)   if the accounting period is an 'ADP exempt period', 20 months after the end of the accounting period.

The elections, and any variations in the reliefs which the CFC is to be assumed to have claimed, may be made effective by a notice made under *ICTA 1988, 24 Sch 4(2)*. The Inland Revenue will also accept elections made by the CFC itself or, if the secretary or director of the CFC gives specific authority, by a UK company which alone or jointly with other UK companies has a majority interest in the CFC (see Inland Revenue Tax Bulletin for June 1995 at page 223).

Insurance companies

Introduction

12.29   UK insurance companies come within the definition of 'qualifying companies' (see 3.4 above) and so prima facie must apply the foreign exchange tax rules. Special rules and exemptions are however required to deal with the unique characteristics of insurance business.

Exemptions from the foreign exchange tax rules

12.30   Monetary assets, liabilities and currency contracts held, or owed, in respect of long-term insurance business and mutual general insurance business are effectively excluded from the main foreign exchange tax rules. [*FA 1993, 15 Sch 2*]. The Revenue have confirmed that such businesses do not need to compute what would have been the taxable amount had the regime applied.

12.31   Mutual general insurers are taxed on investment income plus chargeable gains, so they continue to be taxed on exchange differences arising on their investments on disposal thereof.

12.32   For life assurance business, the life tax regime (following reform in *FA 1989* and *FA 1990*) was considered to deal satisfactorily with foreign exchange differences. It was also felt unnecessary to include the other classes of long-term business in the foreign exchange tax rules. Capital redemption fund business is taxed on a similar basis to life assurance. Permanent health insurance ('PHI') is also excluded and so obviates any need to allocate exchange gains and losses on investments between PHI and life assurance business and thus at least achieves a significant administrative benefit, not least as PHI business is for many companies not a substantial proportion of their long-term business.

12.33 Where an asset, liability or currency contract is held only partly for the purposes of long-term insurance business and/or mutual insurance business the taxable exchange difference is proportionately reduced (using the 'alternative method' as mentioned in Chapter 9).

12.34 Effectively these exemptions mean that only monetary assets, liabilities and currency contracts held in respect of proprietary general insurance business are within the foreign exchange tax rules.

12.35 The exclusions from the main regime of exchange differences on mutual and long-term business had to be revisited following the introduction of the corporate and government debt regime. Prior to that, exchange differences would have been taxable with market value profits and losses, either on realisation under the CGT regime or as a trading profit, or as recognised in the annual DTI regime depending upon the type of business.

12.36 The corporate and government debt regime now taxes the market value fluctuations but excludes exchange fluctuations. New provisions were required to ensure the latter remained subject to tax at some point. Exchange differences taxable as recognised within the DTI regime are still taxed on that basis, but special provisions apply in other cases [*SI 1996 No 673* and *SI 1996 No 1485*].

12.37 For life and mutual general business, currency bonds are not qualifying corporate bonds. [*TCGA 1992, s 117A*]. The exchange differences on such assets are brought into tax by *SI 1996 No 673* which provides for a capital gain to be calculated and taxed on disposal, equal to the exchange movement on the basic valuation between acquisition and disposal with no indexation allowance. For PHI business, the exchange difference is still taxable upon disposal as a Schedule D Case I profit.

12.38 *SI 1996 No 1485* which amends *SI 1994 No 3231 (ICR)* permits an insurer to elect, in respect of all of its currency assets held for the purposes of long-term or mutual insurance business, for the annual exchange differences to be taxable under the corporate and government debt rules and not otherwise. The purpose of the election is to simplify compliance matters, eliminating the need to apportion the annual accounts amount between the exempt foreign exchange amount and the taxable corporate and government debt amount.

Qualifying assets and liabilities

12.39 Shares held in 'qualifying circumstances' (i.e. held for trading purposes) are within the definition of assets subject to the foreign exchange tax rules ('qualifying assets' – see 3.8 above). This provision is disapplied for insurance trades so that exchange differences on such shares held in a general insurance trade are taxed under general principles (generally on a realisation basis). [*ICR 3*]. Thus it is only 'true' currency monetary assets which are within the new regime.

12.40 Some general insurers tax the profits arising on investments held for the trade only on realisation as part of their Schedule D Case I trading result. For assets which come within the corporate and government debt regime, this will no longer apply. For such assets which are also subject to the foreign exchange regime, this could potentially give rise to a company needing to separate out the total valuation movement in a period between the exchange difference on the original currency value and the market value fluctuation (the balance). In practice, unless special rules such as the matching election are in point, this separation will not be required and the basis of taxation of the exchange movements on investments will generally be the same as that of the market value movements.

12.41 Insurance claims provisions to the extent allowable for tax purposes are liabilities subject to the foreign exchange tax rules because these are provisions in respect of a potential duty to settle a qualifying debt, any such duty would be owed for trading purposes, and the provision is taken into account in computing the trading profit or loss for tax purposes ('qualifying liabilities' – see 3.18 above). Unearned premium reserves are also qualifying liabilities. [*ICR 2*].

12.42 For insurance companies writing business on a three-year account (e.g. Marine Aviation and Transport business), the tax computations may be prepared on a three-year or one-year basis. With a three-year tax basis, the normal rules will ensure that claims provisions established on closure are qualifying liabilities (to the extent they are tax deductible). For three-year business taxed on a one-year basis, the provisions calculated for tax purposes at the end of the 'open' years are treated as qualifying liabilities. [*ICR 2*].

12.43 The regulations recognise the problem of notification delays for insurers, caused by periodic settlement with e.g. brokers and reinsurers. The date an insurer becomes entitled to an asset or subject to a liability is, if later than the normal date, the date the item is entered in the accounts. [*ICR 5*].

Transitional rules

12.44 The normal transitional rules will apply to chargeable assets held by insurers and to fixed and fluctuating nothings. Particular problems arise for investments held for trade purposes, for which insurers will in the past have tended to follow one of three main practices in respect of exchange differences:

(*a*) taxing profits or allowing losses on investments only on realisation;

(*b*) taxing all exchange gains and losses as they accrue; or

(*c*) excluding all exchange gains and losses from tax.

12.45 For assets which are currently taxed on realisation within the Schedule D Case I result, the transitional rules provide that the asset is deemed to be disposed of and reacquired at its accounts value immediately prior to Commencement Day. The resulting gain/loss is 'held over' and set against future exchange losses/gains on the same item, on a cumulative basis. On disposal of the item concerned, any remaining deferred gain/loss is treated as an exchange gain/loss of that period (see 6.44 above). As explained in 6.44 and 6.50 above, the foreign exchange transitional rules apply to local currency assets held as Schedule D Case I realisation assets, as well as foreign currency assets. Therefore, the attributed gain or loss, although not including an exchange element, must still be calculated for local currency bonds, and the elections described in 12.46(*a*) and (*b*) below may be made.

12.46 Two issues arise with regard to the transitional provisions for assets taxed on a realisation basis:

(*a*) Firstly, for companies with large holdings of these assets, the 'asset by asset' tracking rules for the utilisation of the Commencement Day deemed gain/loss (on a cumulative basis) gives rise to systems and compliance implications. There was therefore an option under which the company could opt to bring the total Commencement Day gains into charge to tax evenly over six years (see 6.50 above).

(*b*) Secondly, the basic transitional rule effectively crystallises both exchange differences on original currency cost and market revaluations to Commencement Day (i.e. on the whole book value at Commencement Day) with post-commencement exchange differences based for tax purposes upon Commencement Day currency values. An insurance company could elect to crystallise only exchange differences to Commencement Day based on original currency cost with the 'tax' exchange differences thereafter continuing to be based upon original currency cost (see 6.13 above).

The time limit for both of these elections was 30 September 1996. [*SI 1996 No 1349*].

12.47 Such companies may also reflect investments in their accounts at a cost excluding accrued interest ('clean cost' basis) but for tax purposes use the cost inclusive of accrued interest ('dirty cost' basis). Calculations of amounts under the foreign exchange tax rules adopt the accounts valuation as the basic valuation. In such a case the effect of the election under 12.46(*b*) above would be to give an attributed gain or loss equal to the amount of interest accrued on the security when it was purchased.

12.48   If a company made both elections under 12.46(*a*) and (*b*) above then *TR 15(7)* (inserted by *SI 1996 No 1349, Reg 8(c)*) prevents the attributed gains or loss being spread over accounting periods ending on or after 30 June 1996. Instead, the balance of the attributed gain or loss not recognised in earlier periods is recognised on realisation.

12.49   The Inland Revenue have confirmed to the ABI that companies using a full translation basis (12.44(*b*) above) (i.e. on all currency assets and liabilities, irrespective of whether they are monetary or not) may continue to do so and will not need transitional rules. The exclusion basis (12.44(*c*) above) is regarded by the Revenue as having been accepted on the basis of a 'broadly matched' currency position and the new regime applies from Commencement Day with no special transitional arrangements. (There had been concern that, if a company was not precisely matched, transitional rules might be applied to 'surplus' assets.) In either case, companies often needed to make the election discussed at 6.13 above.

Deferral of unrealised gains

12.50   Exchange differences on claims provisions and unearned premium reserves are not included in the net exchange gains part of the calculation of the maximum amount available for deferral (see 8.7 above) as these are trading provisions and not duties of settlement under qualifying debts. Currency monetary assets held for the trade (e.g. US$ Treasury bonds) are, however, included in the net exchange gains figure of the claimant company in the calculation. This means that a net exchange gain of nil overall in accounting terms may result in an exchange loss for the deferral calculations and hence limit the extent to which deferral is possible in a general insurer.

Relief for losses

12.51   Relief for losses, whether under *section 393A* or the group relief provisions against profits arising on life assurance business is limited by *section 434A* – such reliefs cannot be set against the policy holders' share (as defined in *FA 1989*) of such profits. Similar limitations apply to the offset of non-trading exchange losses. [*ICR 6*].

Oil companies

Introduction

12.52   UK oil companies fall within the definition of 'qualifying companies' and so the foreign exchange tax rules apply. However, there are two special provisions in the way that they apply.

Local currency election

12.53   *FA 1993, s 94* and related regulation allows elections for *parts* of the trade of a UK company carried on through overseas branches. This section is disapplied for petroleum extraction companies carrying on a ring fence trade (as defined in *ICTA 1988, s 492*). Such a company may make a local currency election for part of its trade *if* that part consists of activities relating to oil or gas carried on under a petroleum licence in the UK or a designated area. [*FA 1993, s 94A* and *LR 4(2)(b)*].

Non-trading exchange losses

12.54   Under *FA 1988, s 131(4)* a claim may be made to offset non-trading exchange losses arising in an accounting period against other profits arising in that company in that accounting period, subject to this claim not displacing relief for trading losses brought forward from an earlier accounting period. However, for oil companies under *FA 1993, s 133(2)* ring fence profits may not be offset against non-trading exchange losses arising in that period by a claim made under *FA 1993, s 131(4)*.

Partnerships

Introduction

12.55   Partnerships comprising individuals and entities which are not qualifying companies under the foreign exchange and financial instruments legislation are themselves entirely outside the scope of this legislation and continue to determine the tax treatment of foreign exchange gains and losses by reference to the old rules described in Chapter 1.

12.56   If a partnership is made up entirely of members which are qualifying companies, the financial instrument legislation [*FA 1994, s 172*] treats the partnership itself as a qualifying company. The practice of the Inland Revenue [*SP 9/94* and *SP 4/98*] is to follow that approach for exchange differences.

12.57   The rules where a partnership comprises some members which are qualifying companies and others which are not, follow an approach which is broadly parallel to that adopted for the generality of results for tax purposes for a 'mixed' partnership contained in *ICTA 1988, s 114*.

Profit calculation

12.58   To calculate the taxable profit or loss on corporate partners, a tax computation is prepared for the entire partnership as if it were a company and the corporate partners are then allocated their share of this.

12.59   This computation will be on the basis that the partnership is a qualifying company for the purpose of the foreign exchange legislation, with a Commencement Day on the first day of its accounting period. If the accounting period of a corporate partner differs from that of the partnership, then the taxable result will be allocated to the partner, normally on a time basis, between the relevant accounting periods of the company itself. The items apportioned in this way between accounting periods include net non-trading losses on foreign exchange and financial instruments.

12.60   Valuations of assets and liabilities should be made in accordance with the accounting methods used by the partnership. The main benefit and arm's length anti-avoidance rules (see 7.2 *et seq* above) will apply by reference to the circumstances of the partnership.

12.61   For individual partners (and others which are not qualifying companies) a tax computation must be prepared under the old rules for both foreign exchange and financial instruments and these partners will then be allocated their appropriate share of the taxable result.

12.62   Thus, by applying different legislation to the two computations, the total amount of profit or loss allocated to all of the partners may be greater or may be less than the overall profits on either basis.

12.63   For corporate partners, non-trading foreign exchange profits and losses are included with the other non-trading foreign exchange gains and losses of that company for the purposes of charging tax under Schedule D Case III or granting loss relief under the rules set out in Chapter 5.

12.64   The foreign exchange trading gains and losses of corporate partners derived from the partnership will, in the same way as other trading gains and losses from the partnership with which they are aggregated, be treated as arising from a trade separate from any other trade or trades carried on by the company.

Special provisions

12.65   The detailed rules of the treatment of partnerships within the foreign exchange legislation were previously set out in Inland Revenue Statement of Practice SP9/94, published on 20 December 1994 and included in Appendix 2 to this book. This is superseded for accounting periods ending after 31 March 1996 by SP 4/98, which was published on 16 November 1998 and is also included in Appendix 2. SP 9/94 continues to be relevant for accounting periods ending on or before 31 March 1996.

12.66   In SP 9/94 the Inland Revenue's view was that only partnerships consisting entirely of qualifying companies could make a local currency election. This view has been revised by SP 4/98 for accounting periods ending after 31 March 1996, so that a local currency election may now be made by any partnership so long as at least one of the partners is a qualifying company. Any election must satisfy the conditions for a valid election (see 10.36 *et seq* above) applied to the partnership as if it were a company. All partners who are, at the time of the election, subject to UK corporation tax must sign the election in order for it to be valid.

12.67 A partnership may also make a claim to defer a proportion of unrealised exchange gains under the provisions outlined in Chapter 8. In any accounting period the amount of any exchange gain to be deferred will be the proportion of that gain which is appropriate to qualifying members of the partnership. Thus corporate partners may exclude from their share of exchange gains and losses the appropriate part of the deferred gain, provided that the partnership has itself made a claim.

12.68 SP 9/94 limited the range of assets for which a partnership could make a matching election. SP 4/98 confirms that the Inland Revenue now accepts that partnerships which have eligible liabilities may make a matching election for the full range of eligible assets (see 9.4 above). The election must be signed by all partners subject to UK corporation tax in order for it to be valid.

12.69 A company cannot make a claim to match its own liability with an asset held by the partnership.

12.70 Where a matching election has been made by a partnership, there are detailed rules in SP 4/98 for dealing with the situation where a corporate partner leaves the partnership or reduces its asset share ratio before a matched asset is disposed of by the partnership.

Chapter 13

Planning Points and Practical Issues

Introduction

13.1   The legislation described in this book requires careful planning, both in advance of undertaking transactions to ensure that there are no adverse tax consequences and after the event to ensure that the required procedures are followed to give proper tax compliance for the submission of tax returns and making the necessary claims and elections within the specified time-limits. This chapter gives a brief guide to planning aspects of the foreign exchange tax rules and sets out a list of the time-limits which must be observed.

New transactions and business – basic information needed

13.2   Before starting detailed tax planning for new foreign currency transactions and businesses involving foreign currencies, certain basic information needs to be ascertained by taxpayer companies. The following list should provide a reasonable start:

(*a*)   are you a qualifying company?

(*b*)   identify qualifying assets, liabilities and contracts;

(*c*)   ascertain company and group accounting policy for exchange differences;

(*d*)   identify and analyse conversion rights attaching to or associated with any debt instrument assets;

(*e*)   identify the exchange rates (e.g. quarterly in advance, spot) used for accounting purposes;

(*f*)   divide items between trade and non-trade;

(*g*)   identify unremittable income and irrecoverable debts;

(*h*)   analyse all items which were nothings under the old regime between those which are fixed and those which are fluctuating under the terms of the legislation; and (*i*)   ascertain the ability to refinance existing foreign currency debts.

Steps to consider

13.3   Having ascertained the basic information in 13.2 above, you can now start to consider what steps should be taken to ensure that no unexpected tax liabilities arise and that any advantages which may be available are not destroyed. The following list should provide a reasonable start and also highlight areas that should be considered and monitored for existing foreign currency exposures:

(A)   non-trade items – optimise non-trading relief claims and ensure maximum double tax relief is obtained;

(B)   convertibles – take care in drafting convertible debt assets to ensure either within the foreign exchange rules or outside (as the company requires);

(C)   remember that convertible debt liabilities are inside the foreign exchange tax rules;

(D)   if an election to convert capital losses into foreign exchange losses has been made, consider what assets need to be held to use up the converted losses;

(E)   consider whether systems are in place to track all movements at every point in every accounting period for loans which are grandfathered under the transitional provisions;

(F)   consider the thin capitalisation position of overseas subsidiaries and recapitalise as necessary;

(G)   consider whether deferral is worthwhile, whether the necessary systems are in place to gather the required information and identify items which will be defined as long-term capital for this purpose;

(H)   establish intercompany debts to enable matching elections to be made in the company holding overseas subsidiaries;

(I)   if a new overseas subsidiary is being acquired, remember the short time limit (92 days from acquisition) if a matching election is to be immediately effective;

(J)   ensure that the accounting policy of the entity making a matching election follows SSAP 20, paragraph 51 and not paragraph 57 to give hedging for accounts purposes on an individual entity basis;

(K)   identify assets which need to be matched on a multi-currency basis and ensure that appropriate accounting policies are agreed to enable this to be reflected in the statutory accounts at the beginning of the period in which the matching election is to be made;

(L)   identify problems which will arise by virtue of a reserves mismatch on single entity matching and which could create a problem with negative distributable reserves;

(M) for partial matching elections ensure exchange losses on unmatched eligible loans are not taken to reserves as loss relief will be denied;

(N)   take care when borrowing and on-lending in a matching company as loss relief may be deferred;

(O)   identify areas where the conditions exist to enable a local currency election to be made and consider whether this would be advantageous;

(P)   remember the short time limit (92 days) from coming into the UK tax charge if a local currency election is to be immediately effective;

(Q)   ensure that there is careful documentation in place to prove the commercial basis of any foreign exchange transactions which could be considered by the Inland Revenue to be non-arm's length;

(R)   ensure that there is full support for the irrecoverability of bad debts at the relevant date;

(S)   ensure that there is full support for the unremittability of income at the relevant date;

(T)   review the ability of CFCs to meet the acceptable distribution test under the foreign exchange tax rules;

(U)   review the position of CFCs for ease of providing information, fulfilling the arm's length test, the acceptability of local accounting practice for UK purposes, the claims which will be assumed to be made under the foreign exchange tax rules and the restated profit for CFC purposes;

(V)   consider options for restructuring the CFCs or removing them totally from the group;

(W) if entering into foreign currency denominated transactions with UK individuals, remember that the tax treatment of exchange differences for individuals is on the old rules principles and so advantages or disadvantages may arise from the difference in treatment;

(X)   if an oil company, look at the local currency election provisions for ring fence income;

(Y) if a member of a partnership, consider the implications for non-coterminous year ends and possible additional tax exposures; and

(Z) review matching elections to ensure additional liabilties are not drawn in by virtue of their becoming an economic hedge for another asset as a result of the elimination of foreign exchange exposure between eurozone currencies.

Foreign exchange tax issues on acquisitions, reorganisations and disposals

13.4 A large number of foreign exchange tax issues need to be considered when reorganising groups, acquiring new businesses or disposing of existing businesses. These include issues under the following main areas.

(*a*) Are new matching elections needed? (Remember that if the ownership of the overseas shares changes a new election is needed.)

(*b*) Are new local currency elections needed for new businesses?

(*c*) On an acquisition the full transitional rule history and elections position of the company need to be established.

(*d*) Are the effects of the transitional rules removed by the transactions (e.g. grandfathered loan repaid)?

(*e*) Remember that matched exchange differences move with the shares when the ownership of a matched asset changes (see 9.32 to 9.36).

(*f*) There may be other issues depending on the transactions undertaken.

Time-limits

13.5 Having identified the problems, opportunities and compliance requirements, it is essential that the time-limits set out below are adhered to if major tax costs are not to be incurred. They are set out in the order in which they occur in this book. For completeness the following table includes all the transitional time limits although these will have expired for all companies by the date of publication of this book. The very latest possible transitional time limit was by 21 June 1996 (for companies with a Commencement Day of 22 March 1996).

ELECTION & STATUTORY REFERENCE	TIME-LIMIT

Chapter 5 – Non-trading exchange losses

Accounting periods beginning on or after 1 April 1996

Net non-trading deficit set off:	Within two years of end of accounting period to which deficit arose.
● against other profits	
● group relief	
● carry back against Schedule D Case III profits	
● Carry forward against non-trading profits of the next accounting period	Within two years of the end of the accounting period in which the deficit is to be offset.

Accounting periods ending during the period from 23 March 1995 to 31 March 1996

Net non-trading exchange loss set off:	Within two years of end of accounting period to which loss relates (5.29 above).
● group relief	
● against other profits	
● carry back three years	

[*FA 1993, s 131(14)*]

Chapter 6 – Transitional rules

Use original cost instead of pre-commencement book value as basic valuation of qualifying assets [*TR 6(2)*]	30 September 1996. All elections prior may be withdrawn. (SI 1996 No 1349 extended the previous limits which were the later of 92 days from Commencement Day and 183 days from Appointed Day (6.13 above).)
Opt out of grandfathering transitional rule for all fluctuating 'nothings' [*TR 3(5)*]	Later of: ● 92 days from Commencement Day and ● 183 days from Appointed Day to opt out of grandfathering from a company's Commencement Day. Election is irrevocable (6.42 above).

Pre-Commencement Day gains and losses accruing after Commencement Day spread over a six-year period [*TR 15(1)*]	30 September 1996. All elections prior may be withdrawn. (SI 1996 No 1349 extended the previous limits which were the later of 92 days from Commencement Day and 183 days from Appointed Day (6.51 above).)
Residual capital loss treated as exchange loss [*TR 14(5)*]	Within two years of end of accounting period in which disposal occurs. Election is irrevocable (6.66 above).
Pre-Commencement Day capital loss treated as exchange loss under foreign exchange tax rules [*TR 16(1)*]	Later of: ● 92 days after Commencement Day and ● 183 days after Appointed Day The election is irrevocable (6.68 above).

Chapter 8 – Deferral of unrealised exchange gain

Deferral of unrealised exchange gains [*FA 1993, s 139(6)–(8)*]	Within two years of end of accounting period in which gain incurred, unless assessment not final and conclusive by this date (8.15 above).

Chapter 9 – Matching election

Matching election

[*MR 11(4)*]	To be effective from Commencement Day later of: ● 92 days from Commencement Day and ● 183 days from Appointed Day Election is irrevocable (9.21 above).
[*MR 10(1)*]	Otherwise effective from date election is made (9.21 above).
[*MR 11(2)*]	For new asset, for election to be effective from date of acquisition within 92 days of acquisition date (9.21 above).

233

13.5 *Planning Points and Practical Issues*

Election to vary percentage or amount specified in election [*MR 11(3)*]

May specify any day up to 92 days before election is made for election to take effect (9.21 above).

Chapter 10 – Local currency election

Local currency election [*LR 9(2)*]

If within charge to tax on Commencement Day and to be effective from Commencement Day, not later than 92 days from Commencement Day (10.52 above).

[*LR 9(3)*]

If trade comes within charge to tax, election will be effective from day it comes into the charge to tax, provided the election is made within 92 days of that day (10.53 above).

Such elections are irrevocable and apply for all accounting periods from the date the election is made (10.54 above).

Local currency election for overseas branch [*LR 5(7)*]

Within 92 days of Commencement Day, to be effective from Commencement Day (10.50 above).

Chapter 11 – Other special provisions

Non-exchange losses to be treated as an exchange loss [*ER 2(7)*]

Within two years of the end of the accounting period that non-exchange loss accrued to the company (11.5 above).

Chapter 12 – Controlled foreign companies and other special companies

CFC matching election to be effective from start of first accounting period for which direction has effect [*MR 11(5)*]

Within 92 days of the date of the CFC direction (12.26 above).

CFC opt out of grandfathering	Earlier of: • Within 60 days of the issue of the CFC direction • 20 months after end of the accounting period (12.28 above).
CFC excess loss relief	Within 60 days of the issue of the CFC direction (12.28 above) or if later within 20 months of the end of the accounting period in which the loss accrued.

Appendix 1

Primary Legislation

Contents

Appendix 1

Schedules
8   Loan relationships: claims relating to deficits
9   Loan relationships: special computational provisions
15   Loan relationships: savings and transitional provisions

FINANCE (NO 2) ACT 1997
40   Carry-back of loan relationship deficits

FINANCE ACT 2000
         International matters
105   Corporation tax: use of currencies other than sterling
106   Foreign exchange gains and losses: use of local currency

---

Taxes Management Act 1970

[87A Interest on overdue corporation tax etc.

(1)   Corporation tax shall carry interest at the rate applicable under section
       178 of the Finance Act 1989 from the date when the tax becomes due
       and payable (in accordance with [section 59D of this Act]¹¹) until
       payment.

(2)   Subsection (1) above applies even if the date when the tax becomes due
       and payable (as mentioned in that subsection) is a non-business day
       within the meaning of section 92 of the Bills of Exchange Act 1882.

(3)   In relation to corporation tax assessed by virtue of section 346(2) or
       347(1) of the principal Act, 137(4), 139(7) or 179(11) of the 1992 Act or
       [paragraph 75A(2) of Schedule 18 to the Finance Act 1998]¹⁵ (which
       enable unpaid corporation tax assessed on a company to be assessed on
       other persons in certain circumstances), the reference in subsection (1)
       above to the date when the tax becomes due and payable is a reference
       to the date when it became due and payable by the company.

(4)   *[Subject to [subsections (4B) and (7)]⁵ below]² in any case where –*

       *(a)   there is in any accounting period of a company (in this subsection
             referred to as 'the later period') an amount of surplus advance
             corporation tax, as defined in subsection (3) of section 239 of the
             principal Act, and*

       *(b)   pursuant to a claim under the said subsection (3), the whole or any
             part of that amount is treated for the purposes of the said section 239
             as discharging liability for an amount of corporation tax for an
             earlier accounting period (in this subsection referred to as 'the earlier
             period'), and*

       *(c)   disregarding the effect of the said subsection (3), an amount of
             corporation tax for the earlier period would carry interest in
             accordance with this section.*

       *then, in determining the amount of interest payable under this section on
       corporation tax unpaid for the earlier period, no account shall be taken of
       any reduction in the amount of that tax which results from the said
       subsection (3) except so far as concerns interest for any time after the date*

on which any corporation tax for the later period became due and payable (as mentioned in subsection [(8) below]^{12}).]$^{1\ 14}$

[(4A)   In a case where –

(a)   there is for an accounting period of a company ('the later period') [a non-trading deficit on the company's loan relationships]^{8},

(b)   as a result of a claim under [section 83(2)(c) of the Finance Act 1996 or paragraph 4(3) of Schedule 11 to that Act the whole or part of the deficit for the later period is set off against profits]^{9} of an earlier accounting period ('the earlier period'), and]^{4}

[(c)   if the claim had not been made, there would be an amount or, as the case may be, an additional amount of corporation tax for the earlier period which would carry interest in accordance with this section,

then, for the purposes of the determination at any time of whether any interest is payable under this section or of the amount of interest so payable, the amount mentioned in paragraph (c) above shall be taken to be an amount of unpaid corporation tax for the earlier period except so far as concerns interest for any time after the date on which any corporation tax for the later period became (or, as the case may be, would have become) due and payable as mentioned in subsection [(8) below]^{12}.]^{6}

[(4B)   *Where, in a case falling within subsection (4A)(a) and (b) above –*

(a)   *there is in the earlier period, as a result of the claim under [section 83(2)(c) of the Finance Act 1996 or paragraph 4(3) of Schedule 11 to that Act]^{10}, an amount of surplus advance corporation tax, as defined in section 239(3) of the principal Act, and*

(b)   *pursuant to a claim under the said section 239(3), the whole or any part of that amount is to be treated for the purposes of section 239 of the principal Act as discharging liability for an amount of corporation tax for an accounting period before the earlier period,*

the claim under the said section 239(3) shall be disregarded for the purposes of subsection (4A) above but subsection (4) above shall have effect in relation to that claim as if the reference in the words after paragraph (c) to the later period within the meaning of subsection (4) above were a reference to the period which, in relation to the claim under [section 83(2)(c) of the Finance Act 1996 or paragraph 4(3) of Schedule 11 to that Act]^{10}, would be the later period for the purposes of subsection (4A) above.]$^{7\ 14}$

[(5)   A sum assessed on a company by such an assessment as is referred to in section 252(5) of the principal Act (recovery of payment of tax credit or interest on such a payment) shall carry interest at the rate applicable under section 178 of the Finance Act 1989 from the date when the payment of tax credit or interest was made until the sum assessed is paid.]^{1}

[(6)   In any case where –

(a)   on a claim under section 393A(1) of the principal Act, the whole or any part of a loss incurred in an accounting period ('the later period') has been set off for the purposes of corporation tax against profits of a preceding accounting period ('the earlier period');

(b) the earlier period does not fall wholly within the period of twelve months immediately preceding the later period; and

(c) if the claim had not been made, there would be an amount or, as the case may be, an additional amount of corporation tax for the earlier period which would carry interest in accordance with this section,

then, for the purposes of the determination at any time of whether any interest is payable under this section or of the amount of interest so payable, the amount mentioned in paragraph (c) above shall be taken to be an amount of unpaid corporation tax for the earlier period except so far as concerns interest for any time after the date on which any corporation tax for the later period became (or, as the case may be, would have become) due and payable as mentioned in subsection [(8) below][12].

(7) Where, in a case falling within subsection (6)(a) and (b) above –

(a) there is in the earlier period, as a result of the claim under section 393A(1) of the principal Act, an amount of surplus advance corporation tax, as defined in subsection (3) of section 239 of that Act; and

(b) pursuant to a claim under the said subsection (3), the whole or any part of that amount is to be treated for the purposes of the said section 239 as discharging liability for an amount of corporation tax for an accounting period before the earlier period,

the claim under the said subsection (3) shall be disregarded for the purposes of subsection (6) above but subsection (4) above shall have effect in relation to that claim as if the reference in the words after paragraph (c) to the later period within the meaning of subsection (4) above were a reference to the period which, in relation to the claim under the said section 393A(1), would be the later period for the purposes of subsection (6) above.][3 14]

[(8) In subsections (4), (4A) and (6) above, any reference to the date on which corporation tax for an accounting period became, or would have become, due and payable shall be construed on the basis that corporation tax for an accounting period becomes due and payable on the day following the expiry of nine months from the end of the accounting period.

(9) The power conferred by section 59E of the Act (alteration of date on which corporation tax becomes due and payable) does not include power to make provision in relation to subsection (4), (4A), (6) or (8) above the effect of which would be to change the meaning of references in subsection (4), (4A) or (6) above to the date on which corporation tax for an accounting period became, or would have become, due and payable (as mentioned in subsection (8) above).][13]

---

[1] Inserted by F(No2)A 1987, s 85 (as amended by ICTA 1988, 29 Sch 10(4), FA 1989, s 179(1), FA 1991, 15 Sch 2 and TCGA 1992, 10 Sch 2(9) with effect with respect to accounting periods ending after 30 September 1993 (SI 1992 No 3066 (The Corporation Tax Acts (Provisions for Payment of Tax and Returns) (Appointed Days) Order 1992)).

[2] Inserted by FA 1993, 14 Sch 4(1) with effect as in [1] above.

[3] Substituted by FA 1993, 14 Sch 4(2) with effect as in [1] above.
Previously
'In any case where –

(a) on a claim under section 393A(1) of the principal Act, the whole or any part of a loss incurred in an accounting period (the 'later period') is set off for the purposes of corporation tax against profits of a preceding accounting period (the 'earlier period').

(b) the earlier period does not fall wholly within the period of twelve months immediately preceding the later period, and

(c) if the claim had not been made, an amount of corporation tax for the earlier period would carry interest in accordance with this section.

then, in determining the amount of interest payable under this section on corporation tax unpaid for the earlier period, no account shall be taken of any reduction in the amount of that tax which results from the claim, except so far as concerns interest for any time after the date on which any corporation tax for the later period became (or, as the case may be, would have become) due and payable, as mentioned in subsection (1) above.][a]

a   Inserted by F(No2)A 1987, s 85 with effect as in [1] above.

4   Inserted by FA 1993, 18 Sch 1 and applies
    (i) where a qualifying asset or liability is one to which the company becomes entitled or subject on or after its 'commencement day', or
    (ii) the rights and duties under a currency contract are ones to which it becomes entitled and subject after that day.
    The 'commencement day' for a company is the first day of its first accounting period to begin on or after 23 March 1995 (see FA 1993 section 165 (Appointed Day) Order 1994 (SI 1994 No 3224)).

5   Substituted by FA 1995, 24 Sch 9 with effect as in [4] above.

6   Substituted by FA 1995, 24 Sch 8 with effect as in [4] above.

7   Inserted by FA 1995, 24 Sch 9 with effect as in [4] above.

8   Substituted by FA 1996, 14 Sch 1(1)(a) for corporation tax purposes in relation to accounting periods ending after 31 March 1996 and for income tax purposes in relation to 1996/97 and subsequent years of assessment (but subject to transitional provisions in FA 1996, 15 Sch). Previously 'a relievable amount within the meaning of section 131 of the Finance Act 1993 (non-trading exchange gains and losses)'.

9   Substituted by FA 1996, 14 Sch 1(1)(b) as in [8] above.
    Previously 'subsection (5) or (6) of that section the whole or part of the relievable amount for the later period is set off against the exchange profits (as defined in subsection (10) of that section)'.

10 Substituted by FA 1996, 14 Sch 1(2) as in [8] above.
    Previously 'section 131(5) or (6) of the Finance Act 1993'.

11 Substituted by FA 1994, s 199 and 19 Sch 24 with effect in relation to accounting periods ending on or after the self-assessment appointed day (1 July 1999).
    Previously 'section 10 of the principal Act'.

12 Substituted by FA 1998, 4 Sch 4 with effect as in [11] above.
    Previously '(1) above'.

13 Inserted by FA 1998, 4 Sch 4 with effect as in [11] above.

14 Subsections (4) (4B) and (7) are repealed by FA 1998, 3 Sch 4 with effect in relation to relevant periods beginning after 5 April 1999.

15 Substituted by FA 1999, s 92(5)(7) in relation to accounting periods ending on or after 1 July 1999.
    Previously 'section 96(8) of the Finance Act 1990'.

91   Effect on interest of reliefs

(1)   Where any amount of interest is payable under section 86 [...][9] of this Act in relation to an assessment, and relief from tax charged by the assessment is given to any person by a discharge of any of that tax, such adjustment shall be made of the said amount, and such repayment shall be made of any amounts previously paid under [that section][10] in relation to the assessment, as are necessary to secure that the total sum, if any, paid or payable under [that section][10] in relation to the assessment is the same as it would have been if the tax discharged had never been charged.

[(1A) Where interest is payable under section 87A of this Act in respect of an amount of corporation tax for an accounting period, and relief from tax is given by a discharge of any of that corporation tax –

    (a) such adjustment shall be made of the amount of interest payable under that section in respect of corporation tax for that accounting period, and

    (b) such repayment shall be made of any amounts of interest previously paid under that section in respect of that corporation tax,

as are necessary to secure that the total sum (if any) paid or payable under that section in respect of corporation tax for that accounting period is the same as it would have been if the tax discharged had never been charged.

  (1B) Subsection (1A) above has effect subject to section 87A(4) [(4A), (4B),][8] [(6) and (7)][7] of this Act.][5]

    (2) [Subject to subsection (2A) below][6] where relief from tax paid for any chargeable period is given to any person by repayment, he shall be entitled to require that the amount repaid shall be treated for the purposes of this section, so far as it will go, as if it were a discharge of the tax charged on him (whether alone or together with other persons) by or by virtue of any assessment for or relating to the same chargeable period, so, however, that it shall not be applied to any assessment made after the relief was given and that it shall not be applied to more than one assessment so as to reduce, without extinguishing, the amount of tax charged thereby.

[(2A) In any case where –

    (a) relief from corporation tax is given to any person by repayment, and

    (b) that tax was paid for an accounting period ending after the day which is the appointed day for the purposes of section 10 of the principal Act,

that person shall be entitled to require that the amount repaid shall be treated for the purposes of this section, so far as it will go, as if it were a discharge of the corporation tax charged on him for that period.][6]

    (3) Notwithstanding anything in the preceding provisions of this section, no relief, whether given by way of discharge or repayment, shall be treated for the purposes of this section as –

    (a) [...][1]

    (b) affecting tax charged by any assessment to income tax made under Schedule A or Schedule D if either –

        (i) [...][1]

        (ii) it arises in connection with income taxable otherwise than under Schedule A or Schedule D, or

        (iii) it relates to a source income from which is taxable otherwise than under Schedule A or Schedule D [or

    (c) affecting tax charged at a rate other than the basic rate [the lower rate or the starting rate][4] on income from which tax has been deducted (otherwise than under section [203][3] of the principal Act) or is treated as having been deducted, unless it is a relief from the tax so charged.][2]

(4) For the purposes of this section a relief from corporation tax or capital gains tax shall not be treated as affecting tax charged by any assessment unless the assessment is to the same tax.

---

[1]   Repealed by FA 1971, 6 Sch 81, 88(a) and 14 Sch Part II, with effect for 1973/74 and later years.

[2]   Inserted by FA 1971, 6 Sch 81, 88(b), with effect for 1973/74 and later years.

[3]   Substituted by ICTA 1988, 29 Sch 32, with effect from 6 April 1988.

[4]   Substituted by FA 1999, s 22(11) (12) with effect from the year 1999/2000.
Previously ['or the lower rate'][a].

    [a]   Inserted by F(No 2)A 1992, s 19(2)(7) with effect for the year 1992/93 and subsequent years of assessment.

[5]   Inserted by F(No 2)A 1987, s 86(5) with effect with respect to accounting periods ending after 30 September 1993 (SI 1992 No 3066 (The Corporation Tax Acts (Provisions for Payment of Tax and Returns) (Appointed Days) Order 1992)).

[6]   Inserted by F(No 2)A 1987, s 86(6) (as amended by ICTA 1988, 29 Sch 10(6)) with effect as in [5] above.

[7]   Inserted by FA 1993, 14 Sch 5 with effect as in [5] above.

[8]   Inserted by FA 1995, 24 Sch 10 with effect from 23 March 1995 (SI 1994 No 3224).

[9]   Repealed by FA 1996, 18 Sch 4(2)(b)
(i) as respects 1996/97 onwards (except so far as relating to partnerships whose trades, professions or businesses were set up and commenced before 6 April 1994 when it applies as respects 1997/98 onwards); and
(ii) in relation to any income tax which is charged by an assessment made on or after 6 April 1998 and is for the year 1995/96 or earlier.
Previously 'or section 88'.

[10]   Substituted by FA 1996, 18 Sch 4(2)(b) as in [9] above.
Previously 'those provisions'.

Income and Corporation Taxes Act 1988

CHAPTER IV CONTROLLED FOREIGN COMPANIES

747 Imputation of chargeable profits and creditable tax of controlled foreign companies

(1)   If [. . .][2] in any accounting period a company –

(a) is resident outside the United Kingdom, and

(b) is controlled by persons resident in the United Kingdom, and

(c) is subject to a lower level of taxation in the territory in which it is resident,

[. . .][3], the provisions of this Chapter shall apply in relation to that accounting period.

(2)   A company which falls within paragraphs (a) to (c) of subsection (1) above is in this Chapter referred to as a 'controlled foreign company'.

(3)   [Subject to section 748, where][4] the provisions of this Chapter apply in relation to an accounting period of a controlled foreign company, the chargeable profits of that company for that period and its creditable tax (if any) for that period shall each be apportioned in accordance with section 752 among the persons (whether resident in the United Kingdom or not) who had an interest in that company at any time during that accounting period.

(4) Where, on such an apportionment of a controlled foreign company's chargeable profits for an accounting period as is referred to in subsection (3) above, an amount of those profits is apportioned to a company resident in the United Kingdom then, subject to subsection (5) below –

(a) a sum equal to corporation tax at the appropriate rate on that apportioned amount of profits, less the portion of the controlled foreign company's creditable tax for that period (if any) which is apportioned to the resident company, shall be [chargeable on]⁵ the resident company as if it were an amount of corporation tax chargeable on that company; and

(b) if, apart from this paragraph, section 739 would deem any sum forming part of the company's chargeable profits for that accounting period to be the income of an individual for the purposes of the Income Tax Acts, that section shall not apply to such portion of that sum as corresponds to the portion of those chargeable profits which is apportioned to companies which are resident in the United Kingdom and which, by virtue of paragraph (a) above, have a liability to tax in respect thereof;

and for the purposes of paragraph (a) above 'the appropriate rate' means the rate of corporation tax applicable to profits of that accounting period of the resident company in which ends the accounting period of the controlled foreign company [which is mentioned in subsection (1) above]⁶ or, if there is more than one such rate, the average rate over the whole of that accounting period of the resident company.

[(4A) Where by virtue of section 747A a company's chargeable profits for an accounting period are to be computed and expressed in a currency other than sterling, for the purposes of subsection (4)(a) above the apportioned amount shall be taken to be the sterling equivalent of the apportioned amount found in the currency other than sterling.

(4B) The translation required by subsection (4A) above shall be made by reference to the London closing exchange rate for the two currencies concerned for the last day of the accounting period concerned.]¹

(5) Tax shall not, by virtue of subsection (4) above, be [chargeable on]⁷ a company resident in the United Kingdom unless, on the apportionment in question, the aggregate of –

(a) the amount of the controlled foreign company's chargeable profits for the accounting period in question which is apportioned to the resident company, and

(b) any amounts of those chargeable profits which are apportioned to persons who are connected or associated with the resident company,

is at least [25 per cent]⁸ of the total of those chargeable profits.

(6) In relation to a company resident outside the United Kingdom –

(a) any reference in this Chapter to its chargeable profits for an accounting period is a reference to the amount which, on the assumptions in Schedule 24, would be the amount of the total profits of the company for that period on which, after allowing for any deductions available against those profits, corporation tax would be chargeable; and

(b) any reference in this Chapter to profits does not include a reference to chargeable gains but otherwise (except as provided by paragraph (a) above) has the same meaning as it has for the purposes of corporation tax.

---

¹   Inserted by FA 1995, 25 Sch 3 with effect from 1 May 1995.

²   Deleted by FA 1998, 17 Sch 1 with effect in relation to accounting periods of companies resident in the UK which end on or after the corporation tax self-assessment appointed day (1 July 1999).
    Previously 'the Board have reason to believe that'.

³   Deleted by FA 1998, 17 Sch 1 with effect as in ² above.
    Previously 'and the Board so direct'.

⁴   Substituted by FA 1998, 17 Sch 1 with effect as in ² above.
    Previously 'where, by virtue of a direction under subsection (1) above,'.

⁵   Substituted by FA 1998, 17 Sch 1 with effect as in ² above.
    Previously 'assessed on and recoverable from'.

⁶   Substituted by FA 1998, 17 Sch 1 with effect as in ² above.
    Previously 'to which the direction under subsection (1) above relates'.

⁷   Substituted by FA 1998, 17 Sch 1 with effect as in ² above.
    Previously 'assessed and recoverable from'.

⁸   Substituted by FA 1998, 17 Sch 1 with effect as in ² above.
    Previously '10 per cent'.

[747A   Special rule for computing chargeable profits

(1) Subsection (2) below applies where for the purposes of this Chapter a company's chargeable profits fall to be determined for –

(a) the first relevant accounting period of the company, or

(b) any subsequent accounting period of the company.

(2) Notwithstanding any other rule (whether statutory or otherwise) the chargeable profits for any such period shall be computed and expressed in the currency used in the accounts of the company for its first relevant accounting period.

(3) Subsection (4) below applies where for the purposes of this Chapter a company's chargeable profits fall to be determined for any accounting period of the company which –

(a) begins on or after the appointed day, and

(b) falls before the company's first relevant accounting period.

(4) Notwithstanding any other rule (whether statutory or otherwise) the chargeable profits for any such period shall be computed and expressed in the currency used in the accounts of the company for the accounting period concerned.

(5) For the purposes of this section the first relevant accounting period of the company shall be found in accordance with subsections (6) to (8) below.

(6) Where [an apportionment under section 747(3) has fallen to be made]⁶ as regards an accounting period of the company which begins before its commencement day, its first relevant accounting period is its accounting period which begins on its commencement day.

(7) [...]²

(8) Where [...]³ subsection (6) above does not apply, [the company's]⁴ first relevant accounting period is its first accounting period which begins on or after its commencement day and as regards which –

245

[(a) an apportionment under section 747(3) has fallen to be made, or

(b) it can reasonably be assumed that such an apportionment would have fallen to be made, but for the fact that the company pursued, within the meaning of Part I of Schedule 25, an acceptable distribution policy,]⁷

[unless the company is a trading company, in which case paragraph (b) above shall be disregarded in the case of its accounting periods beginning before 28 November 1995.]⁵

(9) For the purposes of this section –

(a) a company's commencement day is the first day of its first accounting period to begin after the day preceding the appointed day;

(b) the appointed day [(which, for ease of reference, is 23rd March 1995)]⁸ is such day as may be appointed under section 165(7)(b) of the Finance Act 1993 (which relates to exchange gains and losses).

(10) References in this section to the accounts of a company –

(a) are to the accounts which the company is required by the law of its home State to keep, or

(b) if the company is not required by the law of its home State to keep accounts, are to the accounts of the company which most closely correspond to the individual accounts which companies formed and registered under the Companies Act 1985 are required by that Act to keep;

and for the purposes of this subsection the home State of a company is the country or territory under whose law the company is incorporated or formed.]¹

---

¹ Inserted by FA 1995, 25 Sch 2.

² Deleted by FA 1996, 36 Sch 1(2) in relation to accounting periods of a controlled foreign company beginning on or after 28 November 1995.
Previously
'Where the company is a trading company and subsection (6) above does not apply, its first relevant accounting period is its first accounting period which begins on or after its commencement day and as regards which a direction has been given under section 747.'

³ Deleted by FA 1996, 36 Sch 1(3) as in ² above.
Previously 'the company is not a trading company and'.

⁴ Substituted by FA 1996, 36 Sch 1(3) as in ² above.
Previously 'its'.

⁵ Inserted by FA 1996, 36 Sch 1(3) as in ² above.

⁶ Substituted by FA 1998, 17 Sch 2 with effect in relation to accounting periods of companies resident in the UK which end on or after the corporation tax self-assessment appointed day (1 July 1999)
Previously 'a direction has been given under section 747'.

⁷ Substituted by FA 1998, 17 Sch 2 with effect as in ⁶ above.
Previously
'(a) a direction has been given under section 747, or
(b) it can reasonably be assumed that a direction would have been given under section 747 but for the fact that it pursued, within the meaning of Part I of Schedule 25, an acceptable distribution policy.'

⁸ Inserted by FA 1998, 17 Sch 2 with effect as in ⁶ above.

748   [Cases where section 747(3) does not apply]³

(1)   [No apportionment under section 747(3) falls to be made as regards an accounting period of a controlled foreign company if –]⁴

(a)   in respect of that period the company pursues, within the meaning of Part I of Schedule 25, an acceptable distribution policy; or

(b)   throughout that period the company is, within the meaning of Part II of that Schedule, engaged in exempt activities; or

(c)   the public quotation condition set out in Part III of that Schedule is fulfilled with respect to that period; or

(d)   the chargeable profits of the accounting period do not exceed [£50,000]⁵ or, if the accounting period is less than 12 months, a proportionately reduced amount [; or

(e)   as respects the accounting period, the company is, within the meaning of regulations made by the Board for the purposes of this paragraph, resident in a territory specified in the regulations and satisfies –

(i)   such conditions with respect to its income or gains as may be so specified; and

(ii)   such other conditions (if any) as may be so specified.]⁶

[(1A)   Regulations under paragraph (e) of subsection (1) above may –

(a)   make different provision for different cases or with respect to different territories;

(b)   make provision having effect in relation to accounting periods of controlled foreign companies ending not more than one year before the date on which the regulations are made; and

(c)   contain such supplementary, incidental, consequential and transitional provision as the Board may think fit.]⁶

(2)   [. . .]⁷

(3)   Notwithstanding that none of paragraphs (a) to [(e)]⁸ of subsection (1) above applies to an accounting period of a controlled foreign company, [no apportionment under section 747(3) falls to be made as regards that accounting period if it is the case that]⁹

(a)   in so far as any of the transactions the results of which are reflected in the profits arising in that accounting period [or any two or more transactions taken together, the results of at least one of which are so reflected]², achieved a reduction in United Kingdom tax, either the reduction so achieved was minimal or it was not the main purpose or one of the main purposes of that transaction or, as the case may be, of those transactions taken together to achieve that reduction, and

(b)   it was not the main reason or, as the case may be, one of the main reasons for the company's existence in that accounting period to achieve a reduction in United Kingdom tax by a diversion of profits from the United Kingdom,

and Part IV of Schedule 25 shall have effect with respect to the preceding provisions of this subsection.

[(4) Where by virtue of section 747A a company's chargeable profits for an accounting period are to be computed and expressed in a currency other than sterling, for the purposes of subsection (1)(d) above its chargeable profits for the period shall be taken to be the sterling equivalent of its chargeable profits found in the currency other than sterling.

(5) The translation required by subsection (4) above shall be made by reference to the London closing exchange rate for the two currencies concerned for the last day of the accounting period concerned.]¹

---

¹ Inserted by FA 1995, 25 Sch 4 with effect from 1 May 1995.

² Substituted by FA 1996, 36 Sch 2 in relation to accounting periods of a controlled foreign company beginning on or after 28 November 1995.
Previously 'or any two or more of those transactions taken together'.

³ Substituted by FA 1998, 17 Sch 3 with effect in relation to accounting periods of companies resident in the UK which end on or after the corporation tax self-assessment appointed day (1 July 1999)
Previously 'Limitations on direction making powers'.

⁴ Substituted by FA 1998, 17 Sch 3 with effect as in ³ above.
Previously 'No direction may be given under section 747(1) with respect to an accounting period of a controlled foreign company if—'.

⁵ Substituted by FA 1998, 17 Sch 3 with effect as in ³ above.
Previously '£20,000'.

⁶ Inserted by FA 1998, 17 Sch 3 with effect as in ³ above.

⁷ Deleted by FA 1998, 17 Sch 3 with effect as in ³ above.
Previously
'Without prejudice to any right of appeal, nothing in subsection (1) above prevents the Board from giving a direction with respect to an accounting period after the end of that period but before it is known whether the company has paid such a dividend as establishes that it is pursuing an acceptable distribution policy in respect of the profits arising in that period.'

⁸ Substituted by FA 1998, 17 Sch 3 with effect as in ³ above.
Previously '(d)'.

⁹ Substituted by FA 1998, 17 Sch 3 with effect as in ³ above.
Previously 'no direction may be given under section 747(1) with respect to that accounting period if it appears to the Board that –'.

---

750 Territories with a lower level of taxation

(1) Without prejudice to [subsection (5)]³ of section 749, a company which, by virtue of [any of subsections (1) to (4)]⁴ of that section, is to be regarded as resident in a particular territory outside the United Kingdom shall be considered to be subject to a lower level of taxation in that territory if the amount of tax ('the local tax') which is paid under the law of that territory in respect of the profits of the company which arise in any accounting period is less than [three-quarters]¹ of the corresponding United Kingdom tax on those profits.

(2) For the purposes of this Chapter, the amount of the corresponding United Kingdom tax on the profits arising in an accounting period of a company resident outside the United Kingdom is the amount of corporation tax which, on the assumptions set out in Schedule 24 and subject to subsection (3) below, would be chargeable in respect of the chargeable profits of the company for that accounting period.

(3) In determining the amount of corporation tax which, in accordance with subsection (2) above, would be chargeable in respect of the chargeable

profits of an accounting period of a company resident outside the United Kingdom –

[(a) it shall be assumed for the purposes of Schedule 24 that an apportionment under section 747(3) falls to be made as regards that period; and][5]

(b) there shall be disregarded so much of any relief from corporation tax in respect of income as would be attributable to the local tax and would fall to be given by virtue of any provision of Part XVIII other than section 810; and

(c) there shall be deducted from what would otherwise be the amount of that corporation tax –

　(i) any amount which (on the assumptions set out in Schedule 24) would fall to be set off against corporation tax by virtue of section 7(2); and

　(ii) any amount of income tax or corporation tax actually charged in respect of any of those chargeable profits.

(4) The references in subsection (3)(c) above to an amount falling to be set off or an amount actually charged do not include so much of any such amount as has been or falls to be repaid to the company whether on the making of a claim or otherwise.

[(5) Subsections (6) and (7) below apply where by virtue of section 747A a company's chargeable profits for an accounting period are to be computed and expressed in a currency other than sterling.

(6) For the purposes of subsection (2) above the company's chargeable profits for the period shall be taken to be the sterling equivalent of its chargeable profits found in the currency other than sterling.

(7) In applying section 13 for the purposes of making the determination mentioned in subsection (3) above, any reference in section 13 to the amount of the company's profits for the period on which corporation tax falls finally to be borne shall be construed as a reference to the sterling sum found under subsection (6) above.

(8) Any translation required by subsection (6) above shall be made by reference to the London closing exchange rate for the two currencies concerned for the last day of the accounting period concerned.][2]

---

[1]　Substituted by FA 1993, s 119(1)(2) in relation to accounting periods beginning on or after 16 March 1993.
Previously 'one-half'.

[2]　Inserted by FA 1995, 25 Sch 5 with effect from 1 May 1995.

[3]　Substituted by FA 1998, 17 Sch 5 with effect in relation to accounting periods of companies resident in the UK which end on or after the corporation tax self-assessment appointed day (1 July 1999).
Previously 'subsection (3)'.

[4]　Substituted by FA 1998, 17 Sch 5 with effect as in [3] above.
Previously 'subsection (1) or subsection (2)'.

[5]　Substituted by FA 1998, 17 Sch 5 with effect as in [3] above.
Previously
'(a) it shall be assumed for the purposes of Schedule 24 –
　(i) that a direction has been given under section 747(1) in respect of that period; and
　(ii) that the Board have made any declaration which they could have made under sub-paragraph (3) of paragraph 11 of that Schedule and of which they gave notice as mentioned in that sub-paragraph; and'.

797 Limits on credit: corporation tax

(1) The amount of the credit for foreign tax which under any arrangements is to be allowed against corporation tax in respect of any income or chargeable gain ('the relevant income or gain') shall not exceed the corporation tax attributable to the relevant income or gain, determined in accordance with subsections (2) and (3) below.

(2) Subject to subsection (3) below, the amount of corporation tax attributable to the relevant income or gain shall be treated as equal to such proportion of the amount of that income or gain as corresponds to the rate of corporation tax payable by the company (before any credit under this Part) on its income or chargeable gains for the accounting period in which the income arises or the gain accrues ('the relevant accounting period').

(3) Where in the relevant accounting period there is any deduction to be made for charges on income, expenses of management or other amounts which can be deducted from or set against or treated as reducing profits of more than one description–

(a) the company may for the purposes of this section allocate the deduction in such amounts and to such of its profits for the period as it thinks fit; and

(b) the amount of the relevant income or gain shall be treated for the purposes of subsection (2) above as reduced or, as the case may be, extinguished by so much (if any) of the deduction as is allocated to it.

[(3A) Where, in a case to which section 797A does not apply, a company has a non-trading deficit on its loan relationships for the relevant accounting period, then for the purposes of subsection (3) above that deficit shall be treated, to the extent that it is an amount to which a claim under–

(a) subsection (2)(a) of section 83 of the Finance Act 1996 (deficit set against current year profits), or

(b) paragraph 4(2) of Schedule 11 to that Act (set-off of deficits in the case of insurance companies),

relates, as an amount that can in that period be set against profits of any description but can be allocated in accordance with subsection (3) above only to the profits against which it is set off in pursuance of the claim.

(3B) For the purposes of subsection (3) above, where–

(a) section 797A does not apply in the case of any company, and

(b) any amount is carried forward to the relevant accounting period in pursuance of a claim under subsection (2)(d) of section 83 of the Finance Act 1996 [. . .]²,

then that amount must be allocated to non-trading profits of the company for that period (so far as they are sufficient for the purpose) and cannot be allocated to any other profits.]¹

250

(4) *[Where in accordance with section 239 any advance corporation tax falls to be set against the company's liability to corporation tax on its profits (within the meaning of that section) for the relevant accounting period–*

(a) *so far as that liability relates to the relevant income or gain, it shall be taken to be reduced by the amount of the credit for foreign tax attributable to that income or gain, as determined in accordance with subsections (2) and (3) above; and*

(b) *the amount of advance corporation tax which may be set against that liability, so far as it relates to the relevant income or gain, shall not exceed whichever is the lower of the limits specified in subsection (5) below;*

and section 239(2) shall have effect in relation only to so much of the profits of the company chargeable to corporation tax for that period as does not include the relevant income or gain.]³

(5) *[In relation to an amount of income or gain in respect of which the company's liability to corporation tax is taken to be reduced as mentioned in paragraph (a) of subsection (4) above, the limits referred to in paragraph (b) of that subsection are–*

(a) *the limit which would apply under section 239(2) if that amount of income or gain were the company's only income or gain for that relevant accounting period; and*

(b) *the amount of corporation tax for which, after taking account of that reduction, the company is liable in respect of that amount of income or gain.]³*

[(6) In this section 'non-trading profits' has the same meaning as in paragraph 4 of Schedule 8 to the Finance Act 1996.]¹

---

¹   Inserted by FA 1996, 14 Sch 42 in relation to accounting periods ending after 31 March 1996 but subject to transitional provisions in FA 1996, 15 Sch.

²   Repealed by FA 1998, 27 Sch 17 and deemed always to have had effect.

³   Sub-sections (4) and (5) repealed by FA 1998 s 31, 3 Sch 35 with effect for accounting periods beginning after 5 April 1999.

797A   Foreign tax on interest brought into account as a non-trading credit

(1) This section applies for the purposes of any arrangements where, in the case of any company–

(a) any non-trading credit relating to an amount of interest is brought into account for the purposes of Chapter II of Part IV of the Finance Act 1996 (loan relationships) for any accounting period ('the applicable accounting period'); and

(b) there is in respect of that amount an amount of foreign tax for which, under the arrangements, credit is allowable against United Kingdom tax computed by reference to that interest.

(2) It shall be assumed that tax chargeable under paragraph (a) of Case III of Schedule D on the profits and gains arising for the applicable accounting period from the company's loan relationships falls to be

computed on the actual amount of its non-trading credits for that period, and without any deduction in respect of non-trading debits.

(3) Section 797(3) shall have effect (subject to subsection (7) below) as if–

(a) there were for the applicable accounting period an amount equal to the adjusted amount of the non-trading debits falling to be brought into account by being set against profits of the company for that period of any description; and

(b) different parts of that amount might be set against different profits.

(4) For the purposes of this section, the adjusted amount of a company's non-trading debits for any accounting period is the amount equal, in the case of that company, to the aggregate of the non-trading debits given for that period for the purposes of Chapter II of Part IV of the Finance Act 1996 (loan relationships) less the aggregate of the amounts specified in subsection (5) below.

(5) Those amounts are–

(a) so much of any non-trading deficit for the applicable accounting period as is an amount to which a claim under subsection (2)(b), (c) or (d) of section 83 of the Finance Act 1996 or paragraph 4(3) of Schedule 11 to that Act (group relief and transfer to previous or subsequent period of deficits) relates; [and]²

(b) so much of any non-trading deficit for that period as falls to be carried forward to a subsequent period in accordance with subsection (3) of that section or paragraph 4(4) of that Schedule; [. . .]³

(c) [. . .]³

[An amount carried forward to the applicable accounting period under section 83(3) of that Act shall not be treated as a non-trading deficit for that period for the purposes of paragraph (a) and (b).]²

(6) Section 797(3) shall have effect as if any amount [carried forward to the applicable accounting period in pursuance of a claim under section 83(2)(d) of that Act]⁴ were an amount capable of being allocated only to any non-trading profits of the company.

(7) Where–

(a) the company has a non-trading deficit for the applicable accounting period,

(b) the amount of that deficit exceeds the aggregate of the amounts specified in subsection (5) above, and

(c) in pursuance of a claim under–

(i) subsection (2)(a) of section 83 of the Finance Act 1996 (deficit set against current year profits), or

(ii) paragraph 4(2) of Schedule 11 to that Act (set-off of deficits in the case of insurance companies),

the excess falls to be set off against profits of any description,

section 797(3) shall have effect as if non-trading debits of the company which in aggregate are equal to the amount of the excess were required to be allocated to the profits against which they are set off in pursuance of the claim.

[An amount carried forward to the applicable accounting period under section 83(3) of the Finance Act 1996 shall be disregarded for the purposes of paragraphs (a) and (b).][2]

(8)   In this section 'non-trading profits' has the same meaning as in paragraph 4 of Schedule 8 to the Finance Act 1996.][1]

---

[1]   Inserted by FA 1996, 14 Sch 43 in relation to accounting periods ending after 31 March 1996 but subject to transitional provisions in FA 1996, 15 Sch.

[2]   Inserted by FA 1998, s 82(2) and deemed always to have had effect.

[3]   Repealed by FA 1998, s 82(2), 27 Sch 17 and deemed always to have had effect.

[4]   Substituted by FA 1998, s 82(2) and deemed always to have had effect.

---

826   Interest on tax overpaid

(1)   In any case where –

(a)   a repayment falls to be made of corporation tax paid by a company for an accounting period which ends after the appointed day; or

[(aa)   a repayment falls to be made under sections 246N and 246Q of advance corporation tax paid by a company in respect of distributions made by it in such an accounting period; or][9]

(b)   a repayment of income tax falls to made in respect of a payment received by a company in such an accounting period; or

(c)   a payment falls to be made to a company of the whole or part of the tax credit comprised in any franked investment income received by the company in such an accounting period,

then, from the material date until [the order for repayment or payment is issued][1], the repayment or payment shall carry interest at the [rate applicable under section 178 of the Finance Act 1989][2].

(2)   [Subject to section 826A(2),][21] in relation to corporation tax paid by a company for an accounting period, the material date for the purposes of this section is the date on which corporation tax was paid or, if it is later, the date on which corporation tax for that accounting period became (or, as the case may be, would have become) due and payable in accordance with [section 59D of the Management Act (payment of corporation tax)][14].

[(2A)   *In relation to advance corporation tax paid by a company in respect of distributions made by it in an accounting period, the material date for the purposes of this section is the date on which corporation tax for that accounting period became (or, as the case may be, would have become) due and payable in accordance with section 10.]*[9]

(3)   In relation to a repayment of income tax falling within subsection (1)(b) above or a payment of the whole or part of a tax credit falling within subsection (1)(c) above, [the material date is the day after the end of the accounting period][25] in which the payment referred to in subsection (1)(b) above or, as the case may be, the franked investment income referred to in subsection (1)(c) above was received by the company.

(4) For the purposes of this section a repayment of tax made on a claim under section 419(4) shall be treated as if it were a repayment of corporation tax for the accounting period in which [the event giving rise to entitlement to relief under section 419(4) occurred][29] but, in relation to such a repayment of tax, the material date for the purposes of this section is –

   (a) [the date when the entitlement to relief in respect of the repayment accrued, that is to say –

      (i) where the repayment [or the release or writing off][30] of the loan or advance (or part thereof) occurred on or after the day mentioned in section 419(4A), the date nine months after the end of that accounting period; and

      (ii) in any other case, the date nine months after the end of the accounting period in which the loan or advance was made; or][15]

   (b) if it is later, the date on which the tax which is to be repaid was in fact paid.

(5) Interest paid under this section –

   [(a)][22] shall be paid without any deduction of income tax; and

   [(b)][22] [subject to subsection (5A) below,][23] shall not be brought into account in computing any profits or income.

[(5A) Paragraph (b) of subsection (5) above does not apply in relation to interest payable to a company within the charge to corporation tax.][24]

(6) Where a repayment of corporation tax is a repayment of tax paid by a company on different dates, the repayment shall so far as possible be treated for the purposes of this section as a repayment of tax paid on a later rather than an earlier date among those dates.

(7) *[Subject to [subsections (7AA) and (7CA)][10] below,][3] in any case where –*

   (a) there is in any accounting period of a company ('the later period') an amount of surplus advance corporation tax, as defined in section 239(3); and

   (b) pursuant to a claim under section 239(3), the whole or any part of that amount is treated for the purposes of section 239 as discharging liability for an amount of corporation tax for an earlier accounting period ('the earlier period'); and

   (c) a repayment falls to be made of corporation tax [paid for the earlier period or of income tax in respect of a payment received by the company in that accounting period][4]

then, in determining the amount of interest (if any) payable under this section on the repayment [referred to in paragraph (c) above, no account shall be taken of so much of the amount of the repayment as falls to be made as a result of the claim under][5] section 239(3) except so far as concerns interest for any time after the date on which any corporation tax for the later period became due and payable (as mentioned in subsection [(7D) below][27]).

[(7A) In any case where –

254

(a) a company carrying on a trade incurs a loss in the trade in an accounting period ('the later period'),

(b) as a result of a claim under section 393A(1), the whole or any part of that loss is set off for the purposes of corporation tax against profits (of whatever description) of an earlier accounting period ('the earlier period') which does not fall wholly within the period of twelve months immediately preceding the later period, and

(c) a repayment falls to be made of corporation tax paid for the earlier period or of income tax in respect of a payment received by the company in that accounting period,

then, in determining the amount of interest (if any) payable under this section on the repayment referred to in paragraph (c) above, no account shall be taken of [so much of the amount of that repayment as falls to be made][6] as a result of the claim under section 393A(1), except so far as concerns interest for any time after the date on which any corporation tax for the later period became (or, as the case may be, would have become) due and payable, as mentioned in subsection [(7D) below][27].

[(7AA) *Where, in a case falling within subsection (7A)(a) and (b) above –*

(a) *there is in the earlier period, as a result of the claim under section 393A(1), an amount of surplus advance corporation tax, as defined in section 239(3); and*

(b) *pursuant to a claim under section 239(3) the whole or any part of that amount is to be treated for the purposes of section 239 as discharging liability for an amount of corporation tax for an accounting period before the earlier period.*

then subsection (7) above shall have effect in relation to the claim under the said subsection (3) as if the reference in the words after paragraph (c) to the later period within the meaning of subsection (7) above were a reference to the period which, in relation to the claim under section 393A(1), would be the later period for the purposes of subsection (7A) above.][7]

(7B) [. . .][20]

[(7C) In a case where –

(a) there is for an accounting period of a company ('the later period') [a non-trading deficit on the company's loan relationships,][16]

(b) as a result of a claim under [section 83(2)(c) of the Finance Act 1996 or paragraph 4(3) of Schedule 11 to that Act the whole or part of the deficit for the later period is set off against profits][17] of an earlier accounting period ('the earlier period'), and

(c) a repayment falls to be made of corporation tax for the earlier period [or of income tax in respect of a payment received by the company in that accounting period][11],

then, in determining the amount of interest (if any) payable under this section on the [repayment referred to in paragraph (c) above, no account shall be taken of so much of the amount of the repayment as falls to be made as a result of][12] the claim under [section 83(2)(c) of that Act or, as the case may be, paragraph 4(3) of Schedule 11 to that Act][18] except so far as concerns interest for any time after the date on which any corporation tax for the later period became (or, as the case may be, would have become) due and payable, as mentioned in subsection [(7D) below][27].]8

[(7CA)   *Where, in a case falling within subsection (7C)(a) and (b) above –*

   (a) *there is in the earlier period, as a result of the claim under [section 83(2)(c) of the Finance Act 1996 or paragraph 4(3) of Schedule 11 to that Act][19], an amount of surplus advance corporation tax, as defined in section 239(3), and*

   (b) *pursuant to a claim under section 239(3), the whole or any part of that amount is to be treated for the purposes of section 239 as discharging liability for an amount of corporation tax for an accounting period before the earlier period,*

   then subsection (7) above shall have effect in relation to the claim under section 239(3) as if the reference in the words after paragraph (c) to the later period within the meaning of subsection (7) above were a reference to the period which, in relation to the claim under [section 83(2)(c) of the Finance Act 1996 or paragraph 4(3) of Schedule 11 to that Act][19], would be the later period for the purposes of subsection (7C) above.][13]

[(7D)   In subsection (7), (7A), (7B) and (7C) above, any reference to the date on which corporation tax for an accounting period became, or would have become, due and payable shall be construed on the basis that corporation tax for an accounting period becomes due and payable on the day following the expiry of nine months from the end of the accounting period.][28]

[(7E)   The power conferred by section 59E of the Management Act (alteration of date on which corporation tax becomes due and payable) does not include power to make provision in relation to subsection (7), (7A), (7B), (7C) or (7D) above the effect of which would be to change the meaning of references in subsection (7), (7A), (7B) or (7C) above to the date on which corporation tax for an accounting period became, or would have become, due and payable (as mentioned in subsection (7D) above).][28]

   (8)   In consequence of the preceding provisions of this section, no repayment supplement (within the meaning of section 825) shall be paid in respect of any repayment of tax or payment of tax credit where the relevant accounting period (within the meaning of that section) ends after the appointed day.

[(8A)   Where–

   (a) interest has been paid to a company under subsection (1)(a) above,

   (b) there is a charge in the company's assessed liability to corporation tax, other than a change which in whole or in part corrects an error made by the Board or an officer of the Board, and

   (c) as a result only of that change (and, in particular, not as a result of any error in the calculation of the interest), it appears to an officer of the Board that the interest ought not to have been paid, either at all or to any extent, the interest that ought not to have been paid may be recovered from the company as if it were interest charged under Part IX of the Management Act (interest on overdue tax).

(8B) For the purposes of subsection (8A) above, the cases where there is a change in a company's assessed liability to corporation tax are those cases where–

    (a) an assessment, or an amendment of an assessment, of the amount of corporation tax payable by the company for the accounting period in question is made, or

    (b) a determination of that amount is made under paragraph 36 or 37 of Schedule 18 to the Finance Act 1998 (which until superseded by a self-assessment under that Schedule has effect as if it were one),

whether or not any previous assessment or determination has been made.

(8C) In subsection (8A)(b) above 'error' includes–

    (a) any computational error; and

    (b) the allowance of a claim or election which ought not to have been allowed.][26]

(9) In this section 'the appointed day' means such day or days, not being earlier than 31st March 1992, as the Treasury may by order appoint for the purposes of this section.

---

[1]   Substituted by FA 1989, s 180(6) and deemed always to have had effect.

[2]   Substituted by FA 1989, s 179(1)(c)(ii) with effect in relation to any period for which FA 1989, s 178(1) has effect for the purposes of this section.
Previously 'rate which, under section 89 of the Management Act, is for the time being the prescribed rate for the purposes of this section'.

[3]   Inserted by FA 1993, 14 Sch 10(1)(a) with effect in relation to accounting periods ending after 30 September 1993 (SI 1992 No 3066).

[4]   Substituted by FA 1993, 14 Sch 10(1)(b) with effect as in [3] above.
Previously 'made for the earlier period'.

[5]   Substituted by FA 1993, 14 Sch 10(1)(c) with effect as in [3] above.
Previously 'of corporation tax for the earlier period, no account shall be taken of any increase in the amount of the repayment resulting from'.

[6]   Substituted by FA 1993, 14 Sch 10(2) with effect as in [3] above.
Previously 'any increase in the amount of that repayment'.

[7]   Inserted by FA 1993, 14 Sch 10(3) with effect, subject to FA 1993, 14 Sch 10(6), in relation to any claim under ICTA 1988, s 393A(1) as a result of which there is an amount of surplus advance corporation tax in an accounting period ending after the appointed day for the purposes of ICTA 1988, s 826.

[8]   Inserted by FA 1993, 18 Sch 5 and applies
(i) where a qualifying asset or liability is one to which the company becomes entitled or subject on or after its 'commencement day', or
(ii) the rights and duties under a currency contract are ones to which it becomes entitled and subject after that day.
The 'commencement day' for a company is the first day of its first accounting period to begin after the day before an appointed day.

[9]   Inserted by FA 1994, 16 Sch 20 with effect in relation to
(a) any dividend paid on or after 1 July 1994;
(b) any foreign source profit consisting of income for, or a chargeable gain for, an accounting period beginning on or after 1 July 1993.

[10]   Substituted by FA 1995, 24 Sch 12 with effect from the day appointed under FA 1993, s 165(7)(b), namely 23 March 1995 (SI 1994 No 3224).
Previously 'subsection (7AA)'.

[11]   Inserted by FA 1995, 24 Sch 11, 12 with effect as in [10] above.

[12]   Substituted by FA 1995, 24 Sch 11 with effect as in [10] above.
Previously 'repayment of corporation tax for the earlier period, no account shall be taken of any increase in the amount of the repayment resulting from'.

[13]   Inserted by FA 1995, 24 Sch 12 in relation to any claim under FA 1993, s 131 (5)(6) as a result of which there is an amount of surplus advance corporation tax in an accounting period ending after 30 September 1993, (subject to FA 1995 24 Sch 12 (5)).

[14]   Substituted by FA 1994, 19 Sch 42 with effect for accounting period ending after the appointed day (1 July 1999).
Previously 'section 10'.

[15]   Substituted by FA 1996, s 173 in relation to any loan or advance made in an accounting period ending on or after 31 March 1996.
Previously
'the date on which the loan or advance (or part thereof) is repaid, or'.

[16]   Substituted by FA 1996, 14 Sch 48 with effect in relation to accounting periods ending after 31 March 1996 but subject to transitional provisions in FA 1996, 15 Sch.
Previously 'a relievable amount within the meaning of section 131 of the Finance Act 1993 (non-trading exchange gains and losses),'.

[17]   Substituted by FA 1996, 14 Sch 48 as in [16] above.
Previously 'subsection (5) or (6) of that section the whole or part of the relievable amount for the later period is set off against the exchange profits (as defined in subsection (10) of that section)'.

[18]   Substituted by FA 1996, 14 Sch 48 as in [16] above.
Previously 'subsection (5) or (6) (as the case may be) of that section'.

[19]   Substituted by FA 1996, 14 Sch 48 as in [16] above.
Previously 'section 131(5) or (6) of the Finance Act 1993'.

[20]   Repealed by F(No 2)A 1997, 8 Sch but only where the earlier period (see (7B)(b) below) begins on or after 2 July 1997.
Previously
In any case where –

(a)   a company carrying on a trade incurs a loss in the trade in an accounting period ('the later period'),

(b)   as a result of a claim under section 242, the whole or any part of a surplus of franked investment income for an earlier accounting period (the 'earlier period') which does not fall wholly within the period of twelve months immediately preceding the later period is treated as there mentioned for the purpose of setting the loss against total profits under section 393A(1), and

(c)   a payment falls to be made of the whole or part of a tax credit comprised in franked investment income received by the company in the earlier period,

then, in determining the amount of interest (if any) payable under this section on the payment referred to in paragraph (c) above, no account shall be taken of [so much of the amount of that payment as falls to be made][b] as a result of the claim under section 242 (to the extent that that section relates to section 393A(1)), except so far as concerns interest for any time after the date on which any corporation tax for the later period became (or, as the case may be, would have become) due and payable, as mentioned in subsection [(7D) be-low][c].][a]

(a)   Inserted by FA 1991, 15 Sch 23 in relation to losses incurred in accounting periods ended after 31 March 1991.

(b)   Substituted by FA 1993 14 Sch 10(4) with effect in relation to accounting periods ending after 30 September 1993 (SI 1992 No 3066). Previously 'any increase in the amount of that payment'.

(c)   Substituted by FA 1998, 4 Sch 5 with effect where the accounting period whose due a payable date falls to be determined is an acconting period ending on or after the corporation tax self-assessment appointed day (1 July 1999);
Previously '(2) above'.

21   Inserted by FA 1998, 4 Sch 1 with effect from 31 July 1998.

22   Inserted by FA 1998, s 34(2) with effect from 31 July 1998.

23   Inserted by FA 1998, s 34(3) with effect in relation to interest payable by virtue of any paragraph of ICTA 1988, s 826(1) if the accounting period mentioned in that paragraph is one which ends on or after the corporation tax self-assessment appointed day (1 July 1999).

24   Inserted by FA 1998, s 34(4) with effect as in²³ above.

25   Substituted by FA 1998, 4 Sch 2 with effect in relation to accounting periods ending on or after the corporation tax self-assessment appointed day (1 July 1999).
      Previously 'the material date is the date on which corporation tax became (or, as the case may be, would have become) due and payable for the accounting period'.

26   Inserted by FA 1998, 4 Sch 3 with effect as in²⁵ above.

27   Substituted by FA 1998, 4 Sch 5 with effect where the accounting period whose due and payable date falls to be determined is an accounting period ending on or after the corporation tax self-assessment appointed day (1 July 1999).
      Previously '(2) above'.

28   Inserted by FA 1998, 4 Sch 5 with effect as in²⁷ above.

29   Substituted by FA 1990, s 90 with effect in relation to the release or writing off of the whole or part of a debt after 5 April 1999.
      Previously 'the repayment of, or of the part in question of, the loan or advance mentioned in section 419(4) was made'.

30   Inserted by FA 1990, s 90 with effect as in²⁹ above

Notes
(a)   The appointed day for the purposes of this section is 30 September 1993 (SI 1992 No 3066 (The Corporation Tax Acts (Provisions for Payment of Tax and Returns) (Appointed Days) Order 1992)).
(b)   Subsection (2A) is repealed by FA 1998, 3 Sch 38 with effect in relation to accounting periods beginning on or after 6 April 1999.
(c)   Subsection (7) is repealed by FA 1998, 3 Sch 38 with effect where the later period mentioned in that subsection begins on or after 6 April 1999.
(d)   Subsections (7AA) and (7CA) are repealed by FA 1998, 3 Sch 38 where the earlier period mentioned in those subsections begins on or after 6 April 1999.

[826A   Interest on payments in respect of corporation tax and meaning of 'the material date'

(1)   The Treasury may by regulations make provision applying section 826, with such modifications as may be prescribed, for the purpose of conferring on companies of such descriptions as may be prescribed a right to interest–

(a)   on such payments made by them in respect of corporation tax as may be prescribed,

(b)   at the rate applicable under section 178 of the Finance Act 1989, and

(c)   for such period as may be prescribed,

and for treating any such interest for the purposes, or prescribed purposes, of the Tax Acts as interest under section 826(1)(a) on a repayment of corporation tax.

(2)   The Treasury may by regulations make provision modifying section 826(2) in relation to companies of such descriptions as may be prescribed.

(3)   Subsections (1) and (2) above do not apply in relation to companies in relation to which section 826(2) is modified or otherwise affected by

regulations under section 59E of the Management Act (alteration of date on which corporation tax becomes due and payable) in relation to the accounting period to which the corporation tax in question relates.

(4) Where the Treasury make regulations under subsection (2) above in relation to companies of any description, they may also make regulations modifying section 59DA(2) of the Management Act in relation to those companies, or any description of such companies, by varying the date before which the claim there mentioned may not be made.

(5) Regulations under this section–

(a) may make different provision in relation to different cases or circumstances or in relation to companies or accounting periods of different descriptions;

(b) may make such supplementary, incidental, consequential or transitional provision as appears to the Treasury to be necessary or expedient.

(6) Regulations under this section may not make provision in relation to accounting periods ending before the day appointed under section 199 of the Finance Act 1994 for the purpose of Chapter III of Part IV of that Act (corporation tax self-assessment).

(7) In this section 'prescribed' means prescribed by regulations made under this section.][1]

---

[1]   Inserted by FA 1998, 4 Sch 1 with effect from 31 July 1998.

SCHEDULE 24
(Section 747(6))

**ASSUMPTIONS FOR CALCULATING CHARGEABLE PROFITS,
CREDITABLE TAX AND CORRESPONDING UNITED KINGDOM
TAX OF FOREIGN COMPANIES**

General

1 (1) The company shall be assumed to be resident in the United Kingdom.

(2) Nothing in sub-paragraph (1) above requires it to be assumed that there is any change in the place or places at which the company carries on its activities.

(3) For the avoidance of doubt, it is hereby declared that, if any sums forming part of the company's profits for an accounting period have been received by the company without any deduction of or charge to tax [and have been so received by virtue of section 154(2) of the Finance Act 1996][1] the effect of the assumption in sub-paragraph (1) above is that those sums are to be brought within the charge to tax for the purposes of calculating the company's chargeable profits or corresponding United Kingdom tax.

[(3A) In any case where–

(a) it is at any time necessary for any purpose of Chapter IV of Part XVII to determine [in the case of any person][3] the chargeable profits of the company for an accounting period, and

(b) at that time–

(i) [it has not been established in the case of that person that that or any earlier accounting period of the company is an accounting period in respect of which an apportionment under section 747(3) falls to be made, and][4]

(ii) it has not been established [in the case of that person][3] that that or any earlier accounting period of the company is an ADP exempt period,

[in determining the chargeable profits of the company for the accounting period mentioned in paragraph (a) above, it shall be assumed, for the purposes of those provisions of paragraphs 2 and 10 below which refer to the first accounting period in respect of which an apportionment under section 747(3) falls to be made or which is an ADP exempt period, that that period (but not any earlier period) is an accounting period in respect of which such an apportionment falls to be made or which is an ADP exempt period.][5]][2]

(4) In any case where –

(a) it is at any time necessary for any purpose of Chapter IV of Part XVII to determine [in the case of any person][3] the chargeable profits of the company for an accounting period, and

(b) [at that time it has not been established in the case of that person that that or any earlier accounting period of the company is an accounting period in respect of which an apportionment under section 747(3) falls to be made,][6]

[in determining the chargeable profits of the company for the accounting period mentioned in paragraph (a) above, it shall be assumed, for
the purposes of those provisions of paragraph 9 below which refer to the
first accounting period in respect of which an apportionment under
section 747(3) falls to be made, that such an apportionment falls to be
made in respect of that period (but not in respect of any earlier
period).]⁷

(5) Nothing in this Schedule affects any liability for, or the computation of,
corporation tax in respect of a trade which is carried on by a company
resident outside the United Kingdom through a branch or agency in the
United Kingdom.

[(6) Any reference in this Schedule to an 'ADP exempt period', in the case
of any company, is a reference to an accounting period of the company–

(a) which begins on or after 28 November 1995; and

(b) in respect of which the company pursued, within the meaning of
Part I of Schedule 25, an acceptable distribution policy.]²

---

¹ Substituted by FA 1996, 28 Sch 6 for income tax purposes from 1996/97 onwards and for
corporation tax purposes for accounting periods ending after 31 March 1996.
Previously 'by virtue of section 47 or 48'.

² Inserted by FA 1996, 36 Sch 3 in relation to accounting periods of a controlled foreign company
beginning on or after 28 November 1995.

³ Inserted by FA 1998, 17 Sch 17 with effect in relation to accounting periods of companies resident
in the UK which end on or after the corporation tax self-assessment appointed day (1 July 1999).
See FA 1998, 17 Sch 37 for details of the commencement and transitional provisions.

⁴ Substituted by FA 1998, 17 Sch 17 with effect as in ³ above.
Previously 'no direction has been given under section 747(1) with respect to that or any earlier
accounting period of the company, and'.

⁵ Substituted by FA 1998, 17 Sch 17 with effect as in ³ above.
Previously 'in determining the chargeable profits of the company for the accounting period
mentioned in paragraph (a) above it shall be assumed, for the purpose of any of the following
provisions of this Schedule which refer to the first accounting period in respect of which a direction
is given under section 747(1) or which is an ADP exempt period, that that period (but not any
earlier period) is an accounting period in respect of which such a direction is given or which is an
ADP exempt period.'

⁶ Substituted by FA 1998, 17 Sch 17 with effect as in ³ above.
Previously 'at that time no direction has been given under section 747(1) with respect to that or any
earlier accounting period of the company,'.

⁷ Substituted by FA 1998, 17 Sch 17 with effect as in ³ above.
Previously '[in determining the chargeable profits of the company of the accounting period
mentioned in paragraph (a) above]ᵃ it shall be assumed, for the purpose of any of the following
provisions of this Schedule which refer to the first accounting period in respect of which a direction
is given under that section, that such a direction has been given for that period (but not for any
earlier period).'

a   Inserted by FA 1995, 25 Sch 6 and deemed always to have had effect.

---

2   (1) The company shall be assumed to have become resident in the United
Kingdom (and, accordingly, within the charge to corporation tax) at the
beginning of the first accounting period

[(a) in respect of which [an apportionment under section 747(3) falls to
be made]², or

(b) which is an ADP exempt period,

and][1] that United Kingdom residence shall be assumed to continue throughout subsequent accounting periods of the company (whether or not [an apportionment falls to be made][3] in respect of all or any of them) until the company ceases to be controlled by persons resident in the United Kingdom.

(2) Except in so far as the following provisions of this Schedule otherwise provide, for the purposes of calculating a company's chargeable profits or corresponding United Kingdom tax for any accounting period which is not the first such period referred to in sub-paragraph (1) above (and, in particular, for the purpose of applying any relief which is relevant to two or more accounting periods), it shall be assumed that a calculation of chargeable profits or, as the case may be, corresponding United Kingdom tax has been made for every previous accounting period throughout which the company was, by virtue of sub-paragraph (1) above, assumed to have been resident in the United Kingdom.

---

[1] Substituted by FA 1996, 36 Sch 3 in relation to accounting periods of a controlled foreign company beginning on or after 28 November 1995.
Previously 'in respect of which a direction is given under section 747(1)'.

[2] Substituted by FA 1998, 17 Sch 18 with effect in relation to accounting periods of companies resident in the UK which end on or after the corporation tax self-assessment appointed day (1 July 1999). See FA 1998, 17 Sch 37 for details of the commencement and transitional provisions.
Previously 'a direction is given under section 747(1)'.

[3] Substituted by FA 1998, 17 Sch 18 with effect as in [2] above.
Previously 'a direction is given'.

---

3 The company shall be assumed not to be a close company.

4 (1) Subject to sub-paragraph (2) below, where any relief under the Corporation Tax Acts is dependent upon the making of a claim or election, the company shall be assumed to have made that claim or election which would give the maximum amount of relief and to have made that claim or election within any time limit applicable to it.

[(1A) Sub-paragraph (2) below applies to any accounting period of the company –

(a) in respect of which [an apportionment under section 747(3) falls to be made][2]; or

(b) which is an ADP exempt period.][1]

(2) [Where this sub-paragraph applies to an accounting period of the company, then][1] if, by notice [given to an officer of the Board][3] at any time not later than the expiry of [the period of twenty months following the end of the accounting period][4] or within such longer period as the Board may in any particular case allow, the United Kingdom resident company which has or, as the case may be, any two or more United Kingdom resident companies which together have, a majority interest in the company so request, the company shall be assumed –

(a) not to have made any claim or election specified in the notice; or

(b) to have made a claim or election so specified, being different from one assumed by sub-paragraph (1) above but being one which (subject to compliance with any time limit) could have been made in the case of a company within the charge to corporation tax; or

(c) to have disclaimed or required the postponement, in whole or in part, of an allowance if (subject to compliance with any time limit) a company within the charge to corporation tax could have disclaimed the allowance or, as the case may be, required such a postponement.

[(2A) [. . .]⁵

(3) For the purposes of this paragraph, a United Kingdom resident company has, or two or more United Kingdom resident companies together have, a majority interest in the company if on the apportionment of the company's chargeable profits for the relevant accounting period under section 747(3) more than half of the amount of those profits –

(a) which are apportioned to all United Kingdom resident companies, and

(b) which give rise to [any liability]⁶ on any such companies under subsection (4)(a) of that section,

are apportioned to the United Kingdom resident company or companies concerned.

[(3A) Sub-paragraph (3) above shall apply in relation to an accounting period which is an ADP exempt period as it would apply if –

(a) that accounting period had instead been one in respect of which [an apportionment under section 747(3) had fallen to be made]⁷, and

(b) [such apportionments as are mentioned in sub-paragraph (3) above had been made and such liabilities as are mentioned in that sub-paragraph had arisen.]⁸]¹

(4) In sub-paragraph (3) above 'the relevant accounting period' means the accounting period or, as the case may be, the first accounting period in which the relief in question is or would be available in accordance with sub-paragraph (1) above.

---

¹   Inserted by FA 1996, 36 Sch 3 in relation to accounting periods of a controlled foreign company beginning on or after 28 November 1995.

²   Substituted by FA 1998, 17 Sch 19 with effect in relation to accounting periods of companies resident in the UK which end on or after the corporation tax self-assessment appointed day (1 July 1999). See FA 1998, 17 Sch 37 for details of the commencement and transitional provisions. Previously 'a direction is given under section 747(1)'.

³   Substituted by FA 1998, 17 Sch 19 with effect as in ¹ above. Previously 'given to the Board'.

⁴   Substituted by FA 1998, 17 Sch 19 with effect as in 1 above. Previously '[the appropriate period]ᵃ.

    a   Substituted by FA 1996, 36 Sch 3 in relation to accounting periods of a controlled foreign company beginning on or after 28 November 1995. Previously 'the time for making of an appeal under section 753'.

⁵   Deleted by FA 1998, 17 Sch 19 with effect as in ¹ above. Previously 'For the purposes of sub-paragraph (2) above, 'the appropriate period'–

    [(a) in the case of an accounting period in respect of which a direction is given under section 747(1), means the time for the making of an appeal under section 753; and

    (b) in the case of an accounting period which is an ADP exempt period, means the period of twenty months following the end of the accounting period.]ᵃ

^a   Inserted by FA 1996, 36 Sch 3 in relation to accounting periods of a controlled foreign company beginning on or after 28 November 1995.

⁶   Substituted by FA 1998, 17 Sch 19 with effect as in ¹ above. Previously 'any liability'.

⁷   Substituted by FA 1998, 17 Sch 19 with effect as in ¹ above. Previously 'a direction had been duly given under section 747(1)'.

⁸   Substituted by FA 1998, 17 Sch 19 with effect as in ¹ above. Previously 'such apportionments and assessments as are mentioned in sub-paragraph (3) above had been made'.

Group relief etc.

5   The company shall be assumed to be neither a member of a group of companies nor a member of a consortium for the purposes of any provision of the Tax Acts.

6   (1)   In relation to section 247 it shall be assumed –

     (a)   that the conditions for the making of an election under subsection (1) are not fulfilled with respect to dividends paid or received by the company; and

     (b)   that the conditions for the making of an election under subsection (4) are not fulfilled with respect to payments made or received by the company.

     (2)   References in sub-paragraph (1) above to *dividends or* payments re-ceived by the company apply to any received by another person on behalf of or in trust for the company, but not to any received by the company on behalf of or in trust for another person.

Note
(a) Subparagraph (1)(a) and in subparagraph (2) the words 'dividends or' are repealed by FA 1998, 3 Sch 24 with effect in relation to accounting periods of companies resident outside the UK which begin on or after 6 April 1999.

---

7   *The company shall be assumed not to be a subsidiary to which the benefit of any advance corporation tax may be surrendered under section 240.*

Note
(a) This paragraph is repealed by FA 1998, 3 Sch 24 with effect in relation to accounting periods of companies resident outside the UK which begin on or after 6 April 1999.

---

8   **Company reconstructions**

Without prejudice to the operation of section 343 in a case where the company is the predecessor, within the meaning of that section, and a company resident in the United Kingdom is the successor, within the meaning of that section –

     (a)   the assumption that the company is resident in the United Kingdom shall not be regarded as requiring it also to be assumed that the company is within the charge to tax in respect of a trade for the purposes of that section, and

(b)   except in so far as the company is actually within that charge (by carrying on the trade through a branch or agency in the United Kingdom), it shall accordingly be assumed that the company can never be the successor, within the meaning of that section, to another company (whether resident in the United Kingdom or not).

9 Losses in pre-direction accounting periods

(1)   [. . .]³ This paragraph applies in any case where the company incurred a loss in a trade in an accounting period –

(a) which precedes the first accounting period in respect of which [an apportionment under section 747(3) falls to be made]⁴ ('the starting period'); and

(b) which ended less than six years before the beginning of the starting period; and

(c) in which the company was not resident [, and is not to be assumed by virtue of paragraph 2(1)(b) above to have been resident,]¹ in the United Kingdom;

and in this paragraph any such accounting period is referred to as a '[pre-apportionment]² period'.

(2)   [. . .]⁵

(3)   If a claim is made for the purpose by the United Kingdom resident company or companies referred to in paragraph 4(2) above, the chargeable profits (if any) of the company for accounting periods beginning with that [pre-apportionment]² period which is specified in the claim and in which a loss is incurred as mentioned in sub-paragraph (1) above shall be determined (in accordance with the provisions of this Schedule other than this paragraph) on the assumption that that [pre-apportionment]² period was the first accounting period in respect of which [an apportionment under section 747(3) fell to be made]⁶.

(4)   [A claim under sub-paragraph (3) above shall be made by notice given to an officer of the Board within the period of twenty months following the end of the starting period or within such longer period as the Board may in any particular case allow.]⁷

(5)   [. . .]⁸

(6)   [. . .]⁹

[(7) Nothing in–

(a) paragraph 10 of Schedule 18 to the Finance Act 1998 (claims or elections in company tax returns), or

(b) Schedule 1A to the Management Act (claims or elections not included in returns),

shall apply, whether by virtue of section 754 or otherwise, to a claim under sub-paragraph (3) above.]¹⁰

---

¹   Inserted by FA 1996, 36 Sch 3 in relation to accounting periods of a controlled foreign company beginning on or after 28 November 1995.

²   Substituted by FA 1998, 17 Sch 19 with effect in relation to accounting periods of companies resident in the UK which end on or after the corporation tax self-assessment appointed day (1 July 1999). See FA 1998, 17 Sch 37 for details of the commencement and transitional provisions. Previously 'pre-direction'.

³   Deleted by FA 1998, 17 Sch 19 with effect as in ² above. Previously 'Subject to sub-paragraph (2) below'.

⁴   Substituted by FA 1998, 17 Sch 19 with effect as in ² above. Previously 'Subject to sub-paragraph (2) below'.

⁵   Deleted by FA 1998, 17 Sch 19 with effect as in ² above. Previously 'This paragraph does not apply in any case where a declaration is made under paragraph 11(3) below specifying an accounting period of the company which begins before, or is the same as, the first pre-direction period in which the company incurred a loss as mentioned in sub-paragraph (1) above.'

⁶   Substituted by FA 1998, 17 Sch 19 with effect as in ² above. Previously 'a direction was given under section 747(1)'.

⁷   Substituted by FA 1998, 17 Sch 19 with effect as in ² above. Previously 'A claim under sub-paragraph (3) above shall be made by notice given to the Board within 60 days of the date of notice under subsection (1) or subsection (3) of section 753 relating to the starting period or within such longer period as the Board may in any particular case allow.'

⁸   Deleted by FA 1998, 17 Sch 19 with effect as in ² above. Previously 'For the purposes of a claim under sub-paragraph (3) above, it shall be assumed that Chapter IV of Part XVII was in force before the beginning of the first of the pre-direction periods.'

⁹   Deleted by FA 1998, 17 Sch 19 with effect as in ² above. Previously 'In determining for the purposes of this paragraph which accounting period of the company is the starting period, no account should be taken of the effect of any declaration under paragraph 11(3) below.'

Capital allowances

10 (1)   [Subject to paragraph 12 below]⁴, if, in an accounting period falling before the beginning of the first accounting period

[(a) in respect of which [an apportionment under 747(3) falls to be made]⁵, or

(b) which is an ADP exempt period,

the]³ company incurred any capital expenditure on the provision of machinery or plant for the purposes of its trade, that machinery or plant shall be assumed, for the purposes of [Part II of the 1990 Act]¹, to have been provided for purposes wholly other than those of the trade and not to have been brought into use for the purposes of that trade until the beginning of that first accounting period, and [section 81 of]² that Act (expenditure treated as equivalent to market value at the time the machinery or plant is brought into use) shall apply accordingly.

(2)   This paragraph shall be construed as one with [Part II of the 1990 Act]¹.

---

¹   Substituted by CAA 1990, 1 Sch 8(42) with effect for chargeable periods ending after 5 April 1990. Previously 'Chapter I of Part III of the Finance Act 1971'.

²   Substituted by CAA 1990, 1 Sch 8(42) with effect as in ¹ above. Previously 'paragraph 7 of Schedule 8 to'.

³   Substituted by FA 1996, 36 Sch 3 in relation to accounting periods of a controlled foreign company beginning on or after 28 November 1995.

Previously 'in respect of which a direction is given under section 747(1), the'.

4   Substituted by FA 1998,17 Sch 21 with effect in relation to accounting periods of companies
     resident in the UK which end on or after the corporation tax self-assessment appointed day (1 July
     1999). See FA 1998, 17 Sch 37 for details of commencement and transitional provisions.
     Previously 'subject to paragraphs 11 and 12 below'.

5   Substituted by FA 1998, 17 Sch 21 with effect as in ⁴ above.
     Previously 'a direction if given under section 747(1)'.

---

11   [. . .]¹

---

¹   Repealed by FA 1998, 17 Sch 22 with effect in relation to accounting periods of companies resident
     in the UK which end on or after the corporation tax self-assessment appointed day (1 July 1999).
     See FA 1998, 17 Sch 37 for details of commencement and transitional provisions.
     Previously

     '(1) This paragraph applies in any case where it appears to the Board that the reason why no
     direction was given under section 747(1) in respect of an accounting period which precedes the
     starting period was that the effect of any allowance which would be assumed for that preceding
     period by virtue of this Schedule would be such that –

     (a) the company would not have been considered to be subject in that accounting period to a
         lower level of taxation in the territory in which it was resident; or

     (b) the company would have had no chargeable profits for that accounting period; or

     (c) the chargeable profits of the company for that accounting period would not have exceeded
         £20,000 or such smaller amount as was appropriate in accordance with section
         748(1)(d).

     (2) In this paragraph 'the starting period' means the first accounting period

     [(a) in respect of which a direction is given under section 747(1), or

     (b) which is an ADP exempt period,

     and]ᵇ, in a case where a claim is made under sub-paragraph (3) of paragraph 9 above, no
     account shall be taken of the effect of that sub-paragraph in determining which accounting
     period is the starting period for the purposes of this paragraph.

     (3) If, in a case where this paragraph applies, the Board so declare by notice given to every
     company to which, in accordance with section 753(1), notice of the making of the direction
     relating to the starting period is required to be given, the chargeable profits of that period and
     every subsequent accounting period and the corresponding United Kingdom tax for every
     subsequent accounting period shall be determined (in accordance with the provisions of this
     Schedule other than this paragraph) on the assumption that the accounting period specified in
     the declaration was the first accounting period in respect of which a direction was given and,
     accordingly, as if allowances had been assumed in respect of that accounting period and any
     subsequent accounting period which precedes the starting period.

     (4) Nothing in sub-paragraph (3) above affects the operation of paragraph 9(3) above in a case
     where the accounting period specified in a claim under paragraph 9(3) above begins before the
     period specified in a declaration under sub-paragraph (3) above.

     (5) Subject to sub-paragraph (6) below, the Board shall not make a declaration under sub-
     paragraph (3) above with respect to an accounting period which precedes the starting period
     unless the facts are such that –

     (a) assuming the company to have been subject in that period to a lower level of taxation in the
         territory in which it was resident, and

     (b) assuming the company to have had in that period chargeable profits of such an amount that
         the condition in section 748(1)(d) would not be fulfilled,

     a direction could have been given in respect of that period under section 747(1).

     (6) In its application to a company falling within section 749(3), sub-paragraph (5) above shall
     have effect with the omission of paragraph (a).

     (7) In this paragraph 'allowance' means an allowance under [Part I or II of the 1990 Act]ᵃ'

a   Substituted by CAA 1990, 1 Sch 8(42) with effect for chargeable periods ending after 5
April 1990.
Previously 'Chapter I of Part I of the 1968 Act or Chapter I of Part III of the Finance Act
1971'.

b   Substituted by FA 1996, 36 Sch 3 in relation to accounting periods of a controlled foreign
company beginning on or after 28 November 1995.
Previously 'in respect of which a direction is given under section 747(1) and,'.

11A   [. . .]¹

---

¹   Repealed by FA 1998, 17 Sch 23 with effect in relation to accounting periods of companies resident
in the UK which end on or after the corporation tax self-assessment appointed day (1 July 1999).
See FA 1998, 17 Sch 37 for details of commencement and transitional provisions.
Previously
'(1) This paragraph applies where by virtue of section 747A the company's chargeable profits for
an accounting period (the period in question) are to be computed and expressed in a currency
(the relevant foreign currency) other than sterling.

(2) For the the purposes of making in relation to the period in question any calculation which –

(a) falls to be made under the enactments relating to capital allowances, and

(b) takes account of amounts arrived at under those enactments in relation to accounting
periods falling before the company's commencement day (within the meaning given by
section 747A(9)),

it shall be assumed that any such amount is the equivalent, expressed in the relevant foreign
currency, of the amount expressed in sterling.

(3) For the purposes of the application in relation to the period in question of paragraph 11(1)(c)
above, it shall be assumed that the company's chargeable profits for the period are the sterling
equivalent of its chargeable profits found in the relevant foreign currency.

(4) For the purposes of the application of section 34, 35 or 96 of the 1990 Act (motor cars and
dwelling-houses) in relation to expenditure incurred in the period in question, it shall be
assumed that any sterling sum mentioned in any of those sections is the equivalent, expressed
in the relevant foreign currency, of the amount expressed in sterling.

(5) The translation required by sub-paragraph (2) above shall be made by reference to the London
closing exchange rate for the two currencies concerned for the first day of the period in
question.

(6) The translation required by sub-paragraph (3) above shall be made by reference to the London
closing exchange rate for the two currencies concerned for the first day of the period in
question.

(7) The translation required by sub-paragraph (4) above shall be made by reference to the London
closing exchange rate for the two currencies concerned for the day on which the expenditure
concerned was incurred.]ᵃ'

a   Inserted by FA 1995, 25 Sch 6(4) with effect from 1 May 1995.

---

12   Unremittable overseas income

For the purposes of the application of section 584 to the company's income
it shall be assumed –

(a)   that any reference in paragraph (a) or paragraph (b) of subsection
(1) of that section to the United Kingdom is a reference to both the
United Kingdom and the territory in which the company is in fact
resident; and

(b)   that a notice under subsection (2) of that section (expressing a wish
to be assessed in accordance with that subsection) may be given on

behalf of the company by the United Kingdom resident company
or companies referred to in paragraph 4(2) above.

Exchange gains and losses

The appointment day for the purposes of the application of FA 1993, Chapter II, Part II is 23 March 1995 (SI 1994 No 3224).

[13   Paragraphs 14 to 19 below apply for the purposes of the application of Chapter II of Part II of the Finance Act 1993.][1]

---

[1]   Inserted by FA 1995, 25 Sch 6 with effect from 1 May 1995.

---

14 (1)   This paragraph applies where –

(a)   by virtue of section 747A the company's chargeable profits for an accounting period are to be computed and expressed in a particular currency (the relevant currency),

(b)   in an accrual period an asset or contract was held, or a liability was owed, by the company, and

(c)   the accrual period falls within or constitutes the accounting period concerned.

(2)   It shall be assumed that –

(a)   the local currency for the purposes of sections 125 to 127 of the Finance Act 1993 is the relevant currency, and

(b)   section 149 of that Act (local currency to be used) does not apply as regards the accrual period concerned.][1]

---

[1]   Inserted by FA 1995, 25 Sch 6 with effect from 1 May 1995.

[15   Where the accounting period mentioned in section 139(1) of the Finance Act 1993 is one for which, by virtue of section 747A, the company's chargeable profits are to be computed and expressed in a currency other than sterling –

(a)   section 142(1) to (4) of that Act shall be assumed not to apply as regards that period;

(b)   section 142(5) and (6) of that Act shall be assumed not to apply as regards the next accounting period of the company.][1]

---

[1]   Inserted by FA 1995, 25 Sch 6 with effect from 1 May 1995.

[16 (1)   This paragraph applies where the last relevant accounting period for the purposes of section 146 of the Finance Act 1993 is one for which by virtue of section 747A the company's chargeable profits are to be computed and expressed in a particular currency (the relevant currency).

(2) Subsections (10), (11) and (14) of section 146 of the Finance Act 1993 shall be assumed not to apply.]¹

---

¹   Inserted by FA 1995, 25 Sch 6 with effect from 1 May 1995.

[17   Where by virtue of section 747A the company's chargeable profits for an accounting period are to be computed and expressed in a particular currency, the references in section 148(9) of the Finance Act 1993 to sterling shall be assumed to be references to that particular currency.]¹

---

¹   Inserted by FA 1995, 25 Sch 6 with effect from 1 May 1995.

[18 (1) This paragraph applies where the accounting period mentioned in paragraph (b) of subsection (11) of section 153 of the Finance Act 1993 is one for which, by virtue of section 747A, the company's chargeable profits are to be computed and expressed in a particular currency (the relevant currency).

(2) That subsection shall have effect as if the reference to the local currency of the trade for the accounting period were a reference to the relevant currency.]¹

---

¹   Inserted by FA 1995, 25 Sch 6 with effect from 1 May 1995.

[19 (1) This paragraph applies where –

(a) Chapter II of Part II of the Finance Act 1993 falls to be applied as regards an accounting period of the company;

(b) under that Chapter, an exchange gain or an exchange loss accrued to the company for an accrual period constituting or falling within an earlier accounting period of the company, and

(c) the accounting period mentioned in paragraph (b) above falls before the company's first relevant accounting period.

(2) It shall be assumed, for the purposes of applying Chapter II of Part II of the Finance Act 1993 as respects the accounting period mentioned in sub-paragraph (1)(a) above, that the exchange gain or loss mentioned in sub-paragraph (1)(b) above never existed.

(3) In sub-paragraph (1) above –

(a) references to an exchange gain are to an exchange gain of a trade or an exchange gain of part of a trade or a non-trading exchange gain;

(b) references to an exchange loss are to an exchange loss of a trade or an exchange loss of part of a trade or a non-trading exchange loss;

(c) the reference in sub-paragraph (1)(b) to an exchange gain or an exchange loss accruing is to the gain or loss accruing before the application of any of sections 131, 136, 137 and 140 of the Finance Act 1993 in relation to the accounting period mentioned in sub-paragraph (1)(b);

(d) references to the first relevant accounting period of the company shall be construed in accordance with section 747A.][1]

---

[1]   Inserted by FA 1995, 25 Sch 6 with effect from 1 May 1995.

[20   Transfer pricing

(1) Sub-paragraph (2) of paragraph 5 of Schedule 28AA (no potential UK tax advantage where both parties are within charge to income or corporation tax etc) shall be assumed not to apply in any case where, apart from that sub-paragraph (and on the assumption in paragraph 1(1) above),–

     (a) paragraph 6 of that Schedule would apply; and

     (b) the company would be the disadvantaged person for the purposes of that paragraph.

(2) Schedule 28AA (transfer pricing etc: provision not at arm's length) shall be assumed not to apply in any case where, apart from this sub-paragraph,–

     (a) the actual provision would (on the assumption in paragraph 1(1) above) confer a potential advantage in relation to United Kingdom taxation on the company;

     (b) the other affected person would be a company resident outside the United Kingdom; and

     (c) each accounting period of that company which falls wholly or partly within the accounting period in question is one as regards which–

         (i) an apportionment under section 747(3) falls to be made; or

         (ii) no such apportionment falls to be made by virtue of the period being an ADP exempt period.

(3) In any case where–

     (a) by virtue of sub-paragraph (2) above, Schedule 28AA is assumed not to apply, and

     (b) the actual provision mentioned in paragraph (a) of that sub-paragraph involves (on the assumption in paragraph 1(1) above) any such interest or other distribution out of assets as would constitute a distribution for the purposes of the Corporation Tax Acts by virtue of paragraph (da) of section 209(2),

that interest or distribution out of assets shall be assumed not to constitute such a distribution by virtue of that paragraph.][1]

---

[1]   Inserted by FA 1998, 17 Sch 24 with effect in relation to accounting periods of companies resident in the UK which end on or after the corporatioin tax self-assessment appointed day (1 July 1999). See FA 1998, 17 Sch 37 for details of commencement and transitional provisions.

Taxation of Chargeable Gains Act 1992

117   Meaning of 'qualifying corporate bond'

[(A1)   For the purposes of corporation tax 'qualifying corporate bond' means (subject to sections 117A and 117B below) any asset representing a loan relationship of a company; and for purposes other than those of corporation tax references to a qualifying corporate bond shall be construed in accordance with the following provisions of this section.]²

(1)   For the purposes of this section, a 'corporate bond' is a security, as defined in section 132(3)(b)–

(a)   the debt on which represents and has at all times represented a normal commercial loan; and

(b)   which is expressed in sterling and in respect of which no provision is made for conversion into, or redemption in, a currency other than sterling,

and in paragraph (a) above 'normal commercial loan' has the meaning which would be given by sub-paragraph (5) of paragraph 1 of Schedule 18 to the Taxes Act if for paragraph (a)(i) to (iii) of that sub-paragraph there were substituted the words 'corporate bonds (within the meaning of section 117 of the 1992 Act)'.

(2)   For the purposes of subsection (1)(b) above–

(a)   a security shall not be regarded as expressed in sterling if the amount of sterling falls to be determined by reference to the value at any time of any other currency or asset; and

(b)   a provision for redemption in a currency other than sterling but at the rate of exchange prevailing at redemption shall be disregarded.

[(2AA)   For the purposes of this section 'corporate bond' also includes any asset which is not included in the definition in subsection (1) above and which is a relevant discounted security for the purposes of Schedule 13 to the Finance Act 1996.]²

(2A)(3)   [. . .]³

(4)   For the purposes of this section 'corporate bond' also includes a share in a building society–

(a)   which is a qualifying share,

(b)   which is expressed in sterling, and

(c)   in respect of which no provision is made for conversion into, or redemption in, a currency other than sterling.

(5)   For the purposes of subsection (4) above, a share in a building society is a qualifying share if–

(a)   it is a permanent interest bearing share, or

(b) it is of a description specified in regulations made by the Treasury for the purposes of this paragraph.

(6) Subsection (2) above applies for the purposes of subsection (4) above as it applies for the purposes of subsection (1)(b) above, treating the reference to a security as a reference to a share.

[(6A) For the purposes of this section 'corporate bond' also includes, except in relation to a person who acquires it on or after a disposal in relation to which section 115 has or has had effect in accordance with section 116(10)(c), any debenture issued on or after 16 March 1993 which is not a security (as defined in section 132) but–

(a) is issued in circumstances such that it would fall by virtue of section 251(6) to be treated for the purposes of section 251 as such a security; and

(b) would be a corporate bond if it were a security as so defined.]¹

[(6B) An excluded indexed security issued on or after 6 April 1996 is not a corporate bond for the purposes of this section; and an excluded indexed security issued before that date shall be taken to be such a bond for the purposes of this section only if–

(a) it would be so taken apart from this subsection; and

(b) the question whether it should be so taken arises for the purposes of section 116(10).

(6C) In subsection (6B) above 'excluded indexed security' has the same meaning as in Schedule 13 to the Finance Act 1996 (relevant discounted securities).]²

(7) Subject to subsections (9) and (10) below, for the purposes of this Act, a corporate bond–

(a) is a 'qualifying' corporate bond if it is issued after 13 March 1984; and

(b) becomes a 'qualifying' corporate bond if, having been issued on or before that date, it is acquired by any person after that date and that acquisition is not as a result of a disposal which is excluded for the purposes of this subsection, or which was excluded for the purposes of section 64(4) of the Finance Act 1984.

(8) Where a person disposes of a corporate bond which was issued on or before 13 March 1984 and, before the disposal, the bond had not become a qualifying corporate bond, the disposal is excluded for the purposes of subsection (7) above if, by virtue of any enactment–

(a) the disposal is treated for the purposes of this Act as one on which neither a gain nor a loss accrues to the person making the disposal; or

(b) the consideration for the disposal is treated for the purposes of this Act as reduced by an amount equal to the held-over gain on that disposal, as defined for the purposes of section 165 or 260.

[(8A) A corporate bond falling within subsection (2AA) above is a qualifying corporate bond whatever its date of issue.]²

(9)(10) [. . .]⁴

(11) For the purposes of this section–

(a) where a security is comprised in a letter of allotment or similar instrument and the right to the security thereby conferred remains provisional until accepted, the security shall not be treated as issued until there has been acceptance; and

(b) 'permanent interest bearing share' has the same meaning as in the Building Societies (Designated Capital Resources) (Permanent Interest Bearing Shares) Order 1991 [as if that Order were still in force, with the modification that, for references to 'the first criterion' wherever they appear (including definitions) there are substituted references to 'the second criterion']⁵.

(12) The Treasury may by regulations provide that for the definition of the expression 'permanent interest bearing share' in subsection (11) above (as it has effect for the time being) there shall be substituted a different definition of that expression, and regulations under this subsection or subsection (5)(b) above may contain such supplementary, incidental, consequential or transitional provision as the Treasury thinks fit.

(13) This section shall have effect for the purposes of section 254 with the omission of subsections (4) to (6), (11) and (12).

---

¹   Inserted by FA 1993, s 84(1) in relation to any chargeable period ending on or after 16 March 1993.

²   Inserted by FA 1996, 14 Sch 61 for corporation tax purposes in relation to accounting periods ending after 31 March 1996 and for income tax purposes in relation to 1996/97 and subsequent years of assessment (but subject to transitional provisions in FA 1996, 15 Sch).

³   Repealed by FA 1996, 41 Sch Part V(3) as in ² above.
     Previously
'[(2A)Where it falls to be decided whether at any time on or after 29 November 1994 a security (whenever issued) is a corporate bond for the purposes of this section, a security which falls within paragraph 2(2)(c) of Schedule 11 to the Finance Act 1989 (quoted indexed securities) shall be treated as not being a corporate bond within the definition in subsection (1) above.]ᵃ

     (3) For the purposes of this section 'corporate bond' also includes a security which is not included in the definition in subsection (1) above, and which–

     (a) is a deep gain security for the purposes of Schedule 11 to the Finance Act 1989 ('the 1989 Act'), or

     (b) by virtue of paragraph 21(2) of Schedule 11 to the 1989 Act falls to be treated as a deep gain security as there mentioned, or

     (c) by virtue of paragraph 22(2) of that Schedule, falls to be treated as a deep gain security as there mentioned, or

     (d) by virtue of paragraph 22A(2) or 22B(3) of that Schedule, falls to be treated as a deep gain security as mentioned in the paragraph concerned.'

     ᵃ   Inserted by FA 1995, s 50.

⁴   Repealed by FA 1996, 41 Sch Part V(3) as in ² above.
     Previously
'(9)   Subject to subsection (10) below, for the purposes of this Act–

     (a)   a corporate bond which falls within subsection (3)(a) above is a qualifying corporate bond, whatever the date of its issue;

     (b)   a corporate bond which falls within subsection (3)(b) above is a qualifying corporate bond as regards a disposal made after the time mentioned in paragraph 21(1)(c) of Schedule 11 to the 1989 Act, whatever the date of its issue;

     (c)   a corporate bond which falls within subsection (3)(c) above is a qualifying corporate bond as regards a disposal made after the time the agreement mentioned in paragraph 22(1)(b) of that Schedule is made, whatever the date of its issue;

(d) a corporate bond which falls within subsection (3)(d) above is a qualifying corporate bond as regards a disposal made after the time mentioned in paragraph 22A(1)(c) or 22B(2)(b) of that Schedule (as the case may be);

and subsections (7) and (8) above shall not apply in the case of any such bond.

(10) A security which is issued by a member of a group of companies to another member of the same group is not a qualifying corporate bond for the purposes of this Act except in relation to a disposal by a person who (at the time of the disposal) is not a member of the same group as the company which issued the security; and references in this subsection to a group of companies or to a member of a group shall be construed in accordance with section 170(2) to (14).'

[5] Inserted by the Capital Gains Tax (Definitions of Permanent Interest Bearing Share) Regulations (SI 1999 No 1953) with effect from 29 July 1999.

---

128 Consideration given or received by holder

(1) Subject to subsection (2) below, where, on a reorganisation, a person gives or becomes liable to give any consideration for his new holding or any part of it, that consideration shall in relation to any disposal of the new holding or any part of it be treated as having been given for the original shares, and if the new holding or part of it is disposed of with a liability attaching to it in respect of that consideration, the consideration given for the disposal shall be adjusted accordingly.

(2) There shall not be treated as consideration given for the new holding or any part of it–

(a) any surrender, cancellation or other alteration of the original shares or of the rights attached thereto, or

(b) any consideration consisting of any application, in paying up the new holding or any part of it, of assets of the company or of any dividend or other distribution declared out of those assets but not made,

and, in the case of a reorganisation on or after 10 March 1981, any consideration given for the new holding or any part of it otherwise than by way of a bargain made at arm's length shall be disregarded to the extent that its amount or value exceeds the relevant increase in value; and for this purpose 'the relevant increase in value' means the amount by which the market value of the new holding immediately after the reorganisation exceeds the market value of the original shares immediately before the reorganisation.

(3) Where on a reorganisation a person receives (or is deemed to receive), or becomes entitled to receive, any consideration, other than the new holding, for the disposal of an interest in the original shares, and in particular–

(a) where under section 122 he is to be treated as if he had in consideration of a capital distribution disposed of an interest in the original shares, or

(b) where he receives (or is deemed to receive) consideration from other shareholders in respect of a surrender of rights derived from the original shares,

he shall be treated as if the new holding resulted from his having for that consideration disposed of an interest in the original shares (but without prejudice to the original shares and the new holding being treated in accordance with section 127 as the same asset).

(4) Where for the purpose of subsection (3) above it is necessary in computing the gain or loss accruing on the disposal of the interest in the original shares mentioned in that subsection to apportion the cost of acquisition of the original shares between what is disposed of and what is retained, the apportionment shall be made in the like manner as under section 129.

129 Part disposal of new holding

Subject to section 130(2), where for the purpose of computing the gain or loss accruing to a person from the acquisition and disposal of any part of the new holding it is necessary to apportion the cost of acquisition of any of the original shares between what is disposed of and what is retained, the apportionment shall be made by reference to market value at the date of the disposal (with such adjustment of the market value of any part of the new holding as may be required to offset any liability attaching thereto but forming part of the cost to be apportioned).

130 Composite new holdings

(1) This section shall apply to a new holding–

(a) if it consists of more than one class of shares in or debentures of the company and one or more of those classes is of shares or debentures which, at any time not later than the end of the period of 3 months beginning with the date on which the reorganisation took effect, or of such longer period as the Board may by notice allow, had quoted market values on a recognised stock exchange in the United Kingdom or elsewhere, or

(b) if it consists of more than one class of rights of unit holders and one or more of those classes is of rights the prices of which were published daily by the managers of the scheme at any time not later than the end of that period of 3 months (or longer if so allowed).

(2) Where for the purpose of computing the gain or loss accruing to a person from the acquisition and disposal of the whole or any part of any class of shares or debentures or rights of unit holders forming part of a new holding to which this section applies it is necessary to apportion costs of acquisition between what is disposed of and what is retained, the cost of acquisition of the new holding shall first be apportioned between the entire classes of shares or debentures or rights of which it consists by reference to market value on the first day (whether that day fell before the reorganisation took effect or later) on which market values or prices were quoted or published for the shares, debentures or rights as mentioned in subsection (1)(a) or (1)(b) above (with such adjustment of the market value of any class as may be required to offset any liability attaching thereto but forming part of the cost to be apportioned).

(3) For the purposes of this section the day on which a reorganisation involving the allotment of shares or debentures or unit holders' rights takes effect is the day following the day on which the right to renounce any allotment expires.

135 Exchange of securities for those in another company

(1) Subsection (3) below has effect where a company ('company A') issues shares or debentures to a person in exchange for shares in or debentures of another company ('company B') and–

    (a) company A holds, or in consequence of the exchange will hold, more than one-quarter of the ordinary share capital (as defined in section 832(1) of the Taxes Act) of company B, or

    (b) company A issues the shares or debentures in exchange for shares as the result of a general offer–

        (i) which is made to members of company B or any class of them (with or without exceptions for persons connected with company A), and

        (ii) which is made in the first instance on a condition such that if it were satisfied company A would have control of company B [, or

    (c) company A holds, or in consequence of the exchange will hold, the greater part of the voting power in company B.][1]

(2) Subsection (3) below also has effect where under section 136 persons are to be treated as exchanging shares or debentures held by them in consequence of the arrangement there mentioned.

(3) Subject to sections 137 and 138, sections 127 to 131 shall apply with any necessary adaptations as if the 2 companies mentioned in subsection (1) above or, as the case may be, in section 136 were the same company and the exchange were a reorganisation of its share capital.

---

[1]   Inserted by F(No 2)A 1992, s 35(1) and always deemed to have had effect.

---

136 Reconstruction or amalgamation involving issue of securities

(1) Where—

    (a) an arrangement between a company and the persons holding shares in or debentures of the company, or any class of such shares or debentures, is entered into for the purposes of or in connection with a scheme of reconstruction or amalgamation, and

    (b) under the arrangement another company issues shares or debentures to those persons in respect of and in proportion to (or as nearly as may be in proportion to) their holdings of shares in or debentures of the first-mentioned company, but the shares in or debentures of the first-mentioned company are either retained by those persons or cancelled,

    then those persons shall be treated as exchanging the first-mentioned shares or debentures for those held by them in consequence of the arrangement (any shares or debentures retained being for this purpose regarded as if they had been cancelled and replaced by a new issue), and subsections (2) and (3) of section 135 shall apply accordingly.

(2) In this section 'scheme of reconstruction or amalgamation' means a scheme for the reconstruction of any company or companies or the amalgamation of any 2 or more companies, and references to shares or

debentures being retained include their being retained with altered rights or in an altered form whether as the result of reduction, consolidation, division or otherwise.

(3) This section, and section 135(2), shall apply in relation to a company which has no share capital as if references to shares in or debentures of a company included references to any interests in the company possessed by members of the company.

Finance Act 1993

Interest: general

60   Certain interest not allowed as a deduction

(1) This section applies where—

    (a) a qualifying company becomes subject to a qualifying debt, and

    (b) the interest payable exceeds a commercial return on the capital repayable, expressing that capital in the settlement currency of the debt.

(2) In computing the corporation tax chargeable for an accounting period of the company, so much of the excess interest as is paid in the accounting period shall not be allowed as a deduction against the total profits for the period (if it would be allowed apart from this section).

(3) In this section—

"qualifying company" has the meaning given by section 152 below;
"qualifying debt" has the meaning given by section 153(10) below;
"settlement currency", in relation to a debt, shall be construed in accordance with section 161 below.

(4) This section applies where the company becomes subject to the debt 000(whether as the original debtor or otherwise) on or after the day which is its commencement day for the purposes of section 165 below.

[92   The basic rule: sterling to be used

(1) Where a company carries on a business, the profits or losses of the business for an accounting period shall for the purposes of corporation tax be computed and expressed in sterling; but this is subject to section 93 below.

(2) In this section—

'losses' includes management expenses and any allowances falling to be made under section 28 or 61(1) of the Capital Allowances Act 1990;
'profits' includes gains, income and any charges falling to be made under section 28 or 61(1) of that Act.

93   Use of currency other than sterling

(1) This section applies where in an accounting period a company carries on a business and either the first condition or the second condition is fulfilled.

(2) The first condition is that—

(a) the accounts of the company as a whole are prepared in a currency other than sterling in accordance with normal accounting practice; and

(b) in the case of a company which is not resident in the United Kingdom, the company makes a return of accounts for its branch in the United Kingdom prepared in such a currency in accordance with such practice.

(3) The second condition is that—

(a) the accounts of the company as a whole are prepared in sterling but, so far as relating to the business, they are prepared, using the closing rate/net investment method, from financial statements prepared in a currency other than sterling; or

(b) in the case of a company which is not resident in the United Kingdom, the company makes a return of accounts for its branch in the United Kingdom prepared in sterling but, so far as relating to the business, it is prepared, using that method, from financial statements prepared in such a currency.

(4) The profits or losses of the business for an accounting period shall for the purposes of corporation tax be found by—

(a) taking the amount of all the profits and losses of the business for the period computed and expressed in the relevant foreign currency;

(b) taking account of any of the following which are so computed and expressed—

(i) any management expenses brought forward under section 75(3) of the Taxes Act 1988 from an earlier accounting period;

(ii) any losses of the business brought forward under section 392B or 393 of that Act from such a period; and

(iii) any non-trading deficits on loan relationships brought forward under section 83 of the Finance Act 1996 from the previous accounting period; and

(c) taking the sterling equivalent of the amount found by applying paragraphs (a) and (b) above.

(5) In the application of section 22B, 34, 35, 38C, 38D or 79A of the Capital Allowances Act 1990 for the purposes of subsection (4)(a) or (b) above, it shall be assumed that any sterling amount mentioned in any of those sections is its equivalent expressed in the relevant foreign currency.

(6) Where in an accounting period—

(a) a company carries on different parts of a business through different branches (whether within or outside the United Kingdom); and

(b) this section would apply differently in relation to different parts if they were separate businesses,

those parts shall be treated for the purposes of this section as if they were separate businesses for that period.

(7) In this section, unless the context otherwise requires—

'accounts', in relation to a company, means—

(a) the annual accounts of the company prepared in accordance with Part VII of the Companies Act 1985 or Part VIII of the Companies (Northern Ireland) Order 1986; or

(b) if the company is not required to prepare such accounts, the accounts which it is required to keep under the law of its home State; or

(c) if the company is not so required to keep accounts, such of its accounts as most closely correspond to accounts which it would have been required to prepare if the provisions of that Part applied to it;

'branch' includes any collection of assets and liabilities;
'the closing rate/net investment method' means the method so called as described under the title 'Foreign currency translation' in the Statement of Standard Accounting Practice issued in April 1983 by the Institute of Chartered Accountants in England and Wales;
'home State', in relation to a company, means the country or territory under whose laws the company is incorporated;
'losses' has the same meaning as in section 92 above except that it does not include allowable losses within the meaning of the Taxation of Chargeable Gains Act 1992;
'profits' has the same meaning as in section 92 above except that it does not include chargeable gains within the meaning of that Act;
'the relevant foreign currency' means the currency other than sterling or, where the first condition is fulfilled and two different such currencies are involved, the currency in which the return of accounts is prepared;
'return of accounts', in relation to a branch in the United Kingdom, means a return of such accounts of the branch as may be required by the Inland Revenue under paragraph 3 of Schedule 18 to the Finance Act 1998 (company tax returns, assessments and related matters).

94 Rules for ascertaining currency equivalents

(1) Any receipt or expense which is to be taken into account in making a computation under subsection (1) of section 92 above for an accounting period, and is denominated in a currency other than sterling, shall be translated into its sterling equivalent—

(a) if either of the conditions mentioned in subsection (2) below is fulfilled, by reference to the rate used in the preparation of the accounts of the company as a whole for that period;

(b) if neither of those conditions is fulfilled, by reference to the London closing exchange rate for the relevant day.

(2) The conditions are—

(a) that the rate is an arm's length exchange rate for the relevant day;

(b) that the rate is an average arm's length exchange rate for a period ending with that day, or for a period not exceeding three months which includes that day, and the arm's length exchange rate for any day in that period (except the first) is not significantly different from that for the preceding day.

(3) Subject to subsections (5) and (7) below, any amount found by applying paragraphs (a) and (b) of subsection (4) of section 93 above shall be translated into its sterling equivalent by reference to the London closing exchange rate for the relevant day.

(4) The following—

(a) any receipt or expense which is to be taken into account in making a calculation for the purposes of subsection (4)(a) or (b) of section 93 above, and is denominated in a currency other than the relevant foreign currency; and

(b) any such sterling amount as is referred to in subsection (5) of that section,

shall be translated into its equivalent expressed in the relevant foreign currency by reference to the London closing exchange rate for the relevant day.

(5) Where section 93 above applies by virtue of the first condition mentioned in that section, then, as regards the business or part of the business, the company—

(a) may elect, by a notice given to an officer of the Board, that as from the first day of the accounting period in which the notice is given, an average arm's length exchange rate shall be used for the purposes of subsection (3) above instead of the rate there mentioned; and

(b) may withdraw such an election, by a notice so given, as from the first day of the first accounting period beginning on or after the date of the notice.

(6) Where an election under subsection (5) above is withdrawn, no further election may be made under that subsection so as to take effect before the third anniversary of the day on which the withdrawal takes effect.

(7) Where—

(a) section 93 above applies by virtue of the second condition mentioned in that section; and

(b) the accounts of the company, so far as relating to the business or part of the business, are prepared by reference to an average arm's length exchange rate,

that exchange rate shall be used for the purposes of subsection (3) above instead of the rate there mentioned.

(8) In this section—

'accounts' has the same meaning as in section 93 above;
'arm's length exchange rate' means such exchange rate as might reasonably be expected to be agreed between persons dealing at arm's length;
'average arm's length exchange rate', in relation to a period, means the rate which represents an appropriate average of arm's length exchange rates for the period;

'the relevant day' means—

(a) for the purposes of subsections (1),(2) and (4)(a) above, the day on which the company becomes entitled to the receipt or incurs (or is treated as incurring) the expense;

(b) for the purposes of subsection (3) above, the last day of the accounting period in question;

(c) for the purposes of subsection (4)(b) above, the day on which the company incurs the capital expenditure.

(9) Nothing in this section affects the operation of Chapter IV of Part VII of the Taxes Act 1988 (controlled foreign companies) or Chapter II of this Part.

(10) Nothing in paragraph 88 of Schedule 18 to the Finance Act 1998 (company tax returns, assessments and related matters) shall be taken to prevent any amount which is taken to be conclusively determined for the purposes of the Corporation Tax Acts from being translated under this section by reference to an exchange rate which was not used to determine the amount which can no longer be altered.]¹

---

¹   Substituted for sections 92 to 95 by FA 2000, s 105(1) with effect for accounting periods beginning on or after 1 January 2000 and ending on or after 21 March 2000 (subject to subsection (5) of FA 2000, s 105).
Previously
'Corporation tax: currency

92   The basic rule: sterling to be used

Where a company carries on a trade, the profits or losses of the trade for an accounting period shall for the purposes of corporation tax be computed and expressed in sterling; but this is subject to any regulations under section 93 or 94 below.

93   Currency other than sterling for trades

(1) Regulations may provide that where a company carries on a trade the basic profits or losses of the trade for an accounting period shall for the purposes of corporation tax be computed and expressed in such currency (other than sterling) as is found in accordance with prescribed rules, in a case where –

(a) prescribed conditions are fulfilled, and

(b) an election is made by the company in accordance with the regulations and has effect for the accounting period concerned by virtue of the regulations.

(2) For the purposes of this section the basic profits or losses of a trade for an accounting period are all the profits or losses of the trade for the period, but leaving out of account –

(a) any trading receipt of the trade in the period, and any trading expense of the trade in the period, that arises by virtue of section 144(2) of the Capital Allowances Act 1990 (which makes provision about giving effect to allowances and charges);

(b) any amount mentioned in section 142(4) below and treated as received in respect of the trade and in respect of the period.

(3) Subsections (4) and (5) below apply where the basic profits or losses of a trade for an accounting period are for the purposes of corporation tax to be computed and expressed in a currency other than sterling.

(4) The amount of the basic profits or losses shall be treated for the purposes of corporation tax as the sterling equivalent of their amount expressed in the other currency.

(5) The profits or losses of the trade for the period shall for the purposes of corporation tax be found by taking the amount of the basic profits or losses found in sterling under subsection (4) above and then –

    (a) taking account of any trading receipt of the trade in the period, and any trading expense of the trade in the period, that arises by virtue of section 144(2) of the Capital Allowances Act 1990, and

    (b) taking account (as provided by section 142 below) of any amount mentioned in section 142(4) and treated as received in respect of the trade and in respect of the period.

(6) For the purposes of subsection (4) above the sterling equivalent of an amount is the sterling equivalent calculated by reference to –

    (a) such rate of exchange as is found under prescribed rules, or

    (b) if no such rules apply in the case concerned, the London closing exchange rate for the last day of the accounting period concerned.

94 Parts of trades

(1) Regulations may make provision under this section as regards a case where in an accounting period –

    (a) a company carries on part of a trade in the United Kingdom, and carries on a different part of the trade through an overseas branch or different parts through different overseas branches, or

    (b) a company carries on different parts of a trade through different overseas branches;

and 'overseas branch' means a branch outside the United Kingdom.

(2) Regulations may provide that the basic profits or losses of different parts of the trade for an accounting period shall for the purposes of corporation tax be computed and expressed in such different currencies as are found in accordance with prescribed rules, in a case where –

    (a) prescribed conditions are fulfilled, and

    (b) an election is made by the company in accordance with the regulations and has effect for the accounting period concerned by virtue of the regulations.

(3) The regulations must be so framed that –

    (a) one currency is used for each part;

    (b) at least two currencies are used;

    (c) subject to paragraph (b) above, the same currency may be used for more than one part;

    (d) if no election is made as regards a particular part, sterling is to be used for that part.

(4) For the purposes of this section the basic profits or losses of part of a trade for an accounting period are all the profits or losses of the part for the period; but this is subject to subsections (5) and (6) below.

(5) No account shall be taken of any trading receipt of the trade in the period, and any trading expense of the trade in the period, that arises by virtue of section 144(2) of the Capital Allowances Act 1990 (which makes provision about giving effect to allowances and charges).

(6) Where the basic profits or losses of the part of the trade for the period are for the purposes of corporation tax to be computed and expressed in a currency other than sterling, no account shall be taken of any amount mentioned in section 142(4) below and treated as received in respect of the part of the trade and in respect of the period.

(7) Where the basic profits or losses of different parts of a trade for an accounting period are for the purposes of corporation tax to be computed and expressed in two or more different currencies, subsections (8) to (10) below have effect for finding the profits or losses of the trade for the period for the purposes of corporation tax.

(8) Where the basic profits or losses of any part are for the purposes of corporation tax to be computed and expressed in a currency other than sterling –

    (a) find the sterling equivalent of their amount expressed in the other currency, then

    (b) take account (as provided by section 142 below) of any amount mentioned in section 142(4) and treated as received in respect of the part and in respect of the period, then

    (c) call the result the accountable profits or losses of the part for the period.

(9) Where the basic profits or losses of any part are for the purposes of corporation tax to be computed and expressed in sterling, take those profits or losses and call them the accountable profits or losses of the part for the period.

(10) The profits or losses of the trade for the period for the purposes of corporation tax shall then be found by –

    (a) taking account of the accountable profits or losses of the different parts for the period, and

    (b) then taking account of any trading receipt of the trade in the period, and any trading expense of the trade in the period, that arises by virtue of section 144(2) of the Capital Allowances Act 1990.

(11) For the purposes of subsection (8) above the sterling equivalent of an amount is the sterling equivalent calculated by reference to –

    (a) such rate of exchange as is found under prescribed rules, or

    (b) if no such rules apply in the case concerned, the London closing exchange rate for the last day of the accounting period concerned.

[94A   Parts of trades: petroleum extraction companies

(1) If a trade carried on by a petroleum extraction company is a ring fence trade –

    (a) subsection (1) of section 94 above shall not apply as regards the trade, but

    (b) regulations may make provision under that section as regards a case where in an accounting period the company carries on the trade and the condition mentioned in subsection (2) below is fulfilled.

(2) The condition is that –

    (a) part of the trade consists of activities which relate to oil and are carried on under the authority of a petroleum licence in the United Kingdom or a designated area, and

    (b) part of the trade consists of activities which relate to gas and are carried on under the authority of a petroleum licence in the United Kingdom or a designated area.

(3) For the purposes of this section –

    (a) a petroleum licence is a licence granted under [Part I of the Petroleum Act 1998][2] or the Petroleum (Production) Act (Northern Ireland) 1964;

    (b) a petroleum extraction company is a company which carries on activities under the authority of such a licence;

    (c) a designated area is an area designated by Order in Council under section 1(7) of the Continental Shelf Act 1964.

(4) For the purposes of this section 'ring fence trade' means activities which –

    (a) fall within any of paragraphs (a) to (c) of subsection (1) of section 492 of the Taxes Act 1988 (oil extraction etc.), and

    (b) constitute a separate trade (whether by virtue of that subsection or otherwise).

(5) For the purposes of this section –

    (a) 'oil' means such substance as falls within the meaning of oil contained in section 502(1) of the Taxes Act 1988 and is not gas:

    (b) 'gas' means such substance as falls within the meaning of oil contained in section 502(1) of the Taxes Act 1988 and is gas of which the largest component by volume, measured at a temperature of 15 degrees centigrade and a pressure of one atmosphere, is methane or ethane or a combination of those gases.][1]

[1]   Inserted by FA 1994, s 136(1).

[2]   Substituted by Petroleum Act 1998, 4 Sch 36 with effect from 11 June 1998.
       Previously 'the Petroleum (Production) Act 1934'.

95   Currency to be used: supplementary

(1) Regulations under section 93 or 94 above may include –

    (a) provision that an election may in prescribed circumstances have effect from a time before it is made;

    (b) provision that prescribed conditions shall be treated as fulfilled in prescribed circumstances (subject to any provision under paragraph (c) below);

    (c) provision that prescribed conditions shall be treated as not having been fulfilled if the inspector notifies the company that he is not satisfied that they are fulfilled;

    (d) provision for an appeal from the inspector's notification;

and any provision under paragraph (c) above may allow a notification to be made after the accounting period ends.

(2) The power to make regulations under section 93 or 94 above shall be exercisable by the Treasury by statutory instrument subject to annulment in pursuance of a resolution of the House of Commons.

(3) In sections 93 and 94 above 'prescribed' means prescribed by regulations made under the section concerned.

(4) Where as regards a trade and for an accounting period –

    (a) an election is made under regulations made under section 93 above, or

    (b) an election is made under regulations made under section 94 above,

no election may be made as regards the trade for the period under regulations made under the other section.

(5) For the purposes of sections 93 and 94 above the ecu shall be regarded as a currency other than sterling; and the reference here to the ecu is to the European currency unit as defined for the time being in Council Regulation No. 3180/78/EEC or in any Community instrument replacing it.

(6) Sections 92 to 94[A][1] above apply in relation to any accounting period beginning on or after the day appointed under section 165(7)(b) below.

Notes
(a) The appointed day under subsection (6) above is 23 March 1995 (see Finance Act 1993, section 165 (Appointed Day) Order (SI 1995 No 3224)).'

CHAPTER II   EXCHANGE GAINS AND LOSSES

Accrual of gains and losses

125   Accrual on qualifying assets and liabilities

(1)   Subsection (2) below applies where a qualifying company holds a qualifying asset and there is a difference between–

    (a)   the local currency equivalent, at the translation time with which an accrual period as regards the asset begins, of the basic valuation of the asset, and

   (b) the local currency equivalent, at the translation time with which the accrual period ends, of the basic valuation of the asset.

(2) There is as regards the asset an exchange difference for the accrual period, and –

   (a) if the difference represents an increase over the period, an initial exchange gain of an amount equal to the difference accrues to the company as regards the asset for the period;

   (b) if the difference represents a decrease over the period, an initial exchange loss of an amount equal to the difference accrues to the company as regards the asset for the period.

(3) Subsection (4) below applies where a qualifying company owes a qualifying liability and there is a difference between –

   (a) the local currency equivalent, at the translation time with which an accrual period as regards the liability begins, of the basic valuation of the liability, and

   (b) the local currency equivalent, at the translation time with which the accrual period ends, of the basic valuation of the liability.

(4) There is as regards the liability an exchange difference for the accrual period, and –

   (a) if the difference represents a decrease over the period, an initial exchange gain of an amount equal to the difference accrues to the company as regards the liability for the period;

   (b) if the difference represents an increase over the period, an initial exchange loss of an amount equal to the difference accrues to the company as regards the liability for the period.

126 Accrual on currency contracts

(1) This section applies where a qualifying company enters into a contract (a currency contract) under which –

   (a) it becomes entitled to a right and subject to a duty to receive payment at a specified time of a specified amount of one currency (the first currency), and

   (b) it becomes entitled to a right and subject to a duty to pay in exchange and at the same time a specified amount of another currency (the second currency).

[(1A) In deciding whether a contract falls within subsection (1) above it is immaterial that the rights and duties there mentioned may be exercised and discharged by a payment made to or, as the case may require, by the qualifying company of an amount (in whatever currency) designed to represent any difference in value at the specified time between the two payments referred to in that subsection.][1]

(2) Subsection (3) below applies if there is a difference between –

   (a) the local currency equivalent, at the translation time with which an accrual period as regards the contract begins, of the amount of the first currency, and

    (b) the local currency equivalent, at the translation time with which the accrual period ends, of the amount of the first currency.

(3) There is as regards the contract an exchange difference for the accrual period, and –

    (a) if the difference represents an increase over the period, an initial exchange gain of an amount equal to the difference accrues to the company as regards the contract for the period;

    (b) if the difference represents a decrease over the period, an initial exchange loss of an amount equal to the difference accrues to the company as regards the contract for the period.

(4) Subsection (5) below applies if there is a difference between –

    (a) the local currency equivalent, at the translation time with which an accrual period as regards the contract begins, of the amount of the second currency, and

    (b) the local currency equivalent, at the translation time with which the accrual period ends, of the amount of the second currency.

(5) There is as regards the contract an exchange difference for the accrual period, and –

    (a) if the difference represents a decrease over the period, an initial exchange gain of an amount equal to the difference accrues to the company as regards the contract for the period;

    (b) if the difference represents an increase over the period, an initial exchange loss of an amount equal to the difference accrues to the company as regards the contract for the period.

[(6) Subsection (7) below applies where –

    (a) under a contract a qualifying company becomes entitled to a right and subject to a duty to receive or make a payment at a specified time, and

    (b) the amount of the payment (in whatever currency) is computed in such a way as to be equal to the amount of the payment referred to in subsection (1A) above which would have fallen to be computed if –

        (i) the qualifying company had been entitled and subject as mentioned in subsection (1) above, and

        (ii) a payment such as is referred to in subsection (1A) above were to be made to or by the qualifying company.

(7) For the purposes of this Chapter –

    (a) the qualifying company shall be deemed to have become entitled and subject as mentioned in subsection (1) above under the contract referred to in subsection (6) above;

    (b) the payment made under the contract shall be treated as if it were a payment falling within subsection (1A) above in the exercise and discharge of the rights and duties to which the qualifying company is deemed to have become entitled and subject by virtue of paragraph (a) above.][2]

---

127   Accrual on debts whose amounts vary

(1)   In a case where –

   (a) a qualifying company holds an asset consisting of a right to settlement under a qualifying debt or owes a liability consisting of a duty to settle under such a debt, and

   (b) the nominal amount of the debt outstanding varies during an accrual period (whether because of an increase or a decrease or both),

   the following provisions of this section shall apply for the period and section 125 above shall not.

[(1A) For the purposes of this section if, in the case of any debt–

   (a) an amount in respect of any discount or premium relating to that debt is treated, on an accruals basis of accounting, as accruing at any time for the purposes of Chapter II of Part IV of the Finance Act 1996 (loan relationships), or

   (b) any such amount would be treated as so accruing if the authorised method of accounting used for those purposes as respects the loan relationship relating to that debt were an accruals basis of accounting, instead of a mark to market basis,

   then, for the purposes of this section, there shall be deemed to be such a variation at that time of the nominal amount of the debt outstanding as is specified in subsection (1B) below.

(1B) That variation is–

   (a) if the amount mentioned in paragraph (a) or (b) of subsection (1A) above relates to a discount, a variation that increases the nominal amount of the debt outstanding by the amount so mentioned; and

   (b) if the amount so mentioned relates to a premium, a variation that decreases the nominal amount of the debt outstanding by the amount so mentioned.]¹

(2)   In such a case –

   (a) take the local currency equivalent, at the translation time with which the accrual period begins, of the nominal amount of the debt then outstanding;

   (b) take the local currency equivalent, at each time (if any) immediately after the nominal amount of the debt outstanding increases in the accrual period, of the amount by which it then increases;

   (c) take the local currency equivalent, at each time (if any) immediately after the nominal amount of the debt outstanding decreases in the accrual period, of the amount by which it then decreases;

289

(d) take the figure found under paragraph (a) above, add each figure found under paragraph (b) above, subtract each figure found under paragraph (c) above, and call the resulting figure the first amount;

(e) take the local currency equivalent, at the translation time with which the accrual period ends, of the nominal amount of the debt then outstanding, and call the figure so found the second amount.

(3) Where the qualifying company has a right to settlement under the debt the following provisions apply in relation to the asset consisting of the right –

(a) if the second amount exceeds the first an initial exchange gain of an amount equal to the difference between them accrues to the company as regards the asset for the accrual period;

(b) if the second amount is less than the first an initial exchange loss of an amount equal to the difference between them accrues to the company as regards the asset for the accrual period.

(4) Where the qualifying company has a duty to settle under the debt the following provisions apply in relation to the liability consisting of the duty –

(a) if the second amount is less than the first an initial exchange gain of an amount equal to the difference between them accrues to the company as regards the liability for the accrual period;

(b) if the second amount exceeds the first an initial exchange loss of an amount equal to the difference between them accrues to the company as regards the liability for the accrual period.

(5) If the first amount has a negative value, for the purposes of this section the second amount (however small its value) shall be taken to exceed the first amount (however large its value).

(6) Subsection (7) below modifies the preceding provisions of this section in their application to an asset or liability where there is a difference between –

(a) the basic valuation of the asset or liability, and

(b) the nominal amount of the debt outstanding at the translation time with which the accrual period begins.

(7) In such a case –

(a) the reference in subsection (2)(a) above to the nominal amount of the debt outstanding shall be taken to be a reference to the basic valuation of the asset or liability;

(b) the reference in subsection (2)(c) above to the amount by which the nominal amount of the debt outstanding decreases shall be taken to be a reference to the amount found under subsection (8) below;

(c) the reference in subsection (2)(e) above to the nominal amount of the debt outstanding shall be taken to be a reference to the amount found under subsection (10) below.

(8)   The amount referred to in subsection (7)(b) above is the amount given by the formula –

$$A \times \frac{B}{C}$$

(9)   For the purposes of subsection (8) above –

A is the basic valuation of the asset or liability;

B is the amount by which, at the time of the decrease mentioned in subsection (2)(c) above, the nominal amount of the debt outstanding then decreases;
C is the nominal amount of the debt outstanding at the translation time with which the accrual period begins.

(10) The amount referred to in subsection (7)(c) above is the amount given by the formula –

$$D + E - F$$

(11) For the purposes of subsection (10) above –

D is the basic valuation of the asset or liability;

E is the amount (if any) by which the nominal amount of the debt outstanding has at any time increased in the accrual period or, if it has increased more than once, the aggregate of such amounts;

F is the amount (if any) found under subsection (8) above or, if the nominal amount of the debt outstanding has decreased more than once in the accrual period, the aggregate of the amounts so found.

---

[1]   Inserted by FA 1996, 14 Sch 67 in relation to accounting periods ending after 31 March 1996 but subject to transitional provisions in FA 1996, 15 Sch.

Trading gains and losses

128 Trading gains and losses

(1)   Subsections (2) to (4) below apply where –

(a)   as regards an asset, liability or contract an initial exchange gain accrues to a qualifying company for an accrual period, and

(b)   at any time in the period the asset or contract was held, or the liability was owed, by the company for the purposes of a trade or part of a trade carried on by it.

(2)   If throughout the accrual period the asset or contract was held, or the liability was owed, by the company solely for the purposes of the trade or part the whole of the gain is an exchange gain of the trade or part for the period.

(3)   In any other case the gain shall be apportioned on a just and reasonable basis and so much as is attributable to the trade or part is an exchange gain of the trade for the period.

(4) The company shall be treated for the purposes of the Tax Acts as–

   (a) receiving in respect of the trade or part an amount equal to the exchange gain of the trade or part for the accrual period, and

   (b) receiving the amount in respect of the accounting period which constitutes the accrual period or in which the accrual period falls.

(5) Subsections (6) to (8) below apply where –

   (a) as regards an asset, liability or contract an initial exchange loss accrues to a qualifying company for an accrual period, and

   (b) at any time in the period the asset or contract was held, or the liability was owed, by the company for the purposes of a trade or part of a trade carried on by it.

(6) If throughout the accrual period the asset or contract was held, or the liability was owed, by the company solely for the purposes of the trade or part the whole of the loss is an exchange loss of the trade or part for the period.

(7) In any other case the loss shall be apportioned on a just and reasonable basis and so much as is attributable to the trade or part is an exchange loss of the trade or part for the period.

(8) The company shall be treated for the purposes of the Tax Acts as–

   (a) incurring in the trade or part a loss of an amount equal to the exchange loss of the trade or part for the accrual period, and

   (b) incurring the loss in respect of the accounting period which constitutes the accrual period or in which the accrual period falls.

[(9) For the purposes of this section a part of a trade is any part of a trade which is treated for the purposes of section 93 above as if it were a separate business for the relevant accounting period; and the relevant accounting period is the accounting period which constitutes the accrual period concerned or in which that accrual period falls.]²

(10) The preceding provisions of this section apply –

   (a) whether the asset or contract is at any time held, or the liability is at any time owed, on revenue account or capital account, and

   (b) notwithstanding anything in section 74 of the Taxes Act 1988 (general rules as to deductions not allowable).

[(10A) In a case where –

   (a) an exchange gain of a trade or part of a trade or an exchange loss of a trade or part of a trade would (apart from this subsection) accrue to a company as regards a liability consisting of a duty to settle under a qualifying debt, and

   (b) a charge is allowed to the company in respect of the debt under section 338 of the Taxes Act 1988 (allowance of charges on income and capital),

   the exchange gain or loss shall be treated as not accruing.

(10B) A charge shall be treated as allowed as mentioned in subsection (10A) above if –

(a) it would be so allowed if the company's total profits were sufficient,

(b) it would be so allowed if the duty mentioned in that subsection were settled, and if in settling it payment were made out of the company's profits brought into charge to corporation tax, or

(c) it would be so allowed if the facts were as mentioned in both paragraph (a) and paragraph (b) above.][1]

(11) In a case where –

(a) an accounting period of a qualifying company begins on or after its commencement day, and

(b) but for this subsection, a gain or loss falling within subsection (12) below would be taken into account in calculating for the purposes of corporation tax the profits or losses for the period of a trade carried on by the company,

the gain or loss shall be left out of account in calculating the profits or losses.

(12) A gain or loss falls within this subsection if it –

(a) accrues to the company, otherwise than by virtue of this Chapter, as regards a qualifying asset or liability or a currency contract, and

(b) is attributable to fluctuations in currency exchange rates;

and it is immaterial whether the gain or loss is realised.

---

[1]   Inserted by FA 1995, 24 Sch 2 and deemed to have been part of the original enactment.

[2]   Substituted by FA 2000, s 106(6) in relation to accounting periods beginning on or after 1 January 2000 and ending on or after 21 March 2000.
Previously
'(9)   For the purposes of this section a part of a trade is any part of a trade whose basic profits or losses for the relevant accounting period are by virtue of regulations under section 94 above to be computed and expressed in a particular currency for the purposes of corporation tax; and the relevant accounting period is the accounting period which constitutes the accrual period concerned or in which that accrual period falls.'.

Non-trading gains and losses

129   Non-trading gains and losses: general

(1) In a case where–

(a) as regards an asset, liability or contract an initial exchange gain accrues to a qualifying company for an accrual period, and

(b) the whole or part of the gain is not an exchange gain of a trade or part of a trade for the period,

the whole or part (as the case may be) is a non-trading exchange gain for the period.

(2) The company shall be treated as –

(a) receiving in respect of the asset, liability or contract an amount equal to the non-trading exchange gain for the accrual period, and

(b) receiving the amount in the accounting period which constitutes the accrual period or in which the accrual period falls;

[and the rule in section 130(1) below shall apply.]³

(3) In a case where –

(a) as regards an asset, liability or contract an initial exchange loss accrues to a qualifying company for an accrual period, and

(b) the whole or part of the loss is not an exchange loss of a trade or part of a trade for the period,

the whole or part (as the case may be) is a non-trading exchange loss for the period.

(4) The company shall be treated as –

(a) incurring in respect of the asset, liability or contract a loss of an amount equal to the non-trading exchange loss for the accrual period, and

(b) incurring the loss in the accounting period which constitutes the accrual period or in which the accrual period falls;

[and the rule in section 130(2) below shall apply.]³

(5)(6) [. . .]⁴

(7) In a case where –

(a) a non-trading exchange gain or loss would (apart from this subsection) accrue as regards an asset consisting of a right to settlement under a qualifying debt, and

(b) the right is a right to receive income [that is not interest falling to be brought into account for the purposes of Chapter II of Part IV of the Finance Act 1996 (loan relationships) as interest accruing, or (according to the authorised method of accounting used) becoming due and payable, in an accounting period ending after 31 March 1996]⁵,

the non-trading exchange gain or loss shall be treated as not accruing.

(8) In a case where –

(a) a non-trading exchange gain or loss would (apart from this subsection) accrue to a company as regards a liability consisting of a duty to settle under a qualifying debt, and

(b) a charge is allowed to the company in respect of the debt under section 338 of the Taxes Act 1988 (allowance of charges on income and capital) [. . .]¹.

the non-trading exchange gain or loss shall be treated as not accruing.

[(8A) A charge shall be treated as allowed as mentioned in subsection (8) above if –

(a) it would be so allowed if the company's total profits were sufficient,

(b) it would be so allowed if the duty mentioned in that subsection were settled, and if in settling it payment were made out of the company's profits brought into charge to corporation tax, or

(c) it would be so allowed if the facts were as mentioned in both paragraph (a) and paragraph (b) above.][2]

(9) Section 396 of the Taxes Act 1988 (Case VI losses) shall not be taken to apply to a loss which a company is treated as incurring by virtue of this section; and an amount which a company is treated as receiving by virtue of this section shall not be regarded, for the purposes of subsection (1) of section 396, as income arising as mentioned in that subsection.

---

[1]   Inserted by FA 1995, 24 Sch 3.

[2]   Repealed by FA 1995, 29 Sch Part VIII (16). Previously 'or the circumstances are such that a charge would be so allowed if the duty were settled'.

[3]   Substituted by FA 1996, 14 Sch 68 in relation to accounting periods ending after 31 March 1996 but subject to transitional provisions in FA 1996, 15 Sch.
      Previously 'and (subject to subsection (6) below) the rules in sections 130 to 133 below shall apply.'

[4]   Deleted by FA 1996, 14 Sch 68 as in [3] above.
      Previously
      '(5) For the purposes of subsection (6) below and sections 130 to 133 below, in relation to an accounting period–

      (a) amount A is the amount a company is treated as receiving in the accounting period by virtue of this section or (if it is treated as so receiving two or more amounts) the aggregate of those amounts;

      (b) amount B is the amount of the loss a company is treated as incurring in the accounting period by virtue of this section or (if it is treated as so incurring two or more losses) the aggregate of the amounts of those losses.

      (6) In a case where–

      (a) a company is treated as receiving in an accounting period an amount or amounts by virtue of this section,

      (b) it is treated as incurring in the accounting period a loss or losses by virtue of this section, and

      (c) amount A is equal to amount B,

      the rules in sections 130 to 133 below shall not apply.'

[5]   Substituted by FA 1996, 14 Sch 68 as in [3] above.
      Previously '(whether interest, dividend or otherwise)'.

---

130   [Non-trading gains and losses

(1) Where a company is treated by virtue of section 129 above as receiving any amount in an accounting period, that amount shall be brought into account for that accounting period as if it were a non-trading credit falling for the purposes of Chapter II of Part IV of the Finance Act 1996 (loan relationships) to be brought into account in respect of a loan relationship of the company.

(2) Where a company is treated by virtue of section 129 above as incurring any loss in an accounting period, the amount of the loss shall be brought into account for that accounting period as if it were a non-trading debit falling for the purposes of Chapter II of Part IV of the Finance Act 1996 to be brought into account in respect of a loan relationship of the company.][1]

Inserted by FA 1996, 14 Sch 69 in relation to accounting periods ending after 31 March 1996 but subject to transitional provisions in FA 1996, 15 Sch.

Note. The provisions of section 130 above replaced the original provisions in sections 130 to 133 of the Act which read as follows.

130 Non-trading gains and losses: charge to tax

(1) Subsection (2) below applies where –

    (a) a company is treated as receiving in an accounting period an amount or amounts by virtue of section 129 above, and

    (b) it is not treated as incurring in the accounting period any loss by virtue of that section.

(2) The company shall be treated as receiving in the accounting period annual profits or gains of an amount equal to amount A, and the profits or gains shall be chargeable to tax under Case VI of Schedule D for the accounting period.

(3) Subsection (4) below applies where –

    (a) a company is treated as receiving in an accounting period an amount or amounts by virtue of section 129 above,

    (b) it is treated as incurring in the accounting period a loss or losses by virtue of that section, and

    (c) amount A exceeds amount B.

(4) The company shall be treated as receiving in the accounting period annual profits or gains of an amount equal to amount A minus amount B, and the profits or gains shall be chargeable to tax under Case VI of Schedule D for the accounting period.

131 Non-trading gains and losses: relief

(1) This section applies where –

    (a) a company is treated as incurring in an accounting period a loss or losses by virtue of section 129 above, and

    (b) it is not treated as receiving in the accounting period any amount by virtue of that section;

and where this section applies by virtue of this subsection references to the relievable amount for the accounting period are to an amount equal to amount B.

(2) This section also applies where –

    (a) a company is treated as incurring in an accounting period a loss or losses by virtue of section 129 above,

    (b) it is treated as receiving in the accounting period an amount or amounts by virtue of that section, and

    (c) amount B exceeds amount A;

and where this section applies by virtue of this subsection references to the relievable amount for the accounting period are to an amount equal to amount B minus amount A.

(3) The company may claim under this subsection that the whole or part of the relievable amount for an accounting period shall be treated for the purposes of section 403(1) of the Taxes Act 1988 (group relief) as if it were a loss incurred by the company in the period in carrying on a trade, and in such a case section 403(2) (exclusions) shall not apply.

(4) The company may claim under this subsection that the whole or part of the relievable amount for an accounting period shall be set off for the purposes of corporation tax against profits (of whatever description) of that accounting period; and in such a case, subject to any relief for a loss incurred in a trade in an earlier accounting period, those profits shall then be treated as reduced accordingly.

(5) Where a company has made no claim under subsection (3) or (4) above as regards the

relievable amount for an accounting period, the company may claim under this subsection that–

(a)   the whole of the relievable amount, or

(b)   where the relievable amount exceeds the relevant exchange profits, so much of the relievable amount as is equal to those profits,

shall be treated as mentioned in subsection (7) below.

(6)   Where a company has made a claim under subsection (3) or (4) above as regards the relievable amount for an accounting period, the company may claim under this subsection that –

(a)   such part of the relievable amount as is not the subject of any such claim, or

(b)   where that part exceeds the relevant exchange profits, so much of that part as is equal to those profits.

shall be treated as mentioned in subsection (7) below.

(7)   Where a company claims under subsection (5) or (6) above as regards the whole or part of the relievable amount for an accounting period, the whole or part concerned shall be set off for the purposes of corporation tax against the exchange profits of preceding accounting periods falling wholly or partly within the permitted period; and (subject to any relief for an earlier loss) the exchange profits of any of those accounting periods shall then be treated as reduced by the whole or part concerned or by so much of it as cannot be set off under this subsection against the exchange profits of a later accounting period.

(8)   For the purposes of subsections (5) and (6) above 'the relevant exchange profits' means the total of the following –

(a)   the exchange profits, as reduced by any reliefs for earlier losses and any reliefs falling within subsection (9) below, of all those accounting periods falling wholly within the permitted period, and

(b)   such part of the exchange profits, as so reduced, of any accounting period falling partly before the beginning of the permitted period as is proportionate to the part of the accounting period falling within the permitted period.

(9)   The reliefs falling within this subsection are –

(a)   any relief under section 338 of the Taxes Act 1988 (charges on income) in respect of payments made wholly and exclusively for the purposes of a trade;

(b)   where the company is an investment company for the purposes of Part IV of the Taxes Act 1988, any relief under that section in respect of payments made wholly and exclusively for the purposes of its business.

(10)   For the purposes of subsections (7) and (8) above –

(a)   the exchange profits of an accounting period are the annual profits or gains the company is treated as receiving in that period under section 130 above,

(b)   the permitted period is the period of three years immediately preceding the accounting period first mentioned in subsection (7) above, and

(c)   an earlier loss is a loss incurred, or treated as incurred, in an accounting period earlier than that first mentioned in subsection (7) above.

(11)   The amount of the reduction that may be made under subsection (7) above in the exchange profits of an accounting period falling partly before the beginning of the permitted period shall not exceed a part of those profits proportionate to the part of the accounting period falling within the permitted period.

(12)   If the whole or part of the relievable amount for an accounting period is not dealt with under a claim under this section –

(a)   the company shall be treated as incurring by virtue of section 129 above a loss of an amount equal to the whole or part (as the case may be),

(b)   the company shall be treated as incurring the loss in the next succeeding accounting period, and

(c)   in relation to that accounting period references to amount B shall be construed accordingly.

(13)   A company –

    (a)   may not claim under more than one of subsections (3) and (4) above as regards the same part of a relievable amount, and

    (b)   where it has claimed under subsection (5)(b) or (6) above as regards part of a relievable amount, may not later claim under subsection (3) or (4) above as regards part of the relievable amount.

(14)   A claim under any of subsections (3) to (6) above must be made within the period of two years immediately following the accounting period to which the relievable amount relates or within such further period as the Board may allow.

132   Modifications where loss carried forward

(1)   This section applies where section 131(12) above treats a company as incurring a loss in an accounting period by virtue of section 129 above.

(2)   In this section references to amount C are to so much of amount B as the company is treated as incurring in the accounting period otherwise than by virtue of section 131(12).

(3)   Where section 131 above applies by virtue of section 131(1) and this section applies, then, as regards the accounting period –

    (a)   if amount C is nil section 131(3) to (6) shall not apply;

    (b)   if amount C exceeds nil the references to the relievable amount in section 131(3) to (7), (13) and (14) shall be construed as references to so much of that amount as equals amount C.

(4)   Where section 131 above applies by virtue of section 131(2) and this section applies, then, as regards the accounting period –

    (a)   if amount C does not exceed amount A section 131(3) to (6) shall not apply;

    (b)   if amount C exceeds amount A the references to the relievable amount in section 131(3) to (7), (13) and (14) shall be construed as references to so much of that amount as equals amount C minus amount A.

133   Interaction with ICTA

(1)   Section 131(4) above shall apply before section 393A(1) of the Taxes Act 1988 in relation to profits of the accounting period first mentioned in section 131(4) above.

(2)   Relief shall not be given under section 131(4) above against any ring fence profits of the company; and in this subsection 'ring fence profits' has the same meaning as in Chapter V of Part XII of the Taxes Act 1988.

(3)   Where the company incurs a loss in a trade in the accounting period first mentioned in subsection (7) of section 131 above, that subsection shall apply after section 393A(1) of the Taxes Act 1988 in relation to exchange profits of a particular accounting period.

(4)   Relief shall not be given by virtue of section 131(7) above so as to interfere with –

    (a)   any relief under section 338 of the Taxes Act 1988 (charges on income) in respect of payments made wholly and exclusively for the purposes of a trade, or

    (b)   where the company is an investment company for the purposes of Part IV of the Taxes Act 1988, any relief under that section in respect of payments made wholly and exclusively for the purposes of its business.

(5)   The reference in subsection (3) above to exchange profits of an accounting period shall be construed in accordance with section 131(10) above.

Alternative calculation

134   Alternative calculation

Schedule 15 to this Act (which provides for the amount of an initial exchange gain or loss to be found in accordance with an alternative method of calculation in certain cases) shall have effect.

Main benefit test

135 Loss disregarded if the main benefit

(1) In a case where –

    (a) an exchange loss would (apart from this section) accrue to a company for an accrual period,

    (b) the loss would accrue as regards an asset or liability falling within section 153(1)(a) or (2)(a) below, [and][1]

    (c) the nominal currency of the asset or liability is such that the main benefit or one of the main benefits that might be expected to arise from the company's holding the asset or owing the liability is the accrual of the loss, [. . .][2]

    (d) [. . .][3]

the loss shall be treated as not accruing.

(2) References in subsection (1) above to an exchange loss are to an exchange loss of a trade or an exchange loss of part of a trade or a non-trading exchange loss.

---

[1]   Inserted by FA 1998, s 109 with effect in relation to transactions entered into at any time as respects accounting periods ending on or after the day appointed by FA 1994, s 199 for the purposes of Chapter III of Part IV of that Act (1 July 1999).

[2]   Deleted by FA 1998, s 109 with effect as in [1] above.
Previously 'and'.

[3]   Deleted by FA 1998, s 109 with effect as in [1] above.
Previously 'the Board direct that this subsection shall apply,'.

Note
(a) Where a direction given on or after 17 March 1998 under FA 1993 s 135(1)(d) relates to any accounting period before the appointed day (1 July 1999) all such adjustments shall be made, whether by assessment, repayment of tax or otherwise, as are necessary to give effect to that direction.

[135A Sterling used if avoidance of gain is the main benefit

(1) This section applies where, as regards qualifying assets and liabilities of a company—

    (a) a currency other than sterling would (apart from this section) be the local currency for the purposes of sections 125 to 129 above; and

    (b) the main benefit that might be expected to accrue from that currency being the local currency is that no net exchange gain would accrue to the company for those purposes.

(2) If a net exchange gain would accrue to the company if sterling were the local currency for the purposes of sections 125 to 129 above, then, as regards the assets and liabilities concerned, sterling shall be the local currency for those purposes.

(3) For the purposes of this section a net exchange gain accrues to a company if its initial exchange gains (as determined in accordance with this Chapter) exceed its initial exchange losses (as so determined).][1].

---

1   Inserted by FA 2000, s 106(7) in relation to accounting periods beginning on or after 1 January
2000 and ending on or after 1 March 2000.

Arm's length test

136   Arm's length test: assets and liabilities

(1)   Subject to the following provisions of this section, subsection (2) below
applies where –

     (a)   a qualifying company becomes entitled to a qualifying asset falling
within section 153(1)(a) below or subject to a qualifying liability
falling within section 153(2)(a) below,

     (b)   the transaction as a result of which the company becomes entitled
or subject to the asset or liability would not have been entered into
at all if the parties to the transaction had been dealing at arm's
length, or the transaction's terms would have been different if they
had been so dealing, [and]¹

     (c)   as regards the asset or liability an exchange loss accrues to the
company for an accrual period (or would so accrue apart from this
section), [. . .]²

     (d)   [. . .]³

and any reference in this section to an exchange loss is to an exchange
loss of a trade or an exchange loss of part of a trade or a non-trading
exchange loss.

(2)   The exchange loss shall be treated as not accruing to the company for
the accrual period.

(3)   Where subsection (2) above applies and the accrual period is not the last
to occur as regards the asset or liability while it is held or owed by the
company –

     (a)   an amount equal to the amount of the loss shall be set off against
appropriate exchange gains accruing to the company as regards the
asset or liability for subsequent accrual periods, and

     (b)   any such gain shall then be treated as reduced by that amount or by
so much of it as cannot be set off under this subsection against any
such gain accruing for an earlier accrual period;

and an appropriate exchange gain is an exchange gain of the trade
concerned (if the exchange loss is an exchange loss of a trade) or an
exchange gain of the part of the trade concerned (if the exchange loss is
an exchange loss of part of a trade) or a non-trading exchange gain (if
the exchange loss is a non-trading exchange loss).

(4)   Subsection (5) below applies where the circumstances are such that, had
the parties to the transaction been dealing at arm's length, its terms
would have been the same except that the amount of the debt would
have been an amount (the adjusted amount) greater than nil but less
than its actual amount.

(5)   In such a case –

     (a)   subsection (2) above shall not apply, and

(b) the exchange loss accruing to the company for the accrual period shall be treated as reduced to the amount it would have been if the amount of the debt had been the adjusted amount;

$[\ldots]^4$

(6) Where subsection (5)(b) above applies and the accrual period is not the last to occur as regards the asset or liability while it is held or owed by the company –

(a) an amount equal to the amount by which the loss is treated as reduced shall be set off against appropriate exchange gains accruing to the company as regards the asset or liability for subsequent accrual periods, and

(b) any such gain shall then be treated as reduced by that amount or by so much of it as cannot be set off under this subsection against any such gain accruing for an earlier accrual period;

and an appropriate exchange gain is an exchange gain of the trade concerned (if the exchange loss is an exchange loss of a trade) or an exchange gain of the part of the trade concerned (if the exchange loss is an exchange loss of part of a trade) or a non-trading exchange gain (if the exchange loss is a non-trading exchange loss).

(7) Subsection (2) above shall not apply in a case where –

(a) the right constituting the asset mentioned in subsection (1) above arises under a loan made by the company,

(b) the circumstances are such that, had the parties to the transaction been dealing at arm's length, its terms would have been the same except that interest would have been charged on the loan or, as the case may be, charged at a higher rate, and

(c) in computing for tax purposes the profits or losses of the company for the accounting period which constitutes the accrual period or in which the accrual period falls the whole of the loan [falls to be treated in accordance with Schedule 28AA to]^5 the Taxes Act 1988 (undervalue or overvalue) as if interest had been charged on it or, as the case may be, charged at a higher rate.

(8) Subsection (9) below applies where –

(a) paragraphs (a) and (b) of subsection (7) above apply, and

(b) in computing for tax purposes the profits or losses of the company for the accounting period which constitutes the accrual period or in which the accrual period falls part of the loan [falls to be treated in accordance with Schedule 28AA to]^5 the Taxes Act 1988 as if interest had been charged on it or, as the case may be, charged at a higher rate;

and in subsection (9) below the reference to the adjusted amount is to an amount equal to the part of the loan that has been so treated.

(9) In such a case –

(a) subsection (2) above shall not apply, and

(b) the exchange loss accruing to the company for the accrual period shall be treated as reduced to the amount it would have been if the amount of the loan had been the adjusted amount;

$[\ldots]^4$

(10) Where subsection (9)(b) above applies and the accrual period is not the last to occur as regards the asset while it is held by the company –

(a) an amount equal to the amount by which the loss is treated as reduced shall be set off against appropriate exchange gains accruing to the company as regards the asset for subsequent accrual periods, and

(b) any such gain shall then be treated as reduced by that amount or by so much of it as cannot be set off under this subsection against any such gain accruing for an earlier accrual period;

and an appropriate exchange gain is an exchange gain of the trade concerned (if the exchange loss is an exchange loss of a trade) or an exchange gain of the part of the trade concerned (if the exchange loss is an exchange loss of part of a trade) or a non-trading exchange gain (if the exchange loss is a non-trading exchange loss).

(11) Subsections (2) to (10) above shall not apply where –

(a) the transaction is entered into by the company mentioned in subsection (1) above (company A) and another company (company B),

(b) the companies are members of the same group when the transaction is entered into and throughout the accounting period which constitutes the accrual period mentioned in subsection (1) above or in which the accrual period falls,

(c) as a result of the transaction, not only does company A become entitled or subject to the asset or liability falling within section 153(1)(a) or (2)(a) below but company B also becomes subject or entitled to the corresponding liability or asset (as the case may be) falling within section 153(2)(a) or (1)(a) below,

(d) as regards that liability or asset an appropriate exchange gain accrues to company B for an accrual period coterminous with that mentioned in subsection (1) above,

(e) throughout the accrual period concerned company A holds or owes the asset or liability either for the purposes of one trade or for non-trading purposes,

(f) throughout the accrual period concerned company B owes or holds the liability or asset either for the purposes of one trade or for non-trading purposes, and

(g) amount X is the same as amount Y.

(12) For the purposes of subsection (11) above –

(a) an appropriate exchange gain is an exchange gain of a trade or a non-trading exchange gain found (in either case) in the currency in which the exchange loss mentioned in subsection (1) above is found;

(b) amount X is the amount of the exchange loss mentioned in subsection (1) above;

(c) amount Y is the amount of the exchange gain mentioned in subsection (11)(d) above, found without regard to section 139 below;

(d) companies are members of the same group if by virtue of section 170 of the Taxation of Chargeable Gains Act 1992 they are members of the same group for the purposes of sections 171 to 181 of that Act.

(13) Where the exchange loss mentioned in subsection (1) above represents the whole or part of an initial exchange loss accruing under section 127 above, this section shall have effect as if subsections (4) to (12) were omitted.

(14) Regulations may make provision designed to supplement this section in its application to a case where the exchange loss mentioned in subsection (1) above represents the whole or part of an initial exchange loss accruing under section 127 above; and the regulations may in particular contain provision based on subsections (4) to (12) above but differing from those subsections to such extent as the Treasury think fit.

(15) In applying subsections (1)(b), (4) and (7)(b) above all factors shall be taken into account including any interest or other sums that would have been payable, any currency that would have been involved, and the amount that any loan would have been.

---

[1]   Inserted by FA 1998, s 109 with effect in relation to transactions entered into at any time as respects accounting periods ending on or after the day appointed by FA 1994, s 199 for the purposes of Chapter III of Part IV of that Act (1 July 1999).

[2]   Deleted by FA 1998, s 109 with effect as in [1] above.
Previously 'and'.

[3]   Deleted by FA 1998, s 109 with effect as in [1] above.
Previously 'the Board direct that subsection (2) below shall apply,'.

[4]   Deleted by FA 1998, s 109 with effect as in [1] above.
Previously 'but paragraph (b) above shall only apply if the Board so direct.'

[5]   Substituted by FA 1998, s 108 with effect (in relation to provision made or imposed at any time)

(i) for corporation tax purposes as in [1] above; and

(ii) for income tax purposes, as respects any year of assessment ending on or after 1 July 1999.
Previously 'has been treated under section 770 of'.

Note
(a) Where a direction is given on or after 17 March 1998 under FA 1993 s 136(1)(d), (5) or (9) relates to any accounting period ending before the appointed day (1 July 1999), all such adjustments shall be made, whether by assessment, repayment of tax or otherwise, as are necessary to give effect to that direction.

[136A   Arm's length test: debts of varying amounts

(1) The provisions of this section shall have effect in relation to any exchange loss mentioned in section 136(1) above which represents the whole or part of an initial exchange loss accruing under section 127 above.

(2) Subsection (3) below applies where the circumstances are such that, had the parties to the transaction referred to in section 136(1)(b) above been dealing at arm's length, the terms of the transaction would have been

the same except that the amount of the debt at any time during the accrual period referred to in section 136(1)(c) would have been an amount (in subsection (3) below referred to as 'the adjusted amount') less than its actual amount at that time.

(3) Where this subsection applies in relation to a debt –

    (a) section 136(2) above shall not apply, and

    (b) the exchange loss accruing to the company for the accrual period shall be treated as reduced to the amount it would have been if the amount of the debt had, at any time in the accrual period when the actual amount of the debt exceeded the adjusted amount, been equal to the adjusted amount;

[. . .]²

(4) Where subsection (3)(b) above applies and the accrual period is not the last to occur as regards the asset or liability while it is held or owed by the company –

    (a) an amount equal to the amount by which the loss is treated as reduced shall be set off against appropriate exchange gains accruing to the company as regards the asset or liability for subsequent accrual periods, and

    (b) any such gain shall then be treated as reduced by that amount or by so much of it as cannot be set off under this subsection against any such gain accruing for an earlier accrual period;

and an appropriate exchange gain is an exchange gain of the trade concerned (if the exchange loss is an exchange loss of a trade) or an exchange gain of the part of the trade concerned (if the exchange loss is an exchange loss of part of a trade) or a non-trading exchange gain (if the exchange loss is a non-trading exchange loss).

(5) Section 136(2) above shall not apply in a case where –

    (a) the right constituting the asset mentioned in section 136(1)(a) above arises under a loan made by the company,

    (b) the circumstances are such that, had the parties to the transaction been dealing at arm's length, its terms would have been the same except that interest would have been charged on the loan or, as the case may be, charged at a higher rate, and

    (c) in computing for tax purposes the profits or losses of the company for the accounting period which constitutes the accrual period or in which the accrual period falls the whole of the loan [falls to be treated in accordance with Schedule 28AA to]³ the Taxes Act 1988 (transactions at an undervalue or overvalue) as if interest had been charged on it or, as the case may be, charged at a higher rate.

(6) Subsection (7) below applies where –

    (a) paragraphs (a) and (b) of subsection (5) above apply, and

    (b) in computing for tax purposes the profits or losses of the company for the accounting period which constitutes the accrual period or in which the accrual period falls, part of the loan [falls in relation to any time in that accrual period to be treated in accordance with Schedule 28AA to]⁴ the Taxes Act 1988 as if interest had been charged on it or, as the case may be, charged at a higher rate;

and in subsection (7) any reference to the adjusted amount is to an amount equal to the part of the loan that has been so treated.

(7) In any case where subsection (6) applies –

(a) section 136(2) above shall not apply, and

(b) the exchange loss accruing to the company for the accrual period shall be treated as reduced to the amount it would have been if the amount of the debt had, at any time in the accrual period when the actual amount of the debt exceeded the adjusted amount at that time, been equal to that adjusted amount (and if there is no adjusted amount at any time, the actual amount of the debt at that time shall be taken to be zero);

[. . .]²

(8) Where subsection (7)(b) above applies and the accrual period is not the last to occur as regards the asset while it is held by the company –

(a) an amount equal to the amount by which the loss is treated as reduced shall be set off against appropriate exchange gains accruing to the company as regards the asset for subsequent accrual periods, and

(b) any such gain shall then be treated as reduced by that amount or by so much of it as cannot be set off under this subsection against any such gain accruing for an earlier accrual period;

and an appropriate exchange gain is an exchange gain of the trade concerned (if the exchange loss is an exchange loss of a trade) or an exchange gain of the part of the trade concerned (if the exchange loss is an exchange loss of part of a trade) or a non-trading exchange gain (if the exchange loss is a non-trading exchange loss).

(9) Section 136(2) and subsections (2) to (8) above shall not apply where –

(a) the transaction is entered into by the company mentioned in section 136(1) above (company A) and another company (company B),

(b) the companies are members of the same group when the transaction is entered into and throughout the accounting period which constitutes the accrual period mentioned in section 136(1) above or in which the accrual period falls,

(c) as a result of the transaction, not only does company A become entitled or subject to the asset or liability falling within section 153(1)(a) or (2)(a) below but company B also becomes subject or entitled to the corresponding liability or asset (as the case may be) falling within section 153(2)(a) or (1)(a) below,

(d) as regards that liability or asset an appropriate exchange gain accrues to company B for an accrual period coterminous with that mentioned in section 136(1) above,

(e) throughout the accrual period concerned company A holds or owes the asset or liability either for the purposes of one trade or for non-trading purposes,

(f) throughout the accrual period concerned company B owes or holds the liability or asset either for the purposes of one trade or for non-trading purposes, and

(g) amount X is the same as amount Y.

(10)   For the purposes of subsection (9) above –

   (a)   an appropriate exchange gain is an exchange gain of a trade or a
         non-trading exchange gain found (in either case) in the currency in
         which the exchange loss mentioned in section 136(1) above is
         found;

   (b)   amount X is the amount of the exchange loss mentioned in section
         136(1) above;

   (c)   amount Y is the amount of the exchange gain mentioned in
         subsection (9)(d) above, found without regard to section 139
         below; and

   (d)   companies are members of the same group if by virtue of section
         170 of the Taxation of Chargeable Gains Act 1992 they are mem-
         bers of the same group for the purposes of sections 171 to 181 of
         that Act.

(11)   In applying subsections (2) and (5)(b) above all factors shall be taken
       into account including any interest or other sums that would have been
       payable, any currency that would have been involved, and the amount
       that any loan would have been.][1]

---

[1]   Inserted by SI 1994 No 3232 (The Exchange Gains and Losses (Debts of Varying Amounts)
      Regulations 1994) with effect from 23 March 1995.

[2]   Deleted by FA 1998, s 109 with effect in relation to transactions entered into at any time as respects
      accounting periods ending on or after the day appointed by FA 1994, s 199 for the purposes of
      Chapter III of Part IV of that Act (1 July 1999).
      Previously 'but paragraph (b) above shall only apply if the Board so direct'.

[3]   Substituted by FA 1998, s 108 with effect (in relation to provision made or imposed at any time)

      (i) for corporation tax purposes as in [1] above; and

      (ii) for income tax purposes, as respects any year of assessment ending on or after 1 July 1999.
      Previously 'has been treated under section 770 of'.

[4]   Substituted by FA 1998, s 108 with effect as in [3] above.
      Previously 'has at any time in the accrual period been treated under section 770 of'

Note
(a) Where a direction is given on or after 17 March 1998 under FA 1993 s 135(1)(d) relates to any
    accounting period before the appointed day (1 July 1999) all such adjustments shall be made,
    whether by assessment, repayment of tax or otherwise, as are necessary to give effect to that
    direction.

---

137   Arm's length test: currency contracts

   (1)   Subsection (2) below applies where –

      (a)   a qualifying company enters into a currency contract,

      (b)   the contract would not have been entered into at all if the parties to
            it had been dealing at arm's length, or the contract's terms would
            have been different if they had been so dealing, [and][1]

      (c)   as regards the contract an exchange loss accrues to the company for
            an accrual period (or would so accrue apart from this section),
            [. . .][2]

      (d)   [. . .][3]

and any reference in this section to an exchange loss is to an exchange loss of a trade or an exchange loss of part of a trade or a non-trading exchange loss.

(2) The exchange loss shall be treated as not accruing to the company for the accrual period.

(3) Where subsection (2) above applies and the accrual period is not the last to occur as regards the contract while it is held by the company –

   (a) an amount equal to the amount of the loss shall be set off against appropriate exchange gains accruing to the company as regards the contract for subsequent accrual periods, and

   (b) any such gain shall then be treated as reduced by that amount or by so much of it as cannot be set off under this subsection against any such gain accruing for an earlier accrual period;

and an appropriate exchange gain is an exchange gain of the trade concerned (if the exchange loss is an exchange loss of a trade) or an exchange gain of the part of the trade concerned (if the exchange loss is an exchange loss of part of a trade) or a non-trading exchange gain (if the exchange loss is a non-trading exchange loss).

(4) In applying subsection (1)(b) above all factors shall be taken into account including any currency that would have been involved and any amounts that would have been involved.

---

[1] Inserted by FA 1998, s 109 with effect in relation to transactions entered into at any time as respects accounting periods ending on or after the day appointed by FA 1994, s 199 for the purposes of Chapter III of Part IV of that Act (1 July 1999).
Previously 'but paragraph (b) above shall only apply if the Board so direct.

[2] Deleted by FA 1998, s 109 with effect as in [1] above.
Previously 'and'.

[3] Deleted by FA 1998, s 109 with effect as in [1] above.
Previously 'the Board direct that subsection (2) below shall apply,'.

Note
(a) Where a direction is given on or after 17 March 1998 under FA 1993 s 136(1)(d), (5) or (9) all be   to any accounting period ending before the appointed day (1 July 1999), all such adjustme o that made, whether by assessment, repayment of tax or otherwise, as are necessary to give direction.

---

138 Arm's length test: non-sterling trades

(1) Subsection (2) below applies where –   Je, accruing to a uced by virtue of

   (a) an exchange gain of a trade, or of p d company for an accrual period fall n a currency (the first section 136(3), (6) or (10) or 137 ich the gain is expressed

   (b) the amount falling to be set o currency) different from the (10) or 137(3) the amount (the second currency). e equivalent, expressed in the ed in the first currency.

(2) For the purposes of secti falling to be set off sha second currency, of t

(3)   The translation required by subsection (2) above shall be made by reference to the London closing exchange rate for the two currencies concerned for the first day of the accounting period which constitutes the relevant accrual period or in which that accrual period falls; and the relevant accrual period is the accrual period mentioned in subsection (1)(a) above.

(4)   Subsection (2) above shall have effect subject to the application for succeeding accrual periods of this section as regards an amount falling to be set off.

(5)   References in subsections (1) and (2) above to the amount falling to be set off include references to so much of that amount as remains after any application of section 136(3), (6) or (10) or 137(3) for earlier accrual periods.

Deferral of unrealised gains

139   Claim to defer unrealised gains

(1)   This section applies where (apart from a claim under this section as regards an accounting period) an unrealised exchange gain would accrue to a company –

(a)   for an accrual period constituting or falling within the accounting period, and

(b)   as regards a long-term capital asset or a long-term capital liability;

and the reference here to an exchange gain is to an exchange gain of a trade or an exchange gain of part of a trade or a non-trading exchange gain.

(2)   This section does not apply unless an amount is available for relief under this section for the accounting period.

(3)   The company may claim that –

(a)   the gain, or part of it, shall be treated in accordance with section 140(3) below, and

(b)   an amount shall be treated in accordance with section 140(4) to (10) below as regards the asset or liability.

(4)   claim must –

ɔulate the amount of the gain or part to be treated as mentioned (b bsection (3)(a) above;

e the amount to be treated as mentioned in subsection (c) ᴵ ᴼve;

(5)   The fol asset or liability concerned.

(a)   only whereapply to a claim –

would a y be made as regards an accounting period, but constitut pplies in relation to two or more gains which be made pany for an accrual period or accrual periods ithin the accounting period the claim may re than one of the gains;

(3) The translation required by subsection (2) above shall be made by reference to the London closing exchange rate for the two currencies concerned for the first day of the accounting period which constitutes the relevant accrual period or in which that accrual period falls; and the relevant accrual period is the accrual period mentioned in subsection (1)(a) above.

(4) Subsection (2) above shall have effect subject to the application for succeeding accrual periods of this section as regards an amount falling to be set off.

(5) References in subsections (1) and (2) above to the amount falling to be set off include references to so much of that amount as remains after any application of section 136(3), (6) or (10) or 137(3) for earlier accrual periods.

Deferral of unrealised gains

139 Claim to defer unrealised gains

(1) This section applies where (apart from a claim under this section as regards an accounting period) an unrealised exchange gain would accrue to a company –

   (a) for an accrual period constituting or falling within the accounting period, and

   (b) as regards a long-term capital asset or a long-term capital liability;

and the reference here to an exchange gain is to an exchange gain of a trade or an exchange gain of part of a trade or a non-trading exchange gain.

(2) This section does not apply unless an amount is available for relief under this section for the accounting period.

(3) The company may claim that –

   (a) the gain, or part of it, shall be treated in accordance with section 140(3) below, and

   (b) an amount shall be treated in accordance with section 140(4) to (10) below as regards the asset or liability.

(4) The claim must –

   (a) stipulate the amount of the gain or part to be treated as mentioned in subsection (3)(a) above;

   (b) stipulate the amount to be treated as mentioned in subsection (3)(b) above;

   (c) identify the asset or liability concerned.

(5) The following rules apply to a claim –

   (a) only one claim may be made as regards an accounting period, but where this section applies in relation to two or more gains which would accrue to a company for an accrual period or accrual periods constituting or falling within the accounting period the claim may be made in relation to more than one of the gains;

and any reference in this section to an exchange loss is to an exchange loss of a trade or an exchange loss of part of a trade or a non-trading exchange loss.

(2) The exchange loss shall be treated as not accruing to the company for the accrual period.

(3) Where subsection (2) above applies and the accrual period is not the last to occur as regards the contract while it is held by the company –

   (a) an amount equal to the amount of the loss shall be set off against appropriate exchange gains accruing to the company as regards the contract for subsequent accrual periods, and

   (b) any such gain shall then be treated as reduced by that amount or by so much of it as cannot be set off under this subsection against any such gain accruing for an earlier accrual period;

   and an appropriate exchange gain is an exchange gain of the trade concerned (if the exchange loss is an exchange loss of a trade) or an exchange gain of the part of the trade concerned (if the exchange loss is an exchange loss of part of a trade) or a non-trading exchange gain (if the exchange loss is a non-trading exchange loss).

(4) In applying subsection (1)(b) above all factors shall be taken into account including any currency that would have been involved and any amounts that would have been involved.

---

[1] Inserted by FA 1998, s 109 with effect in relation to transactions entered into at any time as respects accounting periods ending on or after the day appointed by FA 1994, s 199 for the purposes of Chapter III of Part IV of that Act (1 July 1999).
Previously 'but paragraph (b) above shall only apply if the Board so direct.

[2] Deleted by FA 1998, s 109 with effect as in [1] above.
Previously 'and'.

[3] Deleted by FA 1998, s 109 with effect as in [1] above.
Previously 'the Board direct that subsection (2) below shall apply,'.

Note
(a) Where a direction is given on or after 17 March 1998 under FA 1993 s 136(1)(d), (5) or (9) relates to any accounting period ending before the appointed day (1 July 1999), all such adjustments shall be made, whether by assessment, repayment of tax or otherwise, as are necessary to give effect to that direction.

---

138   Arm's length test: non-sterling trades

(1) Subsection (2) below applies where –

   (a) an exchange gain of a trade, or of part of a trade, accruing to a company for an accrual period falls to be reduced by virtue of section 136(3), (6) or (10) or 137(3) above, and

   (b) the amount falling to be set off is expressed in a currency (the first currency) different from the currency in which the gain is expressed (the second currency).

(2) For the purposes of section 136(3), (6) or (10) or 137(3) the amount falling to be set off shall be treated as the equivalent, expressed in the second currency, of the amount expressed in the first currency.

(4) If throughout the second accrual period the asset is held, or the liability is owed, by the company solely for the purposes of a trade or part of a trade –

    (a) an exchange gain of the trade or part for the accrual period shall be treated as accruing to the company as regards the asset or liability,

    (b) the amount of the gain shall be the amount stipulated under section 139(4)(b) above as regards the asset or liability, and

    (c) section 128(4) above shall apply.

(5) If throughout the second accrual period the asset is held, or the liability is owed, by the company solely for purposes other than trading purposes –

    (a) a non-trading exchange gain for the accrual period shall be treated as accruing to the company as regards the asset or liability,

    (b) the amount of the gain shall be the amount stipulated under section 139(4)(b) above as regards the asset or liability, and

    (c) section 129(2) above shall apply.

(6) Where as regards the second accrual period neither subsection (4) nor subsection (5) above applies –

    (a) the amount stipulated under section 139(4)(b) above as regards the asset or liability shall be apportioned for the period on a just and reasonable basis, and

    (b) subsections (7) and (8) below shall apply.

(7) Where for the second accrual period part of an amount is attributed to a trade or part of a trade under subsection (6) above –

    (a) an exchange gain of the trade or part for the accrual period shall be treated as accruing to the company as regards the asset or liability,

    (b) the amount of the gain shall be the amount of the part so attributed, and

    (c) section 128(4) above shall apply.

(8) Where for the second accrual period part of an amount is attributed to purposes other than trading purposes under subsection (6) above –

    (a) a non-trading exchange gain for the accrual period shall be treated as accruing to the company as regards the asset or liability,

    (b) the amount of the gain shall be the amount of the part so attributed, and

    (c) section 129(2) above shall apply.

(9) In a case where –

    (a) an exchange gain of a trade or of part of a trade for the second accrual period is treated as accruing to a company by virtue of the preceding provisions of this section (or would be so treated apart from this subsection), and

    (b) in that period the asset or liability is to any extent held or owed by the company in exempt circumstances,

(b) the amount stipulated under subsection (4)(b) above as regards an asset or liability must be the same as, and must be expressed in the same currency as, the amount of the gain or part stipulated under subsection (4)(a) above as regards the asset or liability;

(c) the amount (or total of the amounts) stipulated under subsection (4)(a) above as regards an accounting period must not exceed the amount available for relief under this section for the accounting period.

(6) A claim may not be made or withdrawn as regards an accounting period if –

(a) the company has been assessed to corporation tax for the period, and

(b) the assessment has become final and conclusive;

but the preceding provisions of this subsection do not apply if the claim or withdrawal is made before the expiry of the period of two years beginning with the end of the accounting period.

(7) In a case where –

(a) the period of six years beginning with the end of an accounting period expires, and

(b) no assessment of the company to corporation tax for the accounting period has become final and conclusive,

a claim may not be made or withdrawn as regards that accounting period.

(8) In a case where –

(a) subsection (6) or (7) above would otherwise prevent a claim being made in a particular case, and

(b) the Board make a determination under this subsection,

a claim may be made on or before such day as the Board allow.

Cross-references. See SI 1994 No 3228, Reg 4 for an amendment to subsection (5) above which has effect where a claim is made under section 139 by a company for an accounting period for the whole or part of which it is a member of a group.

---

140   Deferral of unrealised gains

(1) This section applies where a claim is made under section 139 above as regards an asset or liability.

(2) For the purposes of this section –

(a) the first accrual period is the accrual period mentioned in section 139(1) above, and

(b) the second accrual period is the accrual period next occurring as regards the asset or liability while it is held or owed by the company.

(3) Any gain or part whose amount is stipulated under section 139(4)(a) above as regards the asset or liability shall be treated as not accruing as regards the asset or liability for the first accrual period.

to that extent the gain shall be treated as a non-trading exchange gain (and not as a gain of the trade or part) and section 129(2) above shall apply.

(10) Any apportionment required by subsection (9) above shall be made on a just and reasonable basis.

(11) Subsections (4) to (10) above shall have effect subject to any further application of section 139 above as regards the asset or liability.

[(12) For the purposes of this section a part of a trade is any part of a trade which is treated for the purposes of section 93 above as if it were a separate business for the relevant accounting period; and the relevant accounting period is the accounting period which constitutes the second accrual period or in which that accrual period falls.]¹

---

¹   Substituted by FA 2000, s 106(8) in relation to accounting periods beginning on or after 1 January 2000 and ending on or after 21 March 2000.
Previously
'(12) For the purposes of this section a part of a trade is any part of a trade whose basic profits or losses for the relevant accounting period are by virtue of regulations under section 94 above to be computed and expressed in a particular currency for the purposes of corporation tax; and the relevant accounting period is the accounting period which constitutes the second accrual period or in which that accrual period falls.'.

---

141   Deferral: amount available for relief

(1) An amount is available for relief under section 139 above for an accounting period if amount A is exceeded by amount B or (if amount C is lower than amount B) amount A is exceeded by amount C; and the amount available for relief for the period is the amount of the difference between amount A and amount B or (as the case may be) between amount A and amount C.

(2) Amount A is one tenth of the amount falling within subsection (3) below.

(3) The amount falling within this subsection is an amount equal to the amount of the company's profits for the accounting period on which corporation tax would fall finally to be borne apart from–

(a) a claim under section 139 above as regards the accounting period, and

(b) section 402 of the Taxes Act 1988 (group relief);

and section 238(4) of the Taxes Act 1988 (amount of profits on which corporation tax falls finally to be borne) shall apply for the purposes of this subsection.

(4) Amount B is the amount found by deducting amount B(2) from amount B(1) where–

(a) amount B(1) is the total amount of unrealised exchange gains which accrue or would (apart from a claim under section 139 above as regards the accounting period) accrue to the company, in an accrual period or accrual periods constituting or falling within the accounting period, as regards long-term capital assets or long-term capital liabilities or both;

(b) amount B(2) is the total amount of unrealised exchange losses accruing to the company in such an accrual period or accrual periods as regards such assets or liabilities or both.

(5) Amount C is the amount found by deducting amount C(2) from amount C(1) where–

(a) amount C(1) is the total amount of exchange gains which accrue or would (apart from a claim under section 139 above as regards the accounting period) accrue to the company, in an accrual period or accrual periods falling within the accounting period, as regards relevant items;

(b) amount C(2) is the total amount of exchange losses accruing to the company in such an accrual period or periods as regards relevant items.

(6) In subsections (4) and (5) above the references to exchange gains and losses are to exchange gains and losses of a trade and exchange gains and losses of part of a trade and non-trading exchange gains and losses.

(7) For the purposes of subsection (5) above relevant items are–

(a) assets falling within section 153(1)(a) below;

(b) liabilities falling within section 153(2)(a) below;

(c) currency contracts.

Cross-references. See SI 1994 No 3228, Reg 4 for amendments to this section which have effect where a claim is made under section 139 above by a company for an accounting period for the whole or part of which it is a member of a group.

---

142 Deferral: non-sterling trades

(1) Where apart from this subsection –

(a) a gain falling within section 139(1) above would be expressed in a currency other than sterling, or

(b) a gain or loss falling within section 141(4) or (5) above would be expressed in a currency other than sterling,

the amount of the gain or loss shall be treated for the purposes of sections 139 to 141 above as the sterling equivalent of its amount expressed in the other currency.

[(2) For the purposes of subsection (1) above the sterling equivalent of an amount is the sterling equivalent calculated by reference to such rate of exchange as applies by virtue of section 94 above in the case of the profits or losses for the accounting period concerned of the business or part of which the gain or loss is a gain or loss (or would be apart from section 139 above)][1]

(3) Subsection (4) below applies where –

(a) part of an exchange gain of a [business][2], or part of an exchange gain of part of a [business][2], is treated as not accruing to a company for an accrual period by virtue of section 140(3) above, and

(b) the local currency of the [business]² or part for the accounting period which constitutes the accrual period or in which it falls is a currency other than sterling.

(4) The amount the company is treated as receiving under section 128(4) [or 129(2)]³ above in respect of the accounting period and by virtue of the gain (as reduced) shall be [the amount computed and expressed in that currency.]⁴.

(5) In a case where –

(a) an exchange gain of a [business]², or of part of a [business]², for an accrual period is treated as accruing to a company under section 140 above, and

(b) the local currency of the [business]² or part for the accounting period which constitutes the accrual period or in which it falls is a currency other than sterling,

the amount of the gain shall be treated as the local currency equivalent of its amount expressed in sterling.

(6) The translation required by subsection (5) above shall be made by reference to the London closing exchange rate for the two currencies concerned –

(a) for the last day of the accrual period mentioned in subsection (5) above, or

(b) if that accrual period does not end with the end of a day, for the day on which that accrual period ends.

---

¹ Substituted by FA 2000, s 106(a), in relation to accounting periods beginning on or after 1 January 2000 and ending on or after 21 March 2000.
Previously
'(2) For the purposes of subsection (1) above the sterling equivalent of an amount is –

   (a) the sterling equivalent calculated by reference to such rate of exchange as applies by virtue of section 93(6) above in the case of the basic profits or losses for the accounting period concerned of the trade of which the gain or loss is a gain or loss (or would be apart from section 139 above), or

   (b) the sterling equivalent calculated by reference to such a rate of exchange as applies by virtue of section 94(11) above in the case of the basic profits or losses for the accounting period concerned of the part of the trade of which the gain or loss is a gain or loss (or would be apart from section 139 above).'.

² Substituted by FA 2000, s 106(10), as in ¹ above.
Previously
'business'.

³ Inserted by FA 2000, s 106(11), as in ¹ above.

⁴ Substituted by FA 2000, s 106(11), as in ¹ above.
Previously
'taken into account after the basic profits or losses of the trade or part for the accounting period are found in sterling for the purposes of corporation tax.'.

---

143 Deferral: supplementary

(1) For the purposes of sections 139 and 141 above and this section an exchange gain or loss is unrealised if the accrual period concerned is one

which ends solely by virtue of an accounting period of the company coming to an end.

(2) In a case where –

(a) an unrealised exchange gain would accrue as mentioned in section 139(1) above,

(b) the gain represents the whole or part of an initial exchange gain accruing under section 127 above, and

(c) the whole or part of the unrealised exchange gain is attributable to any part by which the nominal amount of the debt has decreased,

the company may not claim under section 139 above as regards so much of the unrealised exchange gain as is so attributable.

(3) In applying subsection (2)(c) above the gain shall be apportioned on a just and reasonable basis.

(4) For the purposes of sections 139 and 141 above an asset or liability is a long-term capital asset or liability if the following conditions are fulfilled –

(a) the asset or liability falls within section 153(1)(a) or (2)(a) below,

(b) the debt under which it subsists is such that, under the terms as originally entered into, the time for settlement is not less than one year from the time when the debt was created, and

(c) the asset or liability represents capital throughout the accounting period mentioned in section 139(1) above;

and the time for settlement is the earliest time at which the creditor can require settlement if he exercises all available options and rights.

(5) For the purposes of section 140 above an asset is held, or a liability is owed, in exempt circumstances at a given time if it is then held or owed –

(a) for the purposes of long term insurance business;

(b) for the purposes of mutual insurance business;

(c) for the purposes of the occupation of commercial woodlands;

(d) by a housing association approved at that time for the purposes of section 488 of the Taxes Act 1988;

(e) by a self-build society approved at that time for the purposes of section 489 of that Act.

(6) In subsection (5) above –

'long term insurance business' means insurance business of any of the classes specified in Schedule 1 to the Insurance Companies Act 1982;

'commercial woodlands' means woodlands in the United Kingdom which are managed on a commercial basis and with a view to the realisation of profits.

(7) Regulations may –

(a) make provision modifying the effect of sections 139 to 142 above and the preceding provisions of this section in a case where the debt under which a long-term capital asset or liability subsists is settled and replaced to any extent by another debt under which (or other debts under each of which) such an asset or liability subsists;

(b) make provision modifying the effect of sections 139 to 142 above and the preceding provisions of this section in a case where a group of companies is involved;

(c) provide that the amount falling within section 141(3) above shall be treated as reduced in accordance with prescribed rules;

and any provision under paragraph (a) above may include provision that realised gains or losses are to be treated as wholly or partly unrealised.

Irrecoverable debts

144 Irrecoverable debts

(1) In a case where –

(a) a qualifying company holds an asset consisting of a right to settlement under a qualifying debt or owes a liability consisting of a duty to settle under such a debt, and

(b) [...]¹ as regards any accounting period of the company, [...]² all of the debt outstanding immediately before the end of the period could at that time reasonably have been regarded as irrecoverable,

the company shall be treated for the purposes of this Chapter as if immediately before the end of that accounting period it ceased to be entitled to the asset or subject to the liability.

(2) Subsection (3) below applies in a case where –

(a) paragraph (a) of subsection (1) above applies, and

(b) [...]¹ as regards any accounting period of the company, [...]² part of the debt outstanding immediately before the end of the period could at that time reasonably have been regarded as irrecoverable.

(3) The company shall be treated for the purposes of this Chapter as if –

(a) immediately after the beginning of the accounting period next following the accounting period mentioned in subsection (2) above there were a decrease in the nominal amount of the debt outstanding, and

(b) the decrease were of an amount equal to so much of the debt, expressed in its settlement currency, as was outstanding immediately before the end of the accounting period mentioned in subsection (2) above and [...]³ could at that time reasonably have been regarded as irrecoverable.

(4) [...]⁴

---

¹ Deleted by FA 1996, 20 Sch 68 in respect of accounting periods ending on or after a date to be appointed (intended to be no later than 31 March 1998). Previously 'the inspector is satisfied'.

²   Deleted by FA 1996, 20 Sch 68 as in ¹ above.
     Previously 'that'.

³   Deleted by FA 1996, 20 Sch 68 as in ¹ above.
     Previously 'in the opinion of the inspector'.

⁴   Deleted by FA 1996, 20 Sch 68 as in ¹ above.
     Previously
     'Where there is an appeal, this section shall be construed as if–
     (a) 'inspector is satisfied' (in each place) read 'Commissioners concerned are satisfied', and
     (b) 'opinion of the inspector' read 'opinion of the Commissioners concerned'.'

---

145   Irrecoverable debts that become recoverable

(1)   Subsection (2) below applies where –

    (a)   a company has been treated as mentioned in section 144(1) above as regards a debt,

    (b)   at a time (the later time) falling after the end of the accounting period mentioned in section 144(1)(b) above all or part of the debt is actually outstanding, and

    (c)   [...]¹ all or part of the amount actually outstanding at the later time could at that time reasonably have been regarded as recoverable.

(2)   The company shall be treated for the purposes of this Chapter as if –

    (a)   immediately after the later time it had become entitled to an asset consisting of a right to settlement under the debt or (as the case may be) subject to a liability consisting of a duty to settle under the debt, and

    (b)   the nominal amount of the debt outstanding, at the time the company became entitled or subject to the asset or liability, were an amount equal to so much of the debt, expressed in its settlement currency, as was actually outstanding at the later time and [...]² could at that time reasonably have been regarded as recoverable.

(3)   Subsections (4) and (5) below apply where –

    (a)   a company has been treated as mentioned in section 144(3) above as regards a debt, or

    (b)   a company has been treated as mentioned in subsection (2) above as regards a debt by virtue of the fact that [...]² part of the debt could, at the later time, reasonably have been regarded as recoverable.

(4)   In a case where –

    (a)   at a time (the relevant time) falling after the end of the accounting period mentioned in section 144(2)(b) above or (as the case may be) falling after the later time all or part of the debt is actually outstanding,

    (b)   [...]¹ all or part of the amount actually outstanding at the relevant time could at that time reasonably have been regarded as recoverable, and

316

(c) the recoverable amount exceeds the amount which (taking into account section 144(3) above, subsection (2) above and any previous application of this subsection) is the nominal amount of the debt outstanding at the relevant time,

the company shall be treated for the purposes of this Chapter as if, immediately after the relevant time, there were an increase in the nominal amount of the debt outstanding and the increase were of an amount equal to the excess mentioned in paragraph (c) above.

(5) For the purposes of subsection (4) above the recoverable amount is an amount equal to so much of the debt, expressed in its settlement currency, as was actually outstanding at the relevant time and [...]² could at that time reasonably have been regarded as recoverable.

(6) [...]³

---

¹   Deleted by FA 1996, 20 Sch 69 in respect of accounting periods ending on or after a date to be appointed (intended to be no later than 31 March 1998).
Previously 'the inspector is satisfied that'.

²   Deleted by FA 1996, 20 Sch 69 as in ¹ above.
Previously 'in the opinion of the inspector'.

³   Deleted by FA 1996, 20 Sch 69 as in ¹ above.
Previously
'Where there is an appeal, this section shall be construed as if–
(a) 'inspector is satisfied' (in each place) read 'Commissioners concerned are satisfied', and
(b) 'opinion of the inspector' (in each place) read 'opinion of the Commissioners concerned'.'

Currency contracts: special cases

146   Early termination of currency contract

(1) This section applies where –

   (a) a qualifying company ceases to be entitled to rights and subject to duties under a currency contract, and

   (b) at the time it so ceases it has neither received nor made payment of any currency in pursuance of the contract.

[(1A) This section also applies where –

   (a) a qualifying company ceases to be entitled to rights and subject to duties under a currency contract, and

   (b) it so ceases by virtue of the making of a payment to or by the company of an amount (in whatever currency) designed to represent any difference in value at the specified time between the two payments referred to in section 126(1) above.]¹

(2) If the company has a net contractual gain of a trade it shall be treated for the purposes of the Tax Acts as –

   (a) incurring in the trade a loss of an amount equal to that gain, and

   (b) incurring the loss in respect of the last relevant accounting period.

(3) If the company has a net contractual loss of a trade it shall be treated for the purposes of the Tax Acts as –

    (a) receiving in respect of the trade an amount equal to that loss, and

    (b) receiving the amount in respect of the last relevant accounting period.

(4) If the company has a net contractual non-trading gain –

    (a) it shall be treated as incurring by virtue of section 129 above a loss of an amount equal to the amount of that gain,

    (b) it shall be treated as incurring the loss in the last relevant accounting period, and

    (c) in relation to that accounting period references to amount B shall be construed accordingly.

(5) If the company has a net contractual non-trading loss –

    (a) it shall be treated as receiving by virtue of section 129 above an amount equal to the amount of that loss,

    (b) it shall be treated as receiving the amount in the last relevant accounting period, and

    (c) in relation to that accounting period references to amount A shall be construed accordingly.

(6) For the purposes of this section –

    (a) the termination time is the time mentioned in subsection (1)(b) above;

    (b) the last relevant accounting period is the company's accounting period in which the termination time falls;

    (c) the relevant accounting periods are that accounting period and the company's accounting periods preceding it.

(7) This is how to find out whether the company has a net contractual gain or loss of a trade and (if it has) its amount –

    (a) take the aggregate of the amounts (if any) the company is treated as receiving under section 128(4) above in respect of the trade and the contract and the relevant accounting periods;

    (b) take the aggregate of the amounts (if any) of the losses the company is treated as incurring under section 128(8) above in the trade and in respect of the contract and the relevant accounting periods;

    (c) if the amount found under paragraph (a) above exceeds that found under paragraph (b) above the company has a net contractual gain of the trade of an amount equal to the excess;

    (d) if the amount found under paragraph (b) above exceeds that found under paragraph (a) above the company has a net contractual loss of the trade of an amount equal to the excess;

and in applying paragraphs (a) and (b) above ignore the effect of subsections (2) and (3) above.

(8) This is how to find out whether the company has a net contractual non-trading gain or loss and (if it has) its amount –

(a) take the aggregate of the amounts (if any) the company is treated as receiving under section 129(2) above in respect of the contract in the relevant accounting periods;

(b) take the aggregate of the amounts (if any) of the losses the company is treated as incurring under section 129(4) above in respect of the contract in the relevant accounting periods;

(c) if the amount found under paragraph (a) above exceeds that found under paragraph (b) above the company has a net contractual non-trading gain of an amount equal to the excess;

(d) if the amount found under paragraph (b) above exceeds that found under paragraph (a) above the company has a net contractual non-trading loss of an amount equal to the excess;

and in applying paragraphs (a) and (b) above ignore the effect of subsections (4) and (5) above;

(9) For the purposes of subsection (7) above –

(a) an amount the company is treated as receiving under section 128(4) above in respect of part of the trade concerned shall be treated as received in respect of the trade;

(b) a loss the company is treated as incurring under section 128(8) above in part of the trade shall be treated as incurred in the trade.

(10) Where any amount or loss the company is treated as receiving or incurring as mentioned in subsection (7)(a) or (b) above would (apart from this subsection) be expressed in a currency other than the local currency of the trade for the last relevant accounting period, it shall be treated for the purposes of this section as being the local currency equivalent of the amount or loss expressed in that other currency.

(11) For the purposes of subsection (10) above the local currency equivalent of an amount is the equivalent –

(a) expressed in the local currency of the trade for the last relevant accounting period, and

(b) calculated by reference to the London closing exchange rate for the day in which the termination time falls.

(12) Subsection (13) below applies where the company has (apart from that subsection) a net contractual gain or loss of a trade and –

(a) the trade concerned has ceased before the termination time, or

(b) the company carries on exempt activities immediately before the termination time.

(13) In such a case the company shall be treated for the purposes of this section as if –

(a) it did not have the net contractual gain or loss of the trade, and

(b) it had a net contractual non-trading gain or loss (as the case may be) equal to the amount which would have been the amount of the net contractual gain or loss of the trade apart from paragraph (a) above.

(14) Where any amount found under subsection (13)(b) above would (apart from this subsection) be expressed in a currency other than sterling, it shall be treated for the purposes of this section as being the sterling equivalent of the amount expressed in that other currency; and any translation required by this subsection shall be made by reference to the London closing exchange rate for the currencies concerned for the day in which the termination time falls.

(15) For the purposes of this section a company carries on exempt activities at a given time if –

    (a) the activities it then carries on are or include any of the activities mentioned in subsection (16) below,

    (b) it is a housing association approved at that time for the purposes of section 488 of the Taxes Act 1988, or

    (c) it is a self-build society approved at that time for the purposes of section 489 of that Act.

(16) The activities referred to in subsection (15)(a) above are –

    (a) the activity of long term insurance business;

    (b) the activity of mutual insurance business;

    (c) the activity of the occupation of commercial woodlands;

and section 143(6) above applies for the purposes of this subsection.

---

¹ Inserted by FA 1994, s 115(2).

---

147 Reciprocal currency contracts

(1) This section applies where –

    (a) a qualifying company enters into a currency contract (the first contract), and

    (b) the company closes out that contract by entering into another currency contract (the second contract) with rights and duties which are reciprocal to those under the first contract.

(2) For the purposes of this Chapter the company shall be treated as ceasing, at the time it enters into the second contract, to be entitled to rights and subject to duties under the first contract without having received or made payment of any currency in pursuance of the first contract.

(3) For the purposes of this Chapter the second contract shall be ignored (except in applying the preceding provisions of this section).

Excess gains or losses

148 Excess gains or losses

(1) Regulations may provide that where prescribed conditions are fulfilled as regards an asset or liability relief from tax shall be afforded in respect

of it; and subsections (2) to (4) below shall apply for the purposes of the regulations.

(2) The prescribed conditions must be or include ones that are met where it can reasonably be said that –

(a) a loss other than an exchange loss has accrued to a qualifying company as regards the asset or liability and no relief from tax is available under the Tax Acts in respect of the loss, and

(b) exchange gains have accrued to the company as regards the asset or liability without being matched (or fully matched) by exchange losses accruing to the company as regards the asset or liability.

(3) The relief shall take such form as is prescribed and shall be such that the amount relieved does not exceed the amount of the unmatched gains.

(4) The regulations may provide that if the loss mentioned in subsection (2)(a) above is made good to any extent the relief afforded by the regulations shall be cancelled (to the extent prescribed) by an assessment to tax.

(5) Regulations may provide that where prescribed conditions are fulfilled as regards an asset or liability a charge to tax shall be imposed in respect of it; and subsections (6) and (7) below shall apply for the purposes of the regulations.

(6) The prescribed conditions must be or include ones that are met where it can reasonably be said that –

(a) a gain other than an exchange gain has accrued to a qualifying company as regards the asset or liability and no charge to tax is imposed under the Tax Acts in respect of the gain, and

(b) exchange losses have accrued to the company as regards the asset or liability without being matched (or fully matched) by exchange gains accruing to the company as regards the asset or liability.

(7) The charge shall take such form as is prescribed and shall be such that the amount charged does not exceed the amount of the unmatched losses.

(8) Regulations under this section may include provision that the relief –

(a) is subject to a claim being made;

(b) is not available in prescribed circumstances.

(9) Where (apart from this subsection) an exchange gain or loss would be expressed in a currency other than sterling, the amount of the gain or loss shall be treated for the purposes of this section as the sterling equivalent of its amount expressed in the other currency.

(10) The translation required by subsection (9) above shall be made by reference to the London closing exchange rate for the two currencies concerned –

(a) for the last day of the accrual period for which the gain or loss accrues, or

(b) if that accrual period does not end with the end of a day, for the day on which that accrual period ends.

(11)   In this section –

    (a)   references to an exchange gain are to an exchange gain of a trade or an exchange gain of part of a trade or a non-trading exchange gain;

    (b)   references to an exchange loss are to an exchange loss of a trade or an exchange loss of part of a trade or a non-trading exchange loss.

Local currency to be used

149   Local currency to be used

(1)   Subject to the following provisions of this section, the local currency for the purposes of sections 125 to 127 above is sterling.

(2)   Subsections (4) to (6) below apply where –

    (a)   at any time in an accrual period an asset or contract was held, or a liability was owed, by a qualifying company for the purposes of a [business or businesses]¹ carried on by it or of part or parts of a [business or businesses]¹ carried on by it, and

    (b)   the local currency of any such [business]² or part for the relevant accounting period is a currency other than sterling.

(3)   References in this section to the relevant accounting period are to the accounting period which constitutes the accrual period or in which the accrual period falls.

(4)   If throughout the accrual period [. . .]³ only one local currency is involved, sections 125 to [129]⁴ above shall be applied by reference to that currency.

(5)   If throughout the accrual period [. . .]⁵ more than one local currency is involved, sections 125 to [129]⁶ above shall be applied separately by reference to each local currency involved and any exchange gain or loss of a [business]⁷ or part shall be ignored unless found in the currency which is the local currency of the [business]⁷ or part for the relevant accounting period.

[(6)   In any other case –

    (a)   sections 125 to 129 above shall be applied by reference to sterling;

    (b)   those sections shall then be applied separately by reference to each local currency involved (other than sterling); and

    (c)   any exchange gain or loss of a business or part shall be ignored unless found in the currency which is the local currency of the business or part for the relevant accounting period (whether sterling or otherwise).]⁸

[(7)   For the purposes of this section a part of a business is any part of a business which is treated for the purposes of section 93 above as if it were a separate business for the relevant accounting period.]⁹

---

¹   Substituted by FA 2000, s 106(1) in relation to accounting periods beginning on or after 1 January 2000 and ending on or after 21 March 2000.

Previously
'trade or trader'.

²   Substituted by FA 2000, s 106(1), as in ¹ above.
Previously
'trade'.

³   Repealed by FA 2000, s 106(2), as in ¹ above.
Previously
'the asset or contract was held, or the liability was owed, by the company solely for trading purposes and'.

⁴   Substituted by FA 2000, s 106(2), as in ¹ above.
Previously
'128'.

⁵   Repealed by FA 2000, s 106(3), as in ¹ above.
Previously
'the asset or contract was held, or the liability was owed, by the company solely for trading purposes and'.

⁶   Substituted by FA 2000, s 106(3), as in ¹ above.
Previously
'128'.

⁷   Substituted by FA 2000, s 106(3), as in ¹ above.
Previously
'trade'.

⁸   Substituted by FA 2000, s 106(4), as in ¹ above.
Previously
'(6)   In any other case –

     (a)   sections 125 to 128 above shall be applied by reference to sterling and sections 129 to 133 above shall be applied to any non-trading exchange gain or loss;

     (b)   sections 125 to 128 above shall then be applied separately by reference to each local currency involved (other than sterling);

     (c)   any exchange gain or loss of a trade or part shall be ignored unless found in the currency which is the local currency of the trade or part for the relevant accounting period (whether sterling or otherwise).'.

⁹   Substituted by FA 2000, s 106(5), as in ¹ above.
Previously
'(7)   For the purposes of this section a part of a trade is any part of a trade whose basic profits or losses for the relevant accounting period are by virtue of regulations under section 94 above to be computed and expressed in a particular currency for the purposes of corporation tax.'.

Exchange rate to be used

150   Exchange rate at translation times

(1)   This section has effect to determine the exchange rate to be used in finding for the purposes of this Chapter the local currency equivalent at a translation time of –

     (a)   the basic valuation of an asset or liability,

     (b)   the nominal amount of a debt outstanding, or

     (c)   an amount of currency.

(2)   References in this section to the two currencies are to –

     (a)   the local currency and the nominal currency of the asset or liability concerned (where this section applies by virtue of subsection (1)(a) or (1)(b) above), or

    (b) the local currency and the currency mentioned in subsection (1)(c) above (where this section applies by virtue of subsection (1) (c) above).

(3) References in this section to an arm's length rate are to such exchange rate for the two currencies as might reasonably be expected to be agreed between persons dealing at arm's length.

(4) Subsections (5) to (7) below apply where the translation time is a translation time solely by virtue of an accounting period of the company coming to an end.

(5) In a case where –

    (a) an exchange rate for the two currencies is used (as regards the asset, liability or currency contract concerned) in the accounts of the company for the last day of the accounting period, and

    (b) the rate is an arm's length rate,

that is the exchange rate to be used as regards the asset, liability or contract.

(6) In a case where –

    (a) the provision for whose purposes the local currency equivalent falls to be found is section 126 above,

    (b) an exchange rate for the two currencies is not used (as regards the currency contract concerned) in the accounts of the company for the last day of the accounting period,

    (c) the fact that such an exchange rate is not so used conforms with normal accountancy practice, and

    (d) the exchange rate for the two currencies that is implied by the currency contract concerned is an arm's length rate,

the exchange rate mentioned in paragraph (d) above is the exchange rate to be used as regards the contract.

(7) In a case where neither subsection (5) nor subsection (6) above applies, the London closing exchange rate for the two currencies for the last day of the accounting period is the exchange rate to be used.

(8) Subsections (9) to (14) below apply where the translation time is a translation time otherwise than solely by virtue of an accounting period of the company coming to an end.

(9) In a case where –

    (a) an exchange rate for the two currencies is used (as regards the asset, liability or currency contract concerned) in the accounts of the company at the translation time,

    (b) the rate represents the average of arm's length rates for all the days falling within a period, and

    (c) the arm's length rate for any given day (other than the first) falling within the period is not significantly different from the arm's length rate for the day preceding the given day,

that is the exchange rate to be used as regards the asset, liability or contract.

(10) In a case where –

   (a) subsection (9) above does not apply,

   (b) an exchange rate for the two currencies is used (as regards the asset, liability or currency contract concerned) in the accounts of the company at the translation time, and

   (c) the rate is an arm's length rate,

   that is the exchange rate to be used as regards the asset, liability or contract.

(11) In a case where –

   (a) the provision for whose purposes the local currency equivalent falls to be found in section 126 above,

   (b) an exchange rate for the two currencies is not used (as regards the currency contract concerned) in the accounts of the company at the translation time,

   (c) the fact that such an exchange rate is not so used conforms with normal accountancy practice, and

   (d) the exchange rate for the two currencies that is implied by the currency contract concerned is an arm's length rate,

   the exchange rate mentioned in paragraph (d) above is the exchange rate to be used as regards the contract.

(12) In a case where –

   (a) none of subsections (9) to (11) above applies,

   (b) it is the company's normal practice, when using an exchange rate in its accounts, to use a rate which represents an average of exchange rates obtaining for a period, and

   (c) the London closing exchange rate for the two currencies for any given day (other than the first) falling within the relevant period is not significantly different from the London closing exchange rate for the two currencies for the day preceding the given day,

   the rate which represents the average of the London closing exchange rates for the currencies for all the days falling within the relevant period is the exchange rate to be used.

(13) In a case where none of subsections (9) to (12) above applies, the London closing exchange rate for the day in which the translation time falls is the exchange rate to be used.

(14) References in subsection (12) above to the relevant period are to the period which –

   (a) begins when the relevant accounting period begins, and

   (b) ends at the end of the day in which the translation time falls;

   and the relevant accounting period is the accounting period in which the translation time falls.

151 Exchange rate for debts whose amounts vary

   (1) Subsection (2) below has effect to determine the exchange rate to be used in finding for the purposes of this Chapter the local currency

equivalent, at a time immediately after the nominal amount of a debt outstanding increases or decreases, of any amount.

(2)   Subsections (9) to (14) of section 150 above (ignoring subsection (11)) shall apply for that purpose, but in so applying them –

(a)   references to the translation time shall be construed as references to the time mentioned in subsection (1) above;

(b)   references to the two currencies shall be construed as references to the local currency and the settlement currency of the debt.

Interpretation: companies

152   Qualifying companies

(1)   Subject to the following provisions of this section, any company is a qualifying company.

(2)   […]¹

(3)   Where a unit trust scheme is an authorised unit trust as respects an accounting period the trustees (who are deemed to be a company for certain purposes by section 468(1) of the Taxes Act 1988) are not a qualifying company as regards that period.

(4)   A company which is approved for the purposes of section 842 of the Taxes Act 1988 (investment trusts) for an accounting period is not a qualifying company as regards that period.

(5)   In this section –

'unit trust scheme' has the same meaning as in section 469 of the Taxes Act 1988;

'authorised unit trust' has the same meaning as in section 468 of that Act.

---

¹   Repealed by FA 1996, 41 Sch Part V (3) in relation to accounting periods ending after 31 March 1996 but subject to transitional provisions in FA 1996, 15 Sch.
Previously 'A company established for charitable purposes is not a qualifying company.'

Interpretation: assets, liabilities and contracts

153   Qualifying assets and liabilities

(1)   As regards a qualifying company, each of the following is a qualifying asset –

(a)   a right to settlement under a qualifying debt (whether or not the debt is a debt on a security);

(b)   a unit of currency;

(c)   a share held in qualifying circumstances;

but paragraph (a) above shall have effect subject to subsections (3) and (4) below.

(2)   As regards a qualifying company, each of the following is a qualifying liability –

(a) a duty to settle under a qualifying debt (whether or not the debt is a debt on a security);

(b) a liability that takes the form of a provision made by the company in respect of a duty to which it may become subject and which (if it were to become subject to it) would be a duty to settle under a qualifying debt;

(c) a duty to transfer a right to settlement under a qualifying debt on a security, where the duty subsists under a contract and the company is not entitled to the right;

(d) a duty to transfer a share or shares, where the duty subsists under a contract and the company is not entitled to the share or shares;

but paragraphs (a) to (d) above shall have effect subject to subsections (5) to (9) below.

(3) A right to settlement under a qualifying debt is not a qualifying asset if it is a right under a currency contract.

(4) [A right to settlement under a qualifying debt is not a qualifying asset where the company having the right holds an asset representing the debt and that asset is –

(a) an asset to which section 92 of the Finance Act 1996 applies (convertible securities); or

(b) an asset representing a loan relationship to which section 93 of that Act (relationships linked to the value of chargeable assets) applies.][1]

(5) A duty to settle under a qualifying debt is not a qualifying liability if it is a duty under a currency contract.

(6) [...][2]

(7) A liability falling within subsection (2)(b) above is not a qualifying liability unless –

(a) the duty to settle would (if the company were to become subject to it) be owed for the purposes of a trade, and

(b) the provision falls to be taken into account (apart from this Chapter) in computing the profits or losses of the trade for corporation tax purposes.

(8) A duty falling within subsection (2)(c) above is not a qualifying liability unless the right would be a qualifying asset if the company were entitled to it.

(9) A duty falling within subsection (2)(d) above is not a qualifying liability unless the share (or each of the shares) would be a qualifying asset if the company were entitled to it.

(10) For the purposes of this section each of the following is a qualifying debt –

(a) a debt falling to be settled by the payment of money;

(b) a debt falling to be settled by the transfer of a right to settlement under another debt, itself falling to be settled by the payment of money;

and for the purposes of this subsection an ecu shall be regarded as money.

(11) For the purposes of subsections (1)(c) and (4) above qualifying circumstances, in relation to an asset consisting of a share or a right to settlement, are circumstances where the qualifying company carries on a trade and –

(a) if the company were to transfer the asset, the transfer would fall to be taken into account (apart from this Chapter) in computing the profits or losses of the trade for corporation tax purposes, and

(b) if the asset were held by the company at the end of an accounting period, the valuation of the asset to be shown in the company's accounts for that time would fall to be found by taking the local currency equivalent at that time of the valuation put on the asset by the company (whether at that time or earlier) expressed in the nominal currency of the asset;

and the reference here to the local currency is to the local currency of the trade for the accounting period.

[...][3]

(12) Interest accrued in respect of a debt shall not be treated as part of the debt.

---

[1]   Substituted by FA 1996, 14 Sch 70 in relation to accounting periods ending after 31 March 1996 but subject to transitional provisions in FA 1996, 15 Sch.
Previously
'A right to settlement under a qualifying debt is not a qualifying asset if the debt is a debt on a security [and did not represent a normal commercial loan when it was created][a], but the preceding provisions of this subsection do not apply if the security is a deep gain security or the right is held in qualifying circumstances.'
[a]   Substituted by FA 1995, 24 Sch 4.
Previously 'which under the terms of issue can be converted into or exchanged for a share or shares'.

[2]   Deleted by FA 1996, 14 Sch 70 as in [1] above.
Previously
'A duty to settle under a qualifying debt is not a qualifying liability if the debt is a debt on a security [and did not represent a normal commercial loan when it was created][a], but the preceding provisions of this subsection do not apply if the security is a deep gain security.'
[a]   Substituted by FA 1995, 24 Sch 4.
Previously 'which under the terms of issue can be converted into or exchanged for a share or shares'.

[3]   Repealed by FA 1996, 41 Sch Part V(3) as in [1] above.
Previously
'[(11A) In subsections (4) and (6) above 'normal commercial loan' has the meaning which would be given by sub-paragraph (5) of paragraph 1 of Schedule 18 to the Taxes Act 1988 if–
(a) for paragraph (a)(i) to (iii) of that sub-paragraph there were substituted the words 'corporate bonds (within the meaning of section 117 of the Taxation of Chargeable Gains Act 1992)', and
(b) paragraphs (b) and (c) of that sub-paragraph were omitted.][a]
[a]   Inserted by FA 1995, 24 Sch 4.

---

154   Definitions connected with assets

(1) Subject to the following provisions of this section, a company becomes entitled to an asset when it becomes unconditionally entitled to it.

(2) In determining whether or not a company is unconditionally entitled to an asset, any transfer by way of security of the asset or of any interest or right in or over the asset shall be ignored.

(3) Where a company agrees to acquire an asset by transfer it becomes entitled to it when the contract is made and not on a later transfer made pursuant to the contract; but the preceding provisions of this subsection do not apply where the agreement is by way of a currency contract.

(4) Where a company agrees to dispose of an asset by transfer it ceases to be entitled to it when the contract is made and not on a later transfer made pursuant to the contract.

(5) If a contract is conditional (whether on the exercise of an option or otherwise) for the purposes of subsections (3) and (4) above it is made when the condition is satisfied.

[(5A) The question whether a company becomes unconditionally entitled at a particular time to an asset falling within section 153(1)(a) above shall be determined without reference to the fact that there is or is not a later time when, or before which, the whole or any part of the debt is required to be paid.

(5B) Where an asset falling within section 153(1)(a) above consists of a right to interest –

(a) a company becomes unconditionally entitled to the asset at the time when or (as the case may be) before which the interest is required to be paid to the company, and

(b) subsection (5A) above shall not apply.]¹

(6) Where a company ceases to be entitled to an asset and at a later time becomes entitled to the same asset, with effect from the later time the asset shall be treated as if it were a different asset.

(7) In a case where –

(a) at different times a company becomes entitled to rights to settlement under debts on securities, and

(b) the rights are of the same kind,

the rights shall be treated as different assets and not part of the same asset.

(8) Whether a transaction involves a company becoming entitled to –

(a) one asset consisting of a right to settlement under a debt on a security, or

(b) a number of such assets,

shall be determined according to the facts of the case concerned.

(9) For the purpose of deciding whether rights to settlement under debts on securities of a particular kind are held by a company, rights of that kind acquired earlier shall be treated as disposed of before rights of that kind acquired later; and references here to acquisition and disposal are references to becoming entitled and ceasing to be entitled.

(10) For the purpose of deciding whether shares of a particular kind are held by a company, shares of that kind acquired earlier shall be treated as

disposed of before shares of that kind acquired later; and references here to acquisition and disposal are references to becoming entitled and ceasing to be entitled.

(11)   In a case where –

(a)   a rule is used for the purpose mentioned in subsection (9) or (10) above when the company's accounts are prepared,

(b)   the rule differs from that contained in the subsection, and

(c)   the accounts are prepared in accordance with normal accountancy practice,

the rule used when the accounts are prepared (and not the rule in the subsection) shall be used for the purpose.

(12)   In a case where –

(a)   a company would (apart from this subsection) become entitled to an asset at a particular time (the later time) by virtue of the preceding provisions of this section,

(b)   the asset falls within section 153(1)(a) above,

(c)   the time at which the company, in drawing up its accounts, regards itself as becoming entitled to the asset is a time (the earlier time) earlier than the later time, and

(d)   the accounts are drawn up in accordance with normal accountancy practice,

the company shall be taken to have become entitled to the asset at the earlier time and not at the later time.

[(12A)   So much of any asset as consists in a right to receive interest as respects which any sums fall to be brought into account for the purposes of Chapter II of Part IV of the Finance Act 1996 (loan relationships) shall be taken to be an asset to which the company became entitled at the following time (instead of the time for which subsection (12) above provides), that is to say–

(a)   where the sums fall to be brought into account for the purposes of that Chapter in accordance with an authorised accruals basis of accounting, the time when the interest is taken for those purposes to have accrued, and

(b)   where the sums fall to be brought into account for the purposes of that Chapter in accordance with an authorised mark to market basis of accounting, the time when the interest is taken for those purposes to have become due and payable.][2]

(13)   Where subsection (12) above applies, as regards any time beginning with the earlier time and ending immediately before the later time the nominal amount of the debt shall be taken to be –

(a)   such amount as the company treats as the nominal amount in its accounts, or

(b)   such amount as it would so treat in accordance with normal accountancy practice (if that amount is different from the amount found under paragraph (a) above).

[(13A)　In a case where –

(a)　a company would (apart from this subsection) become entitled to an asset at a particular time (the earlier time) by virtue of subsections (1) to (11) above,

(b)　the asset falls within section 153(1)(a) above and the debt concerned is a debt on a security, or the asset is a share,

(c)　the time at which the company, in drawing up its accounts, regards itself as becoming entitled to the asset is a time (the later time) later than the earlier time, and

(d)　the accounts are drawn up in accordance with normal accountancy practice,

the company shall be taken to become entitled to the asset at the later time and not at the earlier time.

(13B)　In a case where –

(a)　a company would (apart from this subsection) cease to be entitled to an asset at a particular time (the earlier time) by virtue of subsections (1) to (11) above,

(b)　the asset falls within section 153(1)(a) above and the debt concerned is a debt on a security, or the asset is a share,

(c)　the time at which the company, in drawing up its accounts, regards itself as ceasing to be entitled to the asset is a time (the later time) later than the earlier time, and

(d)　the accounts are drawn up in accordance with normal accountancy practice,

the company shall be taken to cease to be entitled to the asset at the later time and not at the earlier time.]¹

(14)　A company holds an asset at a particular time if it is entitled to it at that time.

---

¹　Inserted by FA 1994, s 114(1)(2).

²　Inserted by FA 1996, 14 Sch 71 in relation to accounting periods ending after 31 March 1996 but subject to transitional provisions in FA 1996, 15 Sch.

155　Definitions connected with liabilities

(1)　Subject to the following provisions of this section, a company becomes subject to a liability falling within section 153(2)(a) above when it becomes unconditionally subject to it.

(2)　Where a company agrees to acquire a liability falling within section 153(2)(a) above by transfer it becomes subject to it when the contract is made and not on a later transfer made pursuant to the contract.

(3)　Where a company agrees to dispose of a liability falling within section 153(2)(a) above by transfer it ceases to be subject to it when the contract is made and not on a later transfer made pursuant to the contract.

(4)　If a contract is conditional (whether on the exercise of an option or otherwise) for the purposes of subsections (2) and (3) above it is made when the condition is satisfied.

[(4A) The question whether a company becomes unconditionally subject at a particular time to a liability falling within section 153(2)(a) above shall be determined without reference to the fact that there is or is not a later time when, or before which, the whole or any part of the debt is required to be paid.

(4B) Where a liability falling within section 153(2)(a) above consists of a duty to pay interest –

(a) a company becomes unconditionally subject to the liability at the time when or (as the case may be) before which the company is required to pay the interest, and

(b) subsection (4A) above shall not apply.][1]

(5) Where a company ceases to be subject to a liability falling within section 153(2)(a) above and at a later time becomes subject to the same liability, with effect from the later time the liability shall be treated as if it were a different liability.

(6) A company becomes subject to a liability falling within section 153(2)(b) above at the time with effect from which it makes the provision.

(7) A company ceases to be subject to a liability falling within section 153(2)(b) above at the time with effect from which it deletes the provision or (if different) the time with effect from which it would delete the provision under normal accountancy practice.

(8) Where a company makes a provision falling within section 153(2)(b) above and later changes the amount, the company shall be treated as –

(a) deleting (with effect from the time when the change becomes effective) the provision representing the amount before the change, and

(b) making (with effect from that time) a new provision representing the amount as changed;

and so on for further changes.

(9) A company ceases to be subject to a liability falling within section 153(2)(c) above when it becomes entitled to the right concerned, unless it ceases to be subject to the liability earlier apart from this subsection.

(10) A company ceases to be subject to a liability falling within section 153(2)(d) above when it becomes entitled to the share or shares, unless it ceases to be subject to the liability earlier apart from this subsection.

(11) In a case where –

(a) a company would (apart from this subsection) become subject to a liability at a particular time (the later time) by virtue of the preceding provisions of this section,

(b) the liability falls within section 153(2)(a) above,

(c) the time at which the company, in drawing up its accounts, regards itself as becoming subject to the liability is a time (the earlier time) earlier than the later time, and

(d) the accounts are drawn up in accordance with normal accountancy practice,

the company shall be taken to have become subject to the liability at the earlier time and not at the later time.

[(11A) So much of any liability consisting in a liability to pay interest as respects which debits fall to be brought into account for the purposes of Chapter II of Part IV of the Finance Act 1996 (loan relationships) shall be taken to be a liability to which the company became subject at the following time (instead of at the time for which subsection (11) above provides), that is to say–

(a) where the debits fall to be brought into account for the purposes of that Chapter in accordance with an authorised accruals basis of accounting, the time when the interest is taken for those purposes to have accrued, and

(b) where the debits fall to be brought into account for the purposes of that Chapter in accordance with an authorised mark to market basis of accounting, the time when the interest is taken for those purposes to have become due and payable.]²

(12) Where subsection (11) above applies, as regards any time beginning with the earlier time and ending immediately before the later time the nominal amount of the debt shall be taken to be –

(a) such amount as the company treats as the nominal amount in its accounts, or

(b) such amount as it would so treat in accordance with normal accountancy practice (if that amount is different from the amount found under paragraph (a) above).

(13) A company owes a liability at a particular time if it is subject to it at that time.

---

¹   Inserted by FA 1994, s 114(3).

²   Inserted by FA 1996, 14 Sch 72 in relation to accounting periods ending after 31 March 1996 but subject to transitional provisions in FA 1996, 15 Sch.

---

156 Assets and liabilities: other matters

(1) Each of the following questions shall be determined according to the facts of the case concerned –

(a) whether a transaction (or series of transactions) involves the creation of one asset consisting of a right to settlement under a debt or a number of assets consisting of a number of such rights;

(b) whether a transaction (or series of transactions) involves the creation of one liability consisting of a duty to settle under a debt or a number of liabilities consisting of a number of such duties;

(c) whether a transaction (or series of transactions) involves the creation of both an asset (or assets) held and a liability (or liabilities) owed by the same company.

(2) Subsection (3) below applies where –

   (a) a company, in drawing up its accounts, regards itself as becoming
        entitled or subject to an asset or liability at a particular time,

   (b) the company, in drawing up its accounts, regards itself as ceasing to
        be entitled or subject to the asset or liability at a later time,

   (c) at the time mentioned in paragraph (a) above it could reasonably
        be expected that the company would become entitled or subject to
        such an asset or liability,

   (d) the asset or liability does not in fact come into existence before the
        later time but (if it did) it would fall within section 153(1)(a) or
        (2)(a) above, and

   (e) the accounts are drawn up in accordance with normal accountancy
        practice.

(3) The company shall be taken to –

   (a) become entitled or subject to such an asset or liability at the time it
        regards itself as becoming so entitled or subject, and

   (b) cease to be entitled or subject to such an asset or liability at the time
        it regards itself as ceasing to be so entitled or subject.

(4) Where subsection (3) above applies, as regards any time beginning with
     the time mentioned in subsection (3)(a) and ending with the time
     mentioned in subsection (3)(b) the nominal amount of the debt shall be
     taken to be –

   (a) such amount as the company treats as the nominal amount in its
        accounts, or

   (b) such amount as it would so treat in accordance with normal
        accountancy practice (if that amount is different from the amount
        found under paragraph (a) above).

157 Definitions connected with currency contracts

(1) A company becomes entitled to rights and subject to duties under a
     currency contract when it enters into the contract.

(2) A company holds a currency contract at a particular time if it is then
     entitled to rights and subject to duties under the contract; and it is
     immaterial when the rights and duties fall to be exercised and per-
     formed.

Interpretation: other provisions

158 Translation times and accrual periods

(1) Where a qualifying company holds a qualifying asset the following are
     translation times as regards the asset –

   (a) the time immediately after the company becomes entitled to the
        asset;

   (b) the time immediately before the company ceases to be entitled to
        the asset;

   (c) any time which is a time when an accounting period of the company
        ends and which falls after the time mentioned in paragraph (a)
        above and before the time mentioned in paragraph (b) above.

(2) Where a qualifying company owes a qualifying liability the following are translation times as regards the liability –

(a) the time immediately after the company becomes subject to the liability;

(b) the time immediately before the company ceases to be subject to the liability;

(c) any time which is a time when an accounting period of the company ends and which falls after the time mentioned in paragraph (a) above and before the time mentioned in paragraph (b) above.

(3) Where a qualifying company enters into a currency contract the following are translation times as regards the contract –

(a) the time immediately after the company becomes entitled to rights and subject to duties under the contract;

(b) the time immediately before the company ceases to be entitled to those rights and subject to those duties;

(c) any time which is a time when an accounting period of the company ends and which falls after the time mentioned in paragraph (a) above and before the time mentioned in paragraph (b) above.

(4) As regards a qualifying asset, a qualifying liability or a currency contract an accrual period is a period which –

(a) begins with a time which is a translation time (other than the last to fall) as regards the asset, liability or contract, and

(b) ends with the time which is the next translation time to fall as regards the asset, liability or contract.

159   Basic valuation

(1) Subject to the following provisions of this section, the basic valuation of an asset or liability is –

(a) such valuation as the company puts on it with regard to the time immediately after the company becomes entitled or subject to it, or

(b) such valuation as the company would put on it with regard to that time under normal accountancy practice, if that valuation is different from that found under paragraph (a) above.

(2) Where (apart from this subsection) the valuation under subsection (1) above would be in a currency (the actual currency) other than the nominal currency, it shall be taken to be the equivalent, expressed in terms of the nominal currency, of the valuation in the actual currency; and the translation required by this subsection shall be made by reference to the London closing exchange rate for the two currencies concerned for the day in which the time mentioned in subsection (1) above falls.

(3) The basic valuation of a liability falling within section 153(2)(c) or (d) above is the consideration for the company becoming subject to the liability; and any consideration or part that is not pecuniary shall be taken to be equal to its open market value –

(a) found at the time when the company becomes subject to the liability, and

(b) if part of the consideration is pecuniary, expressed in the same currency as that part.

(4) Where (apart from this subsection) the valuation under subsection (3) above would be in a currency (the actual currency) other than the nominal currency, it shall be taken to be the equivalent, expressed in terms of the nominal currency, of the valuation in the actual currency; and the translation required by this subsection shall be made by reference to the London closing exchange rate for the two currencies concerned for the day on which the company becomes subject to the liability.

[(5) Where—

(a) a company becomes entitled, on any transfer by virtue of which it becomes a party to a loan relationship, to a right of settlement under a qualifying debt on a security, and

(b) that transfer is a transfer with accrued interest,

the basic valuation of that right shall be found by taking the consideration for the company's becoming entitled to the right and then deducting the amount of the accrued interest the right to which is transferred.]¹

(10) Subsections (11) and (12) below apply where –

(a) section 127 above applies as regards an asset or liability for an accrual period (the earlier period), and

(b) section 125 or 127 above applies as regards the asset or liability for the next accrual period (the later period).

(11) As regards the later period the basic valuation of the asset or liability shall be taken to be –

(a) the nominal amount of the debt outstanding immediately before the beginning of the later period, or

(b) if section 127(7) above also applies as regards the earlier period, the amount found under section 127(10) for that period.

(12) As regards an accrual period which falls after the later period the basic valuation of the asset or liability shall be the amount found under subsection (11) above, subject to any subsequent application of that subsection.

---

¹   Substituted for subsections (5) to (9) by FA 1996, 14 Sch 73 in relation to accounting periods ending after 31 March 1996 but not to apply in relation to transfers before 1 April 1996 and subject to transitional provisions in FA 1996, 15 Sch.
    Previously
    '(5) Subsections (6) to (9) below apply where–
        (a) the company becomes entitled to a right to settlement under a qualifying debt on a security, and
        (b) the circumstances are such that section 713(2)(b) or (3)(b) of the Taxes Act 1988 applies (transferee treated as entitled under accrued income scheme to relief or a sum found in sterling).
    (6) In such a case the basic valuation of the right shall be found by taking the consideration for the company becoming entitled to the right and–

(a) subtracting such of the amount found under section 713(2)(b) as is attributable to the right, or

(b) adding such of the amount found under section 713(3)(b) as is attributable to the right;

and any apportionment of consideration or of the amount found under section 713(2)(b) or (3)(b) shall be made on a just and reasonable basis.

(7) The following rules apply for the purposes of subsection (6) above—

(a) any consideration or part that is pecuniary shall be expressed in sterling (if not otherwise so expressed);

(b) any consideration or part that is not pecuniary shall be taken to be equal to its open market value, found at the time when the company becomes entitled to the right and expressed in sterling.

(8) Where the nominal currency of the right mentioned in subsection (5) above is not sterling, the valuation found in sterling under subsection (6) above shall be taken to be its equivalent expressed in terms of the nominal currency.

(9) Any translation required by subsection (7) or (8) above shall be made by reference to the London closing exchange rate for the currencies concerned for the day on which the company becomes entitled to the right.'

160 Nominal currency of assets and liabilities

(1) As regards an asset mentioned in section 153(1)(a) above, or a liability mentioned in section 153(2)(a) or (b) or (c) above, the nominal currency is the settlement currency of the debt mentioned in the paragraph concerned.

(2) As regards an asset mentioned in section 153(1)(b) above, the nominal currency is the currency concerned.

(3) As regards an asset mentioned in section 153(1)(c) above, the nominal currency is the currency in which the share is denominated.

(4) As regards a liability mentioned in section 153(2)(d) above, the nominal currency is the currency in which the share is (or shares are) denominated.

161 Settlement currency of a debt

(1) Subject to the following provisions of this section, the settlement currency of a debt is the currency in which ultimate settlement of the debt falls to be made.

(2) In a case where –

(a) ultimate settlement of a debt falls to be made in a particular currency, but

(b) the amount of the currency falls to be determined by reference to the value at any time of an asset consisting of or denominated in another currency,

the settlement currency of the debt is the other currency.

(3) As regards a debt mentioned in section 153(2)(b) above, and as regards a case where section 156(3) above applies, in subsections (1) and (2) above 'falls' (in each place) shall be read as 'would fall'.

(4) Where the settlement currency of a debt cannot be determined under subsections (1) to (3) above, the settlement currency of the debt is the currency that can reasonably be regarded as the most appropriate –

(a) deeming the state of affairs at settlement to be the same as the state of affairs at the material time, and

(b) having regard to subsections (1) to (3) above;

and the material time is the time immediately after the company becomes entitled to the asset mentioned in section 153(1)(a) above or subject to the liability mentioned in section 153(2)(a) or (b) or (c) above.

(5) For the purposes of this section the ecu shall be regarded as a currency.

162 Nominal amount of debt

(1) The nominal amount of debt outstanding at any time is the amount of the debt outstanding at that time, expressed in terms of the settlement currency of the debt.

(2) In a case where –

(a) a payment or repayment is made at any time in a currency other than the settlement currency of a debt, and

(b) it falls to be decided whether there is in consequence an increase or decrease in the nominal amount of the debt outstanding,

the amount of the payment or repayment shall be taken to be its equivalent expressed in terms of the settlement currency of the debt.

(3) Any translation required by this section shall be made by reference to the London closing exchange rate for the currencies concerned for the day in which the time concerned falls.

163 Local currency of a trade

(1) Subject to subsection (2) below, the local currency of a [business][1] for an accounting period is sterling.

[(2) Where by virtue of section 93 above the profits or losses of a business or part of a business for an accounting period are to be computed and expressed in a currency other than sterling for the purposes of corporation tax, that other currency is the local currency of the business or part of a business for the period.][2]

(4) For the purposes of this section the ecu shall be regarded as a currency other than sterling; and references in this Chapter to a currency other than sterling shall be construed accordingly.

---

[1] Substituted by FA 2000, s 106(12) in relation to accounting periods beginning on or after 1 January 2000 and ending on or after 21 March 2000. Previously 'trade'.

[2] Substituted by FA 2000, s 106(13) as in [1] above. Previously
'(2) Where by virtue of regulations under section 93 above the basic profits or losses of a trade for an accounting period are to be computed and expressed in a currency other than sterling for

the purposes of corporation tax, that other currency is the local currency of the trade for the period.

(3) Where by virtue of regulations under section 94 above the basic profits or losses of part of a trade for an accounting period are to be computed and expressed in a particular currency for the purposes of corporation tax, that currency is the local currency of the part for the period'.

---

164 Interpretation: miscellaneous

(1) References to –

    (a) initial exchange gains and losses,

    (b) exchange gains and losses of a trade or of part of a trade,

    (c) non-trading exchange gains and losses, and

    (d) the accrual of gains and losses mentioned in paragraphs (a) to (c) above,

shall be construed in accordance with sections 125 to 129 above and Schedule 15 to this Act.

(2) References to a currency contract shall be construed in accordance with section 126(1) [and (1A)]¹ above.

(3) References to a qualifying debt shall be construed in accordance with section 153(10) above.

(4) References to a company's commencement day shall be construed in accordance with section 165(7) below.

(5) The local currency equivalent of a valuation of an asset or liability, or of an amount, is that valuation or amount expressed in terms of the local currency (a process sometimes known as translation).

(6) [...]³

(7) [...]³

(8) References to a share are to a share in a company (whether or not the qualifying company).

(9) Shares are of the same kind if they are treated as being of the same kind by the practice of a recognised stock exchange or would be so treated if dealt with on such a stock exchange.

(10) Rights to settlement under debts on securities are of the same kind if the securities are treated as being of the same kind by the practice of a recognised stock exchange or would be so treated if dealt with on such a stock exchange.

(11) 'Security' in the expression 'debt on a security' has the meaning given by section 132 of the Taxation of Chargeable Gains Act 1992.

(12) [...]²

(13) References to the ecu are to the European currency unit as defined for the time being in Council Regulation No. 3180/78/EEC or in any Community instrument replacing it.

(14) 'Prescribed' means prescribed by regulations made under this Chapter.

(15) A reference to this Chapter includes a reference to regulations made under it and a reference to a provision of this Chapter includes a reference to regulations made under the provision, unless otherwise required by the context or regulations.

(16) Sections 152 to 163 above, and the preceding provisions of this section, apply for the purposes of this Chapter.

---

¹ Inserted by FA 1994, s 115(3).

² Repealed by FA 1996, 41 Sch Part V(3) in relation to accounting periods ending after 31 March 1996 but subject to transitional provisions in FA 1996, 15 Sch.
Previously
'References to deep gain securities shall be construed in accordance with Schedule 11 to the Finance Act 1989.'

³ Repealed by FA 2000, s 106(14) in relation to accounting periods beginning on or after 1 January 2000 and ending on or after 21 March 2000.
Previously
'(6) References to the basic profits or losses of a trade for an accounting period shall be construed in accordance with section 93(2) above.

(7) References to the basic profits or losses of part of a trade for an accounting period shall be construed in accordance with section 94(4) above.'.

Miscellaneous

165 Commencement and transitionals

(1) This Chapter applies where –

(a) a qualifying asset is one to which the company becomes entitled on or after the company's commencement day;

(b) a qualifying liability is one to which the company becomes subject on or after that day;

(c) the rights and duties under a currency contract are ones to which the company becomes entitled and subject on or after that day.

(2) Where a qualifying asset or liability is held or owed by a qualifying company both immediately before and at the beginning of its commencement day, for the purposes of this Chapter the company shall be treated as becoming entitled or subject to the asset or liability at the beginning of its commencement day.

(3) Where both immediately before and at the beginning of its commencement day a qualifying company is entitled to rights and subject to duties under a currency contract, for the purposes of this Chapter the company shall be treated as becoming entitled and subject to them at the beginning of its commencement day.

(4) Regulations may provide that where –

(a) a qualifying asset or liability is held or owed by a qualifying company both immediately before and at the beginning of its commencement day, and

(b) the asset or liability is of a prescribed description,

subsection (2) above shall not apply and for the purposes of this Chapter the company shall be treated as becoming entitled or subject to the asset or liability at such time (falling after its commencement day) as is found in accordance with prescribed rules.

(5) Regulations may provide that any rule made under subsection (4) above shall not apply, and that subsection (2) above shall accordingly apply, in a case where the company so elects in accordance with prescribed rules.

(6) Schedule 16 to this Act (which contains transitional provisions) shall have effect.

(7) For the purposes of this section –

(a) a company's commencement day is the first day of its first accounting period to begin after the day preceding the appointed day;

(b) the appointed day is such day as may be appointed by order.

(8) Subsections (1) to (6) above do not apply for the purposes of construing Schedule 17 to this Act (which contains its own commencement provisions).

Notes
(a) The day appointed for the purposes of subsection (7) above is 23 March 1995 (SI 1994 No 3224).

---

166 Anti-avoidance: change of accounting period

(1) This section applies where –

(a) a company changes the date on which any accounting period is to begin,

(b) if the change had not been made an exchange gain or gains not accruing to the company would have accrued or an exchange loss or losses accruing to the company would not have accrued or an exchange gain or gains accruing would have been bigger or an exchange loss or losses accruing would have been smaller, and

(c) the change mentioned in paragraph (a) above was made for the purpose, or for purposes which include the purpose, of securing the non-accrual or reduction of the gain or gains or the accrual or increase of the loss or losses.

(2) In such a case the inspector or on appeal the Commissioners concerned –

(a) may in arriving at the exchange gains and losses accruing to the company assume that there had been no such change as is mentioned in subsection (1)(a) above, and

(b) may accordingly make, with regard to the accounting period mentioned in subsection (1)(a) above, such adjustment to the company's corporation tax liability as is just and reasonable.

(3) For the purposes of this section –

(a) an exchange gain is an exchange gain of a trade or an exchange gain of part of a trade or a non-trading exchange gain;

(b) an exchange loss is an exchange loss of a trade or an exchange loss of part of a trade or a non-trading exchange loss.

167 Orders and regulations

(1) Any power to make an order or regulations under this Chapter shall be exercisable by the Treasury.

(2) Any power to make an order under this Chapter shall be exercisable by statutory instrument.

(3) Any power to make regulations under this chapter shall be exercisable by statutory instrument subject to annulment in pursuance of a resolution of the House of Commons.

(4) Any power to make regulations under this Chapter –

(a) may be exercised as regards prescribed cases or descriptions of case;

(b) may be exercised differently in relation to different cases or descriptions of case.

(5) Regulations under this Chapter may make provision in such way as the Treasury think fit, and in particular may amend or modify the effect of any enactment (whether or not contained in this Chapter).

[(5A) Without prejudice to the generality of any power of the Treasury to amend regulations made under this Chapter, every such power shall include power to make such modifications of any regulations so made as the Treasury consider appropriate in consequence of

[(a) the provisions of Chapter II of Part IV of the Finance Act 1996 (loan relationships); or

(b) the provisions of sections 105 and 106 of the Finance Act 2000 (use of local currency).][2].

(5B) The power to make any such modifications as are mentioned in subsection [(5A)(a)][3] above shall be exercisable so as to apply those modifications in relation to any accounting period of a company ending on or after 1 April 1996.][1]

[(5C) The power to make any such modifications as are mentioned in subsection (5A)(b) above shall be exercisable so as to apply those modifications in relation to any accounting period of a company beginning on or after 1 January 2000.][4]

(6) Regulations under this Chapter may include such supplementary, incidental, consequential or transitional provisions as appear to the Treasury to be necessary or expedient.

(7) No specific provision of this Chapter about regulations shall prejudice the generality of subsections (4) to (6) above.

---

[1]   Inserted by FA 1996, 14 Sch 74 in relation to accounting periods ending after 31 March 1996 but subject to transitional provisions in FA 1996, 15 Sch.

[2]   Substituted by FA 2000, s 106(15)(a) in relation to accounting periods beginning on or after 1 January 2000 and ending on or after 21 March 2000.
Previously
'the provisions of Chapter II of Part IV of the Finance Act 1996 (loan relationships).'.

[3]   Substituted by FA 2000, s 106(15)(b), as in [1] above.
Previously
'(5A)'.

[4]   Inserted by FA 2000, s 106(15)(c), as in [1] above.

168 Insurance companies

(1) Subject to the following provisions of this section, this Chapter shall apply in relation to insurance companies as it applies in relation to other qualifying companies.

(2) Regulations may make provision about the treatment for corporation tax purposes of exchange differences arising as regards assets and liabilities held or owed by insurance companies.

(3) Any such provision may be made –

(a) about exchange differences arising as regards assets or liabilities (or both) generally or about a proportion of such differences;

(b) about exchange differences arising as regards prescribed descriptions of assets or liabilities (or both) or about a proportion of such differences;

(c) about exchange differences arising as regards individual assets or liabilities.

(4) Any such provision may be made about assets or liabilities that are qualifying assets or liabilities, or about those that are not, or about both.

(5) Regulations under this section may –

(a) contain exceptions (whether by reference to categories of insurance business or otherwise);

(b) contain provision about the circumstances in which a charge or relief is to arise, its amount, and other matters relating to it;

(c) provide for consequential adjustments in a company's corporation tax liability;

(d) exclude or modify the effect of any of the provisions of this Chapter.

(6) References in this section to exchange differences are to gains and losses attributable to fluctuations in currency exchange rates.

(7) For the purposes of this section an insurance company is [any company which carries on any insurance business (within the meaning of the Insurance Companies Act 1982).][1]

---

[1] Substituted by FA 1995, s 52(2) with effect in relation to any accounting period ending after 30 June 1994.
Previously 'a company to which Part II of the Insurance Companies Act 1982 applies'.

[168A Application of Chapter to certain companies becoming resident in the United Kingdom

(1) In a case where –

(a) by virtue of section 751 of the Taxes Act 1988, an exchange gain or an exchange loss accrues to a company for an accrual period constituting or falling within an accounting period during which the company is resident outside the United Kingdom, and

(b) the company subsequently becomes resident in the United Kingdom,

the company shall be treated, for the purposes of applying this Chapter to accounting periods beginning on or after the date when the company becomes resident in the United Kingdom, as if the exchange gain or loss mentioned in paragraph (a) above never existed.

(2) In this section –

(a) references to an exchange gain are to an exchange gain of a trade or an exchange gain of part of a trade or a non-trading exchange gain;

(b) references to an exchange loss are to an exchange loss of a trade or an exchange loss of part of a trade or a non-trading exchange loss;

(c) the reference in paragraph (a) of subsection (1) above to an exchange gain or an exchange loss accruing is to the gain or loss accruing before the application of any of sections 131, 136, 137 and 140 above in relation to the accounting period mentioned in that paragraph.]¹

---

¹   Inserted by FA 1995, 25 Sch 7.

---

169 Chargeable gains

Schedule 17 to this Act (provisions which relate to the taxation of chargeable gains and are connected with other provisions of this Chapter) shall have effect.

170 Amendments

Schedule 18 to this Act (which contains amendments) shall have effect.

SCHEDULE 15
(Section 134)

EXCHANGE GAINS AND LOSSES: ALTERNATIVE CALCULATION

1 Introduction

(1) This paragraph applies where regulations under this Schedule provide that the amount of an initial exchange gain or initial exchange loss accruing to a company as regards an asset, liability or contract for an accrual period shall be found in accordance with the alternative method of calculation.

(2) In such a case the amount shall not be found in accordance with section 125(2) or (4) of this Act or section 126(3) or (5) or section 127(3) or (4) (as the case may be) but shall be found by –

(a) taking the accrued amount for each day in the accrual period, and

(b) adding the amounts found under paragraph (a) above.

(3) Subject to regulations under this Schedule, the accrued amount for a day in the accrual period shall be found by –

    (a) taking the amount of the initial exchange gain or initial exchange loss found in accordance with section 125(2) or (4) of this Act or section 126(3) or (5) or section 127(3) or (4) (as the case may be), and

    (b) dividing it by the number of days in the period.

(4) Where an accrual period does not begin at the beginning of a day, the part of the day that falls within the accrual period shall be treated for the purposes of this Schedule as a complete day.

(5) Where an accrual period does not end at the end of a day, the part of the day that falls within the accrual period shall be treated for the purposes of this Schedule as a complete day.

2 Exempt circumstances

(1) Regulations may provide that where –

    (a) as regards an asset, liability or contract an initial exchange gain or initial exchange loss accrues to a company for an accrual period under section 125, 126 or 127 of this Act or would so accrue apart from regulations under this Schedule,

    (b) at any time on a day in the period the asset or contract was held, or the liability was owed, by the company in exempt circumstances, and

    (c) such other conditions as may be prescribed are fulfilled,

the amount of the gain or loss shall be found in accordance with the alternative method calculation.

(2) Regulations may also provide that as regards any such day as is mentioned in sub-paragraph (1) above the accrued amount shall be ascertained in accordance with prescribed rules.

(3) Regulations may be so framed that the accrued amount as regards a day depends on the extent to which an asset or contract is held, or a liability is owed, in exempt circumstances.

(4) For the purposes of this paragraph an asset or contract is held, or a liability is owed, in exempt circumstances at a given time if it is then held or owed –

    (a) for the purposes of long term insurance business;

    (b) for the purposes of mutual insurance business;

    (c) for the purposes of the occupation of commercial woodlands;

    (d) by a housing association approved at that time for the purposes of section 488 of the Taxes Act 1988;

    (e) by a self-build society approved at that time for the purposes of section 489 of that Act.

(5) In this paragraph –

'long term insurance business' means insurance business of any of the classes specified in Schedule 1 to the Insurance Companies Act 1982;

'commercial woodlands' means woodlands in the United Kingdom which are managed on a commercial basis and with a view to the realisation of profits.

3 Unremittable income

(1) Regulations may provide that where –

(a) as regards an asset falling within section 153(1)(a) or (b) of this Act an initial exchange gain or initial exchange loss accrues to a company for an accrual period under section 125 or 127 of this Act or would so accrue apart from regulations under this Schedule,

(b) at any time on a day in the period income represented by the asset was unremittable, and

(c) such other conditions as may be prescribed are fulfilled,

the amount of the gain or loss shall be found in accordance with the alternative method of calculation.

(2) Regulations may also provide that as regards any such day as is mentioned in sub-paragraph (1) above the accrued amount shall be ascertained in accordance with prescribed rules.

(3) Regulations may be so framed that the accrued amount as regards a day depends on the extent to which the income represented by an asset is unremittable.

(4) For the purposes of this paragraph income is unremittable if –

[(a) a claim under subsection (2) of section 584 of the Taxes Act 1988 (relief for unremittable income) has been made in relation to the income,

(b) paragraphs (a) and (b) of that subsection apply to it, and

(c) those paragraphs have not ceased to apply to it.]¹

---

¹ Substituted by FA 1996, 20 Sch 70 with effect for accounting periods ending on or after an appointed day (intended to be no later than 31 March 1998).
Previously
'(a) in relation to the income, a notice under subsection (2) of section 584 of the Taxes Act 1988 (relief for unremittable overseas income) has been delivered to the inspector in accordance with subsection (6) of that section,

(b) it has been shown to the satisfaction of the Board that the conditions mentioned in paragraphs (a) and (b) of section 584(2) are satisfied with respect to the income, and

(c) those conditions have not ceased to be satisfied with respect to it.'

---

4 Matched liabilities

(1) Regulations may provide that where –

(a) as regards a liability an initial exchange gain or initial exchange loss accrues to a company for an accrual period under section 125 or 127 of this Act or would so accrue apart from regulations under this Schedule,

(b) the liability falls with section 153(2)(a) of this Act,

(c) the liability is eligible to be matched on any day in the accrual period with an asset held by the company, and such other conditions as may be prescribed are fulfilled, and

(d) an election is made in accordance with the regulations to match the liability with the asset on any such day and the election has effect by virtue of the regulations,

the amount of the gain or loss shall be found in accordance with the alternative method of calculation.

(2) Regulations may also provide that as regards any day in respect of which an election has effect the accrued amount shall be ascertained in accordance with prescribed rules.

(3) The question whether a liability is eligible to be matched with an asset shall be determined in accordance with prescribed rules, and in particular regulations may include provision that –

(a) only liabilities of a prescribed description are eligible to be matched with assets;

(b) only assets of a prescribed description are eligible to be matched with liabilities;

(c) liabilities of a prescribed description are eligible to be matched only with assets of a prescribed description.

(4) Regulations may include provision that on any day –

(a) a liability may be partially matched;

(b) an asset may be partially matched;

(c) one asset may be matched with two or more liabilities (wholly or partially);

(d) one liability may be matched with two or more assets (wholly or partially).

(5) Regulations may include provision that an election relating to an asset or assets shall be treated as made in relation to another asset or other assets (as where assets are replaced by others).

(6) Regulations may include provision –

(a) that an election may in prescribed circumstances have effect from a time before it is made;

(b) that an election may be varied;

(c) that an election may not be revoked;

(d) that an election must be made by the company (subject to any provision under sub-paragraph (7) below).

(7) Regulations may provide that where the company is a relevant controlled foreign company an election may be made by a United Kingdom resident company which has (or may be made jointly by United Kingdom resident companies which together have) a majority interest in the company; and –

    (a) a company is a relevant controlled foreign company in Chapter IV of Part XVII of the Taxes Act 1988 applies in relation to the accounting period of the company which constitutes the accrual period or in which the accrual period falls;

    (b) paragraph 4(3) of Schedule 24 to that Act (majority interest) applies for the purposes of this sub-paragraph.

(8) Regulations may include provision –

    (a) that prescribed conditions shall be treated as fulfilled in prescribed circumstances (subject to any provision under paragraph (b) below);

    (b) that prescribed conditions shall be treated as not having been fulfilled if the inspector gives notification that he is not satisfied that they are fulfilled;

    (c) for an appeal from the inspector's notification;

    (d) for a notification to be given to the company or companies making the election.

(9) Regulations may be so framed that the accrued amount as regards a day depends on the extent to which a liability is matched.

(10) Regulations may also provide as mentioned in one or more of the following paragraphs –

    (a) that a chargeable gain (or chargeable gains) shall be treated as accruing to a relevant person for the purposes of the Taxation of Chargeable Gains Act 1992;

    (b) that an allowable loss (or allowable losses) shall be treated as accruing to a relevant person for the purposes of that Act;

    (c) that the operation of that Act as regards a relevant person shall be otherwise adjusted in accordance with prescribed rules (whether the adjustment results in the incidence of tax on the person being greater or smaller).

(11) For the purposes of sub-paragraph (10) above each of the following is a relevant person –

    (a) the company mentioned in sub-paragraph (1) above;

    (b) any person who has at any time acquired a matched asset (or part of a matched asset) since the company acquired it;

and a matched asset is an asset which has at any time been to an extent matched with a liability in pursuance of an election.

(12) Regulations may make provision –

    (a) as to the occasion on which a chargeable gain or allowable loss mentioned in sub-paragraph (10) above is to be treated as accruing as to the amount to be treated as the amount of the gain or loss, and as to other matters relating to the gain or loss;

    (b) as to the timing and extent of any adjustment mentioned in sub-paragraph (10)(c) above and as to other matters relating to the adjustment.

[4A Currency contracts: matching

(1) Regulations may provide that where –

    (a) as regards a contract an initial exchange gain or initial exchange loss accrues to a company for an accrual period under section 126(5) of this Act or would so accrue apart from regulations under this Schedule,

    (b) the relevant duty is eligible to be matched on any day in the accrual period with an asset held by the company, and such other conditions as may be prescribed are fulfilled, and

    (c) an election is made in accordance with the regulations to match the duty with the asset on any such day and the election has effect by virtue of the regulations,

the amount of the gain or loss shall be found in accordance with the alternative method of calculation.

(2) Regulations may also provide that as regards any day in respect of which an election has effect the accrued amount shall be ascertained in accordance with prescribed rules.

(3) The reference in sub-paragraph (1) above to the relevant duty is to the duty to which, under the contract, the company becomes subject as regards the second currency (within the meaning given by section 126 of this Act).

(4) Where regulations are made under this paragraph, sub-paragraphs (3) to (12) of paragraph 4 above shall apply as they apply where regulations are made under that paragraph; but in the application of those sub-paragraphs by virtue of this sub-paragraph –

    (a) the references to a liability in sub-paragraphs (3),(4),(9) and (11) shall be construed as references to a duty,

    (b) the references to liabilities in sub-paragraphs (3) and (4) shall be construed as references to duties, and

    (c) the reference in sub-paragraph (11)(a) to sub-paragraph (1) of paragraph 4 shall be construed as a reference to sub-paragraph (1) above.][1]

---

[1]   Inserted by FA 1994, s 116(2).

Combination of circumstances

5   (1) This paragraph applies where regulations under more than one of paragraphs 2 to 4 above apply –

    (a) as regards the same asset or liability, and

    (b) for the same accrual period.

(2) Regulations may provide that, as regards any day falling within the period and identified in accordance with prescribed rules, the accrued

amount shall be ascertained in accordance with rules prescribed under this paragraph (rather than provisions made under any of those paragraphs).

[5A(1) This paragraph applies where regulations under both paragraph 2 and paragraph 4A above apply –

(a) as regards the same contract, and

(b) for the same accrual period.

(2) Regulations may provide that, as regards any day falling within the period and identified in accordance with prescribed rules, the accrued amount shall be ascertained in accordance with rules prescribed under this paragraph (rather than provisions made under either of those paragraphs).]¹

---

¹   Inserted by FA 1994, s 116(3).

---

6   Arm's length test

Where regulations make provision under any of [the relevant paragraphs]¹, they may provide that for the purposes of section 136(11) of this Act amounts X and Y shall be found without regard to matters which are prescribed and would otherwise have had to be taken into account under the regulations [; and the relevant paragraphs are paragraphs 2,3,4 and 5 above]².

---

¹   Substituted by FA 1994, s 116(4).
     Previously 'paragraphs 2 to 5 above'.

²   Inserted by FA 1994, s 116(4).

---

7   Local currency

Where regulations make provision under any of paragraphs 2 to 5[A]¹ above, section 149 of this Act shall have effect as if the references to sections 125 to 127 included references to this Schedule and the provisions of the regulations.

---

¹   Inserted by FA 1994, s 116(5).

General

8   Regulations may be so framed that the accrued amount as regards a day is nil (so that, depending on the circumstances, an initial exchange gain or initial exchange loss may be extinguished).

9   Regulations may make different provision about exchange gains (on the one hand) and exchange losses (on the other).

SCHEDULE 16

(Section 165)

EXCHANGE GAINS AND LOSSES: TRANSITIONALS

1 Introduction

For the purposes of this Schedule an existing asset, liability or contract is an asset, liability or contract to which this Chapter applies by virtue of section 165(2) or (3) of this Act or by virtue of regulations under section 165(4) of this Act.

2 General provision

(1) Regulations may make such provision as the Treasury think fit with regard to the application of this Chapter to an existing asset, liability or contract (such as provision for finding the basic valuation of an asset or liability).

(2) Nothing in the following provisions of this Schedule shall prejudice the generality of sub-paragraph (1) above.

3 Attributed gain or loss

(1) Regulations may provide that –

   (a) an amount found in accordance with prescribed rules shall be attributed to an existing asset or liability, and

   (b) the amount shall be characterised as a gain or loss in accordance with prescribed rules.

(2) The regulations may provide that an attributed gain or loss shall be set off against exchange losses or exchange gains accruing as regards the asset or liability; and for this purpose –

   (a) an exchange gain is an exchange gain of a trade or an exchange gain of part of a trade or a non-trading exchange gain;

   (b) an exchange loss is an exchange loss of a trade or an exchange loss of part of a trade or a non-trading exchange loss.

(3) The regulations may provide that if an event of a prescribed description occurs as regards the asset or liability at a time falling on or after the commencement day of the company concerned and at a time when all or part of an attributed gain or loss is outstanding –

   (a) an initial exchange gain or initial exchange loss of an amount found in accordance with prescribed rules shall be treated as accruing to the company as regards the asset or liability, or

   (b) a chargeable gain or allowable loss of an amount found in accordance with prescribed rules shall be treated as accruing to the company as regards the asset or liability for the purposes of the Taxation of Chargeable Gains Act 1992.

(4) The regulations may provide that where –

   (a) apart from provision under this sub-paragraph, an allowable loss would be treated as accruing by virtue of provision made under sub-paragraph (3)(b) above, and

351

(b) the company concerned makes an election in accordance with prescribed rules,

the loss shall not be treated as accruing and relief of an amount equal to it shall be given to the company in such form and manner as may be prescribed.

(5) The regulations may provide that where provision under this paragraph has effect the outstanding attributed gain or loss shall be treated as reduced or extinguished.

(6) The regulations may make provision –

(a) as to the time when an initial exchange gain or initial exchange loss is to be treated as accruing and as to the extent to which it is to be treated as an exchange gain or loss of a trade or of part of a trade or as a non-trading exchange gain or loss;

(b) as to the occasion on which chargeable gain or allowable loss is to be treated as accruing;

(c) as to other matters relating to setting off against, or the accrual of, gains or losses as mentioned in this paragraph.

4 Adjustment of exchange gain or loss

(1) Regulations may provide that where an exchange gain or exchange loss accrues to a company as regards an existing asset or liability (or would so accrue apart from the regulations) –

(a) the amount of the gain or loss shall be deemed to be increased in accordance with prescribed rules,

(b) the amount of the gain or loss shall be deemed to be reduced in accordance with prescribed rules, or

(c) the gain or loss shall be deemed not to accrue.

(2) For the purposes of this paragraph –

(a) an exchange gain is an exchange gain of a trade or an exchange gain of part of a trade or a non-trading exchange gain:

(b) an exchange loss is an exchange loss of a trade or an exchange loss of part of a trade or a non-trading exchange loss.

(3) The regulations may be framed by reference to –

(a) exchange differences arising as regards the asset or liability at any time while the company actually holds or owes it (whether any such time falls before, on or after the company's commencement day);

(b) such other factors as the Treasury think fit;

and for this purpose exchange differences are gains and losses attributable to fluctuations in currency exchanges rates.

(4) The regulations may include provision designed to prevent provision under them being avoided by the replacement (or partial replacement) of assets or liabilities by other assets or liabilities.

5 Allowable losses

(1) Regulations may provide that where –

   (a) an allowable loss of a prescribed description has accrued to a qualifying company for the purposes of the Taxation of Chargeable Gains Act 1992,

   (b) the loss has accrued before the company's commencement day,

   (c) all or part of the loss has not been allowed as a deduction under that Act, and

   (d) prescribed conditions (whether relating to the making of a claim or otherwise) are fulfilled,

   the loss shall be set off against exchange gains accruing to the company.

(2) For the purposes of this paragraph an exchange gain is an exchange gain of a trade or an exchange gain of part of a trade or a non-trading exchange gain.

(3) The regulations may provide that the loss may only be set off –

   (a) to the extent that it has not been allowed as a deduction under the Taxation of Chargeable Gains Act 1992;

   (b) against exchange gains accruing as regards assets or liabilities of a prescribed description.

(4) The regulations may include rules for ascertaining whether an allowable loss of a prescribed description has or has not been allowed as a deduction under the Taxation of Chargeable Gains Act 1992.

6 Miscellaneous

(1) Regulations may provide –

   (a) that provision under paragraph 3 above or provision under paragraph 4 above or provision under neither of them shall apply in the case of an asset or liability according to the circumstances of the case;

   (b) that provision under paragraph 3(3)(a) above or provision under paragraph 3(3)(b) above shall apply in the case of an asset or liability according to the circumstances of the case.

(2) The circumstances may be framed by reference to –

   (a) whether, and how, exchange differences arising as regards the asset or liability would be taken into account for tax purposes apart from this Chapter;

   (b) such other factors as the Treasury think fit;

   and for this purpose exchange differences are gains and losses attributable to fluctuations in currency exchange rates.

SCHEDULE 17
(Section 169)

EXCHANGE GAINS AND LOSSES: CHARGEABLE GAINS

1 Introduction

In this Schedule 'the 1992 Act' means the Taxation of Chargeable Gains Act 1992.

2 Currency

(1) In a case where –

    (a) there is for the purposes of the 1992 Act a disposal of currency other than sterling by a qualifying company, and

    (b) immediately before the disposal the company did not hold the currency in exempt circumstances (within the meaning given by paragraph 3 below),

for the purposes of that Act no chargeable gain or allowable loss shall accrue on the disposal.

(2) This paragraph applies to disposals on or after the company's commencement day.

3 (1) For the purposes of paragraph 2 above a company holds currency in exempt circumstances at a given time if –

    (a) the purposes for which it then holds the currency are or include any of the purposes mentioned in sub-paragraph (2) below,

    (b) it is a housing association approved at that time for the purposes of section 488 of the Taxes Act 1988, or

    (c) it is a self-build society approved at that time for the purposes of section 489 of that Act.

(2) The purposes referred to in sub-paragraph (1)(a) above are –

    (a) the purposes of long term insurance business;

    (b) the purposes of mutual insurance business;

    (c) the purposes of the occupation of commercial woodlands.

(3) In this paragraph –

'long term insurance business' means insurance business of any of the classes specified in Schedule 1 to the Insurance Companies Act 1982;

'commercial woodlands' means woodlands in the United Kingdom which are managed on a commercial basis and with a view to the realisation of profits.

4 Debts other than securities

[...]¹

---

¹   Repealed by FA 1996, 41 Sch Part V(3) in relation to accounting periods ending after 31 March 1996 but not to have effect in relation to any disposals before 1 April 1996 [FA 1996, 15 Sch 22(6)] and subject to transitional provisions in FA 1996, 15 Sch.

Previously

'(1) In a case where –

(a) there is for the purposes of the 1992 Act a disposal of a debt by a qualifying company,

(b) the right to settlement under the debt is a qualifying asset,

(c) the settlement currency of the debt is a currency other than sterling,

(d) immediately before the disposal the company did not hold the debt in exempt circumstances, and

(e) the debt is not a debt on a security,

for the purposes of that Act no chargeable gain or allowable loss shall accrue on the disposal.

(2) Paragraph 3 above applies for the purposes of this paragraph as if references to currency were references to a debt.

(2A) In sub-paragraph (1)(e) above 'security' includes a debenture that is deemed to be a security for the purposes of section 251 of the 1992 Act by virtue of subsection (6) of that section (debentures issued on reorganisation etc.)].[a]

(3) This paragraph applies to disposals on or after the company's commencement day.'

[a]   Inserted by FA 1995, 24 Sch 5.

---

5   Debts on securities: disposals

[...][1]

---

[1]   Repealed by FA 1996, 41 Sch Part V(3) in relation to accounting periods ending after 31 March 1996 but not to have effect in relation to any disposals before 1 April 1996 [FA 1996, 15 Sch 22(6)] and subject to transitional provisions in FA 1996, 15 Sch.

Previously

'[(1) This paragraph applies where –

(a) a right to settlement under a debt on a security is a qualifying asset,

(b) there occurs in relation to the security an event which is a disposal of it for the purposes of the 1992 Act by a qualifying company or which would be such a disposal but for section 127 of that Act (reorganisations),

(c) the event occurs on or after the company's commencement day, and

(d) immediately before the occurrence of the event the company did not hold the right in exempt circumstances.

(2) In applying section 117 of that Act (qualifying corporate bonds) in relation to the event mentioned in sub-paragraph (1) above or to a transaction (if any) falling within sub-paragraph (4) below, that section shall be construed as if subsection (1)(b) (corporate bond must be in sterling) were omitted.

(3) Where the settlement currency of the debt is a currency other than sterling, then, in applying section 117 of the 1992 Act in relation to the event mentioned in sub-paragraph (1) above or to a transaction (if any) falling within sub-paragraph (4) below –

(a) the definition of normal commercial loan for the purposes of section 117(1)(a) shall have effect, and be treated as always having had effect, as if paragraphs (b) and (c) of paragraph 1(5) of Schedule 18 to the Taxes Act 1988 had always been omitted;

(b) section 117 shall be construed as if subsection (10) (securities issued within group) were omitted.

(4) A transaction falls within this sub-paragraph if –

(a) it is a transaction in relation to which sections 127 to 130 of the 1992 Act apply by virtue of any provision of Chapter II of Part IV of that Act, or would apply apart from section 116 of that Act,

(b) it is a transaction under which the qualifying company becomes entitled to the right,

(c) it occurs on or after the company's commencement day but before the event mentioned in sub-paragraph (1) above, and

(d) the company holds the right at all times following the time when it becomes entitled to it and preceding the event mentioned in sub-paragraph (1) above.

(5) Paragraph 3 above applies for the purposes of this paragraph as if references to currency were references to a right.]ᵃ'

Substituted by FA 1995, 24 Sch 6.
Previously
'(1) In a case where –

(a) a right to settlement under a debt on a security is a qualifying asset,

(b) there is for the purposes of the 1992 Act a disposal of the security by a qualifying company, and

(c) immediately before the disposal the company did not hold the security in exempt circumstances,

in applying section 117 of that Act (qualifying corporate bonds) in relation to the disposal, subsection (1)(b) (corporate bond must be in sterling) shall be ignored.

(2) Sub-paragraph (3) below applies where –

(a) the conditions in sub-paragraph (1)(a) to (c) above are fulfilled, and

(b) the settlement currency of the debt is a currency other than sterling.

(3) In applying section 117 of the 1992 Act in relation to the disposal –

(a) the definition of normal commercial loan for the purposes of subsection (1)(a) shall have effect as if paragraphs (b) and (c) of paragraph 1(5) of Schedule 18 to the Taxes Act 1988 were omitted;

(b) subsection (10) (securities issued within group) shall be ignored.

(4) Paragraph 3 above applies for the purposes of this paragraph as if references to currency were references to a security.

(5) This paragraph applies to disposals on or after the company's commencement day.'

6 Debts on securities: relief

[...]¹

¹ Repealed by FA 1996, 41 Sch Part V(3) in relation to accounting periods ending after 31 March 1996 but not to have effect in relation to any disposals before 1 April 1996 [FA 1996, 15 Sch 22(6)] and subject to transitional provisions in FA 1996, 15 Sch.
Previously
'(1) This paragraph applies where –

(a) a qualifying company has made a loan,

(b) the debt is a debt on a security, and

(c) the right to settlement under the debt is a qualifying asset.

(2) In applying section 117 of the 1992 Act (qualifying corporate bonds) for the purposes of section 254 of that Act (relief for debts on qualifying corporate bonds) section 117(1)(b) (corporate bond must be in sterling) shall be ignored.

(3) If the settlement currency of the debt is a currency other than sterling, in applying section 117 of that Act for the purposes of section 254 of that Act –

(a) the definition of normal commercial loan for the purposes of section 117(1)(a) shall have effect as if paragraphs (b) and (c) of paragraph 1(5) of Schedule 18 to the Taxes Act 1988 were omitted;

(b) section 117(10) (securities issued within group) shall be ignored.

(4) In applying section 254(6) of that Act in the case of a security which would not be a qualifying corporate bond apart from sub-paragraph (2) or (3) above, the allowable amount shall be found by taking what that amount would be apart from this sub-paragraph and deducting an amount equal to the amount of any exchange loss (or the aggregate amount of any exchange losses) accruing to the company as regards the asset for a period or periods ending on or before the relevant date.

(5) For the purposes of sub-paragraph (4) above –

    (a) an exchange loss is an exchange loss of a trade or an exchange loss of part of a trade or a non-trading exchange loss;

    (b) the relevant date is the date when the security's value became negligible or the outstanding amount of the principal of the loan was irrecoverable or proved to be irrecoverable (as the case may be).

(6) Where apart from this sub-paragraph the amount of an exchange loss would be an amount expressed in a currency other than the basic currency, it shall be treated for the purposes of this paragraph as the basic currency equivalent on the day the claim is made of the amount so expressed; and the basic currency is the currency in which the allowable amount is expressed.

(7) For the purposes of sub-paragraph (6) above the basic currency equivalent of an amount on a particular day is the basic currency equivalent calculated by reference to the London closing exchange rate for that day.

(8) This paragraph applies to claims made on or after the company's commencement day (whenever the loan was made).'

---

7 Reconstructions, groups etc.

(1) This paragraph applies where there is for the purposes of the 1992 Act a disposal or acquisition of an asset which is –

    (a) currency,

    (b) a debt which is not a debt on a security and the right to settlement under which is a qualifying asset,

    (c) a security (as defined in section 132 of the 1992 Act) where the right to settlement under the debt on the security is a qualifying asset, or

    (d) an obligation which by virtue of section 143 of the 1992 Act (futures and options) is regarded as an asset to the disposal of which that Act applies and which is a duty under a currency contract.

(2) In a case where –

    (a) the condition mentioned in sub-paragraph (3) below is fulfilled, and

    (b) section 139, 171 or 172 of the 1992 Act (reconstructions, groups etc.) would, apart from this paragraph, apply as regards the disposal or acquisition,

the section concerned shall not apply as regards the disposal and the corresponding acquisition or (as the case may be) shall not apply as regards the acquisition and the corresponding disposal.

(3) The condition is that stated in paragraph (a) or (b) below (as the case may be) –

    (a) the disposal is by a qualifying company and immediately before the disposal the asset is held wholly for qualifying purposes;

    (b) the acquisition is by a qualifying company and immediately after the acquisition the asset is held wholly for qualifying purposes.

(4) For the purposes of this paragraph qualifying purposes are purposes which constitute one or both of the following –

    (a) purposes of long term insurance business;

(b) purposes of mutual insurance business;

and 'long term insurance business' means insurance business of any of the classes specified in Schedule 1 to the Insurance Companies Act 1982.

(5) This paragraph applies where the disposal or acquisition (as the case may be) is made on or after the commencement day of the company mentioned in sub-paragraph (3)(a) or (b) above (as the case may be).

8 [...]¹

---

¹   Repealed by FA 1994, 26 Sch Part V(8) with effect in relation to disposals made on or after 30 November 1993.
Previously
'Indexation allowance
In construing section 103(7) of the 1992 Act (restriction on availability of indexation allowance; non-chargeable assets) the effect of paragraphs 2 and 4 above shall be ignored.'

Finance Act 1995, s 131

PART III Exchange gains and losses: transitional provision

131 (1) The provisions specified in subsection (2) below, so far as they require a disposal to be treated, for the purposes of the Taxation of Chargeable Gains Act 1992, as a disposal on which neither a gain nor a loss accrues, shall not apply in relation to any disposal of a qualifying asset which is made –

(a) by one qualifying company to another such company; and

(b) at a time before the commencement day of the company making the disposal and on or after the commencement day of the company to which the disposal is made.

(2) The provisions referred to in subsection (1) above are –

(a) sections 139, 140A, 171, 172, 215, 216 and 217A of the Taxation of Chargeable Gains Act 1992; and

(b) section 486(8) of the Taxes Act 1988.

(3) In this section –

'commencement day', in relation to a qualifying company, means that company's commencement day for the purposes of section 165 of the Finance Act 1993;

'qualifying asset', in relation to a disposal, means anything which, after the disposal, is by virtue of section 153 of that Act a qualifying asset in relation to the company to which the disposal was made; and

'qualifying company' means any company which is a qualifying company within the meaning of section 152 of that Act.

(4)   This section has effect in relation to any disposal of an asset taking place on or after 1st January 1995.

Finance Act 1996

Taxation of profits and gains and relief for deficits

82   Method of bringing amounts into account

(1)   For the purposes of corporation tax–

(a)   the profits and gains arising from the loan relationships of a company, and

(b)   any deficit on a company's loan relationships,

shall be computed in accordance with this section using the credits and debits given for the accounting period in question by the following provisions of this Chapter.

(2)   To the extent that, in any accounting period, a loan relationship of a company is one to which it is a party for the purposes of a trade carried on by it, the credits and debits given in respect of that relationship for that period shall be treated (according to whether they are credits or debits) either–

(a)   as receipts of that trade falling to be brought into account in computing the profits [. . .]^1 of that trade for that period; or

(b)   as expenses of that trade which are deductible in computing those profits [. . .]^1.

(3)   Where for any accounting period there are, in respect of the loan relationships of a company, both–

(a)   credits that are not brought into account under subsection (2) above ('non-trading credits'), and

(b)   debits that are not so brought into account ('non-trading debits'),

the aggregate of the non-trading debits shall be subtracted from the aggregate of the non-trading credits to give the amount to be brought into account under subsection (4) below.

(4)   That amount is the amount which for any accounting period is to be taken (according to whether the aggregate of the non-trading credits or the aggregate of the non-trading debits is the greater) to be either–

(a)   the amount of the company's profits and gains for that period that are chargeable under Case III of Schedule D as profits and gains arising from the company's loan relationships; or

(b)   the amount of the company's non-trading deficit for that period on its loan relationships.

(5)   Where for any accounting period a company has non-trading credits but no non-trading debits in respect of its loan relationships, the aggregate amount of the credits shall be the amount of the company's profits and

gains for that period that are chargeable under Case III of Schedule D as profits and gains arising from those relationships.

(6) Where for any accounting period a company has non-trading debits but no non-trading credits in respect of its loan relationships, that company shall have a non-trading deficit on its loan relationships for that period equal to the aggregate of the debits.

(7) Subsection (2) above, so far as it provides for any amount to be deductible as mentioned in paragraph (b) of that subsection, shall have effect notwithstanding anything in section 74 of the Taxes Act 1988 (allowable deductions).

---

¹ Deleted by FA 1998, 7 Sch 11 with effect from 31 July 1998. Previously 'and gains'.

Notes
(a) The above provisions apply in relation to accounting periods ending after 31 March 1996 but subject to transitional provisions in FA 1996, 15 Sch [FA 1996, s 105].

---

83 Non-trading deficit on loan relationships

(1) This section applies for the purposes of corporation tax where for any accounting period ('the deficit period') there is a non-trading deficit on a company's loan relationships.

(2) The company may make a claim for the whole or any part of the deficit to be treated in any of the following ways, that is to say–

   (a) to be set off against any profits of the company (of whatever description) for the deficit period;

   (b) to be treated as eligible for group relief;

   (c) to be carried back to be set off against profits for earlier accounting periods; or

   (d) to be carried forward and set against non-trading profits for the next accounting period.

[(3) So much of the deficit for the deficit period as is not the subject of a claim under subsection (2) above shall be carried forward and treated as a deficit for the next accounting period.

(4) An amount carried forward to an accounting period under subsection (3) above–

   (a) may be the subject of a claim under paragraph (d) of subsection (2) above, but not under any other paragraph of that subsection, and

   (b) shall be disregarded for the purposes of any claim under that subsection relating to a deficit arising in that period.]¹

(5) No part of any non-trading deficit of a company established for charitable purposes only shall be set off against the profits of that or any other company in pursuance of a claim under subsection (2) above.

(6) A claim under subsection (2) above must be made within the period of two years immediately following the end of the relevant period, or within such further period as the Board may allow.

(7) In subsection (6) above 'the relevant period'–

    (a) in relation to a claim under subsection (2)(a), (b) or (c) above, means the deficit period; and

    (b) in relation to a claim under subsection (2)(d) above, means the accounting period immediately following the deficit period.

(8) Different claims may be made under subsection (2) above as respects different parts of a non-trading deficit for any period, but no claim may be made as respects any part of a deficit to which another claim made under that subsection relates.

(9) Schedule 8 to this Act (which makes provision about what happens where a claim is made under subsection (2) above) shall have effect.

---

[1] Substituted by FA 1998, s 82 and deemed always to have had effect.

Notes
(a) The above provisions apply in relation to accounting periods ending after 31 March 1996 but subject to transitional provisions in FA 1996, 15 Sch [FA 1996, s 105].

SCHEDULE 8
(Section 83)

LOAN RELATIONSHIPS: CLAIMS RELATING TO DEFICITS

Notes
(a) The provisions of this Schedule apply in relation to accounting periods ending after 31 March 1996 but subject to transitional provisions in FA 1996, 15 Sch [FA 1996, s 105].

---

1 Claim to set off deficit against other profits for the deficit period

(1) This paragraph applies where a claim is made under section 83(2)(a) of this Act for the whole or any part of the deficit to be set off against profits of any description for the deficit period.

(2) Subject to the following provisions of this paragraph–

    (a) the amount to which the claim relates shall be set off against the profits of the company for the deficit period that are identified in the claim; and

    (b) those profits shall be treated as reduced accordingly.

(3) Any reduction by virtue of sub-paragraph (2) above shall be made–

    (a) after relief has been given for any loss incurred in a trade in an earlier accounting period; and

    (b) before any relief is given against profits for that period either–

        (i) [under section 392A(1) or 393A(1) of the Taxes Act 1988 (losses set against profits for the same or preceding accounting periods); or][1]

        (ii) by virtue of any claim made, in respect of a deficit for a subsequent period, under section 83(2)(c) of this Act.

(4) Relief shall not be given by virtue of a claim under section 83(2)(a) of this Act against any ring fence profits of the company within the meaning of Chapter V of Part XII of the Taxes Act 1988 (petroleum extraction activities).

---

[1] Substituted by FA 1998, 5 Sch 64 with effect for 1998/99 and subsequent years of assessment for income tax, and from 1 April 1998 for corporation tax.
Previously 'under section 393A(1) of the Taxes Act 1988 (trading losses set against profits for the same or preceding accounting periods); or'.

---

2 Claim to treat deficit as eligible for group relief

(1) This paragraph applies where the company makes a claim under section 83(2)(b) of this Act for the whole or any part of the deficit to be treated as eligible for group relief.

(2) Section 403 of the Taxes Act 1988 (amounts which may be surrendered by way of group relief) applies in accordance with section 4032C(2) of that Act.

---

[1] Substituted by FA 1998, 5 Sch 64 with effect for 1998/99 and subsequent years for income tax, and from 1 April 1998 for corporation tax.
Previously
'The amount to which the claim relates shall be treated as if, for the purposes of subsection (1) of section 403 of the Taxes Act 1988 (group relief for trades)–

(a) it were a loss incurred in the deficit period by a company carrying on a trade; and

(b) the exclusions in subsection (2) of that section did not apply'.

---

3 Claim to carry back deficit to previous accounting periods

(1) This paragraph applies where a claim is made under section 83(2)(c) of this Act for the whole or any part of the deficit to be carried back to be set off against profits for earlier accounting periods.

(2) The claim shall have effect only if it relates to an amount that is equal to whichever is smaller of the following amounts, that is to say–

    (a) so much of that deficit as is neither–

        (i) an amount in relation to which a claim is made under subsection (2)(a) or (b) of section 83 of this Act, nor

        (ii) an amount excluded by virtue of subsection (4) of that section from the amounts in relation to which claims may be made under subsection (2) of that section;

    and

    (b) the total amount of the profits available for relief under this paragraph.

(3) Where the claim has effect, the amount to which the claim relates shall be set off against the profits available for relief under this paragraph–

    (a) by treating those profits as reduced accordingly; and

    (b) to the extent that those profits are profits for more than one accounting period, by applying the relief to profits for a later period before setting off any remainder of the amount to which the claim relates against profits for an earlier period.

(4) Subject to sub-paragraph (5) below, the profits available for relief under this paragraph are the amounts which, for accounting periods ending within the permitted period, would be taken–

  (a) apart from any relief under this paragraph, and

  (b) after the giving of every relief which under sub-paragraph (6) below falls to be given in priority to relief under this paragraph,

to be chargeable under Case III of Schedule D as profits and gains arising from the company's loan relationships.

(5) Where any accounting period begins before the beginning of the permitted period but ends in the course of it–

  (a) any amount chargeable in respect of that accounting period under Case III of Schedule D as profits and gains of the company's loan relationships shall be apportioned according to the proportions of the accounting period falling before and after the beginning of the permitted period; and

  (b) the amount attributable, on that apportionment, to before the beginning of the permitted period shall not be available for relief under this paragraph.

(6) The reliefs which fall to be given in priority to relief under this paragraph in respect of any loss are–

  (a) any relief in respect of a loss or deficit incurred or treated as incurred in an accounting period before the deficit period;

  (b) any relief under section 338 of the Taxes Act 1988 (charges on income) in respect of payments made wholly and exclusively for the purposes of a trade;

  (c) where the company is an investment company for the purposes of Part IV of that Act–

    (i) any allowance under section 28 of the Capital Allowances Act 1990 (machinery and plant of investment companies);

    (ii) any deduction in respect of management expenses under section 75 of the Taxes Act 1988; and

    (iii) any relief under section 338 of the Taxes Act 1988 in respect of payments made wholly and exclusively for the purposes of its business;

  (d) any relief under section 393A of the Taxes Act 1988 (trading losses set against profits of the same or any preceding accounting periods); and

  (e) any relief in pursuance of a claim under section 83(2)(a) or (b) of this Act.

(7) In this paragraph 'the permitted period' means the period of [twelve months][1] immediately preceding the beginning of the deficit period so far as that [twelve months][2] period falls after 31 March 1996.

¹ Substituted by F(No 2)A 1997, s 40(2) in relation to any deficit for a deficit period ending on or after 2 July 1997.
Previously 'three years'.

² Substituted by F(No 2)A 1997, s 40(2) as in ¹ above.
Previously 'three year'.

Notes
(a) See also F(No 2)A 1997, s 40(8)(10)–(12).

4 Claim to carry forward deficit to next accounting period

(1) This paragraph applies where a claim is made under section 83(2)(d) of this Act for the whole or any part of the deficit to be carried forward and set against non-trading profits for the next accounting period.

(2) The amount to which the claim relates shall be set off against the non-trading profits of the company for the accounting period immediately following the deficit period, and those profits shall be treated as reduced accordingly.

(3) In this paragraph 'non-trading profits', in relation to a company, means so much of any profits of the company (of whatever description) as do not consist in trading income for the purposes of section 393A of the Taxes Act 1988 (setting-off of trading losses against profits of the same or an earlier period).

5 Construction of Schedule

In this Schedule 'the deficit' and 'the deficit period' shall be construed by reference to section 83(1) of this Act.

SCHEDULE 9
(Section 84)

LOAN RELATIONSHIPS: SPECIAL COMPUTATIONAL PROVISIONS

4 Foreign exchange gains and losses

(1) The credits and debits to be brought into account for the purposes of this Chapter shall be computed disregarding so much of any authorised accounting method as, by requiring the translation or conversion of amounts from one currency into another, has the effect that credits and debits produced by that method include sums in which profits, gains or losses arising from fluctuations in the value of a currency are to any extent represented.

(2) This paragraph is without prejudice to the provisions of Chapter II of Part II of the Finance Act 1993 (exchange gains and losses).

Notes
(a) The above provisions apply in relation to accounting periods ending after 31 March 1996 but subject to transitional provisions in FA 1996, 15 Sch [FA 1996, s 105].

SCHEDULE 14
(Section 104)

LOAN RELATIONSHIPS: MINOR AND CONSEQUENTIAL AMENDMENTS

1–41	[Not relevant to this book]
42	[Amends ICTA 1988, s 797]
43	[Inserts ICTA 1988, s 797A]
44–47	[Not relevant to this book]
48	[Amends ICTA 1988, s 826]
49–60	[Not relevant to this book]
61	[Amends TCGA 1992, s 117]
62–66	[Not relevant to this book]
67	[Amends FA 1993, s 127]
68	[Amends FA 1993, s 129]
69	[Substitutes new FA 1993, s 130 for previous FA 1993, ss 130–133]
70	[Amends FA 1993, s 153]
71	[Amends FA 1993, s 154]
72	[Amends FA 1993, s 155]
73	[Amends FA 1993, s 159]
74	[Amends FA 1993, s 167]
75–79	[Not relevant to this book]

SCHEDULE 15
(Section 105)

LOAN RELATIONSHIPS: SAVINGS AND TRANSITIONAL PROVISIONS

22 Transitional and savings for Chapter II of Part II of the Finance Act 1993

(1) Chapter II of Part II of the Finance Act 1993 (exchange gains and losses) shall have effect in the case of any continuing loan relationship as follows.

(2) Subsection (1A) of section 127 of that Act (deemed variation of debt in respect of amounts accruing in respect of discounts and premiums) shall have effect in relation to the debt by reference to which the continuing loan relationship at any time subsists as if that debt is one to which the company became subject or entitled on 1 April 1996; and, accordingly, that subsection shall require the nominal amount of the debt outstanding to be treated as varied only where the time of the deemed variation is on or after 1 April 1996.

(3) Where section 127 of that Act has effect in relation to any debt by reference to which a continuing loan relationship at any time subsists, it shall so have effect, so far as the debt is one to which the company is deemed by virtue of sub-paragraph (2) above to have become subject or entitled on 1 April 1996, as if the nominal amount of the debt outstanding on that date were an amount equal to what it would have been if–

(a) sub-paragraph (2) above did not apply; and

(b) section 127(1A) of the Finance Act 1993 and the provisions to which it refers had always had effect.

365

(4) The amendment by this Act of section 153(4) of the Finance Act 1993 (assets excluded from being qualifying assets) shall not apply as respects times before 1 April 1996; and, where a company holds an asset immediately before and on 1 April 1996 and that asset is one which falls to be treated as a qualifying asset by virtue of that amendment–

(a) the company shall be treated as having become entitled to that asset on that date; and

(b) the basic valuation of the asset shall be taken to be its market value on 31 March 1996 (instead of any amount given by section 159 of that Act of 1993);

and in this sub-paragraph 'market value' has the same meaning as in the 1992 Act.

(5) The repeal by this Act of section 153(6) of the Finance Act 1993 (liabilities excluded from being qualifying liabilities) shall not have effect as respects times before 1 April 1996, and, where a company is subject to a liability immediately before and on 1 April 1996 and that liability is one which falls to be treated as a qualifying liability by virtue of that repeal, the company shall be treated as having become subject to that liability on that date.

(6) The repeal by this Act of paragraphs 4 to 6 of Schedule 17 to the Finance Act 1993 (exchange gains and losses) shall not have effect in relation to any disposal before 1 April 1996.

23 Carrying back non-trading losses against exchange profits etc.

(1) Subject to sub-paragraph (2) below, for the purpose of setting any amount against exchange profits for an accounting period beginning before 1 April 1996–

(a) a claim may be made under section 131(5) or (6) of the Finance Act 1993 (treatment of exchange gains and losses) in relation to any relievable amount for an accounting period ending on or after 1 April 1996; and

(b) the provisions of sections 129 to 133 of that Act shall be deemed to have effect for the purposes of that claim without the amendments made by Schedule 14 to this Act.

(2) If any claim is made by virtue of sub-paragraph (1) above in respect of the relievable amount for an accounting period beginning on or after 1 April 1996, then an amount equal to the amount to which the claim relates shall be deemed, for the purposes of the computation falling to be made for that accounting period under section 82 of this Act, to be brought into account for that period as a non-trading credit.

(3) The references in this paragraph and paragraph 24 below to provisions of the Finance Act 1993 shall have effect as including references to those sections as applied by the provisions of Chapter II of Part IV of the Finance Act 1994.

(4) Sub-paragraph (3) above is without prejudice to the generality of section 20(2) of the Interpretation Act 1978 (references to other enactments).

Notes
(a) See also F(No 2)A 1997, s 40(9)–(12).

24   Exchange losses etc. carried forward from before 1 April 1996

Where there is any amount which apart from this Chapter would fall under section 131(12) of the Finance Act 1993 (carrying forward of exchange gains and losses) to be carried forward to an accounting period ending on or after 1 April 1996, that amount shall be treated in relation to that period as an amount carried forward to that period in pursuance of section 83(3) of this Act.

Finance (No 2) Act 1997, s 40

40   Carry-back of loan relationship deficits

(1)   Chapter II of Part IV of the Finance Act 1996 (loan relationships) shall be amended as follows.

(2)   [Amends FA 1996, 8 Sch 3].

(3)   [Amends FA 1996, 11 Sch 4].

(4)   [Amends FA 1996, 11 Sch 5].

(5)   [Amends FA 1996, 11 Sch 8].

(6)   [Amends FA 1996, 11 Sch 9 and inserts FA 1996, 11 Sch 9A].

(7)   Subject to subsection (8) below, this section has effect in relation to any deficit for a deficit period ending on or after 2nd July 1997.

(8)   Paragraph 3 of Schedule 8 to the Finance Act 1996 shall have effect in relation to any deficit for a deficit period beginning before but ending on or after 2nd July 1997 as if the permitted period in relation to the pre-commencement part of the deficit were the period beginning with 1st April 1996 and ending immediately before the beginning of the deficit period.

(9)   Where for the purposes of paragraph 23 of Schedule 15 to the Finance Act 1996 (transitional provision in connection with the carrying back of exchange losses) there is a relievable amount for an accounting period ending on or after 2nd July 1997, that paragraph shall have effect, except in relation to any pre-commencement part of that amount, as if, in section 131(10)(b) of the Finance Act 1993 (the permitted period) as applied by that paragraph, the words "twelve months" were substituted for the words "three years".

(10)   In this section "pre-commencement part", in relation to the deficit for any deficit period or the relievable amount for any accounting period, means the part (if any) of that deficit or relievable amount which, on an apportionment in accordance with subsection (11) or, as the case may be, (12) below, is attributable to such part (if any) of that period as falls before 2nd July 1997.

(11) Except in a case where subsection (12) below applies, an apportionment for the purposes of subsection (10) above shall be made on a time basis according to the respective lengths of the part of the deficit period or, as the case may be, accounting period falling before 2nd July 1997 and the remainder of that period.

(12) Where the circumstances of a particular case are such that the making of an apportionment on the time basis mentioned in subsection (11) above would work in a manner that would be unjust or unreasonable in relation to any person, the apportionment shall be made instead (to the extent only that is necessary in order to avoid injustice and unreasonableness) in such other manner as may be just and reasonable.

Finance Act 2000

International matters

105 Corporation tax: use of currencies other than sterling

(1) For sections 92 to 95 of the Finance Act 1993 there shall be substituted –

'92 The basic rule: sterling to be used

(1) Where a company carries on a business, the profits or losses of the business for an accounting period shall for the purposes of corporation tax be computed and expressed in sterling; but this is subject to section 93 below.

(2) In this section –

'losses' includes management expenses and any allowances falling to be made under section 28 or 61(1) of the Capital Allowances Act 1990;

'profits' includes gains, income and any charges falling to be made under section 28 or 61(1) of that Act.

93 Use of currency other than sterling

(1) This section applies where in an accounting period a company carries on a business and either the first condition or the second condition is fulfilled.

(2) The first condition is that –

(a) the accounts of the company as a whole are prepared in a currency other than sterling in accordance with normal accounting practice; and

(b) in the case of a company which is not resident in the United Kingdom, the company makes a return of accounts for its branch in the United Kingdom prepared in such a currency in accordance with such practice.

(3) The second condition is that –

(a) the accounts of the company as a whole are prepared in sterling but, so far as relating to the business, they are prepared, using the closing rate/net investment method, from financial statements prepared in a currency other than sterling; or

(b) in the case of a company which is not resident in the United Kingdom, the company makes a return of accounts for its branch in the United Kingdom prepared in sterling but, so far as relating to the business, it is prepared, using that method, from financial statements prepared in such a currency.

(4) The profits or losses of the business for an accounting period shall for the purposes of corporation tax be found by –

(a) taking the amount of all the profits and losses of the business for the period computed and expressed in the relevant foreign currency;

(b) taking account of any of the following which are so computed and expressed –

    (i) any management expenses brought forward under section 75(3) of the Taxes Act 1988 from an earlier accounting period;

    (ii) any losses of the business brought forward under section 392B or 393 of that Act from such a period; and

    (iii) any non-trading deficits on loan relationships brought forward under section 83 of the Finance Act 1996 from the previous accounting period; and

(c) taking the sterling equivalent of the amount found by applying paragraphs (a) and (b) above.

(5) In the application of section 22B, 34, 35, 38C, 38D or 79A of the Capital Allowances Act 1990 for the purposes of subsection (4)(a) or (b) above, it shall be assumed that any sterling amount mentioned in any of those sections is its equivalent expressed in the relevant foreign currency.

(6) Where in an accounting period –

(a) a company carries on different parts of a business through different branches (whether within or outside the United Kingdom); and

(b) this section would apply differently in relation to different parts if they were separate businesses,

those parts shall be treated for the purposes of this section as if they were separate businesses for that period.

(7) In this section, unless the context otherwise requires—

'accounts', in relation to a company, means –

(a) the annual accounts of the company prepared in accordance with Part VII of the Companies Act 1985 or Part VIII of the Companies (Northern Ireland) Order 1986; or

(b) if the company is not required to prepare such accounts, the accounts which it is required to keep under the law of its home State; or

(c) if the company is not so required to keep accounts, such of its accounts as most closely correspond to accounts which it would have been required to prepare if the provisions of that Part applied to it;

'branch' includes any collection of assets and liabilities;
'the closing rate/net investment method' means the method so called as described under the title 'Foreign currency translation' in the Statement of Standard Accounting Practice issued in April 1983 by the Institute of Chartered Accountants in England and Wales;
'home State', in relation to a company, means the country or territory under whose laws the company is incorporated;
'losses' has the same meaning as in section 92 above except that it does not include allowable losses within the meaning of the Taxation of Chargeable Gains Act 1992;
'profits' has the same meaning as in section 92 above except that it does not include chargeable gains within the meaning of that Act;
'the relevant foreign currency' means the currency other than sterling or, where the first condition is fulfilled and two different such currencies are involved, the currency in which the return of accounts is prepared;
'return of accounts', in relation to a branch in the United Kingdom, means a return of such accounts of the branch as may be required by the Inland Revenue under paragraph 3 of Schedule 18 to the Finance Act 1998 (company tax returns, assessments and related matters).

94 Rules for ascertaining currency equivalents

(1) Any receipt or expense which is to be taken into account in making a computation under subsection (1) of section 92 above for an accounting period, and is denominated in a currency other than sterling, shall be translated into its sterling equivalent –

(a) if either of the conditions mentioned in subsection (2) below is fulfilled, by reference to the rate used in the preparation of the accounts of the company as a whole for that period;

(b) if neither of those conditions is fulfilled, by reference to the London closing exchange rate for the relevant day.

(2) The conditions are –

(a) that the rate is an arm's length exchange rate for the relevant day;

(b) that the rate is an average arm's length exchange rate for a period ending with that day, or for a period not exceeding three months which includes that day, and the arm's length exchange rate for any day in that period (except the first) is not significantly different from that for the preceding day.

(3) Subject to subsections (5) and (7) below, any amount found by applying paragraphs (a) and (b) of subsection (4) of section 93

above shall be translated into its sterling equivalent by reference to the London closing exchange rate for the relevant day.

(4) The following –

(a) any receipt or expense which is to be taken into account in making a calculation for the purposes of subsection (4)(a) or (b) of section 93 above, and is denominated in a currency other than the relevant foreign currency; and

(b) any such sterling amount as is referred to in subsection (5) of that section,

shall be translated into its equivalent expressed in the relevant foreign currency by reference to the London closing exchange rate for the relevant day.

(5) Where section 93 above applies by virtue of the first condition mentioned in that section, then, as regards the business or part of the business, the company –

(a) may elect, by a notice given to an officer of the Board, that as from the first day of the accounting period in which the notice is given, an average arm's length exchange rate shall be used for the purposes of subsection (3) above instead of the rate there mentioned; and

(b) may withdraw such an election, by a notice so given, as from the first day of the first accounting period beginning on or after the date of the notice.

(6) Where an election under subsection (5) above is withdrawn, no further election may be made under that subsection so as to take effect before the third anniversary of the day on which the withdrawal takes effect.

(7) Where –

(a) section 93 above applies by virtue of the second condition mentioned in that section; and

(b) the accounts of the company, so far as relating to the business or part of the business, are prepared by reference to an average arm's length exchange rate,

that exchange rate shall be used for the purposes of subsection (3) above instead of the rate there mentioned.

(8) In this section –

'accounts' has the same meaning as in section 93 above;
'arm's length exchange rate' means such exchange rate as might reasonably be expected to be agreed between persons dealing at arm's length;
'average arm's length exchange rate', in relation to a period, means the rate which represents an appropriate average of arm's length exchange rates for the period;
'the relevant day' means –

(a) for the purposes of subsections (1),(2) and (4)(a) above, the day on which the company becomes entitled to the receipt or incurs (or is treated as incurring) the expense;

(b) for the purposes of subsection (3) above, the last day of the accounting period in question;

(c) for the purposes of subsection (4)(b) above, the day on which the company incurs the capital expenditure.

(9) Nothing in this section affects the operation of Chapter IV of Part VII of the Taxes Act 1988 (controlled foreign companies) or Chapter II of this Part.

(10) Nothing in paragraph 88 of Schedule 18 to the Finance Act 1998 (company tax returns, assessments and related matters) shall be taken to prevent any amount which is taken to be conclusively determined for the purposes of the Corporation Tax Acts from being translated under this section by reference to an exchange rate which was not used to determine the amount which can no longer be altered.'.

(2) Where any of the items referred to in section 93(4)(b) of the Finance Act 1993 (as substituted by subsection (1) above) fall to be taken into account in the first accounting period in relation to which this section has effect, the amounts of those items shall be computed and expressed in the relevant currency by reference to the London closing exchange rate for the last day of the immediately preceding accounting period.

(3) Where any of the items referred to in section 25(1) of the Capital Allowances Act 1990 which fall to be taken into account for the first accounting period in relation to which this section has effect relate to expenditure which was incurred before the beginning of that period, the amounts of those items shall be computed and expressed in the relevant currency by reference to the London closing exchange rate for the last day of the immediately preceding accounting period.

(4) Subject to subsection (5) below, this section has effect for accounting periods beginning on or after 1st January 2000 and ending on or after 21st March 2000.

(5) Any company which did not, for the accounting period immediately preceding the first accounting period falling within subsection (4) above, make an election in respect of a trade or part of a trade under the Local Currency Elections Regulations 1994 may, by notice given to an officer of the Board on or before 31st August 2000, elect that this section shall not have effect in relation to it until the first accounting period beginning on or after 1st July 2000.

106   Foreign exchange gains and losses: use of local currency

(1) In subsection (2) of section 149 of the Finance Act 1993 (local currency to be used) –

(a) for 'trade or trades', in both places where they occur, there shall be substituted 'business or businesses'; and

(b) for 'any such trade' there shall be substituted 'any such business'.

(2) In subsection (4) of that section –

(a) the words 'the asset or contract was held, or the liability was owed, by the company solely for trading purposes and' shall cease to have effect; and

(b) for 'sections 125 to 128' there shall be substituted 'sections 125 to 129'.

(3) In subsection (5) of that section –

    (a) the words 'the asset or contract was held, or the liability was owed, by the company solely for trading purposes and' shall cease to have effect;

    (b) for 'sections 125 to 128' there shall be substituted 'sections 125 to 129'; and

    (c) for 'trade', in both places where it occurs, there shall be substituted 'business'.

(4) For subsection (6) of that section there shall be substituted –

'(6) In any other case –

    (a) sections 125 to 129 above shall be applied by reference to sterling;

    (b) those sections shall then be applied separately by reference to each local currency involved (other than sterling); and

    (c) any exchange gain or loss of a business or part shall be ignored unless found in the currency which is the local currency of the business or part for the relevant accounting period (whether sterling or otherwise).'.

(5) For subsection (7) of that section there shall be substituted –

'(7) For the purposes of this section a part of a business is any part of a business which is treated for the purposes of section 93 above as if it were a separate business for the relevant accounting period.'.

(6) For subsection (9) of section 128 of the Finance Act 1993 (trading gains and losses) there shall be substituted –

'(9) For the purposes of this section a part of a trade is any part of a trade which is treated for the purposes of section 93 above as if it were a separate business for the relevant accounting period; and the relevant accounting period is the accounting period which constitutes the accrual period concerned or in which that accrual period falls.'.

(7) After section 135 of that Act there shall be inserted –

'135A Sterling used if avoidance of gain is the main benefit

(1) This section applies where, as regards qualifying assets and liabilities of a company –

    (a) a currency other than sterling would (apart from this section) be the local currency for the purposes of sections 125 to 129 above; and

    (b) the main benefit that might be expected to accrue from that currency being the local currency is that no net exchange gain would accrue to the company for those purposes.

(2) If a net exchange gain would accrue to the company if sterling were the local currency for the purposes of sections 125 to 129 above,

then, as regards the assets and liabilities concerned, sterling shall be the local currency for those purposes.

(3) For the purposes of this section a net exchange gain accrues to a company if its initial exchange gains (as determined in accordance with this Chapter) exceed its initial exchange losses (as so determined).'.

(8) For subsection (12) of section 140 of that Act (deferral of unrealised gains) there shall be substituted –

'(12) For the purposes of this section a part of a trade is any part of a trade which is treated for the purposes of section 93 above as if it were a separate business for the relevant accounting period; and the relevant accounting period is the accounting period which constitutes the second accrual period or in which that accrual period falls.'.

(9) For subsection (2) of section 142 of that Act (deferral non-sterling trades) there shall be substituted –

'(2) For the purposes of subsection (1) above the sterling equivalent of an amount is the sterling equivalent calculated by reference to such rate of exchange as applies by virtue of section 94 above in the case of the profits or losses for the accounting period concerned of the business or part of which the gain or loss is a gain or loss (or would be apart from section 139 above).'.

(10) In subsections (3) and (5) of that section, for 'trade', in each place where it occurs, there shall be substituted 'business'.

(11) For subsection (4) of that section there shall be substituted –

'(4) The amount the company is treated as receiving under section 128(4) or 129(2) above in respect of the accounting period and by virtue of the gain (as reduced) shall be the amount computed and expressed in that currency.'.

(12) In subsection (1) of section 163 of that Act (local currency of a trade), for 'trade' there shall be substituted 'business'.

(13) For subsections (2) and (3) of that section there shall be substituted –

'(2) Where by virtue of section 93 above the profits or losses of a business or part of a business for an accounting period are to be computed and expressed in a currency other than sterling for the purposes of corporation tax, that other currency is the local currency of the business or part for that period.'.

(14) In section 164 of that Act (interpretation: miscellaneous), subsections (6) and (7) shall cease to have effect.

(15) In section 167 of that Act (orders and regulations) –

(a) in subsection (5A), for 'the provisions of Chapter II of Part IV of the Finance Act 1996 (loan relationships)' there shall be substituted –

'(a) the provisions of Chapter II of Part IV of the Finance Act 1996 (loan relationships); or

(b) the provisions of sections 105 and 106 of the Finance Act 2000 (use of local currency).';

(b) in subsection (5B), for 'subsection (5A)' there shall be substituted 'subsection (5A)(a)'; and

(c) after that subsection there shall be inserted –

'(5C) The power to make any such modifications as are mentioned in subsection (5A)(b) above shall be exercisable so as to apply those modifications in relation to any accounting period of a company beginning on or after 1st January 2000.'.

(16) In subsection (4)(b) of section 110 of the Finance Act 1998 (determinations requiring the sanction of the Board), after 'section 135,' there shall be inserted '135A,'.

(17) This section has effect for accounting periods beginning on or after 1st January 2000 and ending on or after 21st March 2000.

Inland Revenue Statements of Practice

Contents

Application of Foreign Exchange and Financial Instruments Legislation to Partnerships which include Companies (SP 9/94, 20 December 1994)

General

1. Finance Act 1993 (sections 125–170) and Finance Act 1994 (sections 147–177) provide rules for the assessment and relief for most companies of exchange differences and profits or losses deriving from interest rate contracts and options and currency contracts and options. No special provisions are needed to apply the legislation to partnerships consisting wholly of companies but some modifications are needed to deal with the application of the new rules to partnerships which have both corporate and individual members.

2. Section 172 Finance Act 1994 provides a framework for the application of the financial instruments rules to partnerships which include companies. This Statement of Practice supplements that framework and describes the approach which the Inland Revenue intend to apply to the treatment of exchange differences. The essence of the approach both for financial instruments and foreign exchange is that the provisions in Finance Acts 1993 and 1994 should be applied to corporate members but that those rules should not apply to individual members.

Partnerships consisting wholly of qualifying companies

3. A partnership which includes a qualifying company under the financial instruments rules is treated by section 172 Finance Act 1994 as a qualifying company. No additional rules are provided or needed where all partners are qualifying companies. The practice of the Inland Revenue will be to follow exactly the same approach for exchange differences.

Partnerships of which one or more members are not companies

Basic framework

4. Section 114 Taxes Act 1988 requires (broadly) that profits and losses of the partnership are charged to corporation tax for the shares arising to corporate partners and to income tax for the shares arising to individual partners. Section 215 Finance Act 1994 (treatment of partnerships under self-assessment) ensures, or will ensure, that section 114 applies not just to trades or professions but also to other businesses so that both trading and non-trading partnerships are brought into the self-assessment rules. It also ensures that the computation under section 114(1) for corporate partners and the computation under section 114(3) for individual partners are free-standing.

5. Section 172 Finance Act 1994 describes a partnership, one or more of whose members is a qualifying company (as defined in section 154 Finance Act 1994), as a qualifying partnership and then applies the legislation as if that qualifying partnership were a qualifying company. Section 172(4) requires two separate computations for the purposes of the corporation tax computation within section 114(1) to cater for the (unusual) situation where a corporate member is not a qualifying company.

Practice on partnership assets, liabilities and contracts

6. In law in England, Wales and Northern Ireland the partnership itself does not hold direct interests in partnership assets (nor is it subject directly to liabilities). The effect of section 172 Finance Act 1994 however is to treat the partnership as entitled to rights or subject to duties under interest rate contracts or options or currency contracts or options for the purposes of Chapter II Part IV Finance Act 1994.

7. The practice of the Inland Revenue in relation to exchange differences accruing to a partnership one or more of whose members is a qualifying company (as defined in section 152 Finance Act 1993) will be to follow the approach in section 172 Finance Act 1994 on the basis that this will give results broadly equivalent to a strict application of the law. As for interest rate and currency contracts and options the Inland Revenue will accept computations on the basis that the partnership (rather than the individual members) holds qualifying assets or is subject to qualifying liabilities or is entitled to rights or subject to duties under a currency contract for the purposes of Chapter II Part II Finance Act 1993.

Shares of partnership profits and losses

8. In practice therefore partnerships may submit computations under section 114 Taxes Act 1988

● firstly, on the basis that both Chapter II Part II Finance Act 1993 and Chapter II Part IV Finance Act 1994 apply and

● secondly, on the basis that neither Chapter II Part II Finance Act 1993 nor Chapter II Part IV Finance Act 1994 apply.

When this approach is adopted the first computation will be used to determine the shares of profits and losses appropriate to corporate members which are qualifying companies and the second computation to determine the shares of profits and losses appropriate to individual members.

Interaction with capital gains tax

9. Certain assets which prior to Finance Act 1993 and Finance Act 1994 were subject to capital gains tax (eg foreign currency, certain debts and some interest rate and currency contracts and options) are no longer subject to capital gains tax in the hands of qualifying companies. They will however remain subject to capital gains tax in the hands of persons (including individuals) who are not qualifying companies and section 59 TCGA 1992 (application of capital gains tax to the disposal of partnership assets) will continue to apply to the disposal of shares in partnership assets to which members of the partnership who are not qualifying companies are entitled.

Consequential effects

10. For corporate members of partnerships the effect of section 114(2) under this practice will be to treat the profits or losses derived from the partnership's activities as a trade or business separate and distinct from any other trade or business carried on by the company. For trading losses a company can make its own loss relief claims for its apportioned share of any loss. Because trading profits and losses deriving from section 128 Finance Act 1993 (exchange differences) or section 159 Finance Act 1994 (financial instruments) are incorporated into the computation of trading profit section 114(2) will operate without the need for any additional clarification.

11. Non-trading profits and losses deriving from financial instruments are treated by virtue of section 160 Finance Act 1994 in the same way as non-trading gains and losses deriving from exchange differences the rules for which are provided in sections 129–133 Finance Act 1993. The practice of the Inland Revenue will be to merge a company's share of net non-trading gains or losses deriving from its interest in a partnership with any other non-trading gains and losses accruing to it in its own right by virtue of section 160 Finance Act 1994 and sections 130–133 Finance Act 1993. If as a result of this merged computation there are net non-trading gains then the company will be assessed under Case VI of Schedule D (section 130 Finance Act 1993). If there are net non-trading losses then the company (and not the partnership) will be able to claim relief under

- section 131(1) (group relief)

- section 131(4) (relief against profits of the current accounting period)

- section 131(5) (relief against past exchange or financial instruments profits)

any balance of non-trading loss would be available to the company (and not the partnership) to carry forward as provided in section 131(12) Finance Act 1993.

Differing accounting periods

12. A partnership may draw up its accounts to a different date from that adopted by a qualifying corporate member of the partnership. The profits or losses deriving from the first computation under section 114(1) Taxes Act 1988 should be allocated as necessary (normally on a time basis) between the relevant accounting periods of the company itself. In particular net non-trading losses attributable to exchange differences or financial instruments should be apportioned to the company's relevant accounting periods before merging with other non-trade items attributable to the company in its own right as described in the preceding paragraph.

Partnership changes

13. Where a qualifying company either joins or leaves a partnership part way through an accounting period the partnership will be treated for the purposes of the computations required under section 114 as if it were a qualifying company with the company treated as entitled to an appropriate reduced share of the partnership profit or loss.

Commencement provisions

14. The relevant statutory provisions and therefore this Statement of Practice will come into effect from 23 March 1995. In the unusual situation where a partnership does not draw up accounts the partnership's commencement date under this Statement of Practice will be either the first day of any period to begin on or after 23 March 1995 for which the partnership draws up any financial statements, or the earliest of the commencement days of qualifying corporate members of the partnership.

Provisions specific to the foreign exchange rules

Local currency

15. Sections 93–95 Finance Act 1993 provide (via regulations) for certain profits of certain companies to be computed in a currency other than sterling. There are no equivalent statutory provisions for individuals and this Statement of Practice applies only for the purposes of Chapter II Part II Finance Act 1993 and Chapter II Part IV Finance Act 1994. It follows that it will not be open to partnerships not consisting wholly of qualifying companies to make local currency elections.

Deferral

16. Under sections 139–143 Finance Act 1993 qualifying companies may claim to defer a proportion of unrealised exchange gains. This facility would also be available to qualifying partnerships and the practice of the Inland Revenue will be to consider claims to deferral made by the partnership (rather than individual company members) based on the first computation prepared under section 114(1) Taxes Act 1988. In any accounting period the amount of any exchange gain to be deferred will be the proportion of that gain which is appropriate to qualifying corporate members of the partnership. In any subsequent period the Inland Revenue practice will be to treat any amount deferred as an amount to be allocated (in appropriate shares) to qualifying corporate members of the partnership only. The intention of the practice is to ensure that all amounts deferred under the statutory provisions are subsequently recovered.

Matching

17. Under Regulations 4–11 of The Exchange Gains and Losses (Alternative Method of Calculation of Gain or Loss) Regulations 1994 qualifying companies can elect, in effect, to defer recognition of exchange differences on certain liabilities matching certain assets (principally shares in associated or subsidiary companies, net investments in branches outside the UK and ships or aircraft). The Inland Revenue consider that the matching should be available (as far as applicable) to partnerships involving qualifying companies but that the concept only has relevance in relation to assets described in Regulation 5(6)(d) (ships or aircraft) and Regulation 5(7) (assets subject to capital gains tax) held by a branch outside the United Kingdom where no local currency election has been made. (As explained in paragraph 15 above a partnership not consisting wholly of qualifying companies would not be able to make a local currency election.)

18. Where a partnership does make a matching election in respect of any assets described in the preceding paragraph then the amount of the initial exchange gain or exchange loss will, following Regulation 5(2) and the first computation required under section 114(1) Taxes Act 1988, be reduced to nil. The practice of the Inland Revenue in operating Regulation 7 (recovering matched gains or losses on disposal of assets) will be to defer for later recovery the proportion of deferred gains or losses which was appropriate to qualifying corporate members of the partnership in the relevant accounting periods. These deferred amounts, carried forward separately, will be recovered in periods when the relevant assets are disposed of. The amounts will be allocated in appropriate shares to the then qualifying company members of the partnership. As with deferral the intention is that all amounts deferred as a result of an election under the matching arrangements are ultimately brought to account.

Anti-avoidance rules

19. The practice of the Inland Revenue will be to apply the rules in sections 165–168 Finance Act 1994 and sections 135–138 Finance Act 1993 to the partnership as though it were a qualifying company.

Application of Loan Relationships, Foreign Exchange and Financial Instruments Legislation to Partnerships which include Companies (SP 4/98, 16 November 1998)

General

1. This Statement of Practice supersedes an earlier statement (SP 9/94). That statement dealt with the application of the foreign exchange and financial instruments legislation to partnerships of which at least one partner was a company within the charge to corporation tax. It did not deal with the effect of the loan relationships legislation introduced by FA 1996. That legislation made a major reform to the corporation tax treatment of government and corporate debt. SP 9/94 will continue to be relevant for accounting periods ending on or before 31 March 1996. This Statement of Practice should be applied to later periods.

2. This revised Statement of Practice describes the Inland Revenue's view of how the rules for partnerships apply where profits, losses and other amounts arise to the partnership from loan relationships (corporate and government debt), exchange differences and financial instruments and to transactions between a partnership and its members in these areas.

Statutory framework

3. ICTA 1988, s 8(2) provides that a company is chargeable on profits arising to it under any partnership.

4. ICTA 1988, s 114 gives the rules for computing profits and losses of a trade or business where one or more of the partnership members is a company. The profits and losses of the partnership are computed, for the purposes of corporation tax, as if the partnership were a company, separate from any company which is a partner. The trade or business carried on is also treated as separate from any trade etc, which the company member carries on on its own account.

5. These basic rules therefore apply to the computation of profits and losses under—

–   the loan relationships legislation in FA 1996, Part IV Ch II;

–   the foreign exchange gains and losses (FOREX) legislation in FA 1993, Part II Ch II; and

-   the financial instruments (FI) legislation in FA 1994, Part II Ch II.

Some modifications and consequential adaptations, described in this Statement of Practice, are needed to address particular situations.

6. The effect of ICTA 1988, s 114 is to treat the partnership for tax purposes as itself—

-   a party to loan relationships for the purposes of FA 1996, Part IV Ch II;

-   as entitled to assets and subject to liabilities for the purposes of the FOREX legislation; and

-   entitled to rights, or subject to duties, under interest rate, currency or debt contracts or options for the purposes of the FI legislation; whatever the position under the general law relating to the partnership.

7. FA 1994, s 172 provides a special rule for partnerships, one or more of whose members is a 'qualifying company' for the purposes of the legislation in that Act on financial instruments. A qualifying company for that purpose is any company but it does not include the trustees of an authorised unit trust (even though they are treated as if they were a company for other purposes), nor does it include an open-ended investment company ('OEIC'). It does include an approved investment trust company in relation to interest rate and debt contracts but not in relation to currency contracts. Where a partnership includes both at least one qualifying company and at least one company which is not a qualifying company, s 172(4) operates to require two separate corporation tax computations for the purposes of s 114(1). Otherwise it does no more than reinforce the requirements of s 114.

8. Although there is a similar definition in FA 1993, s 153 (exchange differences) of 'qualifying company' (although for the FOREX legislation an investment trust company is never a qualifying company), there is no specific rule equivalent to FA 1994, s 172. The practice of the Inland Revenue in the rare cases where a non-qualifying company is a member of a partnership will be to follow FA 1994, s 172 as if it applied to exchange differences.

9. There is no concept of qualifying company in FA 1996, Part IV Ch II (loan relationships). However the trustees of an authorised unit trust and an OEIC, although treated as companies for many purposes of the Tax Acts, are treated for the purposes of the loan relationships legislation as if they were subject to income tax rules (FA 1996, Sch 10 para 2(2) and Open-ended Investment Companies (Tax) Regulations 1997 Part II). It follows that where the trustees of an authorised unit trust are, or an OEIC is, a member of a partnership, they will not be treated as companies to whom credits and debits under the loan relationships legislation can be attributed under s 114.

Computation of partnership profits and losses

10. In any case where one or more companies is a member of a partnership, and they are not all excluded from the application of the relevant legislation by paras 7 to 9 above, partnerships should prepare computations of profits and losses from any trade or business under ICTA 1988, s 114 on the basis that the foreign exchange gains and losses, financial instruments and loan relationships legislation apply to the partnership as if it were a company. This computation will be used to determine the shares of profits and losses appropriate to members subject to corporation tax and who are neither investment trusts (except in relation to interest rate and debt contracts), OEICs nor the trustees of authorised unit trusts.

11. Where any member of the partnership is an investment trust, an OEIC or the trustees of an authorised unit trust, another computation should be prepared on the basis that corporation tax rules ignoring the FOREX and FI legislation apply (except where an investment trust is a party to interest rate or debt contracts), and in the case of an authorised unit trust or OEIC, that the rules in FA 1996, Sch 13 rather than the rest of FA 1996, Part IV Ch II, apply. This computation will be used to determine the shares of profits and losses appropriate to those members.

12. Where there are members of the partnership who are neither companies, nor the trustees of an authorised unit trust, a computation of profits and losses for the purposes of income tax, made under ICTA 1988, s 111 will also be required.

13. Profits and losses (including interest) on loan relationships are treated by FA 1996, Part IV Ch II as credits and debits. The debits and credits for the partnership should be computed following the rules in that Chapter. In particular—

– The authorised accounting method used should be that used in the partnership accounts, with an authorised accruals method being used if the partnership accounts do not conform with either authorised method — FA 1996, s 86.

– A claim under FA 1996, s 91 to set off income tax in the period of receipt rather than accrual may be made.

– The special rules for convertible, asset linked and index-linked gilt-edged securities may apply — FA 1996, ss 92–94.

– Exchange differences are left out of account — FA 1996, Sch 9 para 4.

– The bad debt rules in FA 1996, Sch 9 para 5 apply.

– The anti-avoidance rules on imported losses (FA 1996, Sch 9 para 10), transactions not at arm's length (para 11) and loan relationships for unallowable purposes (para 13) will apply.

But —

–   The rules in FA 1996, Sch 9 para 12 about continuity of treatment where loan relationships are transferred between members of a group of companies will not apply where a loan relationship is transferred to or by a partnership.

–   A change in partnership profit sharing ratios, including a case where a company joins or leaves a partnership does not of itself give rise to a related transaction in a loan relationship to which the partnership is a party.

14. Trading profits and losses deriving from exchange differences — FA 1993, s 128 and non-trading profits or losses treated by FA 1993, ss 129, 130 as non-trading debits or credits under the loan relationships legislation should also be computed as set out in para 10 above. In particular—

–   Valuations of assets and liabilities should be made in accordance with the accounting methods used by the partnership — FA 1993, s 159.

–   The main benefit and arm's length rules in FA 1993, ss 133–135 will apply by reference to the circumstances of the partnership.

–   FA 1993, ss 140–143 (deferral of certain gains) may apply. In computing the amount which may be deferred, the whole of the profits and of various types of exchange gains and losses of the partnership, as computed for the purposes of corporation tax, will be taken into account.

15. Trading profits and losses on financial instruments — FA 1994, s 159 — and non-trading profits or losses treated by FA 1994, s 160 as non-trading debits or credits under the loan relationships legislation should also be computed as set out in para 10 above. In particular—

–   Valuations of assets and liabilities should be made in accordance with the accounting methods used by the partnership — FA 1994. ss 156, 157.

–   The transfer of value, arm's length and transactions with non-resident rules in FA 1994, ss 165–168 will apply.

Share of partnership profits and losses for corporation tax purposes

16. The resulting partnership trading profit or loss, excess of non-trading credits over debits assessable under Case III or non-trading deficit, should then be apportioned to the partners according to the partnership agreement. The partners receive a share of the overall result, they do not receive an allocation of individual debits and credits. The partnership itself is not assessable to corporation tax and cannot, for example, carry forward non-trading deficits.

17. Each corporate member of the partnership will be assessed and charged to corporation tax on its share of any trading profit or loss (which

will include all loan relationship, foreign exchange and financial instruments trading profits and losses) as if its share derived from a trade it carried on alone, and which is separate from any trade it carries on on its own account.

18. The corporate members of the partnership should incorporate their allocation of any Case III profit or non-trading deficit into their own Case III or non-trading deficit computation. It will not form a separate 'pot'. The company will be able to claim under FA 1996, s 83 if the result of combining the two amounts is a net non-trading deficit. It should not claim separately for its allocation of a partnership non-trading deficit.

19. For example a company has a non-trading deficit on its own activities of £10,000. It has a share in a partnership Case III profit of £5,000. The company is treated as having an overall deficit of £5,000. It cannot surrender as group relief the amount of £10,000 under FA 1996, s 83(2) and submit to a charge to tax on the £5,000. Similarly if the £5,000 Case III income arose on its own account, and its share of a partnership deficit was £10,000 it could not surrender the deficit of £10,000.

Differing accounting periods

20. A partnership may draw up its accounts to a different date from that adopted by the corporate members of the partnership. The profits or losses deriving from the corporation tax computations under ICTA 1988, s 114(1) should be allocated as necessary (normally on a time basis) between the relevant accounting periods of the company members themselves.

Interaction with capital gains tax

21. For companies which are within the charge to corporation tax and, for the purposes of the foreign exchange or financial instruments legislation, are qualifying companies, certain assets (e.g. foreign currency, certain debts and some interest rate and currency contracts and options) no longer give rise to chargeable gains following FA 1993, FA 1994 and FA 1996. However, these assets may still give rise to chargeable gains in the hands of persons (including individuals) who are not subject to corporation tax. These assets may also, in certain circumstances, give rise to chargeable gains in the hands of some insurance companies. TCGA 1992, s 59 (treatment of partnership assets) and Statement of Practice D12 will continue to apply to the disposal of shares in partnership assets to which members of the partnership who are not companies subject to corporation tax are entitled. In certain circumstances qualifying companies will also be treated as having chargeable gains and losses on liabilities where corresponding matched assets are disposed of—see para 31 onwards below.

Connected persons and FA 1996 s 87

22. ICTA 1988, s 832 defines a company as excluding a partnership. ICTA 1988, s 114 however provides that where at least one of the partners is a company, the profits of any trade, profession or business carried on by the partnership shall be computed for the purposes of corporation tax as if the partnership were a company. The Inland Revenue takes the view that this statutory fiction does not extend to making a partnership a "company" for the purposes of FA 1996, s 87(3) (accounting method for connected parties). It also takes the view that a partnership is neither a participator nor an associate of a participator within the meaning of ICTA 1988, s 417. A partnership is not therefore connected for the purposes of FA 1996, s 87 with any of its members which provide loans to the partnership. Companies making loans to connected parties are usually denied bad debt relief by FA 1996, Sch 9 para 6. But when a loan is made from a corporate member of a partnership to the partnership (or vice versa) it follows from the Inland Revenue view on FA 1996, s 87 that bad debt relief may be available depending on the circumstances of the debtor. It also follows that where a partnership releases a company member from repaying a debt, or vice versa, the relevant party must recognise a credit equal to the amount released.

23. Example — two independent and unconnected companies, A, and B, go into partnership to develop a new product. The partnership, X, is initially funded by loan capital of £50,000, interest free, from each of the two companies. The profit/loss share is 50:50, between the two partners. Company A then injects a further £500,000 into the partnership to fund the production process. This is a five year loan which carries interest of 5 per cent per annum. The business does not do quite as well as expected and eventually the production facility and business is sold to another party for £200,000. This entire amount is paid to Company A in full satisfaction of its debt of £500,000. What are the debits and credits?

24. The Inland Revenue would treat the partnership as a separate person to compute profits and losses. The partnership will accrue interest of £25,000 per year which is an allowable debit in its Case I computation. The overall Case I profit or loss for each accounting period is allocated 50:50 to the partners. On the sale of the business the partnership would have a £300,000 credit for the Case I computation when it satisfied its debt of £500,000 with a payment of £200,000. A and B release the remaining debt of £50,000 each, resulting in a further £100,000 credit for the partnership.

25. Company A would accrue interest of £25,000 per year which is a credit in its Case III computation. In the period the business was sold Company A would bring in 50 per cent of the trading profit of the partnership (including the credits of £300,000 and £100,000). Company A would be entitled to bad debt relief for £300,000 on the loan of £500,000 and of £50,000 on the other loan. This would be given as a debit in its Case III computation.

26. In the period the business was sold Company B would bring in 50 per cent of the trading profit of the partnership (including the credits of £300,000 and £100,000). Company B would be entitled to relief of £50,000 as a debit in its Case III computation.

Interest paid or received under deduction of income tax

27. Yearly interest paid by or on behalf of a partnership in which a company is a member should, subject to s 349(3), be paid under deduction of tax — ICTA 1988, s 349(2)(b).

28. Where a partnership of which a company is member receives interest under deduction of tax, the Inland Revenue practice will be to accept that the income tax suffered should be apportioned amongst the company partners in the same proportion as the interest under the loan relationship is apportioned.

Local currency elections

29. FA 1993, s 92 lays down a general rule that the profits of a trade are to be expressed in sterling. This codified the existing law that still applies to all other computations of income and profits. However, FA 1993, ss 93–95 allow companies to elect (via regulations) for trading profits of certain companies to be computed by translating a figure of profit calculated in a currency other than sterling, without requiring a translation of qualifying assets and liabilities denominated in that currency. In Statement of Practice SP 9/94 the Inland Revenue took the view that unless a partnership consisted wholly of qualifying companies it could not make this local currency election. The revised Inland Revenue view is that because ICTA 1988, s 114 (partnerships involving companies) provides for computations to be prepared as if a partnership were a company, then where at least one of the partners is a qualifying company it is open to that partnership to make a local currency election. Any election must satisfy the conditions in the Local Currency Elections Regulations (SI 1994/3230) applied to the partnership as if it were a company. All partners who are, at the time of the election, subject to UK corporation tax should sign any election. Without all the signatures, the Inland Revenue will treat the election as not effective. In cases where an effective election is made that election will be regarded as irrevocable and will not cease to be valid on subsequent partnership changes.

Deferral

30. Under FA 1993, ss 139–143 qualifying companies may claim to defer a proportion of unrealised exchange gains. This facility will also be available to qualifying partnerships and the practice of the Inland Revenue will be to consider claims to deferral made by the partnership (rather than individual company members) based on the computation prepared

under TA 1988 s 114(1). In any accounting period the amount of any exchange gain to be deferred will be the proportion of that gain which is appropriate to qualifying corporate members of the partnership. In other words each of the corporate partners which is a qualifying company will be able to exclude from its share of exchange gains and losses the appropriate part of the deferred gain. The same approach will be taken to amounts treated as accruing by virtue of FA 1993, s 140(4) in the period to which the gains have been deferred.

31. It follows that a company member of a partnership cannot make a deferral claim in respect of a gain attributed to it under s 114 if the partnership has not itself made a claim. But it can make a claim in respect of its own gains arising otherwise than through the partnership, whether or not a partnership claim has been made for the partnership gains, and no account will be taken of partnership gains or losses in establishing the amount of the company's own gains that may be deferred.

32. The complex rules for companies which are members of groups set out in para 4 of the Exchange Gains & Losses (Deferral of Gains and Losses) Regulations (SI 1994/3228) will not however apply to partnerships. The treatment of the partnership as a company by ICTA 1988, s 114 does not extend to deeming the partnership as such to be a member of a group.

Matching

33. Under regs 4–11 of the Exchange Gains and Losses (Alternative Method of Calculation of Gain or Loss) Regulations (SI 1994/3227) qualifying companies can elect to reduce to nil exchange differences on liabilities which match certain assets (shares in associated or subsidiary companies, net investments in branches outside the UK and ships or aircraft). The Inland Revenue has revised the view expressed in Statement of Practice SP 9/94 which limited the range of assets for which a partnership may make a matching election. It will now accept that partnerships which have eligible liabilities as described in regulation 5(4) or (5) can make a matching election for the full range of eligible assets described in SI 1994/3227 reg 5(6). Where an election is made, the Inland Revenue will not treat it as effective unless it is signed by all partners subject to UK corporation tax.

34. It follows that since a partnership is treated as if it were a company for the purposes of computing exchange gains and losses, and in particular for computing what gains and losses in liabilities may be deferred under the matching rules, a company cannot make a claim to match its own liability (one which is not its share of a partnership liability) with an asset held by the partnership, whether or not the partnership has made an election to match the asset.

35. Under reg 7 of the Alternative Method regulations, disposal of a matched asset triggers the calculation of the aggregate exchange gains and losses on the corresponding liability which have not been taken into

account for tax purposes because they have been reduced to nil by reg 5(2).

36. The net exchange gain or loss thus found is treated as a chargeable gain or allowable loss accruing at the same time as the asset was disposed of. If the matched asset was however a ship or aircraft, the net gain or loss is treated as an exchange gain or loss.

37. In cases where there has been no change in the partnership, or in any partner's asset share ratio, between the date the matching election for the asset has effect and the date the asset is disposed of, any chargeable gain or allowable loss produced by reg 7 will accrue to the partners in accordance with TCGA 1992, s 59 and Statement of Practice D12 in the same way as the chargeable gain or allowable loss on the matched asset will accrue.

38. If the reg 7 gain or loss is an exchange gain or loss then it will be allocated to the partners in the manner described in para 15 onwards.

39. There may be cases however where a corporate partner in a partnership which has made a matching election leaves the partnership or reduces its asset share ratio before the matched asset is disposed of by the partnership. Where this happens, the partner is treated as disposing of the whole or part of his share in the matched asset—Statement of Practice D12 para 4 and the appropriate calculation of excluded exchange gain or loss should be made under reg 7. A proportionate part of the gain or loss will then be allocated to the partner leaving or reducing its asset share. On a subsequent actual disposal of the asset by the partnership an appropriate adjustment should be made to the reg 7 calculation.

40. It is a condition of the Inland Revenue accepting a matching election at partnership level that each partner which is a qualifying company for the purposes of the FOREX legislation at the time the matching election has effect should also undertake to return any reg 7 gain accruing to it in accordance with this statement if it has left the partnership or reduced its asset share ratio.

Anti-avoidance rules

41. As mentioned in paras 13–15 above, the practice of the Inland Revenue will be to apply the rules in FA 1994, ss 165–168, FA 1993, ss 135–138 and FA 1996, Part IV Ch II to the partnership as though it were a qualifying company. But it will also apply these rules where appropriate to individual partnership members.

DRAFT

Application of Local Currency Rules in Finance Act 2000 to Partnerships which include Companies (SP /2000/   )

General

1. This Statement of Practice supplements, and in one respect supersedes, an earlier statement (SP 4/98) in so far as it relates to partnerships with corporate members where either the company or the partnership is subject to sections 93 and 94 Finance Act ('FA')1993 as amended by section 105 FA 2000. The pre-FA 2000 legislation provided for the right to elect to use a currency other than sterling in certain circumstances for restricted aspects of the calculation of trading profits or losses for tax purposes. The FA 2000 amendments replace this elective approach with a more widely drawn rule setting out the circumstances in which profits and losses for the purposes of corporation tax should be computed in a currency other than sterling. Accordingly, paragraph 29 of SP 4/98, which deals with the making of local currency elections, ceases to be relevant for periods governed by the amended version of sections 93 and 94 FA 1993. Otherwise, that earlier Statement of Practice continues to apply in full.

2. The amended legislation takes effect generally for the purposes of corporation tax in relation to accounting periods of companies beginning on or after 1 January 2000 and ending on or after 21 March 2000. However, any company which did not make a local currency election under The Local Currency Election Regulations 1994 (SI 1994/3230) for the immediately preceding accounting period may elect that sections 93 and 94, as amended, should not apply to it until its first accounting period beginning on or after 1 July 2000. Such an election must be made on or before 31 August 2000. This Statement of Practice applies for all accounting periods to which the amended version of sections 93 and 94 FA 1993 applies. This means both the accounting periods of corporate members of partnerships and accounting periods of partnerships of which a company is a member.

Statutory framework

3. Section 8(2) Income and Corporation Taxes Act 1988 ('ICTA') provides that a company is chargeable to corporation tax on profits arising to it under any partnership wherever it would be so chargeable if the profits accrued to the company directly.

4. Section 114 ICTA 1988 gives the rules for computing profits and losses of a trade, profession or business carried on by persons in partnership where one member or more of the partnership is a company. The profits and losses of the partnership are computed, for the purposes of corporation tax, as if the partnership is a company, separate from any company

which is a partner. The trade, profession or business carried on is also treated as separate from any trade or business which the company member carries on individually on its own account.

5. For the purposes of corporation tax, section 114 provides that the profits or losses of a partnership with a UK resident corporate member are to be computed as if the partnership were a UK resident company. The corporate member's share of the resultant figure is determined in accordance with its interest in the partnership for the relevant period and charged on the company as if it had been carrying on the business itself.

6. If a corporate member of a partnership is not UK resident, section 114 (read with section 115) provides that the computation of partnership profits is to be made on the basis that the partnership is a non-UK resident company. The corporate member's share of the profit determined in accordance with its interest in the partnership for the period is to be charged on the company as if it was carrying on the business itself through a UK branch. Accordingly, in a partnership involving both UK resident and non-UK resident companies, the profits and losses of the partnership have to be computed on two separate bases for the purposes of arriving at the profits and losses of these two types of corporate partner.

7. The effect of section 114 is to switch on sections 93 and 94 FA 1993 for partnerships with a UK resident corporate member, a non-UK resident corporate member or both for the purposes of computing each company's share of profits from the partnership for corporation tax purposes.

8. Sections 93 and 94 FA 1993, as amended by section 105 FA 2000, set out the circumstances in which profits and losses of a business or part of a business for the purposes of corporation tax should be computed in a currency other than sterling and provide for the ways in which this computation may be made. The rules for computing any proportion of chargeable gains or capital losses for corporation tax remain as before, namely all are to be computed in sterling.

9. Paragraph 12 of Schedule 18, FA 1998 provides that the corporate member's company return must include any amount which in 'a relevant partnership statement', within the meaning of section 12AB Taxes Management Act ('TMA') 1970, is stated to be its share of the partnership results for the period. That statement is not directly concerned with the underlying accounts. But the statement is to form part of the partnership return required by section 12AA TMA 1970. In accordance with subsections (2) and (3) of the latter section an officer of the Board may require the partners, or one of them, to deliver a return of relevant information which may include 'accounts, statements and documents'.

10. Such a partnership return is only required where the partnership is a UK partnership or a foreign partnership which carries on business in the UK through a branch or agency. A UK company may be a member of a

foreign partnership which does not carry on business in the UK. In that case the company's corporation tax return requires it to enclose a copy of the partnership accounts and tax computations showing its share of the partnership's taxable profits and losses for the relevant period.

Election to defer application of the amended legislation

11. For the purposes of corporation tax, the profits and losses of partnerships to which section 114 applies for the accounting periods referred to in paragraph 2 above will have to be computed on the basis that sections 93 and 94 FA 1993 apply to the partnership. It is the view of the Inland Revenue that, because section 114 ICTA 1988 provides for computations to be prepared as if a partnership were a company, where at least one of the partners is a qualifying company it is open to that partnership to make an election to defer the application of the new rules to it until its first accounting period beginning on or after 1 July 2000. Such an election must be made on or before 31 August 2000 and be signed by all partners who, at the time of the election, are subject to United Kingdom corporation tax. Without all the signatures, the Inland Revenue will treat the election as not effective.

Cases where amended sections 93 and 94 FA 1993 apply to a partnership with company members

12. For the purposes of applying section 114 ICTA 1988 to a UK resident corporate member of a (UK or foreign) partnership, it will be necessary to compute the profits and losses of the partnership's business, or part of its business, in accordance with the rules in sections 93 and 94 FA 1993 (as amended) if

- the partnership prepares its accounts as a whole in a currency other than sterling in accordance with normal accounting practice; or,

- although preparing partnership accounts as a whole in sterling, so far as relating to the business or part of its business the partnership accounts are prepared using the closing rate/net investment method from financial statements prepared in a currency other than sterling.

13. For the purposes of applying section 114 ICTA 1988 to a non-UK resident corporate member of a partnership, it will be necessary to compute the profits and losses of the partnership's business or part of its business in accordance with the rules in sections 93 and 94 FA 1993 (as amended) if

- the partnership prepares its accounts as a whole in a currency other than sterling and uses that, or another, foreign currency in the accounts of the UK part of the business which may be required by section 12AA TMA 1970; or

- the partnership prepares its accounts as a whole in sterling but, so far as relates to part of its UK business, the accounts are prepared using the closing rate/net investment method from financial statements prepared in a currency other than sterling; or

- the accounts supporting the partnership return required by section 12AA TMA 1970 are in sterling but, so far as they relate to part of its UK business, they are prepared using the closing rate/net investment method from financial statements prepared in a currency other than sterling.

14. It is the view of the Inland Revenue that the profits and losses of the business or part business for the period, as computed in the relevant foreign currency, should be allocated to corporate members of the partnership in accordance with their entitlement to share in the profits of the partnership for that period. This sum should then be adjusted to take account of the corporate partner's share of any of the items mentioned in subsection (4)(b) of section 93 FA 1993 as determined in accordance with its entitlement by reference to its partnership interest in the relevant preceding period. (Paragraph 16 of SP 4/98 sets out the Inland Revenue view that the partnership itself cannot carry forward items such as non-trading deficits.)

15. The sterling equivalent of the amount computed as a result of the process outlined in the preceding paragraph should then be found in accordance with the rules in section 94 FA 1993 as amended to the extent necessary to find the company's profits or losses for the period for the purposes of corporation tax.

16. The election to use an average arm's length exchange rate and the notice of withdrawal of such an election for which section 94(5) provides will only be accepted by the Revenue where it is signed by all partners who, at the time of the election, are subject to United Kingdom corporation tax. Without all the signatures, the Inland Revenue will treat the election or notice of withdrawal as not effective. A valid election once made will not cease to be effective on subsequent partnership changes, unless validly withdrawn by all partners who at the time of the withdrawal are subject to United Kingdom corporation tax.

17. Where the accounting period of the partnership differs from the accounting period of a corporate member of the partnership, the sterling figure of the company's share of the results of the partnership's business for the period should be allocated between the company's relevant accounting periods on a just and reasonable basis (normally on a time basis).

18. To the extent that a corporate member of a partnership is entitled to a share of losses (within the meaning of section 93(7) FA 1993) computed in the relevant foreign currency which are not utilised for the purposes of corporation tax by the company in the company's relevant accounting period or periods, it is the view of the Inland Revenue that these losses

should be carried forward in the tax computations of the company to the next accounting period in that currency.

Cases where amended sections 93 and 94 apply to non-partnership income of a company member of a partnership

19. A company which carries on business in partnership may separately carry on its own business or part of its business in a currency other than sterling and, accordingly, be within the scope of sections 93 and 94 FA 1993 as amended in respect of that business or part business. It is possible that the company keeps its own accounts in the same currency as the currency used by the partnership or each may use a different non-sterling currency. Alternatively the company may account in foreign currency for its own business, but the business of the partnership may be accounted for in sterling.

20. Irrespective of the way in which the company accounts for its share of the partnership in any of these situations it is the view of the Inland Revenue that, because section 114 ICTA 1988 treats the business carried on in partnership as an entirely separate business of the company, it is necessary for the purposes of corporation tax to arrive at the company's share of the partnership profits and losses for the relevant accounting period or periods in sterling (by conversion of non-sterling profits and losses as computed above where the figure is not already in sterling). This sterling figure must then be combined with the profits and losses of the company in respect of its non-partnership business as computed in any non-sterling currency and then converted to sterling in accordance with sections 93 and 94 FA 1993 so far as these are brought into account for corporation tax purposes for the accounting period.

Appendix 3

Inland Revenue Explanatory Statement: Exchange Gains and Losses and Financial Instruments

Introduction

This Statement gives the Revenue's views on certain aspects of the legislation in Finance Acts 1993 and 1994 and associated regulations which deal with the taxation of exchange gains and losses and profits and losses on certain financial instruments. These new rules will come into effect for companies on the first day of their first accounting period to begin on or after 23 March 1995. This statement draws together various assurances that have been given by the Inland Revenue during the extensive consultations that have taken place during the development of this legislative package. However it is not intended to cover every possible circumstance that could arise; points that emerge in the future will be considered on their merits at that time.

Whilst the Statement sets out the approach that will normally be taken when applying the new legislation, it has to be recognised that particular cases may turn on their own facts, or context, and accordingly there may be circumstances where the interpretation given here will not apply. Of course the content of this Statement is not a substitute for the statutory language and it will be the words enacted by Parliament which determine a company's tax liability. Nothing in this Statement affects a company's right of appeal on any point.

Since the publication of this document in draft form on 7 October 1994, there have been some minor changes to the text. These changes are summarised in an appendix to this document.

Section 1: Outline of the Forex provisions[1]

1.1 The provisions apply to qualifying companies from the first day of their first accounting period to begin on or after 23 March 1995 – that is, to any company within the charge to corporation tax except a charity, authorised unit trust or approved investment trust (section 152).

1.2 Qualifying assets and liabilities are defined in section 153.

- Qualifying assets include currency in the form of cash, and debts (including foreign currency bank accounts). Debts are qualifying assets only to the extent that they are recoverable (section 144). Shares held on trading account are also qualifying assets in cases where the company's practice is to include translation exchange differences on the shares in its profit and loss account (section 153(11)).

- Qualifying liabilities include debts and, in certain circumstances, provisions for contingent liabilities. They also include contractual obligations to deliver securities and shares before the assets are acquired ('short' sales).

1.3 For qualifying assets and liabilities and forward contracts to buy or sell currency, exchange gains and losses are recognised as they accrue between one 'translation time' and the next (sections 125 to 127 and 158).

1.4 Trading exchange gains and losses are taken into account in the computation of trading profits or losses (section 128).

1.5 Net non-trade exchange gains are assessed under Case VI of Schedule D (sections 129 and 130), and there are special rules for non-trade exchange losses (sections 129 and 131 to 133) – these can be set off against other profits of the same accounting period, group relieved, carried back for set-off against exchange profits of the past three years, or carried forward for set-off against exchange profits.

1.6 In broad terms, where unrealised exchange gains on long-term capital items exceed one tenth of the profit of an accounting period, a company may be able to claim to defer the excess until the following accounting period (sections 139 to 143 and the The Exchange Gains and Losses (Deferral of Gains and Losses) Regulations 1994). A further claim may be made in respect of that subsequent accounting period if appropriate. The regulations provide for net exchange gains – and in some instances the profits measure – to be calculated on an aggregate basis where the claimant is a member of a UK group of companies.

1.7 Exchange differences are generally to be calculated by reference to sterling, but

---

[1]   Statutory references in this Section are to Finance Act 1993 unless otherwise stated.

- trading profits or losses before capital allowances may be calculated by reference to other currencies in certain circumstances (sections 149 and 92 to 95, and the Local Currency Elections Regulations 1994) for companies resident in the UK or carrying on a trade here; and

- the chargeable profits of a controlled foreign company are to be computed by reference to the currency of its accounts (legislation to be included in Finance Bill 1995 – announced in Press Release dated 29 September 1994).

1.8 A company can elect for 'matching' of exchange differences on borrowings with exchange differences on certain non-qualifying assets (The Exchange Gains and Losses (Alternative Method of Calculation) Regulations 1994). Matched exchange differences are left out of account until the asset is disposed of, and are then treated as capital gains or allowable losses under the CGT rules.

1.9 Exchange gains and losses relating to exempt activities (mainly long-term and mutual insurance business) are disregarded. (The Exchange Gains and Losses (Alternative Method of Calculation) Regulations 1994).

1.10 There are detailed anti-avoidance provisions at sections 135 to 138.

1.11 Qualifying assets which are currently subject to capital gains tax (CGT) will cease to be so (section 169 and Schedule 17).

1.12 The Exchange Gains and Losses (Excess Exchange Gains and Losses) Regulations 1994 provide for a balancing adjustment to restrict, in certain circumstances, the amount taxed or relieved in respect of exchange gains and losses so as to take account of the overall gain or loss on an asset or liability.

1.13 There are special rules for exchange differences relating to insurance business (The Exchange Gains and Losses (Insurance Companies) Regulations 1994).

1.14 The scheme applies from the first day of a company's first accounting period to begin on or after 23 March 1995 (section 165). There is a special anti-avoidance rule in section 166 to allow a 'just and reasonable' adjustment where a company changes its accounting date, and hence its commencement day, for the purpose of securing a tax advantage.

1.15 Where a qualifying asset, liability or contract is held or owed on the commencement date the company is to be treated as if it became entitled or subject to the asset or liability on that date (section 165(2) and (3)). The Exchange Gains and Losses (Transitional Provisions) Regulations 1994 provide a number of transitional rules for such items.

Section 2: Forex – some questions answered

Finance Act 1993 provisions

Q. Will the new rules mean exchange gains and losses have to be computed separately for each individual transaction?

2.1 No. Although the legislation has to set out how exchange gains and losses are to be computed on any particular asset, liability, or currency contract, the effect is simply to mirror normal accountancy practice. Where exchange differences are already included in the trading profit or loss shown in the accounts on the translation basis – as will generally be the case – no adjustments will be needed in the tax computation to comply with the basic rules described in paragraphs 1.1 to 1.4 above. Where exchange differences on non-trade items are included in the accounts on the translation basis, the aggregate figures from the accounts will correspond to the amounts assessable under Case VI or relievable under the special rules described in paragraph 1.5 above.

2.2 When introducing the provisions on exchange gains and losses in the Finance Bill 1993, the Economic Secretary said (Hansard Col 9, Standing Committee A on 19 May 1993):

'It is important to note that the rules mirror what is achieved by applying normal accountancy practice. Where exchange differences are already included in a company's accounts on the translation basis – as will generally be the case – no adjustment will be needed for exchange differences in the tax computation. Therefore no adjustment will be necessary in the majority of cases involving translation. That is the legislation's intention and, we believe, its effect.'

Q. Will the detailed provisions on exchange rates in section 150 prevent companies from using the figures in the accounts?

2.3 No. Provided normal accountancy practice is followed, the rules are designed to allow companies to use any arm's length rate they have used for a particular date in preparing their accounts, whether this is a spot or a forward rate. Translation of transactions using average rates is also permitted. (The average rate may be the average for any period – so for example monthly or quarterly averages will be permitted).

Q. What is meant by the term 'London closing exchange rate'?

2.4 This term is used elsewhere in the Taxes Acts to denote any of the London rates published by reputable independent bodies such as Reuters, the Bank of England, or the Financial Times. Any of these published rates would be acceptable.

Q. If a non-resident company does not carry on a trade in the UK, but borrows or deposits funds here, will the Forex rules apply to it?

2.5 No. The Forex provisions do not extend the territorial scope of UK taxation in any way, and apply only to companies within the charge to UK corporation tax (subject to special considerations as regards controlled foreign companies). Non-resident investors in UK properties financed by foreign currency mortgages will not be within the provisions unless they are carrying on a trade in the UK.

Q. Why are there different rules for trading and non-trading exchange gains and losses, although their treatment is very similar?

2.6 Dealing with trading exchange gains and losses under the rules for non-trading exchange gains and losses would mean that exchange differences would have to be carved out of the computation of trading profits: this could cause compliance difficulties for companies. Conversely, categorising non-trading exchange differences as trading items could also cause problems, particularly where the company is not actually trading.

2.7 When introducing (as Clause 125) the provision which became section 128 Finance Act 1993, the Economic Secretary said in connection with the requirement to distinguish between trading and non-trading items (Hansard Col 47–8, Standing Committee A on 19 May 1993):

'The provision is not expected to cause difficulty in practice, because under the new rules for relief of non-trade items in subsequent clauses ... the dividing line between trade and non-trade items will be much less important than under the present rules.'

Q. How are exchange differences on qualifying indexed securities, deep discount securities, and deep gain securities computed under the new rules?

2.8 For a deep discount security, deep gain security or qualifying indexed security exchange differences are computed (as for other qualifying assets and liabilities) by reference to the local currency equivalent of the basic valuation of the security. This will normally be the issue price (possibly net of issue costs) or cost of acquisition under section 159 Finance Act 1993. Where a debt on such a security is held or owed at a company's commencement date then the Exchange Gains and Losses (Transitional Provisions) Regulations 1994 deem the basic valuation to be the appropriate valuation under section 159 when the security was either issued or acquired and again this will normally be the issue price or cost at acquisition. These securities are not subject to the computational rules in section 127 (debts which vary).

2.9 For a deep discount security computation of the income elements under the rules in Schedule 4 Taxes Act 1988 are carried out in the nominal currency and converted into local currency –

- for the issuer: at the end of the relevant income period
- for the investor: on redemption or disposal.

Exchange differences to be assessed or relieved under the Forex provisions will not normally arise on income elements.

2.10 For a deep gain security the whole profit accruing to the investor is brought to account on redemption or disposal under the rules in Schedule 11 Finance Act 1989 and paragraph 5A of Schedule 11 (inserted by paragraph 7 of Schedule 18 Finance Act 1993) ensures that any exchange differences which have accrued under the foreign exchange rules are not counted again.

Q. Will it be necessary for a company carrying on exempt activities (within the meaning of paragraph 2 Schedule 15 FA 1993) to prepare computations showing the exchange gains or losses that would have been chargeable in respect of those exempt activities.

2.11 No.

Q. Paragraph 6(4) of Schedule 17 provides for amounts claimed under section 254(6) TCGA to be reduced by the amount of any exchange losses. Are exchange losses to be computed net of exchange gains?

2.12 Yes.

Q. Section 60 Finance Act 1993 extends the circumstances in which the Taxes Acts prevent a deduction for interest that exceeds a reasonable rate of return on a loan. What is this provision aimed at?

2.13 Interest which exceeds a commercial rate of return on the principal advanced is already disallowed under other provisions of the Taxes Acts. The purpose of section 60 is to disallow interest which exceeds a commercial rate on the principal repayable, where the amount repayable is determined by reference to a currency other than that in which the advance was made. For example, if a loan is advanced in cruzeiros, but repayable by reference to a sum fixed in US dollars, the lender is exposed to exchange rate movements against the dollar rather than against the cruzeiro. The interest rate charged should therefore be the rate appropriate to a dollar loan rather than the higher rate which would be required if the amount repayable was fixed in cruzeiros.

2.14 When introducing this provision as clause 60 of the Finance Bill 1993, the Economic Secretary said (Hansard Col 102–103, Standing Committee A on 19 May 1993):

' ... I assure the hon. Gentleman that clause 60 covers only the narrow range of circumstances in which a loan made in one currency is repayable by reference to another currency. The hon. Gentleman asked whether the clause will apply only when loans are not at arm's length. That is not quite the case; it is true that the clause will apply where interest is not at a commercial rate, but it will apply both to arm's length and non-arm's length situations. The circumstances described by and provided for in the clause will by their nature, arise rarely if not infrequently. There is no prospect of the Revenue coming down hard or using the clause widely, but it is necessary to make such provision for the reasons I have given.'

Q. Can perpetual debt be a qualifying asset or liability within Forex?

2.15 Yes. Provided there is at least a contingent right or duty to settle the debt – for example where there is provision for repayment at the borrower's option, or on liquidation of one of the parties – it will be a qualifying asset or liability under Section 153(1)(a) or (2)(a) Finance Act 1993. Section 154(12) and 155(11) ensure that such a debt may be recognised, following normal accountancy practice, before there is an unconditional right or duty.

Regulations

Q. What is the meaning of 'financial statements' in regulation 5 of the Local Currency Elections Regulations 1994?

2.16 Financial statements are statements of account drawn up by a company relating to a trade or part trade which fall short of the definition of 'accounts' in regulation 2 of the regulations (in particular, they are not the statutory accounts), but nevertheless are drawn up on normal accountancy principles. Financial statements might be drawn up for the trade carried on by a branch of a company and then used in the preparation of the accounts of the company as a whole.

Q. How will section 149 Finance Act 1993 be applied where a local currency election has been made in respect of a trade which it is carrying on through an overseas branch?

2.17 Section 149 Finance Act 1993 includes any liability owed by the company for the purposes of the branch trade subject to the local currency election, regardless of whether the loan is owed by the branch or by 'Head Office'

2.18 Where a company has borrowings which it has passed on to the branch (whether in the form of dotation capital via the head office account or as a commercial loan) for use in its trade, the intra-company 'loan' and 'borrowing' are to be ignored (a company cannot lend money to itself and such amounts cannot be qualifying assets or liabilities). However, so much of the real external borrowings as correspond to the intra-company loan are covered by the local currency election. Exchange differences on these borrowings will then be computed by reference to the branch local currency. Because the intra-company advances to the branch will actually reflect the extent of use for the branch trade, the accounting treatment should produce precisely the result which is required under section 149 Finance Act 1993.

2.19 In practical terms this means that a company which has a currency liability at least equal to the amounts advanced by it to its local currency branch will not have to make any computational adjustment in order to determine the consequence of eliminating the intra-company 'asset' and 'liability' because these have equal and opposite effect. In such a case the branch local currency profit (before capital allowances) will be based on the branch local currency accounts.

Q. What scope is there for a matching election in the situation referred to in the previous question?

2.20 A matching election will be available in respect of the net investment in the branch as shown in the company books. For this purpose, 'net investment' will be interpreted in the sense of SSAP 20. Amounts advanced by the company to its branch, which are funded by company local currency liabilities accorded local currency treatment in the manner discussed in paragraphs 2.17 to 2.19 above, will not be regarded as part of the net investment. Thus the net investment will generally only comprise net accumulated branch profits and any sums advanced to the branch which are not funded by liabilities owed by the company for the purposes of the branch trade. This means that where a company has translation differences in respect of the net investment in its local currency branch, which are not covered by the local currency election, they can be matched with differences on currency liabilities designed to hedge that net investment.

2.21 In exceptional circumstances it may be that a branch holds an asset which is unrelated to the branch trade and whose translation to local currency is not therefore eligible to be included in the local currency election. Where the value of such an asset is hedged for accounting purposes by a company liability, a matching election in respect of the net investment may be made – this will enable the accounting treatment to be followed for tax purposes.

Q. How will regulation 10(2)(c) in the matching regulations (The Exchange Gains and Losses (Alternative Method of Calculation) Regulations 1994) be interpreted?

2.22 This regulation will enable a company to elect to match a proportion or amount of an asset according to a formula specified at the time when the matching election is made. So, for example, it will enable a company to match:

- that proportion of the shares in a subsidiary which corresponds to the proportion of the subsidiary's net underlying assets in a particular currency at the relevant time; or

- such part of an asset as corresponds to the value of the asset (or the proportion of the asset established as above) less an amount equal to the part of the asset which is funded by share capital.

Q. How will regulation 5(4)(b) of The Exchange Gains and Losses (Alternative Method of Calculation of Gains and Losses) Regulations 1994 be interpreted in relation to a liability which is matching a share-holding in a company whose assets are denominated in more than one currency?

2.23 Regulation 5(4)(b) requires that the nominal currency of the liability is such that borrowing in that currency could reasonably be expected to eliminate or substantially reduce the economic risk of holding the asset which is attributable to fluctuations in exchange rates. Amongst the circumstances in which the test will be regarded as satisfied are the following illustrative situations:

The UK holding company eligible to make a matching election holds shares in a Dutch holding company which in turn has operating subsidiaries in Germany, France and Hong Kong. Each operating subsidiary trades principally in the country in which it is established so that, for example, a German subsidiary will be a DM asset etc.

Scenario 1. The UK holding company borrows deutschmarks, French francs, and Hong Kong dollars in amounts equivalent to the net asset values of the three operating companies. Each borrowing completely eliminates the exchange risk associated with holding the subsidiary in a particular country. Regulation 5(4)(b) is regarded as satisfied.

Scenario 2. The UK holding company borrows French francs equivalent to the net asset value of the French operating company – and leaves that part of the shareholding equivalent to the net asset values of the other operating companies unhedged. The borrowing completely eliminates the exchange risk on that part of the shareholding associated with holding the French subsidiary. Regulation 5(4)(b) is regarded as satisfied; the closing words of regulation 5(4) allow for only part of the asset to be matched. This would apply even where the relevant part of the shareholding was a small proportion of the total value of the shares.

Scenario 3. The UK holding company borrows deutschmarks equivalent to the net asset values of the German and French subsidiaries. Provided that the company can reasonably expect that, because of the close link between the exchange rate of the deutschmark and that of the French franc, the borrowing in deutschmarks substantially reduces the exchange risk on that part of the shareholding associated with holding the French subsidiary, the test in regulation 5(4)(b) is regarded as satisfied. This will apply to any borrowing in a currency which is different from the currency of the asset (or the underlying asset) as long as the exchange rates of the two currencies are closely linked.

Scenario 4. The UK holding company borrows deutschmarks equivalent to the net asset values of the three operating companies. Provided the net asset value of the Hong Kong subsidiary is not substantial in relation to the net asset values of the three operating companies, the test in regulation 5(4)(b) will be regarded as satisfied on the basis that the borrowing *substantially* reduces the economic risk of holding the asset which is attributable to fluctuations in the exchange rates of the underlying currencies.

Q. The matching provisions apply only where both asset and liability are held/owed by a single company. If intra-group loans are made, is there a risk of interest being imputed on the loans under the transfer pricing legislation?

2.24 The matching provisions do not allow matching where the asset and the liability are in different companies within a group. In such a case, to enable a matching election to be made, the company which has borrowed the funds may on lend them, on an interest free basis, to another UK company which holds the asset. Concern has been expressed that in these circumstances the transfer pricing legislation at section 770 and section 773 of the Taxes Act 1988 may apply. This legislation is however normally only applied to wholly domestic transactions within a UK group where there is a tax advantage or avoidance. While the facts and circumstances of each case must be considered, it is confirmed that the transfer pricing legislation will not be invoked where the Board is satisfied that an interest free loan is made within a group primarily for the purposes of the matching arrangements or where the main reason for no interest being charged is to maximise the use of foreign tax credits. And the position is not affected where the funds lent to the company which holds the asset (in foreign currency) are lent back in sterling to the group lending company which has the original foreign currency borrowing or currency contract.

Q. When do profits have to be computed on an aggregate group basis under the deferral regulations?

2.25 The amount to be deferred is calculated by reference to the aggregate profits of the claimant and certain other group companies where the claimant company's allocated share of the group exchange gains represents more than half of its own profits (new subsection (3A) of section 141). A group company's results will enter into this computation where at any time during the accounting period it owes the claimant company, or is owed by the claimant company, a qualifying debt (excluding trade debts) which represents more than one tenth of the total qualifying debts (excluding trade debts) of the creditor (new subsection (3B)). 'Qualifying debt' has the same meaning as in section 153(10) of the Finance Act 1993, and includes sterling debts as well as debts denominated in other currencies.

Q. In the rules for computing amounts available for relief for group companies, what items are excluded from the computation of amounts C1 and C2 by the new subsection (5) of section 141?

2.26 The new subsection (5) excludes exchange gains and losses on all items on which profits would be taxable under current law – for example debts due for goods, services or assets supplied to or by the company in the course of the trade, currency contracts undertaken to hedge such debts and bank accounts forming part of the circulating capital of the trade. (The question of whether any gain or loss on an item would be taxable under current law is to be determined without regard to the fact that the gain or loss might be 'matched' by a gain or loss on a capital asset or liability following principles established in the case of Pattison v Marine Midland.)

Q. How do the transitional regulations apply to controlled foreign companies?

2.27 Where in the last accounting period before the Forex rules come into effect a controlled foreign company was effectively within the UK tax net, because either:

- a direction under Section 747 Taxes Act 1988 had effect for that accounting period; or

- no direction was made under Section 747 because the acceptable distribution test was satisfied;

the company is treated under the transitional regulations in the same way as a UK resident company within the charge to corporation tax, so that regulation 3 (grandfathering) and Parts III and IV (set-off of certain pre-commencement gains and losses) apply.

Q. A debt is regarded as fixed in term for the purposes of the transitional regulations if it is provided (in accordance with Regulation 3(6)(b)) that certain conditions are satisfied. Do these conditions have to be expressly provided for in the terms of any relevant documentation?

2.28 No. Provided that conditions (for example on the redrawing of principal repaid) are implied by the terms of the relevant agreement they will be satisfied.

Q. If an asset is not fully matched at the time of making a matching election must the election be made only in respect of the matched part of the asset under Regulation 10(2)(c)?

2.29 No. In principle an election can always be made in respect of a whole asset under Paragraph 10(2)(b) even when only a small part of the asset is matched. Where such an election is made all liabilities eligible to be matched with the asset will automatically be taken into account and if they are sufficient to result only in partial matching then only the initial exchange gains and losses on those eligible liabilities can be left out of account. Gains will be left out of account only if they are taken to reserves in the accounts of the company making the election (see Regulation 10(4)).

Section 3: Guidance note on Forex anti-avoidance provisions

Description of provisions

Main benefit test

3.1 Section 135 Finance Act 1993 provides for exchange losses on a foreign currency loan to be disallowed where the accrual of an exchange loss is the main benefit, or one of the main benefits, that might be expected to arise from borrowing or lending in the particular currency. The section applies only where a direction is made by the Board of Inland Revenue.

Arm's length test

3.2 Sections 136 to 138 Finance Act 1993 provide for the 'ring-fencing' of exchange losses on a loan or forward currency contract which is entered into otherwise than on arm's length terms. Such losses will be available for relief only against future exchange gains arising on the same loan or contract. For loans, the application of section 136 is limited by subsections (4) to (10):

- where the amount of a loan is the only respect in which the terms of a loan would have differed had the parties been dealing at arm's length (i.e. a lower amount would have been advanced), the only exchange differences to be ring-fenced are those which arise on the excess of the actual loan over the amount which would have been advanced at arm's length; and

- where a loan is regarded as not on arm's length terms solely because interest has not been charged, or has been charged at lower than a commercial rate, the restriction will not apply if interest, or additional interest, is treated as having been charged on the whole of the loan under section 770 Taxes Act 1988. Where interest is imputed under section 770 on part of a loan, the restriction will not apply to exchange losses on that part.

3.3 In addition, section 136 is not to apply where the loan transaction is between members of a UK group of companies and a corresponding taxable exchange gain accrues to the other group member (subsections (11) and (12)). This will provide automatic exclusion from restriction for most intra-UK group loans.

3.4 Subsection (13) prevents the exclusions from the arm's length test from applying automatically to debts that vary in amount – but The Exchange Gains and Losses (Debts of Varying Amount) Regulations

1994 will apply the exclusions to such debts in exactly the same way as they apply to debts which do not vary.

3.5 As with section 135, the arm's length test will only be applied on a direction given by the Board. This should ensure that the provision does not hit trivial or inappropriate cases and that it is applied even-handedly to all taxpayers. Wherever possible the company will be given an opportunity to put forward any facts or circumstances which it thinks ought to be taken into consideration by the Board.

Some questions answered

Q. The 'main benefit' test in section 135 is very widely drafted. Will it catch commercial transactions?

3.6 No. The provision needs to be widely drafted to ensure that transactions do not escape because the company can show some commercial purpose – however spurious – for the transaction. But it only applies where obtaining relief for an exchange loss is the main benefit, or one of the main benefits, of borrowing, lending or entering into a transaction in a particular currency. If the transaction is entered into primarily for commercial reasons, and the accrual of an exchange loss is merely incidental – even if it is obvious from the outset that an exchange loss is likely to accrue – no direction will be given and the section will not apply.

Q. The arm's length tests in sections 136, 137 and 138 apply where the terms of a transaction are different from those which would have been agreed at arm's length. Will this result in transactions being caught because of minor divergences from arm's length terms?

3.7 No. The arm's length tests are designed to deter avoidance and to catch cases where it would clearly be inappropriate to allow relief for exchange losses on a general basis without ring-fencing. It is expected that they will apply mainly to exchange losses on:

- borrowings by a thinly capitalised UK company; or

- loans to an overseas subsidiary, situated in a country with which the UK has an appropriate Double Taxation Convention, which are regarded as fulfilling an equity function and where no transfer pricing direction has been made in respect of interest on the loan; or

- circular, loss multiplying, or otherwise abusive transactions.

3.8 No direction will be given by the Board in cases where:

- the transaction's terms differ, but not materially, from those which would have been agreed at arm's length; or

409

- the substantive terms of the transaction are at arm's length, but are not documented in the same detail or manner as would be expected between parties acting at arm's length; or

- given the particular facts and circumstances it would be unreasonable or inappropriate for a direction to be made.

Q. Section 136(7) and (8) provide an exclusion for cases where there has been a transfer pricing adjustment on an outward loan which produces the same tax result as if the transaction had been at arm's length. There is no corresponding provision for inward loans – does this mean the transfer pricing adjustment in such cases will be ignored?

3.9 No. Where there has been an adjustment to an inward loan under section 770 or 773 Taxes Act 1988, or where a corresponding adjustment has been agreed by the UK competent authority, then for the purposes of section 136 the terms to be considered will be *as adjusted for tax purposes*. So if a company borrows at 10 per cent and the arm's length rate is 8 per cent, the transfer pricing adjustment would reduce the allowable expense to the 8 per cent level, and if this was the only deviation from arm's length terms then the loan would not be caught by section 136.

Q. Ring-fenced losses can only be carried forward and not back – does this mean that a company can be taxed on gains in years 1 and 2, and then denied effective relief for a loss in year 3?

3.10 The Board's direction making power relates to each accrual period, and gains taxed in earlier accounting periods will be one of the most significant factors to be taken into account in deciding whether section 136 will apply. For example, no direction would normally be given in respect of a loss on a transaction where net gains in excess of that loss on the same transaction had been taxed in earlier years.

Q. How will the amount which could be borrowed at arm's length be established?

3.11 The amount which could be borrowed by an overseas associate will be determined by reference to what a company operating in that overseas jurisdiction could have borrowed at arm's length on a stand-alone basis. It is accepted that, for example, general debt/equity ratios in the UK might differ from those seen in Japan or the United States, and that it would be wrong to apply UK criteria for determining arm's length borrowing globally.

3.12 In addition, the fact that for prudential reasons a bank may demand a parental guarantee before lending to a subsidiary will not, on its own, prevent the loan being regarded as made at arm's length: the test will be whether an independent company in the same circumstances could have borrowed on the same terms.

Q. If a loan is made to a thinly capitalised overseas associate will it be caught automatically by section 136?

3.13 No. The Board will take all factors in account. Even where it appears that a loan has been made to a thinly capitalised overseas associate, the Board would not make a direction where the UK company making the loan receives a market rate of interest, unless it appears that the transaction may be part of a scheme to avoid or defer UK tax.

Q. If a company borrows funds and on-lends them, and one or both transactions are on non-arm's length terms, will the Board take into account the fact that the exchange loss on the borrowing is 'cancelled out' by an equal and opposite exchange gain on the lending?

3.14 Yes. Where there is a clear linkage between a borrowing and lending in this way, the exchange loss on one is cancelled out by an equivalent exchange gain on the other, and there are no other related transactions forming part of a scheme which avoids or defers UK tax, no direction will be made by the Board.

Q. Will a direction be made in relation to on-lending arrangements as described in paragraph 2.24 above?

3.15 No! Even if none of the specific exemptions from the application of section 136(2) apply, no direction will be made unless it appears that the transactions may be part of a scheme to avoid or defer UK tax.

Q. Can the exceptions in subsections (4) to (12) of section 136 to the application of subsection (2) also apply to the application of section 137 in relation to currency contracts?

3.16 It is considered that the circumstances outlined in subsections (4) to (12) of section 136 are unlikely to apply to currency contracts and, therefore, they are not relevant to the application of section 137. However, if this proves not to be so, and circumstances do arise in relation to a currency contract which are equivalent to any of those set out in subsections (4) to (12) of section 136, no direction will be made by the Board under section 137(1)(d).

Section 4: Guidance note on Forex local currency provisions

Interpretation of Regulation 6 of The Local Currency Elections Regulations 1994

4.1 One of the primary conditions to be satisfied before a local currency election can be validly made is set out in Regulation 5(2)(a) of The Local Currency Elections Regulations 1994 which require the currency to be that of the 'primary economic environment' in which the trade or part is carried on. Regulation 6 then sets out guidance on how the primary economic environment is to be determined.

4.2 All relevant circumstances are to be considered but Regulation 6 sets out a number of factors which have to be considered in particular insofar as they are relevant. The Regulations do not require a majority or any particular number of factors to be present and the relevance and importance of each factor needs to be considered separately for each trade (or part). These may vary with the type of trade and the manner and particular market in which the company operates. These notes look at each of the factors set out in Regulation 6 and describe circumstances in which they would be relevant and in which the relative importance of each factor may also be a consideration.

The currency in which the net cash flows of a trade or part are generated or expressed in the relevant accounting records (factor (a))

4.3 SSAP20 describes local currency as the currency of the primary economic environment in which the company operates and generates net cash flows. The Regulations do not just talk about generating cash flows because a company may generate income in a variety of currencies none of which might represent a majority even of its income let alone its net cash flows. For a company which earned 40% of its income in dollars with the remaining income spread amongst other non-sterling currencies but which paid its administration expenses (including salaries) in sterling, the currency of generation of cash flows would have little relevance. However despite the mix of currencies contributing to net cash flows the company may well record its transactions in its records by translating them immediately into what it regards as its local currency. If this happens then clearly factor (a) is relevant in terms of the currency in which cash flows are expressed.

4.4 A company may adopt multi-currency accounting by which it may mean that transactions are initially recorded in the currency in which they are carried out (in which case there might be separate records for dollar, yen etc. transactions). The relevance of factor (a) in this situation would depend on the extent to which net cash flows expressed in the relevant records contributed to overall net cash flows.

4.5 Alternatively a company might keep parallel records in both dollars and sterling. In this situation factor (a) would not enable a choice to be made between the two, and other factors would need to be considered.

The currency in which the company manages the profitability of the trade or part so far as it is affected by currency exposure (factor (b))

4.6 This factor is likely to be relevant for all companies and for some companies it may be the only relevant factor or may be so important that it dominates any other relevant factors. Companies will need to know by reference to which currency they are trying to manage their profits for a variety of reasons. For example they may be required by the parent company or the head office (for a branch) to measure their profitability in a particular currency or bonuses or profit-sharing arrangements may be based on profitability in that currency. There is more however to this factor than mere measurement of profit in a particular currency because the factor refers to the *management* of profitability. Companies will normally have a clear policy on the hedging of exchange risk from which it should be clear by reference to which currency profitability is being managed. This is not to say that all risk would have to be hedged back to, say, the dollar. The company may take the view that the dollar profit would be higher if it left certain transactions unhedged. Most companies preparing their accounts in a particular currency are likely to be managing their profitability by reference to that currency but companies ought if necessary to be able to produce some evidence of what it is actually doing to manage profitability in a particular currency.

For companies resident in the United Kingdom the currency in which the company's share capital and its reserves are denominated (factor (c))

4.7 The currency in which share capital is denominated will be a relevant factor for companies (but not branches). It may not however be an important factor where a company is thinly capitalised or it uses hedging transactions to avoid or alter currency exposure on finance raised through the issue of share capital. If a company has $2 share capital but borrowings of £1,000,000 then factor (c) will be relevant but insignificant in terms of its importance.

The currency to which the company or branch is exposed in its long-term capital borrowing (factor (d))

4.8 The currency risk to which a company depending on significant borrowings is exposed will be relevant. Where borrowings in a specific currency hedge currency assets there will normally be no currency exposure and as far as that borrowing is concerned, factor (d) will not be relevant. Similarly, it will not necessarily be the case that the denomination of the original borrowing will determine the relevant currency for the purposes of factor (d). A company may borrow in say dollars but use a currency swap effectively to swap the borrowing into deutschmarks. In this case the currency exposure would be to deutschmarks. There is a strong likelihood that the currency for factor (d) would be the same as that for factor (b) – the currency in which the company is managing its profitability. Long-term capital borrowings for the purposes of this factor should be taken to be borrowings for a period of more than one year.

The currency which is the generally recognised currency in which trade in the principal market of the trade or part is carried on (factor (e))

4.9 For certain specialised trades there may be a global market in a particular currency. The most obvious example is oil which is internationally traded in dollars. This factor is likely to be of importance where other factors do not give a conclusive steer. Not all oil companies for example account in dollars presumably because they consider themselves to be managing their profitability in a different currency (factor (b)).

Cases in which functional currency approach adopted pre-commencement day

4.10 Inspectors may have accepted a functional currency approach to the calculation of basic profits for corporation tax for periods prior to the appointed day. It is anticipated that the tests set out in regulations will be satisfied in such cases to enable a valid election to be made to cover periods following a company's commencement day.

Section 5: Outline of the financial instruments provisions[2]

5.1 The provisions apply where a qualifying company – that is, any company within the charge to corporation tax except an authorised unit trust (section 154) – enters into a qualifying contract.

5.2 A qualifying contract is defined in section 147 as a contract which is either an interest rate contract or option or a currency contract or option:

a.   an interest rate contract must provide for a qualifying company to pay or receive at least one variable rate payment in exchange for one or more variable rate payments, fixed rate payments, or fixed payments (section 149);

b.   an interest rate option is an option to enter into an interest rate contract, or an option to enter into such an option (for example a swaption) (section 149);

c.   the definition of a currency contract in section 150 follows that in section 126 Finance Act 1993 and covers contracts which provide for an exchange of specified amounts of currencies (whether settled by an actual exchange or by a net payment) at a specified time. The definition is extended by The Currency Contracts and Options (Amendment of Enactments) Order 1994 to cover contracts which provide for a net payment calculated by reference to the movement of one currency against another;

d.   a currency option is defined as:

●   an option to enter into a currency contract (section 151), or

●   an option to buy or sell currency within a specified period or at a specified time (section 151(7)); or

●   an option which automatically settles into cash if it is valuable to the holder at termination (section 151(8)).

5.3 In determining whether a contract is a qualifying contract, provisions which are of minor economic or commercial significance in the context of the contract as a whole are to be disregarded (section 152).

5.4 Qualifying payments under a qualifying contract are defined in section 153, and profits or losses are taxed or relieved on an accruals or mark to market basis under the new rules (section 156). The provisions are designed to secure that the measure of taxable profits on qualifying contracts follows the accounting measure as long as the accounting method adopted does not provide scope for manipulation of the timing of taxable profits or losses.

5.5 Where a mark to market basis is acceptable under section 156, profits

[2]   Statutory references in this Section are to Finance Act 1994 unless otherwise stated.

or losses on the qualifying contract will be determined under section 155(1) and (2) by comparing:

• the aggregate of receipts falling due and payable in the period and any increase in the value of the contract for the period with

• the aggregate of payments falling due and payable in the period with any decrease in value for the period (section 155(4)).

5.6 Where an accruals basis is used under section 156, profits or losses on the qualifying contract will be determined under section 155(1) and (2) by comparing:

• the aggregate of receipts allocated to the period with

• the aggregate of payments allocated to the period (section 155(5)).

5.7 The profits or losses thus identified are either treated as profits or losses arising in the course of the trade (section 159), or as non-trading profits or losses which are taxed or relieved following the mechanism for taxing or relieving non-trading exchange gains and losses in sections 130 to 133 Finance Act 1993 (section 160 Finance Act 1994). Net non-trading gains are assessed under Case VI of Schedule D (sections 129 and 130 Finance Act 1993), and there are special rules for non-trading losses (sections 129 and 131 to 133 Finance Act 93) – these can be set off against other profits of the same accounting period, group relieved, carried back for set-off against profits from qualifying contracts or exchange profits of the past three years, or carried forward for set-off against future net profits from qualifying contracts or exchange profits.

5.8 There are anti-avoidance provisions in sections 165 to 168 to deal with contracts written on non-arm's length terms and those entered into with residents of certain countries.

5.9 Section 169 and Schedule 18 adapt the provisions for insurance and mutual trading companies. Sections 170 to 176 provide special rules concerning investment trusts, charities, partnerships and offshore funds.

5.10 There are transitional arrangements in sections 147 and 148 for qualifying contracts which are in existence on a company's commencement day. In addition, section 158, which provides for adjustments for changes in basis of accounting, is also used (by virtue of subsections (6) and (7)) to make an appropriate adjustment at a company's commencement day to compare amounts taken into account for corporation tax under the old rules with what would have been taken into account had the new rules applied. The result is that over the life of the contract, the correct commercial profit or loss should be recognised. For currency contracts, there are modifications to these basic rules in section 175 (see Section 7 below).

Section 6: Financial instruments – some questions answered

Q. What is the treatment of guarantees?

6.1 A reasonable fee paid by a qualifying company for a guarantee will be a reasonable cost within section 151(2)(b). The Revenue's understanding is that guarantees can take different forms and the obligations of the guarantor may vary accordingly. This has caused problems in the drafting of a specific provision to cover guarantees and in the event it has not proved possible to include anything in the legislation. However, the Revenue has concluded that in certain circumstances payments by the guarantor will be within the provisions (where, for example, the qualifying contract is completely taken over by the guarantor). In any case, consultation suggests that payments under guarantees are a matter of relatively little practical importance because it is only rarely that guarantees are called.

Q. Will ESC C17 continue to apply to swaps falling outside the new rules?

6.2 Yes – for a limited period. Extra-statutory concession C17 will continue to apply to swaps falling outside the new rules during the grandfathering period (ie the six-year period within section 148(2)). At the end of that period, it will be withdrawn. Any swaps that are within the concession will be within the new legislation.

Q. Does tax have to be deducted at source from payments under swaps that are not within the new legislation?

6.3 The mutual obligations which arise under a swap will normally mean that payments and receipts cannot be treated as annual payments. It follows that where this is the case there is no statutory requirement to deduct tax at source. This is also strictly the position for swaps within ESC C17 during the grandfathering period. Where however swap fees are dealt with as if they were annual payments in accordance with ESC C17 then, during the grandfathering period, tax should still be deducted at source unless the payments are to a recognised bank or swaps dealer.

Q. Section 148 – is the 3 month period long enough?

6.4 Companies will have the periods up to the appointed day and between the appointed day and their commencement day to take stock of their quasi-qualifying contracts.

Q. How are automatically cash-settled instruments included in the new regime?

6.5 Automatically cash-settled interest rate 'options' (such as an interest rate cap) are covered by the definition of an interest rate contract in section 149(1). In the case of a cap, for example, the difference between say LIBOR and the strike price will be a variable rate of interest and hence the contingent payments under the cap will be variable rate payments as defined in section 149(6). The structure in section 150 dealing with currency instruments is slightly different. Automatically cash-settled currency 'options' are dealt with in section 150(8).

Q. What is the position of fixed/fixed swaps?

6.6 There was some concern that so called fixed/fixed swaps might not be covered by the legislation because section 149(2) requires an interest rate contract to make provision for at least one variable rate payment. If a fixed/fixed swap provides for an ultimate exchange of currencies then it will be a currency contract as defined in section 150. The fixed interest-based payments will be covered by section 150(3) and the exchange by section 150(2). It is difficult to see how other sorts of fixed/fixed swaps might be used for risk management.

Q. What is the treatment if payments between the same counterparties over a number of contracts are netted under the terms of a Master Agreement?

6.7 The Revenue have considered the question of netting of payments in the context of the Master Agreement of the International Swaps and Derivatives Association. Although the Master Agreement and all Confirmations which govern the transactions are to form a single agreement between the parties, the Revenue's view is that prior to default, each transaction may fairly be regarded as being a separate agreement giving rise to a separate profit or loss.

6.8 This analysis is capable of applying equally where there is an election for netting under the terms of the Master Agreement on the basis that, in such a case, the transactions may be regarded as involving constructive payments of the gross amounts.

6.9 The analysis does not, however, run counter to the view that in certain events, a single payment flows in respect of all agreements between the same counterparties under the netting provisions contained in the ISDA Master Agreement.

6.10 The position under other Master Agreements may be less certain, particularly if, every time a fresh transaction is entered into, that agreement seeks to subsume that transaction into previous transactions between the same parties and under the same Master Agreement so as to produce a single resulting agreement. However, provided it is possible to compute separately the components of net cash flows and rights and obligations under such a Master Agreement and allocate them to the individual transactions, the legislation will be applied to individual qualifying contracts in the same way that it would have applied had the individual transaction been wholly free-standing.

Q. Does the exercise of an interest rate option, such as a swaption, give rise to a separate interest rate contract within section 149?

6.11 Yes, it does. Payments immediately following exercise are either within the terms of sections 149 and 150 or within section 151(1).

Q. What are the Revenue's views on various terms used in the definition of 'fixed payment', 'fixed rate payment' and 'variable rate payment' in section 149(6)?

6.12

– **references to the singular**. Under the Interpretation Act the singular includes the plural unless the context indicates otherwise. The Revenue's view is that the singular includes the plural in a number of the definitional sections. In particular, this applies to the references to 'time', 'payment', 'amount', 'period' and 'rate' where they appear in section 149(2), (3) and (6), 150(2), (3) and (4), and 151(1) and (2). That means, for example, that contracts which provide for an interest rate or rates to be applied to a specific amount or amounts for a specified period or periods will be covered by the new rules.

– **specified in the contract**. The reference to 'a fixed amount specified in the contract' in the definitions of fixed payment covers amounts, such as a premium paid for a cap, which are fixed and identifiable in amount at the outset of the contract.

However, in the Revenue's view, the references to an amount specified in the contract in the definitions of fixed rate and variable rate payments and in section 150(2), (3) and (4) also cover amounts which may not be capable of being identified as numbers at the outset of the contract, but which depend upon a calculation deriving from a formula included in the terms of the contract. For example, a contract which applies a variable interest rate to an amortising amount of notional principal will be within the definition of an interest rate contract. Range forward contracts and Asian options, for example, will also normally be covered by the definitions in section 150.

– **wholly or mainly**. This phrase is included in the definition of fixed rate and variable rate payments and in the definition of the interest based payments in section 150(3) to ensure that contracts are not excluded simply because, for example, those payments need to be grossed up to take account of withholding tax.

– **a rate the value of which**. These words are needed because the value of a rate, such as LIBOR, may vary as the rate moves.

– a rate of interest. A rate of interest is not defined in the legislation and so must take its ordinary meaning. It will therefore encompass rates which are generally regarded as a rate of interest by the commercial world. Further, even where this is not so, it will cover indices used as a measure where the specific circumstances and context mean that the index can be so regarded. For example, if the interest a company pays on a loan is computed by reference to the FT-SE 100 index, then that index would be an interest rate if included in a contract used to manage the risk on the interest being paid.

– variable rate of interest/fixed rate of interest

(i)   The terms 'variable rate of interest' and 'fixed rate of interest' are mutually exclusive.

(ii) A fixed rate of interest might be, say 8% or, say, the fixed yield on a specified Treasury bond. Either *could* (but will not necessarily) be stated in the contract as a percentage.

(iii) A variable rate of interest on the other hand has the potential to vary through time and could not be stated in the contract as a percentage. Examples would be, say, overnight LIBOR, 3 month LIBOR, 3 month LIBOR + 6%, and so on. All these rates may be different tomorrow. They all have the potential to vary from day to day and are all therefore variable rates of interest. The fact that today's 3 month LIBOR holds good for deposits made today for a 3 month period does not make 3 month LIBOR a fixed rate of interest.

(iv) Section 149(6) latches onto the value of the fixed or variable rate of interest and applies that to an amount of notional principal for a specified period. To take two examples:

a. A 3 year contract provides for 12 months LIBOR at a reference date (say 31/12) to be applied to notional principal of £1m.

12 month LIBOR is a variable rate of interest and therefore the payments will be variable rate payments. It turns out that the value of 12 month LIBOR at each reference date is as follows:

31.12.94	5%	therefore variable rate payment – 50K
31.12.95	6%	therefore variable rate payment – 60K
31.12.96	7%	therefore variable rate payment – 70K

b. Another contract (or perhaps the other leg to the contract above) provides a fixed rate of 5% to be applied to notional principal of £1m for 1994, then a fixed rate of 6% for 1995 and finally a fixed rate of 7% for 1996. The rates are all fixed and cannot vary and give rise to fixed rate payments of 50K, 60K and 70K.

Q. How will the words 'at the same time' in subsections (2) and (4) of section 150 be interpreted?

6.13 The phrase 'at the same time' refers to the entitlement and obligation to receive and make payments of the two currencies arising at the same time. The fact that actual payments may be made at different times is irrelevant.

Q. How will the words 'at a specified time' in subsections (2)(a) and (4)(a) of section 150 be interpreted?

6.14 The Revenue considers that 'at a specified time' can cover a number of specified times (see 'references to the singular' above) among which the company can choose. There might be an initial exchange (within section 150(4)) with provision for the final re-exchange on one of a number of specified times (within section 150(2)) with recurrent payments (within section 150(3)) throughout the period up to the time chosen for the re-exchange. It is considered that the condition in section 150(2) and the timing condition in section 150(5)(a) can be applied successively to the various possible re-exchange dates.

6.15 The point can be further illustrated using the example of a cross-currency amortising swap. There would be an initial exchange (within section 150(4)) with provision for re-exchange in, say, three tranches (within section 150(2)), with recurrent payments (within section 150(3)) based on the reducing principal. Each re-exchange is within section 150(2) and the requirement in section 150(5) is that the entitlement and obligation for the section 150(3) payments on each tranche arise before the re-exchange of that tranche.

Q. What mechanism is there for ensuring that the same treatment is afforded to both parties under a contract, provisions of which are disregarded under section 152?

6.16 The aim will be to arrive at a consistent treatment for both parties to the contract. In the event of an appeal against the Revenue decision, the Special Commissioners (Jurisdiction and Procedures) Regulations 1994 (SI 1994 No. 1811) and The General Commissioners (Jurisdiction and Procedures) Regulations 1994 (SI 1994 No. 1812) contain provisions for joining of additional parties to any appeal proceedings. This will ensure that both parties to a contract have a right to be heard and that the decision is binding on both.

Q. What is the meaning of 'small' in section 152(1)(b)?

6.17 During the Parliamentary debate on this provision, the Economic Secretary stated that he would normally expect a value to be small if it were less than 5% of the aggregate value of the qualifying payments. This does not, however, rule out the possibility of a company successfully arguing that a value of more than 5% is small on the facts of a particular case.

Q. Examples of the payments that will be included in section 151?

6.18 Section 151(1) includes yield adjustment fees. Stamp duty, indemnity fees and capital adequacy payments, for example, will be reasonable costs within section 151(2)(b) provided that they are reasonable in amount. The grossing up of arrangement fees and other payments within section 151 for withholding tax will not prevent them from being qualifying payments.

Q. Does section 154 (and section 160(4)) extend the scope of companies within the UK tax net with regard to payments under qualifying contracts?

6.19 There has been some concern that the new provisions impose a Case VI income tax charge on non-resident companies not within the charge to corporation tax because the definition of a qualifying company in section 154(1) embraces any company. However, the new rules are limited to companies which have an accounting period (see for example sections 147 and 155(1)). For this purpose, accounting period has the same meaning as it does for the foreign exchange legislation (section 177(5)). Since it is not separately defined in that legislation it takes its meaning from section 12 Taxes Act 1988 (see section 834(1) Taxes Act 1988) which limits the scope of both the foreign exchange and financial instruments legislation to companies within the charge to corporation tax (subject to special considerations as regards controlled foreign companies).

Q. Are decreases in value taken into account under section 155(4)?

6.20 Yes, negative values are to be taken into account under section 155(4). For example, the change in value from a negative value to a larger negative value will be a decrease in value, and a change from a larger negative value to a smaller one will be an increase in value.

Q. How are lump sum payments dealt with under section 155(4)?

6.21 Lump sum payments must be brought into the accounting period in which they become due for payment and this will be reflected in the value of the contract. For example, suppose a qualifying company holds a fixed/floating swap and receives a lump sum payment of £30m in return for a payment in the first year of £6m. The fair value of the obligation at the end of the accounting period is £23m. Amount A is £30m and amount B is £29m giving a net profit of £1m for the accounting period.

Q. How will section 156(3) be interpreted?

6.22 Companies may use different methods of arriving at a mark to market valuation and may incorporate adjustments for factors such as credit risk and liquidity. The Revenue will, as now, be happy to follow any reasonable method of valuation provided it is in accordance with generally accepted market and accounting practice and is followed consistently.

Q. On the basis that the Inland Revenue accept that a credit risk factor may be incorporated in a mark to market valuation, do they also accept that a claim under Section 163(1)(b) is not required to establish the credit risk element of that mark to market valuation?

6.23 Yes.

Q. How can lump sum payments be spread so as to satisfy the terms of section 156(4)?

6.24 These can be spread on any basis which has the effect of matching costs with benefits in any period. This will include spreading on a straight-line basis or an economic accruals basis which achieves this effect.

Q. Can non-trading losses on qualifying contracts be carried back to set against exchange gains of previous post-commencement periods?

6.25 Yes. Section 160(2) will work for each accounting period feeding into amount A in section 129 Finance Act 1993 any non-trading profit on a qualifying contract and into amount B any non-trading loss on a qualifying contract and therefore into the definition of exchange profits in section 131(10) Finance Act 1993. This is done for each successive accounting period so that if in any accounting period there is an overall loss, that loss can then be carried back against the exchange profits (defined as exchange gains less losses), and the non-trading profits less losses on qualifying contracts, of that period.

Q. What rights of appeal are there if the inspector is not satisfied under section 163(1)(b)?

6.26 There are the normal rights of appeal against a decision of an inspector on a claim.

Q. How does Section 165 apply to an option which is granted on arm's length terms but is not exercised because of adverse price movements during its term?

6.27 Section 165 will not apply on the grant of an option at arm's length because there is no transfer of value. Neither will it apply on the expiry of an option which is out of the money: there is no transfer of value as a result of the expiry of the option. Any overall transfer of value from the holder to the writer (resulting from the payment of the option premium) stems from price movements during the term of the option. Section 165(1)(b) is primarily designed to address the situation where an option which would normally be exercised, i.e. it is in the money and therefore valuable in the holder's hands, is not exercised and there is a transfer of value as a result of the decision not to exercise.

Q. How does section 165(3)(b) work in relation to a transfer of value through an associated third party?

6.28 Section 165(3) focuses on the transaction or the expiry of an option between the qualifying company and the associated third party. It asks the question: immediately after the transaction or expiry, is the value of the associated third party's net assets more than it would have been but for the transaction or expiry? 'The transaction' is that between the qualifying company and the third party. The fact that there is a second transfer of value from the associated third party to the associated company – section 165(8) – is not relevant to the answering of that question. It is the position immediately after the transaction or expiry which is relevant in determining whether there is a transfer of value.

Q. Is it clear that section 167(8)(a) eliminates any element of double counting between sections 165 and 167?

6.29 In the Revenue's view, yes. The clear intention of section 167(8)(a) is to eliminate any possibility of an adjustment under both section 167 and 165 and that is what the legislation achieves.

Q. How will agents acting for a principal be treated under section 168?

6.30 The Revenue's understanding is that generally where an agent is acting for a disclosed principal then it is the principal which will be entitled to rights and subject to duties under the contract. Therefore, it is the principal and not the agent which is party to the contract for the purposes of the new rules and section 168(3) and (4) focuses on the principal in these circumstances.

Q. Will the ecu be a currency for the purposes of this legislation?

6.31 Yes! This is achieved by section 177(5).

Q. Are payments under a swap within Section 123 Taxes Act 1988?

6.32 No! The Revenue do not consider that section 123 extends to the recurrent payments under a swap.

Q. In what circumstances will the regulatory power in section 177(6) be exercised?

6.33 The power is to authorise the making of an order to allow the legislative definition of the instruments covered to keep pace with commercial developments.

The Government have confirmed that this is not intended to be a means of surreptitiously extending the scope of the legislation and it is expected that any order made under this power would be preceded by appropriate consultation. The power is drafted to allow for suitable transitional arrangements to be made.

Q. How will the transitional rules under the financial instruments legislation apply to controlled foreign companies?

6.34 Where in the last accounting period before the Financial Instruments rules come into effect for a particular contract, a controlled foreign company was effectively within the UK tax net, because either:

- a direction under Section 747 Taxes Act 1988 had effect for that accounting period; or

- no direction was made under Section 747 because the acceptable distribution test was satisfied;

the company will be treated in the same way as a UK resident company within the charge to corporation tax. This means, for example, that section 158 Finance Act 1994 will apply to make any appropriate adjustment. This parallels the treatment under the Forex rules, outlined in paragraph 2.27 above.

Section 7: Currency contracts – foreign exchange and financial instruments legislation – some questions answered

Q. What are the definitions of 'currency contract' contained in sections 126 Finance Act 1993 and section 150 Finance Act 1994 intended to cover?

7.1 The definitions are intended to cover most common forms of currency contract involving the exchange of one currency for another. Thus they would include forward purchases and sales of currency (whether settled by delivery or cash difference), exchange traded futures, over the counter forward contracts or exchanges of principal under a currency swap. Further guidance on various terms used in the detailed definitions is contained in paragraph 6.12 of Section 6 (Financial Instruments).

Q. Will companies be able to follow for tax purposes the treatment of currency contracts which they adopt in their accounts?

7.2 In most cases, yes. The legislation will permit the following of accounts treatment in a number of circumstances all of which represent normal accountancy practice. In particular the following methods are catered for:

- marking to market

- use of forward exchange rates

- use of underlying spot rates (with the consequential recognition of a forward premium or discount)

- use of the exchange rate implied in a contract where:

  - that rate is used in valuing a related asset or liability which is a qualifying asset or liability (e.g. a trade debt or a bond issue see paragraphs 7.9 to 7.10 below) or
  - it is used in valuing a related asset or liability which is not a qualifying asset or liability and normal accounting practice is followed or
  - there is no related transaction but normal accountancy practice is followed (for example in relation to anticipated sales).

7.3 Accounts figures are unlikely to be followed where the transitional or anti-avoidance rules apply or where cash or realisation basis is adopted.

7.4 Annex I to this Section explains how the detail of the legislation works.

Q. How does the legislation deal with a currency contract terminated without delivery of the underlying currencies (for example by sale, payment of a cash difference or the entering into of a reciprocal contract)?

7.5 The rules operate to ensure that overall the commercial profit or loss is recognised. Any termination payment is relieved or assessed via section 153(1)(b) or (d) Finance Act 1994. Section 161 Finance Act 1994 and section 147 Finance Act 1993 operate to reverse out in the year of termination any amounts accrued (but not paid) and any unrealised exchange differences.

Q. Will periodic payments under a currency swap be regarded as payments of currency as described in section 146(1)(b) Finance Act 1993 and if so will section 146 and 147 Finance Act 1993 still operate as intended only on termination to ensure recognition of the economic profit?

7.6 Sections 146 and 147 will operate as intended when a contract is terminated without delivery of the underlying currency. Periodic payments under a currency swap do not affect the operation of these rules because they are not payments of currency relevant to the definition of a currency contract for the purposes of the foreign exchange legislation in section 126 Finance Act 1993.

Q. Where a currency contract is fully closed out by entering into a reciprocal contract as described in section 153(3) Finance Act 1993 is it clear that section 161 Finance Act 1994 operates to deal correctly with any accrued forward premium or discount?

7.7 Sections 146 and 147 Finance Act 1993 ensure that the closing out of a contract by entering into a reciprocal contract is a termination event and the Inland Revenue will regard such an event as within section 161(1)(a) or (c) Finance Act 1994 so that Section 161(2) of that Act will apply. This should ensure that the taxation treatment will follow commercial practice.

Q. Do the periodic payments under a currency swap represent debts requiring translation under section 126 Finance Act 1993?

7.8 Normally, no. Companies will not hold a qualifying asset or be subject to a qualifying liability (sections 153(1)(a) and 153(2)(a) Finance Act 1993) until the amounts become due and payable (sections 154(14) and 155(13) Finance Act 1993). Full relief and assessment of these payments will normally follow from the rules in Chapter II Finance Act 1994. Any possibility of double counting is precluded by section 173 Finance Act 1994.

Q. If a company makes a bond issue and the proceeds of that issue are swapped into another currency (using a currency swap) will the company be able to follow for tax purposes an accounting treatment which allows both transactions to be recorded at the exchange rate implied in the swap agreement?

7.9 Yes – provided that the bond represents a qualifying liability under section 153(2)(a), the swap agreement is a currency contract for the purposes of section 126 Finance Act 1993 and the exchange rate implied in the contract is an arm's length rate in accordance with the relevant provisions in section 150 Finance Act 1993. Thus a company borrows $150m and swaps into sterling receiving £100m. If, as a result, it is accepted for accounting purposes that the liability of $150m should be treated as a liability of £100m the value will be accepted as the local currency equivalent for both the liability and the currencies underlying the swap so that, in this example, no exchange differences would arise.

7.10 A bond which is not a qualifying asset under section 153(1)(a) (e.g. a convertible) may remain subject to tax on chargeable gains. The normal chargeable gains rules would apply here to such an asset and the use of the rate implied in the contract would be inappropriate. The acceptability of the use here by a qualifying company of the implied rate in valuing a related currency contract will depend on whether such treatment represents normal accounting practice – see paragraph 7.2 above.

Q. Will Section 153(4) and (5) Finance Act 1994 operate to compute a forward premium or discount where no such amount is shown in a company's accounts?

7.11 Generally, no. A company will recognise a forward premium or discount where it accounts for the currencies underlying a currency contract at the inception of the contract at spot rates. Section 153(4) and (5) operate to pick up the same figure. Where contracts are accounted for by marking to market, by using the rate implied in the contract or by the use of forward rates companies will not recognise a forward premium or discount and there will be no amount to be picked up under section 153(4) and (5) Finance Act 1994. Annex I explains in more detail how the provisions operate.

7.12 Section 153(4) and (5) may operate to produce a forward premium or discount on transition not recognised in a company's accounts as explained at paragraph 7.13 below and in more detail in Annex II.

Q. How do the transitional rules for currency contracts work?

7.13 The intention of the legislation is to ensure that over the life of a contract entered into before a company's commencement date the overall commercial profit or loss is recognised for tax purposes.

7.14 Section 165(3) Finance Act 1993 provides that a company is treated as becoming entitled to rights and subject to duties under a currency contract at the beginning of its commencement day using the valuations of the underlying currencies adopted by the company in preparing its accounts. It follows that for post-commencement gains and losses companies can normally expect to recognise for tax purposes the profits or losses shown in their accounts.

7.15 Where profits or losses on a currency contract would have been recognised in computing trading profits under existing legislation, companies can expect to continue to adopt accounts figures for tax purposes. Where under existing legislation pre-commencement profits or losses would not be recognised in computing trading profits (and any profit or loss would therefore be subject to tax on chargeable gains) there are separate rules to ensure that overall the whole commercial profit or loss is recognised. Annex II to this note explains in more detail how the provisions operate. See also paragraphs 7.16 and 7.17 below.

Q. If a company has entered into a currency contract before its commencement date and generally accepted accounting practice permits the use of the exchange rate implied in the contract (so that no exchange differences arise after commencement) will any deemed forward premium or discount arise because of the operation of the transitional rules?

7.16 No. In these circumstances there will be no difference computed in accordance with sections 153(4) and (5) to be taken into account.

Q. A deemed forward premium or discount may arise at commencement because of the operation of the transitional rules and section 153(4) and (5) Finance Act 1994. How will such a deemed amount be treated given that it does not appear in a company's accounts?

7.17 Any deemed forward premium or discount should be subject to the same acceptable accruals test provided in section 156 Finance Act 1994 as would have applied to any forward premium or discount actually recognised in a company's accounts. The Inland Revenue would expect such a premium to be spread (probably on a straight line basis) over the life of the contract in accordance with section 156(4) and (5) Finance Act 1994. Any deemed forward premium or discount should normally therefore be spread over the period from commencement (the date on which the company is treated as becoming entitled to rights and subject to duties under the contract following section 165(3) Finance Act 1993) to the date to which the contract matures.

Annex 1

Interaction of foreign exchange and financial instruments legislation with normal accounting practice

Examples

This Annex describes a number of accounting practices and how the legislation operates to enable these treatments to be followed for tax purposes. The examples are based on the following contract terms.

1st January year 1 (after commencement of new legislation) company agrees to acquire $100 for £55 in 2 years time.

Spot values of $100 are

– 1st January Year 1	£52
– 31st December Year 1	£60
– 31st December Year 2	£75

Forward values of $100 are

– 2 years from 1st January year 1 (as contract terms)	£55
– 1 year from 31st December year 1	£65

Mark to market valuations of contract are

– 31st December Year 1	£14
– 31st December Year 2	£20

1. Accounting using forward rates

Accounts figures

In the company's accounts the following exchange gains will be recognised.

Year 1	£65 − £55 =	£10
Year 2	£75 − £65 =	£10
Total Profit		£20

No forward premium would be recognised at inception because, being valued at forward rates, the amount payable and the forward rate value are the same.

Figures for tax purposes

Provided that the forward rates were arm's length rates the exchange gains appearing in the company's accounts would be followed. No

430

forward premium would arise at inception of the contract because there would be no difference between the two amounts described in Section 153(4) and (5) Finance Act 1994 – both of them would be £55.

2. Use of rate implied in the contract

Accounts entries

SSAP 20 allows the use of the rate implied in a contract to value a trading transaction related to that forward contract. Suppose in the above example that in addition the company owed $100 which it repaid on maturity of a contract on 1st January Year 3. Following SSAP 20 the company could book the borrowing at the contract rate of £55 throughout. The currency contract would not be specifically recognised in the accounts. When the debt is repaid the dollars necessary to make the repayment will only cost the company £55 and no profit or loss need therefore be recognised on either the currency contract or the related borrowing.

Figures for tax purposes

Under the foreign exchange legislation the Inland Revenue take the view that the use of the contract rate (assuming that it is an arm's length rate) in valuing the related borrowing represents the use of that exchange rate in the company's accounts. Both for the borrowing and for the dollars to be delivered under the contract the legislation will permit the adoption of the contract rate throughout so that no profit or loss need be recognised under the contract.

3. Contract accounted for using spot rates

Accounts figures

Exchange gains Year 1	£60 − £52 =	£8
Exchange gains Year 2	£75 − £60 =	£15
Forward premium		
Spot value at commencement	£52	
Contract rate	£55	
Forward premium	£ 3	
Allocation:		
Year 1		(£1.50)
Year 2		(£1.50)
Overall profit		£20

Where spot rates are adopted a forward premium or discount must be recognised in a company's accounts if the correct overall profit (£75 − £55 = £20) is to be recognised.

Figures for tax purposes

Provided the exchange rates adopted in the accounts are arm's length rates the exchange gains recognised under the Forex legislation will be the same as those recognised in the company's accounts. The forward premium recognised in the accounts is also recognised under the financial instruments legislation via sections 153(4) and (5) Finance Act 1994. In this example the local currency equivalent of the dollars to be delivered ($100) at the inception of the contract (the amount to be found under section 153(4)(a)) is £52 and the local currency equivalent of the currency to be paid in exchange (sterling) is £55 (the amount to be found under section 153(4)(b)). The difference of £3 is the amount to be treated as a qualifying payment made by the company under section 153(5)(b). The accounts treatment – spreading this premium over the life of the contract – would be an acceptable accruals basis of accounting for the purposes of section 156 Finance Act 1994.

4. Accounting on a mark to market basis

Accounts and tax figures

Provided that a company is marking to market on a basis which satisfies the conditions in Section 156 Finance Act 1994 the following accounting profits will be recognised under the financial instruments rules

Year 1	£14 − £0	=	£14
Year 2	£20 − £14	=	£6
Overall profit			£20

Section 162 Finance Act 1994 ensures that any underlying exchange differences are not counted twice (under both the foreign exchange and financial instruments legislation). Although section 162 is drafted in terms of deducting exchange gains and adding exchange losses to amounts to be taken into account under the financial instruments legislation in practice the Inland Revenue expects to accept computations based on acceptable mark to market valuations without the need separately to identify the exchange differences.

No forward premium or discount of course arises in a company's accounts where it is marking to market and similarly there is no additional amount to be taken into account under section 153(4) and (5) Finance Act 1994 because at the inception of the contract any valuations of currencies underlying the contract for the purposes of marking to market will have regard to forward rather than spot rates. As explained in the preceding examples no forward premium or discount arises where forward rates are employed.

5. Termination of contracts without delivery

The contract in the example described above might be closed out or otherwise terminated at say 31st December year 2 without delivery of the underlying currencies but instead a receipt of £20. The company would expect to recognise the overall profit on the contract of £20 in its accounts and the foreign exchange and financial instruments rules will achieve the same result. The payment of £20 would be a qualifying payment received either under section 150(9) or section 151(2)(c) Finance Act 1994. The legislation then reverses out in the period of termination the exchange differences previously assessed or relieved (following section 146 Finance Act 1993) and any forward premium (following section 161 Finance Act 1994). This leaves just the overall profit of £20 assessable over the 2 year period.

If the contract had been marked to market, section 155(4) and (7) Finance Act 1994 would produce a loss on the contract of £14 by treating the value of the contract immediately before termination as nil. The payment of £20 would be a qualifying receipt, giving net income in year 2 of £6 and again an overall assessable profit of £20.

Annex 2

Currency contracts – Transitional arrangements

The explanations provided in this Annex are based on the specimen contract described in Annex I but on the basis that the company's commencement date (from which the new legislation applies) is 1 January in year 2.

Contract previously dealt with in computing trading profits

1. If any profit or loss on the contract had been dealt with in computing trading profits for year 1 under existing legislation then the Revenue would expect to recognise exactly the same profits as those shown in the accounts both for year 1 and year 2. The new legislation does not affect year 1 and the company would expect the profits shown by its accounts to be adopted for tax purposes. In year 2 the company is treated as becoming entitled to rights and subject to dues under the currency contract at its commencement date following section 165(3) Finance Act 1993 and section 147(2)(b) Finance Act 1994. Regulation 5 of The Exchange Gains and Losses (Transitional Provisions) Regulations 1994 provides that the values adopted by the company for the currencies underlying the contract are the values to be taken into account at commencement date. So, from commencement the exchange differences shown in a company's accounts will normally be those taken into account under the foreign exchange legislation. It follows that whether a company accounts using spot rates, forward rates or the rate implied in a contract exactly the same exchange differences will be recognised post-commencement as shown in the examples in Annex I.

2. Where a company accounts using spot rates, the company will receive relief for the part of the forward premium allocated to year 1 under existing legislation (here £1.50). The balance of the premium will be recognised in year 2 under the new legislation. Section 175(1)(b) Finance Act 1994 ensures that the forward premium continues to be calculated for the purposes of the legislation by reference to currency values at inception of the contact (ie following accounts values). Only the portion appropriate to the post commencement period (£1.50) is allocated to that period in accordance with section 156 Finance Act 1994 so that accounts figures will be followed for tax.

Contracts not taken into account in computing trading profits

3. Where profits or losses in the example in Annex I would not be taken into account in computing trading profits in period 1 under existing legislation, the currency acquired or sold under the contract would be dealt with under the Capital Gains code or Section 143 TCGA would

apply to the contract itself. The new legislation is intended to ensure that the commercial profit is brought to account and that there is no double counting.

4. In the example, exchange differences are computed for period 2 in exactly the same way as in the example in Annex I whichever method of accounting is adopted. But no exchange differences or (where spot values are adopted) any part of the forward premium is recognised for tax purposes in period 1. Section 153(4) and (5) Finance Act 1994 are applied as if the contract had been entered into on the company's commencement day (in contrast to the position with contracts dealt with in computing trading profits where any forward premium recognised in the accounts is also recognised under the legislation). This means that a deemed forward premium or discount is calculated at a company's commencement date and that any forward premium or discount actually shown in the company's accounts is ignored.

The following paragraphs look at the examples in Annex I.

(i) Contract accounted for using spot rates

Exchange Gain period 2 £75 − £60 =		£15
Deemed forward discount at commencement		
Local currency value of $100 in company's accounts at commencement:	£60	
Local currency value of £55 in company's accounts at commencement:	£55	
Deemed forward discount		£5
Total profit to be recognised		£20

In this case the whole of the deemed forward discount will be recognised in period 2 and the actual premium recognised in the company's accounts for the year to 31 December Year 1 of £1.50 would be ignored. Had the contract run for a further year then the deemed forward discount should be spread over the two years from commencement in the same way that the company would spread a premium or discount which it did recognise in its accounts. This spreading will be an acceptable accruals basis for the purposes of Section 156(4) Finance Act 1994.

(ii) Accounting using forward rates

Exchange Gain year 2 £75 − £65 =		£10
Local currency equivalent of $100 at commencement in company's accounts	£65	
Local currency equivalent of £55 at commencement in company's accounts	£55	
Forward discount to be assessed		£10
Total profit		£20

435

Again the correct overall profit is recognised and the deemed forward discount would be allocated to year 2.

(iii) Accounting using rate implied in the contract

No exchange gains would be recognised in year 2 because $100 would be valued at £55 throughout.

Also no deemed forward premium would arise because the local currency equivalent of the $100 recognised in the company's accounts at commencement would be £55 equalling the value of the sterling to be paid of £55.

Where therefore the rate implied in the contract is used by the company to account for a contract entered into before commencement, no deemed forward premium arises (see paragraph 7.16 above).

Interaction with capital gains rules

5. The new legislation will tax all gains and losses on a contract entered into before a company's commencement date but running on afterwards. In most circumstances a combination of paragraph 2 of schedule 17 Finance Act 1993 and section 173 Finance Act 1994 ensures that no chargeable gain arises and therefore that there is no double counting.

Where an unconditional contract to *dispose* of foreign currency is entered into before commencement but the currency is delivered after commencement there is a disposal for the purposes of computing tax on chargeable gains at the date of the contract. The following paragraphs explain how double counting is avoided here.

Example

Suppose a company agrees one year prior to commencement to sell at arm's length $1,000 in two years time for £600. The contract is one to which capital gains rules would have applied. Spot values of $1,000 as follows are used in the company's accounts:

at inception of contract	£400
at commencement	£550
at maturity	£450

The company will make a profit of £150 when it sells for £600 dollars worth £450.

Figures for tax purposes

Exchange Gain to be recognised in period 2 £550 − £450 =   £100
Deemed forward discount calculated under Section 153(4)
Finance Act 1994.
    Value of $1,000 at commencement   £550
    Value of £600 at commencement   £600
    Deemed forward discount   50
        Total profit assessable   £150

Because the currency contract is unconditional there is a disposal for the purposes of computing chargeable gains of $1,000 at the inception of the contract with disposal proceeds £600. Assuming that there are no other currency transactions and that the currency necessary to meet this contract is only acquired at maturity the acquisition cost of $1,000 will be £450 and there would be a chargeable gain of £150. But all the commercial profit on the contract has been recognised in computing profits for corporation tax under the new legislation. Here, the Inland Revenue will accept that the whole of the consideration and any acquisition cost which would have been taken into account in computing a chargeable gain have in fact been taken into account in computing either exchange differences or the deemed forward discount in circumstances such that section 37(1) and section 39(1) TCGA 1992 prevent those amounts being taken into account again in computing chargeable gains.

A capital gain may still, however, arise. For example, where the rate implied in a contract is an appropriate exchange rate under the foreign exchange rules, different valuations are likely to be needed for capital gains purposes. If, as a result, a chargeable gain does arise in a period prior to a company's commencement date, section 158(3) Finance Act 1994 will operate to compute an equivalent income loss at commencement. Similarly, if a pre-commencement capital loss arises, section 158(5) will produce an equivalent income gain.

Section 8: Statement of Practice – Application of foreign exchange and financial instruments legislation to partnerships which include companies

[Reproduces text of Inland Revenue Statement of Practice SP9/94. See Appendix 2 above.]

Appendix 4

Statutory Instruments

Contents

The Exchange Gains and Losses (Transitional Provisions) Regulations 1994 (SI 1994 No 3226)

Made: 15th December 1994
Laid before the House of Commons: 16th December 1994
Coming into force: 23rd March 1995

ARRANGEMENT OF REGULATIONS

The Treasury, in exercise of the powers conferred on them by sections 164(14), 165(4) and (5) and 167(1) and (4) to (6) of, and Schedule 16 to, the Finance Act 1993, hereby make the following Regulations:

PART I   INTRODUCTORY PROVISIONS

1   Citation, commencement and interpretation

(1) These Regulations may be cited as the Exchange Gains and Losses (Transitional Provisions) Regulations 1994.

(2) These Regulations shall come into force on 23rd March 1995.

(3) In these Regulations, subject to any contrary intention –

(a) 'the 1992 Act' means the Taxation of Chargeable Gains Act 1992;

(b) 'the 1993 Act' means the Finance Act 1993;

[(ba) 'discounted debt' has the same meaning as 'relevant discounted security' as that term is defined for the purposes of Schedule 13 to the Finance Act 1996 by paragraphs 3 and 14(1) of that Schedule;]¹

(c) any reference to Chapter II is a reference to Chapter II of Part II of the 1993 Act;

(d) any reference to a particular section is a reference to that section of that Act;

(e) any reference to an exchange gain or loss is a reference to an exchange gain or loss of a trade or part of a trade or a non-trading exchange gain or loss;

(f) any reference to an exchange difference is a reference to any gain or loss which is attributable to fluctuations in currency exchange rates;

(g) 'a regulation 6(3) asset' means an existing asset the basic valuation of which is determined in accordance with regulation 6(3); and

(h) 'the regulation 2(2) provisions' means the provisions specified in regulation 2(2).

(4) In determining for the purposes of these Regulations whether any gain or loss or other amount has or has not been taken into account for the purposes of corporation tax in computing a company's profits and gains (or the profits and gains of a trade) for an accounting period, or would have been or would not have been so taken into account if the company had been within the charge to corporation tax at the time the gain or loss accrued, there shall be disregarded, subject to any contrary intention, any insufficiency of profits or gains for that period.

(5) In computing the chargeable profits for an accounting period of a controlled foreign company as respects which –

(a) a direction under section 747 of the Income and Corporation Taxes Act 1988 has been given for the company's accounting period which includes the day preceding the day on which these Regulations come into force, or

(b) it can reasonably be assumed that such a direction would have been given for that accounting period but for the fact that the company pursues, within the meaning of Part I of Schedule 25 to that Act, an acceptable distribution policy, it shall be assumed for the purposes of these Regulations (if it would not otherwise be so assumed) that the company is resident in the United Kingdom for the period as respects which the computation is being made for any other period (whether earlier or later than the period referred to in paragraph (a) or (b) above), and any gain or loss or other amount which is, or has been, taken into account in computing the company's chargeable profits for any period (or which would have been so taken into account if such a computation had been made) shall be treated for those purposes as being, or having been, taken into account for the purposes of corporation tax in computing the company's profits and gains for that period.

---

[1]   Inserted by SI 1996 No. 1349 (The Exchange Gains and Losses (Transitional Provisions) (Amendment) Regulations 1996), Reg 3 with effect from 30 June 1996.

---

2   Interaction with other Exchange Gains and Losses provisions

(1)   Subject to any provision to the contrary, in any case where a calculation falls to be made in relation to an existing asset, liability or contract in accordance with any of these Regulations and at the same time or in relation to the same event a calculation also falls to be made in relation to that asset, liability or contract in accordance with any of the provisions specified in paragraph (2) below, then the calculation to be made in accordance with these Regulations shall be made first and shall have effect for the purposes of the calculation falling to be made in accordance with any of those provisions.

(2)   The provisions referred to above are the following –
Sections 136, 137 and 139 to 141 of the 1993 Act;

The Exchange Gains and Losses (Alternative Method of Calculation of Gain or Loss) Regulations 1994;

The Exchange Gains and Losses (Deferral of Gains and Losses) Regulations 1994.

PART II   MISCELLANEOUS TRANSITIONAL PROVISIONS

3   Delayed application of Chapter II in relation to certain fluctuating debts

(1)   Subject to paragraph (5) below, paragraph (2) below applies in relation to an asset or liability which is held or owed by a company and falls within section 165(4)(a) where–

(a)   any exchange difference accruing to the company on a disposal or settlement by the company of the asset or liability immediately before the company's commencement day would not have been taken into account for the purposes of corporation tax in computing the company's profits and gains of that accounting period or would not be so taken into account if the company had been within the charge to corporation tax at the time the gain or loss accrued,

(b)   the company was within the charge to corporation tax immediately before the company's commencement day,

(c) the asset or liability is the right to settlement of a debt or the duty to settle a debt, and

(d) the amount of the debt or the term of the debt (or both) are not fixed.

(2) In any case where this paragraph applies, the company shall be treated for the purposes of Chapter II –

(a) if before the sixth anniversary of the company's commencement day the amount of the debt is increased (whether or not it has previously been reduced or after the increase is lower than its original amount), as becoming entitled to the asset or subject to the liability in question, at the beginning of the day on which the amount of the debt is increased;

(b) if paragraph (a) does not apply and the company is entitled to the asset or subject to the liability in question at the beginning of the day which is the sixth anniversary of the company's commencement day, as becoming entitled to the asset or subject to the liability at the beginning of that day;

(c) if neither paragraph (a) nor paragraph (b) apply, as never having been entitled to the asset or subject to the liability in question;

and accordingly section 165(2) shall not apply in relation to that asset or liability.

(3) In relation to an asset or liability falling within paragraph (2)(a) above, the amount of any initial exchange gain or loss which accrues to the company for any accrual period which ends before the sixth anniversary of the company's commencement day shall be reduced by an amount equal to the amount found in accordance with paragraph (4) below.

(4) There shall be calculated the amount of any exchange gain or loss which would have accrued as respects the asset or liability for the accrual period in question if the amount of the debt outstanding at any time in that period had been equal to the lowest amount at which the debt had stood at any time on or after the company's commencement day and before the end of that period.

(5) Paragraph (2) above shall not apply in relation to any company which elects that section 165(2) should apply in relation to all the assets or liabilities held or owed by the company and which apart from the election would fall within that paragraph, and an election under this paragraph –

(a) shall be made by notice to the inspector before the expiry of the period of 92 days beginning with the company's commencement day or, if later, the expiry of the period of 183 days beginning with 23rd March 1995, and

(b) shall have effect as from the beginning of the company's commencement day and shall be irrevocable.

(6) For the purposes of this regulation the term of a debt is fixed if (and only if) –

(a) it falls within paragraph (9) below, or

(b) it is provided that –

(i) the principal is to be repayable in total on one specified date or in specified amounts or proportions on specified dates; and

(ii) any part of the principal once repaid cannot be redrawn; and

(iii) any interest which, if not paid when due, is to be capitalised or rolled-up, is to be added to the principal on the due date and repayable on the same terms as the principal.

(7) For the purposes of paragraph (6)(b) above there shall be disregarded any provision –

(a) for the repayment of the debt on the occurrence of an event which at the beginning of the term is neither certain nor likely to occur, or

(b) for the early repayment of the debt at the option of the borrower.

(8) For the purposes of this regulation the amount of a debt is fixed (and only if) –

(a) it falls within paragraph (9) below, or

(b) the maximum amount of the principal is specified at the commencement of the term of the debt and the principal cannot be increased beyond that maximum amount (except as mentioned in paragraph (6)(b)(iii) above).

In determining whether a debt falls within this paragraph there shall be disregarded any term in so far as it provides for the principal or any interest to be calculated by reference to any withholding or other tax (including foreign tax).

(9) A debt falls within this paragraph if –

(a) it is a debt on a deep gain security for the purposes of paragraph 1 of Schedule 11 to the Finance Act 1989 and the amount payable on redemption is payable on one specified date, or

(b) it is a debt on a qualifying indexed security for the purposes of that paragraph, or

(c) it is a debt on a deep discount security for the purposes of paragraph 1 of Schedule 4 to the Income and Corporation Taxes Act 1988.

(10) In relation to any asset or liability to which paragraph (2) above applies, any reference in Chapter II or in any Regulations made under that Chapter (including the following provisions of these Regulations) –

(a) to an existing asset or liability shall include a reference to that asset or liability as from the day on which the company is treated as becoming entitled to the asset or subject to the liability;

(b) to the company's commencement day shall be construed as a reference to that day.

4 Bad debts

(1) Section 144(1) shall have effect in any case where –

(a) the asset or liability referred to in subsection (1)(a) is an existing asset or liability held or owed by a qualifying company, and

(b) the accounting period referred to in subsection (1)(b) is the company's accounting period ending immediately before the company's commencement day,

subject to paragraph (2) below.

(2) Subsection (1) shall have effect as if for the words following paragraph (b) there shall be substituted –

'the company shall be treated for the purposes of this Chapter as if it ceased to be entitled or subject to the asset or liability immediately before the end of the company's commencement day, and any exchange gain or loss accruing to the company on that day shall be deemed not to accrue.'

5 Exchange rate at translation times

Section 150 shall apply in relation to a translation time which is the first translation time as respects an existing asset, liability or contract held or owed by a company –

(a) with the omission in subsection (1) of 'at a translation time';

(b) with the omission of subsections (4) and (8) to (14) and, in the case of a regulation 6(3) asset, of subsection (5);

(c) with the substitution in subsections (5) and (6)(b) for 'the last day of the accounting period' of 'the day immediately preceding the company's commencement day or, if that day is not the last day of an accounting period of the company, in the company's accounting records for that day'; and

(d) with the substitution in subsection (7) for the 'last day of the accounting period' of 'the day immediately preceding the company's commencement day'.

6 Basic valuation

(1) Subject to paragraph (2) below, for the purposes of determining the basic valuation of an existing asset or liability held or owed by a company, other than an asset to which paragraph (3) below applies or a debt to which paragraph (6) below applies. Section 159 shall have effect –

(a) with the substitution in subsection (1)(a) for 'after the company becomes entitled or subject to it' of 'before the company's commencement day'; and

(b) with the omission of subsections (3) to (12).

(2) Paragraph (1) above shall not apply in relation to any company which elects that section 159 should apply in relation to all qualifying assets which are either debts on a security or shares held by the company and which apart from the election would fall within that paragraph, and an election under this paragraph –

(a) shall be made by notice to the inspector before [30th September 1996][1], and

(b) shall have effect as from the beginning of the company's commencement day and [, subject to Paragraph (2A) below][2] shall be irrevocable,

445

but in the application of section 159 in relation to any asset by virtue of an election under this paragraph, section 165(2) shall be disregarded.

[(2A) An election under paragraph (2) above may be withdrawn, with effect from the beginning of the company's commencement day, by notice by the company to the inspector before 30th September 1996.][2]

(3) In the case of any existing asset held by a qualifying company a disposal of which in the open market by that company immediately before its commencement day at the asset's market value at that time would have given rise to a chargeable gain or allowable loss –

(a) section 159 shall not apply, but

(b) the basic valuation of the asset shall be taken to be equal to its market value immediately before the company's commencement day,

and for the purposes of this paragraph the market value shall be computed in accordance with the provisions of the 1992 Act but in the nominal currency of the asset.

(4) For the purposes of determining under paragraph (3) above whether a gain or a loss would have accrued on any disposal (but not for the purposes of computing the basic valuation or for any other purpose) –

(a) it shall be assumed that the disposal was not in such circumstances that by virtue of any provision of the 1992 Act neither a gain nor a loss would accrue on the disposal, and

(b) if the market value is such that neither a gain nor a loss would accrue on the disposal, the market value shall be increased by £100.

(5) Any expression used in paragraph (3) or (4) which is not defined in Chapter II shall have the same meaning as in the 1992 Act.

(6) Paragraph (1) above does not apply in relation to –

(a) a debt on a deep gain security for the purposes of paragraph 1 of Schedule 11 to the Finance Act 1989, or

(b) a debt on a qualifying indexed security for the purposes of that paragraph, or

(c) a debt on a deep discount security for the purposes of paragraph 1 of Schedule 4 to the Income and Corporation Taxes Act 1988;

but in the application of section 159 in relation to any such debt, section 165(2) shall be disregarded.

---

[1]   Substituted by SI 1996 No 1349 (The Exchange Gains and Losses (Transitional Provisions) (Amendment) Regulations 1996), Reg 4 with effect from 30 June 1996.
Previously 'the expiry of the period of 92 days beginning with the company's commencement day or, if later, the expiry of the period of 183 days beginning with 23 March 1995'.

[2]   Inserted by SI 1996 No 1349 as in [1] above.

PART III PRE-COMMENCEMENT GAINS AND LOSSES: CASE I ASSETS AND LIABILITIES AND CAPITAL ASSETS

7 Interpretation

(1) For the purposes of any computation required to be made for the purposes of regulation 10 or 11 below, an amount which is a gain shall be taken to be a positive figure and an amount which is a loss shall be taken to be a negative figure, but for the purposes of regulations 12 and 13 all amounts shall be taken to be positive.

(2) In this Part –

'attributed gain', in relation to any asset or liability, means a gain which is attributed to the asset or liability under regulation 8(3) or 9(2) below;

'attributed loss', in relation to any asset or liability, means a loss which is attributed to the asset or liability under regulation 8(3) or 9(2) below;

'current period' has the meaning given by regulation 10 below;

'the cumulative gain' has the meaning given by regulation 10 below;

'the cumulative loss' has the meaning given by regulation 10 below;

'the cumulative taxed gain' has the meaning given by regulation 11 below;

'the cumulative taxed loss' has the meaning given by regulation 11 below;

and any reference to exempt circumstances shall be construed as if it were contained in paragraph 2 of Schedule 15 to the 1993 Act.

8 Attributed gains and losses: trade assets and liabilities

(1) Paragraph (3) below applies in relation to an existing asset held by a qualifying company –

(a) if a profit or loss would have accrued to the company if it had disposed of the asset immediately before the company's commencement day for a consideration equal to the asset's basic valuation; and

(b) that profit or loss would have been taken into account in computing for the purposes of corporation tax the profits and gains of a trade carried on by the company for the accounting period which includes the day immediately before the company's commencement day.

(2) Paragraph (3) below applies in relation to an existing liability owed by a qualifying company –

(a) if a profit or loss would have accrued to the company –

(i) in a case falling within section 153(2)(a), if the liability had been satisfied in full by the company immediately before the company's commencement day, or

(ii) in a case falling within section 153(2)(c) or (d), if the right to settlement or the share or shares in question (as the case may be) had been acquired by the company immediately before the company's commencement day for a consideration equal to the consideration for the company becoming subject to the liability, and

  (b) that profit or loss (if it had accrued) would have been taken into account in computing for the purposes of corporation tax the profits and gains of a trade carried on by the company for the accounting period ending immediately before the company's commencement day.

(3) The amount of any such profit or loss as is mentioned in paragraph (1) or (2) above reduced in accordance with paragraph (4) below if applicable, shall be attributed to the asset or liability (as the case may be) and –

  (a) in the case of a profit shall be attributed as a gain, and

  (b) in the case of a loss shall be attributed as a loss.

(4) In any case where unrealised exchange differences which have accrued in respect of the asset or liability are taken into account for the purposes of corporation tax for the accounting period ending immediately before the company's commencement day or any earlier accounting period, the amount of the profit or loss referred to in paragraph (3) above shall be reduced by an amount equal to the amount of those differences.

(5) Section 159 applies for the purposes of this regulation as modified by regulation 6 above.

9 Attributed gains and losses: regulation 6(3) assets

(1) This regulation applies in relation to any regulation 6(3) asset held by a qualifying company a disposal of which by that company immediately before its commencement day at the asset's market value at that time would have given rise to a chargeable gain or allowable loss, but does not apply in any case where any such disposal of the asset by the company would fall within section 116(10)(b) of the 1992 Act.

(2) Subject to paragraph (3) below, an amount equal to any chargeable gain or allowable loss (as the case may be) which would have accrued to the company had it disposed of the asset as mentioned in paragraph (1) above shall be attributed to the asset and –

  (a) if a chargeable gain would have accrued, it shall be attributed as a gain, and

  (b) if an allowable loss would have accrued, it shall be attributed as a loss.

(3) In any case where –

  (a) the asset was held by a company which at any time before its commencement day was not resident in the United Kingdom, and

  (b) if the asset had been disposed of at that time and a gain had accrued to the company on that disposal, it would not have been included in the company's chargeable profits by virtue of section 10(3) of the 1992 Act, then for the purposes of paragraph (1) above the company shall be deemed to have acquired the asset, at market value, on the first day on which any gain which would have accrued to the company if the asset had been disposed of on that day (assuming that the disposal gave rise to a gain and disregarding any allowable losses which might be available for deduction under section 8(1) of, or Schedule 7A to, the 1992 Act would have been included in the company's chargeable profits for the purposes of corporation tax (whether because the company became resident or the asset became situated in the United Kingdom on that day or for any other reason).

(4) In any case where the company referred to in paragraph (1) above acquired the asset on a no gain/no loss disposal, then the reference in paragraph (3) above to a company includes the company from which it acquired the asset, and if that company also acquired the asset on such a disposal to the company from which it acquired the asset, and so on for a series of such disposals.

(5) The disposal referred to in paragraph (1) above shall be taken not to be a no gain/no loss disposal, and for the purposes of this regulation a disposal is a no gain/no loss disposal if, by virtue of any enactment specified in section 35(3)(d) of the 1992 Act, neither a gain nor a loss accrues to the person making the disposal.

(6) In any case where section 176 of the 1992 Act would have applied in relation to the disposal referred to in paragraph (1) above if that disposal had actually taken place, that section shall apply for the calculation of any allowable loss for the purposes of that paragraph.

(7) Any expression used in this regulation which is not defined in Chapter II shall have the same meaning as in the 1992 Act.

10   The cumulative gain and the cumulative loss

(1) Subject to regulation 15, in the case of any existing asset or liability held or owed by a company as respects which an initial exchange gain or loss accrues to the company for an accrual period ('the current period'), there shall be calculated the aggregate amount of initial exchange gains and losses which have accrued as respects the asset or liability in question for all earlier accrual periods and for the current period, and that aggregate amount –

 (a) if positive, shall be the cumulative gain for that asset or liability for the current period, and

 (b) if negative, shall be the cumulative loss for that asset or liability for the current period,

but in cases where that aggregate amount is zero there shall be either a cumulative gain or a cumulative loss equal to zero for the period, according to whether there was a cumulative gain or a cumulative loss of any amount (including zero) for the accrual period immediately preceding the current period.

(2) For the purposes of paragraph (1) above, the amount of any initial exchange gain or loss shall be determined disregarding the following provisions of this Part and the regulation 2(2) provisions.

[(3) Where–

449

    (a) the asset held or the liability owed by the company consists of a discounted debt, and

    (b) the company did not cease on 31st March 1996 to be entitled to the asset or (as the case may be) subject to the liability, it shall be regarded, for the purposes of paragraph (1) above and section 158 (translation times and accrual periods), as ceasing on that date to be so entitled or subject, and references in this regulation and in regulations 11 and 12 to accrual periods (including references to an accrual period as the current period) shall, as respects that asset or liability, be construed accordingly.][1]

---

[1]   Inserted by SI 1996 No 1349 (The Exchange Gains and Losses (Transitional Provisions) (Amendment) Regulations 1996), Reg 5 with effect from 30 June 1996.

---

11   The cumulative taxed gain and the cumulative taxed loss

(1)   In the case of any asset or liability to which regulation 10 applies, there shall be calculated the aggregate amount of the initial exchange gains and losses which have accrued to the company as respects the asset or liability for accrual periods earlier than the current period, and –

    (a) if that aggregate amount is positive it shall be the cumulative taxed gain for that asset or liability for the current period,

    (b) if it is negative it shall be the cumulative taxed loss for that asset or liability for the current period, and

    (c) if that aggregate amount is zero or, by virtue of regulation 12, there is no aggregate amount, there shall be taken to be a cumulative taxed loss equal to zero for the period.

(2)   For the purposes of paragraph (1) above –

    (a) the question whether any initial exchange gain or loss has accrued for any period other than the current period shall be determined in accordance with this Part but as if the regulation 2(2) provisions had never come into force; and

    (b) there shall be disregarded any gain or loss which accrued for an accrual period other than the current period unless –

        (i) it has been taken into account in computing the profits or gains of the company holding or owning the asset or liability for the purposes of corporation tax for accounting periods ending before the beginning of the current period, or

        (ii) it would have been so taken into account if the regulation 2(2) provisions had never come into force; or

        (iii) it is equal to zero.

12   Assets and liabilities as respects which there is an attributed gain or loss

(1)   Subject to regulation 15, in relation to an asset or liability held or owed by a company as respects which –

    (a) there is an attributed gain, E, or an attributed loss, F, and

(b) an initial exchange gain or loss ('the actual gain or loss') accrues to the company for the current period.

Table A or Table B below (as appropriate) shall apply and in any case falling within the first column of that Table, the actual gain or loss shall be deemed not to accrue but, subject to any conditions specified in the second column, the gain or loss specified in relation thereto in the third column shall be deemed to accrue and shall be an initial exchange gain or loss (as the case may be) accruing in the place of the actual gain or loss.

(2) For the purposes of paragraph (1)(b) above, the question whether any initial exchange gain or loss has accrued shall be determined disregarding this Part and the regulation 2(2) provisions.

Table A
If there is an attributed gain E

Case for the current period	Condition	Deemed gain or loss
1 Cumulative loss B and no cumulative taxed gain or loss	B is greater than E	Loss equal to $B - E$
2 Cumulative loss B and a cumulative taxed loss C	i) B is not greater than E and C is greater than zero	i) Gain equal to C
	ii) B is greater than E and C is less than $(B - E)$	ii) Loss equal to $(B - E) - C$
	iii) B is greater than E and C is greater than $(B - E)$	iii) Gain equal to $C - (B - E)$
3 Cumulative loss B and a cumulative taxed gain D	i) B is greater than E	i) Loss equal to $(B - E) + D$
	ii) B is not greater than E	ii) Loss equal to D
4 Cumulative gain A and a cumulative taxed gain D	i) A is greater than D	i) Gain equal to $A - D$
	ii) D is greater than A	ii) Loss equal to $D - A$
5 Cumulative gain A and a cumulative taxed loss C		Gain equal to $C + A$

Table B
If there is an attributed loss F

Case for the current period	Condition	Deemed gain or loss
1 Cumulative gain A and no cumulative taxed gain or loss	A is greater than F	Gain equal to A − F
2 Cumulative gain A and a cumulative taxed gain D	i) A is not greater than F	i) Loss equal to D
	ii) A is greater than F and D is less than (A − F)	ii) Gain equal to (A − F) − D
	iii) A is greater than F and D is greater than (A − F)	iii) Loss equal to D − (A − F)
3 Cumulative gain A and a cumulative taxed loss C	i) A is greater than F	i) Gain equal to (A − F) + C
	ii) A is not greater than F and C is greater than zero	ii) Gain equal to C
4 Cumulative loss B and a cumulative taxed loss C	i) B is greater than C	i) Loss equal to B − C
	ii) C is greater than B	ii) Gain equal to C − B
5 Cumulative loss B and a cumulative taxed gain D		Loss equal to B + D

13   Gains and losses on disposal of assets and liabilities

(1)   Subject to regulations 14(1) and 15(1), paragraph (2) or (3) below applies where –

   (a)   an accrual period ends as respects an existing asset or liability held or owed by a company which is the last accrual period as respects that asset or liability, and

   (b)   there is as respects the asset or liability an attributed gain or loss.

(2)   If there is an attributed gain, E, as respects the asset or liability, then –

   (a)   if there is a cumulative gain, A, as respects the asset or liability for the last period, an amount equal to E shall be deemed to be a relevant gain, accruing to the company as respects that asset or liability immediately before the end of the last accrual period;

   (b)   if there is a cumulative loss, B, as respects the asset or liability for the last period, and E exceeds B, an amount equal to the excess shall be deemed to be a relevant gain, accruing to the company as respects that asset or liability immediately before the end of the last accrual period; and

(c) if there is neither a cumulative loss nor a cumulative gain as respects the asset or liability for the last period, an amount equal to E shall be deemed to be a relevant gain, accruing to the company as respects that asset or liability immediately before the end of the last accrual period.

(3) If there is an attributed loss, F, as respects the asset or liability, then –

(a) if there is a cumulative loss, B, as respects the asset or liability for the last period, an amount equal to F shall be deemed to be a relevant loss, accruing to the company as respects that asset or liability immediately before the end of the last accrual period.

(b) if there is a cumulative gain, A, as respects the asset or liability for the last period, and F exceeds A, an amount equal to the excess shall be deemed to be a relevant loss, accruing to the company as respects that asset or liability immediately before the end of the last accrual period; and

(c) if there is neither a cumulative loss nor a cumulative gain as respects the asset or liability for the last period, an amount equal to F shall be deemed to be a relevant loss, accruing to the company as respects that asset or liability immediately before the end of the last accrual period.

(4) In paragraphs (2) and (3) above any reference to a relevant gain or loss is –

(a) in relation to a regulation 6(3) asset, a chargeable gain or an allowable loss; and

(b) in relation to any other asset or any liability, an initial exchange gain or an initial exchange loss;

and in relation to a regulation 6(3) asset, those paragraphs have effect subject to regulation [14(5) to (9) and (11)][1].

(5) If the asset or liability has in whole or in part been held or owed by the company in exempt circumstances at any time during the last accrual period, then any initial exchange gain or loss which accrues as respects that asset or liability by virtue of paragraph (2) or (3) above shall be treated as not being an exchange gain or loss of a trade or part of a trade for that accrual period, and section 129 shall apply accordingly.

(6) Subject to paragraph (7) below, if the asset or liability is one as respects which section 127 applies and the debt has been reduced during an accrual period, then –

(a) the debt shall be treated as if it were two debts (all the terms and conditions of which are the same as those of the actual debt except as to principal) one equal to the amount outstanding at the end of the accrual period and the other equal to the difference between that amount and the amount of the debt at the beginning of the period, and

(b) the attributed gain or loss, the cumulative taxed gain or loss and the cumulative gain or loss (if any) which is found as respects the asset or liability for that accrual period shall each be divided proportionately into two parts according to the proportion by which the debt has been reduced, and

(c) that part of each of those gains or losses which bears the same proportion to the actual gain or loss as the amount of the debt outstanding at the end of the period bears to the amount of the debt at the beginning of the period shall be taken into account under regulation 12 and the other part shall be taken into account under paragraphs (1) to (5) above.

(7) Paragraph (6) shall not apply –

(a) where the amount of the debt increased before the reduction occurred unless the debt was reduced to an amount less than the amount it was before the increase (or if there has been more than one, the first increase) occurred; or

(b) as respects the last accrual period for the asset or liability if an initial exchange gain or loss does not accrue (disregarding this Part) as respects the asset or liability for that period.

(8) Paragraph (6) may apply in relation to an asset or liability for more than one accrual period if the debt is reduced in more than one accrual period.

---

¹   Substituted by SI 1996 No 1349 (The Exchange Gains and Losses (Transitional Provisions) (Amendment) Regulations 1996), Reg 6 with effect from 30 June 1996. Previously '14(2) to (11)'.

---

14 Further provisions relating to regulation 6(3) assets

(1) Where the asset in question is a regulation 6(3) asset then –

(a) regulation 13 does not apply if, immediately before the relevant transaction, it was held by the company in exempt circumstances, and

(b) the following provisions of this regulation shall not apply if section 127 has applied in relation to the asset for any accrual period:

and in this regulation any reference to the relevant transaction is a reference to the transaction by virtue of which the company ceased to be entitled to the asset.

(2)–(4) [...]¹

(5) In any case where apart from this paragraph an allowable loss would accrue to a company as respects a regulation 6(3) asset by virtue of [regulation 13]², then, subject to paragraph (7) below –

(a) the company may elect, by notice to the inspector within two years of the end of the accounting period in which the disposal in question occurs, that this paragraph shall apply as respects the asset, and

(b) where such an election is made, an amount equal to the amount of that loss (or that reduced loss) shall be set against the amount of any exchange gains accruing to the company in the accounting period which is or includes the last accrual period or in subsequent accounting periods, and

(c) if a reduction is made under paragraph (7)(b) below in the amount available under sub-paragraph (b) above to be set against any gains, the allowable loss or the reduced loss shall be deemed to be equal to the amount of that reduction, and

(d) if such a reduction is not made, the allowable loss, or reduced loss, shall not be deemed to accrue.

An election under this paragraph shall be irrevocable.

(6) Paragraph (7) below applies in any case where a reorganisation within the meaning of section 127 of the 1992 Act, or any other transaction to which that section applied, took place before the company's commencement day in relation to which –

(a) the original shares (within the meaning of that section) were or included one or more shares which would not have been qualifying assets had the company been entitled to them on its commencement day or, if the company was still entitled to them on that day, are not qualifying assets; and

(b) the new holding (within the meaning of that section) was or included an asset –

(i) which is a regulation 6(3) asset held by the company (whether or not the company held it in pursuance of the reorganisation or other transaction in question or in pursuance of a subsequent no gain/no loss disposal), or

(ii) which would have been a regulation 6(3) asset had the company held it on its commencement day and which has been exchanged for, or converted into, the regulation 6(3) asset which the company held on its commencement day in pursuance of one or more transactions to which section 127 of the 1992 Act applied or one or more no gain/no loss disposals (or both).

In relation to any transaction within section 136 of the 1992 Act, the reference in sub-paragraph (b) to an exchange shall be construed in accordance with that section.

(7) Where this paragraph applies in relation to a reorganisation within the meaning of section 127 of the 1992 Act, or any other transaction to which that section applied –

(a) any election under paragraph (5)(a) above must be made in relation to all regulation 6(3) assets derived from shares which –

(i) in relation to that reorganisation or transaction are the original shares (within the meaning of that section), and

(ii) are held by the company on its commencement day, and

(b) the amount available to be set against any exchange gains in accordance with paragraph (5)(b) above shall be reduced by an amount equal to the excess (if any) of A over B where –

A is the aggregate of the attributable losses referable to those regulation 6(3) assets which have been found under regulation 9, and

B is the aggregate of those losses which would have been found under regulation 9 if section 127 of the 1992 Act had not applied in relation to the reorganisation or other transaction, and where the excess is greater than the amount available, that amount shall be taken to be zero, and

(c) where the company ceases to be entitled to all those regulation 6(3) assets in pursuance of more than one transaction –

(i) the election must be made in relation to the first of those transactions, and

(ii) shall have effect in relation to subsequent relevant transactions relating to any of those assets (notwithstanding paragraph (5)(a) above), and

(iii) sub-paragraph (b) above shall apply in relation to each relevant transaction as respects those regulation 6(3) assets which are the subject of that transaction.

(8) Paragraph (6)(b) does not apply if the company acquired the asset in pursuance of a transaction to which section 127 of the 1992 Act did not apply and which is not a no gain/no loss disposal.

(9) For the purposes of this regulation, a transaction is a no gain, no loss disposal if, by virtue of any enactment specified in section 35(3)(d) of the 1992 Act, neither a gain nor a loss accrues to the person transferring the asset in question.

(10) [...]³

(11) Any expression used in this regulation which is not defined in Chapter II shall be construed as if this regulation were included in the 1992 Act.

---

¹ Deleted by SI 1996 No 1349 (The Exchange Gains and Losses (Transitional Provisions) (Amendment) Regulations 1996), Reg 7 with respect to any disposal of an asset to which Reg 6(3) above applies that is made on or after 1 April 1996.
Previously

'(2) If there was an attributed gain as respects a regulation 6(3) asset and the basic valuation of the asset exceeds its market value at the time of the relevant transaction, then, subject to paragraph (4) below, an amount equal to the amount of the excess shall be set against the amount of the chargeable gain, if any, which (disregarding this paragraph) is deemed to accrue by virtue of regulation 13 and-

(a) if the two amounts are equal, the chargeable gain shall not be deemed to accrue;

(b) if the excess is the greater, an allowable loss shall be deemed to accrue to the company at the time of the relevant transaction of an amount equal to the difference between the excess and the amount of that chargeable gain, and that gain shall not be deemed to accrue;

(c) if the chargeable gain is the greater, it shall be reduced by an amount equal to the amount of the excess.

(3) If there was an attributed loss as respects a regulation 6(3) asset and the market value of the asset at the time of the relevant transaction exceeds the basic valuation of the asset, then, subject to paragraph (4) below, an amount equal to the amount of the excess shall be set against the amount of the allowable loss, if any, which (disregarding this paragraph) is deemed to accrue by virtue of regulation 13 and-

(a) if the two amounts are equal, the allowable loss shall not be deemed to accrue;

(b) if the excess is the greater, that loss shall not be deemed to accrue but a chargeable gain shall be deemed to accrue to the company at the time of the disposal of an amount equal to the difference between the excess and the amount of that loss, and

(c) if the allowable loss is the greater, it shall be reduced by an amount equal to the amount of the excess.

(4) The amount of the excess for the purposes of paragraph (2) or (3) above shall not exceed an amount equal to the aggregate of-

(a) the cumulative taxed gain or loss, and

(b) the initial exchange gain or loss (if any) accruing as respects the asset for its last accrual period, and

(c) any chargeable gain or allowable loss which (disregarding paragraphs (2) and (3)) accrues by virtue of regulation 13;

and for the purposes of paragraph (2) section 176 of the 1992 Act shall apply in relation to that excess as if it were an allowable loss accruing on the relevant transaction (and if apart from this paragraph that section would not apply in relation to that transaction, it shall so apply for this purpose).'

²   Substituted by SI 1996 No 1349, Reg 7 with effect as in ¹ above.
Previously 'paragraph (2) above or, if that paragraph does not apply, by virtue of regulation 13 or the amount of the allowable loss is reduced by virtue of paragraph (3) above'.

³   Deleted by SI 1996 No 1349, Reg 7 with effect as in ¹ above.
Previously
'For the purposes of paragraphs (2) to (4) above, the amount of any excess shall be expressed in the nominal currency and shall be translated into sterling using the London closing exchange rate for the day immediately preceding the company's commencement day.'

---

15   Elections to treat pre-commencement day gains and losses as accruing after commencement day over 6 year period

(1)   A company may elect by notice to the inspector, before [30 September 1996]¹, that the provisions of this regulation shall apply, subject to [paragraphs (6) and (7)]² below, in relation to all existing assets and liabilities held or owed by the company, and where an election has effect under this regulation –

(a)   it shall have effect as from the beginning of the company's commencement [day and, subject to paragraph (1A) below,]³ shall be irrevocable, and

(b)   regulations 10 to 14 shall not apply in relation to any such existing asset or liability.

[(1A)   An election under paragraph (1) above may be withdrawn, with effect from the beginning of the company's commencement day, by notice by the company to the inspector before 30th September 1996.]⁴

(2)   In any case where an election has effect under this regulation and as respects any existing asset or liability held or owed by the company there is an attributed gain or loss, then for the purposes of Chapter II the amount of that gain or loss shall be divided into 6 equal parts of which –

(a)   each shall be deemed to be an initial exchange gain or loss (as the case may be) accruing as respects that asset or liability, and

(b)   the first shall be deemed to accrue to the company at the beginning of the company's commencement day, and

(c)   subject to paragraph (3) below, the remaining 5 shall be deemed to accrue (severally) to the company at the beginning of each of the following 5 anniversaries of that day.

(3)   If the company ceases to be within the charge to corporation tax before the fifth anniversary of its commencement day, any exchange gain or

loss which (by virtue of paragraph (2)(c) above) has not accrued before the company ceases to be within the charge to corporation tax, shall be deemed to accrue to the company immediately before it so ceases.

(4) Any initial exchange gain or loss which is deemed to accrue to the company by virtue of this regulation shall be deemed to accrue for an accrual period which is identical to the accounting period of the company which includes the day on which the gain or loss is treated as accruing.

(5) This regulation and sections 128 and 129 shall continue to apply in relation to an asset or liability as respects which the gain or loss is deemed to accrue by virtue of this regulation notwithstanding a disposal of the asset or liability by the company before the fifth anniversary of the company's commencement day, and for the purposes of those sections the asset or liability shall be deemed to continue to be held or owed until that anniversary by the company for the same purposes as those for which it was held or owed immediately before the disposal.

(6) An election under this regulation shall not apply in relation to a regulation 6(3) asset or an asset which is held by the company on its commencement day in exempt circumstances.

[(7) Where in relation to an existing asset held by the company-

(a) an election has effect under regulation 6(2),

(b) an election has effect under this regulation,

(c) there is an attributed gain or loss computed in accordance with paragraph (2) of this regulation as respects the asset, and

(d) any of the dates referred to in sub-paragraphs (b) and (c) of that paragraph falls in an accounting period of the company ending on or after 30th June 1996,

no part of the attributed gain or loss shall be taken into account for the purposes of corporation tax for that accounting period, but the amount of the attributed gain or loss which would have been taken into account for that period but for this paragraph shall be treated for the purposes of regulation 13 as a relevant gain or loss falling within that regulation.]⁴

---

[1]   Substituted by SI 1996 No 1349 (The Exchange Gains and Losses (Transitional Provisions) (Amendment) Regulations 1996), Reg 8 with effect from 30 June 1996. Previously 'the expiry of the period of 92 days beginning with the company's commencement day or, if later, the expiry of the period of 183 days beginning with 23rd March 1995'.

[2]   Substituted by SI 1996 No 1349, Reg 8 as in ¹ above. Previously 'paragraph (6)'.

[3]   Substituted by SI 1996 No 1349, Reg 8 as in ¹ above. Previously 'day, and'.

[4]   Inserted by SI 1996 No 1349, Reg 8 as in ¹ above.

---

16   Set off of certain pre-commencement losses against exchange gains

(1) A company may elect by notice to the inspector, before the expiry of the period of 92 days beginning with the company's commencement day or, if later, the expiry of the period of 183 days beginning with 23rd March

1995, that available losses shall be available to be set against the company's exchange gains in accordance with paragraphs (9) to (11) below, and an election under this paragraph –

(a) may be made in relation to the whole of the available losses or such amount, less than the whole of the available losses, as may be specified in the election; and

(b) shall be irrevocable.

(2) Subject to paragraphs (4) to (8) below, in this regulation 'available losses', in relation to any company, means allowable losses which –

(a) accrued to the company before its commencement day at a time when it was within the charge to corporation tax, and

(b) accrued either –

   (i) on the disposal of assets which if they had not been disposed of before the company's commencement day would have been qualifying assets, or

   (ii) by virtue of section 143 of the 1992 Act in respect of a currency contract, a currency option, an interest rate contract or an interest rate option, (and this provision shall be construed as one with Chapter II of Part IV of the Finance Act 1994),

   other than losses which are attributable to assets which would not have been qualifying assets if they had been held by the company on its commencement day.

(3) For the purposes of paragraph (2) above, a loss is attributable to an asset ('the first asset') if and to the extent that –

(a) it accrued on the disposal of another asset by the company ('the second asset'), and

(b) the first asset was the subject of a reorganisation or other transaction to which section 127 of the 1992 Act applied, and

(c) either –

   (i) the second asset was held by the company in pursuance of that reorganisation or other transaction, or

   (ii) the second asset was held by the company in pursuance of a transaction which is the last in a series of transactions, the first of which is the transaction referred to in sub-paragraph (b) above, and all of which are either transactions to which section 127 of the 1992 Act applied or no gain/no loss disposals (within the meaning of regulation 14(9)) so that the loss has been calculated by reference to the acquisition or other costs of the first asset.

   References in this paragraph to a reorganisation or other transaction to which section 127 of the 1992 Act applied include a reference to any reorganisation or other transaction to which that section would have applied but for section 116 of that Act.

(4) A loss which has accrued to a company on the disposal of an asset is not an available loss if –

(a) had a gain instead accrued on that disposal, the company would not have been chargeable to corporation tax in respect of that gain; or

(b) it has been deducted, or is deductible, under section 8(1) of, or Schedule 7A to, the 1992 Act from any chargeable gains which have accrued to the company in accounting periods ending before the company's commencement day.

(5) Paragraph (6) below applies in any case where –

(a) an allowable loss has accrued to a company on the disposal of an asset, and

(b) the asset was held by the company at any time when it was not resident in the United Kingdom, and

(c) if the asset had been disposed of at that time and a gain had accrued to the company on that disposal, it would not have been included in the company's chargeable profits by virtue of section 10(3) of the 1992 Act.

(6) Where this paragraph applies –

(a) there shall be computed the amount of the allowable loss (if any) which would have accrued to the company on the disposal if it had acquired the asset, at market value, on the first day on which any gain which would have accrued to the company if the asset had been disposed of on that day (assuming that the disposal gave rise to a gain and disregarding any allowable losses which might be available for deduction under section 8(1) of or Schedule 7A to the 1992 Act) would have been included in the company's chargeable profits for the purposes of corporation tax (whether because the company became resident or the asset became situated in the United Kingdom on that day or for any other reason); and

(b) if there is neither a loss nor a gain or there is a gain on that computation, there shall be taken to be a loss of zero;

and the available losses shall be reduced by an amount equal to the excess of the amount of the allowable loss referred to in paragraph (5)(a) above over the amount of the loss found under paragraph (a) or (b) above.

(7) In any case where the company acquired the asset on a no gain/no loss disposal, then references in paragraph (5)(b) and (c) and (6)(a) above to a company include the company from which it acquired the asset, and if that company also acquired the asset on such a disposal, to the company from which it acquired the asset, and so on for a series of such disposals.

For the purposes of this paragraph an asset is acquired on a no gain/no loss disposal if, by virtue of any enactment specified in section 35(3)(d) of the 1992 Act, neither a gain nor a loss accrues to the person making the disposal.

(8) Where losses have accrued to a company for accounting periods ending before the company's commencement day (but after the last accounting period, if any, as respects which the company did not have a surplus of allowable losses available to be carried forward to the next accounting

period under section 8(1)(b) of or Schedule 7A to the 1992 Act) in respect of assets falling within paragraph (2)(b) above and also in respect of other assets, the losses accruing in respect of those other assets shall not be available losses, and for the purposes of determining in such a case which losses are available and which are not –

(a) losses which have accrued as respects assets falling within paragraph (2)(b) above shall be taken to have been set off first against gains accruing on such assets, and

(b) losses which have accrued as respects other assets shall be taken to have been set off first against gains accruing on such other assets.

(9) Losses as respects which an election made by a company has effect under this regulation shall be set against any exchange gain which accrues to the company –

(a) in an accounting period beginning on or after the company's commencement day, and

(b) either –

(i) in respect of a regulation 6(3) asset or an asset which would be a regulation 6(3) asset if it were an existing asset held by the company; or

(ii) in respect of a currency contract which before the company's commencement day (assuming the contract to have been in existence then) would have fallen within section 143 of the 1992 Act;

and losses shall be set against gains accruing in earlier accounting periods rather than later periods.

(10) Where a loss is to be set against a gain under this regulation the amount of the loss shall be deducted from the gain before the application of section 128(4) or 129(2) (whichever is applicable).

(11) Any reference in paragraphs (1), (9) and (10) above to an exchange gain in relation to a company is a reference to a gain which has accrued (or been deemed to accrue) to the company for an accrual period as respects any asset, liability or contract after regulations 12 and 13 and the regulation 2(2) provisions have applied (if they are applicable) as respects the asset, liability or contract for that accrual period; but computations under regulations 12 and 13 shall be made disregarding any set-off under this regulation.

(12) Where allowable losses have accrued on disposals occurring at different times, and the election is made in relation to an amount rather than to the whole of the allowable losses, the losses constituting that amount shall be taken for all purposes to be those losses accruing on earlier disposals rather than those accruing on later disposals, and any allowable losses which constitute an amount specified in an election under this regulation shall not be available for deduction under section 8(1) of, or Schedule 7A to, the 1992 Act.

(13) In this regulation –

(a) any reference to a company's commencement day in relation to any company which, by virtue of regulation 3, has more that one commencement day, is a reference to the first such day; and

(b) any expression which is not defined in Chapter II shall have the same meaning as in the 1992 Act.

PART IV PRE-COMMENCEMENT GAINS AND LOSSES: DEBTS OF FIXED AMOUNTS

17 Application, etc. of Part IV

(1) This Part applies in relation to an existing asset or liability held or owed by a company which immediately before its commencement day was within the charge to corporation tax where –

(a) the asset or liability is the right to settlement of a debt or the duty to settle a debt which in either case is fixed (within the meaning of regulation 3) as to [both its amount and term][1], and

(b) any exchange difference accruing to the company on a disposal or settlement by the company of the asset or liability immediately before the company's commencement day would not have been taken into account, or would not have been wholly taken into account, for the purposes of corporation tax in computing the company's profits and gains of that accounting period or would not be so taken into account if the company had been within the charge to corporation tax at the time the gain or loss accrued.

(2) For the purposes of the Tables set out in regulation 20, all amounts shall be taken to be positive, but for all other computations for the purposes of this Part, an amount which is a gain shall be taken to be a positive figure and an amount which is a loss shall be taken to be a negative figure.

(3) Regulations 18 to 20 have effect subject to regulations 21 and 22, and in regulations 18, 19 and 21 'the current period' has the same meaning as in regulation 20.

---

[1] Substituted by SI 1995 No 408 (The Exchange Gains and Losses (Transitional Provisions) (Amendment) Regulations 1995 with effect from 23 March 1995. Previously 'its amount or its terms (or both)'.

---

18 Post-commencement net gains and losses and pre-commencement gains and losses

(1) Where this Part applies, there shall be calculated the aggregate amount of the initial exchange gains and losses which have accrued as respects the asset or liability for all accrual periods including the current period, and that aggregate amount is referred to in this Part, if positive, as 'the post-commencement net gain' and if negative as 'the post-commencement net loss'.

(2) Where the aggregate amount found under paragraph (1) above for all accrual periods including the current period is zero, then –

(a) if the aggregate amount for all accrual periods preceding the current period was a post-commencement net gain, there shall be a post-commencement net gain equal to zero; and

(b) if the aggregate amount for all accrual periods preceding the current period was a post-commencement net loss, or there is no such aggregate amount, there shall be a post-commencement net loss equal to zero.

(3) Where this Part applies, there shall be calculated the aggregate amount of the exchange differences which have accrued as respects the asset or liability for accounting periods before the company's commencement day, disregarding realised exchange differences and any unrealised exchange difference which has been taken into account in computing the profits or gains of the company for the purposes of corporation tax for any such accounting period, and the result is referred to in this Part, if positve, as 'the pre-commencement gain' and if negative as 'the pre-commencement loss'.

(4) In any case where the asset or liability is held at the end of the current period for the purposes of a trade or part of a trade the local currency of which is not sterling, that local currency shall be used in making the calculations required by paragraphs (1),(2) and (3) above.

(5) For the purposes of paragraph (1) above, the question whether any initial exchange gain or loss has accrued, and if so its amount, shall be determined disregarding regulations 20 to 22 and the regulation 2(2) provisions.

[(6) Where

(a) the asset held or the liability owed by the company consists of a discounted debt, and

(b) the company did not cease on 31st March 1996 to be entitled to the asset or (as the case may be) subject to the liability,

it shall be regarded, for the purposes of paragraph (1) above and section 158, as ceasing on that date to be so entitled or subject, and references in this regulation, and in regulations 19 and 20, to accrual periods (including references to an accrual period as the current period) shall, as respects that asset or liability, be construed accordingly.]¹

---

¹ Inserted by SI 1996 No 1349 (The Exchange Gains and Losses (Transitional Provisions) (Amendment) Regulations 1996), Reg 9 with effect from 30 June 1996.

---

19 Overall exchange gains and losses and cumulative taxed gains and losses

(1) Where this Part applies, there shall be calculated the aggregate amount of –

(a) the pre-commencement gain or loss, and

(b) the post-commencement net gain or loss.

(2) The aggregate amount found in accordance with paragraph (1) above is referred to in this Part, if positive, as 'the overall exchange gain', Z, and if negative as 'the overall exchange loss', W, and if the aggregate is zero there shall be an overall exchange loss of zero.

(3) In the case of any asset or liability to which this Part applies and as respects which an initial exchange gain or loss has accrued for the

current period, there shall be calculated the aggregate amount of the initial exchange gains and losses which have accrued to the company as respects the asset or liability for the accrual periods earlier than the current period, and –

(a) if that aggregate amount is positive it shall be the cumulative taxed gain, G, for that asset or liability for the current period.

(b) if it is negative it shall be the cumulative taxed loss, L, for that asset or liability for the current period, and

(c) in cases where that aggregate amount is zero there shall be taken to be a cumulative taxed loss equal to zero for the period.

(4) For the purposes of paragraph (3) above –

(a) the question whether any initial exchange gain or loss has accrued for the current period shall be determined disregarding regulations 20 to 22 and the regulation 2(2) provisions;

(b) the question whether any initial exchange gain or loss has accrued for any period other than the current period shall be determined in accordance with this Part but as if the regulation 2(2) provisions had never come into force; and

(c) there shall be disregarded any gain or loss which has accrued for an accrual period other than the current period unless –

(i) it has been taken into account in computing the profits or gains of the company holding or owing the asset or liability for the purposes of corporation tax for accounting periods ending before the beginning of the current period, or

(ii) it would have been so taken into account if the regulation 2(2) provisions had never come into force; or

(iii) it is equal to zero.

20 Deemed gains and losses

Table C or D set out below (as appropriate) shall apply in relation to an asset or liability as respects which an initial exchange gain or loss accrues to a company for an accrual period ('the current period'), determined disregarding this regulation and regulations 21 and 22 and the regulation 2(2) provisions, and as respects which there is –

(a)   a post-commencement net gain, X, or

(b)   a post-commencement net loss, Y,

and if the primary condition and the secondary condition (if any) are satisfied, any initial exchange gain of loss which (apart from this regulation) would accrue to the company for the current period ('the actual gain or loss') shall be deemed not to accrue but the gain or loss specified in the third column of the Table in relation to those conditions shall be deemed to accrue and shall be an initial exchange gain or loss (as the case may be) accruing in the place of the actual gain or loss.

Table C
If there is a post-commencement net gain X

Primary condition	Secondary condition	Deemed gain or loss
1 Overall exchange again Z and no cumulative taxed gain or loss	X is greater than Z	Gain equal to Z
2 Overall exchange gain Z and a cumulative taxed gain G	i) Z is not greater than G and X is greater than Z	i) Loss equal to G-Z
	ii) Z is greater than G and X is greater than Z	ii) Gain equal to Z-G
	iii) X is not greater than Z nor greater than G	iii) Loss equal to G-X
	iv) X is not greater than Z but is greater than G	iv) Gain equal to X-G
3 Overall exchange gain Z and a cumulative taxed loss L	i) X is greater than Z	i) Gain equal to Z+L
	ii) X is not greater than Z	ii) Gain equal to X+L
4 Overall exchange loss W and no cumulative taxed gain or loss		Loss equal to zero
5 Overall exchange loss W and a cumulative taxed gain G		Loss equal to G
6 Overall exchange loss W and a cumulative taxed loss L		Gain equal to L

Table D
If there is a post-commencement net loss Y

Primary condition	Secondary condition	Deemed gain or loss
1 Overall exchange loss W and no cumulative taxed gain or loss	Y is greater than W	Loss equal to W
2 Overall exchange loss W and a cumulative taxed loss L	i) W is not greater than L and Y is greater than W	i) Gain equal to L − W
	ii) W is greater than L and Y is greater than W	ii) Loss equal to W − L
	iii) Y is not greater than W nor greater than L	iii) Gain equal to L − Y
	iv) Y is not greater than W but is greater than L	iv) Loss equal to Y − L
3 Overall exchange loss W and a cumulative taxed gain G	i) Y is greater than W	i) Loss equal to W + G
	ii) Y is not greater than W	ii) Loss equal to Y + G
4 Overall exchange gain Z and no cumulative taxed gain or loss		Loss equal to zero
5 Overall exchange gain Z and a cumulative taxed loss L		Gain equal to L
6 Overall exchange gain Z and a cumulative taxed gain G		Loss equal to G

21 Modification of regulations 18 to 20 where nominal amount of debt increases after commencement

(1) This regulation applies where the existing asset or liability to which this Part applies is the right to settlement of a debt, or a duty to settle a debt, the nominal amount of which is or has been increased on or after the company's commencement day, and in this regulation 'the original debt' means the debt as at the beginning of that day.

(2) Where this regulation applies –

(a) the calculations required to be made by regulations 18 and 19 shall first be made in relation to the original debt (on the assumption that it had not been increased on or after the company's commencement day), and there shall be found the amount of any deemed gain or loss under regulation 20(1) basing the computations on the amounts found in accordance with those calculations, and

    (b) there shall then be calculated the amount of the initial exchange gain or loss (if any) which would have accrued as respects the asset or liability if –

        (i) Parts I to III of these Regulations were disregarded, and

        (ii) the company had become entitled to the asset or subject to the liability at the beginning of its commencement day, and

        (iii) the amount of the debt at the beginning of the company's commencement day had been zero,

and the amount of any such gain or loss is referred to in this regulation as the 'notional gain' or the 'notional loss', as the case may be.

(3) The amount of the notional gain or loss shall be aggregated with the amount of the deemed gain or loss found, in accordance with paragraph (2)(a) above, under regulation 20(1) and –

    (a) if that aggregate amount is positive it shall be deemed to be the initial exchange gain accruing to the company as respects the asset or liability for the current period;

    (b) if that aggregate amount is negative it shall be deemed to be the initial exchange loss accruing to the company as respects the asset or liability for the current period;

    (c) if that aggregate amount is zero there shall be deemed to be neither an initial exchange gain nor an initial exchange loss accruing to the company as respects the asset or liability for the current period;

and any initial exchange gain or loss which disregarding this Part would accrue to the company as respects the asset or liability for the current period shall (in accordance with regulation 20(1)) be deemed not to accrue.

(4) Where this regulation applies, regulation 20(1) shall effect (in accordance with paragraph (2) above) with the omission of the words 'and shall be an initial exchange gain or loss (as the case may be) accruing in the place of the actual gain or loss'.

(5) Where the debt in question is not wholly repaid at one time, then for the purposes of this Part any amount repaid after commencement shall be taken to reduce the amount of the original debt first, before any amount by which that debt has been increased is reduced.

22 Replacement loans

(1) In any case where –

    (a) a debt to which this Part applies otherwise than by virtue of this regulation ('the original debt') is settled before final settlement of the debt is due, and

    (b) the company owing the original debt incurs another debt ('the new debt') not earlier than 30 days before the day on which the original debt is settled and not later than 30 days after that day,

then, subject to paragraphs (3) to (7) below, regulations 18 to 21 shall continue to apply in relation to the new debt as if it were the original debt (disregarding regulation 17(1)(b)) except that regulation 21 shall not apply in relation to any debt as respects which paragraph (5) below applies.

(2)   Any reference in this regulation to the settlement amount is a reference to the amount of the settlement referred to in paragraph (1)(a) above.

(3)   For the purposes of this regulation –

(a)   any debt due for goods or services supplied to or by the company in the course of its trade shall be disregarded for the purposes of paragraph (1)(a) and (b) above;

(b)   a debt shall be disregarded for the purposes of paragraph (1)(b) above unless –

(i)   it is held or owed for the purpose of a trade or part of a trade and is in a currency other than the local currency of the trade or part; or

(ii)   it is not held for the purposes of a trade or part of a trade and is in a currency other than sterling:

(whether or not it is the same as the currency of the original debt);

and paragraph (1) above shall not apply in relation to any person who is party to the agreement under which the new debt is incurred if he was not party to the agreement under which the original debt was incurred.

(4)   In any case where the settlement amount exceeds the amount of the new debt at the time it is incurred, then, for the purposes of computing the amount of any post-commencement net exchange gain or loss and the overall exchange gain or loss for the new debt, the amount of any initial exchange gain or loss and any exchange difference which has accrued as respects the original debt shall be proportionately reduced.

(5)   In any case where the amount of the new debt, at the time it is incurred, exceeds the settlement amount, then for any accrual period for the new debt –

(a)   there shall be found the amount of any initial exchange gain or loss which would have accrued as respects the new debt in accordance with this Part if the amount of the new debt at the time it was incurred had been equal to the settlement amount;

(b)   there shall be found the amount of any initial exchange gain or loss which would have accrued as respects the new debt in accordance with Chapter II –

(i)   if regulations 18 to 21 did not apply, and

(ii)   the amount of the new debt at the time it was incurred had been equal to the amount by which it exceeds the settlement amount;

(c)   the amounts found in accordance with sub-paragraphs (a) and (b) above shall be aggregated and the aggregate amount so found –

(i)   if positive shall be the initial exchange gain accruing to the company as respects the new debt for the accrual period in question, and

(ii) if negative shall be the initial exchange loss accruing to the company as respects the new debt for the accrual period question;

and any initial exchange gain or loss which would apart from this paragraph so accrue shall be deemed not to accrue.

(6) In any case where the amount of the new debt, at the time it is incurred, exceeds the settlement amount, then –

   (a) if that debt is partly repaid at any time, the repayment shall be taken into account so as to reduce the amount of the debt first for the purposes of paragraph (5)(b) above and only secondly for the purposes of paragraph (5)(a) above, and

   (b) if that debt is increased at any time, the increase shall be taken into account so as to increase the amount of the debt for the purposes of paragraph (5)(b) above unless the debt has been reduced to an amount less than the settlement amount in which case –

      (i) the increase shall first increase the amount of the debt for the purposes of paragraph (5)(a) above, but not so as to increase the debt for those purposes beyond the settlement amount, and

      (ii) if the increase exceeds the amount by which the debt was less than the settlement amount, the amount of that excess shall increase the amount of the debt for the purposes of paragraph (5)(b).

(7) For the purposes of paragraph (8) below 'the relevant time' means the time when the terms of the original debt required it to be repaid.

(8) Regulations 18 to 21, and paragraphs (4) to (6) above, shall not apply to the new debt in relation to any time after the relevant time and accordingly, if the new debt has not been wholly repaid by the relevant time, then –

   (a) for the purposes of this Part, and of Chapter II as it applies for the purposes of any calculation required to be made in accordance with any provision of this Part, the company shall be deemed to cease to be entitled or subject to the debt at the relevant time, and

   (b) for the purposes of Chapter II as it applies otherwise than in accordance with sub-paragraph (a) above, the company shall be deemed to become entitled or subject to the new debt at the relevant time, to the extent that the new debt has not been repaid at that time.

(9) This regulation shall also apply, subject to any necessary modifications –

   (a) where part only of the original debt is settled before final settlement of that part is due, and not earlier than 30 days before the day it is settled and not later than 30 days after that day the company owing that debt incurs another debt (so that where this paragraph applies, this Part shall continue to apply to the old debt and to the new debt); and

   (b) where a debt to which this Part applies by virtue of this regulation is settled (in whole or in part), and not earlier than 30 days before the day on which it is settled and not later than 30 days after that day the company owing that debt incurs another debt.

The Exchange Gains and Losses (Alternative Method of Calculation of Gain or Loss) Regulations 1994 (SI 1994 No 3227)

Made: 15th December 1994
Laid before the House of Commons: 16th December 1994
Coming into force: 23rd March 1995

ARRANGEMENT OF REGULATIONS

General

The Treasury, in exercise of the powers conferred on them by sections 164(14), 167(1) and (4) to (6) of, and Schedule 15 to, the Finance Act 1993, hereby make the following Regulations:

General

1   Citation, commencement and interpretation

(1)   These Regulations may be cited as the Exchange Gains and Losses (Alternative Method of Calculation of Gain or Loss) Regulations 1994.

(2)   These Regulations shall come into force on 23rd March 1995.

(3)   In these Regulations 'the 1993 Act' means the Finance Act 1993.

Assets etc. held in exempt circumstances

2   Reduction in exchange gains and losses

(1)   This regulation applies in any case where an asset, liability or contract is held or owed during the whole or part of an accrual period ('the current period') by a company wholly or partly in exempt circumstances.

(2)   In any case where this regulation applies, the amount of the initial exchange gain or initial exchange loss which, apart from this regulation, would accrue to the company as respects that asset, liability or contract for the current period shall be found in accordance with the alternative method of calculation but subject to paragraph (5) below.

(3)   The accrued amount for each day in that period during which the asset, contract or liability is wholly held or owed in exempt circumstances shall be reduced to nil.

(4)   In any case where during an accrual period an asset, contract or liability is held or owed –

     (a)   partly for the purposes of long term insurance business, mutual insurance business or the occupation of commercial woodlands, and

     (b)   partly for other purposes (not also being exempt),

the accrued amount for each day in that period shall be correspondingly apportioned between the different purposes, and the amount so apportioned to the purposes of long term insurance business, mutual insurance business or the occupation of commercial woodlands (as the case may be) shall be reduced to nil.

(5)   In any case where –

     (a)   at any time during the current period there is a major change in the extent to which the asset, contract or liability is held or owed, or is not held or owed, in exempt circumstances, and

     (b)   there is a significant change in the rate of exchange relevant to the computation of the accrued amounts during that period and

     (c)   that time is not (disregarding this regulation) a translation time as respects the asset, liability or contract,

then the initial exchange gain or loss as respects the asset, contract or liability for the current period shall be calculated as if that time were a translation time, (but not so as to create more than one accrual period), so that separate calculations are made for different parts of the period and paragraphs (3) and (4) above (if applicable) are applied separately in relation to each such part.

(6)   This regulation does not apply in relation to any gain which is treated as a non-trading exchange gain by virtue of section 140(9) of the 1993 Act.

Unremittable income

3   Reduction in exchange gains and losses

(1)   This regulation applies in any case where –

(a) an asset falling within section 153(1)(a) or (b) of the 1993 Act is held by a company, and

(b) income represented by the asset is unremittable on any day which falls in an accrual period of that asset.

(2) In any case where this regulation applies, the amount of the initial exchange gain or initial exchange loss which, apart from this regulation, would accrue to the company as respects the asset for the period in question shall, subject to paragraph (3) and (4) below, be found in accordance with the alternative method of calculation.

(3) The accrued amount for each day in that period during which the income is unremittable shall –

(a) if all the income represented by the asset is unremittable on that day, be reduced to nil, or

(b) if only a proportion of the income represented by the asset is unremittable on that day, be reduced by a corresponding proportion.

(4) Where income which has been unremittable during an accrual period becomes remittable at any time during that period, the initial exchange gain or loss as respects the asset for that period shall be calculated as if the time when income becomes remittable were a translation time, (but not so as to create more than one accrual period) so that –

(a) separate amounts are found for different parts of the period, and

(b) paragraph (3) above is applied in relation to each such amount.

Matching

4 Interpretation

(1) This regulation has effect for the interpretation of regulations 5 to 11.

(2) In those regulations –

'the Taxes Act' means the Income and Corporation Taxes Act 1988;

'the 1992 Act' means the Taxation of Chargeable Gains Act 1992;

'accounts', in relation to a company, means the accounts of the company prepared in accordance with normal accountancy practice being either –

(i) the annual accounts of the company prepared in accordance with Part VII of the Companies Act 1985, or

(ii) if the company is not required to prepare such accounts, the accounts which it is required to keep under the law of its home State or, if it is not so required to keep accounts, such of its accounts as most closely correspond to accounts which it would have required to prepare if the provisions of that Part applied to the company;

'a local currency election' means an election under the Local Currency Elections Regulations 1994;

'chargeable gain' has the same meaning as it has for the purposes of the 1992 Act;

'a liability' means –

(a) a liability falling within section 153(2) (a) of the 1993 Act, or

(b) in relation to a currency contract held by a company, the duty of the company under that contract to pay in exchange for one currency an amount of a second currency;

and in relation to a currency contract references to initial exchange gains or losses shall be construed as references to initial exchange gains and losses accruing as regards the second currency.

['qualifying asset' shall be construed in accordance with subsection (1) of section 153 of the 1993 Act, read with subsections (3) and (4) of that section.][1]

(3) For the purposes of this regulation and regulations 5 to 11, any reference to an asset being matched in part only shall include a reference to any asset matched in accordance with an election under regulation 10(2)(c).

(4) A liability is matched by an asset at any time only to the extent that the value of the liability at that time is matched by the value of the asset at that time, and subject to that, if the election concerned is made under regulation (10)(2)(c) so that the asset is matched in part only, the liability shall be taken to be matched only to a corresponding extent.

(5) The value of a company's asset or liability at any time shall be taken to be the value attributed to the asset or liability as at that time by the company for the purposes of its accounts for the accounting period which includes that time (expressed in the currency in which those accounts are prepared).

(6) Any reference to the disposal of an asset and to the time of the disposal of an asset shall be construed as a reference to any event which is a disposal for the purposes of the 1992 Act and the time at which the disposal occurs for the purposes of that Act, and for the purposes of the foregoing, any reference to a disposal includes a part disposal.

---

[1]   Inserted by SI 1996 No 1347 (The Exchange Gains and Losses (Alternative Method of Calculation of Gain or Loss) (Amendment) Regulations 1996), Reg 3 with effect from 30 June 1996.

---

5   Gains and losses accruing as regards matched liabilities to be found by the alternative method of calculation

(1) This regulation applies in any case where –

(a) a liability is owed by a company, and

(b) the liability is eligible to be matched with an asset on a day which falls within an accrual period for that liability, and

(c) an election made under regulation 10 is in effect for that day matching the liability (wholly or in part) with an eligible asset held by the company;

and in this regulation 'the current period' means that accrual period.

(2) In any case where this regulation applies, then, subject to [paragraphs (3) and (3A)][1] below –

(a) the amount of the initial exchange gain or initial exchange loss which, apart from this regulation, would accrue to the company for the current period as respects the liability shall be found in accordance with the alternative method of calculation, and

(b) the accrued amount for each day in that period during which the liability and asset are matched shall –

    (i) if the whole of the liability is matched, be reduced to nil, or

    (ii) if only a proportion of the liability is matched, be reduced by a corresponding proportion.

(3) If in any case where this regulation applies –

(a) at any time during the current period there is a major change in the extent to which the liability is matched, and

(b) there is a significant change in the rate of exchange relevant to the computation of the accrued amounts during the current period, and

(c) that time is not (disregarding this regulation) a translation time as respects the liability,

then [, subject to paragraph (3A) below,]² the initial exchange gain or loss as respects the liability for the current period shall be calculated, in accordance with paragraph (2) above, as if that time were a translation time (but not so as to create more than one accrual period) so that separate calculations are made for different parts of the period.

[(3A) If in a case where this regulation applies—

(a) only a proportion of a liability owed by the company is matched with an asset, not being an asset that is a ship or an aircraft, or

(b) another liability owed by the company is eligible to be matched with that asset at the time the election is made, but is not matched, and

(c) an exchange loss in relation to-

    (i) the whole of the liability referred to in sub-paragraph (a) or (b), or

    (ii) a proportion of that liability, being in the case of the liability referred to in sub-paragraph (a), a greater proportion than the proportion matched,

is shown in the company's accounts for the period which is or includes the current period, in the reserves,

the amount of the initial exchange loss as respects that liability for the current period, calculated in accordance with this regulation, shall be reduced by the amount by which the exchange loss shown in the reserves and relating to that liability exceeds the exchange loss relating to the proportion (if any) of the liability that was matched.]²

(4) A liability (not being a duty under a currency contract) is eligible to be matched with an asset if –

(a) the liability does not represent either –

    (i) a duty to settle under a debt in respect of goods or services supplied to the company in the ordinary course of its trade, or

       (ii) accrued interest, and

  (b) the nominal currency of the liability is such that borrowing in that currency could reasonably be expected to eliminate or substantially reduce the economic risk of holding the asset which is attributable to fluctuations in exchange rates.

Where the asset is matched in part only, references in this paragraph to the asset are to the part matched.

(5) In the case of a liability which is a duty under a currency contract, the liability is eligible to be matched with an asset if the second currency to which it relates is such that the company could by entering into that contract reasonably expect to eliminate or substantially reduce the economic risk of holding the asset which is attributable to fluctuations in exchange rates.

Where the asset is matched in part only, references in this paragraph to the asset are to the part matched.

(6) An asset held by a company is an eligible asset at any time if at that time –

  (a) it is shares in a company which is not resident in the United Kingdom, but this sub-paragraph only applies if at the time the election is made the company is an associated company of the company making the election; or

  (b) it is shares in a company which –

      (i) is resident in the United Kingdom, and

      (ii) has made a local currency election and is entitled, by virtue of that election, to have the basic profits and losses of a trade, or part of a trade, which it carries on in the United Kingdom computed in a currency other than sterling, and

      (iii) is a 90 per cent subsidiary (within the meaning of paragraph (7) below) of the company making the election; or

  (c) it is a debt on a security which under the terms of issue can be converted into or exchanged for shares falling within sub-paragraph (a) or (b) above [and which is not a qualifying asset][2]; or

  (d) it is the company's net investment in a branch outside the United Kingdom through which the company carries on a trade or part of a trade and the company has made a local currency election and is entitled, by virtue of that election, to have the basic profits and losses of that trade or that part computed in a currency other than sterling; or

  (e) it is a ship or an aircraft.

(7) For the purposes of paragraph (6) above –

  (a) 'shares' includes stock but does not include any asset which is a qualifying asset, [...][3]

  [(aa) all shares in the same company shall constitute a single asset,

  (ab) all debts on a security issued by the same company shall constitute a single asset, and][2]

(b) a company is a 90 per cent subsidiary of another company if it is a 90 per cent subsidiary of that other within the meaning of section 838 of the Taxes Act or would be if 'directly or indirectly' were substituted for 'directly' in subsection (1)(c) of that section.

(8) An asset held by a company is also an eligible asset at any time (whether or not it also falls within any provision of paragraph (6)) if at that time –

    (a) a gain accruing on the disposal of the asset by a person resident in the United Kingdom would be a chargeable gain, and

    (b) the asset –

        (i) is not a qualifying asset, and

        (ii) is held by a branch of the company outside the United Kingdom through which the company carries on a trade or part of a trade and the company is not entitled to have the basic profits and losses of that trade or that part computed in a currency other than sterling by virtue of a local currency election.

(9) For the purposes of paragraphs (6) and (8) above –

    (a) a company is an associated company of another if that other directly controls 20 per cent or more of the voting power in the company;

    (b) the net investment of a company in a branch is the value of the assets of that branch less the liabilities of the branch and any other liabilities owed by the company for the purposes of the trade or part trade carried on through the branch.

---

[1] Substituted by SI 1996 No 1347 (The Exchange Gains and Losses (Alternative Method of Calculation of Gain or Loss) (Amendment) Regulations 1996), Reg 4 with effect as respects accrual periods ending on or after 30 June 1996.
Previously 'paragraph (3)'.

[2] Inserted by SI 1996 No 1347, Reg 4 with effect as in [1] above.

[3] Deleted by SI 1996 No 1347, Reg 4 with effect as in [1] above.
Previously 'and'.

---

6 Controlled foreign companies

(1) Where an accounting period of a controlled foreign company is or includes an accrual period, then, for the purposes of computing in accordance with Schedule 24 to the Taxes Act the company's chargeable profits for the accounting period, an election for matching may be made by a company resident in the United Kingdom which has, or jointly by companies resident in the United Kingdom which together have, a majority interest in the foreign company, notwithstanding that in such a case the company owing any liability or acquiring or holding any asset will not be the company making the election.

(2) Paragraph 4(3) and (4) of that Schedule shall apply for the purposes of determining whether one or more companies has a majority interest in another company and, for that purpose, the relevant accounting period is the accounting period referred to in paragraph (1) above.

7 Deemed gains and losses on disposal of matched assets

(1) Subject to paragraph (2) below, paragraphs (3) to (8) below apply in any case where there is a disposal of an asset by a company at any time ('the disposal time') and at any time before the disposal time it was (to any extent) a matched asset for the purposes of an election for matching made by the company ('the relevant election').

(2) Paragraphs (3) to (8) below do not apply –

(a) if the asset is re-acquired by the company under a contract made not more than 30 days before or 30 days after the disposal time; or

(b) if the relevant election specified the company's net investment in a branch as the asset to be matched and the asset disposed of was immediately before the disposal time included in that investment.

(3) There shall be found as respects the liability or liabilities matched with the asset for each accrual period for which the relevant election has had effect –

(a) the amount of the initial exchange gain (if any) calculated in accordance with the preceding regulations, and

(b) the amount of the initial exchange gain which would have accrued if the relevant election had not had effect;

and the excess of the amount found under sub-paragraph (b) over that found under sub-paragraph (a), or if no amount is found under sub-paragraph (a) the amount found under sub-paragraph (b), for each period is referred to below as the amount by which the initial exchange gain for the period has been reduced.

(4) There shall be found as respects the liability or liabilities matched with the asset for each accrual period for which the relevant election has had effect –

(a) the amount of the initial exchange loss (if any) calculated in accordance with the preceding regulations, and

(b) the amount of the initial exchange loss which would have accrued if the relevant election had not had effect;

and the excess of the amount found under sub-paragraph (b) over that found under sub-paragraph (a), or if no amount is found under sub-paragraph (a) the amount found under sub-paragraph (b), for each period is referred to below as the amount by which the initial exchange loss for the period has been reduced.

(5) There shall be found –

(a) the aggregate of the amounts by which the initial exchange gains accruing as respects the liability for accrual periods for which the relevant election has effect have been reduced, and

(b) the aggregate of the amounts by which the initial exchange losses accruing as respects the liability for accrual periods for which the relevant election has effect have been reduced.

(6) Subject to regulation 8 and paragraphs (7) and (8) below –

(a) if the amount found under paragraph (5)(a) above exceeds the amount found under paragraph (5)(b) above, then for the purposes of the 1992 Act (and in addition to any chargeable gain or allowable loss which accrues otherwise than by virtue of this regulation) a chargeable gain shall be deemed to accrue to the company at the disposal time and the amount of the gain shall be equal to the amount of that excess;

(b) if the amount found under paragraph (5)(b) above exceeds the amount found under paragraph (5)(a) above, then for the purposes of the 1992 Act (and in addition to any chargeable gain or allowable loss which accrues otherwise than by virtue of this regulation) an allowable loss shall be deemed to accrue to the company at the disposal time and the amount of the loss shall be equal to the amount of that excess.

(7) Paragraph (6) above shall not apply if the asset disposed of is a ship or an aircraft, but instead, subject to regulation 8 and paragraph (8) below –

(a) if the amount found under paragraph (5)(a) above exceeds the amount found under paragraph (5)(b) above, an initial exchange gain, equal to the amount of that excess, shall be deemed to accrue to the company as respects the asset immediately before the disposal time;

(b) if the amount found under paragraph (5)(b) above exceeds the amount found under paragraph (5)(a) above, an initial exchange loss, equal to the amount of that excess, shall be deemed to accrue to the company as respects the asset immediately before the disposal time.

(8) Where there is a part disposal of the asset, the amount of the deemed gain or loss found under paragraph (6) or (7) above shall be reduced proportionately.

8 Deferral etc. of deemed gains and losses in certain cases

(1) Paragraph (2) below applies in any case where a company ('the disposing company') disposes of a matched asset to another company and neither a gain nor a loss accrues on that disposal by virtue of section 139, 140A, 171, 215 or 216 of the 1992 Act ('a no gain/no loss disposal'), and references below to the relevant disposal are references to that disposal.

(2) In any case where this paragraph applies, any deemed gain or loss which would (apart from this regulation) be deemed to accrue to the disposing company at the time of the relevant disposal by virtue of paragraph (6) or (7) of regulation 7 ('the deferred gain or loss') shall not accrue at that time, but paragraph (3) or (4) below (as the case may be) shall apply.

(3) If the deferred gain or loss would have accrued by virtue of regulation 7(6), then for the purposes of the 1992 Act a chargeable gain or allowable loss (as the case may be) equal in amount to the amount of the deferred gain or loss shall be deemed to accrue –

(a) on the first disposal (after the relevant disposal) of the asset which is not a no gain/no loss disposal,

(b) to the company making that disposal.

(4) If the deferred gain or loss would have accrued by virtue of regulation 7(7), then an initial exchange gain or loss (as the case may be) equal in amount to the amount of the deferred gain or loss shall be deemed to accrue –

   (a) on the first disposal (after the relevant disposal) of the asset which is not a no gain/no loss disposal,

   (b) to the company making that disposal.

(5) In any case where paragraph (3) or (4) above applies on a subsequent disposal which is a part disposal of the asset in question, the amount of any deferred gain or loss shall be apportioned as between the part disposed of and the part retained and the amount of any gain or loss which is deemed to accrue on that part disposal by virtue of paragraph (3) or (4) shall be equal to the amount apportioned to the part disposed of.

(6) Paragraph (7) below applies where a disposal of a matched asset falls within regulation 7(1) and is also part of a transfer to which section 140 of the 1992 Act applies (or would apply disregarding this regulation).

(7) In any case where this paragraph applies, any gain or loss which would (apart from this paragraph) be deemed to accrue to the disposing company at the time of that disposal by virtue of paragraph (6) or (7) of regulation 7 ('the deferred gain or loss') shall not accrue at that time but in computing any chargeable gain or allowable loss accruing as respects the matched asset the amount of the consideration for the transfer of that asset –

   (a) if apart from this paragraph there would have been a deferred gain of any amount under regulation 7(6) or (7), shall be increased by an equal amount;

   (b) if apart from this paragraph there would have been a deferred loss of any amount under regulation 7(6) or (7) shall be reduced by an equal amount;

   and if sub-paragraph (b) applies and the amount of that deferred loss exceeds the amount of the consideration, an allowable loss equal to that excess shall be deemed to accrue as respects the asset on the disposal (in addition to any other loss which may accrue as respects that asset).

9 Transactions to which section 116 or 127 of the 1992 Act applies

(1) This regulation applies where a transaction occurs to which section 127 of the 1992 Act applies, or would apply but for section 116 of that Act and section 116(10) of that Act applies, and as respects which the original shares are or include a matched asset ('the relevant transaction'), and any reference to the original shares and to the new holding shall be construed in accordance with section 126 of that Act.

(2) In any case where this regulation applies there shall be calculated the amount of any chargeable gain or allowable loss which would have been deemed to accrue by virtue of paragraph (6) of regulation 7 if the relevant transaction had been a disposal for the purposes of the 1992 Act as respects which that paragraph applied, and the amount of any such gain or loss is referred to below as the deferred gain or the deferred loss.

(3) If there is a deferred gain, then –

    (a) if section 127 applies, in computing the amount of any chargeable gain or allowable loss accruing on a subsequent disposal of the new holding, the consideration received on that disposal of the new holding shall be increased by an amount equal to the amount of the deferred gain;

    (b) if section 116 applies and the amount of a chargeable gain or allowable loss which would have accrued at the time of that transaction falls to be calculated under section 116(10)(a), the market value of the matched asset shall for the purposes of section 116(10)(a) of the 1992 Act be increased by an amount equal to the amount of the deferred gain.

(4) If there is a deferred loss, then –

    (a) if section 127 applies, in computing the amount of any chargeable gain or allowable loss accruing on a subsequent disposal of the new holding, the consideration received on that disposal of the new holding shall be reduced by an amount equal to the amount of the deferred loss;

    (b) if section 116 applies and the amount of a chargeable gain or allowable loss which would have accrued at the time of that transaction falls to be calculated under section 116(10)(a), the market value of the asset shall for the purposes of section 116(10)(a) of the 1992 Act be reduced by any amount equal to the amount of the deferred loss,

and if the amount of the deferred loss exceeds the amount of that consideration or market value, an allowable loss equal in amount to that excess shall be deemed to accrue as respects the new holding at the time of the subsequent disposal.

(5) In any case where section 127 applies, or would but for section 116 apply, in relation to a transaction involving original shares which are or include an asset as respects which paragraph (2), but not paragraph (3), of regulation 8 has applied, then paragraphs (3) and (4) above shall also apply in relation to that asset and the loss or gain deferred under that regulation.

(6) In any case where there is a disposal of part of the asset in question and paragraphs (1) to (5) above apply to that disposal, the amount of any deferred gain or loss shall be apportioned as between the part disposed of and the part retained and those paragraphs shall apply (with any necessary modifications) separately in relation to the different parts.

10 Elections for matching

(1) Subject to the provisions of these Regulations, an election under this regulation –

    (a) may be made by notice given to the inspector by the company which owes the liability to be matched by the election,

    (b) shall have effect as from the day on which it is made, and

    (c) shall be irrevocable.

(2) An election for matching must identify –

(a) [...]¹

(b) the asset to be matched;

(c) if the liability [to be matched by the election]³ is not being matched with the whole of the asset either –

　　(i) a fixed percentage of the asset which is to be available for matching; or

　　(ii) the value of the whole asset as at the time the election is made and a specific amount which is to be available for matching; or

　　(iii) a proportion or part of the asset which is to be available for matching where the value of the proportion or part is to be determined by reference to a formula or other method of calculation specified in the election and may vary from time to time in accordance with that formula or other method of calculation;

(d) [...]²

(e) the provision of these Regulations by virtue of which the asset is an eligible asset.

(3) An election under paragraph (2)(c)(i) or (ii) above may be varied by a subsequent election under this regulation so as to increase the percentage or amount which is specified in the election.

(4) An election to match a liability with an asset falling within regulation 5(6)(a), (b), (c) or (d) or 5(8), shall not have effect for any accrual period for which an initial exchange gain accrues as respects the liability unless –

(a) any exchange difference arising in relation to the asset, and

(b) at least part of any exchange difference arising in relation to the liability,

are shown, in the company's accounts for the period which is or includes the accrual period in which those differences arise, in the reserves, and if only part of the exchange differences relating to the liability are shown in the reserves, the election shall have effect for that period only to that part.

Where the liability or asset (or both) are matched in part only, references in this paragraph to the liability or asset are to the part matched.

(5) An election shall not cease to have effect at any time by reason only that the liability [matched by]⁴ the election ceased at that time to match the asset to which the election refers either at all or to the same extent to which it matched it at the time the election was made (either by reason of its ceasing to be owed by the company or because it is reduced or its value changes), but where [in any such case at any time after the election is made or, in the case of an election to which regulation 11(2) applies, has effect, the company is subject to another eligible liability]⁵ which might have been [matched by]⁴ the election if the election had been made at that time, the election shall continue to have effect in relation to that other liability.

This paragraph shall apply with the necessary modifications in relation to any such other liability as it applies in relation to the liability originally [matched by][4] the election.

(6) In any case where the asset to which the election refers was original shares as defined by section 126 of the 1992 Act and by reason of a reorganisation (as so defined) the asset ceased at any time to match the liability [matched by][4] the election, then if the whole or any part of the new holding (as so defined) might have been [matched by][4] the election if the election had been made at the time of the reorganisation, the election shall not cease to have effect but shall continue to have effect in relation to the new holding or part as the case may be.

(7) Any question as to which liability is matched with which asset shall be determined on a just and reasonable basis.

---

[1]   Deleted by SI 1996 No 1347 (The Exchange Gains and Losses (Alternative Method of Calculation of Gain or Loss) (Amendment) Regulations 1996), Reg 5 with effect from 30 June 1996. Previously 'the liability to be matched'.

[2]   Deleted by SI 1996 No 1347, Reg 5 with effect as in [1] above. Previously 'the reasons why the company considers that regulation 5(4)(b) or (5) (as the case may be) is satisfied as respects the liability'.

[3]   Inserted by SI 1996 No 1347, Reg 5 with effect as in [1] above.

[4]   Substituted by SI 1996 No 1347, Reg 5 with effect as in [1] above. Previously 'specified in'.

[5]   Substituted by SI 1996 No 1347, Reg 5 with effect as in [1] above. Previously 'the liability ceases to be owed by the company at any time, then if the company owes any other liability'.

---

11   Effectiveness of elections

(1) An election which does not comply with regulation 10(2) shall be of no effect.

(2) Notwithstanding regulation 10(1) above, if an election –

(a) specifies as an eligible asset an asset which the company acquired not more than 92 days before the day on which the election is made, and

(b) specifies the date of acquisition as the date as from which the election is to have effect,

the election shall have effect, so far as it relates to that asset and any liability to be matched with that asset, as from that date.

(3) Notwithstanding regulation 10(1) above, an election under regulation 10(3) may specify a day not more than 92 days earlier than the day on which the election is made as the date as from which the election is to have effect, and in such a case the election shall have effect as from that date.

(4) Notwithstanding regulation 10(1) above, if an election specifies an asset as an eligible asset which the company held on its commencement day and the election is made before the expiry –

(a) of the period of 183 days beginning with 23rd March 1995, or

(b) of the period of 92 days beginning with the company's commencement day,

whichever is the later, and the election specifies the company's commencement day as the date as from which the election is to have effect, the election shall have effect, so far as it relates to that asset and any liability to be matched with that asset, as from that specified day.

(5) Notwithstanding regulation 10(1) above, an election expressed to be made under this paragraph and made –

(a) in pursuance of regulation 6 above in relation to a controlled foreign company as respects which a direction under section 747 of the Taxes Act is given on or after 23rd March 1995 for an accounting period of the company, whenever beginning, (and a direction under that section has not been given with respect to an earlier accounting period of that company [or, where the direction is given on or after 1st April 1996, no earlier accounting period of that company is an ADP exempt period][1]), and

(b) before the expiry of the period of 92 days beginning with the date of that direction,

shall have effect from the latest of the following days, that is to say, the first day of the first accounting period as respects which the direction has effect, the first day of the first accounting period beginning on or after 23rd March 1995, and the day on which the asset in question is acquired by the company.

[(6) In paragraph (5) above 'ADP exempt period' means an accounting period of the company –

(a) which begins on or after 28th November 1995, and

(b) in respect of which the company has pursued, within the meaning of Part I of Schedule 25 to the Taxes Act, an acceptable distribution policy.][1]

---

[1]   Inserted by SI 1996 No 1347 (The Exchange Gains and Losses (Alternative Method of Calculation of Gain or Loss) (Amendment) Regulations 1996), Reg 6 with effect from 30 June 1996.

Transactions not at arm's length

12   Disregard of regulations 2 and 4 to 11

(1) For the purposes of section 136(11) of the 1993 Act –

(a) the question whether an appropriate exchange gain accrues to a company as mentioned in paragraph (d) of that subsection, and

(b) the amount of any such gain,

shall be determined as if regulations 2 and 4 to 11 were not and never had been in force.

(2) For the purposes of section 136A(9) of the 1993 Act –

(a) the question whether an appropriate exchange gain accrues to a company as mentioned in paragraph (d) of that subsection, and

(b) the amount of any such gain,

shall be determined as if regulations 2 and 4 to 11 were not and never had been in force.

The Exchange Gains and Losses (Deferral of Gains and Losses) Regulations 1994 (SI 1994 No 3228)

Made: 15th December 1994
Laid before the House of Commons: 16th December 1994
Coming into force: 23rd March 1995

The Treasury, in exercise of the powers conferred on them by sections 143(7), 164(14) and 167(1) of the Finance Act 1993, hereby make the following Regulations:

1 Citation, commencement and interpretation

(1) These Regulations may be cited as the Exchange Gains and Losses (Deferral of Gains and Losses) Regulations 1994.

(2) These Regulations shall come into force on 23rd March 1995.

(3) In these Regulations, 'the 1993 Act' means the Finance Act 1993 and any reference to a particular section, without more, is a reference to that section of that Act.

2 Settlement and replacement of debts

(1) This regulation applies where –

(a) a debt held or owed by a company ('the original debt') under which a long term capital asset or liability ('the original asset or liability') subsists is settled and replaced to any extent by another debt ('the replacement debt') under which another such asset or liability ('the replacement asset or liability') subsists, and

(b) (apart from this regulation) an exchange gain or loss accrues to the company for an accrual period ('the settlement period') as respects the original asset or liability which (where the debt is not wholly settled) is attributable to that part of the debt by which its nominal amount is decreased:

and in these Regulations 'the replacement debt date' is the date on which that company becomes entitled or subject to the replacement debt.

(2) Subject to paragraph (6) below, in any case where this regulation applies –

(a) if the settlement period is the last accrual period as respects the original asset or liability, subject to paragraph (3) below, any exchange gain or loss which accrued for that period as respects that asset or liability shall be deemed to be unrealised, and any such exchange gain shall be deemed not to accrue as respects that asset or liability for that period;

(b) if the settlement period is not the last accrual period as respects the original asset or liability, subject to paragraph (3) below, any exchange gain which accrued for that period as respects that asset or liability shall be deemed not to accrue as respects that asset or liability for that period;

(c) an amount equal to the amount of any exchange gain falling within sub-paragraph (a) or (b) above shall be deemed to be an exchange gain accruing as respects the replacement asset or liability for its first accrual period and section 143(2) shall not apply in relation to any gain deemed to accrue by this sub-paragraph;

and sections 139 to 143 (apart from section 143(7)) shall have effect accordingly.

(3) Paragraph (2) does not apply –

    (a) in relation to any debt unless it falls within paragraph (10) or (11) below;

    (b) in relation to any debt unless the replacement debt date falls in the period beginning 30 days before the date on which the original debt or part of the original debt was settled and ending 30 days after that date;

    (c) in relation to any debt as the replacement debt as respects another debt if or to the extent that, for the purposes of this regulation and sections 139 to 143, it replaces a third debt.

(4) Where this regulation applies and the amount by which the original debt is settled exceeds the amount of the replacement debt, then the exchange gain referred to in paragraph (1)(b) above shall be apportioned according to the proportion which that excess bears to the amount by which that debt is replaced, and paragraph (2) shall not apply to so much of the exchange gain as corresponds to the excess.

(5) In any case where paragraph (2) above applies and the replacement debt date falls in one accounting period and the settlement of the whole or part of the original debt occurred in a later accounting period, then the reference in paragraph (2)(c) above to the first accrual period for the replacement debt shall be construed as a reference to the accrual period for that debt which falls within that later accounting period.

(6) In any case where paragraph (2) above would (but for this paragraph) apply and the settlement of the original debt occurred in one accounting period and the replacement debt date falls in a later accounting period, then that paragraph shall not apply but –

    (a) if the settlement period is the last accrual period for the asset or liability in question, the exchange gain or loss shall be deemed to be unrealised, and

    (b) for the purposes of making a claim under section 139 as respects the original debt (or so much of it as is replaced) and the earlier accounting period –

        (i) the first accrual period for the replacement debt shall be taken to be the second accrual period for the original debt, and

        (ii) section 143(2) shall not apply; and

    (c) references in section 140(4) to (9) to the asset or liability shall be construed as references to the replacement asset or liability;

and sections 139 to 143 (apart from section 143(7)) shall have effect accordingly.

(7) For the purposes of paragraph (3)(c) above –

(a) if the whole or part of the original debt is settled but there is more than one new debt held or owed by the company which may be taken to be the replacement debt, then the first of those new debts to which the company became entitled or subject shall be taken to replace the original debt and any later debt may only be taken to replace the original debt if and to the extent that the amount replaced of the original debt exceeds the amount of the earlier debt, and

(b) if there is more than one debt which another debt could be taken to replace, that other debt shall be taken to replace the debt which was settled first and shall only be taken to replace the debt settled later if and to the extent that its amount exceeds the amount of the debt settled earlier.

(8) The company may notify the inspector that it wishes one debt to be taken to replace another debt otherwise than in accordance with para- graph (7) above (but subject to paragraph (3)), and if the [notice states]¹ that the first mentioned debt in fact replaced the other debt, paragraph (7) shall not apply and that debt shall be taken to replace the other debt in accordance with the notice.

(9) Where paragraph (6), (7) or (8) above applies all such apportionments of gains shall be made for the purposes of this regulation and sections 139 to 143 as may be just and reasonable.

(10) A debt falls within this paragraph if –

(a) the maximum amount of the principal is specified at the com- mencement of the term of the debt and the principle cannot be increased beyond that maximum amount (except as mentioned in sub-paragraph (c) below), and

(b) any part of the principal once repaid cannot be redrawn, and

(c) any interest which, if not paid when due, is to be capitalised or rolled-up, is to be added to the principal on the due date and repayable on the same terms as the principal.

In determining whether a debt falls within this paragraph there shall be disregarded any term in so far as it provides for the principal or any interest to be calculated by reference to any withholding or other tax (including foreign tax).

(11) A debt falls within this paragraph if –

(a) it is a debt on a deep gain security for the purposes of paragraph 1 of Schedule 11 to the Finance Act 1989 and the amount payable on redemption is payable on one specified date, or

(b) it is a debt on a qualifying indexed security for the purposes of that paragraph, or

(c) it is a debt on a deep discount security for the purposes of paragraph 1 of Schedule 4 to the Income and Corporation Taxes Act 1988;

and for the purposes of this regulation the amount of any such debt on the replacement debt date shall be taken to be equal to its basic valuation.

---

[1] Substituted by SI 1996 No 1348 (The Exchange Gains and Losses (Deferral of Gains and Losses) (Amendment) Regulations 1996), Reg 3 with respect to accounting periods of companies ending on or after 30 June 1996.
Previously 'inspector is (or on appeal the Commissioners are) satisfied'.

---

3   Disregard of certain profits in section 141(3) computation

(1)   This regulation applies in any case where a company's profits for an accounting period which are to be taken into account under section 141(3) of the 1993 Act include any income or chargeable gains which are relevant income or gains for the purposes of section 797 of the Income and Corporation Taxes Act 1988 ('the relevant income or gains').

(2)   Where this regulation applies then, for the purposes of section 141(3), the company's profits for the accounting period shall be reduced by an amount equal to the excess of X over Y where –

X is the amount of the relevant income and gain, and
Y is the amount (if any) found under paragraph (4) below.

(3)   There shall be found the amount which would be the amount of corporation tax attributable to the relevant income or gains under section 797 if Chapter IV of Part X of the 1988 Act had not been enacted, and the excess of that amount over the amount of the credit for foreign tax allowable against the corporation tax in fact attributable to the relevant income or gain determined in accordance with section 797(2) and (3) shall be the net corporation tax attributable to the relevant income or gain.

(4)   There shall be found the gross amount (if any) of income and gains on which an amount of corporation tax equal to that net corporation tax would be charged if the income and gains were chargeable to tax as income and gains of the company for that accounting period at the rate payable by the company (before any credit under Part XVIII of the 1988 Act).

4   Groups of companies

(1)   For the purposes of this regulation companies are members of a group if by virtue of section 170 of the Taxation of Chargeable Gains Tax Act 1992 they are members of a group for the purposes of sections 171 to 181 of that Act.

(2)   This regulation applies to a claim made under section 139 of the 1993 Act as regards an accounting period of the claimant company for the whole or part of which it is a member of a group, and in relation to such a claim subsection (5) of that section shall have effect with the addition at the end of paragraph (c) of the words –

'and if the claim is made by a member of a group (within the meaning of section 141 below) it must contain a statement of that fact'.

(3) In relation to a claim to which this regulation applies, section 141 shall have effect subject to the following modifications.

(4) The following subsections shall be substituted for subsection (1)–

'(1) Subject to subsection (1A) below, where a company ("the claimant company") makes a claim under section 139 above ("the current claim") as regards an accounting period of the claimant company for the whole or part of which it is a member of a group ("the relevant accounting period")–

(a) an amount is available for relief under that section for that accounting period which is equal to the amount (if any) by which amount A is exceeded by the appropriate proportion of the group B amount, or of the group C amount, if it is lower than the group B amount, and

(b) the appropriate proportion is that proportion which amount B3 (as found for the claimant company) bears to amount $\Sigma B3$.

(1A) In any case where there is no group B amount or no group C amount, no amount shall be available for relief under section 139.

(1B) For the purposes of this section a company is a member of a group if by virtue of section 170 of the Taxation of Chargeable Gains Tax Act 1992 it is a member of the group for the purposes of sections 171 to 181 of that Act, and references below to a "group company" and "group", in relation to the claimant company, are references to companies belonging to the same group as that company and to that group.'

(5) After subsection (3) there shall be inserted–

'(3A) In any case where an amount equal to the appropriate proportion found under subsection (1) above for the claimant company is equal to at least half of the amount of that company's profits (within the meaning of subsection (3) above disregarding this subsection), subsection (3) shall have effect as if for the reference to the company's profits there were substituted a reference to the [aggregate of the profits of the claimant company and][1] of those group companies to which subsection (3B) below applies for the relevant accounting period.

(3B) This subsection applies as respects a group company for an accounting period if at any time during that period–

(a) that group company owes the claimant company qualifying debts the amount outstanding under which is equal to at least one-tenth of the total value outstanding of all the qualifying debts owed by that group company; or

(b) the claimant company owes that group company qualifying debts the amount outstanding under which is equal to at least one-tenth of the total value outstanding of all the qualifying debts owed by the claimant company;

and for the purposes of this subsection "qualifying debts" do not include debts due for goods or services supplied to or by the company in the course of its trade.'

(6) The following subsections shall be substituted for subsections (4) and (5)–

'(4) There shall be found for each group company during the relevant accounting period amounts B1 and B2 where–

    (a) B1 is the total amount of–

        (i) unrealised exchange gains which accrue or would (apart from a claim under section 139 above) accrue to the company in an accrual period constituting or falling within the relevant accounting period as regards long-term capital assets or long-term capital liabilities or both,

        (ii) less any such exchange gain in so far as it is attributable to that part of the debt by which its nominal amount is decreased, and

    (b) B2 is the total amount of–

        (i) unrealised exchange losses which accrue to the company in an accrual period constituting or falling within the relevant accounting period as regards long-term capital assets or long-term capital liabilities or both,

        (ii) less any such exchange loss in so far as it is attributable to that part of the debt by which its nominal amount is decreased,

and the excess of B1 over B2 (if any) is called B3, and the excess of B2 over B1 (if any) is called B4.

(4A) There shall be found the aggregate of the B3 amounts for the group, called ΣB3, and the aggregate of the B4 amounts for the group, called ΣB4, and the excess of ΣB3 over ΣB4 (if any) is called the group B amount.

(4B) There shall be found for each group company during the relevant accounting period amounts C1 and C2 where–

    (a) C1 is the total amount of the exchange gains which accrue or would (apart , from a claim under section 139 above) accrue to the company in an accrual period constituting or falling within the relevant accounting period as regards relevant items, and

    (b) C2 is the total amount of the exchange losses which accrue to the company in an accrual period constituting or falling within the relevant accounting period as regards relevant items,

and the excess of C1 over C2 (if any) is called C3, and the excess of C2 over C1 (if any) is called C4.

This subsection is subject to subsection (5) below.

(4C) There shall be found the aggregate of the C3 amounts for the group, called ΣC3, and the aggregate of the C4 amounts for the group, called ΣC4, and the excess of ΣC3 over ΣC4 (if any) is called the group C amount.

(4D) In any case where an accrual period for a company falls partly within and partly outside the relevant accounting period, any exchange gains or losses which accrue or would (apart from a claim under section 139) accrue to the company in that accrual period shall be apportioned according to the respective lengths of that part of the accrual period which falls within the relevant accounting period and the remainder of the accrual period, and the proportion of the exchange gains and losses corresponding to the remainder of that period shall be disregarded for the purposes of this section.

(4E) In any case where a company (including the claimant company) ceases to be or becomes a group company during the relevant accounting period–

(a) references in subsections (1), (3), (3A), (3B), (4) and (4B) above to that accounting period shall as respects that company be construed as references to that part of that period during which the company was a group company, and

(b) the company's profits for that period shall be apportioned according to the respective lengths of that part of the relevant accounting period during which the company was a group company and of the remainder of the accounting period, and

(c) the proportion of the profits corresponding to that remainder shall be disregarded for the purposes of this section;

but if it appears that such an apportionment would produce an unreasonable or unjust result, such other method of apportionment shall be used as appears just and reasonable.

(4F) In any case where the accounting period of a group company other than the claimant company does not coincide with the relevant accounting period–

(a) references in subsections (1), (3), (3A), (3B), (4) and (4B) above to that accounting period shall as respects that group company be construed as references to so much of its accounting period or periods which fall within the relevant accounting period, and

(b) that group company's profits for that period or periods shall be apportioned according to the respective lengths of that part of its accounting period which coincides with the relevant accounting period and the remainder of the accounting period, and

(c) the proportion of the profits corresponding to the remainder of that period or periods shall be disregarded for the purposes of this section.

(4G) In any case where subsection (3) or (3A) above has effect subject to regulation 3 of the Exchange Gains and Losses (Deferral of Gains and Losses) Regulations 1994, subsections (4E) and (4F) above shall each have effect with the addition of a reference to that regulation in paragraph (a).

(5) For the purposes of subsection (4B) above, in computing the amounts C1 and C2 for any group company which is not the claimant company, there shall be disregarded any exchange gain or loss which has accrued (disregarding section 139 above) as regards an asset, liability or contract if, by virtue of subsection (11) of section 128 above, any gain or loss falling within subsection (12) of

that section and accruing to the company as respects that asset, liability or contract would not be taken into account in calculating for the purposes of corporation tax the profits or losses of any period of a trade carried on by the company during the relevant accounting period.'

(7) In subsection (6) for 'subsections (4) and (5) above' there shall be substituted 'this section'.

(8) In subsection (7) for 'subsection (5) above' there shall be substituted 'this section'.

---

[1] Substituted by SI 1996 No 1348 (The Exchange Gains and Losses (Deferral of Gains and Losses) (Amendment) Regulations 1996), Reg 4 with respect to accounting periods of companies ending on or after 30 June 1996.
Previously 'aggregate profits'.

The Exchange Gains and Losses (Excess Gains and Losses) Regulations 1994 (SI 1994 No 3229)

Made: 15th December 1994
Laid before the House of Commons: 16th December 1994
Coming into force: 23rd March 1995

The Treasury, in exercise of the powers conferred on them by sections 148, 164(14) and 167(1) of the Finance Act 1993, hereby make the following Regulations:

1 Citation, commencement and interpretation

(1)   These Regulations may be cited as the Exchange Gains and Losses (Excess Gains and Losses) Regulations 1994.

(2)   These Regulations shall come into force on 23rd March 1995.

(3)   In these Regulations 'the 1993 Act' means the Finance Act 1993.

2 Non-exchange losses and gains

(1)   In any case where as respects an asset or liability –

(a)   an exchange gain has accrued to a qualifying company, and

(b)   a loss which is not an exchange loss ('the non-exchange loss') subsequently accrues to the company –

(i)   at the time the company ceases to be entitled or subject to the asset or liability or to part of the asset or liability, and

(ii)   by virtue of an arm's length transaction, and

(c)   relief from tax is not (apart from this regulation) available under the Tax Acts in respect of the non-exchange loss,

then, on a claim being by the company, an initial exchange loss equal in amount to the excess (if any) of A over B or, if less, the amount of the non-exchange loss shall be treated as accruing to the company as respects that asset or liability for the appropriate accrual period.

(2)   Paragraph (1) above does not apply in relation to any asset or liability as respects which the loss referred to in paragraph (1)(b) accrues to the company if the company acquired the asset or became subject to the liability in pursuance of a transaction which was not an arm's length transaction.

(3)   For the purposes of this regulation the amount of any non-exchange loss shall be reduced by the amount, if any, of any insurance or compensation moneys or other sum to which the company is entitled in respect of the loss which do not fall to be taken into account in computing the company's profits for the purposes of corporation tax.

(4)   In any case where as respects an asset or liability –

(a)   an exchange loss has accrued to a qualifying company, and

(b)   a gain which is not an exchange gain ('the non-exchange gain') subsequently accrues to the company at the time the company ceases to be entitled or subject to the asset or liability or to part of the asset or liability, and

(c) the non-exchange gain is not (apart from this regulation) chargeable to tax under the Tax Acts,

then an initial exchange gain equal in amount to the excess (if any) of B over A or, if less, the amount of the non-exchange gain shall be treated as accruing to the company as respects that asset or liability for the appropriate accrual period.

(5) For the purposes of paragraphs (1) and (4) above –

A is the aggregate amount of any exchange gains which have accrued to the company as respects the asset or liability for all accrual periods since the company's commencement day;

B is the aggregate amount of any exchange losses which have accrued to the company as respects the asset or liability for all accrual periods since the company's commencement day;

'the appropriate accrual period', in relation to any asset or liability –

(i)   if the company ceases to be entitled or subject to part only of the asset or liability, means the accrual period in which it ceases to be so entitled or subject, and

(ii) in any other case, means the last accrual period as respects that asset or liability; and

'an arm's length transaction' is any transaction the terms of which are such as might reasonably be expected to have been agreed between parties at arm's length.

(6) The amount of any exchange gain or exchange loss shall not be taken into account under paragraph (1) or (4) above unless by virtue of section 128(4) or (8) or 129(2) or (4) of the 1993 Act the company has been treated as receiving an amount equal to that amount or incurring a loss equal to that loss.

(7) A claim under paragraph (1) above must be made to the inspector before the expiry of the period of two years beginning with the end of the accounting period in which the non-exchange loss accrued to the company.

3 Cancellation of relief where loss is recovered

(1) Where –

(a) by virtue of regulation 2(1) an initial exchange loss has been treated as accruing to a company ('the loss making company') as respects an asset or liability by reason of a non-exchange loss accruing as respects that asset or liability, and

(b) the whole or part of that non-exchange loss is subsequently recovered by the loss making company, or by another company in the same group, in an accounting period of the loss making company,

an initial exchange gain equal in amount to the amount of the net exchange loss found in accordance with paragraphs (3) and (4) below shall be deemed to accrue to the loss making company.

For the purposes of this paragraph, companies are members of a group if by virtue of section 170 of the Taxation of Chargeable Gains Act 1992 they are members of a group for the purposes of sections 171 to 181 of that Act.

(2) Any initial exchange gain deemed to accrue under paragraph (1) above shall –

(a) if the initial exchange loss referred to above was an exchange loss of a trade or part of a trade and the loss making company carries on that trade or part at the time of the recovery, be deemed to be an exchange gain of that trade or part, and section 128 of the 1993 Act shall apply accordingly,

(b) if sub-paragraph (a) above does not apply, be deemed to be a non-trading exchange gain, and section 129 of the 1993 Act shall apply accordingly,

and in either case the gain shall be deemed to accrue as respects the asset or liability for an accrual period identical to the accounting period in which the time of recovery falls.

(3) For the purposes of paragraph (1) above the net exchange loss shall (subject to paragraph (4) below) be equal to the excess (if any) of A over (B–C) where –

A is the amount of loss recovered, translated into the company's local currency (if it is not in that currency) using the London closing exchange rates for the two currencies for the date of the recovery,

B is the amount of the non-exchange loss referred to in paragraph (1) above, and

C is the amount of the initial exchange loss deemed to accrue to the company by virtue of regulation 2(1).

(4) Where parts of the loss are recovered at different times, then in relation to any recovery after the first –

(a) amount A shall include any amount recovered earlier;

(b) the net exchange loss found in accordance with paragraph (3) above shall be reduced by the amount (or aggregate amount, if more than one) of any initial exchange gain deemed to accrue (under paragraph (1) above) in relation to any earlier recovery.

The Local Currency Elections Regulations 1994 (SI 1994 No 3230)

Made: 15th December 1994
Laid before the House of Commons: 16th December 1994
Coming into force: 23rd March 1995

The Treasury, in exercise of the powers conferred on them by sections 93(1) and (6), 94(1), (2), (3) and (11) and 95(1), (2) and (3) of the Finance Act 1993, hereby make the following Regulations:

1   Citation and commencement

(1)   These Regulations may be cited as the Local Currency Elections Regulations 1994.

(2)   These Regulations shall come into force on 23rd March 1995.

2   Defintions

In these Regulations, except where the context otherwise requires –

'the 1993 Act' means the Finance Act 1993;

'accounts' in relation to a company, means –

(i)   the annual accounts of the company prepared in accordance with Part VII of the Companies Act 1985, or

(ii)   if the company is not required to prepare such accounts, the accounts which it is required to keep under the law of its home State or, if it is not so required to keep accounts, such of its accounts as most closely correspond to accounts which it would have been required to prepare if the provisions of that Part applied to the company;

'commencement day', in relation to any company, means the first day of the company's first accounting period beginning on or after 23rd March 1995;

'local currency' means a currency other than sterling;

'overseas branch' means a branch outside the United Kingdom;

'specified', in relation to an election, means specified in the election; and references to an election are references to an election under regulation 3 or 4.

3   Elections for trades

(1)   Subject to the following provisions of these Regulations, a company carrying on a trade may by notice given to the inspector elect to have the basic profits and losses of the trade computed and expressed for the purposes of corporation tax in a specified local currency.

(2)   A company may not make an election under this regulation for a trade for an accounting period if there is in force an election under regulation 4 for that accounting period and any part of that trade.

Cross references. See European Single Currency (Taxes) Regulations (SI 1998/3177). Reg 43 (an election made under this regulation in relation to the ecu or a currency participating in the euro shall have effect, inter alia, as if it were made in relation to the euro as well as the ecu or participating currency as the case may be).

Notes

(a) The regulation has effect as if para (2) is substituted and a new para (3) inserted in accordance with the European Single Currency (Taxes) Regulations (SI 1998/3177), Reg 45 in relation to local currency elections affected by the euro.

---

4 Elections for part trades

(1) Subject to the following provisions of these Regulations, a company carrying on a trade may by notice given to the inspector elect to have the basic profits and losses of a specified part of the trade computed and expressed for the purposes of corporation tax in a specified local currency.

(2) A company may make an election under this regulation –

(a) for a trade which it carries on, wholly or in part, through one or more overseas branches, or

(b) for a ring fence trade as respects which the condition mentioned in section 94A(2) of the 1993 Act is fulfilled,

but not in relation to any other trade (and accordingly an election under paragraph (1) of this regulation may, subject to these Regulations, be made for a part of the trade which is carried on in the United Kingdom).

(3) An election under this regulation may specify different currencies for different parts of the trade but if the company makes an election for each part of the trade, at least two currencies must be specified.

(4) Where a company makes more than one election for different parts of one trade, paragraph (3) above shall apply cumulatively to the elections.

(5) Where a company carries on part of a trade through two or more branches situated in the same country, an election under paragraph (2)(a) above for that part of the trade must specify the same currency to be used for all those branches, and for the purposes of this paragraph the United Kingdom shall be taken to be one country.

(6) In any case where a company makes an election under this regulation for one or more parts of a trade but not for all the parts of the trade, the basic profits and losses of any part of the trade for which there is no election shall be computed and expressed for the purposes of corporation tax in sterling.

(7) A company may not make an election under this regulation for part of a trade for an accounting period if there is in force an election under regulation 3 for that trade and that accounting period.

Cross references. See European Single Currency (Taxes) Regulations (SI 1998/3177), Reg 43 (an election made under this regulation in relation to the ecu or a currency participating in the euro shall have affect, inter alia, as if it were made in relation to the euro as well as the ecu or participating currency as the case may be).

---

5   Factors affecting determination of local currency

(1)   This regulation applies in relation to any election made by a company for the purpose of determining what currency (if any) may be specified in the election.

(2)   A currency may be specified in an election as a local currency if, but only if –

   (a)   it is the currency of the primary economic environment in which the trade or part of the trade is carried on, and

   (b)   one of the conditions set out in paragraphs (3), (4), (5) and (6) below is satisfied.

(3)   A currency may be specified in any election as a local currency if the accounts are prepared in that currency in accordance with normal accountancy practice.

(4)   A currency may be specified in an election made by a company resident in the United Kingdom as a local currency if the accounts, so far as they relate to the trade or part in question, are prepared from the financial statements relating to the trade or part using the closing rate/net investment method, and those statements are prepared in that currency.

The reference above to the closing rate/net investment method is a reference to that method as described under the title 'Foreign currency translation' in the Statement of Standard Accounting Practice issued in April 1983 by the Institute of Chartered Accountants in England and Wales.

(5)   A currency may be specified in an election made by a company not resident in the United Kingdom as a local currency if it is the currency in which the financial statements relating to that trade or part are prepared in accordance with normal accountancy practice.

(6)   Subject to paragraph (7) below, a currency may be specified as a local currency in any election which is not for a trade or part of a trade carried on in the United Kingdom if –

   (a)   the company making the election was within the charge to corporation tax as respects the trade or part in question immediately before its commencement day, and

   (b)   for accounting periods ending within the two years before that day, the basic profits and losses of the trade or part were computed and expressed for corporation tax purposes in that currency.

(7)   An election made by virtue of paragraph (6) above shall be of no effect unless it is made before the expiry of the period of 92 days beginning with the company's commencement day.

Notes

(a)   This regulation has effect as if para (2) is amended in accordance with the European Single Currency (Taxes) Regulations (SI 1998/3177, Reg 42) in relation to local currency elections affected by the introduction of the euro.

6 Factors relevant to the determination of the primary economic environment

In determining whether a currency is the currency of the primary economic environment in which a trade or any part of a trade is carried on, regard shall be had to all relevant circumstances including in particular (in so far as they may be relevant) the following factors, that is to say –

(a) the currency in which the net cash flows of the trade or part are generated or expressed in the relevant accounting records;

(b) the currency in which the company manages the profitability of the trade or part so far as it is affected by currency exposure;

(c) in the case of a company which is resident in the United Kingdom, the currency in which the company's share capital and its reserves are denominated;

(d) the currency to which the company, or, where the trade or part is carried on through a branch, that branch, is exposed in its long term capital borrowing (of any kind whatsoever);

(e) the currency which is the generally recognised currency in which trading in the principal market of the trade or part is carried on.

Notes

(a) This regulation has effect as if the words 'for the purpose of regulation 5(2)(a)' were inserted after the words 'In determining' in relation to local currency elections affected by the introduction of the euro; see the European Single Currency (Taxes) Regulations (SI 1998/3177, Reg 42).

7 Provisions supplementary to regulations 4, 5 and 6

(1) Where the election specifies more than one currency for parts of a trade, regulations 4, 5 and 6 shall apply separately in relation to each currency and each part of the trade.

(2) In regulations 4, 5 and 6, except where the context otherwise requires –

(a) any reference to accounts, in relation to an election, is a reference to the accounts of the company making the election for the accounting period for which the election is to have effect; and

(b) any reference to relevant accounting records, in relation to an election, is a reference to the accounting records, relating to the trade or that part of a trade to which the election refers, for the accounting period for which the election is to have effect.

8 Determination of rate of exchange

(1) A company may in an election for a trade or part of a trade state that for accounting periods for which the election has effect an average arm's length exchange rate will be used in translating the basic profits or losses of the trade or part into sterling for the purposes of section 93(4) or 94(8) of the 1993 Act (as the case may be).

(2) In paragraph (1) above –

'arm's length exchange rate' means such exchange rate as might reasonably be expected to be agreed between persons dealing at arm's length; and 'average arm's length exchange rate' means the rate which represents the average of the arm's length exchange rates for all the days in the accounting period in question.

(3) Subject to paragraph (4) below, where an election contains a statement in accordance with paragraph (1) above, the average arm's length exchange rate shall be used in translating the basic profits or losses of the trade or part into sterling for the purposes of section 93(4) or 94(8) of the 1993 Act (as the case may be) for all accounting periods for which the election has effect.

(4) The company may by notice given to the inspector terminate the statement referred to above with effect from the first day of the first accounting period beginning on or after the date of the notice.

Notes

(a) This regulation has effect in accordance with the modifications made by the European Single Currency (Taxes) Regulations (SI 1998/3177) Reg 46 in relation to local currency elections affected by the introduction of the euro.

9 Periods for which elections have effect

(1) Subject to the following provisions of these Regulations, an election for a trade or part of a trade shall have effect as respects that trade or part for all accounting periods beginning on or after the date on which the election is made.

(2) Subject to the following provisions of these Regulations, an election for a trade or part of a trade made by a company which, as respects that trade or part, is within the charge to corporation tax immediately before its commencement day shall have effect as respects that trade or part of all accounting periods beginning on or after that day if the election is made before the end of the period of 92 days beginning with that day.

(3) Subject to the following provisions of these Regulations, an election for a trade or part of a trade made by a company which, as respects that trade or part, is not within the charge to corporation tax immediately before its commencement day shall have effect as respects that trade or part for all accounting periods beginning on or after the first day on which it comes within that charge as respects that trade or part if the election is made before the end of the period of 92 days beginning with that first day.

Notes

(a) This regulation has effect in accordance with the modifications made by the European Single Currency (Taxes) Regulations (SI 1998/3177) Reg 47 in relation to local currency elections affected by the introduction of the euro.

10 Information to be submitted with elections and effectiveness of elections

(1) An election by a company for a trade or part of a trade shall include –

(a) a statement of the reasons why the company believes that such of the requirements of these Regulations as are applicable to the election will be met as respects that trade or part for the first accounting period of the company for which the election is to have effect; and

(b) particulars of the nature of the trade or part and the place where it is carried on.

(2) An election which does not comply with paragraph (1) above and regulation 5(7) (if applicable) shall be of no effect.

(3) Without prejudice to paragraphs (1) and (2) above, an election made by a company for a trade or part of a trade shall be of no effect if the requirements of regulation 5 (so far as they are applicable to the election) are not complied with as respects that trade or part for the first accounting period of the company for which the election is intended to have effect.

(4) If at any time in an accounting period of the company, the currency specified in an election made by the company ceases to be eligible to be specified in an election as the local currency of the trade or part, the election shall cease to have effect at the end of that accounting period.

(5) In any case where an election has ceased to have effect by virtue of paragraph (4) above, the company shall notify the inspector in writing of that fact as soon as is reasonably practicable after becoming aware of it.

(6) In a case where paragraph (4) above applies the inspector may notify the company in writing that by virtue of that paragraph the election is no longer effective.

The Exchange Gains and Losses (Insurance Companies) Regulations 1994 (SI 1994 No 3231)

Made: 15th December 1994
Laid before the House of Commons: 16th December 1994
Coming into force: 23rd March 1995

The Treasury, in exercise of the powers conferred on them by sections 167(1) and 168(2) to (5) of the Finance Act 1993, hereby make the following Regulations:

1 (1) These Regulations may be cited as the Exchange Gains and Losses (Insurance Companies) Regulations 1994.

(2) These Regulations shall come into force on 23rd March 1995.

(3) [In these Regulations unless the context otherwise requires–

'basic valuation' shall be construed in accordance with section 159(1) of the 1993 Act;

'loan relationship' shall be construed in accordance with the Corporation Tax Acts, except that a relationship shall not be a loan relationship where the profits or gains chargeable to tax under Case III of Schedule D which arise from the relationship are confined to interest;

'new holding' and 'original shares' have the meanings given by section 126(1) of the 1992 Act;

'regulation 7 asset' shall be construed in accordance with regulation 7(1);

'the Taxes Act' means the Income and Corporation Taxes Act 1988;

'the 1992 Act' means the Taxation of Chargeable Gains Act 1992;

'the 1993 Act' means the Finance Act 1993.]¹

---

¹ Substituted by SI 1996 No 673 (The Exchange Gains and Losses (Insurance Companies) (Amendment) Regulations 1996), Reg 3 with effect from 31 March 1996. Previously 'In these Regulations "the 1993 Act" means the Finance Act 1993'.

---

2 (1) For corporation tax purposes, Chapter II of Part II of the 1993 Act (and regulations made under that Chapter including the following provisions of these Regulations) shall apply –

(a) in relation to insurance companies' unearned premium reserves as if –

(i) the unearned premium reserve of any insurance company were a liability owed by the company, and

(ii) the reference in paragraph (b) of section 153(2) of that Act to provision made by the company in respect of a duty to which it may become subject and which (if it were to become subject to it) would be a duty to settle under qualifying liability included the unearned premium reserve (disregarding section 153(7)(a)); and

(b) as if any item (not being a provision apart from this subparagraph) –

    (i) which is included in any accounts for any period prepared by the company for tax purposes, and

    (ii) which, if it were included in the company's statutory accounts for the same period, would be a provision within section 153(2)(b),

were a provision within section 153(2)(b).

(2) In paragraph (1)(b) above 'statutory accounts', in relation to a company, means –

    (a) the annual accounts of the company prepared in accordance with Part VII of the Companies Act 1985, or

    (b) if the company is not required to prepare such accounts, the accounts which it is required to keep under the law of its home State or, if it is not so required to keep accounts, such of its accounts as most closely correspond to accounts which it would have been required to prepare if the provisions of that Part applied to the company.

3 Any exchange difference which arises as regards a qualifying asset which is a share held by a qualifying company which is an insurance company shall be disregarded for the purposes of Chapter II of Part II of the 1993 Act (including regulations made under that Chapter), and accordingly –

    (a) an exchange gain or loss which (apart from this regulation) would accrue as regards that asset shall be taken not to accrue for the purposes of that Chapter; and

    (b) section 128(11) of that Act shall not apply in relation to any gain or loss which accrues as regards that asset.

4 (1) Paragraph (2) below shall apply where –

    (a) a gain or loss accrues to an insurance company as regards an asset or liability at any time when the asset or liability is held or owed by the company wholly or partly in exempt circumstances (within the meaning of paragraph 2 of Schedule 15 to the 1993 Act), and

    (b) apart from paragraph (2) below, that gain or loss would fall within section 128(11) of that Act, and

    (c) by virtue of paragraph 1 of that Schedule and regulation 2 of the Exchange Gains and Losses (Alternative Method of Calculation of Gains and Losses) Regulations 1994 the amount of an initial exchange gain or loss accruing to the company as regards the asset or liability for the accrual period which includes or ends immediately before that time is to be found in accordance with the alternative method of calculation.

(2) In any case where this paragraph applies –

    (a) if by virtue of regulation 2 of those Regulations the amount of the initial exchange gain or loss referred to in paragraph (1)(c) above is reduced to zero, then section 128(11) of the 1993 Act shall not apply in relation to the gain or loss referred to in paragraph (1)(a) above;

(b) if by virtue of regulation 2 of those Regulations the amount of that initial exchange gain or loss is reduced by a proportion so that it is less than it would have been if that regulation had not applied, then section 128(11) of the 1993 Act shall not apply in relation to a corresponding proportion of the gain or loss referred to in paragraph (1)(a) above.

[5A (1) In any case where, immediately before 1st April 1996, an insurance company holds an asset in exempt circumstances, the definition of 'relevant qualifying asset' in paragraph 5(8) of Schedule 15 to the Finance Act 1996 shall be modified so as to except from that definition, in relation to an insurance company, an asset held in exempt circumstances immediately before 1st April 1996.

(2) References in paragraph (1) above to exempt circumstances shall be construed in accordance with paragraph 3 of Schedule 17 to the 1993 Act, but as if references in that paragraph to a currency were references to an asset.][1]

---

[1]   Inserted by SI 1996 No 1485 (The Exchange Gains and Losses (Insurance Companies) (Amendment No 2) Regulations), Reg 3 in relation to accounting periods ending on or after 30 June 1996.

---

6   […][1]

---

[1]   Revoked by SI 1996 No 673 (The Exchange Gains and Losses (Insurance Companies) (Amendment) Regulations 1996), Reg 5 in relation to accounting periods ending after 31 March 1996. Previously

(1) Relief under subsection (4) or (7) of section 131 of the 1993 Act, so far as those subsections have effect in relation to losses other than losses treated as non-trading losses for the purposes of section 160 of the Finance Act 1994, shall not be allowable against the policy holders' share of the relevant profits for any accounting period.

(2) In this regulation 'the policy holders' share of the relevant profits' has the same meaning as in section 88 of the Finance Act 1989.

[7 (1) An asset specified by this regulation is an asset to which regulations 8 to 12 apply; and any such asset is referred to in those regulations as a 'regulation 7 asset'.

(2) An asset is specified by this regulation if it is an asset which, at the time of its disposal–

(a) represents a loan relationship of a company;

(b) is an asset to which paragraph (3), (4), (5) or (6) below applies; and

(c) is held in exempt circumstances.

(3) This paragraph applies to an asset if–

(a) the settlement currency of the debt to which it relates is a currency other than sterling; and

(b) that debt is not a debt on a security.

(4) This paragraph applies to an asset if the debt to which it relates is a debt on a security and is in a foreign currency.

(5) This paragraph applies to an asset if it is comprised in a relevant holding and is denominated in a currency other than sterling.

(6) This paragraph applies to an asset if–

(a) it is a qualifying corporate bond,

(b) it would not, apart from this paragraph, be a regulation 7 asset,

(c) it constitutes a new holding, and

(d) the original shares, in relation to the new holding, consisted of a regulation 7 asset by virtue of paragraph (3), (4) or (5) above.

(7) For the purposes of paragraph (4) above a debt is a debt in a foreign currency if it is–

(a) a debt expressed in a currency other than sterling;

(b) a debt the amount of which in sterling falls at any time to be determined by reference to the value at that time of a currency other than sterling; or

(c) subject to paragraph (8) below, a debt as respects which provision is made for its conversion into, or redemption in, a currency other than sterling.

(8) A debt is not a debt in a foreign currency for the purposes of paragraph (4) above by reason only that provision is made for its redemption on payment of an amount in a currency other than sterling equal, at the rate prevailing at the date of redemption, to a specified amount in sterling.

(9) For the purposes of paragraph (5) above an asset is comprised in a relevant holding if it consists of–

(a) a unit in a unit trust scheme, or

(b) a relevant interest in an offshore fund [, or

(c) a share in an open-ended investment company]²

to which section 212 of the 1992 Act does not apply or would not apply if the asset were an asset of the company's long term business fund.

(10) For the purposes of paragraph (5) above–

(a) a unit in a unit trust scheme, or

(b) a right (other than a share in a company) which constitutes a relevant interest in an offshore fund,

shall be taken to be denominated in a currency other than sterling if the price at which it may be acquired from, or disposed of to, persons concerned in the management of the trust or fund is fixed by those persons in a currency other than sterling.

(11) For the purposes of paragraph (5) above shares constituting a relevant interest in an offshore fund shall be taken to be denominated in a currency other than sterling if their nominal value is expressed in such a currency. [and shares of a given class in an open-ended investment company shall be taken to be denominated in a currency other than sterling if the price at which they may be acquired from, or disposed of to, the company or its authorised corporate director is fixed by the company or director in a currency other than sterling, or (as the case may be) the price or prices at which they are quoted in The Stock Exchange Daily Official List is in a currency other than sterling.]²

(12) The reference in paragraph (2) (c) above to exempt circumstances shall be construed in accordance with paragraph 3 of Schedule 17 to the 1993

Act, but as if references in that paragraph to a currency were references to the debt to which the relationship relates.

(13)   In this regulation–

'debt on a security' shall be construed in accordance with section 132 of the 1992 Act;

'long term business fund' has the meaning given by section 431 (2) of the Taxes Act;

['open-ended investment company' and 'authorised corporate director' in relation to such a company have the meanings given by subsection (10) of section 468 of the Taxes Act, read with subsections (11) to (18) of that section, as those subsections are added in relation to open-ended investment companies by regulation 10(4) of the Open-ended Investment Companies (Tax) Regulations 1997; and accordingly references in subsections (11) to (16) of that section to 'the Tax Acts' shall be construed as if they included references to these Regulations;][2]

'qualifying corporate bond' has the same meaning as in the 1992 Act;

'relevant interest in an offshore fund' has the meaning given by section 212 (5) of the 1992 Act;

'security' includes a debenture that is deemed to be a security for the purposes of section 251 of the 1992 Act by virtue of subsection (6) of that section;

'unit trust scheme' shall be construed in accordance with section 99 of the 1992 Act.][1]

---

[1]   Inserted by SI 1996 No 673 (The Exchange Gains and Losses (Insurance Companies) (Amendment) Regulations 1996), Reg 4 in relation to disposals taking place on or after 1 April 1996.

[2]   Inserted by SI 1997 No 1155 (Exchange Gains and Losses (Insurance Companies) (Amendment) Regulations 1997), Regs 3–5 with effect from 28 April 1997.

[8   (1)   The amount of the chargeable gain accruing on the disposal of a regulation 7 asset shall, subject to paragraphs (5) and (6) below and to [regulations 8A to 12][2], be computed by ascertaining the amount specified in paragraph (3) below ('the first amount') and the amount specified in paragraph (4) below ('the second amount').

(2)   Where the second amount exceeds the first amount the excess shall be a chargeable gain; where the first amount exceeds the second amount the excess shall be an allowable loss; and where the first amount and the second amount are equal there shall be neither a chargeable gain nor an allowable loss.

(3)   The first amount is the basic valuation of the asset translated into sterling at the time immediately after the company becomes entitled to the asset.

(4)   The second amount is the basic valuation of the asset translated into sterling at the time immediately before the company ceases to be entitled to the asset.

(5)   Where any profit on the sale of a regulation 7 asset would be treated wholly as a receipt falling to be brought into account in computing profits or gains charged under Case I of Schedule D, neither a chargeable gain nor an allowable loss shall be treated as arising.

(6) Where any profit on the sale of a regulation 7 asset would be treated partly as a receipt falling to be brought into account in computing profits or gains charged under Case I of Schedule D, any chargeable gain or allowable loss accruing by virtue of this regulation shall be reduced on a just and reasonable basis.

(7) Any translation into sterling required by this regulation shall be made by reference to the London closing rate.

(8) The provisions of Chapters III and IV of Part II of the 1992 Act shall not apply to any computation required by this regulation.

(9) All regulation 7 assets which are the subject of the computation required by this regulation shall be treated as relevant securities within the meaning given by subsection (1) of section 108 of the 1992 Act; and that section shall apply accordingly.

(10) Nothing in this regulation shall be taken as preventing any gain or loss which is deemed to accrue by virtue of section 116(10)(b) of the 1992 Act from being brought into charge to tax.]¹

---

¹   Inserted by SI 1996 No 673 (The Exchange Gains and Losses (Insurance Companies) (Amendment) Regulations 1996), Reg 4 in relation to disposals taking place on or after 1 April 1996.

²   Substituted by SI 1996 No 1485 (The Exchange Gains and Losses (Insurance Companies) (Amendment No 2) Regulations 1996), Reg 4 with effect from 30 June 1996. Previously 'regulations 9 to 12'.

[8A (1) An insurance company may elect that the enactments specified in paragraph (2) below shall not apply on the disposal of regulation 7 assets, and that, in its application to the loan relationships represented by those assets, Chapter II of Part IV of the Finance Act 1996 shall apply with the modification that paragraph 4 of Schedule 9 to that Act shall be omitted.

(2) The enactments specified in this paragraph are regulation 8 and sections 117A and 117B of the 1992 Act.

(3) An election under this regulation —

(a) shall have effect in relation to all regulation 7 assets (whether held on 1st April 1996 or acquired subsequently),

(b) shall be made by notice in writing given to an officer of the Board, either by 30th September 1996 or within three months of the end of the accounting period of the company in which it acquired a regulation 7 asset for the first time, whichever is the later, and

(c) shall be irrevocable.]¹

---

¹   Inserted by SI 1996 No 1485 (The Exchange Gains and Losses (Insurance Companies) (Amendment No 2) Regulations 1996), Reg 5 with effect from 30 June 1996.

[9 (1) This regulation applies in any case where –

(a) an insurance company has acquired a regulation 7 asset, and

(b) the asset was held by the company immediately before 1st April 1996.

(2) Regulation 8 shall apply on the disposal of the asset with the modification that the first amount shall be the basic valuation of the asset translated into sterling by reference to the London closing rate on 1st April 1996.]¹

¹   Inserted by SI 1996 No 673 (The Exchange Gains and Losses (Insurance Companies) (Amendment) Regulations 1996), Reg 4 in relation to disposals taking place on or after 1 April 1996.

[10 (1) This regulation applies in any case where, for the purposes of sections 126 to 131 of the 1992 Act–

(a) a regulation 7 asset constitutes the original shares, and

(b) another regulation 7 asset constitutes the new holding.

(2) Regulation 8 shall apply on the disposal of the new holding with the modifications specified in paragraphs (3) and (4) below.

(3) The modification specified in this paragraph is that the first amount shall be the aggregate of–

(a) the basic valuation of the original shares translated into sterling at the time immediately after the company became entitled to the original shares, and

(b) the basic valuation of the new holding translated into sterling at the time immediately after the company became entitled to the new holding.

(4) The modification specified in this paragraph is that the second amount shall be the aggregate of–

(a) the basic valuation of the original shares translated into sterling at the time immediately before the company became entitled to the new holding, and

(b) the basic valuation of the new holding translated into sterling at the time immediately before the company ceased to be entitled to the new holding.]¹

¹   Inserted by SI 1996 No 673 (The Exchange Gains and Losses (Insurance Companies) (Amendment) Regulations 1996), Reg 4 in relation to disposals taking place on or after 1 April 1996.

[11 (1) This regulation applies in any case where–

(a) an asset is a regulation 7 asset by virtue of paragraph (5) of that regulation, and

(b) the asset has at any time after 31st March 1996 and during the company's period of ownership been an asset which did not represent a loan relationship.

(2) Regulation 8 shall apply on the disposal of the asset with the modification that the first amount shall be the basic valuation of the asset translated into sterling at the beginning of the accounting period in which the asset first became a regulation 7 asset by virtue of paragraph (5) of that regulation.]¹

¹   Inserted by SI 1996 No 673 (The Exchange Gains and Losses (Insurance Companies) (Amendment) Regulations 1996), Reg 4 in relation to disposals taking place on or after 1 April 1996.

[12 (1) This regulation applies in any case where an asset is a regulation 7 asset by virtue of paragraph (6) of that regulation.

(2) Regulation 8 shall apply on the disposal of the asset with the modifications that–

(a) the first amount shall be the basic valuation of the original shares in relation to the asset translated into sterling at the time immediately after the company became entitled to the original shares, and

(b) the second amount shall be the basic valuation of the original shares in relation to the asset translated into sterling at the time immediately before the company ceased to be entitled to the original shares.]¹

---

¹   Inserted by SI 1996 No 673 (The Exchange Gains and Losses (Insurance Companies) (Amendment) Regulations 1996), Reg 4 in relation to disposals taking place on or after 1 April 1996.

The European Single Currency (Taxes) Regulations 1998 (SI 1998 No 3177)

Made: 17th December 1998
Laid before the House of Commons: 17th December 1998
Coming into force: 1st January 1999

ARRANGEMENT OF REGULATIONS

Part VI Repurchases and Stock Lending – Stamp Duty and Stamp Duty Reserve Tax

Part VII Accrued Income Scheme

Part VIII Chargeable Gains

Part IX Controlled Foreign Companies

Part X Amendments to the Local Currency Elections Regulations

The Treasury, in exercise of the powers conferred on them by sections 93(1) and (6), 94(1), (2), (3) and (11) and 95 (1), (2) and (3) of the Finance Act 1993 and section 163 of the Finance Act 1998, hereby make the following Regulations:

PART I INTRODUCTORY

1   Citation and commencement

These Regulations may be cited as the European Single Currency (Taxes) Regulations 1998 and shall come into force on 1st January 1999.

2   Interpretation

(1)   In these Regulations unless the context otherwise requires –

'commodity or financial futures' has the meaning given by subsection (2)(a) of section 143 of the 1992 Act, and references in these Regulations to commodity or financial futures include references to a commodity or financial futures contract referred to in subsection (7)(a) or (b);

'debt', other than a debt on a security, includes a debt owed by a bank which is not in sterling and which is represented by a sum standing to the credit of a person in an account in the bank;

'derivative' means any commodity or financial futures or an option;

'ecu' shall be construed in accordance with section 95(5) of the Finance Act 1993;

'euro' means the single currency adopted or proposed to be adopted as its currency by a member State in accordance with the Treaty establishing the European Community;

'euroconversion' has the meaning given by regulation 3;

'long-term capital asset' and 'long-term capital liability' have the meaning given in relation to both those expressions by section 143(4) of the Finance Act 1993;

'member State' means a member State other than the United Kingdom;

'participating member State' means a member State that adopts the euro as its currency;

'qualifying contract' shall be construed in accordance with sections 147, 147A and 148 of the Finance Act 1994;

'reconventioning' in relation to a relevant asset means a change, consequent on simple redenomination, in the terms of the asset as a result of which the new terms become aligned to the prevailing terms of equivalent marketable relevant assets denominated in euro;

'relevant asset' means a debt (whether or not a debt on a security), a long-term capital asset, a long-term capital liability, an option, a qualifying contract, or any commodity or financial futures;

'renominalisation' in relation to a relevant asset means a change, consequent on simple redenomination, in the minimum nominal amount in which the asset can be held or traded to a new round amount;

'security' has the meaning given by section 132(3)(b) of the 1992 Act;

'simple redenomination' means the conversion of the currency in which an asset, liability, contract or instrument is expressed from the currency of a participating member State into euro, and any rounding of the resulting amount to the nearest euro cent;

'the Taxes Act' means the Income and Corporation Taxes Act 1988;

'the 1992 Act' means the Taxation of Chargeable Gains Act 1992.

(2) In these Regulations references to an option, without more, are references to an option to which section 144 or 144A of the 1992 Act applies.

3 Definition of euroconversion

(1) 'Euroconversion' means

    (a) in relation to any currency, or an amount expressed in any currency, of a participating member State, the conversion or restating of that currency or that amount into euro and any rounding of the resulting amount within a euro;

    (b) in relation to any asset, liability, contract or instrument

        (i) the simple redenomination of that asset, liability, contract or instrument, or

        (ii) in the case of a relevant asset, the simple redenomination of that asset accompanied by either or both of renominalisation and reconventioning, or

        (iii) the substitution (whether by way of exchange, conversion, replacement or otherwise) for the asset, liability, contract or instrument of an equivalent replacement asset, liability, contract or instrument.

(2) An equivalent replacement asset, liability, contract or instrument means an asset, liability, contract or instrument whose amount, terms and conditions are identical to what it is reasonable to assume would be the amount, terms and conditions of the original asset, liability, contract or instrument were it to undergo a simple redenomination, or (in the case of a relevant asset) a simple redenomination accompanied by either or both of renominalisation and reconventioning.

(3) For the purposes of paragraphs (1) and (2) a simple redenomination is accompanied (in the case of a relevant asset) by renominalisation or reconventioning if either –

    (a) the renominalisation or reconventioning is effected simultaneously, or

    (b) it is effected within a period of time following the simple redenomination which is such as to enable it reasonably to be inferred that the renominalisation or reconventioning is associated with the simple redenomination.

PART II DEDUCTIBILITY OF COSTS OF EUROCONVERSION OF SHARES AND OTHER SECURITIES

4 Interpretation

References in this Part of these Regulations to a euroconversion in relation to shares and other securities of a company ('the original shares and other securities') are references to a euroconversion that is effected solely by the issue of shares and other securities in replacement of the original shares and other securities.

5 Trading companies

Costs incurred in respect of a euroconversion of its shares or other securities by a company carrying on a trade shall be deductible in computing the amount of its profits chargeable to corporation tax under Case I of Schedule D as if those costs constituted money wholly and exclusively laid out or expended for the purposes of the trade within section 74(1)(a) of the Taxes Act.

6 Investment companies and insurance companies – deemed expenses of management

(1) Costs which –

    (a) are incurred by an investment company or a company carrying on life assurance business in respect of a euroconversion of its shares or other securities, and

    (b) except where the costs are referable to life assurance business of a company whose profits in relation to that business are charged to tax otherwise than under Case I of Schedule D, are not deductible under regulation 5,

shall be treated as sums disbursed as expenses of management to which section 75(1) of the Taxes Act (deduction in computing total profits of an investment company for an accounting period) applies.

(2) Costs incurred by a company carrying on life assurance business in respect of a euroconversion of its shares or other securities shall be deductible in computing the profits of that company chargeable to corporation tax under Case VI of Schedule D as if those costs were allowances falling to be made under Part II of the Capital Allowance Act 1990 and referred to in subsection (4) of section 434D of the Taxes Act; and accordingly those costs shall be apportioned in accordance with that subsection between the different classes of life assurance business carried on by that company.

(3) Section 76 of the Taxes Act (expenses of management: insurance companies) shall have effect as if the reference in subsection (1)(d) of that section (disallowance of certain expenses as expenses of management) to expenses referable to different classes of life assurance business included a reference to costs apportioned to those classes of business under paragraph (2).

(4) In this regulation –

'investment company' has the meaning given by section 130 of the Taxes Act;

'life assurance business' shall be construed in accordance with section 431(2) of the Taxes Act.

PART III EXCHANGE GAINS AND LOSSES, INTEREST RATE AND CURRENCY CONTRACTS AND OPTIONS, DEBT CONTRACTS AND OPTIONS, AND RELEVANT DISCOUNTED SECURITIES

7 Deferral of unrealised gains

(1) Where, as a result of a euroconversion of a long-term capital asset or of a long-term capital liability, that asset ('the original long-term capital

asset') or that liability ('the original long-term capital liability') is replaced by a new long-term capital asset or a new long-term capital liability –

(a) the new long-term capital asset or the new long-term capital liability shall be treated as if it were the same asset or liability as the original long-term capital asset or the original long-term capital liability, acquired when the original long-term capital asset or the original long-term capital liability was acquired; and

(b) any gain which accrued as respects the original long-term capital asset or the original long-term capital liability for the accrual period in which the euroconversion of that asset or liability took place shall, without prejudice to regulation 2 of the Exchange Gains and Losses (Deferral of Gains and Losses) Regulations 1994 (settlement and replacement of debts), be deemed to be un-realised, and sections 139 to 143 (apart from section 143(7)) of the Finance Act 1993 shall have effect accordingly.

(2) In paragraph (1) 'accrual period' shall be construed in accordance with section 158(4) of the Finance Act 1993.

8 Interest rate contracts (including options) change in rate of interest

Where, as a result of the adoption of the euro by a member State –

(a) there is a change in the variable rate of interest resulting in a change in the variable rate payment specified in a contract ('the original contract') in accordance with subsection (2) of section 149 of the Finance Act 1994, and

(b) the change in the variable rate payment is such as to result in the rescission of the original contract and the making of a new contract,

the new contract shall be treated for the purposes of that section as if it were the same contract as the original contract, made when the original contract was made.

9 Currency contracts (including options) – change in rate of interest

Where, as a result of the adoption of the euro by a member State

(a) there is a change in the rate of interest specified in a currency contract ('the original contract') in accordance with subsection (3) of section 150 of the Finance Act 1994, and

(b) the change is such as to result in the rescission of the original contract and the making of a new contract,

the new contract shall be treated for the purposes of that section as if it were the same contract as the original contract, made when the original contract was made.

10 Currency contracts (including options) conversion into euro

(1) This regulation applies in a case where, as a result of the adoption of the euro by member States –

(a) the amounts of both the currencies specified in a currency contract referred to in section 126 of the Finance Act 1993 ('section 126'), or in a currency contract referred to in section 150 of the Finance Act 1994 ('section 150'), are converted into euro, and

(b) the effect is that the currency contract ('the original currency contract') is rescinded and replaced by a new contract which, but for the adoption of the euro, would have been a currency contract.

(2) This regulation also applies in a case where –

(a) one of the currencies ('the former currency') specified in a currency contract referred to in section 126 or section 150 is in a currency other than euro and the other currency is either in euro or expressed to be in the single currency,

(b) as a result of the adoption of the euro by a member State, the former currency is converted into euro, and

(c) the effect is that the currency contract ('the original currency contract') is rescinded and replaced by a new contract which, but for the adoption of the euro, would have been a currency contract.

(3) In each of the cases referred to in paragraphs (1) and (2) the new contract shall be treated for the purposes of section 126 or, as the case may be, section 150 as if it were a currency contract and were the same contract as the original currency contract, made when the original currency contract was made.

11 Debt contracts (including options) – conversion into euro

(1) Where as a result of the adoption of the euro by a member State –

(a) there is a euroconversion of the loan relationship to which, under a debt contract, a qualifying company has any entitlement, or is subject to any duty, to become a party, or

(b) a qualifying company has any entitlement, or is subject to any duty, to become treated as a person with rights and liabilities corresponding to those of a party to a loan relationship and there is a euroconversion of any of those rights and liabilities, and

(c) in either of the cases referred to in sub-paragraphs (a) and (b) the effect is that the original debt contract is rescinded and replaced by a new debt contract,

the new debt contract shall be treated for the purposes of section 150A of the Finance Act 1994 (debt contracts and options) as if it were the same contract as the original debt contract, made when the original debt contract was made.

(2) In paragraph (1) –

'debt contract' has the meaning given by section 150A(1) and (2) of the Finance Act 1994;

'loan relationship' has the meaning given by section 81 of the Finance Act 1996, read with section 150A(10) of the Finance Act 1994;

'qualifying company' shall be construed in accordance with section 154 of the Finance Act 1994.

12 Exchange or conversion of relevant discounted securities

(1) A euroconversion of relevant discounted securities that is effected solely by means of an exchange or conversion of those securities shall be treated as not constituting either –

    (a) a transfer of those securities within the meaning of paragraph 4 of Schedule 13 to the Finance Act 1996 ('Schedule 13'), or

    (b) a conversion of those securities for the purposes of paragraph 5 of Schedule 13.

(2) The relevant discounted securities ('the new securities') resulting from the exchange or conversion referred to in paragraph (1) shall be deemed for the purposes of Schedule 13 to have been acquired for the amount resulting from the formula –

$$A - B$$

where

A is the amount equal to the acquisition cost of the relevant discounted securities replaced by the new securities, and

B is the amount of any cash payment received by a person in respect of the euroconversion, to the extent that that amount does not exceed A.

(3) Where a cash payment is received by a person in respect of relevant discounted securities as a result of a euroconversion of those securities which –

    (a) involves a simple redenomination of those securities, accompanied by either or both of renominalisation and reconventioning as a consequence of that simple redenomination, and

    (b) is effected otherwise than by means of –

        (i) a transfer of those securities, or

        (ii) an exchange or conversion of those securities,

    those securities shall be deemed for the purposes of Schedule 13 to have been acquired for the amount resulting from the formula–

$$C - D$$

where –

C is the amount equal to the acquisition cost of the relevant discounted securities, and

D is the amount of the cash payment received, to the extent that that amount does not exceed C.

(4) Where –

    (a) the amount of the cash payment referred to in the description of B in paragraph (2) exceeds the amount referred to in the description of A in that paragraph, or

    (b) the amount of the cash payment referred to in the description of D in paragraph (3) exceeds the amount referred to in the description of C in that paragraph,

an amount equal to the excess in either case shall constitute a profit realised by a person from the discount on a relevant discounted security for the purposes of paragraph 1 of Schedule 13 (charge to tax on realised profit comprised in discount).

(5) In this regulation 'relevant discounted security' has the meaning given by paragraph 3 of Schedule 13.

PART IV AGREEMENTS FOR SALE AND REPURCHASE OF SECURITIES

13 Interpretation

In this Part of these Regulations –

'capital payment' means any payment on the euroconversion of securities other than any interest, dividend or other annual payment payable in respect of the securities;

'original owner' and 'interim holder' shall be construed in accordance with section 730A(1)of the Taxes Act;

'transferor' shall be construed in accordance with sections 727A(1) and 737A(1) of the Taxes Act.

14 Replacement of securities in a euroconversion

(1) This regulation applies in a case where –

(a) there is an agreement for the sale of securities, and

(b) there is a euroconversion of the securities to which the agreement relates ('the old securities'), effected wholly or in part by the issue of new securities to replace them.

(2) The new securities which replace the old securities shall be regarded for the purposes of sections 727A(1), 730A(1) and 737A(1) of the Taxes Act, and section 263A(1) of the 1992 Act, as similar securities in relation to the old securities.

(3) In paragraph (2) the reference to similar securities shall be construed in accordance with section 727A(4), 730B(4) or 737B(6), as the case may be.

15 Payment or benefit received by interim holder on euroconversion

(1) This regulation applies in a case where –

(a) there is an arrangement for the sale and repurchase of securities to which section 263A(1) of the 1992 Act applies,

(b) a capital payment, but for the arrangement, would be received by the original owner on the euroconversion of those securities,

(c) the interim holder is not required under the arrangement to pay to the original owner an amount representative of that capital payment, and an amount representative of that capital payment is not required under the arrangement to be taken into account in computing the repurchase price of the securities, and

(d) the amount of the capital payment would not exceed 500 euros.

(2) The interim holder shall not be regarded, for the purposes of section 263A of the 1992 Act, as receiving a benefit under subsection (3)(b) of that section equal to the amount of the capital payment.

16 Payment deemed to be made by interim holder on euroconversion

(1) This regulation applies in a case where –

    (a) there is an arrangement for the sale and repurchase of securities to which section 730A(1) of the Taxes Act, or section 263A(1) of the 1992 Act, applies, or to which section 730A(1) of the Taxes Act would apply if the sale price and the repurchase price were different,

    (b) there is a euroconversion of those securities prior to their being repurchased, and

    (c) it is reasonable to assume that an amount that is representative of a capital payment in respect of the euroconversion is taken into account in computing the repurchase price of those securities.

(2) The amount referred to in paragraph (1)(c) shall be treated as if it were a separate representative payment in respect of the euroconversion made by the interim holder to the person required or entitled under the arrangement to repurchase the securities.

(3) The repurchase price of the securities shall be treated, for the purposes of section 730A of the Taxes Act and the 1992 Act, as increased by an amount equal to the amount of the separate payment treated as made by paragraph (2).

17 Renominalisation resulting in new minimum denomination in which securities can be held or traded

(1) This regulation applies in a case where –

    (a) there is an arrangement for the sale and repurchase of securities to which section 730A(1) or 737A(1) of the Taxes Act, or section 263A(1) of the 1992 Act, applies, or to which section 730A(1) of the Taxes Act would apply if the sale price and the repurchase price were different,

    (b) there is a euroconversion of those securities prior to their being repurchased,

    (c) the aggregate nominal value (expressed in euros) of the securities sold, or of securities issued to replace them in a euroconversion is, as a result of renominalisation, not a whole multiple of the new minimum denomination in which those securities can be traded at the time of repurchase under the arrangement,

    (d) securities the aggregate nominal value of which is equal to the largest whole multiple of the new minimum denomination which does not exceed the aggregate nominal value referred to in subparagraph (c) are required under the arrangement to be sold back to the original owner or the transferor or a person connected with him, and

    (e) the interim holder is required under the arrangement to pay to the original owner or transferor, or person connected with him, an amount which either –

        (i) is equal to the amount of what would, but for the arrangement, have been the proceeds of disposal of the remainder of the

520

securities on the renominalisation received by the original owner, or

    (ii) is equal to the value, at the time of the repurchase of securities pursuant to the arrangement, of the remainder if the remainder could still be held at that time though not traded.

(2)   Where this regulation applies, the requirement for payment of the amount specified in paragraph (1)(e) is to be regarded for the purposes of sections 727A, 730A and 737A of the Taxes Act, and section 263A of the 1992 Act, as equivalent to a requirement on the original owner, transferor or person connected with him to repurchase the remainder of the securities.

(3)   The value referred to in paragraph (1)(e)(ii) is the appropriate proportion (based on nominal value) of the market value of the minimum amount of the original securities that, at the time of the repurchase of the securities pursuant to the arrangement, could be traded.

(4)   Where the amount calculated in accordance with sub-paragraph (e) of paragraph (1) does not exceed 500 euros, and the arrangement does not require payment of a sum equal to this amount, this regulation shall have effect as if the amount calculated in accordance with that sub-paragraph were nil and the requirement specified in that sub-paragraph were satisfied.

(5)   Where, in a case to which paragraph (1)(a) to (d) applies –

    (a) no amount is paid as mentioned in paragraph (1)(e) by the interim holder to the original owner, transferor or person connected with him in respect of securities that, as a result of the renominalisation, could not be traded, but

    (b) it is reasonable to assume that an amount that is representative of an amount that could have been paid as mentioned in sub-paragraph (a) was taken into account in computing the repurchase price of the securities,

that amount shall be treated as if it were a separate payment made by the interim holder to the original owner, transferor or person connected with him that is representative of a capital payment on the euroconversion of the securities, and the repurchase price of the securities shall be treated as increased by an amount equal to the amount of that separate payment so treated as made.

18   Payment made or deemed to be made by interim holder in respect of euroconversion – chargeable gains consequences

(1)   This regulation applies in a case where –

    (a) there is an arrangement for the sale and repurchase of securities to which section 263A(1) of the 1992 Act applies, and

    (b) as a result of a euroconversion of those securities, a payment representative of a capital payment is made, or treated under regulation 16(2) or 17(5) as made ("deemed payment"), by the interim holder to the original owner or the transferor or a person connected with him.

(2)   The payment or deemed payment shall be treated, for the purposes of the 1992 Act –

    (a) where the original owner and the repurchaser are the same person, as a capital payment received by the original owner in respect of the euroconversion of the securities concerned on such date as, on a just and reasonable view, may be inferred from the terms of the arrangement to be the date when the original owner would, but for the arrangement, have received a capital payment in respect of which the payment or deemed payment is made;

    (b) where the original owner and the repurchaser are not the same person and so far as concerns persons other than the interim holder, as reducing the repurchase price; and

    (c) as deductible by the interim holder in computing any capital gain arising –

       (i) on a disposal of the securities received by the interim holder under the arrangement, or

      (ii) where there has been an exchange of those securities as a result of the euroconversion, on a disposal of the securities received by the interim holder in exchange for the original securities received by him under the arrangement.

19 Euroconversion-loan relationships consequences

(1) Paragraph 15 of Schedule 9 to the Finance Act 1996 (loan relationships – repo transactions and stock-lending) shall have effect as if the definition of 'repo or stock-lending arrangements' in sub-paragraph (3) of that paragraph also included provision under an agreement or series of agreements for the original owner, or a person connected with him, subsequently to be or become entitled, or required, to have transferred to him either –

    (a) the rights accruing on a euroconversion of the loan relationship, or

    (b) where the rights include a payment on the euroconversion, other than interest, of an amount which, when aggregated with all other payments on the euroconversion of loan relationships with equivalent rights which are the subject of the same repo or stock-lending arrangement, results in an aggregate amount that does not exceed 500 euros, either the whole of those rights or the whole of those rights apart from that payment.

(2) In paragraph (1)(b) 'equivalent rights' shall be construed in accordance with paragraph 15(4) of Schedule 9 to the Finance Act 1996.

PART V STOCK LENDING ARRANGEMENTS

20 Interpretation

In this Part of these Regulations –

'capital payment' means any payment on the euroconversion of securities other than any interest, dividend or other annual payment payable in respect of the securities;

'stock lending arrangement', 'borrower' and 'lender' have the meanings given by section 263B(1) of the 1992 Act.

21 Deemed capital payment

(1) This regulation applies in a case where –

(a) there is a stock lending arrangement in relation to securities,

(b) a capital payment resulting from the euroconversion of those securities would, but for the arrangement, be received by the lender, and

(c) the stock lending arrangement does not include a requirement for the borrower to make a payment to the lender that is representative of the capital payment referred to in sub-paragraph (b).

(2) Subject to paragraph (3), the lender shall be treated, for all purposes of the Taxes Acts, as having received a capital payment in respect of the euroconversion of the securities concerned –

(a) on such date as it is reasonable to assume would have been, but for the arrangement, the first date on which the lender could have received the payment mentioned in paragraph (1)(b), and

(b) in an amount equal to the amount of the payment he could have received.

(3) Paragraph (2) shall not apply where the amount of the capital payment that the lender could have received is less than 500 euros.

22 Renominalisation resulting in new minimum amount in which securities can be held or traded

(1) This regulation applies in a case where – –

(a) there is a stock lending arrangement in relation to securities,

(b) there is a euroconversion of those securities prior to their being transferred back to the lender under the arrangement,

(c) the aggregate nominal value (expressed in euros) of the securities transferred to the borrower under the arrangement, or of the securities issued to replace them in the euroconversion, is, as a result of renominalisation, not a whole multiple of the new minimum denomination in which those securities can be traded at the time of the transfer of securities back to the lender under the arrangement,

(d) securities the aggregate nominal value of which is equal to the largest whole multiple of the new minimum denomination which does not exceed the aggregate nominal value referred to in sub-paragraph (c) are transferred back to the lender pursuant to the arrangement, and

(e) the borrower is required under the arrangement to pay to the lender an amount which either –

(i) is equal to the amount of what would, but for the arrangement, have been the proceeds of disposal of the remainder of the securities on the renominalisation received by the lender, or

(ii) is equal to the value, at the time of the transfer of securities back to the lender under the arrangement, of the remainder of the securities if the remainder could still be held at that time though not traded.

(2) Where this regulation applies, the requirement for payment of the amount specified in paragraph (1)(e) is to be regarded for the purposes of section 263B of the 1992 Act as a requirement on the part of the borrower to transfer the remainder of the securities back to the lender.

(3) The value referred to in paragraph (1)(e)(ii) is the appropriate proportion (based on nominal value) of the market value of the minimum amount of the original securities that, at the time of the transfer back of securities to the lender under the arrangement, could be traded.

(4) Where the value, or proceeds of disposal, of the remainder of the securities referred to in sub-paragraph (e) of paragraph (1) does not exceed 500 euros, and the arrangement does not require payment of a sum equal to this amount, this regulation shall have effect as if the amount calculated in accordance with that sub-paragraph were nil and the requirement specified in that sub-paragraph were satisfied.

23 Payment made by borrower to lender in respect of euroconversion – chargeable gains consequences

(1) This regulation applies in a case where –

(a) there is a stock lending arrangement in relation to securities, and

(b) a payment representative of a capital payment resulting from a euroconversion of those securities is made by the borrower to the lender.

(2) The representative payment shall be treated, for all purposes of the Taxes Acts –

(a) as a capital payment received by the lender in respect of the euroconversion of the securities concerned on such date as it is reasonable to assume would have been, but for the arrangement, the first date on which the lender could have received the capital payment, and

(b) as deductible by the borrower in computing any capital gain arising –

    (i) on a disposal of the securities received by the borrower under the arrangement, or

    (ii) where the euroconversion is effected by means of an exchange of securities, on a disposal of the securities received by the borrower in exchange for the original securities received by him under the arrangement.

PART VI REPURCHASES AND STOCK LENDING – STAMP DUTY AND STAMP DUTY RESERVE TAX

24 Interpretation

In this Part of these Regulations 'capital payment' means any payment on the euroconversion of securities other than any interest, dividend or other annual payment payable in respect of the securities.

25   Replacement of stock in a euroconversion

(1)   This regulation applies in a case where –

(a)   there is an arrangement involving the transfer of stock to which subsection (1)(a) of section 80C of the Finance Act 1986 (repurchases and stock lending exemption from stamp duty) applies, and

(b)   there is a euroconversion of that stock ('the old stock'), effected wholly or in part by the issue of new stock to replace the old stock.

(2)   The new stock shall be regarded, for the purposes of section 80C of the Finance Act 1986, as stock of the same kind and amount as the old stock.

26   Replacement of chargeable securities in a euroconversion

(1)   This regulation applies in a case where –

(a)   there is an arrangement involving the transfer of chargeable securities to which subsection (1)(a) of section 89AA of the Finance Act 1986 (repurchases and stock lending exemption from stamp duty reserve tax) applies, and

(b)   there is a euroconversion of those chargeable securities ('the old chargeable securities'), effected wholly or partly by the issue of new chargeable securities to replace the old chargeable securities.

(2)   The new chargeable securities shall be regarded, for the purposes of section 89AA of the Finance Act 1986, as chargeable securities of the same kind and amount as the old chargeable securities.

27   Payment or benefit received by transferee of stock on euroconversion

(1)   This regulation applies in a case where –

(a)   there is an arrangement involving the transfer of stock to which subsection (1) of section 80C of the Finance Act 1986 applies,

(b)   a capital payment would, but for the arrangement, be received by the person referred to as B in that section or by his nominee on the euroconversion of that stock,

(c)   neither the person referred to as A in that section nor his nominee is required under the arrangement to pay to B or to B's nominee an amount equivalent to the amount of that capital payment, and an amount equivalent to the amount of that capital payment is not required under the arrangement to be taken into account in computing the price of stock to be transferred to B or his nominee under the arrangement, and

(d)   the amount of the capital payment would not exceed 500 euros.

(2)   A shall not be regarded, for the purposes of section 80C of the Finance Act 1986, as a person to whom a benefit consisting of an amount equal to the capital payment referred to in paragraph (1) accrues as mentioned in subsection (4)(b) of that section.

28 Payment or benefit received by transferee of chargeable securities on euroconversion

(1) This regulation applies in a case where –

(a) there is an arrangement involving the transfer of chargeable securities to which subsection (1) of section 89AA of the Finance Act 1986 applies,

(b) a capital payment would, but for the arrangement, be received by the person referred to as Q in that section or by his nominee on the euroconversion of those chargeable securities,

(c) neither the person referred to as P in that section nor his nominee is required under the arrangement to pay to Q or to Q's nominee an amount equivalent to the amount of that capital payment, and an amount equivalent to the amount of that capital payment is not required under the arrangement to be taken into account in computing the price of the chargeable securities to be transferred to Q or his nominee under the arrangement, and

(d) the amount of the capital payment would not exceed 500 euros.

(2) P shall not be regarded, for the purposes of section 89AA of the Finance Act 1986, as a person to whom a benefit consisting of an amount equal to the capital payment referred to in paragraph (1) accrues as mentioned in subsection (4)(b) of that section.

29 Renominalisation resulting in new minimum denomination in which stock can be held or traded

(1) This regulation applies in a case where –

(a) there is an arrangement involving the transfer of stock to which subsection (1) of section 80C of the Finance Act 1986 applies,

(b) there is a euroconversion of that stock prior to the transfer of stock under the arrangement by A or his nominee to B or his nominee as mentioned in subsection (1)(b) of that section,

(c) the aggregate nominal value (expressed in euros) of the stock transferred by B to A or his nominee as mentioned in subsection (1)(a) of that section, or of stock issued to replace that stock in a euroconversion is, as a result of renominalisation, not a whole multiple of the new minimum denomination in which that stock can be traded at the time of the transfer of stock referred to in sub-paragraph (b),

(d) stock the aggregate nominal value of which is equal to the largest whole multiple of the new minimum denomination which does not exceed the aggregate nominal value referred to in sub-paragraph (c) is required under the arrangement to be transferred by A or his nominee to B or his nominee, and

(e) A or his nominee is required under the arrangement to pay to B or his nominee an amount which either –

(i) is equal to the amount of what would, but for the arrangement, have been the proceeds of disposal of the remainder of the stock on the renominalisation received by B, or

       (ii) is equal to the value, at the time of the transfer of stock referred to in sub-paragraph (b), of the remainder of the stock if the remainder could still be held at that time though not traded.

(2) Where this regulation applies, the requirement for payment of the amount specified in paragraph (1)(e) is to be regarded, for the purposes of section 80C of the Finance Act 1986, as equivalent to a requirement for the remainder of the stock to be transferred by A or his nominee to B or his nominee.

(3) The value referred to in paragraph (1)(e)(ii) is the appropriate proportion (based on nominal value) of the market value of the minimum amount of the original stock that, at the time of the transfer of stock referred to in sub-paragraph (b), could be traded.

(4) Where the amount calculated in accordance with sub-paragraph (e) of paragraph (1) does not exceed 500 euros, and the arrangement does not require payment of a sum equal to this amount, this regulation shall have effect as if the amount calculated in accordance with that sub-paragraph were nil and the requirement specified in that sub-paragraph were satisfied.

30 Renominalisation resulting in new minimum denomination in which chargeable securities can be held or traded

(1) This regulation applies in a case where –

    (a) there is an arrangement involving the transfer of chargeable securities to which subsection (1) of section 89AA of the Finance Act 1986 applies,

    (b) there is a euroconversion of those chargeable securities prior to the transfer of chargeable securities under the arrangement by P or his nominee to Q or his nominee as mentioned in subsection (1)(b) of that section,

    (c) the aggregate nominal value (expressed in euros) of the chargeable securities transferred by Q to P or his nominee as mentioned in subsection (1)(a) of that section, or of chargeable securities issued to replace those chargeable securities in a euroconversion is, as a result of renominalisation, not a whole multiple of the new minimum denomination in which those chargeable securities can be traded at the time of the transfer of chargeable securities referred to sub-paragraph (b),

    (d) chargeable securities the aggregate nominal value of which is equal to the largest whole multiple of the new minimum denomination which does not exceed the aggregate nominal value referred to in sub-paragraph (c) are required under the arrangement to be transferred by P or his nominee to Q or his nominee, and

    (e) P or his nominee is required under the arrangement to pay to Q or his nominee an amount which either –

       (i) is equal to the amount of what would, but for the arrangement, have been the proceeds of disposal of the remainder of the chargeable securities on the renominalisation received by Q, or

        (ii) is equal to the value, at the time of the transfer of chargeable securities referred to in sub-paragraph (b), of the remainder of the chargeable securities if the remainder could still be held at that time though not traded.

(2)   Where this regulation applies, the requirement for payment of the amount specified in paragraph (1)(e) is to be regarded, for the purposes of section 89AA of the Finance Act 1986, as equivalent to a requirement for the remainder of the chargeable securities to be transferred by P or his nominee to Q or his nominee.

(3)   The value referred to in paragraph (1)(e)(ii) is the appropriate proportion (based on nominal value) of the market value of the minimum amount of the original chargeable securities that, at the time of the transfer of chargeable securities referred to in paragraph (1)(b), could be traded.

(4)   Where the amount calculated in accordance with sub-paragraph (e) of paragraph (1) does not exceed 500 euros, and the arrangement does not require payment of a sum equal to this amount, this regulation shall have effect as if the amount calculated in accordance with that sub-paragraph were nil and the requirement specified in that sub-paragraph were satisfied.

PART VII ACCRUED INCOME SCHEME

31 Interpretation

In this Part of these Regulations –

'the accrued amount' has the meaning given by section 713(4) of the Taxes Act;

'the accrued income provisions' means sections 710 to 728 of the Taxes Act;

'interest period' shall be construed in accordance with section 711(3) and (4) of the Taxes Act except that, where securities are issued on an exchange of securities to which regulation 32 (exchange of securities resulting from euroconversion) applies, paragraph (a) of section 711(3) of that Act (commencement of interest period) shall have effect for the purposes of regulation 33 as if the reference in that paragraph to the day following that on which securities are issued were a reference to the day on which they are issued;

'the rebate amount' has the meaning given by section 713(5) of the Taxes Act;

'securities' has the meaning given by section 710(2) to (4) of the Taxes Act;

'transfer' in relation to a transfer of securities has the meaning given by subsection (5), read with subsection (13), of section 710 of the Taxes Act.

32 Disapplication of accrued income provisions in respect of an exchange or conversion of securities resulting from a euroconversion

An exchange or conversion of securities that arises solely as a result of actions to effect a euroconversion of those securities shall not constitute, or be treated as, a transfer of those securities for the purposes of the accrued income provisions.

33 Disapplication of variable interest rate provision in certain circumstances

(1) This regulation applies in a case where, solely to provide for actions reasonably required to effect a euroconversion of a security –

    (a) there may be a change in the rate of interest carried by the security in relation to the interest period in which the euroconversion occurs, or

    (b) there may be a change in the rate of interest carried by the security in relation to subsequent periods but, throughout the subsequent periods, the new rate of interest falls within one, and one only, of the categories specified in paragraphs (a) to (c) of section 717(2) of the Taxes Act, or

    (c) there may be a change in the rate of interest as mentioned in sub-paragraph (a) and a change in the rate of interest as mentioned in sub-paragraph (b).

(2) The provision for change in the rate of interest referred to in paragraph (1)(a) or (b) shall not cause the security concerned to be one to which section 717 of the Taxes Act applies.

34 Calculation of accrued amount or rebate amount in the event of a euroconversion of securities

(1) This regulation applies in a case where –

    (a) there is a transfer of securities at any time in an interest period, and

    (b) at any time in that interest period there is a euroconversion of the securities transferred in that period.

(2) The accrued amount or, as the case may be, the rebate amount arising in respect of the transferred securities on the transfer shall be such amount as is just and reasonable.

35 Treatment of capital sum receivable on euroconversion of securities

(1) This regulation applies in a case where –

    (a) otherwise than as a result of a transfer of securities that is not an exchange or conversion of securities to which regulation 32 applies, a person becomes entitled in an interest period to a capital sum in connection with a euroconversion of securities, and

    (b) any part of that sum is, on a just and reasonable view –

        (i) attributable to a reduction in the interest payable on those securities, or

        (ii) by way of compensation for a deferral of the interest payable on those securities.

(2) The person entitled to a capital sum in an interest period as mentioned in paragraph (1)(a) shall be regarded as entitled in that interest period to a sum on the securities, for the purposes of section 713(2)(a) or (3)(a), in an amount equal to the part of the sum referred to in paragraph (1)(b).

PART VIII CHARGEABLE GAINS

36 Equation of holding of non-sterling currency with new euro holding on euroconversion

A euroconversion of currency ('the original currency') shall not be treated for the purposes of the 1992 Act as involving any disposal of the original currency or any acquisition of the new euro holding or any part of it, but the original currency (taken as a single asset) and the new euro holding (taken as a single asset) shall be treated for those purposes as the same asset acquired as the original currency was acquired.

37 Equation of debt (other than a debt on a security) on euroconversion

A euroconversion of a debt other than a debt on a security ('the original debt') shall not be treated for the purposes of the 1992 Act as involving any disposal of that debt by the creditor or any acquisition by him of a new debt or any part of it, but the original debt and the new debt shall be treated for those purposes (to the extent that they are not already so treated) as the same asset acquired as the original asset was acquired.

38 Derivatives over assets the subject of euroconversion

(1) This regulation applies where –

(a) a derivative represents rights or obligations in respect of any asset or liability or other amount ('the underlying asset'),

(b) there is a euroconversion of the underlying asset,

(c) a transaction is entered into in relation to that derivative that would, but for this regulation, result in a disposal for the purposes of the 1992 Act of the derivative ('the original derivative') and the acquisition of a new derivative,

(d) the terms of the new derivative differ from the terms of the original derivative only to the extent necessary to reflect the euroconversion of the underlying asset, and

(e) no party to the transaction receives any consideration in respect of the original derivative other than the new derivative.

(2) The transaction described at paragraph (1)(c) shall not be treated for the purposes of the 1992 Act as involving any disposal of the original derivative or any acquisition of the new derivative, but the original derivative and the new derivative shall be treated for those purposes as the same asset acquired as the original derivative was acquired.

39 Cash payments received on euroconversion of securities

Chapter II of Part IV of the 1992 Act shall have effect as if after section 133 of that Act (premiums on conversion of securities) there were inserted the following section –

"133A Cash payments received on euroconversion of securities

(1) This section applies where, under a euroconversion of a security that does not involve a disposal of the security and

accordingly is not a conversion of securities within section 132(3)(a), a person receives, or becomes entitled to receive, any sum of money ('the cash payment').

(2) If the cash payment is small, as compared with the value of the security concerned –

(a) receipt of the cash payment shall not be treated for the purposes of this Act as a disposal of part of the security, and

(b) the cash payment shall be deducted from any expenditure allowable under this Act as a deduction in computing a gain or a loss on a disposal of the security by the person receiving or becoming entitled to receive the cash payment.

(3) Where the allowable expenditure is less than the cash payment (or is nil) –

(a) subsection (2) above shall not apply, and

(b) if the recipient so elects (and there is any allowable expenditure) –

(i) the amount of the cash payment shall be reduced by the amount of the allowable expenditure, and

(ii) none of that expenditure shall be allowable as a deduction in computing a gain accruing on the occasion of the euroconversion or on any subsequent occasion.

(4) In this section –

(a) 'allowable expenditure' means expenditure which immediately before the euroconversion was attributable to the security under paragraphs (a) and (b) of section 38(1);

(b) 'euroconversion' has the meaning given by regulation 3 of the European Single Currency (Taxes) Regulations 1998."

PART IX CONTROLLED FOREIGN COMPANIES

40 Replacement of currency used in accounts of controlled foreign company by euro

(1) This regulation applies in a case where, as a result of the adoption of the euro by a participating member State, the currency used in the accounts of a controlled foreign company for the first relevant accounting period of the company is to be replaced by the euro.

(2) Section 747A(2) of the Taxes Act shall have effect as if it provided that –

(a) where the currency used in the accounts of the controlled foreign company for the first relevant accounting period was the ecu, the chargeable profits for any subsequent accounting period ending on or after 1st January 1999 should be computed and expressed in the euro;

(b) where the currency used in the accounts of the controlled foreign company for the first relevant accounting period was a currency other than the ecu –

    (i) the chargeable profits for any subsequent accounting period in which, or in any part of which, the currency continues to exist as a legal sub-unit of the euro should be computed and expressed in either the currency so used or the euro;

    (ii) the chargeable profits for any accounting period beginning after the end of the latest accounting period referred to in paragraph (i) should be computed and expressed in the euro.

PART X AMENDMENTS TO THE LOCAL CURRENCY ELECTIONS REGULATIONS

41 Introductory

(1) The Local Currency Elections Regulations 1994 (the 1994 Regulations) shall have effect in relation to the adoption of the euro by a member State with the modifications specified in regulations 42 to 47.

(2) Except where otherwise defined in these Regulations, expressions used in this Part of these Regulations have the meanings given by the 1994 Regulations, and references to a regulation in regulations 42 to 47 are references to a regulation of the 1994 Regulations.

42 Period for determining validity of elections

(1) In regulation 5(2) –

    (a) in sub-paragraph (a) after the words 'trade is carried on' there shall be inserted
    ', determined –

        (i) at the beginning of the first accounting period to which the election applies and at any time thereafter, or

        (ii) where the election is for a part of a trade which the company begins to carry on at a time in the first accounting period to which the election applies which is not the beginning of that accounting period, at the time the part of the trade commences and at any time thereafter';

    (b) in sub-paragraph (b) there shall be added at the end 'as regards the first accounting period to which the election applies and subsequent accounting periods'.

(2) In regulation 6 after the words 'In determining' there shall be inserted 'for the purposes of regulation 5(2)(a)'.

43 Existing election for ecu or participating currencies

(1) An election made by a company under regulation 3 or 4 in relation to –

    (a) the ecu, or

    (b) a currency participating in the euro,

shall have effect for the purposes of the 1994 Regulations on and after 1st January 1999 or, if later, the date on which the euro is adopted by the participating member State concerned, as if the election –

(a) continued on or after that date, and

(b) was made in relation to the euro as well as in relation to the ecu or, as the case may be, the participating currency concerned.

(2) In paragraph (1) the reference to a currency participating in the euro (or the participating currency) is a reference to the currency of a participating member State which, as a result of the adoption of the euro by that member State, is replaced by the euro but continues to exist as a legal sub-unit of the euro.

44 Treatment of existing part trade elections in participating currencies

(1) Where prior to 1st January 1999, or, if later, prior to the date on which the euro is adopted by the participating member State concerned –

(a) a company makes more than one election under regulation 4 for different parts of its trade,

(b) the currency specified in each election –

(i) as at 1st January 1999, is a participating currency, or

(ii) as at the later date on which the euro is adopted by the participating member State concerned, is either a participating currency or the euro, and

(c) the elections taken together cover the whole of the company's trade,

the elections shall be treated on and after 1st January 1999 or, as the case may be, the later date referred to above, for the purposes of the 1994 Regulations, as if they together constituted a single election for the euro as well as for the participating currency concerned under regulation 3 in respect of the whole of the company's trade.

(2) Where prior to 1st January 1999 or, if later, prior to the date on which the euro is adopted by the participating member State concerned –

(a) a company makes more than one election under regulation 4 for different parts of its trade,

(b) the currency specified in more than one of its elections –

(i) as at 1st January 1999, is a participating currency, or

(ii) as at the later date on which the euro is adopted by the participating member State concerned, is either a participating currency or the euro, and

(c) the elections taken together do not cover the whole of the company's trade,

all the elections referred to in sub-paragraph (b) shall be treated on and after 1st January 1999 or, as the case may be, the later date referred to above, for the purposes of the 1994 Regulations, as if they together constituted a single election for the euro as well as for the participating currency concerned under regulation 4 in respect of part of the company's trade.

45 Election for whole trade where part trade election already exists

For regulation 3(2) there shall be substituted –

'(2) An election made by a company under this regulation for a trade for an accounting period shall be of no effect if –

(a) an election ('the previous election') has previously been made by the company under regulation 4 in a different currency for that accounting period and any part of that trade, and

(b) the previous election remains in force as respects that trade and that accounting period.

(3) Where –

(a) an election ('the new election') is made by a company under this regulation for a trade for an accounting period, and

(b) an election ('the previous election') has previously been made by the company under regulation 4 in the same currency for that accounting period and any part of that trade,

the new election shall be taken to replace the previous election with effect from the beginning of the first accounting period to which the new election applies.'

46 Determination of rate of exchange where part trade election replaced by whole trade election or combined part trade election

In regulation 8 –

(a) in paragraph (1) at the beginning there shall be inserted '"Subject to paragraph (5) below,';

(b) after paragraph (4) there shall be added –

'(5) Where, as a result of the adoption of the euro by one or more participating member States –

(a) elections by a company for parts of its trade under regulation 4 are treated under regulation 44 of the European Single Currency (Taxes) Regulations 1998 as a single election by the company for the euro under regulation 3 in respect of the whole of its trade for an accounting period beginning on or after 1st January 1999 or, if later, on or after the date of adoption of the euro by the member State concerned,

(b) elections by a company for parts of its trade under regulation 4 are treated under regulation 44 of those Regulations as a single election by the company for the euro under regulation 4 in respect of part of its trade for an accounting period beginning on or after 1st January 1999 or, if later, on or after the date of adoption of the euro by the member State concerned,

the company shall, unless it makes a new statement under paragraph (1) above for that accounting period not later than the date specified in paragraph (6) below, be treated in relation to that accounting period and thereafter as using for the purposes of that paragraph the London closing exchange rate.

(6) The date specified is the date which is 92 days after the date of adoption of the euro by the member State concerned.

(7) In paragraphs (5) and (6) above references to the euro are references to the single currency adopted by a member State other than the United Kingdom in accordance with the Treaty establishing the European Community.'

47 Part trade elections for new part trades

In regulation 9 after paragraph (3) there shall be added –

'(4) Subject to the following provisions of these Regulations, an election for a part of a trade which a company begins to carry on at a time ('the relevant time') in an accounting period that is not the beginning of that accounting period shall have effect as respects that part for all accounting periods beginning on or after the relevant time if the election is made before the relevant time.'

The Exchange Gains and Losses (Miscellaneous Modifications) Regulations 2000 (Draft)

The Treasury, in exercise of the powers conferred upon them by sections 164(14), 167(1) and (4) to (6) of, and Schedules 15 and 16 to, the Finance Act 1993 and section 163 of the Finance Act 1998, hereby make the following Regulations:

1 Citation and commencement

(1) These Regulations may be cited as the Exchange Gains and Losses (Miscellaneous Modifications) Regulations 2000 and shall come into force on   2000.

(2) Regulations 2 to 9 shall have effect in relation to any accounting period of a company beginning on or after 1st January 2000 for which sections 105 and 106 of the Finance Act 2000 have effect.

2 Modification of the Exchange Gains and Losses (Transitional Provisions) Regulations 1994

Apply the Exchange Gains and Losses (Transitional Provisions) Regulations 1994 with the modifications set out in regulations 3 and 4.

3 In regulation 18(4) for 'a trade or part of a trade' substitute 'a business or part of a business'.

4 In regulation 22(3) for sub-paragraph (b) substitute –

'(b) a debt shall be disregarded for the purposes of paragraph (1)(b) above unless it is held or owed for the purposes of a business or part of a business and is in a currency other than the local currency of the business or part (whether or not it is the same as the currency of the original debt);'.

5 Modification of the Exchange Gains and Losses (Alternative Method of Calculation of Gain or Loss) Regulations 1994

Apply the Exchange Gains and Losses (Alternative Method of Calculation of Gain or Loss) Regulations 1994 with the modifications set out in regulations 6 to 8.

6 In regulation 4(2) –

(a) after the definition of 'accounts' insert –

' "branch" shall be construed in accordance with section 93(7) of the 1993 Act;';

(b) omit the definition of 'a local currency election';

(c) after the definition of 'qualifying asset' add –

' "the relevant foreign currency" has the meaning given by section 93(7) of the 1993 Act.'

7 (1) In regulation 5(6) –

(a) after 'An asset held by a company' insert 'which prepares its accounts as a whole in sterling';

(b) for sub-paragraph (b)(ii) substitute –

'(ii) is a company to which section 93 of the 1993 Act applies by virtue of its accounts as a whole being prepared in a currency other than sterling in accordance with normal accounting practice, and';

(c) in sub-paragraph (d) for 'in a branch' to 'other than sterling' substitute 'in a branch through which the company carries on a business or part of a business and, by virtue of section 93 of the 1993 Act, the profits and losses of that business or that part are to be computed and expressed in a currency other than sterling'.

(2) After regulation 5(6) insert –

'(6A) An asset held by a company which prepares its accounts as a whole in a currency other than sterling is an eligible asset at any time if at that time –

(a) it is shares which –

    (i) are denominated in a currency other than the relevant foreign currency for the company making the election; and

    (ii) are in a company that is not resident in the United Kingdom and is, at the time the election is made, an associated company of the company making the election; or

(b) it is shares in a company which –

    (i) is resident in the United Kingdom, and

    (ii) prepares its accounts as a whole either in sterling or in a currency other than sterling which is not the relevant foreign currency for the company making the election, and

    (iii) is a 90 per cent. subsidiary (within the meaning of paragraph (7) below) of the company making the election; or

(c) it is a debt on a security which under the terms of issue can be converted into or exchanged for shares falling within sub-paragraph (a) or (b) above and which is not a qualifying asset; or

(d) it is the company's net investment in a branch through which the company carries on a business or part of a business and, by virtue of section 93 of the 1993 Act, the profits and losses of that business or that part are to be computed and expressed in a currency other than the relevant foreign currency for the company; or

(e) it is a ship or an aircraft.'

(3) For regulation 5(8)(b) substitute –

'(b) the asset is not a qualifying asset, and

(c) the asset is held by a branch of the company outside the United Kingdom through which the company carries on a business or part of a business, and

    (i) where the company prepares its accounts as a whole in sterling, the profits and losses of that business or that part are not to be computed and expressed in a currency other than sterling by virtue of section 93 of the 1993 Act, or

(ii) where the company prepares its accounts as a whole in a currency other than sterling, the profits and losses of that business or that part are not to be computed and expressed in a currency other than the relevant foreign currency for the company by virtue of that section.'

(4) In regulation 5(9) –

(a) For '(6) and (8)' substitute '(6), (6A) and (8)';

(b) for 'trade' in both places where it occurs substitute 'business'.

8 In regulation 10(4) after 'regulation 5(6)(a), (b), (c) or (d)' insert 'or 5(6A)(a), (b), (c) or (d)'.

9 Revocation of the European Single Currency (Taxes) Regulations 1998

Part X of the European Single Currency (Taxes) Regulations 1998 is revoked to the extent that it is not previously revoked.

10 Modification of the effect of section 146 of the Finance Act 1993

(1) This regulation shall have effect in any case where –

(a) paragraph (2)(b) of regulation 5 of the Exchange Gains and Losses (Alternative Method of Calculation of Gain or Loss) Regulations 1994 applies so as to reduce the amount of an initial exchange gain or initial exchange loss which, apart from that regulation, would accrue to a company as respects a liability, and

(b) section 146 of the Finance Act 1993 ('section 146') applies.

(2) Section 146 shall have effect as if the reduction referred to in paragraph (1)(a) had not been made.

Appendix 5

Extracts from Inland Revenue Bulletins

Contents

Tax Bulletin contains certain qualifications which appear on the back page of each issue. These should be referred to before reliance is placed on an interpretation.

Foreign exchange and financial instruments (Issue 17, June 1995)

Currency contracts and transition – board's direction under ICTA 1988, s 747

A company may hold a currency contract for a period which straddles its commencement day (the first day of the company's first accounting period to start on or after 23 March 1995) and on which any profit or loss does not fall to be dealt with in computing trading profits. Here, the transitional provisions at FA 1994, s 175 enable FA 1994, s 153(4) and (5) to operate to bring in unrealised pre-commencement foreign exchange gains or losses as a deemed forward premium or discount. This is intended to ensure that the commercial profit or loss over the life of the contract is recognised for tax purposes. Concern has, however, been expressed that the operation of these provisions alone might inappropriately result in a company becoming subject to a direction under the Controlled Foreign Company ('CFC') legislation. This is because, prior to the FOREX legislation, such a contract would have been subject to capital gains rules which do not apply to CFCs.

Paragraphs 2.27 and 6.34 of the Inland Revenue's Explanatory Statement [see Appendix 3 above] explain how the transitional provisions will apply to CFCs. Broadly, where a CFC would have been subject to a direction under ICTA 1988, s 747 (or would have been, had it not paid an acceptable distribution) in the accounting period prior to it becoming subject to the FOREX rules, it is treated in the same way as a UK resident company for the purposes of both the foreign exchange and the financial instrument transitional rules. However, where this is not the case, but the CFC might otherwise become subject to a direction under ICTA 1988, s 747 in the following accounting period, purely because of FA 1994, s 153(4) and (5) operating to impute a deemed receipt in respect of pre-commencement exchange gains, then the Board will take this factor into account when considering whether a direction should be made.

[FA 1994, s 148(2)(3), 153(4)(5) and 175; ICTA 1988, s 747]

Grandfathering and other elections

'Grandfathering' is a feature of both the new Foreign Exchange Regulations supporting the FOREX legislation in the 1993 Finance Act and the new Financial Instrument legislation in the 1994 Finance Act, both of which came into force on 23 March 1995.

Where a qualifying company holds 'fluctuating' debts at its commencement day (the first day of its first accounting period to start on or after 23 March 1995), subject to certain conditions, these are kept out of the new FOREX tax regime for six years (i.e. they are 'grandfathered'), unless the company elects otherwise (Exchange Gains and Losses (Transitional Provisions) Regulations 1994 (SI 1994 No 3226), Reg 3(2) and (5)). Similarly, if a qualifying company holds an interest rate contract or option at its commencement day, this is also kept out of the new Financial Instrument regime for six years, again unless the company elects otherwise (FA 1994, s 148(2) and (3)).

Such elections should be made by the company concerned. However, it is appreciated that in the case of a Controlled Foreign Company ('CFC') this requirement may cause practical difficulties. Therefore, the Inland Revenue will be prepared to accept an election made on behalf of the CFC, by a company resident in the UK which alone or jointly with other companies resident in the UK has a majority interest in the CFC, as long as the secretary or director of the CFC has given specific authority to this effect.

This same principle will be applied for elections under Exchange Gains and Losses (Transitional Provisions) Regulations 1994 (SI 1994 No 3226), Regs 6(2) and 15(1). (Under Regulation 6(2), a company may elect to adopt the original cost price as the basic valuation for certain qualifying assets. Under Regulation 15(1), it can elect for certain pre-commencement exchange gains or losses to be treated as accruing over the six years following commencement.)

[Exchange Gains and Losses (Transitional Provisions) Regulations 1994 (SI 1994 No 3226); FA 1994, s 148]

Exchange gains and losses (Issue 21, February 1996)

Transitional provisions

This article clarifies our views on the treatment of deep discount and qualifying indexed securities under the transitional rules for the foreign exchange (FOREX) legislation in Finance Act 1993.

Tax Bulletin Issue 15 (February 1995) referred to the introduction of a new legislative package for Exchange Gains and Losses and Financial Instruments. It also gave details of an Explanatory Statement containing clarifications which had been given during the consultative process about the operation of the scheme.

The scheme applies to the corporate sector and will apply from the first day of a company's first accounting period beginning on or after 23 March 1995 – its 'commencement day'. Under the scheme, exchange gains and losses are computed by reference to the 'basic valuation' of an asset or liability. The Exchange Gains and Losses (Transitional Provisions) Regulations (SI 1994 No 3226) provide rules:

- to establish the basic valuation of an asset or liability which was held or owed immediately before and at the beginning of a company's commencement day, and

- to deal with pre-commencement gains and losses on such assets and liabilities.

Where a deep discount or qualifying indexed security held by a qualifying company would have given rise to a chargeable gain or allowable loss, had it been disposed of at market value immediately before the company's commencement day, then Regulation 6(3) of the transitional rules will apply: its basic valuation will be its market value immediately before commencement day. As a 'Regulation 6(3) asset' any pre-commencement gain or loss will be dealt with under Part III of the Transitional Provisions Regulations which provides rules for cumulative set-off against post-commencement exchange differences.

Where a deep discount or qualifying indexed security would not have given rise to a chargeable gain or allowable loss pre-commencement because, for example, it was a liability owed by the company or a qualifying corporate bond held by the company, then Regulation 6(3) will not be in point. Instead, the basic valuation will be established by Regulation 6(6). This will normally be the issue price (possibly net of issue costs) or cost of acquisition. Because such debts are defined in Regulation 3(9) as fixed debts for the purposes of the Transitional Provisions Regulations, pre-commencement exchange differences will be dealt with under Part IV of those regulations which provides the rules for the operation of a 'kink test'.

Further detail of the treatment of deep discount and qualifying indexed securities outside Regulation 6(3) is included in paragraph 2.8 of the Explanatory Statement [see Appendix 3 above].

[The Exchange Gains and Losses (Transitional Provisions) Regulations (SI 1994 No 3226)]

The Exchange Gains and Losses (Alternative Method of Calculation of Gain or Loss) (Amendment) Regulations 1996 (SI 1996/1347) (Issue 24, August 1996)

These Regulations were laid before the House of Commons on 21 May 1996 and came into force on 30 June 1996. They introduce amendments to that part of the Exchange Gains and Losses (Alternative Method of Calculation of Gain or Loss) Regulations 1994 (Statutory Instrument (SI) 1994/3227) which deals with matched assets and liabilities ('the matching regulations'). One change – designed to block an avoidance loophole – has given rise to concern that its effects go further that intended.

The matching regulations are designed to enable tax treatment broadly to follow normal accounting practice. Normally exchange differences on monetary assets and liabilities (for instance, cash or debt) are dealt with for accounting purposes through a company's profit and loss account and generally this is followed for tax purposes. The off-set method permitted by Statement of Standard Accounting Practice (SSAP) 20 allows exchange differences on liabilities used to fund or hedge equity investments to be dealt with as a reserve movement set against exchange differences arising on the translation of the net investment. As a result the exchange differences are not recognised in the profit and loss account. Where the exchange movements on the liability are brought to account for tax purposes on a translation basis following Finance Act (FA) 1993, but those on the asset are not because it is not a 'monetary asset' (for example shares rather than debt) then without special provision, accountancy treatment and tax treatment would diverge. The matching regulations aim to mirror as far as possible the accounting treatment permitted by SSAP 20 by providing for an election to enable exchange differences on certain matched liabilities (i.e. certain debt and duties under currency contracts) to be deferred or in certain circumstances to be left out of account altogether. The regulations allow the whole or a specified part of an asset to be matched in this way.

Regulation 4 of SI 1996/1347 inserts a new Regulation 5(3A) into SI 1994/3227. This is designed to prevent companies taking advantage of these matching regulations by using the time limits for making an election or increasing the proportion of an asset to be matched to defer the recognition of exchange gains for tax purposes but obtaining immediate tax relief for exchange losses. It does this by preventing companies gaining immediate relief for exchange losses where for accounting purposes they have been taken to reserves to offset exchange gains on an equity investment or foreign enterprise, but which would otherwise be recognised as they accrue for tax purposes. It is intended to operate where less than 100% of an asset is the subject of a matching election. It is not intended to deny relief for losses arising on liabilities on which exchange differences are taken to reserves in accordance with SSAP 20 where no matching election has been made in respect of an asset.

Concern has been expressed that the new Regulation 5(3A) goes too far, that it:

● disallows completely those losses which would have been recognised on disposal of the matched asset under the original regulations,

● disallows exchange losses dealt with as an adjustment to reserves to offset exchange gains on long term loans, inter-company balances or other assets not subject to a matching election which have also been dealt with as a movement to reserves in accordance with normal accounting practice.

To allay these concerns, the Inland Revenue can offer reassurance that in applying new Regulation 5 (3A):

(a) Where the matched asset is one to which Regulation 7 of SI 1994/3227 would otherwise apply, so that deferred exchange differences on matched liabilities would have been recognised on disposal of the asset under the original regulations, then any exchange loss not recognised as it accrues as a result of Regulation 5(3A) will also be relieved on disposal of the asset.

(b) New Regulation 5(3A) will only be applied where an asset is partially matched. In that case, it will only be applied to deny immediate tax recognition for exchange losses on one or more liabilities matching that asset to the extent that such losses relate to the excess of:

● the amount of such liabilities which hedge or fund that asset (and in respect of which exchange differences are consequently taken to reserves in accordance with SSAP20); over

● the amount of such liabilities matched for tax purposes.

(c) New Regulation 5(3A) will only be given effect where such exchange losses taken to reserves remain outside a matching election at a time on or after 30 June 1996. Where, for example, a revised matching election is made before 30 June 1996 bringing the proportion of the asset matched into line with accounting treatment, Regulation 5(3A) will have no effect.

This article sets out how the Revenue will apply new Regulation 5(3A) and will be followed in all circumstances where the regulation is applied.

Appendix 6

SSAP 20
Foreign Currency Translations

(Reproduced with permission from the Accounting Standards Board)

Contents

Foreign currency translation

The provisions of this statement of standard accounting practice should be read in conjunction with the (Explanatory) Foreword to accounting standards and need not be applied to immaterial items. The provisions apply to financial statements prepared under either the historical cost convention or the current cost convention.

This statement sets out the standard accounting practice for foreign currency translation, but does not deal with the method of calculating profits or losses arising from a company's normal currency dealing operations; neither does it deal specifically with the determination of distributable profits.

Part 1 – Explanatory note

Background

1 A company may engage in foreign currency operations in two main ways:

(a) Firstly, it may enter directly into business transactions which are denominated in foreign currencies; the results of these transactions will need to be translated into the currency in which the company reports.

(b) Secondly, foreign operations may be conducted through a foreign enterprise which maintains its accounting records in a currency other than that of the investing company; in order to prepare consolidated financial statements it will be necessary to translate the complete financial statements of the foreign enterprise into the currency used for reporting purposes by the investing company.

Objectives of translation

2 The translation of foreign currency transactions and financial statements should produce results which are generally compatible with the effects of rate changes on a company's cash flows and its equity and should ensure that the financial statements present a true and fair view of the results of management actions. Consolidated statements should reflect the financial results of and relationships as measured in the foreign currency financial statements prior to translation.

Procedures

3 In this statement the procedures which should be adopted when accounting for foreign operations are considered in two stages, namely:

(a) the preparation of the financial statements of an individual company; and

(b) the preparation of consolidated financial statements.

The individual company stage

4 During an accounting period, a company may enter into transactions which are denominated in a foreign currency. The result of each transaction should normally be translated into the company's local currency using the exchange rate in operation on the date on which the transaction occurred; however, if the rates do not fluctuate significantly, an average rate for a period may be used as an approximation. Where the transaction is to be settled at a contracted rate, that rate should be used; where a trading transaction is covered by a related or matching forward contract, the rate of exchange specified in that contract may be used.

5 Once non-monetary assets, e.g., plant, machinery and equity investments, have been translated and recorded they should be carried in the company's local currency. Subject to the provisions of paragraph 30 concerning the treatment of foreign equity investments financed by foreign currency borrowings, no subsequent translations of these assets will normally need to be made.

6 At the balance sheet date monetary assets and liabilities denominated in a foreign currency. e.g., cash and bank balances, loans and amounts receivable and payable, should be translated by using the rate of exchange ruling at that date, or, where appropriate, the rates of exchange fixed under the terms of the relevant transactions. Where there are related or matching forward contracts in respect of trading transactions, the rates of exchange specified in those contracts may be used.

7 An exchange gain or loss will result during an accounting period if a business transaction is settled at an exchange rate which differs from that used when the transaction was initially recorded, or, where appropriate, that used at the last balance sheet date. An exchange gain or loss will also arise on unsettled transactions if the rate of exchange used at the balance sheet date differs from that used previously.

8 Exchange gains or losses arising on settled transactions in the context of an individual company's operations have already been reflected in cash flows, since a change in the exchange rate increases or decreases the local currency equivalent of amounts paid or received in cash settlement. Similarly, it is reasonably certain that exchange gains or losses on unsettled short-term monetary items will soon be reflected in cash flows. Therefore, it is normally appropriate, because of the cash flow effects, to recognise such gains and losses as part of the profit or loss for the year; they should be included in profit or loss from ordinary activities unless they arise from events which themselves would fall to be treated as extraordinary items, in which case they would be included as part of such items.

9 When dealing with long-term monetary items, additional considerations apply. Although it is not easy to predict what the exchange rate will be when a long-term liability or asset matures, it is necessary, when stating the liability or the asset in terms of the reporting currency, to make the best estimate possible in the light of the information available at the time; generally speaking translation at the year-end rate will provide the best estimate, particularly when the currency concerned is freely dealt in on the spot and forward exchange markets.

10 In order to give a true and fair view of results, exchange gains and losses on long-term monetary items should normally be reported as part of the profit or loss for the period in accordance with the accruals concept of accounting; treatment of these items on a simple cash movements basis would be inconsistent with that concept. Exchange gains on unsettled transactions can be determined at the balance sheet date no less objectively than exchange losses; deferring the gains whilst recognising the losses would not only be illogical by denying in effect that any favourable movement in exchange rates had occurred but would also inhibit fair measurement of the performance of the enterprise in the year. In particular, this symmetry of treatment recognises that there will probably be some interaction between currency movements and interest rates and reflects more accurately in the profit and loss account the true results of currency involvement.

11 For the special reasons outlined above, both exchange gains and losses on long-term monetary items should be recognised in the profit and loss account. However, it is necessary to consider on the grounds of prudence whether the amount of the gain, or the amount by which exchange gains exceed past exchange losses on the same items, to be recognised in the profit and loss account should be restricted in the exceptional cases where there are doubts as to the convertibility or marketability of the currency in question.

12 Gains or losses on exchange arising from transactions between a holding company and its subsidiaries, or from transactions between fellow subsidiaries, should normally be reported in the individual company's financial statements as part of the profit or loss for the year in the same way as gains or losses arising from transactions with third parties.

The consolidated financial statements stage

13 The method used to translate financial statements for consolidation purposes should reflect the financial and other operational relationships which exist between an investing company and its foreign enterprises.

14 In most circumstances the closing rate/net investment method, described in paragraphs 15 to 20, should be used and exchange differences accounted for on a net investment basis. However, in certain specified circumstances (see paragraphs 21 to 24) the temporal method should be used.

The closing rate/net investment method

15 This method recognises that the investment of a company is in the net worth of its foreign enterprise rather than a direct investment in the individual assets and liabilities of that enterprise. The foreign enterprise will normally have net current assets and fixed assets which may be financed partly by local currency borrowings. In its day-to-day operations the foreign enterprise is not normally dependent on the reporting currency of the investing company. The investing company may look forward to a stream of dividends but the net investment will remain until the business is liquidated or the investment disposed of.

16 Under this method the amounts in the balance sheet of a foreign enterprise should be translated into the reporting currency of the investing company using the rate of exchange ruling at the balance sheet date. Exchange differences will arise if this rate differs from that ruling at the previous balance sheet date or at the date of any subsequent capital injection (or reduction).

17 Amounts in the profit and loss account of a foreign enterprise should be translated at the closing rate or at an average rate for the accounting period. The use of the closing rate is more likely to achieve the objective of translation, stated in paragraph 2, of reflecting the financial results and relationships as measured in the foreign currency financial statements prior to translation. However, it can be argued that an average rate reflects more fairly the profits or losses and cash flows as they arise to the group throughout an accounting period. The use of either method is therefore permitted, provided that the one selected is applied consistently from period to period.

18 No definitive method of calculating the average rate had been prescribed, since the appropriate method may justifiably vary as between individual companies. Factors that will need to be considered include the company's internal accounting procedures and the extent of seasonal trade variations; the use of a weighting procedure will in most cases be desirable. Where the average rate used differs from the closing rate, a difference will arise which should be dealt with in reserves.

19 The results of the operations of a foreign enterprise are best reflected in the group profit and loss account by consolidating the net profit or loss shown in its local currency financial statements without adjustment (other than for normal consolidation adjustments). If exchange differences arising from the retranslation of a company's net investment in its foreign enterprise were introduced into the profit and loss account, the results from trading operations, as shown in the local currency financial statements, would be distorted. Such differences may result from many factors unrelated to the trading performance or financial operations of the foreign enterprise; in particular, they do not represent or measure changes in actual or prospective cash flows. It is therefore inappropriate to regard them as profits or losses and they should be dealt with as adjustments to reserves.

20 Although equity investments in foreign enterprises will normally be made by the purchase of shares, investments may also be made by means of long-term loans and inter-company deferred trading balances. Where financing by such means is intended to be, for all practical purposes, as permanent as equity, such loans and inter-company balances should be treated as part of the investing company's net investment in the foreign enterprise; hence exchange differences arising on such loans and inter-company balances should be dealt with as adjustments to reserves.

The temporal method

21 For most investing companies in the UK and Ireland foreign operations are normally carried out through foreign enterprises which operate as separate or quasi-independent entities rather than as direct extensions of the trade of the investing company.

22 However, there are some cases in which the affairs of a foreign enterprise are so closely interlinked with those of the investing company that its results may be regarded as being more dependent on the economic environment of the investing company's currency than on that of its own reporting currency. In such a case the financial statements of the foreign enterprise should be included in the consolidated financial statements as if all its transactions had been entered into by the investing company itself in its own currency. For this purpose the temporal method of translation should be used; the mechanics of this method are identical with those used in preparing the accounts of an individual company, as stated in paragraphs 4 to 12.

23 It is not possible to select one factor which of itself will lead a company to conclude that the temporal method should be adopted. All the available evidence should be considered in determining whether the currency of the investing company is the dominant currency in the economic environment in which the foreign enterprise operates. Amongst the factors to be taken into account will be:

(a)   the extent to which the cash flows of the enterprise have a direct impact upon those of the investing company;

(b)   the extent to which the functioning of the enterprise is dependent directly upon the investing company;

(c)   the currency in which the majority of the trading transactions are de-nominated;

(d)   the major currency to which the operation is exposed in its financing structure.

24 Examples of situations where the temporal method may be appropriate are where the foreign enterprise:

(a)   acts as a selling agency receiving stocks of goods from the investing company and remitting the proceeds back to the company;

(b)   produces a raw material or manufactures parts or sub-assemblies which are then shipped to the investing company for inclusion in its own products;

(c)   is located overseas for tax, exchange control or similar reasons to act as a means of raising finance for other companies in the group.

The treatment of foreign branches

25 For the purpose of this statement, foreign operations which are conducted through a foreign branch should be accounted for in accordance with the nature of the business operations concerned. Where such a branch operates as a separate business with local finance, it should be accounted for using the closing rate/net investment method. Where the foreign branch operates as an extension of the company's trade and its cash flows have a direct impact upon those of the company, the temporal method should be used.

Areas of hyper-inflation

26 Where a foreign enterprise operates in a country in which a very high rate of inflation exists it may not be possible to present fairly in historical cost accounts the financial position of a foreign enterprise simply by a translation process. In such circumstances the local currency financial statements should be adjusted where possible to reflect current price levels before the translation process is undertaken.

The special case of equity investments financed by foreign borrowings

27 Under the procedures set out in this statement, exchange gains or losses on foreign currency borrowings taken up by an investing company or foreign enterprise would normally be reported as part of that company's profit or loss from ordinary activities and would flow through into the consolidated profit and loss account.

28 Where an individual company has used borrowings in currencies other than its own to finance foreign equity investments, or where the purpose of such borrowings is to provide a hedge against the exchange risk associated with existing equity investments, the company may be covered in economic terms against any movement in exchange rates. It would be inappropriate in such cases to record an accounting profit or loss when exchange rates change.

29 Therefore, provided the conditions set out in this paragraph apply, the company may denominate its foreign equity investments in the appropriate foreign currencies and translate the carrying amounts at the end of each accounting period at the closing rates of exchange. Where investments are treated in this way, any resulting exchange differences should be taken direct to reserves and the exchange gains or losses on the borrowings should then be offset, as a reserve movement, against these exchange differences. The conditions which must apply are as follows:

(a) in any accounting period, exchange gains or losses arising on the borrowings may be offset only to the extent of exchange differences arising on the equity investments;

(b) the foreign currency borrowings, whose exchange gains or losses are used in the offset process, should not exceed, in the aggregate, the total amount of cash that the investments are expected to be able to generate, whether from profits or otherwise; and

(c) the accounting treatment adopted should be applied consistently from period to period.

30 Similarly, within a group, foreign borrowings may have been used to finance group investments in foreign enterprises or to provide a hedge against the exchange risk associated with similar existing investments. Any increase or decrease in the amount outstanding on the borrowings arising from exchange movements will probably be covered by corresponding changes in the carrying amount of the net assets underlying the net investments (which would be reflected in reserves). Since in this case the group will be covered in economic terms against any movement in exchange rates, it would be inappropriate to record an accounting profit or loss when exchange rates change.

31 In the consolidated financial statements, therefore, subject to certain conditions, the exchange gains or losses on such foreign currency borrowings, which would otherwise have been taken to the group profit and loss account, may be offset as reserve movements against exchange differences on the retranslation of the net investments. The conditions which must apply are as follows:

(a) the relationship between the investing company and the foreign enterprises concerned should be such as to justify the use of the closing rate method for consolidation purposes;

(b)   in any accounting period, exchange gains or losses arising on foreign currency borrowings may be offset only to the extent of the exchange differences arising on the net investments in foreign enterprises;

(c)   the foreign currency borrowings, whose exchange gains or losses are used in the offset process, should not exceed, in the aggregate, the total amount of cash that the net investments are expected to be able to generate, whether from profits or otherwise; and

(d)   the accounting treatment adopted should be applied consistently from period to period.

32   Where the provisions of paragraph 29 have been applied in the investing company's financial statements to a foreign equity investment which is neither a subsidiary nor an associated company, the same offset procedure may be applied in the consolidated financial statements.

Part 2 – Definition of terms

---

33   *Financial statements* are balance sheets, profit and loss accounts, statements of source and application of funds, notes and other statements, which collectively are intended to give a true and fair view of the financial position and profit or loss.

34   *Company* includes any enterprise which comes within the scope of statements of standard accounting practice.

35   *An exempt company* is one which:

(a)   is registered in Great Britain and does not prepare its accounts in accordance with either Sections 149 and 152 of the Companies Act 1948 [now Sections 226 and 227 of the Companies Act 1985]; or

(b)   is registered in Northern Ireland and is exempted from full disclosure by Part 3 of Schedule 6A to the Companies Act (Northern Ireland) 1960 as amended by the Companies (Northern Ireland) Order 1982; or

(c)   is registered in the Republic of Ireland and is exempted from full disclosure by Part 3 of Schedule 6 to the Companies Act 1963.

36   A *foreign enterprise* is a subsidiary, associated company or branch whose operations are based in a country other than that of the investing company or whose assets and liabilities are denominated mainly in a foreign currency.

37   A *foreign branch* is either a legally constituted enterprise located overseas or a group of assets and liabilities which are accounted for in foreign currencies.

38   *Translation* is the process whereby financial data denominated in one currency are expressed in terms of another currency. It includes both the expression of individual transactions in terms of another currency and the expression of a complete set of financial statements prepared in one currency in terms of another currency.

39 A company's *local currency* is the currency of the primary economic environment in which it operates and generates net cash flows.

40 An *exchange rate* is a rate at which two currencies may be exchanged for each other at a particular point in time; different rates apply for spot and forward transactions.

41 The *closing rate* is the exchange rate for spot transactions ruling at the balance sheet date and is the mean of the buying and selling rates at the close of business on the day for which the rate is to be ascertained.

42 A *forward contract* is an agreement to exchange different currencies at a specified future date and at a specified rate. The difference between the specified rate and the spot rate ruling on the date the contract was entered into is the discount or premium on the forward contract.

43 The *net investment* which a company has in a foreign enterprise is its effective equity stake and comprises its proportion of such foreign enterprise's net assets; in appropriate circumstances, intra-group loans and other deferred balances may be regarded as part of the effective equity stake.

44 *Monetary items* are money held and amounts to be received or paid in money and, where a company is not an exempt company, should be categorised as either short-term or long-term. Short-term monetary items are those which fall due within one year of the balance sheet date.

Part 3 – Standard accounting practice

---

45 When preparing the financial statements of an individual company the procedures set out in paragraphs 46 to 51 should be followed. When preparing consolidated financial statements, the procedures set out in paragraphs 52 to 58 should be followed.

Individual companies

46 Subject to the provisions of paragraphs 48 and 51 each asset, liability, revenue or cost arising from a transaction denominated in a foreign currency should be translated into the local currency at the exchange rate in operation on the date on which the transaction occurred; if the rates do not fluctuate significantly, an average rate for a period may be used as an approximation. Where the transaction is to be settled at a contracted rate, that rate should be used. Where a trading transaction is covered by a related or matching forward contract, the rate of exchange specified in that contract may be used.

47 Subject to the special provisions of paragraph 51, which relate to the treatment of foreign equity investments financed by foreign currency borrowings, no subsequent translations should normally be made once non-monetary assets have been translated and recorded.

48 At each balance sheet date, monetary assets and liabilities denominated in a foreign currency should be translated by using the closing rate or, where appropriate, the rates of exchange fixed under the terms of the relevant transactions. Where there are related or matching forward contracts in respect of trading transactions, the rates of exchange specified in those contracts may be used.

49 All exchange gains or losses on settled transactions and unsettled short-term monetary items should be reported as part of the profit or loss for the year from ordinary activities (unless they result from transactions which themselves would fall to be treated as extraordinary items, in which case the exchange gains or losses should be included as part of such items).

50 Exchange gains and losses on long-term monetary items should also be recognised in the profit and loss account; however, it is necessary to consider on the grounds of prudence whether, in the exceptional cases outlined in paragraph 11, the amount of the gain, or the amount by which exchange gains exceed past exchange losses on the same items to be recognised in the profit and loss account, should be restricted.

51 Where a company has used foreign currency borrowings to finance, or provide a hedge against, its foreign equity investments and the conditions set out in this paragraph apply, the equity investments may be denominated in the appropriate foreign currencies and the carrying amounts translated at the end of each accounting period at closing rates for inclusion in the investing company's financial statements. Where investments are treated in this way, any exchange differences arising should be taken to reserves and the exchange gains or losses on the foreign currency borrowings should then be offset, as a reserve movement, against these exchange differences. The conditions which must apply are as follows:

(a)   in any accounting period, exchange gains or losses arising on the borrowings may be offset only to the extent of exchange differences arising on the equity investments;

(b)   the foreign currency borrowings, whose exchange gains or losses are used in the offset process, should not exceed, in the aggregate, the total amount of cash that the investments are expected to be able to generate, whether from profits or otherwise; and

(c)   the accounting treatment adopted should be applied consistently from period to period.

Consolidated financial statements

52 When preparing group accounts for a company and its foreign enterprises, which includes the incorporation of the results of associated companies or foreign branches into those of an investing company, the closing rate/net investment method of translating the local currency financial statements should normally be used.

53 Exchange differences arising from the retranslation of the opening net investment in a foreign enterprise at the closing rate should be recorded as a movement on reserves.

54 The profit and loss account of a foreign enterprise accounted for under the closing rate/net investment method should be translated at the closing rate or at an average rate for the period. Where an average rate is used, the difference between the profit and loss account translated at an average rate and at the closing rate should be recorded as a movement on reserves. The average rate used should be calculated by the method considered most appropriate for the circumstances of the foreign enterprise.

55 In those circumstances where the trade of the foreign enterprise is more dependent on the economic environment of the investing company's currency than that of its own reporting currency, the temporal method should be used.

56 The method used for translating the financial statements of each foreign enterprise should be applied consistently from period to period unless its financial and other operational relationships with the investing company change.

57 Where foreign currency borrowings have been used to finance, or provide a hedge against, group equity investments in foreign enterprises, exchange gains or losses on the borrowings, which would otherwise have been taken to the profit and loss account, may be offset as reserve movements against exchange differences arising on the retranslation of the net investments provided that:

(a)   the relationships between the investing company and the foreign enterprises concerned justify the use of the closing rate method for consolidation purposes;

(b)   in any accounting period, the exchange gains and losses arising on foreign currency borrowings are offset only to the extent of the exchange differences arising on the net investments in foreign enterprises;

(c)   the foreign currency borrowings, whose exchange gains or losses are used in the offset process, should not exceed, in the aggregate, the total amount of cash that the net investments are expected to be able to generate, whether from profits or otherwise; and

(d)   the accounting treatment is applied consistently from period to period.

58 Where the provisions of paragraph 51 have been applied in the investing company's financial statements to a foreign equity investment which is neither a subsidiary nor an associated company, the same offset procedure may be applied in the consolidated financial statements.

Disclosure

59 The methods used in the translation of the financial statements of foreign enterprises and the treatment accorded to exchange differences should be disclosed in the financial statements.

60 The following information should also be disclosed in the financial statements:

(a)   for all companies, or groups of companies, which are not exempt companies, the net amount of exchange gains and losses on foreign currency borrowings less deposits, identifying separately:

    (i)   the amount offset in reserves under the provisions of paragraphs 51, 57 and 58; and

    (ii)   the net amount charged/credited to the profit and loss account;

(b)   for all companies, or groups of companies, the net movement on reserves arising from exchange differences.

Date from which effective

61   The accounting and disclosure requirements set out in this statement should be adopted as soon as possible. They should be regarded as standard in respect of financial statements relating to accounting periods beginning on or after I April 1983.

Part 4 – Legal requirements in UK and Ireland

---

62   Paragraphs 63 to 69 below apply to companies preparing accounts in compliance with Sections 149 and 152 of the Companies Act 1948 [now Sections 226 and 227 of the Companies Act 1985] or with Sections 143 and 146 of the Companies Áct (Northern Ireland) 1960. The references to the Schedule which follow are to Schedule 8 to the Companies Act 1948 (as inserted by Section I of the Companies Act 1981) [now Schedule 4 to the Companies Act 1985]. References to the Schedule will also be to Schedule 6 to the Companies Act (Northern Ireland) 1960, as inserted by Article 3 of the Companies (Northern Ireland) Order 1982, when this is brought into operation on 1 July 1983.

63   Paragraph 12 of the Schedule requires that the amount of any item shall be determined on a prudent basis and, in particular, that only profits realised at the balance sheet date shall be included in the profit and loss account. (Paragraph 90 of the Schedule [see now Section 262(3) of the Companies Act 1985] defines realised profits in relation to a company's accounts as 'such profits of the company as fall to be treated as realised profits for the purposes of those accounts in accordance with principles generally accepted with respect to the determination for accounting purposes of realised profits at the time when those accounts are prepared').

64   Paragraph 15 of the Schedule permits a departure from paragraph 12 of the Schedule if it appears to the directors that there are special reasons for such a departure. Particulars of any departure, the reasons for it and its effect must be given in a note to the accounts.

65   For companies other than exempt companies, all exchange gains taken through the profit and loss account, other than those arising on unsettled long-term monetary items, are realised. For such companies the application of paragraph 50 of this statement may result in unrealised exchange gains on unsettled long-term monetary items being taken to the profit and loss account. In this statement the need to show a true and fair view of results, referred to in paragraph 10 above, is considered to constitute a special reason for departure from the principle under paragraph 15 of the Schedule.

66 This statement is based on the assumption that the process of translation at closing rates for the purposes of this statement does not constitute a departure from the historical cost rules under Section C [now Section B] of the Schedule nor does it give rise to a diminution in value of an asset under Section B of the Schedule.

67 Paragraph 58(1) of the Schedule requires that, where sums originally denominated in foreign currencies are brought into the balance sheet or profit and loss account, the basis on which those sums have been translated into sterling shall be stated.

68 Part I of the Schedule lays down the choice of formats permitted for the presentation of accounts. Distinction is drawn between operating and other income and expense. For this reason it is necessary to consider the nature of each foreign exchange gain or loss and to allocate each accordingly. Gains or losses arising from trading transactions should normally be included under 'Other operating income or expense' while those arising from arrangements which may be considered as financing should be disclosed separately as part of 'Other interest receivable/payable and similar income/expense'. Exchange gains or losses which arise from events which themselves fall to be treated as extraordinary items should be included as part of such items.

69 Paragraph 46 of the Schedule requires the following information to be disclosed about movements on any reserve:

(a)   the amount of the reserve at the date of the beginning of the financial year and as at the balance sheet date respectively;

(b)   any amounts transferred to or from the reserve during that year; and

(c)   the source and application respectively of any amounts so transferred.

70 Paragraphs 1 and 2 of Schedule 2 to the Companies Act 1981 permit certain companies to prepare accounts in compliance with Sections 149A and 152A of and Schedule 8A to the Companies Act 1948 instead of Sections 149 and 152 and Schedule 8 [see now special provisions for banking companies and groups in Schedule 9 to the Companies Act 1985 and for insurance companies in Schedule 9A to that Act]. Paragraph 11(9) of Schedule 8A requires disclosure of the basis on which foreign currencies have been converted into sterling. Schedule 2 to the Companies (Northern Ireland) Order 1982 will permit similar companies registered in Northern Ireland to prepare accounts in accordance with Sections 143A and 146A of and Schedule 6A to the Companies Act (Northern Ireland) 1960 which require the same disclosure.

71 Similar legal requirements are expected to be enacted in the Republic of Ireland.

Part 5 – Compliance with International Accounting Standard No. 21 'Accounting for the effects of changes in foreign exchange rates'

72 Compliance with the requirements of Statement of Standard Accounting Practice No 20 'Foreign currency translation' will automatically ensure compliance with International Accounting Standard No 21 'Accounting for the effects of changes in foreign exchange rates'.

Appendix 7

Inland Revenue Press Releases

Contents

Economic and monetary union (EMU): tax consequences (21 January 1998)

The Government proposes to introduce legislation in the next Finance Bill to deal with some technical tax issues arising out of EMU. In his speech to the Bank of England Symposium 'London as an international financial centre for the euro' the Chancellor of the Exchequer, Gordon Brown MP, said:

'I can announce a further step that the Government is taking to help business prepare. We propose to introduce legislation in the next Finance Bill to help businesses by dealing with technical tax issues arising out of EMU. The introduction of the euro in January 1999 will have implications for some UK businesses and there are some tax obstacles which business has identified and which we propose to remove. The Inland Revenue are today issuing a press release setting out some proposals for change.'

This press release:

● describes some consequences for the calculation of direct taxes which will arise as a result of the start of the single currency in January 1999, despite the UK not joining on that date;

● sets out the Government's proposals for some legislation in the next Finance Bill (which might take the form of an enabling power for appropriate secondary legislation); and

● invites written comments from interested parties on these proposals or other tax issues arising out of EMU, to be sent to the co-ordinator for EMU for the Revenue – Julian Reed, Inland Revenue, Room 507, 22 Kingsway, London, WC2B 6NR.

Details

1 The Revenue have been holding discussions with the Bank of England and certain representative bodies about the tax consequences of EMU. An agreed statement is [reproduced below] which sets out how the Government proposes that the tax system will apply in certain circumstances.

2 When dealing with foreign currency, the corporate tax system broadly follows the accounting treatment. The Government proposes to adopt this approach when dealing with the introduction of the euro. Some technical changes are needed to achieve this result. The Government proposes to bring forward legislation to make the following changes:

● Under existing law a trading company can, subject to certain conditions, elect for its corporation tax liability to be computed on the basis of accounts drawn up in a foreign currency. The Government will bring forward legislation to convert automatically an existing election for a currency which joins EMU into an election for the euro.

- Bonds in currencies which join EMU may be redenominated into the euro. It is the Government's intention that a straightforward redenomination will not normally give rise to a tax charge that would not otherwise have arisen. The Government is considering what legislation will be needed to achieve this result.

- There are special rules applying, for the purposes of the legislation on foreign exchange gains and losses and financial instruments, to contracts involving two currencies ('currency contracts'). The Government proposes to introduce legislation to allow these rules to continue to apply to existing contracts if the currencies both join EMU.

Some tax issues arising as a result of economic and monetary union

The following is a summary of some tax issues arising as a result of EMU, whether or not the UK participates. The issues addressed are not comprehensive, but are those of immediate concern which have been raised with and agreed by the Revenue.

Discussions on remaining issues continue between the Revenue, the Bank of England and representatives of the following bodies – the International Swaps & Derivatives Association, the London Investment Banking Association, the British Bankers' Association, the International Primary Markets Association, the International Securities Markets Association, the Institutional Fund Managers' Association and the American Banking & Securities Association in London.

Foreign exchange legislation

Q The foreign exchange legislation allows a trading company which satisfies certain conditions (an 'eligible company') to adopt a currency other than sterling as its functional currency for tax purposes by making a local election (under *FA 1993, ss 92–94* and the Local Currency Elections Regulations, SI 1994/3230. Will eligible companies be allowed to make local currency election for the euro?

1.1 Yes. The euro will be allowed as the subject of a local currency election.

Q Will an existing local currency election in respect of a participating currency effectively carry over into the euro without any action or consequence for taxpayers?

1.2 The Government proposes to introduce legislation in the next Finance Bill to ensure the continuity of a local currency election for a participating currency.

Q Will a company which has an existing local currency election for non-participating currency be able to re-elect for the euro following monetary union?

1.3 Yes, if it satisfies the conditions in the normal way (that is, if the euro becomes an eligible currency and the existing currency becomes ineligible).

Q When will the revised local currency elections described at 1.2 and 1.3 above become effective?

1.4 The election for a participating currency (1.2) will switch automatically (as a result of the legislation proposed in 1.2) from that currency to the euro for the first accounting period ending after 1 January 1999 when the company in question prepares its accounts in euros.

An election for the euro which replaces an election for a non-participating currency (1.3) will only be effective from the beginning of the next accounting period after it is received. So companies must make an election before the start of the first accounting period to which they want the election to apply.

Q The foreign exchange legislation contains the anti-avoidance legislation in *FA 1993, ss 135, 136* which may be applied at the direction of the Board. Respectively, the sections apply where the main benefit of the asset or liability is the accrual of a loss and where the transactions are entered into otherwise than at arm's length. In cases where the conversion of assets or liabilities occurs, or the main economic purpose of the transaction has fallen away, as a result of the introduction of the euro, will the Board seek to apply these provisions?

1.5 No. *FA 1993, ss 135, 136* will not be invoked as a result of the introduction of the euro, provided that the Board believes that no abuse is taking place. It should also be noted that the Consultative Document on the Modernisation of Transfer Pricing Legislation proposes that under self-assessment the requirement for the Board's direction would be removed, so taxpayers would have an obligation to declare when these provisions applied. If these reforms proceed, then taxpayers may rely on this statement in the preparation of their tax returns.

Q Unrealised exchange gains on debts which are considered 'long-term capital assets or liabilities' may be deferred under *FA 1993, s 139*. If the assets or liabilities are redenominated in such a way as to appear to give rise to a different asset or liability will such gains or losses be considered realised and therefore ineligible for deferral?

1.6 The Government proposes to introduce legislation to prevent the relief in *FA 1993, s 139* being lost as a result of redenomination.

Q A company may choose to hedge a foreign currency asset with a foreign currency liability or currency contract. Under *FA 1993, 15 Sch* and the Exchange Gains and Losses (Alternative Method of Calculation of Gain or Loss) Regulations, SI 1994/3227 exchange movements on an eligible liability or currency contract may, in the circumstances prescribed, be deferred e.g. until the disposal of the matched asset. If such a matched asset is redenomindated in such a way as to appear to give rise to a different asset will it cause the crystallisation of any deferred exchange movements on hedging liabilities or currency contracts?

1.7 It is not the Government's intention that redenomination should cause matching elections to become ineffective. Views are invited on whether legislation is needed to achieve this in practice.

Financial instruments legislation

Q The financial instruments legislation provides inter alia for the taxation of 'currency contracts'. It contains a definition (*FA 1994, s 150*) of 'currency contracts' which requires payment in different currencies. Will currency contracts involving two currencies that convert to the euro no longer be currency contracts as only the euro will be involved?

2.1 No. The Government proposes to introduce legislation to ensure that such contracts will continue to be currency contracts for all purposes of the legislation.

Q The financial instruments legislation provides that 'qualifying payments' may be paid gross by a 'qualifying company' (*FA 1994, s 174*). Will fixed rate swaps of two currencies which convert to the euro lose this protection, becoming subject to withholding as an annuity or annual payments for tax purposes?

2.2 No. The Government's intention is that such contracts will continue to be within the financial instruments legislation provided that no abuse is taking place (e.g. where a transaction is entered into immediately before conversion to exploit this relief).

Q The financial instruments legislation prescribes the payments which may be made under a 'currency contract'. A contract may allow for other transfers of money or money's worth and still be a 'currency contract' provided that the conditions in *FA 1994, s 152* are met, which broadly seek to ensure that the relative value of these transfers at the 'relevant time' is small. Will conversion constitute a 'relevant time' for *FA 1994, s 152*, causing the issue of whether or not a contract is a 'currency contract' to be re-considered?

2.3 No. Conversion, regardless of how it is achieved, will not be a 'relevant time' for these purposes. (Council Regulation (EC) No 1103/97 under art 235 of the Treaty provides for continuity of contract on the introduction of the euro. However conversion may also be achieved through bilateral legal agreement.)

Q The financial instruments legislation contains anti-avoidance provisions, dealing with transfers of value, transactions not at arm's length and qualifying contracts with non-residents (*FA 1994, ss 165–168*). If conversion to the euro causes there to be a new contract, will there be a reconsideration of *FA 1994, ss 165–168* potentially causing adjustments to taxable income to arise under these anti-avoidance provisions?

2.4 No. Conversion to the euro of itself will not cause anti-avoidance provisions to apply, provided the Board believes that no abuse is taking place. (The removal of the requirement for a Board's direction which is referred to in 1.5 above also applies to this legislation.)

Preparing British business for the euro (29 July 1998)

The Government will be consulting British businesses and other tax-payers on how transactions involving participating currencies will be treated for tax purposes following the introduction of the single currency on 1 January 1999, Economic Secretary Helen Liddell has announced.

Announcing the proposals, Mrs Liddell said:

'The introduction of the single currency on 1 January 1999 will change the way in which business is conducted for many British companies, even though the UK will not be a member of EMU.

The Government is determined to assist British business to adjust to these changes as effectively as possible. We are working together with business representatives whenever possible to find out what their requirements are and how we can assist them.

Following earlier consultations, we have already identified some technical changes which need to be made to prevent unintended taxes consequences arising from the introduction of the euro in other EU countries. Today's proposals will be embodied in draft regulations to be published in the Autumn. The consultation will enable British business to ensure that these changes meet their requirements.'

Details

1 In the light of consultations held to date between the Inland Revenue and certain representative bodies, the Government has agreed that technical changes should be made to certain tax provisions. Decisions made after an earlier round of consultations with these bodies were announced in the Revenue Press Release dated 21 January. The summary below covers both new points and those announced earlier. More details, in a set of 'questions and answers' are available in the Annex.

2 The changes proposed will deal with four broad sets of questions:

(i)   the treatment of assets/contracts denominated in participating foreign currencies where re-denomination into euros might otherwise give rise to a disposal or transfer or bring forward a tax charge; and the treatment of derivatives over re-denominated assets;

(ii)   the treatment of financing transactions involving re-denominated assets;

(iii)   the treatment of the costs of re-denomination; and

(iv)   the interpretation of the special rules allowing for accounting in foreign currencies for tax purposes.

In general, the Government's approach is to try to ensure as far as possible that the introduction of the single currency in other member states is tax neutral and therefore does not give rise to a charge of a loss which would not otherwise have arisen.

3   In relation to continuity of assets and contracts – subheading (i) – the Government proposes to introduce regulations to:

- ensure that, where assets are subject to a straightforward re-denomination, there is continuity for the purposes of tax on capital gains both for the assets and any related derivative contracts within the scope of *TCGA 1992*;

- provide for the appropriate treatment of any cash payments received as a result of the re-denomination of bonds in the hands of investors;

- ensure that re-denomination does not disturb the relief on un-realised exchange gains under *FA 1993, s 139*;

- provide for continuity of currency contracts and options involving two currencies which convert to the euro.

4   For financing transactions – subheading (ii) – such as stock loans and sale and repurchase agreements, involving straightforward re-denominations (of bonds), the Government intends to ensure, by regulation if necessary, that the re-denominated bonds will count as the 'same' or 'equivalent' assets for the relevant tax provisions. The Government also intends to introduce a regulation to ensure that intermediaries obtain the appropriate deduction for any charge arising on passing on a cash-payment arising from a re-denomination.

5   On costs of re-denomination – subheading (iii) – the Government proposes to introduce a regulation to allow the costs of re-denomination into euros of existing non-sterling capital assets so long as the re-denomination involves only the replacement of existing stock and not the issue of increased amounts or of greater value. The Government also proposes to make clear in regulations what costs will be allowable in relation to the re-denomination of investments.

6   Finally, in relation to accounting for tax purposes in euro – subheading (iv) – the Government proposes regulations to ensure the continuity of local currency elections for participating currencies to allow companies to make a local currency election for the euro before the euro comes into existence, but only for accounting periods commencing on or after 1 January 1999. In addition, it proposes a regulation amending the special rules for computing the chargeable profits of controlled foreign companies (CFCs). The rules lock a CFC into computing profits in the currency used by it in its first relevant accounting period. The proposed regulation will ensure that, where that currency is replaced by the euro, the currency to be used in computing future profits will switch automatically to the euro.

Other issues

7 Although the consultation with representative bodies has focused mainly on the corporate sector, the Government also intends to use the regulations to deal with any tax issues that may specifically affect other taxpayers, including individuals. It will, for example, take the opportunity to ensure in the regulations that the conversion by UK resident individuals of cash holdings of a foreign participating currency into euro will not give rise to a capital gain or loss.

8 The Government encourages those who have comments or questions relating to these proposals, or to other areas which they think may need to be addressed, whether by regulation or otherwise, to write to Bridget Micklem, Inland Revenue, Room S23, West Wing, Somerset House, Strand, London WC2R 1LB.

Notes

1 Clause 163 of the *Finance Bill* made provision for the introduction of an enabling power which would allow tax changes that are needed as a result of the introduction of the single currency in other member states to be made by regulation.

2 The enabling power covers all taxes for which the Inland Revenue is responsible and provides scope to change the law to prevent unintended tax consequences arising when the single currency starts in other member states.

3 Regulations made under the enabling power will be put into statute by a statutory instrument subject to negative resolution of the House of Commons. This is the normal method used for tax regulations.

4 The consultations which have taken place so far on the content of the regulations have been between the Revenue, the Bank of England and representatives of the following bodies:

- the International Swaps and Derivatives Association,
- the London Investment Banking Association,
- the British Bankers' Association,
- the International Primary Market Association,
- the American Banking & Securities Association in London.

5 Alongside the work on technical tax questions arising from the introduction of the single currency in other member states, the Inland Revenue has been working with Customs and the Treasury to consider practical arrangements relating to the payment of taxes in euro. More detail on these questions will be provided separately in a joint Inland Revenue/Customs press release.

Annex: further tax issues arising as a result of the introduction of the single currency in other member states

The Question and Answer statement below on tax issues arising as a result of the introduction of the single currency in other member states should be read in conjunction with the Revenue Press Release of 21 January 1998 entitled 'Some tax issues arising as a result of economic and monetary union'. The statement deals with certain further tax issues arising as a result of EMU that have been raised with and agreed by the Inland Revenue.

The statement is not intended to address comprehensively all the issues that might arise as a result of the introduction of the single currency in other member states and does not cover possible tax issues that might arise if the UK were to join the single currency.

Continuity of assets

1.1 In what circumstances will the fact of monetary union and/or the re-denomination of an asset (i.e. a debt security, instruments or contracts) from a participating currency into euro be regarded as giving rise to a disposal, transfer, etc of the asset (or a derivative over the asset) and an acquisition of a new asset (or derivative) by a taxpayer and in what circumstances will the taxpayer receive continuity of treatment, i.e. so that the taxpayer is treated as still holding the same asset or derivative that it has always held?

Answer
The issue should not be relevant to a company to the extent that it is taxed in relation to the asset or derivative under the foreign exchange, financial instruments or loan relationship legislation. In those circumstances, the Inland Revenue would expect the accounts to be followed (subject to the specific rules in those provisions).

In other circumstances, under the application of the existing law on capital gains, the re-denomination could give rise to a taxable gain or loss. However, the Government accepts that it is not desirable for a charge to arise on a straightforward re-denomination of an asset consequent on the introduction of the single currency.

It therefore proposes to introduce a regulation to ensure that if an asset is re-denominated in euros and the post re-denomination asset is in all material respects the same as the pre re-denomination asset (ignoring the changes reasonably required to give effect to the re-denomination), then, where this would not otherwise be the case, the re-denomination will not be regarded as involving a disposal or acquisition, and the asset will be regarded as the same for capital gains purposes.

If other changes are simultaneously made to the asset beyond those associated with a straightforward re-denomination, then the question of whether those other changes give rise to a transfer or disposal and an acquisition of a different asset or derivative will need to be considered in accordance with existing principles.

1.2 How will cash-outs received as a result of a re-denomination of bonds be treated in the hands of investors?

Answer
Any cash received as the result of a re-denomination will need to be recognised by the taxpayer. In the case of a person holding the asset as part of its trade or of a company taxed in relation to the asset for example, under the loan relationship or financial instrument provisions, the treatment should follow existing rules.

Where the asset falls under the capital gains regime, under current law cash received may fall to be treated as a part-disposal. However, the Government is willing to accept that small amounts deriving from a straightforward re-denomination should not be taxed, and therefore proposes to introduce a regulation to provide a *de minimis* exemption for cash payments received on re-denomination as a result of the introduction of the single currency. This should tie in with the proposed regulation on continuity of assets and with current provisions such as the part-disposal provisions on the conversion of securities in *TCGA 1992, s 133*. The Government is still considering the question of the appropriate treatment of cash-outs derived from the repackaging of odd-lots and would welcome comments on this subject.

Note: Question & Answer **1.1** and **1.2** do not cover the re-denominations of equities and equity-related instruments, since detailed consideration of this issue can only be given once it becomes clearer how the re-denomination of equities is to be achieved and since it is not likely that many companies will re-denominate their shares in the early days of the single currency. At present, it does not seem that any new capital gains issues are likely to arise in this area, since the UK has existing legislation which deals with the capital gains consequences of reorganisations of share capital.

Equities

2 If a UK company were to re-denominate any of its share capital during the transitional period on the introduction of the single currency into euro and, due to rounding, a payment of cash or an issuance of new stock is required to be made to [a] shareholder, will that payment of cash or issuance of stock give rise to a dividend or distribution?

Answer
The consequences of re-denomination of equities (ordinary shares), preference shares and convertibles, can all be dealt with under the

normal rules. A cash payment in respect of shares would therefore constitute a distribution except where and to the extent that it fell to be treated as a repayment of share capital.

A cash payment in respect of securities within *TA 1988, s 209(2)(e)(ii)* would also more than likely fall to be treated in whole or in part as a distribution. This treatment will apply equally for conversions of any non-£ and £ shares, preference shares or convertibles.

Options and other derivatives

3.1 In paras **2.1** and **2.3** of the Press Release of 21 January, certain guidance is given in relation to 'currency contracts' as defined in *FA 1994, s 150*. Will the same guidance apply to 'currency options' as defined in that section?

Answer
Yes

3.2 An interest rate contract (within *FA 1994, s 149*) must include the right to receive or a duty to make a variable rate payment. A variable rate is one based on a rate the value of which at any time is the same as that of the variable rate of interest specified in the contract, for example PIBOR. Will an interest rate contract, or an option to enter into such a contract which specifies a variable interest rate by reference to a currency which converts to euro such that the original specified rate no longer exists, be regarded as having termination and been replaced by a new contract or option?

Answer
Such a change to the subject matter of a contract may cause the contract to be void, voidable, or possible frustrated. However, the contract may continue to exist for a number of reasons. The changes may be insufficient to cause the contract to be frustrated, by reason of the law under which it is written. Similarly, the change in questions may have been anticipated and be successfully provided for in the original agreement. Alternatively, the contract may remain operative by reason of the bilateral agreement of the counterparties to maintain it, which may or may not technically give rise to a new contract.

It is the Government's intention that a contract which 'continues' for whatever reason (including when the new bilateral agreement gives rise to what is technically a new contract) will not give rise to a taxable event provided that the economic substance of the contract is not materially altered. As for assets in **1.1** above, the economic substance will be considered to be unaltered where there have been no material changes in the relevant factors.

It should be noted that the contract may be in respect of an underlying instrument which itself is not considered to have continued. In these circumstances the contract will be considered in its own right; the question will be whether, in economic substance, the contract has the same effect as before conversion.

In any event, if the contract falls within the *FA 1994* regime, for derivative financial instruments, and so is accounted for on an acceptable accruals or mark to market basis of accounting, it is likely that the tax consequences of a taxable event will be exactly the same as those arising if there had been no such event.

3.3 There may be transactions in futures or options in foreign currencies or in foreign currency denominated equities/debts/other financial instruments which are denominated in foreign currencies which do not fall within *TA 1998, 5AA Sch*. However, the effect of the introduction of the single currency and/or the re-denomination of assets may be to give rise from that time to a fixed return which is from that point a 'guaranteed return'. Will the provision of *5AA Sch* apply in these circumstances?

Answer

TA 1988, 5AA Sch applies where the main or one of the main purposes of the transaction in question is the production of a return that is guaranteed. It follows that one looks to the purposes of the parties at the time of entering into the transaction. Accordingly, the mere fact that the return from a future or option becomes fixed as a result of and from the time of the introduction of the single currency would not result in the provisions of *5AA Sch* being applied, unless, in entering into the transaction in question, that was an intended result within the meaning of *5AA Sch*.

3.4 *TA 1988, 5AA Sch* deals with the taxation of the profits and gains arising from transactions in futures and options that are designed to produce guaranteed returns. Will conversion constitute a disposal for the purposes of *5AA Sch*, causing any inherent profits and gains to be realised for tax purposes at that time?

Answer

The treatment of a conversion for the purposes of *5AA Sch* will follow that proposed at **1.1**.

3.5 *TCGA 1992, ss 143–148* provides, *inter alia*, for the taxation of option contracts which are not taxable under Schedule D (broadly option contracts which do not fall within the financial instruments rules set out in *FA 1994*, or within the anti-avoidance rules set out in *TA 1988, 5AA Sch*, and which are not held on trading account). *TCGA 1992, s 144* will apply for example to an investment company holding an option over shares which qualifies as a financial option. The basic approach (under *TCGA 1992, s 144*) is to treat an option as a separate asset for capital gains purposes except where it is exercised, in which case, its grant (or acquisition) and the acquisition or disposal of the underlying subject matter are treated as one transaction. Will the start of the single currency and/or the re-denomination of either the option or the subject-matter of the option be regarded as giving rise to settlement or lapse without exercise of an existing option and the entering into a new one?

Appendix 7

Answer
The regulation referred to in para 1.1 will provide for the continuity treatment for capital gains purposes, where appropriate, both for assets and for derivatives (including options) over assets.

Financing transactions

4.1   Where a debt security denominated in a participating currency is re-denominated into euros, will the re-denominated security be regarded as similar to/equivalent to/the same description as the original security for repo/stock-lending and related purposes (i.e. for the purposes of the following provisions:

- *FA 1996, ss 80C, 89AA;*
- *TA 1988, ss 730A, 730B, 737A, 737C;*
- *TCGA 1992, s 263B;*
- *FA 1996, 9 Sch 15.*

Answer
In the case of straightforward re-denominations – see **1.1** – the Government will ensure (by regulation if necessary) that re-denominated securities will count as similar to/equivalent to/the same description as the original securities for the tax provisions relating to repo and stocklending for all taxpayers covered by **1.1**. The Government is still considering how the law should apply for financing transactions involving re-denominations which would not meet the proposed 'same asset' tests.

4.2   Where 'cashing out' takes place on re-denomination, for example, due to rounding, will payments representative of the cash amounts be treated as manufactured payments?

Answer
The starting position would be that we would expect the characterisation of the representative payments to mirror that of the payments they represent. To the extent therefore that cash amounts themselves are capital payments, the payments representative of them would not count as manufactured payments.

However, where the person making the representative payment is not taxed on a trading basis, the tax liability may not correspond to the economic effect of his action in receiving cash payment and passing it on.

The Government will introduce a regulation so that where cash-outs due as a result of a re-denomination are passed on, the intermediary obtains the appropriate deduction from any charge. This will only apply, however, where it is clear that no abuse is taking place in relation to credits for tax withheld (if any) or underlying tax relief.

Note: **4.1** and **4.2** do not cover financing transactions involving equities which are re-denominated into euro. The treatment of financing transactions involving re-denominated equities will be addressed, along with continuity questions, when it becomes clearer how share re-denominations are to be achieved. However, insofar as similar issues arise, the Government will wish as far as possible the principles established for transactions involving re-denominated bonds to carry over to equities so that in the case of straightforward re-denominations, the provisions referred to above will apply.

Costs of re-denomination

5.1 Will costs incurred by a company upon re-denomination, as a result of the introduction of the single currency, of securities and equities issued by it be deductible for tax purposes?

Answer
The costs incurred upon re-denomination of a company's loan relationships are already provided for in the existing legislation and will be regarded as charges and expenses within *FA 1996, s 84(3)(a)–(d)*.

For other non-sterling securities or equities, which are re-denominated as a result of the start of the single currency, the Government believes there is a case for legislating a special relief. Accordingly the Government proposes to introduce a regulation to allow the costs of re-denomination into euros of existing non-sterling capital assets (both for traders and investment companies) so long as the re-denomination involves only the replacement of existing stock and not the issue of increased amounts or of greater value. This regulation will not apply to costs attributable to any other factor – e.g. to other changes made to a security or equity at the same time as re-denomination. To the extent that such costs are not attributable to the start of the single currency, their deductibility will be determined in accordance with existing principles.

5.2 Will costs incurred by an investor as a consequence of its investments being re-denominated as a result of the introduction of the single currency be deductible for tax purposes?

Answer
As far as the costs of re-denomination of investments is concerned, some costs may be allowable under current law as a trading expense or as an expense of management of an investment company, but others would not. The Government therefore proposes to make explicit in regulations exactly what will be allowable.

In the particular case of costs attributable to changes to computer software, the Revenue has already given guidance at para IM 664 of the Inspectors' Manual.

Foreign exchange

6.1 Will non-trading companies be able to make a local currency election to adopt the euro as their functional currency rather than sterling?

Answer
No. Non-trading companies will not be able to make a local currency election to adopt the euro as their functional currency.

6.2 It may not be apparent to a trading company that the inauguration of the single currency has made the euro the most appropriate currency for the company's accounts until some time after 1 January 1999 or even the start of its first post-January 1999 accounting period. Are there any plans to introduce a 'window period' (of, say, 92 days, by analogy with the transitional provisions for the commencement of the FOREX provisions) for the making of an election for euro to take effect from the start of the accounting period of the company in which the single currency begins falls or of the first post-January 1999 accounting period of the company?

Answer
The Government does not intend to introduce a window period in respect of the timing rules on local currency elections. However, to facilitate the making of elections for the euro, the Government proposes to introduce a regulation which would amend the existing local currency rules to allow companies to elect, prior to 1 January 1999 (i.e. before the euro actually exists), for the euro for accounting periods commencing on or after that date. This will put beyond doubt the ability of companies with 31 December year-ends to elect for the euro for accounting periods beginning on 1 January 1999. The Government has already announced that it intends to introduce a regulation to ensure that existing local currency elections in participating currencies are converted automatically to the euro.

6.3 Are there any plans to allow a company with euro-denominated share capital and euro-denominated assets to match these under *FA 1993, 15 Sch* or any extension thereto?

Answer
No. There are no plans to extend the circumstances in which a matching election may be made.

Authorised unit trusts – stamp duty and stamp duty reserve tax

7 The start of the single currency is likely to give rise to an opportunity for or commercial desire for significant rationalisation of unit trusts. However, the existing provision (contained in *FA 1997, s 95*) for rationalisations of authorised unit trusts to take place without any stamp duty or stamp duty reserve tax charge arising on the relevant transfer of assets expires on 30 June 1999. Are there any plans to postpone that expiration date?

Answer
An extension of the deadline for these reliefs would require legislation. The Association of Unit Trusts and Investment Funds have asked Ministers to consider an extension, for a variety of reasons of which EMU is one, but no decision has yet been taken.

Index